Buddha Shakyamuni

Guru Rinpoche

The Padmakara Translation Group gratefully acknowledges the generous support of the Tsadra Foundation in sponsoring the translation and preparation of this book.

༄༅། །ཡིན་ཏན་རིན་པོ་ཆེའི་མཛོད་ཀྱི་རྩ་བ་དང་
མཆན་འགྲེལ་ཐེག་གསུམ་བདུད་རྩིའི་སྙིང་པོ་
ཞེས་བྱ་བ་བཞུགས། །

པཧྨ་ཀུ་རའི་སྒྲ་བསྒྱུར་མཐུན་ཚོགས་ནས་
སྒྲ་བསྒྱུར་ལུས།།

TREASURY of PRECIOUS QUALITIES

The Rain of Joy

JIGME LINGPA

WITH *The Quintessence of the Three Paths*
A Commentary by Longchen Yeshe Dorje, Kangyur Rinpoche

BOOK TWO
Vajrayana and the Great Perfection
Translated by the Padmakara Translation Group
Foreword by Jigme Khyentse Rinpoche

SHAMBHALA

Shambhala Publications, Inc.
4720 Walnut Street
Boulder, Colorado 80301
www.shambhala.com

Paperback edition published 2020

Line drawing of Jigme Lingpa by Olivier Philippot

Cover art: Detail from fresco of Jigme Lingpa, used by permission of the Kangyur trust, Orgyen Kunzang Chöling Monastery, Darjeeling.

9 8 7 6 5 4 3 2 1

First Paperback Edition
Printed in the United States of America

∞ This edition is printed on acid-free paper that meets the American National Standards Institute z39.48 Standard.

♻ Shambhala Publications makes every effort to print on recycled paper. For more information please visit www.shambhala.com.

Shambhala Publications is distributed worldwide by Penguin Random House, Inc., and its subsidiaries.

The Library of Congress catalogues the previous edition of this book as follows:
Klong-chen Ye-shes-rdo-rje, Bka'-'gyur Rin-po-che.
[Yon tan rin po che'i mdzod kyi mchan 'grel theg gsum bdud rtsi'i nying khu. English]
Treasury of precious qualities, the rain of joy / by Jigme Lingpa. With the Quintessence of the three paths: a commentary / by Longchen Yeshe Dorje, Kangyur Rinpoche.—1st ed.
p. cm.
In English; includes translation from Tibetan.
Previously published: 2013.
Includes bibliographical references and index.
"Translated by the Padmakara Translation Group; foreword by Jigme Khyentse Rinpoche."
978-157062-598-5 (v. 1, hardcover: alk. paper)
978-159030-711-3 (v. 1, pbk.: alk. paper)
978-161180-045-6 (v. 2, hardcover: alk. paper)
978-161180-099-9 (v. 2, pbk.: alk. paper)
1. 'Jigs-med-gling-pa Rang-byung-rdo-rje, 1729 or 1730–1798.
Yon tan rin po che'i mdzod. 2. Rdzogs-chen—Doctrines,
Rdzogs-chen. I. 'Jigs-med-glin-pa Ran-byun-rdo-rje,
1729 or 30–1798. Yon tan rin po che'i mdzod. English. II. Comiti de traduction Padmakara. III. Title. IV. Title: Rain of joy.
BQ7662.4.J573 K59 2010
294.3/420423—dc23
2009047770

Contents ~

Foreword by Jigme Khyentse Rinpoche ⌇

The *Treasury of Precious Qualities* gives instructions for all the stages of the path to enlightenment according to the capacities of the three kinds of beings. I am very happy that this, the second volume, is now available in English, providing those of us who are interested with instructions that make it possible to reach enlightenment in a single lifetime. It is as though buddhahood were being placed in the palms of our hands.

Of course, the Buddha's teaching, from the preliminaries right up to the practice of the Great Perfection, is not a magical recipe that will simply give us enlightenment right away, so that we can become Buddhas without having to abandon our old habits. To practice the Dharma means to change, and to want to change, for the better. Therefore if we do actually read this book, we should do so with the genuine, heartfelt wish to be free from the samsara of our old ways, and with the wish to attain enlightenment for the sake of all beings.

As this text will show, the practice of the Vajrayana is based upon pure vision and the five perfections. The study, reflection, and meditation on them have produced great accomplished beings like Kyabje Kangyur Rinpoche, Kyabje Dudjom Rinpoche, Kyabje Dilgo Khyentse Rinpoche, Kyabje Trulshik Rinpoche, and many others. Teachings like these are not meant to fill the filing cabinets of our intellects. They are not intended to be the source material for academic research. Neither, on the other hand, are they a holiday brochure for so-called practitioners to daydream about flying to accomplishment. To be no more than an erudite scholar on the one hand, or a "dzogrim or dzogchen dreamer" on the other, are ways to waste our precious human life. For neither of these alternatives is beyond the eight worldly concerns.

These teachings are meant to be taken seriously for what they are. Therefore, it is recommended that this book be read and studied under the guidance of authentic and accomplished teachers, whose compassion inspires us with genuine devotion to the teachings and to the lineage, a devotion that is based on sound reasoning and not just sentiment.

When we read a book like this, we need to take especial care, and to act according to the instructions and guidance of the tradition. This is the only way to ensure that we receive these teachings properly and that we lay the foundations for our freedom—instead of even more delusion and mistaken understanding that are contrary to the Dharma.

I pray that all of us who read and study this book will do so correctly, and that we will be able to receive the blessings of these teachings and of the masters of the lineage, so that we will come to embody their humility, their compassion, and their wisdom.

Translators' Introduction ෴

This book is a translation of the second and concluding section of the *Treasury of Precious Qualities* by Rigdzin Jigme Lingpa, together with the commentary of Longchen Yeshe Dorje, Kangyur Rinpoche. It brings to completion a project begun in 2000 with the publication, as an independent book, of the translation of Kangyur Rinpoche's commentary on the first nine chapters. Fortunately, it became possible in 2010 to reissue this first volume, slightly revised and in more complete form, that is, accompanied by a translation of Jigme Lingpa's root verses.

Despite the length of time separating the appearance of the first and second volumes, they nevertheless belong together as a single work. It is therefore unnecessary to repeat here the introductory material already supplied at the beginning of book 1, which is where the interested reader will find short biographies of Rigdzin Jigme Lingpa and Kangyur Rinpoche, together with general information applicable to the text as a whole.

The *Treasury of Precious Qualities* belongs to the literary genre known in Tibetan as *lam rim*, or stages of the path, in which the way to enlightenment is explained in terms of the system of three levels of spiritual capacity popularized by the great Indian master Atisha Dipamkara, who visited Tibet in the eleventh century. And since, in this exposition, the path is viewed according to the perspective of the Nyingma, or old translation school, of Tibetan Buddhism, its different levels are regarded as steps and stages leading to the teachings of the Great Perfection, which is considered the pinnacle of all vehicles.

The first nine chapters of the *Treasury* (corresponding to the first volume of our translation) cover all the levels of Buddhist teaching up to and including the sutra section of the Mahayana, which, taken together, are referred to as the causal vehicle. The concluding four chapters, translated in the present volume, are an exposition of the resultant vehicle. Chapter 10 is a general exposition of the Vajrayana. After a brief account of the transmission lineages and an explanation of the classification of the tantras according to the old and new translation schools, the main body of the chapter consists of a detailed presentation of the Anuttara or highest level of tantra. It contains lengthy presentations of such topics as the four empowerments, the generation and perfection stages, and the various categories of samaya. The concluding section of the *Treasury* is devoted to the teachings of the Great Perfection, with the eleventh, twelfth, and thirteenth chapters being devoted respectively to an explanation of the ground, path, and result.

As was mentioned in the introduction to book 1, Kangyur Rinpoche's commentary, which is similar in length to those composed by Dodrup Jigme Trinlé Özer and Alak Sogpo Tendar, consists of notes taken in the course of an exposition of Khenpo Yönten Gyamtso's commentary given by his root teacher, Trinlé Jampa Jungné of Riwoche (1856–1922). Unlike the two other commentaries just mentioned, which derive their explanation lineage (*bshad rgyun*) directly from Jigme Lingpa himself, Kangyur Rinpoche's commentary, composed two generations later, is in the lineage, so to speak, of the detailed but highly accessible (and therefore very popular) work of Yönten Gyamtso. It gives a useful summary of the much longer text, while at the same time amplifying and clarifying certain aspects of it with Kangyur Rinpoche's personal insights. Of the three shorter commentaries, moreover, that of Kangyur Rinpoche is distinguished by the fact that it presents in much greater detail the three final chapters on the Great Perfection. The corresponding section in the commentary of Dodrup Jigme Trinlé Özer is by comparison brief and summary, while Sogpo Tendar's explanation is filled with long and difficult quotations from the tantras, expressive of his desire, as it is sometimes said, to demonstrate the truth and authenticity of the Great Perfection to his Gelugpa confreres.

TANTRA, SECRECY, AND RESTRICTED SALES

The practice of Secret Mantra and the Great Perfection is traditionally described as powerful but "perilous." If the teachings and transmissions are granted by authentic masters, and if they are implemented correctly and with diligence by qualified disciples, they have the power greatly to accelerate the process of spiritual development so that—given aptitude, intense effort, and the proper conditions—enlightenment may be achieved in a single lifetime. If however, these teachings are misused—if they are given and received for the wrong reasons, and if they are implemented by those who are unqualified and who have little regard for the sacred pledges associated with them—then the karmic consequences (as the texts frequently and emphatically declare) can be catastrophic.

It is quite true that nowadays, in certain situations, tantric empowerments, such as the Kalachakra, are given to an unrestricted public in which many people may be present who do not intend to implement the associated practices, and who receive the empowerment in the manner of a religious blessing. By contrast, those who wish to practice Secret Mantra, and such teachings as Mahamudra and the Great Perfection, require not merely the reception of the appropriate initiations, but also the reading transmission, and the all-important practical, usually oral, instructions of a qualified master, whose guidance must be sedulously followed. These instructions are often given to groups or individuals in closed retreat, and after lengthy preparation through the practice and accumulation of the traditional preliminaries. Finally, the reception of such teachings, and indeed the empowerments themselves, also imply the taking of the samaya pledge: a commitment that is to be maintained and repaired by daily confession, the recitation of the Vajrasattva mantra, and the regular offering of ganachakra.

Two important reasons are usually given for tantric secrecy. To begin with, there is a concern for the purity and strength of the tradition itself. To explain the Secret Mantra to the idly curious, to those who are unprepared and have little idea of the import and importance of the teachings in question, or to those who have only theoretical interest and have neither the capacity nor intention of submitting to the associated trainings, is understood to result in a dilution and dissipation of the tradition, and a corresponding weakening of the blessing power of the lineage. The only safeguard against such degeneration is the meticulous transmission of the teachings by accomplished masters to suitably qualified disciples who are committed to the practice of the teachings received. Tantra is never presented merely as a body of information or as an object of curiosity or intellectual inquiry. The teachings, their implementation, and the sacred pledges are all inextricably linked. They cannot be separated without danger.

This brings us to the second reason for tantric secrecy, which stems from a concern for the disciples themselves. The various levels of tantric view are subtle and difficult to understand. The practice of tantra is arduous and requires persistent effort, and some of its yogas are potentially dangerous. Without adequate preparation and expert guidance, the risk of misinterpretation is high. This in turn can lead to wrong view and the rejection of the profound teachings, which leads, it is said, to the states of loss for many lives to come. Ill-advised attempts to practice tantra on one's own, on the basis of a private reading of texts and of information gathered here and there from inauthentic sources, can be very detrimental, and may attract adversity and great misfortune. In short, therefore, if one wishes to pursue the tantric path, it is essential to do it properly: to seek teachings from a genuine master and to progress through the different stages of the practice laid down by the tradition.

With regard to the provision of tantric materials and manuals of instruction, important as these are for the transmission of Buddhism to the West, certain authorities and translators—as a means to avoid the difficulties just mentioned—have recourse to a system of restricted sales. That is, texts are translated and printed, but the books themselves are only sold to those who can prove their entitlement to them by supplying information about their teachers, the empowerments and teachings they have received, and so on. This somewhat bureaucratic procedure is in many ways understandable. It is an attempt to prevent the texts from falling into the wrong hands, as well as to protect the author or translator from the serious charge of divulging tantric secrets. This good intention, however, is difficult to implement, since it is obvious that, aside from the fairly limited possibility, on the part of the publisher, of verifying the information submitted, it is clear that the success of such a system of checks relies almost entirely on the sincerity and candor of the would-be purchaser. And it is obvious that the protective device just mentioned can be easily circumvented by the unscrupulous submission of false information.

At the translators' conference hosted by Dzongsar Khyentse Rinpoche in Bir, India, in 2009, when the idea was first drafted to translate the Kangyur or Tibetan canon, the point was made that in compliance with the demands of tantric secrecy, the translations of the tantras should be restricted and not made publicly available. When, however, His Holiness the Dalai Lama was questioned about this, his reply was categorical. "No need!" he said. "They are already published." He meant of course that the texts of the tantras are already freely available in Tibetan, in almost any monastic library. It would of course be disingenuous to overlook the considerable difference in attitude between the majority of Westerners, who have the habit of buying and reading whatever might appear in bookshops, real or virtual, and traditionally minded Tibetans, who have an ingrained respect for their sacred texts and would never dream of reading or even opening a tantric text without the preparations that we have just outlined. Even so, the Dalai Lama was putting his finger on the illogicality of placing restrictions on translations of texts that are in the public domain, so to speak, in the original language—making capital, in other words, out of the ignorance of the Tibetan language on the part of readers who require translations.

By questioning the efficacy or desirability of a system of restricted publication, we do not in any way wish to impugn the principles of tantric secrecy as we have just described them. We wish only to emphasize that in the translation and eventual study of the tantric teachings, everything depends on sincerity and purity of intention, whether on the part of authors, translators, or of the eventual readers. It is important to understand the principles, but what one does afterward is a matter of individual decision.

We wish therefore to state clearly that in translating and preparing this text for publication, it is our intention to be of service to the community of practitioners who sincerely wish to follow the path of Secret Mantra within the context of Mahayana Buddhism, according to tradition and within the respectful observance of its demands. The second volume of Jigme Lingpa's *Treasury* and Kangyur Rinpoche's commentary are, to be sure, of general import. They contain no practical instructions. They are instead a general explanation of the paths of Secret Mantra and the Great Perfection, and are indeed an invaluable presentation of the theoretical structure in which the different levels of teaching and practice are located.

As with the first volume of the complete translation, we have once again supplied, in addition to the translation of Jigme Lingpa's root text, and as an amplification to Kangyur Rinpoche's commentary (which in some places is probably too concise for the majority of Western readers), a considerable number of appendixes and endnotes. These include passages from the great commentary by Khenpo Yönten Gyamtso and clarifications from Khenpo Pema Sherab. Most especially, however, we have been able to include extensive notes of magisterial authority taken from an explanation of Yönten Gyamtso's commentary given by Kyabje Dilgo Khyentse Rinpoche in Bhutan in 1983. We hope by this means to supply readers with a tool of maximum efficacy and an abundant source of help in their study and practice.

TERMS AND MEANINGS

The task of translating into English difficult terms expressive of ideas that find no equivalent in the religious and philosophical cultures of the West, and that are sometimes of a subtlety that defies clear and unequivocal definition even in the original language, is the common predicament of translators of Tibetan Buddhist texts. And their stumbling efforts, the fruit of an often arduous and ungrateful labor, are, however well-intentioned, likely to find "but cold entertainment in the world." Such solutions as one may light upon, especially when trying to negotiate the reefs and shoals created by the difficult but unavoidable terminology of tantra, and even more so of the Great Perfection, are often little more than temporary makeshifts that may or may not please (the second alternative being the more likely). Nevertheless, it is to be hoped that the terms and translations that survive the test of time, and which may, for whatever reason, be sanctified by custom and consistent use, may come at length to indicate, even if they do not adequately express, the subtle content of the original.

In translating the last four chapters of the *Treasury*, we had to deal with a vocabulary of particular difficulty. We would therefore like to take this opportunity, if not to defend (for we are the first to acknowledge the inadequacy of our solutions), then at least to explain our choices in translating a handful of difficult but important expressions. Before doing so, it is important to advert to the fact that Tibetan terms may be highly polyvalent, and that—depending on subject matter, context, and the level of the teachings concerned—the same words may convey a variety of quite different meanings. In particular, even though some of the terms used in the section on the Great Perfection may evoke the Yogachara or Mind Only school, their meaning, it should be understood, is significantly different.

Throughout this text, as in our previous translations, we have consistently maintained the fairly arbitrary convention of translating *shes rab* (Skt. *prajña*) as "wisdom," and *ye shes* (Skt. *jñana*) as "primordial wisdom." The use of the word "wisdom" in both these expressions is justified by the equal presence of the element *shes* ("know," "understand") in both the Tibetan terms. *Shes rab*, which literally means "superior or perfect knowledge," does seem to find an adequate equivalent in the English word "wisdom." In order to translate *ye shes*, however, we have, rather clumsily, added the adjective "primordial" or "primal," thereby attempting to capture the sense of the first syllable of the Tibetan term as it is usually glossed: "knowledge from the beginning" (*ye nas shes pa*).

There is, admittedly, a considerable measure of overlap between both *shes rab* and *ye shes*. Nevertheless, *shes rab* is usually defined as the knowledge or wisdom that derives from study, reflection, and meditation; whereas *ye shes* is the nondual intuition that is said to arise when the mind rests in the state that is free from conceptual elaboration (*spros bral*). Thus defined, and speaking in rather approximate terms, *ye shes* is the equivalent of *rig pa* or *rang rig*, which, in the context of the Great Perfection, we have systematically and exclusively translated as "awareness" or "self-cognizing awareness" respectively. In other places, of course, *rig pa* may have a variety of meanings ("understanding," "science," "perception," "intelligence," and so on) and has therefore been translated in whatever way seemed most appropriate to the context. The negative term *ma rig pa* ordinarily means "ignorance" or "nescience." And although we have found it more natural to retain this translation in all cases, it should be understood that, in the Great Perfection, "ignorance" denotes not merely the state of not knowing, but the lack of *rig pa*, the exalted state of awareness.

The famous trio of terms—*ngo bo, rang bzhin, thugs rje*—which in relation to the way of being of the mind, is constantly cited in Great Perfection texts, is particularly intractable. The first term, *ngo bo*, is usually rendered by "nature," and we have kept this. It is worth pointing out, though, that C. S. Lewis devotes no fewer than fifty pages of his book *Studies in Words* to a discussion of the history and acceptations of this word in the English language. Here, we understand the word "nature" to convey description: "what a thing is like." Therefore, in answer to the question, "What is the mind like?" the Great Perfection replies: "Its nature is empty. It precedes, and is free of, all ascription."

The difficulty in translating *rang bzhin* stems from the fact that both it and *ngo bo* are perfect synonyms. Consequently any difference in the translation must derive not from some difference detectable in the original terms (for there is none), but from that to which they refer. And in the case of *rang bzhin*, the reference is to a quality of the mind that is just as intrinsic and fundamental as its emptiness, namely, its character of luminous clarity and knowing. For the English translation, and as a word that approximates to the descriptive dimension of the word "nature," we have therefore chosen "character." Speaking of the mind therefore, "its nature is emptiness; its character is luminosity."

The third term, *thugs rje,* is the most difficult of all. It is often, but quite misleadingly, translated as "compassion." After all, *thugs rje* is simply the honorific equivalent of *snying rje;* and in those situations where it denotes the inability to tolerate the suffering of other beings, it certainly comes close to the English word "compassion." Even here, however, there is but small equivalence, inasmuch as the Tibetan does not denote the ability or willingness simply to commiserate and to share in another's pain, but rather the heroic intention to destroy it. Be that as it may, even if we accept "compassion," as we probably must, as the translation of *snying rje* and *thugs rje* in this particular context, the fact remains that the etymological sense of the Tibetan words ("lordship, or power, of the mind") gives them a range of meanings in other places that the English word "compassion" cannot possibly cover. In the context of the Great Perfection, *thugs rje* means, in the words of Yönten Gyamtso, "pure and unadulterated awareness that has not yet stirred from its own true condition or state," but which has the potential to do so. In this case, therefore, we have decided to translate *thugs rje* (tentatively and without much euphony), not as "compassion," but as "cognitive potency."

Another important term, frequently encountered in Tibetan Buddhist literature, is *'od gsal,* which one often finds translated as "clarity," "clear light," "luminosity," "radiance," and so on. In the context of tantra and the Great Perfection, we have consistently opted for "luminosity" as a rendering of this term. It should be understood, however, that it refers to a characteristic of the mind and has nothing to do with ordinary, physical light.

In the presentation of the path of the Great Perfection in chapter 12, there is a discussion of the important concept of "subsiding" or "freedom" (*grol ba*). This Tibetan verb, which with all due caution may be regarded as intransitive (*tha mi dad pa*), is occasionally and ill-advisedly translated into English as "to liberate," no doubt through confusion with the similar, but transitive, verbs *'grol ba* and *sgrol ba*. This is not a satisfactory solution since, quite apart from the mistake in meaning, "to liberate," in the sense of "to set free," is certainly a transitive verb in English and requires a direct object. Therefore the invented verb "to self-liberate," used intransitively and found in expressions like "the mind 'self-liberates'" (which is presumably intended to express something different from "the mind liberates itself") is an aberration. It should be dismissed as an unfortunate piece of "Buddhist Hybrid English" and, in our opinion, is to be avoided. In fact, *grol ba* means something like "to dwindle," "to disperse," or "to subside," as when a crowd melts away or when ripples sink back into the surface of a pool. We have therefore translated it as "subside" or "subsiding." There are in fact no fewer than five kinds of "subsiding." For the most part, "subsiding" works well enough. It is awkward, however, in the case of "primordial subsiding" (*ye grol*) since it is difficult to imagine a subsiding that occurs even before anything has arisen! We keep the same term, however, for the sake of consistency, but gloss it with "the primordial state of openness and freedom."

The Tibetan term *rang snang* is notoriously difficult to translate with any degree of economy. At its most basic level, it refers to the environment that appears to any individual mind (*rang ngor snang ba*). Through the ripening of karmic seeds, every living being has a specific and unshared perception of the world, which coincides with that of others to the extent that they share a similar karmic constitution. One sometimes finds *rang snang* translated as "self-appearance." This unfortunately conjures up the notions of self-manifestation, or even self-disclosure, which are quite wide of the mark in that *rang snang* refers to what appears to oneself, and not to the way that oneself appears. We have therefore preferred "self-experience" (in the sense of "that which is experienced by oneself"), and sometimes even "exclusive self-experience."

The use of this term varies slightly at different levels of the teaching, and naturally becomes extremely technical. For example, in the explanation given in the Great Perfection of how appearance arises from the ground nature, the line of demarcation between buddhahood and the unenlightened state lies precisely in the ability or failure to recognize the appearance of the ground as the self-experience of awareness itself (*rig pa'i rang snang*). For if this appearance of the ground is taken as something outside awareness, the dualistic interplay of subject and object, characteristic of the ordinary mind, becomes established—a bifurcation that awareness transcends. Those who fail to recognize the true nature of the ground's appearance are ordinary beings. They experience an external world, act accordingly, and wander in endless samsara, whereas those who recognize the true nature of the appearance of the ground attain the freedom of enlightenment.

In the explanation of the sambhogakaya and nirmanakaya, the Great Perfection teachings introduce a number of subtle distinctions, stating for instance that the sambhogakaya and its buddhafields are actually the exclusive self-experience of the sambhogakaya, and are perceptible to no one else. Accordingly, that which appears to the Bodhisattvas residing on the grounds of realization (who are usually said to enjoy the vision of the sambhogakaya) is not strictly speaking the sambhogakaya, but a form of the nirmanakaya, albeit an exalted one. This is the so-called *rang bzhin sprul pa'i sku*, which one sometimes finds rather unhelpfully translated as the "natural nirmanakaya." In fact, it means the nirmanakaya that displays characteristics of the sambhogakaya and is a sort of halfway house between the two. In a bid for consistency, and taking into account the fact that *rang bzhin* is associated with the luminous character of the mind, as indeed is the sambhogakaya, we have chosen to render *rang bzhin sprul pa'i sku* as the "nirmanakaya of luminous character."

It will be obvious from the above remarks that, in relation to the profound teachings of the Great Perfection, we translators are quite out of our depth. It is worth reflecting that the Great Perfection is not, like other views, a theory or conceptual estimate of the nature of phenomena. It begins with, and consists in, a direct realization of that nature. And without that realization, it is impossible to discourse authoritatively, or even meaningfully, upon it. It was no doubt in reference to this that the great Khenpo Jigme Phuntsok is reported as saying that "the Great Perfection" was an expression he scarcely dared even to pronounce.

For ourselves, and as far as concerns the present translation, we can only say that, after listening to the exposition and explanation of lamas and khenpos, we have done our best to provide the reader with what we hope will be a not unhelpful rendering of an important text. No translation can ever be a spotless and invisible pane through which the original can be seen without distortion. All translators leave traces of their passage, and the original text can only be viewed through the refracting lens of their understanding, which in the present case is very limited. We therefore apologize in advance for all inexactitudes, relying on the patience and indulgence of the reader and, in the spirit of the tradition, imploring the forgiveness of the dakinis and wisdom protectors.

All such imperfections and blemishes have nothing to do with the sublime assistance which, over the years, we have received from our teachers. In particular, we wish to thank Shechen Rabjam Rinpoche and Jigme Khyentse Rinpoche, who began the explanation of the *Treasury of Precious Qualities* at La Sonnerie, Dordogne, in 1995. We are deeply grateful also to Alak Zenkar Rinpoche, who helped us particularly with the first volume of this translation and had given us much inspiration and encouragement throughout this project. Most especially, we wish to thank our teacher, Pema Wangyal Rinpoche, through whose blessing and unfailing kindness we have been able to enter and remain in the

Buddhadharma, and through whom we have also had access to the teaching of his father Kyabje Kangyur Rinpoche, Kyabje Dudjom Rinpoche, Kyabje Dilgo Khyentse Rinpoche, and Kyabje Trulzhik Rinpoche.

As for the actual translation of the two volumes, sutra and tantra, of the root text and commentary, this would have been completely impossible without the full and detailed explanations, and the endlessly patient clarifications, of Khenchen Pema Sherab of Namdroling Monastery, Mysore, India. To him we owe a debt of gratitude that is scarcely within our power to express. We would like to thank also our dear friend Gelong Konchok Tenzin (Matthieu Ricard) for his unfailing help over many years as translator and interpreter and source of much helpful supplementary material. It was he indeed who supplied us with his copious transcriptions of the oral commentary of Dilgo Khyentse Rinpoche on certain passages of the *Treasury* that we have been able to incorporate into the endnotes.

This book was translated by Helena Blankleder and Wulstan Fletcher of the Padmakara Translation Group.

Dordogne, France
February 2012

Treasury of Precious Qualities

by Jigme Lingpa

BOOK TWO

Jigme Lingpa

CHAPTER 10

The Teachings of the Vidyādharas

1. The Bodhisattva mantra vehicle is known
   As the resultant vehicle, the vajra vehicle,
   The vehicle of skillful means, the pitaka of Vidyādharas.
   It is far greater than the causal vehicle.

2. In terms of continuity, we speak of tantra or continuum
   Of ground, of path, and of result.
   Based upon two stages and combining skillful means and wisdom,
   Its approach is vast and is untroubled by austerities.
   For those of sharp acumen,
   Its discipline is swift to bring results.

3. According to four ages of the world:
   Endowed with All Perfection, the Age of Three,
   The Age of Two, and then the Age of Strife;
   According then to caste of priest or king,
   Of merchant, menial, or outcaste;
   According to capacity: meager, moderate, sharp, or very best—
   The teachings are expounded in four tantras:
   Kriya, Charya, Yoga, and Anuttara.

4. The first three are the outer Secret Mantra
   And are mostly like the causal vehicle the Buddha set forth openly:
   They urge a life of purity and of restraint.
   Desire is taken as the path but not as in the Age of Strife:
   The deities are not in union;
   No use is made of the five nectars and five meats.

5. When classified, there are the Kriya and the Charya tantras
Wherein are found both male and female Bodhisattvas,
Deities of vidya- and dharani-mantras.
"Lord and servant" is the style of Kriya,
"Relatives and friends" the Charya mode.

6. Kriya is practiced in the mode of lord and servant:
One does not see oneself as deity but takes a lower place.
To this there are exceptions but the emphasis is placed
On generation of the deity in front.
Important are external deeds of purity and cleansing.
Acting thus, as high and low, is said to bring accomplishment.

7. Charya is so called because it takes as conduct equally
The skillful means of Kriya and the inner ways of Yoga.
Before oneself, samayasattva,
One sees the jnanasattva regarded as a sibling:
Thus one gains accomplishment.

8. The courtyards and the palace of the Yogatantra
Are likened to the vast array of the sambhogakaya.
And yet the deities are not in union.
Generation and perfection, skillful means and wisdom,
Are separate and performed successively.

9. The inner yoga, here, is chief,
With speech and body taught as its auxiliaries.
The wisdom deity is invoked, dissolved,
And fixed by the four seals,
And in the state where visualized and wisdom deities are one,
Accomplishment is gained.
When recitation is complete, the deity is asked to leave.

10. Anuttara, the inner Secret Mantra—according as it stresses
    Generation or perfection or their union,
    Is entitled "father," "mother," or "nondual."
    The deities appear in union,
    Particular samaya substances are used.
    The practice here transcends both clean and unclean,
    Taking and rejecting.

11. Mahayoga, father tantra, path of skillful means,
    Chiefly implements the generation stage
    And cleanses the five winds.
    Anuyoga, mother tantra, path of wisdom,
    Chiefly implements the deeds of the perfection stage:
    The yogas of the essence-drop
    Engendering the bliss deriving from its melting.
    Atiyoga is the path of nondual primal wisdom
    Through which is gained great luminosity that's neither one nor
        many.

12. Vital for them all is to possess
    A body that's equipped with the six elements.
    And when the channels, winds, and essence-drops—
    The bases for the skandhas, dhatus, ayatanas—are refined,
    The qualities of generation and perfection and their union
    Arise upon the Vajrayana path.

13. Concerning the great mandala,
    Naturally, spontaneously present,
    View bestows conviction;
    Meditation brings experience;
    Conduct shuns all dualistic attitudes;
    Result is the attaining of the twofold goal.
    These perfectly relate to tantras of the ground, path, and result.

14. The door to Secret Mantra is empowerment that brings maturity.
    The generation and perfection stages both bring freedom.
    Observance of samaya is the favorable condition.
    These three define the path of Mantra, faultless and supreme.

15. Without reception of empowerment,
    No attainment can there be,
    For that would be like wanting ghee from pressing sand.
    And though one strives in teaching, learning, meditation,
    One will go to hell.
    While those who have empowerment
    Are the Buddha's heirs.

16. Completely freed from sinful deeds
    Through gazing on the mandala,
    Born in stainless families, and after seven lives,
    They surely gain accomplishment, it's said,
    Traversing the ten grounds.

17. Some teachers give empowerment but lack the confidence
    That comes from the two stages.
    They care more for their house and worldly ways,
    And misuse riches pledged for spiritual ends.
    Their ways are dissolute and unrestrained.
    They're meager in compassion, full of clever talk.
    And even though they give empowerment,
    They and their disciples—
    Just like young cows roped together—
    All fall down in the abyss.

18. But masters who have liberated minds,
    Who are endowed with tenfold knowledge—
    Outer, inner, secret—
    Should test the minds of their disciples.
    The latter must be faithful and endowed with tender conscience.
    To them in proper order should empowerments be given.

19. The practice of approach, the ritual of the land, the preparation,
    Admission of disciples to the mandala together with their
        ripening:
    Each of these four rituals has four aspects.
    All must be complete or else
    The rite is spoiled and powerless to mature.

20. Empowerments are classified according to the tantra classes.
    The Kriyatantra has empowerments of water and of crown.
    To these the Charyatantra adds empowerment of the vajra name.
    The Yogatantra has the five empowerments of knowledge,
    The secret empowerment and the empowerment that bestows
    Authority to teach. All are then completed
    With empowerment of consolidation.

21. The Anuttara has four empowerments:
    The vase, the secret, wisdom, and the word.
    The peak of all the vehicles has four particular empowerments:
    Elaborate and unelaborate, extremely, and supremely unelaborate.
    Though generally, empowerments
    Are limitless in classes and divisions,
    All are counted in the four Anuttara empowerments.

22. The ground, path, and result
    Are present from the first in all the four empowerments.
    When the two causes and the four conditions are assembled,
    Empowerments are truly given.
    The channels, winds, and essence-drops (the natural supports)
    Are concomitant cause. This and the cooperative
    Constitute the twofold aspect of the cause.

23. Disciples, as the fitted vessels,
    Constitute the causal condition.
    The master who has realization of the view
    Is dominant condition.
    His knowledge of the empowering ritual
    Is the objective condition.
    The empowerments' interlinking
    Is the condition that immediately precedes.

24. These empowerments are four in number
    According to the antidotes connected with
    The channels, chief constituents of the body,
    Which are in the form of syllables;
    The winds that dwell within the channels;
    The essence-drops supported by the winds;
    And, based upon these essence-drops, the highest bodhichitta.

25. Occupants of the desire realm, common beings,
    Experience four levels of desire.
    And thus, according to what purifies
    And what is to be purified,
    There are four empowerments.

26. The first is antidote to that desire
    That's sated just by looking,
    As in the case of gods who have
    The mastery of others' magical creations.
    The vase empowerment is granted
    Based upon a mandala of colored sand.
    It chiefly purifies the body's obscurations.

27. The universe and beings,
    The stable vessel and its moving contents,
    The aggregates, the elements, and sensorial fields,
    All arise as but the single mandala of the three seats.
    The view has three essential features:
    Appearance, voidness, and their union.
    Supreme attainment is the realization that
    Samsara and nirvana are not two different things.

28. At death, the transference of consciousness
    Is made by means of orb of light and sound.
    Pulsation of the channels ceases;
    Nirmanakayas of the generation stage
    Pervade the whole of space;
    The uncompounded vajra body is achieved.

29. The secret empowerment is granted
    On the basis of the mandala of secret space.
    It cleanses the desire that's sated with a smile,
    Possessed by gods enjoying magical creations.
    It purifies the obscurations linked with speech.
    This is the path of blessings for oneself.
    The tummo practice brings into the central channel
    The dualistic winds from roma and from kyangma,
    And the self-arisen primal wisdom manifests.

30. The supreme attainment of this path
    Is to know all tongues distinctly
    As the perfect speech of Buddhas.
    At death occurs the state of great example luminosity;
    The pulsing of the sounds of speech subsides;
    And the sambhogakaya manifests,
    Together with the vajra speech
    All perfect in its sixty qualities.

31. Based upon the secret mandala of the lovely one
    Whose mandala of the three seats
    Is visualized according to the sadhana,
    The empowerment of wisdom cleanses the desire
    That's satisfied by holding hands,
    Enjoyed by gods of the Tushita heaven.
    The obscurations of the mind are thereby cleansed
    And "light," "increase," and "culmination" all occur.
    The blissful melting of the essence-drop
    Accomplishes the primal wisdom of four joys.

32. This path's supreme attainment
    Is to taste of bliss and emptiness inseparable.
    When death occurs, the vajra mind
    Appears although devoid of real existence.
    The knot upon the channels at the heart is loosed
    And the example wisdom manifests.
    The vajra of enlightened mind, the dharmakaya utterly refined,
    Pervades and fills the whole of space.

33. Based upon the mandala of bodhichitta,
    The empowerment that indicates by word
    The experience of the third initiation
    Purifies desire for union,
    Felt as far as the divine realm Free of Conflict.
    It purifies the veil obscuring the three doors:
    Perception of the separateness of body, speech, and mind.

34. The "essence-drop of voidness" has awareness as its core.
    The path's supreme attainment
    Is primordial wisdom inconceivable.
    At death there is the transfer
    To the greatly secret Mahamudra.
    The result is the svabhavikakaya
    That fills the whole of space.

35. The Sanskrit for "empowerment" contains a double meaning.
    Abhishimcha means the scattering of adventitious obscuration;
    Shekata denotes the pouring out of happy destiny.

36. Supreme empowerment resides within oneself,
    Based on the six elements, endowed with perfect qualities:
    This is the empowerment in aspect of a cause.
    Empowerments of the path comprise
    The empowerments that a master gives by means of ritual
    And those in which one trains through concentration.
    When the mind matures as the four kayas,
    This is the empowerment in the aspect of result,
    Resembling the empowerment of great rays of light
    Referred to in the causal vehicle.

37. On completion of the four empowerments,
    One takes the vows of a Vidyādhara.
    And just as when a seed is placed in soil well tilled,
    Those receiving such empowerments
    Cleanse the four defilements
    Making the four kayas manifest.

38. The path is twofold: generation and perfection.
    The first is taught according to four kinds of birth,
    As means to cleanse the tendencies that lead to them.
    The way of generation, in accordance with samsara's aspects,
    Purifies and cleanses the three realms without exception.

39. The way of generation in accordance with nirvana
    And the features of the deity
    Perfects the fruit abiding in the ground.
    Both these aspects (cleansing and perfecting)
    Produce a ripening as the perfection stage.
    To purify, perfect, and ripen—these three aspects—
    Are most crucial in all generation practices.

40. Just as beings born from eggs are twice-born,
    There exists a generation practice with two aspects:
    Others as the children of oneself, oneself as child of other.
    For *others as the children of oneself,* five stages are required.

41. First, from the seed, the main divinity is generated;
    Then the Buddhas of the ten directions are invoked
    And these dissolve into the secret space;
    Beings are then summoned, their obscurations purified;
    Then one generates great confidence in nonduality;
    And from the secret space the deities emerge
    And take their seat upon the thrones.

42. For *oneself as child of other* eight stages are required.
    Just as from a "ripened" egg a chick appears,
    The principal divinity melts into light, becoming a seed-syllable.
    From this the father-mother deities arise
    Complete in all their features.
    The father's thoughts turn into syllables.
    And from the mother, lights shine forth and supplicate the father.

43. All surrounding deities dissolve into oneself
    And one is filled with pride.
    The father-mother are in union:
    The mandala is generated in the secret space.
    Two and forty thoughts appear as deities
    That, coming forth, are tethered by four mudras
    And then sealed.

44. Briefly, as a deity one should first see oneself,
    And visualize the mandala in the space in front.
    The confession prayer of every day should then be said.
    Deity and mandala then melt into the state of emptiness
    And from this state, one meditates upon
    The mandala of the specific deity, according to the sadhana.

45. For womb-birth to be purified,
    There are the four or five "awakenings."
    The four are in accordance with the sense of the *Heruka Galpo*.
    Death and bardo are both cleansed
    By emptiness and bodhichitta.
    The bardo consciousness is purified
    By the deity's seed-syllable.

46. The mixture of the male and female essences
    With wind and consciousness
    Takes on a round, then elongated, shape
    And this is cleansed by transformation
    Of the syllable into the implement.
    The change from soft to more consistent form is cleansed
    By transformation of the implement into a sphere of light.
    The fish-shape, turtle-shape,
    The stage when all the senses are complete
    Are cleansed by transformation of the sphere of light into the
        deity.

47. The body of the deity relates to the enlightened body.
    The syllable relates to vajra speech.
    The enlightened mind is correlated with the implement.
    These "three vajra methods" are the way of father tantras.

48. Searching for a body in the bardo
    Is like being on the pathway of accumulation.
    Entry of the mind into the womb is like the path of joining.
    Five awakenings on entry to the womb
    Are like the paths of seeing and of meditation.
    The ten months in the womb are like the grounds of realization,
    While birth reflects the path of no more learning and
        nirmanakaya.

49. The first awakening, the lunar disk,
    Purifies the semen that is present in womb-birth,
    Humidity in birth from warmth and moisture,
    The paternal aspect present in egg-birth,
    The voidness aspect of miraculous birth.

50. The second is the solar disk, which likewise purifies
    The female essence present in womb-birth,
    The warmth in birth from warmth and moisture,
    The maternal aspect present in egg-birth,
    The luminosity occurring in miraculous birth.

51. The third awakening, the seed-syllable and implement,
    Purifies the entry of the consciousness
    Amid the male and female essences,
    So too the entrance of the bardo consciousness
    Into the other three environments of birth.

52. The fourth awakening is the merging
    Of the three preceding forms.
    It purifies the merging into one
    Of semen, ovum, consciousness;
    The merging warmth and consciousness
    In birth from warmth and moisture;
    The merging emptiness and luminosity
    Together with the bardo consciousness
    Occurring in miraculous birth.

53. The fifth awakening consists
    In visualization of the body of the deity.
    And when, in the four kinds of birth,
    The senses are completely formed,
    It cleanses their arousal by the objects they encounter
    As well as the appearances of samsara.

54. The elements and aggregates and consciousnesses
Are all innately pure,
They are the deities of the three seats.
According to the way of being of nirvana,
From the cause heruka arises the result heruka.
Semen, ovum, wind, together with the mind are cleansed
And cause the ripening as the perfection stage.

55. In birth from warmth and moisture,
When the consciousness is blended
With the merging of these elements,
Form is instantly produced.
Likewise through the mere recalling of its name and form,
The deity appears with all its attributes,
And then one meditates upon the entire generation stage.

56. And just as in miraculous birth,
The deity arises in a single flash of recollection,
Clearly manifest without depending on its name and form.
Of these four kinds of meditation,
Beginners mainly concentrate
Upon the generation stage that purifies birth from an egg.
Then gradually they train
According to habituation with the practice:
Firm, most firm, and excellently firm.

57. All these practices include the suchness concentration,
The wisdom free from all conceptual constructs.
Its radiance is compassion all-illuminating,
Through the impetus of which, the generation stage occurs.
This is the supreme, unmistaken path of skillful means.

58. From the very instant they appear,
    The deities are free from real existence.
    This is the profound path where appearance and voidness,
    Means and wisdom, are conjoined.
    A generation stage exists where, contrary to this,
    There is a clinging to appearance.
    Even those outside the Dharma, even certain kinds of spirits,
    Have such practices.

59. The Bodhisattva path of seeing is renowned,
    In Mantrayana, as the high accomplishment of Mahamudra.
    The method for its realization is the gathering of merit
    (Through seeing all phenomena as deities),
    And the gathering of wisdom
    (Through the understanding that they lack intrinsic being).

60. Those with sharp capacity,
    Who lean upon these two accumulations
    As contributary cause,
    Ascend the stairway of the four Vidyādharas
    Linked with the five paths.
    And thus they go as if by magic to the fields of the five kayas
    Endowed with the five certainties and all the other qualities.

61. And now we come to the perfection stage.
    The father tantras say that cleansing of the winds of the five
        elements
    Engenders primal wisdom, luminous and empty.
    The mother tantras say that primal wisdom that derives
    From blissful melting of the essence-drop is generated
    Through the skillful path of one's own body,
    Whereas primal wisdom of the four joys comes
    Depending on the body of another.

62. The nondual tantras stress
    The luminosity of the great essence-drop
    Transcending one and many.
    The first two classes are conceptual paths,
    Employing visual forms.
    The third is that of luminosity devoid of forms.

63. The conceptual perfection stage
    Concerns the stationary channels and the mobile winds,
    Together with positioned bodhichitta.
    In these three lies the city of the vajra aggregate.

64. When a place is found inside a human womb,
    The knot of channels at the navel, with the "two eyes," first is
        formed.
    Thence the body grows, in which there are three channels, pillar-
        like,
    Quintessence of the male and female elements.

65. Within them dwell the three seed-syllables,
    Which outwardly support the body, speech, and mind.
    Inwardly they are the basis of the three defilements.
    Secretly, they are the basis of enlightened body, speech, and mind.

66. The central channel's top lies in the brahma-door;
    Its lower tip lies in the secret center.
    Roma, kyangma, white and red, are on the right and left.
    This order is reversed in women:
    They have kyangma on the right.
    The two side channels twist around the pale blue central channel
    Making, in a series, one and twenty knots.

67. The chakras are the same in number
    As the enlightened body, speech, and mind,
    Or as the kayas, whether four or five, or as the six perfections.
    Their channels, petal-like, are in their number great or less.
    For what is to be purified needs various means of cleansing.

68. The channels at the navel number sixty-four;
    Eight are at the heart, and sixteen at the chakra of the throat.
    In the chakra of the crown are thirty-two,
    And seventy-two within the bliss-preserving place.
    The ushnisha has been called the chakra of the realm of space.

69. Both in, and in between, the chakras, there occur
    Twelve transits of the winds, which correspond
    To movements through the twelve celestial mansions
    As well as to the twelve dependent links.
    The essence-drops are drawn up
    By the halting of their transits.
    When they penetrate the chakra of primordial wisdom at the
        secret place,
    One transit of the wind together with the first dependent link are
        halted,
    And the realization of the first ground manifests.

70. By stages and until the chakra of the realm of space is reached,
    Each transit of the wind is stopped as well as each dependent link,
    Whereby the twelve grounds thus are all perfected.
    When finally the essence-drop
    Is mingled with the realm of space,
    Complete enlightenment occurs.
    Such is the tradition of the primordial Buddha.

71. Within the radial channels of the chakras,
    The seeds of the six realms are found as objects to be purified.
    They're cleansed by the Six Sages of Awareness, agents of their
        cleansing,
    And also by the six perfections.
    The five distinct primordial wisdoms
    And the sixth, which mind cannot conceive,
    Are by this means obtained.

72. In the heart, moreover, is the wheel of peaceful deities;
    The wheel of wrathful deities is in the head.
    In both, the deities and radial channels are of equal number.
    There are two paths, of skillful means and liberation.
    The first has two approaches: through the upper and the lower
        doors.
    All this is the assertion of the *Mayajala,* king of tantras.

73. Associated with the elements
    Are the major and the minor moving winds.
    In every day of four and twenty hours,
    Move twenty-one thousand and six hundred major winds.
    And for the eighty-four thousand kinds of thought
    There is an equal quantity of minor winds,
    Which act as vehicles for them.

74. The fundamental winds are: life-supporting,
    Fire-accompanying, all-pervading,
    Upward-moving, downward-voiding—five in all.
    Their respective functions are to maintain life,
    Give heat, produce the body's strength,
    To drive the intake and the outflow of the breath,
    And to enable walking, sitting,
    And elimination of the body's waste.

75. The upward-moving wind is masculine,
    Residing in the body's upper part.
    The downward-voiding wind is feminine and is below.
    The rest are neuter and found equally throughout.
    The "inner" winds possess the hues of the five elements.
    They support the aggregates, the elements, and the sense-fields;
    And they are like the causal base whence five results emerge:
    Five poisons and five primal wisdoms.

76. When, in particular, the five refined winds
    Penetrate the central channel,
    The concentrations of unbounded earth,
    Fire, water, wind, and space,
    And every perfect quality and wondrous power, are gained.
    The "secret" winds are the five primal wisdoms;
    They are the contrary of coarse phenomena.

77. We come now to positioned bodhichitta.
    From roma flows amrita of the moon;
    From kyangma flows the solar blood.
    The kyangma in a man, the roma in a woman,
    Are knotted at their ends
    And therefore the two essences are kept from being lost.

78. The refined essence-drops, both white and red,
    Aside from moving in these channels,
    Spread and dwell in all the channel knots as dakas and yoginis,
    Who, joined in union, receive the offering of empty bliss.

79. In brief, the stationary channels are like irrigation pipes,
    The mobile wind is like the steersman driving to and fro.
    And bodhichitta is like water that collects where it is led.
    Along the "space of Rahu" are six chakras superposed.
    The chariot of "life" and "effort" is conveyed to them.
    And, step-by-step and two by two,
    The knots upon the central channel are undone.

80. When the refined winds and the essence-drops
    Enter Rahu's belly, the first ground is achieved.
    Thence the qualities of all ten grounds increase
    And the refined winds and the essence-drops ascend to the
       ushnisha.

81. Now the special doctrine of the *Mayajala*,
    As it is expounded in the *Secret Essence*,
    Teaches that the world and all that it contains
    Is found complete within ourselves.
    Within the city of the aggregates
    The sugatagarbha neutrally abides
    Throughout the triple time.
    By rendering it manifest do all attain enlightenment.

82. Upon the vajra-throne,
    Within the hollow recess of the heart's eternal knot,
    There are eight channels all refined:
    Three middle ones provide the basis
    Of three kayas and the dharmatā.
    In front, there is a channel whence arises primal wisdom.
    Behind is found the channel of all perfect qualities
    From which arise the buddhafields.
    And to the left are found three channels of the ordinary mind,
    The basis of delusory appearance.

83. In the midst of each of them
    Are the seed-syllables of samsara and nirvana.
    These dwell as objects to be purified
    And agents of their cleansing.
    The syllables of the enlightened body, speech, and mind
    Will cleanse the objects to be purified.

84. In the center of them all a channel runs, refined and white,
    Ten times more slender than a horse's hair,
    In which is found a very subtle light of fivefold hue:
    Quintessence of the mingled breath and female essence.
    This light is basis of the bodhichitta, luminous in nature.
    When the wind-mind all refined collects within the palace
    Where abide Samantabhadra and the Buddhas of five families,
    All nirvanic visions of the buddhafields appear.

85. When the appearance aspect, the five lights,
    Is mingled in a single savor
    With the voidness aspect, dharmakaya,
    The two accumulations of the path reach their completion.
    Akanishtha the immaculate,
    Which has the name of "Dense Array,"
    Is not located in some other place.
    As soon as all the obscurations are removed,
    It automatically appears.

86. Thus this body is the very basis of primordial wisdom.
    And even in samsara, the mind in its true nature
    Is not weakened or impaired.
    Bodhichitta, ultimate, unchanging,
    Permeates all beings like the oil within a grain of sesame.

87. Once the nature of the vajra body
    And the way of being of the primal ground are understood,
    Practitioners exert themselves
    In Tummo, the Illusory Body,
    The Path of Dream (delusions that occur within delusion),
    Luminosity, the Bardo, and the Transference of Consciousness.

88. They gain accomplishment without depending
    On the body of another:
    They take the skillful path of their own bodies.
    Once the channels, winds, and essence-drops are mastered,
    The path of empty bliss, the body of another, may be used.
    It is the skillful path wherein all practices
    Are truly and authentically performed.

89. Now comes that perfection stage
    In which there are no visual forms.
    All the features of the generation and perfection stages—
    The pure appearance of the world and its inhabitants—
    Melt away, dissolving into light.
    The letter in the heart dissolves into the anushvara,
    And this, dissolving from below, turns into emptiness,
    The very nature of the sky.
    One rests then in the sphere of great primordial wisdom.

90. The stage of generation puts an end to clinging
    To the real existence of appearing things,
    And the perfection stage eliminates
    All clinging to them as illusions.
    Bliss, clarity, the state devoid of thought arise,
    And coemergent primal wisdom.
    Such is the profound and unexcelled perfection stage,
    Taught only in the tantras unsurpassed.
    The lower tantras do not speak of it.
    For those with sharpest faculties,
    It is the short and hidden pathway most profound,
    Conducive to the state of Vajradhara in a single life.

91. For this, samaya is our helping friend,
    And those who have embraced the Secret Mantra
    Must preserve its precepts without spoiling them.
    They must correctly use its methods as an antidote
    And in their practice be like peacocks taking deadly poison.

92. Samaya and vow are different things.
    Samaya is a promise not to be transgressed,
    While vow is understood
    In terms both of injunction and of prohibition.
    They share a single nature but are different in their aspect.

93. If the mantra vows, foundation of all trainings,
    Are not received, or if one is deranged and so forth,
    Not in one's right mind,
    No downfall can there be and no accomplishment.
    But those who hold the mantra vows,
    Who do not spoil them or relinquish them,
    Whose minds rest in their proper state,
    Are vessels for both downfalls and accomplishment.

94. Excepting the abandonment of bodhichitta,
    All other downfalls are affected
    By the presence of entanglements:
    The steady wish to perpetrate the act,
    The failure to regret it,
    Absence of a sense of guilt within oneself,
    And absence of a sense of shame regarding others.

95. When, throughout the action till its very end,
    The motivation is at all times tainted by these three,
    The deed becomes a true defeat, possessed of all entanglements.
    But if there is a break in the intention, if it's not continuous,
    Or if one of the three things is absent,
    All components of the action are not present.
    Therefore there arises an infraction.

96. With such an understanding,
    Keep the samayas, root and branch.
    Do not reject them in your mind,
    Nor in your body cast them out.
    In all the six divisions of the day and night together,
    Check to see if any of the fourteen downfalls
    Has occurred or not.

97. If you find that you are stained,
    With sorrow you should think how to repair your error.
    And if you find no fault, rejoice and dedicate your virtue.
    But whether you were stained or were not stained
    In times now past,
    You should maintain a powerful sense
    Of self-restraint, resolving that,
    From now on, and at cost of life or limb,
    No fault will be committed.

98. If, with obfuscated mind, you fail to check
    In any of the six divisions of the day and night together,
    A "grave infraction" is incurred.
    And if these six divisions pass without examination,
    The infraction is increased sixfold.
    If no repair is made throughout that day,
    Then twelve infractions are incurred, so it is said,
    At first light of the following dawn.
    And this applies to branch samayas also.

99. At the outset one should study
The root downfalls, fourteen in their number.
They are of the greatest consequence for all the highest tantras.
The first is to revile and fail to honor
The three kinds of teacher who connect us with the Dharma.
Of teachers who bestow empowerment,
What need is there to speak?
But also there are teachers who explain the scriptures—
Even just a single line of tantric text;
And there are teachers who give deep instructions
That concern the path.
For people who incur this downfall
There is no accomplishment of mantra.

100. The second downfall is to transgress
Buddha's prohibitions and permissions
Given in accordance with the three vows and their precepts.
Included here is scornful disregard
Of an authentic master's teaching
Given in respect of object and of time.

101. The third is to revile and criticize the vajra kindred,
Those with whom one has received empowerment.
Although this rule is so defined,
Yet every living being is linked with us—
For all have buddha-nature.
Therefore all relations are included, near and far.

102. The fourth is to feel pleased on seeing
But a single cruel and wicked being
Suffer through his actions.
To do this is to cast away the loving mind;
And this, for Bodhisattvas, is a very grievous fault.
What need is there to speak
Of wishing to destroy the happiness of others?

103. The fifth is loss of bodhichitta: the pursuit of others' benefit.
As soon as this is given up, the mind of aspiration is abandoned,
And therefore a defeat occurs complete with all entanglements.
This includes the loss of semen
In other than the seven sanctioned circumstances.

104. The sixth is to find fault with Buddha's teachings
That belong to the three vehicles,
Saying that the Buddha did not teach them;
Also to disparage texts that treat of the activities,
And writings able to bring forth accomplishment,
Failing to consider them as teachings authorized and blessed.

105. The seventh is to speak about the deep instructions
Of the Secret Mantra, of its view and action,
With those who have not yet received
The basic and superior empowerments,
With those of spoiled samaya,
With those improper vessels fearful of deep teachings,
With those who have impediments of time and situation.
Although this downfall is so specified,
Yet even to bestow permissions for the practice
Or transmissions of the texts
To such as these is to betray the secret.
Therefore test the vessel.

106. The eighth is not to recognize
The aggregate of form as Buddha Vairochana,
And likewise for the other four;
And not to know as deities the senses and their objects—
Regarding them with sophistry as truths of suffering,
Despising and tormenting them with sharp austerities.

107. The ninth is to have doubts about, and then reject,
     The natural purity, the sense of emptiness
     (The sphere of Buddhas only),
     Which nonetheless resides in beings as their buddha-nature—
     Regarding it as merely indirect instruction.

108. The tenth is to be patient, complacent, and affectionate
     With those who, for example,
     Denigrate the teacher and the Triple Gem
     And who destroy the teaching—
     Beings suitable for taming through ferocious means.

109. Eleventh is to treat with logical assessment
     The nature that exceeds the reach of names.
     The no-self of phenomena runs counter to the intellect.
     For though the mind may take as highest view
     The voidness of the aggregates and so forth,
     This "unborn nature" is the estimate of common thought.

110. The twelfth is not to give
     To those who are the proper vessels of the Mantra,
     Or those who have three kinds of faith,
     The teachings that they seek.
     It is, with bad intention, to discourage them
     And turn them from their aspiration.

111. The thirteenth is to view samaya substances,
     Which are to be consumed
     According to the way that they appear:
     Spurning some and craving others.
     It is to wander into one of two extremes
     Through failure to embrace the proper conduct of the Mantras.

112. The fourteenth is to view as ordinary
    The Yogini and others who transcend the world,
    The mamos, dakinis, and so forth, guardians of the threshold,
    To consider the five elements to be as they appear,
    And to disparage women, basis of empowerment.

113. Eight infractions complement
    The fourteen downfalls.
    They are not complete defeats
    Whereby the vows are utterly destroyed,
    But strongly hinder the attainment of accomplishment.

114. The first infraction is to take as consort
    Someone who is ordinary,
    Whose mind has not been mellowed
    By empowerment, samayas, and the vows.
    The second is to draw, without the proper practices,
    The nectar from a "wellspring of awareness"
    Lacking in the proper attributes.

115. The third is to reveal to those without empowerment,
    Especially to those who have no faith,
    The images of deities, texts, implements, and mudras.
    The fourth is to engage in argument or idle chatter
    At the ganachakra feast, causing thus disturbance in the practice.

116. The fifth is failure to instruct, though one is able,
    Those who ask for holy Dharma and are ready vessels,
    Returning answers meaningless and false.
    The sixth is to sojourn for more than seven days
    Among the Shravakas who judge and criticize
    The view and practice of the Secret Mantra.

117. The seventh is to say, with arrogant pretense,
That one is holder of the Vajrayana teachings,
While knowing nothing of the tantras and their practices.
The eighth is to instruct in secret teachings
Those who, though empowerment is granted them,
Persist in doubt and have no faith in Mantra.

118. This list, which Nagarjuna made,
Resembles those of Shura and of Lakshminkara.
Other points, however, do the latter mention:
To grant empowerment and to perform
The ritual of consecration and the fire offering
Without correctly finishing the mantra recitation,
Gathering disciples prematurely;
To transgress needlessly the pratimoksha
And the bodhisattva rules by actions
Such as eating after noon save for the ganachakra.
These infractions, it is taught, incur disgrace
And steal away accomplishment.
They should therefore be carefully considered.

119. Master Bhawilha has listed under fourteen heads
The root downfalls shared by all the highest yoga tantras.
They belong to all of them and they are widely known.
Moreover, each of the four tantra classes
Has a corresponding list of the fourteen downfalls.
This is clearly shown in tantras like the *Wheel of Time,*
The *Secret Tantra of the General Rites,*
And the *Enlightenment of Vairochana.*

120. It should be easier for yogis to give up their lives and die
Than not to keep samaya constantly.
Aside from hell or buddhahood,
For those who practice Mantra, there's no other destination.
One should strive therefore, at once, with great remorse
In ways of reparation, if a downfall is incurred.

121. The first downfall is particularly grievous.
If it is committed, one should show devoted homage to the teacher,
Making offerings of all one has.
One should again request empowerment and mend one's vow.
And if the teacher is not living close at hand,
One should take repeatedly the self-empowerment.

122. Likewise, in the absence of the teacher,
Basis of one's shame and dread of censure,
Confession should be made to those practitioners
Who have the mantra vows intact and pure.
Prostrating with a sense of inner discipline,
One should declare one's name and then confess
The fault whereby the Vajrayana discipline was spoiled.
Since concealment will prevent the state of bliss,
There should be no disguising of the fault
And one must state one's purpose of amendment.

123. The one to whom confession is addressed
Asks whether the misdeed has been avowed
And when the answer "Yes" has been returned,
Asks whether the same fault
Will be avoided in the future.
One should reply that, following the Dharma,
One will discipline oneself as carefully
As carrying a burden on one's head.
All this should be enacted thrice, concluding with:
"Indeed this is the way!" and "It is well!"

124. If reparation is delayed,
The downfall's strength increases day by day.
To counter this, one should make regular confession
With all four strengths complete,
With recitation of the hundred syllables,
Repeating a confession prayer
Where all the fourteen downfalls are rehearsed.

125. There are particular samayas that belong
      To the traditions of the *General Scripture, Mayajala,* and the Mind.
      The *General Scripture* groups them
      As samayas of the vajra body, speech, and mind, that should be
          kept,
      Samayas of the actions that should be performed,
      Of things that are attractive, things not to be spurned,
      Of things that should be known,
      And things that should be meditated on.
      Together there are twenty-eight samayas that should be observed.

126. The *Mayajala* specifies five root samayas
      Together with ten branches.
      In the root samayas it is said that one should not reject
      The vajra master but show reverence to him;
      Neither should one cut the stream of mudra and of mantra.
      One must cherish those engaged upon the perfect path
      And keep from speaking secret things to others.

127. The branch samayas have been grouped in two divisions.
      The first concerns the nonrejection of the five defilements.
      When their nature's understood, defilements are but suchness.
      When seized with skillful means,
      They are like poison eaten by a peacock.
      When known to be primordially the five enlightened families,
      They are transformed into primordial wisdom.

128. The second group concerns the five great nectars,
      Which are to be accepted eagerly—
      Accepted as the play of dharmatā,
      Accepted in the knowledge
      That they have the nature of the five enlightened families,
      Accepted as samaya substance, bringer of attainment,
      Accepted since they draw the dakinis—
      And swift will be accomplishment,
      Accepted since to do so is the conduct of all Buddhas.

129. When all the various aspects are distinguished
     A total of two hundred branch samayas will be reached,
     Which then, according to the way of the all-seeing Rongpa,
     Are again reduced to twenty.

130. The Mind tradition speaks
     Of nonexistence, single [nature],
     Evenness, spontaneous presence.
     Here there are no precepts to observe,
     For there is nothing to transgress.
     The bonds of these samayas bind us
     To the fundamental state of things—
     A vajra free of defect from the very first.
     Indeed, this is the kingly way.

131. Beginners on this path must purify their minds.
     Their faults, if they occur, should therefore be amended,
     Just as when a precious vessel is repaired.
     The *Arrangement of Samayas* says
     That there are root samayas
     Of the teachers's body, speech, and mind.
     Each is then divided into outer, inner, secret,
     Each one of which is subdivided into three.

132. The three of body are to give up
     Killing, sexual impurity, and theft;
     Contempt for parents and one's siblings,
     Contempt for one's own body,
     And contempt for all who practice Dharma.
     One must not step on the teacher's shadow,
     Nor harm his consort and the vajra kin.

133. The three of speech are to refrain
From lying, violent words, divisive speech;
From disrespect for those who teach the Dharma,
For those who contemplate its meaning,
And for those who meditate upon the fundamental nature.
One must not speak offensively
To teacher, consort, or the vajra kin.

134. The three samayas of the mind consist
In giving up the three faults of the mind;
Defective conduct, meditation, view.
It also means to be at all times mindful
Of the teacher, yidam deity, and vajra kin,
Together with the view and meditation.

135. For those who have the mastery of skillful methods
There are five and twenty branch samayas.
These comprise the five acts that should be performed:
Tana, gana, taking what has not been given,
Lies, and worthless chatter.
Knowing when they are allowed and when forbidden,
All such actions one should do.
The five defilements: craving, hatred, and the rest
Should not be spurned but stripped
Of their "autonomous existence."

136. Excrement and urine, mamsa, rakta, dew:
    These are five things to be willingly accepted,
    Free from dualistic thoughts of clean and of unclean.
    The aggregates, the elements and colors,
    The senses and their objects
    Are five things to be known as deities,
    And thus experienced through strength of wisdom.
    Vajra, jewel, lotus, action, tathāgata
    Are the five things to be meditated on
    And integrated through habituation to the view.
    These twenty-five samayas are taught in the *Elucidation of Samaya.*

137. Likewise there are five and twenty modes of conduct
    Belonging to the *Kalachakra.*
    Then there are the vows belonging to the five enlightened families,
    Occurring equally in tantras of both old and new translations:
    Guhyasamaja, Union with the Buddhas, the *Secret Moon,* and so forth.

138. The vow of Buddha yoga corresponds
    To bodhichitta both in aspiration and in action
    And also to the threefold discipline.
    The vow connected with Akshobhya
    Is to have the bell and vajra
    And to uphold both the mudra and the teacher.
    The vow of Ratnasambhava is to give with open hands
    The gifts of Dharma, riches, fearlessness, and love.
    The vow of Amitabha is to uphold and explain
    The teachings of three vehicles.
    Amoghasiddhi's vow is earnestly to undertake
    All kinds of actions, offerings, and praise.

139. Concerning now the special vows
    Of the five families of yoga unsurpassed,
    Those belonging to the vajra family should kill.
    In addition to the ten fields, this denotes
    The "killing" of the winds and thoughts within the central
        channel.
    Those belonging to the jewel family should steal.
    This means to take a consort who is qualified
    As well as to appropriate the wealth of those devoid of merit.
    It also means to capture perfect buddhahood
    Through one's own strength and power.

140. Those belonging to the lotus family
    Should venerate the one with lovely, deerlike, eyes;
    And Lady Emptiness they should indeed enjoy.
    Karmamudra, dharmamudra, samayamudra, mahamudra—
    On these they should rely.
    Those belonging to the action family
    Should speak lies that are illusion-like.
    And those of the wheel family
    Should taste samaya substances
    And pleasures that derive from objects of the senses
    As being mere illusions.
    The branches of these vows,
    Which here are not explained,
    Are pledges like the promise to set free
    All those who are not free, and all the rest.
    They are the same as those expounded
    In the *Bodhisattva Grounds*.

141. For devas and asuras and the hidden people
     You should show no disrespect.
     Neither should you scorn the mudra or the mount,
     The weapons or symbolic implements.
     The first two here are clear in meaning;
     The hidden people are the yakshas;
     The mudra is the perfect body of the yidam;
     And "mount" denotes the teacher's horse or seat.

142. The weapons are the ones held by the deities,
     The implements are handheld attributes.
     It is forbidden to step over shadows
     That the images, the teachers, and the stupas cast.
     The same is true for offerings that are old and stale.
     Foodstuffs modeled as the attributes of deities
     Are not to be consumed. It is forbidden.

143. Practitioners of Mantra who do not distinguish
     Teachings that are indirect from those that are explicit,
     Regarding killing, stealing, and the rest,
     Will fall down into hell.
     In brief, wherever the elusive secret is not understood,
     Such acts should be avoided.
     They should be concealed and not performed.

144. Even those who murder brahmins every day
     Or perpetrate the evil actions of immediate effect
     May take the mantra vows.
     What need is there to say therefore
     That Secret Mantra is supreme in skillful means?

145. Not to know criteria for the downfalls,
     To lack respect toward one's teacher,
     To be by habit careless, to have strong defilements:
     Such are the four origins of downfall.
     Add to these forgetfulness and lack of clear mindfulness:
     These are the six causes for the ruin of samaya.

146. Their antidotes are mindfulness and introspection.
     And with the same care as a doctor
     Taking cataracts from off a blind man's eyes,
     In all six periods throughout the night and day
     One should examine with the greatest care
     What one should do and what one should not do.

147. When samaya has been damaged,
     It can be more easily restored
     Than misdemeanors in the lower vehicles.
     According to the rules for Shravakas,
     A fault may be repaired as much as seven times,
     Provided that there's no intention to conceal.
     If there is concealment, faults cannot be mended even once:
     It is as when an earthen pot is smashed.

148. To harm the bodhisattva vow
     Is like damaging a precious vessel—
     One must take support of someone else:
     The vow is mended with a master's help.
     But damaging the vow of Secret Mantra
     Is like making dents upon a precious vessel.
     One can with one's own strength repair the fault.

149. If one offends the teacher and the vajra kindred,
     One should make amends at once by pleasing them.
     If one spoils the speech samaya, one should meditate
     On Vajradharma and recite a hundred thousand times
     His mantra of a hundred syllables.
     If one spoils the mind samaya,
     One should rest one-pointedly in meditation,
     Keeping silence for three years:
     Such is the method of repair.

150. If any of the six parts of the day elapse
     Without a remedy applied,
     One speaks of downfalls that exceed the temporal limit.
     For faults left for a day, a month, a year, or for two years,
     One speaks respectively of a transgression,
     A deterioration, a breach of limit, and a tearing.
     They can all be mended,
     Although, turn by turn, they grow in gravity.
     But after three years, none can be redressed.

151. Transgression, if committed, is restored by ganachakra.
     If there is deterioration, it can be repaired by offerings.
     If a breach of limit has occurred, it is redressed by gifts
     Of child and spouse and wealth.
     And if there is a tearing, it can be amended with one's life.
     All is stipulated in the *Vajra Sun Array.*

152. One should furthermore receive repeatedly
     The four empowerments,
     And perform the self-empowerment.
     One should implement the generation and perfection stages,
     Mantra recitation, and the discipline of non-emission,
     The yoga of the essence-drop, and fire oblation,
     The gift of torma, separating mantra,
     Mudra, and lustration,
     Consuming downfalls with the tummo fire.

153. One should confess one's faults in the assembly
    Or in the presence of a blessed support.
    One should save the lives of animals and read the scriptures.
    One should recite the hundred syllables,
    Make offerings of mandala and prayers in seven branches,
    Build stupas, and so forth.
    Endless are the means to purify samaya.
    Especially with the *Confession That Churns Up the Depths of Hell*
    There is nothing that is left uncleansed.
    With all the practices performed conceptually
    To feel remorse is of the highest moment.

154. The consequence of failure to confess
    Is, in this life, the withering of all good fortune
    And then a fall into the vajra hell unparalleled.
    But those who maintain pure samaya
    Will gain in sixteen lifetimes or, more swiftly,
    In this life, at death, or in the bardo state,
    The eight achievements, ten outer and interior powers,
    And the eight qualities of mastery.
    They achieve the levels of the four Vidyādharas.
    Supreme accomplishment they gain:
    The seven qualities of union,
    And reach the buddhafields of the five kayas,
    Spontaneously accomplishing the twofold aim.

CHAPTER 11

The Ground of the Great Perfection

1. In the second turning of the Dharma wheel,
    The Conqueror explained three doors of perfect liberation.
    The essence of this teaching is awareness that is self-cognizing,
    Which, celebrated as the Great Perfection,
    Naturally resides in beings as their buddha-nature.

2. Since all the sublime teachings of the vast and perfect path
    Are solely for the cleansing of the mind,
    The three vows, six perfections, generation and perfection, and the
        rest—
    All are steps that lead us to the path of Great Perfection.

3. This teaches that the things of both samsara and nirvana
    Never wander from the ultimate expanse, becoming something
        else.
    Samsara and nirvana have no real existence.
    Their ground is perfect in three aspects:
    Nature, character, and cognitive potency.

4. Within this ground, pure Buddhas and impure beings,
    The two modes of samsara and nirvana,
    Resemble dreams that never stir from sleep.
    They come from nowhere; nowhere do they go.

5. The way of being of this ground has sometimes been defined
    As primal purity, spontaneous presence, determinate or
        indeterminate.
    Some say that it can change to anything or be defined as anything;
    Some call it manifold variety.

6. The advocates of all these seven views
    Describe the ground exclusively in terms
    Of just one aspect of the nature that is pure primordially.
    They are like seven men who, blind from birth,
    Discuss the contours of an elephant, the color of a swan.

7. But our tradition teaches that within the nature,
    Pure from the beginning, there is of perfect qualities
    A spontaneous presence.
    This nature and this presence
    Are not different or the same.
    Free of every notion of "a thing with properties,"
    The nature is primordially pure. And yet,
    Since luminosity abides unceasingly within its depths
    So too, there is spontaneous presence.

8. Within this single ground,
    They do not contradict, like separate things.
    It is as when the mind is on the verge of sleep
    And later fast asleep.
    The nature of the mind is pure primordially
    And therefore in samsara it has never turned.
    Yet through creative power, spontaneously present,
    A display appears in various forms.

9. Just like a sapphire's inner light
    (A depth of luminosity that does not shine externally
    Except when urged by circumstance),
    The radiance of primal purity
    (Transcending "thing and property")
    Is naturally, spontaneously present.
    As long as there's no breaking of the outer seal,
    It's like a body closed within a vase.

10. By nature it is empty, yet untrammeled is its radiance.
    Wherefore it is the ground whence all appearances arise—
    Though from this ground they never part.
    This pure, accomplished mind does not shine forth
    As things that are on one side or another.

11. It is not "Buddha" and it is not "sentient being."
    It is neither one nor various,
    And does not dwell in the extremes nor in the middle.
    It is neither empty void nor entity.
    It is the unconditioned undividedness
    Of the three aspects.

12. Thence the radiance, the essence of five winds,
    Which have the nature of awareness, is projected outward.
    The seal upon the vase that holds
    The ever-youthful inner luminosity is pierced.
    The ground's appearance manifests
    While never stirring from the ground.

13. Then the radiance of awareness of cognitive potency
    Arises as cognition that examines all appearing things.
    In relation to awareness,
    This has the guise of ignorance.
    So when from limpid primal purity
    That's like a cloudless sky,
    Spontaneous presence stirs, arising in eight ways,
    This is the threshold where samsara and nirvana meet.

14. The tantras of the Atiyoga, peak of all the vehicles,
    And all the pith instructions are the keys to this,
    Which, in this land of snowcapped peaks,
    Has been explained alone by him
    Who is resplendent with a thousand Rays of Stainless Light.

15. At the very instant that Samantabhadra,
     The primordial Buddha,
     Sees the appearance of the ground,
     He knows it as his self-experience,
     Wherefore it does not spread into delusion
     And is higher than the neutral ground.
     The wisdom that thus brings the ground to ripe fruition
     In one instant perfectly discerns its diverse qualities.
     As soon as it discerns them,
     Wisdom comes to ripeness as the kaya.
     Not depending on extraneous factors,
     It remains within its natural place.
     And as the sovereign of a vast array of kayas and of wisdoms,
     Samantabhadra, in that very instant,
     Comes to manifest awakening.

16. Not parting from the ultimate expanse of dharmakaya,
     Unfolding through the portals of spontaneous presence,
     The qualities of freedom manifest as the sambhogakaya,
     Through whose creative power
     Appears the array of "Aeon of Great Brahma."

17. There then appears the pure nirmanakaya of luminous character;
     And according to the varying perceptions
     Of beings manifesting through samsara's impure gate,
     Teachers show their boundless actions, emptying samsara.

18. The recognition of the stainless nature gathers virtue,
     Through perfect mastery of which, great Teachers
     Show forth fields and actions equal to the dharmadhatu.
     Such is the experience and display of buddhahood!

19. Because they have no apprehension of a subject and an object,
They have no thought of one who guides,
Of one who might be guided.
They're like the supreme jewel and mighty tree of miracles:
Their cognitive power appears to others without effort.

20. This the beings of the three worlds do not understand.
Although there's no delusion in the primal ground,
There is no recognition of the nature of the ground's appearance.
This adventitious circumstance
Is ignorance that's one in nature with awareness.

21. As this ignorance increases, there arises coemergent ignorance
And then conceptual ignorance:
All names and meanings and the thought of self.
From these three kinds of ignorance evolve
The four conditions of delusion.

22. The causal condition is the ground itself
Abiding like a dwelling place.
When thoughts arise therein, this is the dominant condition.
Thence arise the object and the subject, the objective condition.
And these three coinciding form the immediately preceding
    condition.

23. Through this confluence, delusion strengthens gradually.
Defilements grow and these give rise
To all the worlds and beings of samsara.
And like a chariot wheel,
The twelve links of dependent coarising turn.

24. Six kinds of beings, four ways to be born—
    All are but illusions, appearing yet unreal.
    From the very moment of appearing
    They are but empty forms without intrinsic being.
    At first, the six investigating intellects arise
    And then six consciousnesses.
    The fetter of the thought that clings to self is very strong.
    It even binds the space-like nature of the mind,
    Which lacks intrinsic being.
    To cling to the existence of a self
    Is like being tricked by whirling firebrands.

25. One being's light, in this world, is another's dark,
    The ambrosia of one, another's fire and water.
    Such contradictory perceptions
    Follow the propensities of beings,
    And in them there is nothing definite.

26. Despite the fact that this is so,
    The *appearing object* is not mind.
    The image of one's countenance is in the mirror,
    But this is simply through dependent coarising:
    Countenance and mirror do not blend together.

27. Phenomena appear, though they are nonexistent;
    The deluded mind fixates on them as this or that.
    When a colored rope is seen, the first initial instant
    Of the consciousness that apprehends it as a snake
    Is called the *apprehended thing.*
    Evaluation follows after and is called the *apprehender.*

28.   If the real snake that appears
      Is said to be the apprehended thing,
      While the apprehender is the mind that apprehends it thus,
      One fails to differentiate perception
      From the appearing object of perception.
      The existence then of beings is made conterminous with what
         appears.

29.   Through ignorance and through duality, arising adventitiously,
      "I" and "mine" occur, the rulers of existence.
      Both are quite unreal. And if one cuts the root of this delusion
      All that has arisen from the "all-creating king"
      Will sink back into it.

CHAPTER 12

The Extraordinary Path of Practice of the Great Perfection

1. The supreme path that leads to union beyond all learning
    Consists of all the six transcendent qualities,
    The power of which depends upon transcendent wisdom.
    This path will never be the cause of something else.

2. Emptiness, the secret of all perfect Buddhas,
    Is the nature, void of every attribute
    And free of all extremes. Not even in the middle is it found.
    This absence of intrinsic being is established as the Great
      Perfection.

3. Pursuing their investigation
    Through their inferential reasoning,
    Philosophers spin out their arguments.
    They are totally at variance with the ultimate.
    Awareness that is self-cognizing
    Lies beyond the reach of words.

4. The primal wisdom of the Conquerors transcends
    The arguments of thinkers who assert existence,
    As well as thoughts of common folk of lower understanding.
    It is primordial freedom and the path of Great Perfection.

5. It is not bound by objects that appear, for it is empty.
    Yet it has a core of natural luminosity.
    It is awareness that with qualities, the wisdoms and the kayas,
    Is conjoined, like sun and sunlight, never to be parted.

6. According to the levels of the mind,
    There are three ways to classify the Great Perfection.
    The mind class speaks of a display
    Arising as creative power.
    The space class speaks of the arrayed adornments
    Of awareness that is self-experiencing.
    The pith instructions say that things have no existence
    Yet appear as empty forms.

7. And these three classes all agree
    That there is nothing to be freed.
    And thus there is no freeing of the pure, accomplished mind.
    The radiance of its natural luminosity has neither ground nor
        root;
    It manifests within the ultimate expanse.

8. It is "primordially subsiding," not contrived or caused,
    "Self-subsiding," for it does not hang upon conditions,
    "Nakedly subsiding," for it is without a basis,
    "Subsiding of extremes," because it cannot be described as one or
        many,
    "Subsiding into one," for it is featureless.

9. Awareness that transcends discursive mind
    Is the Natural Great Perfection's special theme.
    Those who realize it find freedom
    In awareness that arises from the ground.
    Beings who have no such realization
    Circle in that very state.

10. If through examples one distinguishes
    Awareness and discursive mind,
    They are like water and like bubbling foam.
    Now when there are no thoughts,
    Awareness and the mind may seem the same.
    And yet, without intrinsic being,
    Awareness is all-penetrating clarity,
    Whereas the mind is dull,
    Like water in a stagnant pond.

11. Awareness is compared to the new moon
    Whose light is withdrawn deep within.
    The mind is like the full moon with its all-engulfing glow.
    Awareness has the quality of limpid clarity without an object;
    The mind's distinctive feature is a total merging with its object.

12. Awareness is indwelling wisdom.
    It does not depend on methods to engender concentration,
    Yet it is devoid of torpor and disturbance.
    The concentrated mind is fully focused on its object,
    Linked in manner of supported and support.

13. Awareness manifests in objects of the senses,
    Yet, like mercury that falls upon the ground,
    It is not overwhelmed by such appearance.
    But mind is mingled with the source and the sustainer of existence:
    Dualistic, subject-object, thought.

14. Awareness does not push the mind aside;
    Yet with awareness, mind does not keep company.
    For objects and defilements, of one substance with the mind,
    Escape and flee awareness: it's as though they warned each other!
    And when they're gone, one leaves the prison of defilement.
    Such is the special teaching of the pith instruction class.

15. The Shravakas and the Pratyekabuddhas
    Both reject defilements;
    Bodhisattvas tame them with the help of antidotes;
    The general Mantra uses them upon the path.
    In the mind class, they're set free
    Within their true condition.
    In the space class, they are cleansed
    Within the single ultimate reality.
    But in the expanse of awareness—and this is a great wonder—
    They collapse all by themselves.

16. Furthermore, although within the ultimate expanse
    The dharmakaya and the universal ground are one,
    The dharmakaya is compared to a great ocean,
    Whereas that by which it is obscured,
    The consciousness belonging to the universal ground,
    Is like a boatman drifting to samsara or nirvana.

17. From the ground itself come freedom and delusion.
    Their respective characters resemble wakefulness and sleep.
    Delusion is like deep sleep, when the senses are withdrawn;
    Freedom is like waking up from this.

18. The spontaneous presence of the ground
    That, from the first, is indeterminate,
    Is one in substance with the stainless primal purity
    Of the "place of final freedom."
    Yet it is important to distinguish
    That which can, from that which cannot, be
    The ground of subsequent delusion.

19. Likewise primal purity,
    The place of freedom of the ultimate expanse,
    And primal purity,
    Awareness that's experienced on the path,
    Are equal. Neither is confined
    And neither falls into extremes.
    And yet the place of freedom is completely cleansed
    Of wind-mind with its tendencies;
    It is primordially pure of both samsara and nirvana.
    But on the path, the wind-mind is impure
    For it accompanies the senses
    And is thus impaired and burdened
    By the stains of mind and mental factors.
    Only sometimes can one stay in primal purity.

20. In the same way, the illusory body of the deity—
    The radiance of awareness in the bardo state of ultimate reality—
    And the illusory body of the deity on which one meditates
        conceptually
    Are equivalent in being both the body of the deity.
    And yet they're different.
    In the first case, when a deity arises in a buddhafield,
    Freedom comes through recognizing it for what it is.
    In the second case, there's no such freedom.

21. In particular, those with pure samaya,
    Who are engaged upon this path,
    Will soon see the sambhogakaya
    Endowed with marks of buddhahood,
    Perceptible to those on the ten grounds.
    And quickly they attain nirmanakaya fields of luminous character.

22. This consequently is the supreme vajra path.
     Primal pure awareness, free primordially,
     Is empty, free of all intrinsic being;
     It lies beyond the reach of thought and word,
     Transcending every attribute the mind can formulate.
     Awareness, which transcends expectancy,
     Possesses every perfect quality.
     Awareness, furthermore, is not an object to be known,
     It is devoid of everything perceived as "I" and "mine."

23. In its regard, there is no meditation, nothing to be meditated.
     When you settle in the natural state without contrivance,
     You see awareness in its nakedness.
     And since awareness does not change,
     Ignorance and clinging cannot lead you to samsara.

24. Outer objects and fixation on the self
     Are not the work of a creator God.
     They are the fruit of ingrained mental patterns.
     Everything is born from groundlessness and rootlessness.
     And in the moment of its rising, it subsides in unborn nature.

25. Than this you need no other realization.
     To read, to memorize, to meditate and think about the texts:
     All such devices of the mind collapse.
     And this is buddhahood itself, beyond expectancy.

26. More especially, through thögal, highest of all practices,
    One plainly sees the radiance of awareness,
    Thus the chance of erring is but very slight.
    The outer elements, the earth and stones, the hills and rocks—
    Impure material things—subside;
    These elements are cleansed,
    Refined into the great clear light of primal wisdom.
    Thögal is the path on which this is made manifest.
    Trekchö makes the inner elements dissolve,
    They break down into particles, but into light are not refined.
    By contrast, thögal makes the elements transform into
    The vajra body of great transformation,
    Which brings benefit to beings till samsara has been emptied.

27. Thus the thögal teaching is more eminent
    Than all the doctrines on the grounds and paths,
    On conduct and results,
    That other Buddhist schools propose
    Through mind's investigation.
    Its special features are set forth in pith instructions.

28. And yet, until the adventitious factor: apprehension of the "I"
    Subsides in the pure space of dharmadhatu,
    Beings are taken in by it.
    This ordinary way of thoughts and things
    Is lord and ruler of existence.

29. And since beginners in the practice are defiled by it,
    There are two ways whereby they are instructed
    In both calm abiding and deep insight:
    As having the same nature or as different.
    In the first case, concentration is the aspect of quiescence,
    Wisdom that of clarity.
    Calm abiding and deep insight are united—they're not two.
    And thus one rests within a nature free from all extremes.

30. The second case has two approaches:
    Calm abiding and deep insight
    Come from wisdom or from pith instructions.
    When they come from wisdom,
    They are in agreement with the letter of the texts:
    Calm abiding is one-pointed concentration
    On the meaning that is learned,
    While genuine deep insight
    Is the realization of this meaning.

31. When they derive from pith instructions,
    They follow more the spirit of the teachings:
    Calm abiding is the mind devoid of movement,
    Deep insight is the recognition of its nature.

32. Briefly, for the best practitioners,
    Unwholesome thoughts are settled in the dharmakaya.
    Good thoughts, bad thoughts—both are on a level.
    Therefore there's no need for antidotes.
    Those of medium capacity, who stay within the view,
    Become accustomed to the path of limpid union
    Of calm abiding and deep insight.
    Thoughts, both good and bad, subside and melt into the ultimate
        expanse.

33. Those of least capacity at first seek only calm abiding,
    And, having gained stability in concentration,
    They cultivate deep insight, all-discerning wisdom.
    And then by gradual degrees—just as in a land of gold
    No common stones are found—
    Whatever main minds, thoughts, or mental factors manifest,
    They do so as the ground's great openness,
    In which phenomena and mind are never separate.

34. This then is the supreme skillful means:
    Whatever thoughts arise,
    Do not stop them or invite them.
    Do not follow after them.
    If you do not waver from the natural state,
    All qualities of the refined sense powers are gained:
    Divine eye and the other visual powers,
    Preternatural cognition and the rest.

35. If thoughts remain connected with their objects,
    You are still an ordinary being.
    But though in limpid mirrorlike consciousness
    Objects of perception brightly and unceasingly appear,
    Like stars and planets shining on the sea,
    If mind is not attached to them,
    The link that joins the apprehended object
    To the apprehending mind is severed.
    There and then, the ground of unsurpassed primordial wisdom,
    Thought-free, self-cognizing, is attained.

36. In short, the path of ultimate expanse
    Consists in the one nature of all things.
    The path of awareness is extraordinary wisdom.
    The path of luminosity is that of the two lamps.
    The path of trekchö is the simultaneous
    Arising and subsiding of one's thoughts.
    The path of thögal is awareness and the ultimate expanse.

37. I pray you, therefore, understand
    These five uncommon paths
    Belonging to the Natural Great Perfection.

Our companion ignorance and treacherous delusion
Have bound us until now with chains of karma and defilement
In the dreadful wasteland of samsara without end.
Cultivate thereto a weariness of heart!
Rely upon this supreme path, by means of which
We pass beyond all pain into the citadel of supreme peace.

CHAPTER 13

The Ultimate Result, the Kayas and Wisdoms

1. Now that the features of the ground and path
   Have been correctly comprehended,
   The ultimate result will come:
   The kayas and primordial wisdoms.
   These have but a single source:
   The cleansing of the sullied universal ground
   And the sinking back into the dharmadhatu
   Of the mind and mental factors.

2. When from the ground there stirs the ground's appearance,
   The tendency to grasp at "self" gives rise
   To the eight kinds of consciousness
   That grasp at knowledge objects, bringing forth samsara.
   They are like the clouds, and when they're cleared away,
   The sun of primal wisdom—now divested of such veils—
   Shines, by its very nature, bright and clear.

3. Adventitious veils together with their tendencies are shed.
   This is supreme enlightenment endowed with twofold purity,
   Primordial buddhahood, expanse beyond all expectation.
   The light that at the full moon outwardly shines forth
   Is present at the new moon but withdrawn into its depths.
   So too, the dharmatā, unchanging and completely free of thought,
   Is the unchanging vajrakaya, permanent expanse.

4. This peaceful space contains the highest of all attributes.
   Therein the strengths and ocean-like enlightened qualities
   Are all perfected and complete.
   In their appearance they are all distinct.
   Assessed in terms of realization and elimination,
   This space is the abhisambodhikaya.

5. As the mind's pursuit of knowledge objects ceases,
   So too, deluded grasping at a knowing mind is shed.
   Awareness, self-cognizing, does not fall into extremes
   Of permanence or of annihilation.
   Subtle primal wisdom is absorbed within but not obscured;
   It is unceasing knowledge, basis of the kayas and the wisdoms.
   This is seen by those who rest in perfect equipoise
   And it is called the peaceful dharmakaya.

6. Only self-cognizing wisdom knows the buddha-nature.
   Neither one nor many,
   It is neither an existent nor a nonexistent thing.
   It is like space; it is beyond all thought.
   It has no stain—all manifesting radiance is stilled.
   It is beyond the reach of words, belonging to the highest truth.
   No concepts, reasons, metaphors, or arguments depict it,
   For of mind, analogy, and thought, it is the very contrary.
   Not even mighty beings on the tenth ground can encompass it.

7. Only to the Buddhas is it manifest:
   The fair interior of the mansion of the vase,
   Profound and peaceful, ever youthful.
   The Buddhas of the three times always dwell therein,
   And yet, as to their aspect, do not see each other.
   For in the space beyond conceptual construction,
   They constitute a single vast expanse of wisdom.

8. From within the natural radiance of unobstructed knowledge,
   Cognitive power shines out as the sambhogakaya
   Endowed with the five certainties
   Of place, time, Teacher, teaching, company.
   The sambhogakaya and its fields possess
   The major and the minor marks of buddhahood
   Together with an ocean of enlightened qualities.

9. Its place is Akanishtha, perfect and spontaneous.
    It is a Dense Array where lights and rays
    Of the five primal wisdoms blaze with sparkling beams
    That arch and leap like rainbows through the vault of heaven.
    Upon a ground, all soft and yielding to the tread,
    Stand palaces that, measureless and fair,
    Have four doors graced with eight adorning cornices,
    And walls contrived of five primordial wisdoms.
    Each has ledges, pendent strings of jewels,
    A covered terrace and a balustrade,
    And an encircling plinth where Fair-Eyed
    And the goddesses of sensuous pleasure
    Dance their joyful steps
    And send forth offering clouds of empty bliss.
    Each palace is adorned with tail-fans, banners, parasols,
    Jewel-topped flags of victory, awnings, tassels,
    And a shrine equipped with banners.
    Each extends beyond all measure,
    And wheresoever one may turn one's eyes
    Vast palaces, exceeding computation, fill the whole of space.

10. In each of these vast palaces a throne is set
    For the Buddha of each of the five families.
    It is upheld accordingly by lions, elephants,
    Horses, peacocks, shang shang birds.
    Upon each throne are lotuses and disks of sun and moon,
    And here, within Samantabhadra's time
    (For in the ground, the three times are exhausted),
    The five Teachers are enthroned, beyond all change and alteration,
    Exhibiting the marks of buddhahood:
    Vairochana, Vajra Akshobhya, and Ratnasambhava,
    Amitabha and Amoghasiddhi,
    Each united with the consort of his family,
    Endowed with all the seven qualities of union.

11.   Not different from them are their retinues
      Of Bodhisattvas, male and female,
      And the four doorkeepers with their consorts.
      The wheel of Dharma of the Natural Great Perfection turns,
      Transcending common sounds and words.

12.   The upper peaceful palace,
      Where dwells the essence of enlightenment,
      Is ruled by two and forty peaceful deities.
      Of these, Samantabhadra and Samantabhadri,
      Joined in sublime union, provide the ground
      For emanation of the other deities.
      They are all-pervading, thus the dharmakaya,
      Appearing in the six realms as the sages of awareness
      That labor for the benefit of beings.
      Therefore in the buddhafield of the sambhogakaya's
         self-experience,
      There are thirty-four Victorious Ones:
      Ten principal with twenty-four as retinue.
      These deities are symbols of the intrinsic purity
      Of aggregates, of elements, and of sense-fields.
      This is the great mandala of the three seats complete.
      It resembles in its purity all the mandalas
      Residing in the body, as expounded in the highest tantras:
      The *Illusory Net*, the *Union*, and the rest.

13.   The lower palace is the mandala
      Of the *Gathering of the Great Assembly*.
      Measureless, it is ablaze with light and made of nine concentric
         walls.

The four doors of the ninth court outermost
Are marked with cornices
That indicate both karmic cause and fruit.
In the central precinct of the palace,
Upon a rock composed of vajras, and a thousand-petaled lotus,
Are disks of sun and moon,
The signs of skillful means and wisdom.
On these are four and twenty powerful spirits, male and female.
They are arranged in pairs
And on them stand the eight chief animals:
Ferocious tiger, fearful lion, cruel leopard, savage bear,
The mighty elephant, majestic buffalo,
The grasping crocodile, and hateful snake.
They seize and trample down these haughty male and female
   spirits.

14. Above them is the glorious embodiment of samsara and nirvana,
The lord, the supreme Mahottara,
Shining like a sapphire, brilliant like a million suns.
He has one and twenty faces and eight legs;
His two and forty hands uphold
The two and forty peaceful deities.

15. His sublime consort is the Sky-Faced Queen,
Nine-headed, eighteen-armed.
In her main hands she holds a vajra and a blood-filled skull.
Her other hands support the mamos of the sacred lands and places
And the goddesses with heads of animals.
The father and the mother may be one above the other,
Or else they may be joined in union.
All things without exception in samsara and nirvana
Are naturally and perfectly contained
Within this supreme Buddha,
From the throne beneath his feet until the wheel that crowns his
   head.

16. There also is the Heruka of Supreme Power
    With nine resplendent herukas.
    At the four corners of the central platform
    And on the four steps, Gauri stands
    Together with the others of her kind:
    The symbols of the purity of the eight consciousnesses.
    Eight animal-headed goddesses are found
    Within the first court of the mandala.
    In the second are the eight who draw up from the lower states.
    The third is filled with eight and twenty powerful goddesses.
    Each courtyard has its own four door-keepers.
    All is but a blazing, powerful display,
    Resplendent with the nine demeanors of the wrathful deities.
    All this constitutes the mandala
    Of the exclusive self-experience of the sambhogakaya:
    The spontaneously present appearance of the ground,
    The ultimate and actual Akanishtha.

17. In the fourth court are the two and thirty dakinis.
    In the fifth are seven mamos and four sisters,
    In the sixth are gings, six classes, three in each.
    In the seventh are the sixty wrathful male and female deities,
    Two hundred and forty emissaries are in the eighth court
    And in the ninth are sixty mamos.
    All these are apparitions that subdue misleading forces.
    Since they are perceived by these obstructing spirits,
    They do not constitute the mandala of Akanishtha,
    The sambhogakaya's exclusive self-experience.

18. The outward-glowing radiance of the dharmakaya wisdom
    Is home to the sambhogakaya graced with five perfections.
    This is a display encompassed by the Buddha's mind alone,
    From which all obscuration is removed,
    Wherefore the deities and retinues enjoy an equal rank
    Without distinction, high or low.
    The minds of all of them transcend discursiveness,

Their speech is indescribable, their bodies perfect
With the great and lesser marks of buddhahood.
With their pure eyes of primal wisdom,
Which beholds all things as its own self-experience,
They see each other constantly and without hindrance.

19. This sphere of the Victorious Ones, past, present, and to come,
Is unsurpassed, pertaining therefore neither to samsara nor to
     peace.
Thus even great, pure beings cannot see it,
Since they have not, as yet, removed the veils
That counter the primordial wisdom of the Conquerors.
In great Akanishtha that transcends the triple time
(Past, present, and to come),
The Buddhas dwell in the fourth time.
They and all their retinues have but a single nature:
As their own self-experience, they experience each other.

20. From this very sphere and for the sake of beings to be guided,
There emerge three kinds of Teacher who will be their guides:
The nirmanakaya with a character of luminosity,
The nirmanakaya guide of beings, and
The diversified nirmanakaya.
The first is the reflected image
Of the display of the expanse of Akanishtha,
The appearing aspect of the primal wisdom of the Conquerors.
The great and lesser marks of the sambhogakaya
Are as if transferred, reflected in a crystal mirror,
Therefore it is half sambhogakaya, half nirmanakaya.

21. Akanishtha in the center, Abhirati in the east,
Shrimat in the south, and Padmakuta in the west,
Sukarmasiddhi in the north: these are the five fields
Where dwell the five supernal Teachers,
King of Form and all the rest.

They are endowed with all the major and the minor marks,
Together with an ocean of enlightened qualities,
And infinite appearing modes of peaceful and of wrathful deities.

22. Each of the five aspects of primordial wisdom
Is joined by four attendant wisdoms—twenty-five in all.
The primal wisdom of the dharmadhatu is unshakable.
It resembles space, transcends all knowledge objects.
Mirrorlike wisdom is devoid of dualistic concepts:
Apprehended-apprehender.
Devoid of all exertion, it constitutes the ground of the arising
[Of the three wisdoms that come after].
The primal wisdom of equality subsists in the expanse of peace,
Where things lack all defining features,
Where there is no parting of samsara from nirvana.
All-perceiving primal wisdom knows,
At all times and without impediment,
The nature of phenomena
And knowledge objects in their multiplicity.
All-accomplishing primordial wisdom
Altruistically strives for others' good.
Its actions, free from grasping and impediment,
Are spontaneously achieved.

23. The retinues that number only tenth-ground Bodhisattvas
Are instructed through the lights projected from the Teacher's
    form.
And just as stains upon one's face are shown within a glass,
They see what separates the Teacher from themselves:
The obscurations, deep and hard to sound, that veil
    enlightenment.
And, cleansing them, they go to the eleventh ground of Universal
    Light.

24. As for the perfection of the time,
    As long as the great, powerful beings residing on the ten grounds
    Do not have the wisdom of their Teachers,
    Lords of all the world,
    In the expanse of emptiness, the wheel of inexhaustible adornment
    Of enlightened body, speech, and mind,
    These Teachers, having crushed the demon lord of death,
    Remain forever for the weal and profit of the world.

25. The ignorance of beings to be trained
    And all the other of the five defilements
    Are transmuted into the five primal wisdoms—
    A change effected by the greatest antidotes for each:
    The corresponding buddhafields and their enlightened Teachers,
    Who give five kinds of sublime teaching.
    This occurs in sequence from the path of seeing
    Till completion, at the end of the tenth ground,
    When the heart of perfect buddhahood is reached.

26. These buddhafields are only manifest
    To Bodhisattvas who reside on the ten grounds.
    They are not within the range of other beings.
    And though the Teachers are themselves sambhogakayas,
    Their retinues and so forth are not their self-experience only,
    For they are perceived by others.
    Therefore, as is stated in the *Great Conjunction of the Sun and Moon,*
    They are referred to as sambogakayas that are half apparent
    Or nirmanakaya fields of luminous character.

27. Especially, in the Natural Great Perfection,
    Those who have received empowerment
    From a master who has seen
    The supreme nature in the sacred mandala
    Of primal wisdom's self-experience,
    Who train by day with unimpaired samaya
    In the manifest luminosity of the self-experience of awareness,

And who, by night, train in the radiant clarity of the heart—
Although they may not reach the final realization,
Yet, by the truth of ultimate nature
And through the master's blessing,
They equal, in their karmic fortune,
Those upon the grounds of realization.
They go to the nirmanakaya buddhafields
That lie in all the ten directions,
The appearance of the ground, spontaneously present.

28.   In particular, there are five fields bestowing freedom and release.
Therein are palaces contrived successively, beginning in the east,
Of crystal, gold, red ruby, emerald.
They are lit by ox-eyed oval windows.
Their porticoes have ornamental cornices.
At each of the four corners is a stupa made of pearl,
Festooned with chains of bells, both large and small,
Which, moving in the wind, chime out sweet sounds
That tell of the three doors of liberation,
While, in the four directions,
Four banners float on clouds of incense.

29.   Around the palaces are lakes of water
Perfect with eight qualities.
Upon their banks are palms adorned with loops and chains of
    gems.
There the shang shang birds display themselves
With peacocks and katari birds,
With parrots that can speak with human tongues,
And youthful swans, and hoopoes, grouse,
Warblers, cuckoos, kangkaris,
Celestial birds with bell-like voices.
Kritipas there are with golden vajra-forms
And flocks of birds of many colors—
Turquoise, coral, sapphire, conch—
Their throats' sweet lyres sing melody on every side.

30. The Bodhisattvas dwelling in these fields
    Are safe from illness for they bathe in rivers
    That dispel the harms of the defilements.
    A thought suffices for fulfillment of their every wish;
    Their pleasures equal the enjoyments of the gods
    Residing in the Heaven of the Thirty-Three.
    All around there is a fence contrived
    Of jewels of seven kinds surmounted by a ledge.
    Within these sublime fields, the Teachers of four families
    Proclaim the Dharma constantly
    In all four periods of day and night.

31. In the central place, suspended in the air,
    There is the pure field of the glorious heruka,
    The mighty charnel ground, the Mount of Flaming Fire.
    There, surrounded by a cloud of emanated dakas and dakinis,
    Vajrapani and the rest,
    The enlightened Teacher, Youthful Hero,
    The Conqueror, transcendent and accomplished,
    Turns the wheel of Dharma unsurpassed of the resultant vehicle.

32. There are countless Bodhisattvas born from lotuses,
    Accomplished sages in the form of youthful gods and goddesses.
    Devoid of all discursive thought
    And free of the three aspects of the ordinary mind,
    They are free of six defilements and six kinds of intellect,
    Free of ignorance and of its four conditions
    And all that is concomitant with them.

33. These buddhafields are manifested as the character of luminosity
    Through the empowering strength
    Of the enlightened Teacher, Vajradhara.
    Therefore to the Bodhisattvas they are known
    As the nirmanakaya buddhafields of luminous character.

They appear upon the secret path of the Natural Great
    Perfection—
As the *Tantra of Awareness Self-Arisen* has explained.

34.   Then there are the pure fields known
    As the celestial pure lands of great bliss,
    And also the pure lands upon the earth,
    Where dwell the wisdom dakinis
    Who are the mistresses of actual luminosity
    And those who are inhabitants by birth
    Of all the four and twenty sacred lands and all the rest:
    The assemblies of the dakas and the dakinis.
    They have the fortune of Vidyādharas
    And in their ranks they train
    In the remaining portion of their path.
    In the presence of their vajra teachers, holders of awareness,
    They implement the view and powerful practices of Mantra.
    These lands appear exclusively to those who have
    The seeds of virtue and a pure perception—
    Those who have perfected the deep practice
    Of the generation and perfection stages,
    And who have gained accomplishment of Secret Mantra.
    Do not think that these are ordinary domains
    That all might visit if they wish.

35.   Rays of light pour forth from clouds of syllables
    Of the sambhogakaya appearing from the state of suchness.
    There radiate and manifest supreme nirmanakayas,
    Who teach and tame the worlds.
    With different names they manifest
    Concordant with the way that beings in the six existences perceive.
    They are the Munis, guides, the "sages of awareness."

36.   In number equal to the endless worlds
    Of every universe, three-thousandfold,
    In all the ten directions,

Their emanated forms bring benefit
To beings in ways beyond imagining,
By guiding them in the four ways.

37. Through the great merit of the enlightened body,
Whose actions are the twelve great deeds, are beings guided.
The actions of enlightened speech
Consist of three or else a single vehicle
Expounded as a remedy for the defilements
According to the various aptitudes of beings.
Four and eighty thousand doors of teaching may be counted.
They seem to be expounded yet are not composed
Of common sounds and words—
Appearing in the worlds of beings
Through power of blessing and in harmony with aptitude of
    mind.

38. The nirmanakayas guide with their enlightened mind.
In their knowledge they see everything,
Past, present, and to come.
And yet they do not think in terms of the three times:
Theirs is the primordial state: Samantabhadra's time,
Which has the nature of a timeless time.
They have six types of supranormal knowledge
Such as knowledge of the minds of others,
Knowledge of wonders, clairvoyance, and clairaudience.
Their actions thus are ever timely.

39. They are the guides of beings through their enlightened deeds:
At all times through their bodies and their fields,
At all times through their minds,
At all times through their countenances,
At all times through the thought-transcending secret of their
    speech.
Their enlightened body, speech, and mind

Bring direct benefit to beings,
While their enlightened action constantly
Brings benefit direct and indirect.

40. These supreme embodiments,
Which thus are emanated from the ultimate expanse,
Set free the minds of beings to be guided
Through their two primordial wisdoms:
The wisdom that, related to the nature of phenomena,
Knows the nature as it is of everything,
And the wisdom that, related to phenomena themselves,
Knows all things in their multiplicity.
Perfect peace they thus reveal with unique and uncommon
     teachings.

41. Their secondary emanations are beyond enumeration.
They manifest in every state and kind within the six migrations.
They show themselves among the gods to guide them
In the form of Brahma, Indra, Vishnu, and the rest,
In human realms, they come in guise
Of Shravakas, Pratyekabuddhas,
Bodhisattvas, and as Chakravartin kings.
Among asuras, they appear as Vemachitra,
As the Woodpecker among the birds,
And as the lordly lion, Dridhasamadana, for the other beasts.

42. They come, in brief, in any form appropriate
To act as guides for beings, even in the hells and preta-realms.
Their labors never fail through indolence.
Within the spheres of the six worlds these emanations manifest,
In places that, through actions and propensities, both good and
     bad,
Appear as upper states of happiness and lower states of pain.

43. There the teachers show themselves,
    According to the beings' varying perceptions,
    And labor for their sake.
    Their teachings also change to suit the character
    Of those who might be trained,
    According to whose destiny
    The time for teaching also varies.
    So it is that they appear
    For sake of beings in the impure fields.

44. To one who sees the Buddha in a dream,
    A dreamlike Dharma is revealed,
    But neither has reality, neither real existence.
    Hollow, empty, and devoid of self—
    Like this they should be known, as the deep sutras say.
    Samsara and nirvana thus are but the play of dreams,
    And though the Buddhas who appear therein
    Are by their nature pure,
    They manifest according to the beings to be trained,
    And through compassion they appear
    For those who are impure.
    As long as there's samsara,
    They will manifest without reprieve.

45. Then there are diversified nirmanakayas,
    Things contrived or else occurring naturally.
    Sculptures, paintings, temples, mansions, groves,
    Cities in the wilderness that wondrously appear,
    Lotuses and trees of miracles, wish-fulfilling gems;
    Ferries, bridges, carriages, food, clothing, and the rest—
    All that may appear in form inanimate.

46.	There are also animate or "born" nirmanakayas:
	A great fish in a time of dearth;
	And the kind creature that appeared
	For those tormented by disease;
	The wise horse Balaha for those
	Lost in the land of demonesses;
	A golden bee above a filthy swamp.
	All such forms of the diversified nirmanakaya
	Bring happiness to beings
	And do so without striving or intention.
	Glorious they are in all the benefits they bring.

47.	When the time for guiding beings is passed,
	The marks and features of the guides themselves
	Sink back into the ultimate expanse.
	It is as when there are no further water vessels,
	The form of the reflected moon melts back into the moon,
	The ground of its appearance.
	So too, nirmanakayas perceived by beings to be guided
	Sink back again into the space
	Of the sambhogakaya's exclusive self-experience.

48.	As the moon reduces on its waning course
	Until it is occluded on the night of the new moon,
	Each shining phase is not absorbed into the one that follows it.
	Instead, the outer glowing radiance sinks back into the inner space
	From which no radiance emerges.
	Thus it is that the sambhogakaya's exclusive self-experience
	Is gathered back into the great primordial wisdom of the
		dharmakaya.
	Madhyamikas proclaim this as "supreme cessation"
	In which all movements of the mind
	Sink back into the dharmadhatu.

49. Here, it is regarded as the self-cognizing primal wisdom.
This subtle, primal wisdom is the dharmadhatu, inner luminosity,
Absorbed within but not obscured:
The ever-youthful body closed within a vase.
Wherever and whenever there are beings to be trained,
There unfolds from this ground
Primordial wisdom of unceasing potency.
This ultimate reality, in perfect evenness,
Is the result, the state of great spontaneous presence.

Colophon
If I had not completely scrutinized the vessel of my mind,
And saw the face of Drimé Özer, guardian of the world,
And had I not received the sustenance of his compassion,
I would have fallen down the precipice of a false path
And rendered vain this life endowed with freedom.

These teachings, thus, which here are well explained,
Were generated through my teacher's blessing,
And wisdom that proceeds from meditation—
Not through simple cogitation, fruit of study and reflection.
If what they say has contradicted
Views expressed in other tenet systems,
I confess and ask forgiveness.

The meaning of the Dharma,
Like the ocean, deep and hard to fathom,
Is the sphere exclusively of mind that rests in meditative evenness.
It is the domain of primal wisdom that cognizes
Both the nature and the multiplicity of things.
Since this I have correctly seen,
This text will never lead astray.

May I and every living being,
Through this virtue, clear away
The clogging darkness of the twofold veil
That hides the unmistaken path, the teaching of the Conqueror.
And taking ship, may we now sail away
And journey to the isle of precious jewels,
The peace of our enlightenment.

In forest glades, in wholesome vales,
Where creatures of the wild run free,
Where trees put on new raiment as the seasons pass
And make no sound that jars upon the sages dwelling there,
The heart is eased by calls of flocking birds.
The chariot of their peaceful cries draws on the mind
To weary sadness with samsara—
Samsara that is like a coiling vine of deadly snakes—
And to the wish and the decision to depart from it.

May we obtain the glorious state wherein the senses are at peace.
And with a view unshaken by the winds of thought,
With deeds that follow in the footsteps
Of the Buddha's holy heirs,
May we never be a weight upon our fellow beings,
But be their glory through the strength of our activities.

The *Treasury of Precious Qualities* called *The Rain of Joy* was written in glorious Pema Öling, at the request of Chöje Drakpuk-pa of Latö, by the Dzogchen yogi Rangjung Dorje Khyentse Özer, who touched with the crown of his head the dust of the feet of Padmasambhava, the second Buddha.

The Quintessence of the Three Paths

by Longchen Yeshe Dorje, Kangyur Rinpoche

BOOK TWO

Kangyur Rinpoche

THE EXTRAORDINARY PATH
OF BEINGS OF GREAT SCOPE

*The Hidden Teaching of the Path
Expounded in the Vajrayana,
the Vehicle of the Secret Mantra*

and

The Short Path of the Natural Great Perfection

CHAPTER 10

The Teachings of the Vidyādharas

1. The transmission lineages of the Vajrayana

This exposition begins with a brief account of the Vajrayana transmission lineages. With reference to these, it is said in the *Conjunction of the Sun and Moon Tantra*:

> A failure to explain their history
> Will cause the fault of losing faith
> In teachings that are greatly secret and definitive.

And the *Garland of the Teachings of the Aural Lineage* states:

> Outsiders may with evil words
> Disparage the great teachings
> Given by the Buddhas when they came into the world.
> So first describe the Dharma's history.

The three yogas (Maha, Anu, and Ati) of the inner tantras of the old translation school were passed on, generally speaking, in four streams of transmission. The three transmissions of the long lineage of orally transmitted teachings (*kahma*) are taken together and form the first stream. This is followed by the three streams of transmission of the treasure teachings (*terma*): the sixfold, sevenfold, and ninefold lineages.

The three transmissions of kahma[1]

The kahma embodies three kinds of transmission:

1. the mind transmission of the Buddhas,[2]
2. the transmission through symbols of the Vidyādharas,[3] and
3. the hearing transmission of spiritual masters.[4]

The six transmissions of terma[5]

The first three of these transmissions are the same as the three transmissions of kahma. They are followed by:

4. the transmission entrusted to the dakinis,[6]
5. the transmission by empowering prayers,[7] and
6. the transmission by means of script on yellow scrolls.[8]

The seven transmissions of terma

This set of transmissions is the same as the preceding one, except for the transmission by means of script on yellow scrolls, which is replaced by:

6. the transmission by prophetic injunction,[9] and
7. the transmission through the blessings of the practice.[10]

The nine transmissions of terma

These comprise the previous seven, followed by:

8. the hearing transmission of direct quintessential instruction,[11] and
9. the transmission in the form of rubrical instructions for the performance of activities and rituals.[12]

Every class of tantra has its own detailed history, and the above is merely a summary of the different kinds of tantric transmission, all of which have been passed down to our own teachers. The author of the present treatise was the Vidyādhara Jigme Lingpa. He was in truth the Noble Avalokiteshvara appearing in the guise of a spiritual teacher. He received the gift of wisdom of Padmasambhava, Vimalamitra, the all-knowing Longchen Rabjam, and other masters. Their minds mingled inseparably. And by means of the symbols and signs displayed by these great beings, Jigme Lingpa obtained all the teachings, prophecies, ritual instructions, and authorizations. He received, in other words, the transmission through symbols given by the Vidyādharas. All the mind-treasures manifested with a vivid clarity in his mind. Indeed, he received the three kinds of transmission (by mind, by symbol, and by hearing) perfectly and completely in a single instant.[13] Becoming a truly perfect Buddha, he turned the wheel of the teachings in their entirety for fortunate beings. It was as the saying goes:

> Although in body he may be a person (man or god),
> In wisdom he is a truly perfect Buddha.

The Vidyādhara Jigme Lingpa transmitted this excellent treatise of pith instructions orally to Jigme Trinlé Özer,[14] who then transmitted it to Gyalsé Shenphen Thayé,[15] who in turn gave it to Orgyen Jigme Chökyi Wangpo.[16] The latter passed it on to the supremely compassionate Orgyen Tendzin Norbu,[17] who gave it to Yönten Gyamtso.[18] The great khenpo Samten Gyamtso received it from the three aforementioned masters and granted it to Chandra Rasmi, otherwise known as Khenpo Dawö.[19] And from him I (Longchen Yeshe Dorje) received it in its entirety.[20]

1. The main subject of the text
2. The difference between the vehicles of sutra and of mantra

Generally speaking, the Buddha set forth inconceivable systems of teaching[21] for the benefit of beings: the so-called Dharma vehicles, which were attuned to the capacity and orientation of his hearers. All may be condensed into two: the Hinayana and the Mahayana. The Mahayana has in turn two aspects, as specified in the *Proofs of the Mahayana:*

> The Mahayana has two aspects:
> The transcendent virtues and the secret mantras.

The reason for this is that Bodhisattvas, followers of the Mahayana, are of two kinds: those with sharp faculties and those with extremely sharp faculties. Both are equal in having compassion as their motive for practicing in order to attain buddhahood. Their manner of practice is, however, different. In the expository, causal vehicle of the paramitas, the sugatagarbha or buddha-nature is considered to be present in the minds of beings only as a seed. When this is fully developed through circumstantial conditions—in other words, the two accumulations (of merit and wisdom)—buddhahood is attained. And since the cause comes first and its result after, one speaks in this case of a *causal vehicle.*

By contrast, the Mantrayana, the vehicle of mantra, proclaims that all beings are by nature endowed with the sugatagarbha, wherein all enlightened qualities are spontaneously present.[22] The buddha-nature is the ground or basis of purification (*sbyang gzhi*). It is compared with the sun; and like the sun concealed by clouds, the sugatagarbha is veiled by compounded or conditioned states of mind, which are adventitious to it. These are the eight kinds of consciousness, including the alaya, the universal ground. These mental states constitute samsara and are the objects to be purified (*sbyang bya*). The cleansing of these adventitious mental states is effected by empowerment and by meditation on the generation and perfection stages, which thus constitute the agents of purification (*sbyong byed*). Finally, the result of such purification (*sbyangs 'bras*) is described as the full actualization of the enlightened qualities of the mind's nature.

Etymologically, the term "Mantrayana" may be explained as follows. In Sanskrit, "mantra" is a conflation of the elements "manas," which means "mind," and "traya," which means "to protect." In other words, mantra is a protection for the mind.[23] This mind is also described as awareness (*rig pa*), or, speaking in terms of the result, as self-cognizing primordial wisdom (*rig pa'i ye shes*). As it is said in the *Guhyagarbha-tantra* (*the Tantra of the Secret Essence*): "The Bhagavan Creator is the vajra mind, Samantabhadra." And if one were to ask from what it is that mantra protects us, the answer is that it protects from the eight kinds of consciousness, which are marred by the duality of subject and object. And as for the kind of protection that mantra affords, it is a protection that is swift and easy.

The Mantrayana is also described as the *resultant vehicle*. This is because the result itself (buddhahood) is said to dwell in the ground or fundamental nature of the mind. When one settles with certainty in this ground, one discovers an ocean-like infinity of qualities (the kayas and wisdoms) perfect and complete within the mind's nature (the sugatagarbha), of which it is the spontaneous display.[24] When the Mantrayana is practiced, because the meditation is attuned to the kayas and wisdoms, it is the result itself that is taken as the path.[25] And when this result is actualized—here and now in this present body and life—this constitutes the ultimate and highest result of all. For the power of the essential instructions of different paths is distilled in the resultant vehicle, just as the virtues of all medicines are concentrated into the single universal panacea.

Moreover, the vehicle of Secret Mantra principally sets forth the dharmatā itself, referred to as the ultimate and actual vajra. This ultimate reality, the sugatagarbha, of which the vajra is a symbol, is introduced by the teacher. And it is indeed like a vajra in that it irresistibly subdues all dualistic thoughts, while at the same time remaining invulnerable to them. This is why the Secret Mantra is also referred to as Vajrayana, the vajra vehicle.

This vehicle is also called the *vehicle of skillful means,* and this description is used for five reasons. First, the skillful methods with which it is endowed are many, for every practice (generosity, for instance) may be implemented using numerous techniques.[26] Second, the methods used are skillful because they take the five defilements as the path. Third, the methods are easy because they do not require the rejection of the objects of the five senses, which are themselves used as the path. Fourth, the methods are considered profound because only beings equipped with favorable karma and extremely sharp faculties are able to assimilate them. Fifth, the methods are swift because, by using them, the result may be gained within the space of a single life.

Those who never separate from awareness, the ultimate reality of all things (the sugatagarbha), to which they have been introduced by their teachers, are called Vidyādharas, holders of awareness. It is they who are the practitioners of the Secret Mantra. The collection of scriptures on which their practice is based is called the pitaka, or basket, of the

Vidyādharas, and is so called because it is the receptacle of all the different words and meanings of the teachings.

For all these reasons, the resultant vehicle surpasses the expository causal vehicle. As the *Lamp of the Three Modes* declares:

The goal may be the same, and yet by understanding,[27]
Ease, and manifold techniques
To be employed by those of sharp ability,
This Mantrayana is by far superior.

Accordingly, although these two vehicles are the same in that they both result in the attainment of buddhahood, they are different in the understanding or lack of understanding present in the methods for attaining it.[28]

Outwardly, in the expository causal vehicle, one meditates on phenomena as being like illusion and so forth, and this is in order to overthrow one's clinging to their true existence. This however implies a failure to understand the nature of the elements. Inwardly, since there is no notion that the aggregates are the five Buddhas, there is a failure to understand their nature. Secretly, since there is no notion that thoughts and defilements are actually primordial wisdom, there is a failure to understand that they are part of the path. And since there is no notion of the great purity and equality of all phenomena, wherein the two truths are indivisibly united,[29] there is a failure to understand the view that is to be realized.

According to the Mantrayana teachings, which are geared to beings of extremely sharp faculties, the elements, appearing outwardly, are the five female Buddhas; the aggregates, appearing inwardly, are the five male Buddhas; and all thoughts, appearing secretly, are the male and female Bodhisattvas, and have the nature of the five wisdoms. Having established the purity and equality of everything as the great dharmakaya,[30] the practitioners of this path meditate and behave according to the skillful methods explained earlier, free from the dualistic apprehension of phenomena as things to be adopted or rejected. They are therefore quick to achieve the result.

The Sanskrit word "tantra" means "continuum," "continuity," or ² "stream." It may be explained as the continuum [of the ultimate nature] that remains without interruption from the condition of sentient being until the attainment of buddhahood.

The *Subsequent Tantra* says:

"Tantra" is explained as the unbroken stream.
The result lies in the cause and means.[31]

Tantra therefore means an unbroken stream or continuum. It is the continuum of the ground, path, and result: the "ground or cause tantra," which is to be realized; the "tantra of the path or skillful means," whereby one progresses toward the realization of this ground; and the "result tantra," which is the fruit ultimately attained.

The ground tantra or continuum

The ground tantra is the nature of the mind, the sugatagarbha, the fundamental nature, actual primordial wisdom, awareness, bodhichitta, the indivisibility of the two superior truths, the nature that is not within the scope of the ordinary mind. It is beyond bondage and liberation, and it is present primordially in all sentient beings. As the *Guhyagarbhatantra* declares:

Beyond both freedom and enslavement is this buddha-nature.
It is present, it is perfect, from the very first.

The *Extensive Mayajala (Net of Illusory Manifestations)* also adds:

All have bodhichitta, awareness self-cognizing;
This is said on scriptural authority.

The nature of the mind is called the "ground or cause tantra" because, when this nature is not recognized through skillful means, it appears as samsara; and when it is recognized, it appears as nirvana. It is, as it were, the basic source or cause of both these manifestations, and this is the reason for its name. It is said in the *Three Stages:*

Since all phenomena belonging to these two denominations
Arise from it, it is called the ground.

And the unvanquished Maitreya has declared:

As it was before, so later it will be.
It is reality, the ultimate, unchanging.

Simply by way of designation, the ground may be categorized in two ways. On the one hand, the nature of the mind, the sugatagarbha, is the jewellike ground of purification. It is called the ground of the ultimate nature, the fundamental way of being. On the other hand, when it is misperceived,[32] the ground together with its objects is something to be purified like a muddy swamp. Being without true existence, and manifesting adventitiously, it is false and is the so-called ground of imputed reality.[33] It is an empty appearance and is not therefore the genuine cause tantra that carries within itself the result of buddhahood.

The path tantra or continuum

The path tantra consists of the methods whereby all adventitious obscurations, which veil the ground, are removed. These methods are: the view, which is the full recognition of the fundamental nature; the meditation, which focuses on this perfect recognition of the nature of phenomena;[34] and the conduct,[35] which is the support and helper of the view and meditation.

The *Guhyagarbha-tantra* says:

This nature, wonderful and magical,
Is not from elsewhere, comes from nowhere else.
In the state of wisdom it is manifest,
Dependent upon skillful means.

Since this tantra is the cooperative circumstance whereby the result tantra (the goal to be achieved) is actualized, it is called the tantra of skillful means. And since it is the support on the basis of which one moves toward one's destination, it is called the path tantra. As it is said, for instance in the *Compendium of the Scripture's Secret Meaning*, "It is a traveling endowed with attributes."[36] Whereas the extraordinary path of the highest yogas is the tantra of the short path leading to the result, the path of the outer tantras is comparatively long.[37]

The path is known as a tantra or continuum, because it is linked to the ground in the same way that a knowing subject is linked to an object known, and because the path is related to the result in the same way that an agent of accomplishment is related to what is accomplished. It is so called also because the path subsists uninterruptedly, from the beginning of the practice until the accomplishment of the result.[38]

The result tantra or continuum

The result tantra is the name given to the full actualization of the ground nature, when the obscuring veils that cover this fundamental way of being have been totally removed through the practice of the path.[39] It is said in the *Exposition of the Specific Aspects of the Mayajala*:

> Even the "actualization" of the spontaneously accomplished
> (result)
> Occasioned through the yoga of accomplishment,[40]
> And the great yoga,[41] is mere imagination.
> For in reality the ground and the result are not two separate things.
> And this is why we speak of "tantra."

The expression "are not two" means that the ground and result are linked together by their single nature.[42] There is no such thing as a result that is distinct from the ground. But why, in that case, does one speak of the "result tantra"? In this expression, the word "result" refers to the perfect accomplishment of the wish of those who seek the supreme, unsurpassed, final result, while "tantra" indicates that this result is already, uninterruptedly, present within oneself.

Thanks to this way of positing the cause, path, and result tantras, the methods of the actual path tantra surpass the expository causal vehicle in many ways.

The path tantra itself may be subdivided into two aspects: the verbal tantra—that is, the tantra expressed in words—and the actual tantra itself, which the verbal tantras serve to indicate. The verbal tantras are grouped in several ways. They may be classified according to whether they teach the practice of minor activities,[43] the methods to attain the eight ordinary accomplishments, or the methods to attain the supreme accomplishment.[44] They may also be classified as root and branch tantras,[45] or as outer and inner tantras. All these classifications may, however, be subsumed under three groups: the tantra appearing verbally in the wisdom mind of the Tathāgatas and the minds of beings; the spoken tantra, actually uttered by a speaker, such as Vajrapani; and the written tantra or scriptures, from the texts transcribed by Matyaupayika[46] to the manuscripts written down in Indian, Tibetan, or other scripts. The actual tantra, which the verbal tantras indicate, may also be divided into numerous categories.[47]

The Mantrayana view, which establishes the quintessential nature, the fundamental way of being of the ground, is far superior to the view of the causal vehicle. Consequently, the Mantrayana practice is also superior. Generally speaking, the practices of the Sutrayana and Mantrayana are similar in being based on the twofold accumulation of merit and wisdom. Indeed, the practice of all Mahayana schools combines both wisdom and skillful means. In the Secret Mantra, however, when accumulating merit, one does not (as in the causal vehicle) train in generosity and the other paramitas with the understanding that relative phenomena, the aggregates and so forth, are impure. Instead, one practices the generation stage, in which one visualizes the primordially pure nature (of the mind and phenomena) in the form of a deity, and implements the six paramitas according to the Mantrayana. For example, generosity is practiced by making offerings to the mandala; discipline is practiced by refraining from the dualistic apprehension of phenomena; and so on. As for the accumulation of wisdom, in the Secret Mantra one does not merely assert—as one does on the sutra level by means of inferential reasoning—the view of the absence of all conceptual constructs. Instead, one practices the perfection stage, and rests in one's immanent primordial wisdom, to which one has been introduced through the teacher's pith instructions.

It is thus that one implements the extraordinary combination of wisdom and method based on the twin stages of generation and perfection.

And, in contrast with the expository causal vehicle, where such skillful means are unknown, there is no need to endure lengthy and difficult austerities, such as the sacrificing of one's head and limbs. Neither is it necessary to spurn samsaric action and its resultant experience. On the contrary, these very factors[48] are employed on the spiritual path. People who are weighed down with powerful obscurations and negativities, who are impervious to the disciplines and basic methods of the lower vehicles, may enter and train in the path of Mantrayana. For the latter is like a sharp blade that can cut through substances resistant to blunter instruments. The approach of the Mantrayana is thus vast; it is a path to be undertaken by those with very sharp faculties. If, thanks to their profound discernment, such people practice the teachings of the Secret Mantra correctly as explained, uniting the view, meditation, and conduct, then, even if they have committed negativities, they will be unstained by them[49] and will attain the ultimate result, the union (of dharmakaya and rupakaya), in no more than a single lifetime. Consequently, training on the path of the Secret Mantra brings swifter progress than on the path of the sutras.

2. The classification of the tantras
3. A general classification of the tantras into four classes

Although the sugatagarbha is possessed by all, the Buddhas' teachings, which are in accordance with the infinitely pervasive dharmadhatu, are attuned to the varying capacities of infinite beings at the time when they are ready to receive them. The Secret Mantra is the teaching of the sambhogakaya.[50] It is expounded from beginningless time by the great Vajradhara, the embodiment of all the Victorious Ones, in the midst of his boundless retinue. It cannot therefore be identified with the same degree of precision as the teachings of the supreme nirmanakaya, which appear for the sake of specific beings.[51] The places in which the sambhogakaya teachings are set forth, the extent to which they are propagated, the period of their duration from their inception (in other words, Vajradhara's awakening) till their end, the methods designed to correct the functioning of the subtle channels and winds, the vehicles that adopt immanent wisdom as the path, or indeed the number of the classes of tantra—none of these may be precisely defined. The *Tantra of the Ornament of the Vajra Essence* says:

> Secret, greatly secret, and extremely secret;
> Yoga and great yoga, and the great subsequent yoga.

And:

> Secret mantra, greatly secret,
> And the extremely secret (crown of all the tantras).[52]

This clearly indicates the different tantra classes of Atiyoga, Anuyoga, and other tantras. Similarly, the *Tantra Requested by Subahu* says:

> For the benefit of gods, asuras, and of human kind,
> Thirty million and five hundred thousand different secret mantras,
> Vidya-mantras—the pitaka of the Vidyādharas—have appeared.
> This the Conqueror has taught.

The tantra teachings appear in different classes. These correspond to the flow of the male and female essence-drops, and to the movement of the winds, in the seventy-two thousand channels of the human body. The tantra classes have naturally appeared in an equal quantity, prompted by the dominant condition, namely, the sugatagarbha present in the mind of every being. As the explanatory tantra, the *Vajra Garland*, says: "It should be understood that twenty-four thousand classes of tantra correspond to the flow of the red essence. Twenty-four thousand classes correspond to the flow of the bodhichitta, and the remaining twenty-four thousand correspond to the movement of the winds." In a similar fashion, the *Five Stages*, a commentary by Nagarjuna, specifies that "There are seventy-two thousand classes of Secret Mantra."

The tantras of the Mantrayana are also organized into four great classes to facilitate our understanding of how defilements and sense objects are to be harnessed on the path; how the various methods of practice are attuned to the mental dispositions of different practitioners; and for the purposes of organization. The *Established Secrets* says:

For disciples who are fortunate
In being ready to be trained,
The four great classes of the Secret Mantra
Are expounded in the world.

The tantras have been taught in consideration of the cosmic ages, the social castes,[53] and the capacities of beings.

The fourfold classification of the tantras according to cosmic age

For the beings living in this universe, there gradually emerged four ways 3 of relating to desire as an object of purification.[54] In the Age Endowed with Perfection—in the course of which, the life span of beings diminished from infinity to one million six hundred thousand years—there were, as yet, no manifest defilements, and beings were endowed with the following four qualities. They had an immeasurable span of life, a luminous physical form, miraculous abilities, and amrita as their sustenance. During that period, of all the defilements, desire manifested only to a very small degree. Since it was very slight, people obtained satisfaction simply by gazing at each other. However, one of the four qualities mentioned above gradually declined. The period in which this occurred is called the Age of Three, and was a time when people experienced satisfaction from smiling at each other. During the Age of Two, a further quality declined, and people satisfied their desire simply by touching each other and holding each other by the hand. Finally, in the present Age of Strife, when all four qualities have declined, people both fight among themselves and have the wish to embrace and copulate. To remedy these four kinds of desire, the four classes of tantra have been set forth. The *Abridged Kalachakra-tantra* (the *Wheel of Time*) says:

For the first age, Endowed with Perfection, there is Kriyatantra.
For the second age, the Age of Three, there is Charyatantra;
For the third age, the Age of Two, there is Yogatantra;
And for the fourth age, the Age of Strife, there is Anuttaratantra.
The four ages of the world are thus considered,
And thus four tantra classes are set forth.

The fourfold classification of the tantras according to social caste

The fourfold classification of the tantras according to caste takes into account the characteristic behavior of the beings in question. The conduct of the brahmin caste is dominated by a preoccupation with cleanliness and ascetic practice.[55] The conduct of the merchant caste maintains a balance between physical, verbal, and mental activities. The kingly caste is characterized by vast aspirations; and, here, mental activity predominates. Finally, the menial caste comprises those who belong to the common or lowest social rank, who have little interest in cleanliness and whose behavior is strongly marked by defilement. The four classes of tantra were expounded for these four classes of human beings. The *Tantra of the Play of Chakrasamvara* says:

> Kriyatantra fits the cleanly ways of brahmins.
> Charyatantra, higher than the former, fits the merchants' life.[56]
> Yogatantra fits the king with many retinues.
> To the ignorant and to no one else[57]
> I taught primordial freedom.
> Now I set it forth for you, my lovely maid!

The fourfold classification of the tantras according to the capacities of beings

The four classes of tantra are taught in a manner that reflects the four capacities of beings. Those of basic ability attach importance to speech and physical action. They are unable to engage in mental activity on a grand scale. Those of medium capacity are capable of extensive mental undertakings, which they consider to be of equal importance with physical and verbal activities. Those of sharp capacity consider mental activity to be preeminent and busy themselves with physical and verbal activities only as auxiliaries to this. Finally, beings of supreme capacity do not consider physical, verbal, or mental activities as truly existent, some to be adopted, others to be rejected. Such beings are able to combine all actions together. The *Vajra Tent Tantra* says:

> Kriyatantra is for those of least capacity;
> Charyatantra is for those with more than this;

Yogatantra is for sublime beings,
And highest yoga for the ones surpassing all.

The teachings of the Secret Mantra are thus set forth in a graded manner according to the beings to be trained. In the case of Kriyatantra, as a means of harnessing desire and attachment on the path, practitioners depict, and meditate upon, the deity[58] as described in the *Tantra of the Empowerment of Vajrapani:* "In the center, draw the Bhagavan Avalokiteshvara and, on his right, the white-robed lady contemplating him." The *Vajra Ushnisha Tantra* also says:

Of the different deities in the mandala,
The Lord looks on the Lady,
The Lady looks upon the Lord.
Thus are they depicted.

On the level of conduct, practitioners of Kriyatantra earnestly engage in all kinds of purificatory ablutions, and adopt a lifestyle marked by ritual cleanliness. They eat the three white foods, they change their clothes three times a day, and so on. Even though meditation associated with the mind is not absent, Kriya practitioners concentrate on physical and verbal activities.

In the case of Charyatantra, and in order to use desire as an element on the path, practitioners depict and meditate upon the deities as described in the *Tantra of the Enlightenment of Vairochana:*

Depict the great king Vairochana
With slightly smiling lips.
Upon his right, the goddess sits,
Who is renowned as Buddhalochana.
With slightly smiling lips she looks at him.

As far as conduct is concerned, physical, verbal, and mental activities are held in balance. Since Charyatantra practitioners are capable of extensive mental activity and meditation, physical and verbal activities do not occupy a preeminent position for them.

In the case of Yogatantra, as a means to harnessing desire on the path, practitioners depict and meditate upon the deities as the *Tantra of the Glorious and Supreme Primordial Buddha* describes:

> The deities of the mandala are touching slightly.

And:

> To one side there sits Dorje Che,
> Brandishing an arrow.
> He is embraced by Nyema's hand
> In which she holds a monster-headed banner.

It is thus that the deities embrace. As far as conduct is concerned, practitioners regard physical and verbal activities as no more than auxiliaries,[59] whereas meditation is earnestly pursued as their main activity. This meditation consists of a conceptual deity-yoga and a nonconceptual meditation on the ultimate truth.

In the case of Anuttara or highest tantra, as a means to harnessing desire on the path, practitioners visualize the deities (who represent skillful means and wisdom) in union. It is specified in the *Guhyasamaja* that the two sex organs are joined and that all things should be considered in the same way [as the union of skillful means and wisdom, of appearance and emptiness]. And the *Guhyagarbha* says: "Holding different attributes, they are joined with wrathful consorts." As far as conduct is concerned, practitioners are oblivious to the notions of clean and unclean; they neither indulge in defilements, nor do they suppress them. In meditation they are able to rest in a state in which all phenomena are equal, in which there is neither acceptance nor rejection, and in which skillful means and wisdom are united.

The tantras, furthermore, are categorized in four classes in order to accommodate beings who mistakenly adhere to the four Hindu gods, and also to help those who keep to the four Buddhist tenets (of the causal vehicle). Nevertheless, the ultimate view of the sutras and the tantras is identical. The Buddhas, compassionate and skilled in means, for whom every being can be a disciple, may teach beings in different ways according to their individual aspirations. There is therefore no contradiction here. The four Hindu gods are Brahma, Vishnu, Indra, and Ishvara.[60] Brahma is ignorant and propounds cleanliness and purity of life as a spiritual path.[61] Vishnu is wrathful, and aggression is his path.[62] Indra is proud, and his path consists in self-satisfaction deriving from rank and possessions.[63] Ishvara (Mahadeva) is lustful and propounds desire as a spiritual path.[64]

3. An explanation of the three classes of the outer tantras
4. A general exposition

Within the four tantra classes of the Secret Mantra, the first three (Kriya, Charya, and Yoga) are called the outer Secret Mantra, because they are, for the most part, similar to the causal vehicle openly expounded by the Buddha, who appeared in the form of a renunciate, in that they call for a discipline of outer purity of life and abstention from negativity. These tantras are also called the vehicle of knowledge through ascetic practices (*dka' thub rig byed kyi theg pa*) or the vehicle of tantric ascesis (*thub pa rgyud kyi theg pa*).

Although, from the point of view of both skillful means and wisdom, the three outer tantras are superior to the expository causal vehicle, it is nevertheless true that all the practices of the Mahayana, both sutra and tantra, are alike in constituting a path that unites compassion and emptiness, and safeguards the practitioner from being stained by defilement and negativity. This being so, it is necessary to purify one's mind with the vows and methods of the common vehicle, creating a foundation through love, compassion, and bodhichitta. If, on the other hand, one enters the path of Mantra without due care, not only will the extraordinary qualities of the higher path fail to manifest, but one will be brought to ruin.

As we have explained, the outer tantras utilize as the path the kind of desire that is satisfied simply by looking, smiling, or holding hands—quite unlike the physical union characteristic of the Age of Strife. The deities are depicted and meditated upon accordingly and are never considered to be in union. The practitioners of these tantras consume the three white foods and they dress in cotton clothes that are clean and new. They never partake of the five meats,[65] or drink the five nectars,[66] and never make use of human skins and bone ornaments.

4. An exposition dealing specifically with the three classes of the outer tantras
5. The difference between the Kriyatantra and the Charyatantra

5　In general, mantras may be divided into vidya-mantras, dharani-mantras, and secret mantras. These categories refer respectively to skillful means, wisdom, and their nondual union.[67] The *Accomplishment of Wisdom Tantra* says:

> The mantra, you should understand,
> Is subdivided into three.
> The vidya-mantras are, by nature, skillful means;
> Dharani-mantras are, by nature, wisdom;
> Secret mantras are the nondual primal wisdom.

In both Kriyatantra and Charyatantra, the male bodhisattvas are skillful means arising in the form of deities, and the female bodhisattvas are wisdom in the form of deities.[68] Wisdom related to primordial wisdom arises in the form of vidya-mantra deities, while wisdom related to invincible memory arises in the form of dharani-mantra deities. As for the method of practice, when one engages in Kriyatantra, one considers the wisdom deity (jnanasattva) as the lord, and oneself as the servant; but when practicing the Charyatantra, one considers that the wisdom deity and oneself (visualized as a meditational deity or samayasattva) are of equal status without any difference in rank. In Charyatantra, the deity and the practitioner are like siblings or friends.

5. The Kriyatantra or action tantra

6　In the commentary on the *Tantra Requested by Subahu*, the path of Kriyatantra[69] is condensed into four "doors of practice." The first of these is the introductory practice (*'jug pa'i spyod pa*) or empowerment, which renders the practitioner an appropriate vessel. The second is the practice of application (*sbyor ba'i spyod pa*) or approach phase of the meditation on the deities of the three families.[70] The third is the actual practice (*sgrub pa'i spyod pa*), which consists in gathering all the required materials and substances, and the assiduous recitation of the mantra. Finally, the fourth is the practice of proficiency (*grub pa'i spyod pa*), which is the accomplishment of the level of a Vidyādhara enjoying celestial fields,[71] and the achievement, ultimately, of the final result [of buddhahood], whereby the practitioner becomes the equal of the deity.

The first of these four doors of practice, the introduction or empowerment, will be explained in due course.

The second door of practice, that of application, consists, as we have seen, in the approach phase of the meditation upon the deities of the three families. In the Kriyatantra, it is taught that practitioners regard the deities as lords, and themselves as servants. They do not visualize themselves as deities but remain in their ordinary form, considering themselves to be of lower rank. This practice is referred to as elementary or ordinary Kriyatantra.[72] However, there are some Kriyatantras (referred to as special Kriyatantras) in which practitioners do visualize themselves as deities.[73] Chiefly, however, the procedure is to visualize the deity in front of oneself and to request accomplishment.

[In the case of the special Kriyatantras just mentioned,] self-visualization as a deity involves four principles (*de kho na nyid bzhi*), the first two of which belong to the second door of practice.

The first principle is the principle of one's own nature (*bdag gi de kho na nyid*). This means that one must remain in the view proper to Kriyatantra.[74] The "pure deity of dharmatā" is the ultimate nature of one's own mind. It is empty, luminous primordial wisdom, beyond the four conceptual extremes of existence and nonexistence, appearance and emptiness. It is said that for practitioners who directly and fully assimilate this view, and meditate on relative phenomena as being the deity, all dependently arising things will, at the moment of the practitioners' final enlightenment, be "purified into the deity." For phenomena are all, by their very nature, empty. And this practice is like the alchemical process that transmutes base metal into gold.

The second principle is the principle of the deity (*lha'i de kho na nyid*),[75] in reference to which, Buddhaguhya[76] said: "There are six deities: emptiness, letter, sound, form, mudra, and symbol."[77]

One then proceeds to visualize in front of oneself a palace surrounded by a buddhafield, into which the wisdom deity, once invited, enters and is requested to remain. Visualizing oneself in the form of the deity, one should nevertheless consider oneself as a servant and make offerings, praise, and confession to the wisdom deity, regarded as one's superior.

The third door of practice is the practice itself and is associated with the third and fourth of the four principles.

The third principle is that of recitation (*bzlas brjod kyi de kho na nyid*). The *Later Meditation Tantra* says: "Focus on sound, mind, and ground." "Ground" refers both to oneself (visualized as the deity) and the deity visualized in front. "Mind" refers to the visualization of the moon disk in the hearts of these visualized deities. "Sound" refers to the visualization of the garland of the spontaneously resounding mantra on the moon disk, and to its correct recitation.

The fourth principle is that of meditative absorption (*bsam gtan gyi de kho na nyid*). The *Later Meditation Tantra* says:

> Remember that the secret mantras dwelling in the fire
> Bestow accomplishment.
> Dwelling in the sound, they grant meditative equipoise.
> When the sound has vanished, they grant liberation.

"Dwelling in the fire" refers to concentration on the garland of mantra (positioned on the moon disk in the midst of blazing fire) in the heart of oneself visualized as the deity. One performs this meditation while holding the vase breath, and it is on this basis that the four activities are accomplished. The expression "dwelling in the sound" refers to concentration on the syllables of the mantra, which resound spontaneously with bell-like clarity. "Meditative equipoise" is the basis for the cultivation of shamatha or calm abiding. The words "When the sound has vanished, they grant liberation" refer to the gradual diminution in volume of the mantra until its final disappearance, at which point the practitioner rests in a nonreferential state. This causes extraordinary vipashyana, or profound insight, to take birth in the mind.

This is how the meditation is performed inwardly. Outwardly—and this is the principal aspect—one must perform various kinds of purification[78] and keep oneself in a state of cleanliness.[79] In all this, one regards the deity visualized in front as one's superior, and considers oneself to be on a lower level.[80]

The fourth door of practice, that of proficiency, refers to the common attainment of the state of a Vidyādhara enjoying celestial fields. It is said that a Vidyādhara of this kind, who practices the six paramitas of the Mantrayana, will attain the ultimate result: the supreme accomplishment wherein his or her body, speech, and mind become the body, speech, and mind of the deity. The level of vajra holder of the three families will be thereby actualized. The *Heruka Galpo Tantra* says:

> In seven lifetimes, buddhahood is reached.
> And as lord of one of the three families,
> One brings benefit to beings.

5. The Charyatantra or conduct tantra

The Charyatantra (conduct tantra)[81] or Ubhayatantra (the bipartite tantra) is so called because it involves conduct in which the skillful means of purification and cleanliness, as explained in the Kriyatantra, as well as the inner view and meditation of the Yogatantra, are practiced in equal proportion. The *Tantra of Awareness Self-Arisen* says:

> Since Ubhaya is practiced
> With both the view of Yoga
> And the conduct of the Kriya,
> It is called the tantra of both [kinds].[82]

To begin with, one visualizes oneself as the meditational deity (samayasattva) and blesses the visualization with both mantra and mudra. One visualizes the deity in front of oneself, and then invokes the wisdom deity (jnanasattva), requesting it to remain therein. One holds the vase breath, and with one-pointed concentration visualizes in the heart of the wisdom deity the mantra garland on a moon disk. Concentration will thus stabilize. Since the view of the inseparability of the two truths has been refined (more so than on the level of Kriyatantra), the meditational deity and the wisdom deity are regarded as friends or relatives, without distinctions of rank, high or low. It is thus that one gains the accomplishments.

The common siddhis result from conceptual and nonconceptual concentration[83] and so on. In the best case, it is asserted that after five lifetimes or, at the latest, within one or three kalpas, the level of vajra holder of the four families[84] can be actualized.

5. The Yogatantra

8 When one practices the deity-yoga and meditates on the mandala according to Yogatantra,[85] the palace and courtyards, up to and including the outer protection circles, are said to resemble to a large extent the buddhafield called Dense Array together with its palace, which are perceptible only to the sambhogakaya. There are, however, many distinctive features, such as the seat of the deity (a wheel and so forth), the center of the palace in the form of a dome, and the special pinnacle and ornaments. Also, as was explained above, the deities are not in union. To begin with, one must visualize the deities and concentrate on them. Then, one must train oneself in thought-free wisdom of the perfection stage. In this way, one meditates on the yoga of skillful means and the yoga of wisdom in succession and separately. It is said in the *Stages of the Path*:[86]

> Because there is no grasp of spontaneous equality,
> Wherein all things are pure primordial wisdom,
> One meditates successively on skillful means and wisdom.
> Generation and perfection thus are separate.

9 A Yogatantra practitioner endowed with bodhichitta and free from doubt and hesitation,[87] chiefly practices the inner yoga or meditation; all physical and verbal activities, purification, cleanliness, and so forth are shown to be auxiliaries to this.

The yoga of skillful means is practiced with the help of the five factors of awakening (*mngon byang*)[88] and the four powers of manifestation (*cho 'phrul*). In the three lower tantras, generally speaking, one meditates on the five factors of awakening according to the aspects of nirvana.[89] The *Heruka Galpo Tantra* describes the five factors of awakening as:

> Meditation on the thought-free state, the moon, the vajra,
> Which, radiating lights and reabsorbing them, transforms into the
>   deity.[90]

The *Heruka Galpo Tantra* also mentions the four powers of manifestation, specifying them as:

> Concentration, blessing, empowerment, and offering.[91]

Practitioners visualize themselves in the form of the deity. They invoke the wisdom deity from the ultimate expanse and, in the confidence that they and the deity are equal, they dissolve the wisdom deity into themselves inseparably, just like pouring water into water. They seal their body, speech, mind, and activities with the four seals or mudras (respectively, the body of the deity, or mahamudra; the speech of the deity, or dharmamudra; the mind of the deity, or samayamudra; and the emanation and reabsorption of lights, or karmamudra). Thus they are fused—bound indivisibly—with the deity's body, speech, mind, and activities. In the state wherein the meditational deity and the wisdom deity are of a single taste, practitioners endeavor in the recitation of the mantra and gain the two kinds of accomplishment. Practicing in this way, and at the conclusion of the recitation, they receive blessings (or accomplishments), and then request the deity to depart. The stages of generation[92] and of perfection[93] are practiced successively.

The practice results in the attainment of the common accomplishment, namely, the level of a Vidyādhara enjoying celestial fields, and, after three lifetimes, in the attainment of the supreme accomplishment, which is the level of vajra holder of the five families (the four families previously mentioned, together with the karma or activity family). By means of the five factors of awakening, five wisdoms are actualized, and enlightenment occurs in the buddhafield of Dense Array. The *Heruka Galpo Tantra* says:

> In three lives, those who practice Yogatantra
> Are said to gain their freedom in the field of Dense Array,
> Achieving thus their wish.

3. An explanation of the inner tantras
4. A general explanation

10 The inner tantras are superior to the outer tantras in view, meditation, and conduct. Indeed, they are called Anuttara (unsurpassed or highest) because there are no tantras above them. They are, moreover, referred to as "inner Secret Mantra" because in them, skillful means and wisdom—that is, the generation and perfection stages—are practiced inseparably. However, even though these inner tantras set forth a path in which the generation and perfection stages are not separate, they are nevertheless classified according to their emphasis. Some tantras mainly set forth the generation stage. Here the deities are generally male and are profusely arrayed in silken garments, jeweled ornaments, and so on. Some tantras expound the complete perfection stage (whether focused or not focused on characteristics). Here the deities are generally female and they are naked but for the bone ornaments, human skins, ashes, and so forth, with which they are arrayed. Finally, some tantras mainly propound the union of skillful means and wisdom, in other words, the primordial wisdom of luminosity. For this reason, the inner tantras are nominally classified respectively as father tantras, mother tantras, and nondual tantras, although the criteria given above are not the only ones by which the father and mother tantras are differentiated.

The tantras in which the principal male deity in the mandala, but not his consort, may change position, are the father tantras of skillful means. The tantras in which the principal female deity, but not her consort, may change position, are the mother tantras of wisdom. The reason for this kind of change is that if meditators consider as their main deity the deity of the family indicated by the position in the mandala on which their flower fell at the time of empowerment, they will swiftly gain accomplishment. It is therefore important to make the alteration. And when the principal male deity belonging to the family (on which the practitioner's flower fell) changes position and becomes the main deity, whereas the female consort (of the original deity) remains in place, the tantra in question belongs to the father class.[94] The same occurs, *mutatis mutandis,* with the mother tantras.

The male and female deities of the inner tantras are in union, and this symbolizes the inseparability of wisdom and skillful means, namely, primordial wisdom. Moreover, the special samaya substances, which cannot be used in the lower tantras, are adopted here. One is able to enjoy the five meats and five nectars and so on. And because the view of the great purity and equality is realized, no dualistic discrimination is applied to phenomena. Purity, for example, is not prized, and impurity is not spurned; the one is not rejected in favor of the other. And this is reflected in the conduct of the practitioners: all things are regarded as being of the same taste. Generally speaking, the views of the sutra and tantra are different. Even that of the basic Kriyatantra is superior to that of Madhyamaka. Consequently, though the view and conduct of the four tenet systems of the sutra teachings (Vaibhashika, Sautrantika, Chittamatra, and Madhyamaka) appear to resemble those of the four tantra classes, it should be understood that the tantras are superior to them.[95]

4. A specific explanation of the three inner tantras

Practitioners of Mahayoga[96] or father tantra make extensive use of conceptual construction in their meditation. Because of adventitious, dualistic thought, the spontaneous display of primordial wisdom of great bliss (referred to here as skillful means) is perceived as the universe and beings, the aggregates and so forth. The latter are in fact no more than reifications, imputed reality (*kun btags*), misconceived as truly existent things. And in order to purify them, practitioners adopt a view that perfectly recognizes the nature of phenomena, and meditate principally on the generation stage, the path on which the universe is revealed as a buddhafield and a palace, and living beings are perceived as male and female deities.[97]

In the perfection stage [of Mahayoga], on the other hand, thought-free primordial wisdom, which is luminous and empty, is cultivated.

This is done by purifying, in the expanse of the central channel, the five winds (which are the quintessence of the five elements),[98] or by other methods. It is thus that the two accomplishments are gained.

Once meditation on the generation stage has been stabilized, a subsequent practice should be implemented. In other words, mainly in order to cultivate, and draw out, the primordial wisdom of "passion" (*rjes chags kyi ye shes*), one should practice the *subsequent* or *Anu*-yoga, that is, the mother tantra. Here, practitioners first train themselves on the path of skillful means, taking support of their own bodies. By mastering the channels, winds, and essence-drops of the aggregate of their vajra body,[99] they purify the mind and all thoughts or mental factors—namely, dependent reality (*gzhan dbang*)[100]—in the ultimate expanse of the wisdom of emptiness. This brings to birth the primordial wisdom of coemergent bliss and emptiness. Once this has been done, practitioners chiefly implement the perfection stage in which they take support of the body of a partner. Thanks to this method, the essential constituents (*khams*) of the body are refined, and, when melting takes place, the greatly blissful wisdom of the four joys is engendered. It is thus that these practitioners gain the two accomplishments without depending on conceptual meditation. They do so simply by refining their channels, winds, and essence-drops.

In the Atiyoga, the "supreme yoga,"[101] one meditates on primordial wisdom as it is, in its naked state.[102] This is extremely difficult to experience. Here, no difference of emphasis is made between the generation and perfection stages or, in other words, skillful means and wisdom. This path renders manifest the actual nature (*yongs grub*),[103] the primordial wisdom of union. By training in the Atiyoga, one attains the ultimate nature, which is neither one truly existent nature nor a plurality of truly existent natures—in other words, the great, spontaneously present luminosity; and the impure aggregates are refined into the rainbow light that is their quintessence.

2. **An exposition of the Anuttara or highest tantra**
3. **A short general description of the path**

12   It is said that the foundation for the practice of all the highest tantras is the possession of a body belonging to the desire realm, specifically

that of a human being.[104] Such a body is composed of six elements that are gross and manifest (the five physical elements and consciousness),[105] and it can be brought under control through the skillful methods of the generation stage and the wisdom of the perfection stage as taught in the highest tantras. The reason why a body found in the desire realm is a basis for tantric practice is that the gross channels, winds, and essence-drops, together with the buddha-nature in its veiled condition (all of which share the same nature and are the basis for the manifestation of the five aggregates, the eighteen constituents, and the twelve sense-fields) are primordially the vajra body, speech, and mind, inseparable from the primordial wisdom of the four voids[106] and the four lights.[107] This inseparability is expressed by the union of É and WAM.[108]

As it is said the *Tantra of the Sacred Primordial Buddha:*

> The anushvara, the moon, and the male essential fluid are said to be the enlightened body. The visarga, the female essential fluid, and the sun are the enlightened speech.[109] The syllable A is said to be darkness, the enlightened mind. And space abides in É.[110]

When mastery over one's body is achieved, all that it supports will be refined. The channels, purified by the generation stage, are the enlightened body adorned with the major and minor marks. The winds, purified by the perfection stage, are the enlightened speech endowed with sixty melodious aspects. The essence-drops, purified by the practice of the path of union [of these two stages], are the enlightened mind, which is in turn expressed by the five primordial wisdoms. Therefore, since the Vajrayana enables one swiftly to engender all the qualities of the three vajras, it is superior to any other path.

3. A detailed explanation of the actual path of practice of the highest tantras
4. The practice related to the cause tantra or continuum of the universal ground:[111] the view, meditation, conduct, and result

By means of the Vajrayana path, which is profound and short, prac- 13
titioners gain a direct experience of the nature of all phenomena. This

is the nature of the mind, the sugatagarbha, awareness, self-arisen primordial wisdom. This constitutes the spontaneously present primordial mandala of the kayas and wisdoms. This experience may be gained as the gift of one's devotion, or thanks to the introduction to the nature of the mind occurring during an empowerment. It is also possible to gain an experience of it thanks to the generation and perfection stage practices.

One first comes to a clear conviction regarding the ground nature, the fundamental way of being, by means of the *view*—as a result of hearing and reflecting upon the teaching.[112] Within the framework of this view of the authentic, ultimate nature (beyond all mental effort and deliberate action), one gains experience, through *meditation*, of the fact that all phenomena of samsara and nirvana clearly appear and subsist primordially in the great mandala of the three seats. This is the practice in which the generation and perfection stages are indivisibly and inseparably united. Such a practice must be supported by *conduct*. With regard to one's behavior, one must relinquish all the limitations implied in subject-object duality (*gzung 'dzin gyi la dor ba*). One should abandon all ordinary ways of assessing outer and inner phenomena, and the engagement or withdrawal of the mind with regard to "good" and "bad."[113] One must not, through mindless clinging to sense objects, stray into the five ordinary mental poisons. For when approached with skillful means, all are but the display of the great and perfect equality.[114]

Speaking of the view, meditation, and conduct, Patrul Rinpoche said:

Those who hold the fortress of the view, who have a meditation free from dangerous paths, who "set up the life-tree" of conduct, bear the name of practitioners of the Mantrayana.

And we find in the teachings of the accomplished beings of the past:

The view is eighteen kinds of emptiness:
It must be like a fortress, free of doubt.
Meditation is the thirty-seven elements conducive to
    enlightenment:
It must be free from perils of both dullness and excitement.

Conduct is the six transcendent virtues:
It must be like one's life force firmly grounded, free from all self-
 interest.[115]

Alternatively, "fortress" means the generation stage, wherein one is
clearly established in the deity-yoga. "Life force" indicates the perfection stage, wherein one settles in the fundamental way of being, the
union of appearance and emptiness, the ultimate, uncompounded nature. The perils just mentioned refer to the dullness or agitation of the
mind, or simply to the ordinary, inferior mind, from which one must
free oneself. These three (the fortress, the life force, and freedom from
danger) are the "practice of Samantabhadra."

When the proper significance of the view, meditation, and conduct
has been understood, they blend together.[116] When, by means of the
view, one establishes the ground nature and then experiences it in meditation in accordance with the perfection stage, one secures, as a result,
one's own benefit, namely, the dharmakaya. When one meditates on
this in accordance with the generation stage, one secures the benefit of
others, namely, the effortless display of the rupakaya. When conduct is
perfected, one benefits beings with constant, all-pervading, and spontaneous activities, until the very emptying of samsara. It is thus that all
the perfect qualities related to the two objectives are achieved without
difficulty.

The view, meditation, and conduct are unquestionably related to the
tantras of the ground, path, and result. By means of the view,[117] one
establishes the ground tantra, expressed as the spontaneously present
mandala. Through meditation on the union of the generation and perfection stages, the path tantra is brought into experience. With the
assistance of conduct, the result tantra (the mandala of the kayas and
wisdoms)[118] is actually made manifest.

4. **The practice of the path tantra of skillful means: the maturing empowerment and the liberating stages of generation and perfection, together with the support provided by samaya**
5. **A brief exposition**[119]

14   The door of entry to the Secret Mantra is empowerment, the effect of which is to bring to ripeness the (as yet unripened) four vajras, or indestructible states, of the enlightened body, speech, mind, and primordial wisdom.

It is said in the *Fundamental Text:*

> Just as sharpening gives power to a blade,
> Empowerment, when truly gained, gives power.

One must then meditate again and again on the stages of generation and perfection, for they are the skillful means that free one's indwelling primal wisdom from the two kinds of obscuration and habitual tendencies. The favorable circumstance for this is provided by the perfect observance of the samayas related to this path and set forth in the texts of the Mantrayana. If a practitioner is possessed of these three factors (empowerment, practice, and samaya), the path of Secret Mantra is far superior to the vehicle of the paramitas. It is indeed the supreme and unmistaken path. On the other hand, if practitioners do not receive empowerment—which brings them to maturity—but meditate, nevertheless, on the stages of generation and perfection, and perform the [four] activities, this is simply a meaningless pretense.[120]

5. **A detailed explanation**
6. **Empowerment that brings to maturity**
7. **The need for empowerment**

15   The need to receive empowerment as a means of entry into the path of Secret Mantra may be appreciated when one considers that, if one has not first received such an empowerment, then no matter how much effort one makes on the mantra path, no accomplishment will be gained. It is like pressing sand to get ghee: the desired aim will never be achieved. As it is said in the *Tantra of the Enlightenment of Vairochana:*

No accomplishment is gained without empowerment;
No butter comes from pressing sand.
It is as if you punched the sky,
Or drank the water seen in an illusion.

Moreover, not only will there be no accomplishment, but if one usurps the teachings of the Secret Mantra and explains the tantras and instructions to others, committing the fault of divulging the secret, then, no matter how much effort one exerts in listening to the teachings, in meditating on the path of the generation and perfection stages, and in acting without discrimination of what is to be adopted and rejected, it is certain that one will go to hell in the life to come. As the *Kalachakra-tantra* says:

If you explain the tantra but have not received empowerment,
And likewise meditate upon deep suchness,
Then, even if you know the teaching well,
You'll gain no freedom but will go to hell.

The *Guhyagarbha-tantra* speaks extensively in the same vein.

Concerning the benefits of receiving empowerment, it is said that those who, as a preliminary to the reception of empowerment, cultivate bodhichitta in the "yoga of the vajra,"[121] will be considered by the Buddhas as their "close children"—in other words, even closer than the Bodhisattvas on the Mahayana path (of the paramitas). They will be like the royal prince who, out of all the king's sons, is requested to assume the government of the realm. As it is said in the *Guhyagarbha-tantra:*

Henceforth you are the offspring of the Conqueror.
All evil destinies are closed to you.
Instead you will enjoy long life and perfect happiness,
High birth and liberation.

16   This is not all. The mere sight of a mandala effects the purification of all negativities, the five misdeeds of immediate effect and so on. The *Tantra of the Four Seats* says:

> Even those who have committed
> The five sins of immediate consequence
> Are freed when they behold
> A mandala that is painted or is made of colored sand.

It is said that if, after receiving empowerment, one keeps pure samaya, one will be reborn in a "pure family," meaning that, wherever one is born, one will be unspoiled by evil deeds and error.[122] One will again encounter the teachings of the Secret Mantra and, thanks to the fact that one has received empowerment repeatedly, one will surely gain, after no more than seven lives, all the qualities of the generation and perfection stages, through the power of the path—even without practicing with great effort. And progressing through the ten grounds of realization of the Noble Ones, one will attain buddhahood. The *Secret Treasury* says:

> If true empowerment is received,
> Empowerments will be gained in all one's future lives;
> And even if one does not practice,
> After seven births, accomplishment is gained.

And as the *Guhyasamaja* says:

> Through empowerment one reaches the tenth ground.

7. An exposition of the character of authentic teachers and authentic disciples

17   The accomplishment of the Secret Mantra depends on a teacher, who, by bestowing empowerment, must be able to sow in the mind of the disciple the seeds of the four kayas. This simply does not happen in the case of unqualified teachers who have not themselves assimilated the stages of

generation and perfection and do not have the kind of confidence that results from the practice. Instead, they are proud of their pedigree, their paternal and maternal lineages, and they are distracted by the management of their monastic estates and residences. Such teachers make use of the property of their monasteries and communities just as they like. They fail to restrain their thoughts, words, and deeds by means of the three vows, and their behavior is dissolute and disordered. Such teachers have a contemptuous disregard for the karmic principle of cause and effect and, owing to the strength of their greed, are attracted by the worldly lifestyle of their benefactors and so on, and they accumulate riches from the offerings made in the name of the living and dead. They are extremely ill-humored and their compassion is meager. They are completely blind to the wisdom of the tantras and the Tripitaka, and instead are wholly caught up in specious theories and clever talk. If such people have the temerity to bestow empowerments, both they and their disciples will fall into the lower realms like two calves tied together. It is said in the *Wheel of Wisdom Tantra:* "The Buddha has said that to lead a sincere person astray is worse than killing a hundred beings. Therefore one must never teach deceitfully and for reasons of self-interest."

As the *Tantra of the Ornament of the Vajra Essence* describes, one should 18 only follow a teacher who is qualified in the following ten ways. He or she should have an expert knowledge of the mandalas (of the outer tantras); the concentrations (of the generation and perfection stage practices); mudras (manual gestures); the ways of (peaceful and wrathful) treading; the postures (related to the four activities); the recitation (of mantras); the fire-offering ceremony (related to the four activities); offerings (outer, inner, and secret); the activation (of the practice leading to the supreme and common accomplishments); and dissolution (in other words, the dissolution of the visualized forms and the resting in the view of the perfection stage). These are the ten outer characteristics of an authentic master.

On the inner level—that is, in accordance with the inner tantras— these same skills are exemplified, for example, in the teacher's capacity to create mandalas. On the secret level, these ten skills are given in the *Tantra of the Ornament of the Vajra Essence* as the ritual for averting different kinds of obstacles by using protection circles constructed through the power of concentration; the ritual for averting obstacles by means of a material protection circle; the granting of the secret empowerment; the granting of the wisdom empowerment; the ritual of separation ("liberation"); the purification, understanding, and increase of tormas;[123] the vajra recitation; the ritual of powerful practice (quickly and strongly accomplishing what has not been accomplished); the ritual of consecration; and the ritual of creating mandalas. These are the ten skills understood on the secret level.

But a knowledge of the external forms of these rituals is not enough. It is essential to follow a teacher whose mind has been liberated through the view and meditation of the Secret Mantra. As it is said in the *Sambhuti:*

> Through the action of a master who is himself mature,
> Disciples too are brought to perfect maturation.

Such a teacher must examine for as long as twelve years, so it is said, whether disciples, whose characteristics have been described in the sutra section of the present work,[124] have true faith and devotion, and a moral conscientiousness with regard to themselves and others. And if the requisite qualities are present, the teacher should bestow in proper order the four empowerments, beginning with the vase initiation. As it is said in the *Guhyagarbha:*

> Where faith and diligence and yogic aptitude are found,
> The master should bestow in sequence
> First the "benefiting" and then "enabling" empowerments.[125]
> He should care for his disciples with compassion,
> And not allow their talents to be wasted.

7. An explanation of the actual empowerment
8. The preparatory stages of the empowerment

19   In order to purify their own minds, teachers who confer empowerment must first complete the "approach phase" of the practice (*bsnyen pa*).

They must then perform the land ritual (*sa yi cho ga*) in order both to ensure that the place of empowerment is not being appropriated abusively,[126] and to dispel in the ultimate expanse of equality all concepts related to place and place-ownership. The teachers must then implement the preparatory stages (*sta gon gyi rim pa*) of the empowerment, so as to avoid entering the mandala and engaging too abruptly in the activities related to the disciples. Finally, in order to cleanse the minds of their disciples gradually, and bring them to maturity, they must first introduce their disciples into the mandala and then bestow on them the maturing empowerment itself (*slob ma 'jug cing smin byed*). These four ritual practices, all of which must be completed, are each subdivided into four aspects.[127] First, according to the *Guhyagarbha*, the fourfold approach phase of the practice consists of "approach, near-approach, accomplishment, and great accomplishement." Second, the fourfold ritual of the land consists of the leveling of the ground, the request for its use, the appropriation of the ground, and its purification. Third, the four sections of the preparatory stage relate to the earth goddess, the deities of the mandala, the vase, and the disciples. Fourth, the entry into the mandala and the bringing of the disciples to maturity has also four stages. First, the teacher enters the mandala; second, the disciples receive permission to do the same; they then enter; and having entered, they are empowered by their teacher.[128] If any one of these sixteen aspects is missing, or if the teacher is an ordinary being[129] and damages even the slightest element, the blessings and accomplishment of the empowerment will be impaired, and the teacher will be powerless to bring the minds of the disciples to maturity.

8. The empowerment itself
9. A short outline concerning empowerments in general
10. Empowerments classified according to the four classes of tantra

For each of the four classes of tantra, there are numerous empower-   20
ments, which act as doors of entry. They may be briefly described as follows. In the case of Kriyatantra, and with regard to the mandalas of any of the three transmundane families,[130] there are two main empowerments: first, the empowerment with the vase-water and the dharani and,

second, the crown[131] empowerment of the samayamudra, or deity, of the relevant family. As a consolidating conclusion to the giving of the empowerments,[132] the master gives the reading transmission, performs the three rites of cleansing, purification, and protection, and exhibits the eight auspicious substances.

In the case of the Charyatantra, there is the empowerment of the vajra name, in addition to the two empowerments just mentioned. This empowerment is said to be associated with Akshobhya or Vairochana. But there are also the empowerments of vajra, bell, name, mirror, and scalpel, as well as the formal authorization to expound the Dharma,[133] and so forth. These empowerments vary in quantity according to the tantra in question and the individual master.

In the case of Yogatantra, there are empowerments related to the disciple and empowerments related to the master.[134] The former comprise five knowledge empowerments.[135] These are given with the water from the vase, the crown, the vajra, the bell marked with the symbol of the enlightened family, and the name.[136]

Then there are the six empowerments related to the master. First is the empowerment of irreversibility, that is, of holding the three irreversible samayas (of body, speech, and mind). Second is the secret empowerment, which empowers the disciples to enter and, having entered, to see the secret mandala. It is here that the master expounds the principles of the deity and the mandala. Third is the authorization to expound the teachings specific to the Yogatantra. This is also called the "empowerment for expounding the teachings." Fourth is the empowerment of prophecy. Fifth is the empowerment of encouragement. Finally, the sixth is the empowerment of "uplifting through praise." Thus there are eleven empowerments associated with Yogatantra, which, together with the consolidating conclusion, are to be conferred in their entirety.

21   In the Anuttarayoga, there is, to begin with, the actual vase empowerment consisting of seven component empowerments.[137] These are, first, the five knowledge empowerments together with a sixth empowerment of Vajradhara (all of which are related to the disciple). Then there is a vajra master empowerment, which has a further four subsidiary empowerments: authorization to teach, prophecy, encouragement, and "uplifting through praise." Altogether therefore there are eleven em-

powerments related to the vase empowerment. These are followed by the secret empowerment, the wisdom empowerment, and the precious word empowerment. Altogether, this comes to fourteen empowerments belonging to the Anuttarayoga.

It is said in the explanatory tantra, the *Vajra Garland*:

> The first empowerment, you should understand, is principal;
> The second is called secret;
> The third refers to union;
> The fourth implies the ultimate.
> The principal is divided elevenfold.
> The twelfth is secret; and the thirteenth
> Indicates the perfect, pure union;
> The fourteenth is the ultimate.
> Each empowerment is connected with a ground of realization.
> The first three are empowerments of cause;
> The fourth concerns the fruit.

Likewise it is said in the *Essence of Primordial Wisdom*:

> In the yoga called the "unexcelled,"
> "Secret empowerment" is explained as king.
> "Wisdom" is primordial wisdom unsurpassed,
> As also is the "Fourth."

In general, empowerments are enumerated differently according to the class of tantra and the class of sadhana in question.[138] The *Kalachakra* specifies eleven empowerments in all. These are the "seven empowerments in the pattern of childhood," the three higher empowerments on the worldly level, and the fourth empowerment, which is transmundane. The root tantra says:

> Water, crown, silk ribbons, vajra and bell,
> Conduct, name, and king.
> These are seven empowerments
> For the care of childish beings.[139]

Three then follow, relative, mundane,
And then the fourth, the ultimate empowerment:
The empowerments of vase and secret,
Then "primal wisdom of knowledge,"
Then the "primal wisdom of great knowledge"—
These all are perfected.
Designed for those of changing mind
And those whose minds are stable—
For those with obstacles
And those who are unhindered.
There are therefore seventeen.[140]

In the extraordinary tradition of the old translation school, empowerments are classified according to a tripartite system of tantra, elucidatory teachings, and pith instructions,[141] to which is also added the class of sadhanas (sgrub sde). According to the first of these categories, namely, tantra (in other words, the Mayajala), there are ten outer "beneficial empowerments." These are listed as:

Five essences[142] and crown,
Vase, silken ribbons, mala,
Armor, victory banner, parasol and mudra of the deity,
Food and drink—all these empowerments are gradually bestowed.

These are followed by five inner "enabling empowerments," which give the ability to accomplish the twofold goal. To diligent disciples who are able to benefit themselves are granted the empowerment that allows them to hear the teachings and the empowerment that allows them to meditate on the generation and perfection stages. To diligent disciples who are able to benefit others are given the empowerment that allows them to expound the teachings, and the empowerment that allows them to practice the four activities. Finally, to those who are able to benefit both themselves and others a fifth empowerment is given, that of the vajra-king of infinite teachings, which is an empowerment of all the enlightened families together.[143]
Then there are the three profound secret empowerments for the final

perfection stage: the secret empowerment, the empowerment of wisdom, and the empowerment of great bliss. Altogether, these constitute the eighteen sublime empowerments of Mahayoga, according to the *Mayajala.*

In the elucidatory system of the Anuyoga class, there are, according to the *Scripture of All-Inclusive Knowledge,*[144] thirty-six different empowerments. To these belong the ten streams of outer empowerment. These are empowerments conferred using the images of the Buddhas of the five families; their attributes such as the vajra; the picture of the consort or a bell; a vase; the eight auspicious substances; the seven royal attributes; the jewel-throne, lotus-throne, lion-throne, and so on; the eight ornaments such as silken ribbons; the name; and the wheel.

Added to these are the eleven streams of inner empowerment related to the elements.[145] These empowerments are bestowed using a book, which is the implement employed for the empowerment that allows one to listen and study the teachings; the crossed vajra for the empowerment that allows one to perform the four activities; the wheel for the empowerment that allows one to expound the teachings; the nine-pointed vajra for the vajra-king empowerment; the throne; the seven uncommon precious attributes; the complete collection of pictures of the deities[146] for the empowerment, which allows one to meditate on them; the skull ornament; the pictures of the deities of the enlightened body, speech, and mind; the eight substances and symbols for the subjugation of evil forces; and the name.

Then there are thirteen renowned[147] streams of empowerment of the sadhana class. These are given with a lamp, thus empowering one with knowledge of wisdom; the sun and moon, for the symbolic empowerment of compassion; a plowshare arisen from the syllable HUNG;[148] the red (in other words, blood-filled) conch representing the upsurge of the three poisons; weapons that "liberate" the three levels of existence; a lotus flower, unstained by impurity; a corpse-stick indicating the completion of the four activities; a tangle of coiled snakes symbolizing nonduality; the consort for secret union; sense objects empowering one for their enjoyment; the pictures of the main peaceful and wrathful deities, empowering one to meditate on them; the outer, inner, and secret substances required for the practice; the empowerment of the name according to a given family.

Finally, there are two streams that complete and perfect the secret empowerment through the amrita or the double triangular structure symbolizing the secret mandala; and the empowerment of the creative power of awareness. These then are the thirty-six streams of empowerment of Anuyoga.

In the pith instruction system of Atiyoga, the summit of all vehicles,[149] four empowerments are specified: the elaborate vase empowerment; the unelaborate secret empowerment; the extremely unelaborate wisdom empowerment; and the supremely unelaborate word empowerment.[150]

Generally speaking, there are innumerable categories of empowerment according to the various classes of tantra and of sadhana (as for instance, the special profound empowerment given during a drubchen).[151] They may, however, be condensed into four, as Atisha says in his *Summary of Samayas.*[152] They are the empowerment given orally by the teacher, the empowerment through the blessing of the yidam-deity, the empowerment through the prophetic injunction of the vajra dakinis, and the empowerment received through the creative power of the nature of one's own mind.

The first of these four categories includes all empowerments given according to an empowerment ritual. An example of the second was the descent of certain texts onto the roof of King Ja's palace.[153] The third is exemplified by the story of Nagarjuna and Jagadbhadra (*'gro bzang*). Without permission, they took from a Buddhist temple in Oddiyana two texts: the *Two Segments* and the *Tantra of Mahamaya.* They were pursued by the vajra dakinis, who caught them and commanded them to become inheritors of these teachings and to expound them. The fourth kind of empowerment is the empowerment of the creative power of awareness, obtained when one has a direct experience of ultimate reality.

Disciples may attain the result—namely, accomplishment—on the basis of any one of these empowerments. It is therefore important to have a pure perception of all of them and to refrain from thinking, out of partiality for one, that the others are inauthentic, whether in their enumeration or because of the way they are given and received.

All the many categories of empowerment of the Anuttaratantras have one and the same foundation, from which they ramify and into which they can be condensed. This foundation is necessarily composed of the four empowerments of vase, secret, wisdom, and word.

10. An explanation of the causes and conditions whereby empowerment is received

According to the unsurpassable vehicle of the Secret Mantra, the spontaneously present mandala of the ground nature is the basis for the manifestation of all the aggregates, elements, sense powers, and their objects. It is the sugatagarbha expressing itself in the uncontrived, enlightened body, speech, mind, and primordial wisdom—all of which dwell, from the very beginning, in the ground nature as the essence of the vase, secret, wisdom, and word empowerments. These are the four "ground empowerments."[154] These ground empowerments are brought to maturity through the granting of the four empowerments, and they are further enhanced by the four empowerments received during meditative practice. The latter are consequently referred to as "path empowerments." The resultant four kayas, when they are attained, are the four "result empowerments."[155] One speaks of the ground, path, and result empowerments only from the standpoint of the three different situations in which practitioners find themselves, but in point of fact, these empowerments are indivisible in their ultimate nature. And they are primordially present in all sentient beings. As it is said in the *King of Supreme Empowerment Tantra*:

> If these supreme empowerments were not within oneself,
> How could they be gained through someone granting them?
> You may "empower" some wheat to bring forth peas,
> But no such fruit will ever manifest.

Does this mean that all beings are Buddhas? The answer is that they do indeed possess the sugatagarbha as their nature and therefore will all, finally, achieve enlightenment. Consequently, they are all fitting vessels for the Secret Mantra. This is proved by both reasoning and scripture. In practice, however, the appropriate vessels are only those beings whose bodies are endowed with the six elements,[156] and who possess all manifest supports for empowerment.[157] These are the channels (which are the support of the vase empowerment); the winds (which are the support of the secret empowerment); the (substantial) essential constituents or essence-drops,[158] both white and red (which are the support of the wisdom empowerment); and the coarse thoughts of the ordinary mind (the support of the fourth or word empowerment).

The *concomitant* causes[159] of an empowerment are constituted by the above-mentioned innate supports, together with the sugatagarbha, which is supported by them. The *cooperative* causes, which bring to maturity the mind of the disciple endowed with the concomitant causes, are constituted by the implements of initiation empowered through the master's visualization of the deity, the recitation of the mantra, his concentration, and his consort. It is thus that the cause of empowerment has two aspects (concomitant and cooperative).

23 Of the four conditions of empowerment, the first, or *causal* condition, is constituted by faith, devotion, and so forth, thanks to which the disciple becomes a suitable vessel. The *dominant* condition is the vajra master, who has gained mastery of the five principles of the Secret Mantra. These five principles are: first, the master himself, in that he has realized the view; second, the deity; third, the secret mantra; fourth, the recitation; and fifth, the radiation and absorption of lights. If the master has failed to realize the view, he is unable to bestow blessing— just as a stone is unable to support the growth of a seed. The master must also, in accordance with the pith instructions, be fully conversant with the ritual of empowerment, which has the capacity to bring the disciples' minds to maturity. This, the master's knowledge of the ritual, constitutes the *objective* condition, without which, just as in a children's game, no empowerment is received. On entering the mandala, the vase empowerment is granted, which then acts as the basis for the secret empowerment and so forth. Indeed, each subsequent empowerment is dependent on the one preceding it, and is received on that basis, which therefore constitutes the *immediately preceding* condition. If the foregoing empowerment has not been received, the following one cannot occur,

just as it is impossible to paint a fresco until its supporting wall has been built.[160]

When both the concomitant and the cooperative causes, together with the four conditions (causal, dominant, objective, and immediately preceding) are assembled, empowerment is truly bestowed. As it is said in the *Heart-Essence:*

> Where the two causes and the four conditions are all found,
> Empowerment, residing in these six, is gained.
> For these are said to be the essence of empowerment.

10. An explanation of the reason why four empowerments are necessary

Although the methods of the Vajrayana, the supreme antidotes that purify the impure phenomena of samsara into the state of great primordial wisdom, are limitless, they may in fact be condensed into the four empowerments, together with the paths of their respective practices.

Generally speaking, of the bodies possessed by beings in the six realms, those that are composed of the six elements (the support for existence in the higher realms), and specifically the bodies of womb-born humans, take shape gradually, beginning with the knot of channels at the navel. Owing to the propensity for bodily appearance, other bodies are perceived: the "outer body" of the universe and the "intermediate bodies" of other beings. It is clear therefore that the primary object of purification on the bodily level is the network of channels.

The agent of this purification is the vase empowerment. When this is granted, instructions are given for the generation stage practice, in which one meditates on the outer, inner, and intermediate bodies (respectively, the environment, one's own body, and the bodies of other beings) as having the nature of deity. The channels, which are in the form of the seed-syllables of the six classes of beings,[161] are the objects to be purified, whereas the seed-syllables of the enlightened body, speech, mind, wisdom, skillful means, and so on[162] are the agents of purification.

Now the channels are the support for the moving wind, which, when beings are in the state of delusion, fulfills various functions and gives rise to the common languages of the samsaric realms. Therefore the chief object of purification on the level of speech is the wind. The agent of purification is the secret empowerment. When this is granted, instructions are given for the perfection stage practice, the skillful path on which one takes the support of one's own body.

It is the wind that, by moving back and forth, transports and disposes the bodhichitta (the greatly refined essential constituents, both white and red) within the channels. Supported by the wind, these essence-drops are themselves the support of the mind, and this explains why, in order to purify one's mind, it is necessary to gain control of the essential constituents. The agent of purification is the wisdom empowerment. When this is granted, instructions are given for the practice of the perfection stage, the skillful path wherein one relies on the body of a consort and which renders serviceable the essential constituents, the support of the mind.

The nature of the mind (the ultimate bodhichitta, or dharmatā), or rather the defiled element of primordial wisdom,[163] is based upon these essential constituents. In order to actualize ultimate bodhichitta, therefore, it is necessary to purify the habitual propensities that obscure the mind. The agent of purification here is the precious word empowerment. When this is granted, instructions are given for the perfection stage practice of the united level: the meditation on the primordial wisdom of luminosity.

9. A specific explanation of the four empowerments
10. The essence of the four empowerments
11. A brief explanation

25   The Secret Mantra teachings are extremely skillful in the way they use sense objects and defilements as the path. Unlike Noble Beings in their bodies of manifestation, all ordinary individuals of the desire realm have feelings of desire expressed in the wish to look upon, to smile at, to hold hands, and to copulate with others. This fourfold desire is the object of purification—a purification effected by the vase empowerment and the other three empowerments, together with their respective paths

of practice.[164] All of which shows that the four empowerments are indispensable.

11. A detailed explanation of the four empowerments[165]
12. The vase empowerment

The vase empowerment is the greatest antidote for the kind of desire that is satisfied when two members of the opposite sex simply gaze at each other. It is the desire experienced by the gods of the heaven of Mastery over the Magical Creations of Others. The vase empowerment is granted using a mandala made of colored powders.[166] It reveals the nature of the deity, palace, vajra master, and so forth, and when it is granted, together with its supplementary sections, it chiefly purifies the obscurations of the body[167] as well as karmic obscurations. Of the four states,[168] it purifies the waking state together with its coarse appearances, as well as the obscurations of the essence-drop associated with the body.[169] In addition, it vanquishes the demon of the aggregates. 26

This initiation empowers the practitioner to meditate on the generation stage. The inanimate world and living beings are included in the five aggregates, the five elements, and the twelve ayatanas or sense-fields. The five aggregates and the five elements are the seats of the male and female Buddhas. The inner and outer ayatanas—in other words, the sense organs and the sense objects—are the seat respectively of the male and female Bodhisattvas. The four limbs or the body as organ of touch, its object, tactile sensation, and so on, are the seat of the male and female wrathful [door-keepers]. In this single mandala of the three seats, forms are empty appearances, sounds are the resonance of emptiness, and the mind is awareness and emptiness united. All arises as an illusory display. 27

What is the view to be realized when the vase empowerment is received? It is the realization of three essential features (*ngo bo nyid gsum*). The first of these is the "essential feature of appearance." It is the fact that phenomena manifest as the mandala of the deity. This refers to the generation stage. The second is the "essential feature of emptiness," the knowledge that this mandala is by nature empty—with the result that one does not cling to it. This refers to the perfection stage. The third is the "essential feature of union," and consists in the fact that the first two features are inseparable and spontaneously present: there is no need of any intentional effort to unify them. This refers to the union of the generation and perfection stages.[170]

The highest attainment[171] on the path of the vase empowerment is the realization that all the phenomena of samsara and nirvana, being pure and unoriginated, are indivisible in the state of great equality.

28   For those who fail to achieve this in the course of their lives, the pith instruction for the moment of death describes the transference of consciousness visualized in the form of a ball of light.[172] This is done using syllables such as P'ET and HIK.

What result may be obtained through receiving the vase empowerment? When the pulsation of the impure channels has faded,[173]—in other words, when the channels are purified in the state of pure primordial wisdom—the result of the generation stage (namely, the nirmanakaya display) will manifest, pervading and filling the whole of space, in accordance with the rupakaya on which one has previously meditated. And the enlightened body, which is as unchanging as a vajra and uncompounded like space, will be actualized.

12. The secret empowerment

29   The secret empowerment[174] is given on the basis of the mandala of the bhaga. It is the most powerful antidote to the desire felt by the gods of the divine realm of the Enjoyment of Magical Creations, which is satisfied by smiling. It cleanses the obscurations of speech (such as lying) and the obscurations deriving from the defilements. Of the four states, it cleanses the dream state together with its subtle perceptions, and the obscurations of the essence-drop linked with speech, which is the root of the desire to talk.[175] Finally, it vanquishes the demon of defilement.

This initiation empowers one to practice the perfection stage, the path on which, through effort, the channels, essence-drops, and winds[176] are refined and made wholesome, the path whereby one's body, speech, and mind are blessed and transformed into extraordinary primordial wisdom. Thanks to the pith instruction on the tummo practice, all activity of the winds in the channels is harnessed. And through the concentration on the "blazing and dripping" and so forth, the dualistic wind of subject and object is brought into the central channel through the pathways of roma and kyangma.[177] It is thus that one trains according to the methods of specific tantras and their pith instructions.

The view to be realized by the secret empowerment refers here to self-arisen primordial wisdom. This has four degrees.[178] To begin with, the wind-mind[179] gathers in the chakra of defilement at the heart, with the result that the defilements become more pronounced than they were before. This is the defiled self-arisen primordial wisdom. The wind-mind then gathers in the channels of discursiveness, the roma and kyangma, and thoughts become even more pronounced than previously. This is the discursive, self-arisen primordial wisdom. The wind-mind then gathers in certain points where the central channel is traversed horizontally by other channels, and consciousness becomes more muddled than it was before.[180] This is the confused self-arisen primordial wisdom. Finally, when the wind-mind gathers in the central channel, awareness becomes much more luminous and clear than it was before. This is the luminous and vast self-arisen primordial wisdom.[181]

The highest attainment on the path of this empowerment is mastery over the vowels and consonants (ali-kali), which is gained through the purification of one's speech. This brings an understanding of all the sounds and languages uttered in the six realms, loud or soft, pleasant or harsh. They are understood, distinctly and without confusion, as the perfect expression of enlightened speech, which is completely pure.

The pith instruction for the time of death is as follows. When, with the gradual dissolution of the elements at the moment of death, all the winds are about to dissolve in the central channel, practitioners (if they have not already gained accomplishment in this life) maintain the previously mentioned view (of the luminous and vast self-arisen primordial wisdom) with thought-free concentration, and transfer their consciousness into the great "example luminosity."[182]

What is the result to be gained? When the wind sets in motion the syllables or speech-sounds dwelling in the channels, thoughts appear in the aspect of syllables and words, which are then enunciated.[183] When this compounded, impure vibration of the sounds of speech fades into the unborn expanse, the sambhogakaya, which is an uncompounded, spontaneous, and unceasing radiance, is actualized, together with the vajra speech with its sixty melodious aspects[184] and other qualities— which are themselves naturally present and complete within awareness itself.

12. The wisdom empowerment

31 The wisdom empowerment is granted on the basis of the secret mandala of the consort,[185] whose mandala of the three seats (aggregates, elements, and sense-fields) is visualized as a deity according to the sadhana in question, and whose characteristics are described in the tantras.[186] It is the greatest, most purifying antidote to the desire experienced by the gods of the Tushita heaven, which is satisfied by holding hands. It cleanses the obscurations of the mind,[187] and removes coarse conceptual obscurations. And of the four states, it purifies the state of deep sleep wherein the six consciousnesses, together with their perceptions, are halted. It purifies the mind-bearing essence-drop.[188] And finally it vanquishes the demon of the Lord of Death.

The third initiation empowers one to practice the path of the envoy (in other words, the consort), whereby, thanks to the support of the latter's body, the bodhichitta descends from above and is borne up from below. One then meditates on the coemergent primordial wisdom of luminosity induced by the three lights of primordial wisdom: "light" (meaning "skillful means"), "increase of light" (meaning "wisdom"), and "full culmination of light" (meaning the "union of skillful means and wisdom").[189]

The view to be realized refers to the bliss of emptiness, the primordial wisdom of the four joys, accomplished by relying on the skillful method of the blissful melting of the essence-drop, namely, the "gross bodhichitta."[190]

32 The highest attainment on the path of this empowerment is a constant remaining in—that is, a constant experience of—the view of the inseparability of bliss and emptiness, even without the support of the karmamudra, or consort.[191]

The pith instruction for the time of death is as follows. Even if one has not gained accomplishment in the course of one's life, nevertheless, thanks to the stages of dissolution at the moment of death, all the "gross" essence-drops (the support of ultimate bodhichitta) come together and to a slight extent enter the central channel. It is then that primordial wisdom manifests, even though it is without inherent existence. This is the vajra mind. It is the bliss of emptiness, for here, "vajra" stands for emptiness, and "mind" for bliss. When one recognizes this as the ground-luminosity, one is liberated. This means that, as the channel knot at the level of the heart is undone, the example-wisdom manifests and mingles with the ground-luminosity. The two luminosities, the mother and the child, merge, and liberation is achieved.

The result gained is final liberation. The movement of the refined essence-drops in the channels, which is produced by the wind, dissolves into the state of union of the ultimate expanse and primordial wisdom, at which point the vajra of enlightened mind—the union of the immeasurable, space-pervading dharmadhatu and inconceivable primordial wisdom—manifests. Thus is actualized the body of primordial wisdom, the refined body wherein all impurities of the mind and mental factors have subsided.

12. The fourth empowerment or word empowerment

On the basis of the mandala of the example-wisdom of luminosity 33 (which is like an offshoot of ultimate bodhichitta), the disciples who remain therein, in a state of meditative equipoise, experience the primordial wisdom of the third empowerment: the bliss of emptiness, which is the wisdom of the four joys resulting from the descending from above and the bearing up from below of the essence-drops. When the master verbally introduces this as the state of Great Perfection, this constitutes the fourth or word empowerment, the empowerment of great bliss.

The fourth empowerment is the antidote to the desire for sexual union experienced by all beings of the realm of desire up to (and including) the heaven called Free of Conflict. It eliminates the subtle obscurations of the three doors; in other words, the extremely subtle stains whereby the mind perceives body, speech, and mind as separate. It cleanses the utterly subtle conceptual obscurations together with the propensity for movement (the progression from one mental state to another).[192] Of the four states, it purifies that of sexual climax, together with the obscurations of the essence-drop that carries the subtle propensities of body, speech, and mind together. It vanquishes the demon "child of the gods."

34   The view to be realized is that of inconceivable, empty awareness, which has the nature of the three doors of perfect liberation. Its ultimate nature (*ngo bo*), beyond all conceptual constructs, is the "essence-drop of emptiness." Its character (*rang bzhin*) is luminosity, and within this unceasing radiance of awareness, there occurs the display of "cognitive potency" (*thugs rje*)."[193] This display has the kayas and wisdoms as its core.

The fourth initiation empowers one to meditate on the great Mahamudra of luminosity or the Great Perfection of empty awareness. If one receives the fourth initiation according to the common inner tantras, one is empowered to meditate on the latter's corresponding perfection stage. If one receives the fourth initiation proper to the highest vehicle, one is empowered to meditate on the extraordinary path of primordial purity, trekchö (*khregs chod*), and spontaneous presence, thögal (*thod rgal*).

The highest attainment on this path is the realization of inconceivable primordial wisdom, the Mahamudra of blissful emptiness. Thereby one understands fully that samsara is not something to be discarded, and nirvana is not something to be striven for.

The pith instruction for the moment of death consists in the transference into the state of the previously mentioned view, the Mahamudra of the great secret.[194]

The result thus gained is described as the fading away of the movement of the wind of primordial wisdom (the wind that is the quintessence of the elements). All the extremely subtle, adulterated aspects of the wisdom wind, which occur because of the karmic wind, are purified, and thus the wisdom wind is fully actualized. The vajra, the indestructible state, of primordial wisdom (which has the nature of the all-pervading ultimate expanse) is gained together with the svabhavikakaya, the union of the dharmakaya and the rupakaya.[195]

10. The meaning of the term "empowerment"

35   "Abhisheka," the Sanskrit equivalent of the Tibetan word *dbang* (translated into English as "empowerment"), expresses two ideas: the washing

away of impurities and the giving of power. The Sanskrit "abhishim-cha"[196] implies that, through the mere reception of the empowerment, all adventitious impurities, which cast a veil over primordial wisdom, are dispersed, and one is made fortunate—the "pouring out of good fortune" being the meaning of the Sanskrit "shekata."[197] Ultimate reality is naturally endowed with the qualities of the four kayas (the good fortune referred to). These become manifest thanks to the removal of defilements, and this occurs through the practices related to the different empowerments. As soon as one receives empowerment, one is able to meditate on the corresponding path and bring to birth the qualities associated with it. Thus two ideas are implied in the term "abhisheka" (*dbang*, or "empowerment"): the power to remove defilements, and the power to gain all good qualities.

10. Empowerments related to the cause, path, and result[198]

The qualities of the four supreme empowerments—which are by their nature the four vajras of body, speech, mind, and primordial wisdom—are present coemergently within oneself, just as taste, strength, smell, and the effect are present in a medicine. Of the six elements,[199] the element of mind (*sems*), consisting of the four "name-aggregates,"[200] is the support for primordial wisdom.

The supports of the five aggregates are the five elements, and the supports of the elements are the channels. Supported by the channels is the life-wind, and supported by the wind is the bodhichitta. Therefore the concomitant causes[201] of the four empowerments are the channels, the winds, the essence-drops, and the mind—all of which are present within oneself. The nature of all these is the sugatagarbha itself, which is endowed with the qualities of the four empowerments. This is called the cause (or ground) empowerment.

As a means to actualizing the indwelling cause empowerment, a qualified vajra master confers the empowerment by means of an authentic ritual consisting of preparation, main part, and conclusion. This is the path empowerment. In addition, there exist the self-empowerment, the four empowerments of profound guru yoga, and the transfer of the stream of blessings. These are also path empowerments, in which one trains oneself through visualization and repeated practice.

36

Moreover, according to the expository vehicle of causality, it is said that when the path of learning is perfected and the final point of the tenth ground of realization is reached, the "empowerment through great rays of light" is received. Likewise, when all adventitious defilements, which conceal the empowerment primordially present in the nature of the mind, are dispelled through the path empowerments and the practice of the generation and perfection stages, the mind ripens into the four kayas. This is called the empowerment related to the result.[202]

8. The benefits of receiving empowerments

37 When the four empowerments, together with the consolidating conclusion, are completed,[203] the vows of the Vidyādharas are simultaneously received.[204]

Planted in the soil of a field plowed and cleared of stones and hard earth, seeds eventually produce ripe fruit. In the same way, when empowerments are received, the mind, which had been previously unfit for the generation of excellent qualities, is cleared of its "hardness." It receives the seeds of the four kayas, which will then ripen and give fruit. And when such empowerments encounter the proper circumstances—namely, an endeavor in the generation and perfection stage practices that are associated with each of them—they purify, moment by moment, the body, speech, and mind, together with the belief that they are real and distinct entities. At the same time, the karmic obscurations, the obscurations deriving from the defilements, the conceptual obscurations, the obscurations of habitual tendencies, and the obscurations of the four states of waking, deep sleep, dreaming, and sexual climax, are all cleansed. The thirty-seven elements of the four paths of learning leading to enlightenment, the ten paramitas, the two accumulations, and so on, gradually develop and intensify, and the four vajras and the four kayas (nirmanakaya, sambhogakaya, dharmakaya, and svabhavikakaya) are actualized.

6. An explanation of the path of the liberating stages of generation and perfection[205]
7. The generation stage
8. A short exposition

Of the two aspects (generation and perfection) of the path of the pri- 38
mordially pure, ultimate nature, the first is the generation stage,[206] which
is the skillful means whereby birth is used as the path. The four kinds
of generation stage are taught for the purification of all the habitual
tendencies that relate to the four types of birth: birth from a womb,
miraculous birth, birth from an egg, and birth from warmth and moisture. Generally speaking, all four kinds of birth may apply to humans[207]
and animals. Bodhisattvas in the pure fields, celestial beings, the denizens of the hells, and beings in the bardos are born by a process of
miraculous birth. It is possible for pretas to be born from a womb, but
most of them are born in the miraculous way.[208]

8. A detailed exposition of the generation stage
9. Purification, perfection, and ripening

During the generation stage, one meditates on emptiness, which is analogous to death; on compassion, which is analogous to the bardo; on the
seed-syllable, which is analogous to the consciousness in the bardo; and
on the complete (fully visualized) deity, which is analogous to birth,
occurring when all the sense organs of the embryo are fully formed. If
one meditates in conformity with these aspects of samsara—the three
phases of existence (life, death, and the bardo) and the four kinds of
birth—and if one uses the antidotes specific to each of these aspects,
one will, by means of the four generation-stage practices, purify all clinging to phenomena related to body, speech, and mind—as well as all
propensities for birth in the six realms of existence. Consequently, the
practices of the generation stage effect the *purification* of all clinging to
the true existence of the phenomena of the three worlds, which are the
external manifestation of the habitual tendencies of body, speech, and
mind. The perceptible nature of the body corresponds to the world of
desire; the semi-perceptible nature of speech corresponds to the world
of form; and the nonperceptible nature of the mind corresponds to the
world of formlessness.

39   Furthermore, by meditating in harmony with the mode of being of nirvana, using the path of the three kinds of concentration (which conform to the three kayas)[209] and the various aspects of the deity (buddhafield, palace, the major and minor marks, rays of light, and so on), practitioners cultivate an extraordinary ability to bring about the *perfection* of the result: the manifestation in reality of the qualities of the three kayas, which are present primordially in the ground nature. These two aspects of the generation stage (purification and perfection) are the skillful means that indirectly bring under control the channels, winds, and essence-drops of the aggregate of the vajra body. It is a form of meditation that is in accordance with the ultimate nature of the mind, the sugatagarbha. If, having gained a stable practice of the generation stage as just described, one goes on to implement the perfection stage, the example and actual luminosities of primordial wisdom will soon arise. Thus the generation stage comes to *ripeness* as (or ripens into)[210] the perfection stage. These aspects of purification, perfection, and ripening (*dag rdzogs smin gsum*) are extremely important in the common generation stage of the inner tantras.

9. A specific explanation of the purification of the propensities related to the four types of birth
10. The generation-stage practice that purifies birth from an egg
11. A detailed explanation

40   To be born from an egg is an elaborate manner of taking birth in samsara. For it involves being born twice—in the sense that the egg first emerges from the mother bird, and the chick then emerges from the egg. Accordingly, there exists a generation stage that occurs in two steps: [the generation of others as] one's own children and [the generation of oneself as] the child of others. This two-step generation practice is recommended for beginners.[211]

The expression "to generate others as one's children" (*bdag gi sras su gzhan bya ba*) means that the sugatagarbha, the nature of the mind, which is the ground whence all the phenomena of samsara and nirvana arise, is visualized as the principal deity and consort in union. Other tathāgatas proliferate therefrom as though they were their offspring, taking up their position as the surrounding retinue.[212] This visualization passes through five phases.

Based on the pith instructions associated with the three concentra-   41
tions[213]—related for example to the purification into the state of empti-ness of one's body (the ripened effect of one's karma) and of all phenomena—one concentrates on one's awareness in the form of a seed-syllable. One imagines that other seed-syllables emerge from this and transform into the elements stacked one upon the other. Then the syllable DRUM (Skt. *bhrūm*), radiating lights of five colors, transforms into a palace furnished with thrones. Upon the central throne, the seed-syllable descends and transforms into the main deity. This is the "cause heruka"; he is visualized with one face and in the appropriate color.

Rays of wisdom light, emanating from the father-mother deities in union, summon the Buddhas of the ten directions. They enter the father deity through the crown of his head and dissolve into the space of the mother.

Rays of light then summon sentient beings and purify their defile-ments. These beings then dissolve into the space of the mother.

One must then cultivate the pride, or powerful conviction, that one is the deity, the glorious embodiment of the indivisible nature of sam-sara and nirvana.

All the deities then emerge from the secret space and take up their positions on their respective thrones.[214]

The meaning of the expression "to generate oneself as the child of   42
others" (*gzhan gyi sras su bdag bya ba*) is as follows. At the stage when others are visualized as one's children, the "others"—that is, the Tathāga-tas who dissolve into oneself (visualized as the cause heruka) and pass through the door of the consort's womb—becoming thus the retinue, are in fact the wisdom mind of the principal deity.[215] Then [as one visualizes oneself in the form of the principal main deity] one's thoughts, in the form of seed-syllables,[216] descend into the secret space of the consort and take birth as offspring, which are established as the retinue. This process passes through eight phases. It is as when an egg reaches the moment of hatching. It bursts open and a chick emerges with all its limbs and sense organs fully formed. These eight phases are as follows.

The main deity (the cause heruka) in union with the consort melts into light and assumes the appearance of an orb of dark-blue light marked with a seed-syllable and the corresponding attribute.

This transforms and is visualized as the result heruka and consort in union, complete in every detail: [in the present case, Chemchok with] nine heads, eighteen arms, and so forth.

The thoughts of the male deity (that is, the result heruka) transform into seed-syllables, at which point there occurs a state of mind in which there can be no wish for the generation of offspring.[217]

43   Lights then radiate from the consort and entreat the male deity and all the surrounding deities, beseeching them to beget children.

All the surrounding deities dissolve into the heart of the main deity (oneself as the result heruka): they are his wisdom mind. There arises the strong conviction that one is the pervading lord of all mandalas of primordial wisdom.

The main deities remain in union by means of the four mudras, and the secret space is blessed by light rays of bodhichitta. These descend three times into the space of the consort. On the first occasion, they trace out the mandala. On the second occasion, they engender the actual mandala as the support, together with the palace. On the third occasion, the forty-two thoughts existing in the form of seed-syllables transform and appear perfectly as the principal and surrounding deities. And they emerge from the secret space.[218]

From one's heart, there emanate four mudras (goddesses). Merely by touching the support of the wisdom mandala, the goddess with a hook calls the mandala into being from the ultimate expanse.[219] The goddess with the lasso summons the deities and draws them forth from their dwelling place. The goddess with the chain causes them to dissolve into the (visualized) mandala. Finally, the goddess with the bell causes the samayasattvas and jnanasattvas[220] to rejoice, thereby binding them inseparably together.

The surrounding deities, their three centers sealed by the three vajras, are then positioned in their respective places. The main deity (of the wisdom mandala invited from the ultimate expanse) dissolves into the result heruka, the palace into the palace, the thrones into the thrones.

11. A short explanation

The generation stage that purifies the twofold process of birth from an 44
egg can be summarized as follows. First of all, one visualizes oneself as
the "uncontrived" primordial deity.[221] Then one visualizes in the sky in
front of oneself the palace and deities of whichever mandala one is
using for one's meditation. Alternatively, one may consider that this
same mandala emanates from one's own heart. Or again, one may invite
this mandala to arise from the ultimate expanse, considering that it is
present in the space in front of oneself. In the presence of the mandala,
visualized in any of these three ways, one should then perform the daily
confession and the prayers of seven, eight, or ten branches. In conclusion, the field for the accumulation of merit, together with oneself,
dissolves into emptiness. And from within the state of emptiness, the
mandala of the deity is again visualized, in accordance with the practice
one is doing, in order to purify the birth process.[222]

10. The generation-stage practice that purifies birth from a womb
11. The generation-stage practice performed through the four
factors of awakening

In general, a single method of visualization has the power to purify all 45
four kinds of birth. Nevertheless, the practice of meditation attuned to
a specific way of taking birth will first and foremost purify the propensity for the kind of birth in question. This being so, in order to purify
the tendency to be born from a womb, the generation stage is to be
practiced using the four factors of awakening, the three vajra methods,
or a further set of five factors of awakening.

The generation stage that uses the four factors of awakening is set
forth according to the *Heruka Galpo*, where it is written:

> First come emptiness and bodhichitta,
> Second the seed-syllable,
> Third, the perfect form,
> And fourth the placing of the syllables.

Regarding the first of the four factors of awakening, it should be
understood that, in order to purify the moment of death (when,

through the power of delusion the eighty kinds of thought disappear) and in order to purify the wavering, unstable perceptions that manifest in the bardo (when the karmic wind revives), it is necessary to train oneself in emptiness free from all movements of thought, and in the illusion-like compassion of bodhichitta. These two meditations perfect the dharmakaya and sambhogakaya present in the ground[223] and ripen into the practice of luminosity and the illusory body.[224]

The second factor of awakening consists in the clear visualization of the deity's seed-syllable, such as HUNG, which is the symbol of the primordial wisdom of the union of emptiness and compassion. This purifies the entry and merging of the consciousness of the bardo-being with the mingled sperm and ovum of the father and mother. It perfects the nirmanakaya present in the ground, and ripens into the manifestation of the illusory body of the deity from within the state of the example luminosity.

46   The third factor of awakening follows on from the second, namely, the purification effected by the seed-syllable of vajra speech. The mingled sperm, ovum, and consciousness are transformed by the wind into a spherical and then elongated, mucus-like, mass. These stages are purified by the transformation of the seed-syllable into a (visualized) implement, such as a vajra, which is the symbol of the vajra mind. The stages when the embryo is oblong and then ovoid are purified by the transformation of the symbolic implement into a sphere of light. Later, the fetus gradually passes through stages in which it is fish-shaped, then tortoise-shaped, and finally comes to the point where the eyes and the other organs of sense, together with the other limbs, are completely formed. This development is purified by the transformation of the sphere of light into the deity—in other words, the vajra body. This entire meditation perfects the svabhavikakaya of union present in the ground, and ripens into the body of the deity of the level of union, manifesting from within the state of ultimate luminosity.

The fourth factor of awakening is the purification by the seed-syllables (OM, AH, HUNG) of the clinging to the whole array of experienced things that occurs when the child is born and its sense organs awaken to their objects. The syllables radiate either from the womb of the deity or from other positions where they are placed and which they seal (for example, the three centers). It has been said that either of these methods [of visualization] may be used. This perfects the spontaneous enlightened activities present in the ground, and ripens into the manifestation of the body of the perfection-stage deity of the level of union on the path of learning, as well as into the experience, free from clinging, of all objects of desire—the latter then arising as ornaments of awareness. The remaining stages of the sadhanas, such as the emanation of the surrounding deities in the mandala and so on, together with all the concluding sections, are performed according to their respective texts.

11. The generation-stage practice performed through the three vajra methods

The visualization of the great mudra of the deity's body corresponds to the vajra body of all the Tathāgatas; the meditation on the seed-syllable corresponds to vajra speech; and the meditation on the implement marked by the seed-syllable corresponds to the vajra mind.

The stages of the meditation are as follows. When the preliminary stages have been performed as far as the three concentrations, one should meditate on primordial wisdom (the inseparability of appearance and emptiness) in the form of a vajra or some other implement. The merging of the consciousness of the bardo-being with the mingled white and red essences in the womb is thereby purified. Then the five stages of development, through which the mingled sperm, ovum, and mind must pass, are purified by the visualization of the implement's transformation into a seed-syllable, or of its being marked with a seed-syllable (for example, AH, the symbol of enlightened speech). The seed-syllable is then seen to radiate and reabsorb lights that accomplish the twofold aim. The seed-syllable or implement marked thereby then transforms into the complete body of the deity, which is then meditated upon. This purifies the stage in which the sense organs and limbs of the fetus are fully formed. This is the "meditation using the three vajra methods" (*rdo rje'i cho ga gsum*) and is the general tradition of the father tantras.

11. The generation-stage practice performed through the five factors of awakening

12. A general explanation of the correspondence between the ground and the result[225]

48 A correspondence exists between the five paths and the qualities of the result, on the one hand, and the entry and development of a being in the womb, on the other. This is to be understood in the following way. Beings who, while in the bardo, are unable to arise in the sambhogakaya, and those who are able to do so but who, on account of their bodhichitta, do not relinquish the nirmanakaya as a means of helping others, search for a bodily support from within the bardo state. This corresponds to the path of accumulation. When such beings choose the womb-door of a Dharma-practitioner, their consciousness (in the form of a seed-syllable such as HUNG) enters the mother's womb. This corresponds to the path of joining. The semen, ovum, wind, and consciousness, and the blending of these on entry into the womb [the factors to be purified] correspond to the five factors of awakening of the ground.[226] The ordinary process of embryonic development of the fetus as it passes through the five stages of growth (spherical shape, elongated form, and so on) is cleansed by the paths of seeing and meditation—the ten-month period corresponding to the ten grounds of realization.

The birth of the child corresponds to the arising in the form of the supreme yidam-deity. In the words of the root verse, this corresponds to the path of no-more learning and the accomplishment of the body of union of the nirmanakaya.[227] As it is written in the *Luminous Expanse Tantra*:

> On entry to the womb,
> Five factors of awakening occur.
> The ten months correspond to the ten grounds
> And birth accords with the nirmanakaya of luminous character
> Spontaneously endowed with the three kayas.

[Even for ordinary beings, who are without realization,] the search for a bodily support while in the bardo is analogous to the search for the authentic path, through hearing and reflecting on the teachings, while one is on the path of accumulation. The entry of the consciousness into the womb is irreversible, and this is like reaching the level of acceptance on the path of joining.[228] The perfect conjunction of "name and form" (the four mental aggregates and the aggregate of form, respectively), which results from the mingling of semen, ovum, and consciousness, is analogous to the complete realization of no-self on the path of seeing. The gradual passage of the embryo through its five stages of development (spherical form, elongated form, and so on), together with the further development that occurs throughout the ten-month period, corresponds to the gradual progress on the ten grounds that is brought about by the increase of realization on the path of meditation. Once the perfectly formed body has been delivered, there occurs a mastery over the sense organs, their objects, and the six kinds of consciousness. This is analogous to the complete realization that arises on the path of no more learning: the point at which omniscient wisdom awakens and one is empowered to work for the welfare of beings in the six realms.

12. A specific explanation of the five factors of awakening of the path

The five factors of awakening are a feature of the tantras generally. The concentrations for the preliminary and concluding stages of the practice are explained in their respective texts. The five factors of awakening, as constituting the main practice, may be explained as a meditation based on four methods, which are related both to the object, and to the agent, of purification. These methods consist of taking form (*rnam pa*), conviction (*mos pa*), result (*'bras bu*), and power of interdependence (*rten 'brel byin rlabs*) as paths of practice.

In the case of the first factor of awakening, to use "form" as the path means to meditate on the nature of Vairochana as being the disk of the moon arising from the vowels. To use "conviction" as the path means to have the conviction of mirrorlike primordial wisdom that realizes that phenomena arise like reflections in a mirror. The "result" used as the path is the primordial wisdom of the dharmakaya. Thanks to these three methods, the two accumulations are completed. This is referred

49

to as the method that uses the "power of interdependence" as the path.[229] The objects purified are the aggregate of form, the element of earth, the body, the consciousness of the universal ground, and ignorance. The first factor of awakening also purifies the father's semen present in womb-birth, the aspect of humidity in birth from warmth and moisture, the paternal component present in egg-birth, and the emptiness aspect of miraculous birth.

50   In the case of the second factor of awakening, to use "form" as the path means to meditate on the nature of Ratnasambhava as being the disk of the sun arising from the consonants. It is taught that, with regard to these first two factors of awakening, one visualizes garlands of letters in the disks of sun and moon. The vowels (*ali*) are in the moon and are the seeds of the major marks of buddhahood. The consonants (*kali*) are in the sun and are the seeds of the minor marks. To use "conviction" as the path means to have the conviction of the primordial wisdom that realizes the equality of all phenomena. The "result" used as the path is the unobscured luminosity of the primordial wisdom that understands that Buddhas and beings are of the same taste. The objects purified are the aggregate of feeling, the element of fire, the faculty of speech, the defiled consciousness, and pride. The second factor of awakening also purifies the mother's essence present in womb-birth, the aspect of warmth in birth from warmth and moisture, the maternal component present in egg-birth, and the luminosity aspect of miraculous birth.

51   In the case of the third factor of awakening, to use "form" as the path means to meditate on the nature of Amitabha as being the seed-syllable and the implement. To use "conviction" as the path is to have the conviction of the primordial wisdom that discerns all phenomena distinctly and without confusion. The "result" used as the path is the unobscured luminosity of all-discerning primordial wisdom, which knows all phenomena. The objects purified are the aggregate of perception, the element of water, the mental consciousness, and desire. The third factor of awakening also purifies the entry of the bardo consciousness into the mingled semen and ovum occurring in womb-birth, and all other modes of entry by the bardo consciousness into the other places of birth.[230]

In the case of the fourth factor of awakening, to use "form" as the   52
path means to meditate on the nature of Amoghasiddhi as being the
merging of the moon, sun, and implement into a single orb of light. To
use "conviction" as the path is to have the conviction of the primordial
wisdom in which the activities of all Buddhas are united. The "result"
used as the path is the all-accomplishing primordial wisdom. The objects purified are the aggregate of conditioning factors, the element of
air, the activities of the three doors, the five sense consciousnesses, and
jealousy. The fourth factor of awakening also purifies the mingling of
the semen, ovum, and consciousness occurring in both womb-birth and
egg-birth; the mingling of warmth, humidity, and consciousness occurring in birth from warmth and moisture; and the mingling of luminosity
and emptiness with the consciousness of the bardo-being, which occurs
in the case of miraculous birth.

For the fifth factor of awakening, to use "form" as the path is to   53
meditate on the nature of Akshobhya as being the [cause] heruka and
consort in union. To use "conviction" as the path is to have the conviction of the primordial wisdom that realizes that all resultant qualities
are complete and perfect in the dharmadhatu. The "result" used as the
path is the primordial wisdom of the dharmadhatu. The objects purified
are the aggregate of consciousness, the element of space, all the habitual
patterns of the three doors taken together, clinging to the eight kinds
of consciousness as such, and anger. The fifth factor of awakening also
purifies birth (which occurs when the limbs, secondary members, and
sense organs of beings born in any of the four ways are complete and
perfect) and the awakening of the sense powers to their objects as they
enter into contact with them, together with all the delusory appearances
of samsara.

In this way, the five elements, the five aggregates, the eight gatherings   54
(consciousnesses), and the [five] defilements are purified. Indeed, in
their intrinsic purity, they are already perfect as the deities of the three
seats. According to the perspective of nirvana taken as the path (that is,
in terms of the tathāgatas, who are endowed with the major and minor
marks, who bring great benefit to others, and who have perfected all
excellent qualities and wisdoms), the cause-vajradhara and consort in
union transform into a sphere of light from which the result heruka

appears, invoked by the songs of the encircling goddesses, and engages in activities that accomplish the twofold aim.

[According to the perspective of samsara] and by means of the method that uses form as the path, the objects to be purified—semen, ovum, wind, and mind (all of which have the character of samsaric existence)—are completely *purified*. According to the perspective of the Victorious Ones, and through the method that uses conviction as the path, the five qualities of the result—namely, the enlightened body, speech, mind, qualities, and activities, together with all the qualities of the five wisdoms present in the ground—are *perfected*. These two functions, of purifying and perfecting, effect a *ripening* into the perfection stage: the stages of light, increase of light, and culmination of light, luminosity, the level of union, and so on. The method that uses the result as the path ripens in the state endowed with the major and minor marks of enlightenment.

10. The generation-stage practice that purifies birth from warmth and moisture[231]

55 As soon as the consciousness of the bardo-being merges with a conjunction of warmth and moisture, a body is produced. Unlike birth from a womb, this does not take a long time. In the same way, through the simple utterance of a deity's mantra and the simple recollection of its name and form, the mudra or form of the deity, together with the palace (as aspects of the relative truth), appear fully within the empty space of wisdom, the expanse of Samantabhadri. Practitioners then meditate on the complete generation stage. This is called the illusory generation stage of false appearances.

10. The generation-stage practice that purifies miraculous birth

56 The bodies of beings born by way of miraculous birth are completely formed by the mere entry of the consciousness into the factors of luminosity and emptiness. This is even quicker than birth from warmth and moisture. Accordingly, through the simple, instantaneous remembrance of the mantra within the state of meditation on the view, the mandala appears fully perfect. Without depending on conceptual devices, such

as pronouncing the deity's name or mantra, and the gradual concentration on the various aspects of the deity's body, the deity and palace appear vividly present. It is just as when a fish suddenly leaps above the surface of the water.[232]

10. Conclusion

These different ways of meditating on the generation stage, which purify the four kinds of birth, are analogous to the gradual progress of an individual person through the stages of childhood, maturity, and old age. Practitioners train in them according to the strength of their concentration, which depends on their habituation to the practice, slight or extensive as this may be.[233] Fortunate beginners, who are new to this practice, train mainly in the generation stage that purifies egg-birth. Then by degrees, until the moment when their meditation is stable and they are able to visualize the mandala roughly in an instant, they train in the generation stage that purifies birth from a womb. When they have achieved great stability in their meditation and can see all the details clearly, even the white and black of the deity's eyes, they train in the generation stage that purifies birth from warmth and moisture. Finally, when they have a truly excellent meditative stability and the visualization of the entire mandala is done in an instant, they practice the generation stage that purifies miraculous birth.

9. The three concentrations, the basis of the generation stage

All the generation-stage practices of the inner Secret Mantra must be preceded by the three concentrations.[234] The first of these is the *suchness concentration* (*de bzhin nyid kyi ting nge 'dzin*), which consists in resting evenly in the profound state of emptiness, the state of wisdom that cognizes ultimate reality beyond all ontological extremes. When, in the course of an empowerment, a teacher sets forth the pith instructions and gives an introduction to the ground nature (the spontaneously present, fundamental nature of the mind), it is of course possible for disciples to recognize this through the power of the blessings received. But if this does not happen, they need to gain certainty in it through hearing and reflecting on the teachings—whereby it is understood that all phenomena are the appearances of inconceivable suchness.

The radiance of suchness arises as great and universal compassion. This is the *all-illuminating concentration* (*kun tu snang ba'i ting nge 'dzin*). And thanks to the impulse of compassion, there arises the *concentration on the cause* (*rgyu'i ting nge 'dzin*) or seed-syllable. From this, the generation stage, the meditation on the mandala of the deities of the three seats, faultlessly unfolds. The generation stage practice endowed with the three concentrations is the best of all paths of skillful means. It is the unmistaken method of Mantra.[235]

10. The four "life-fastening" nails[236]

The nail of concentration on the deity

58 All mandalas of whatever kind manifest in the manner of an illusory appearance. Although all the deities of the mandala, together with their ornaments, appear perfectly and distinctly, from the very moment of their arising, they are without real existence. To visualize them vividly and clearly as the great union [of appearance and emptiness] is the nail of concentration on the deity (*ting 'dzin lha'i gzer*). In order to purify the karmic tendencies associated with the four kinds of birth, the outer universe is visualized—in the manner of an illusion—as an immeasurable palace. Its inhabitants also are visualized in the form of male and female deities. All appearances, from the central main deity to the mountains of fire [on the mandala's rim], are visualized perfectly and distinctly, even as far as the designs on the deities' garments. Yet from the very moment of their appearing, they are without inherent existence; they are visualized vividly as the great union of appearance and emptiness. The different stages of the sadhana are subsequently pursued, such as the bestowal of the empowerment of the five primordial wisdoms, the sealing of the visualized deities with the seed-syllables of the enlightened body, speech, and mind, and so on.

If the deities are peaceful, they are characterized by nine peaceful expressions (*zhi tshul dgu*); if they are wrathful, they have the nine demeanors (*gar gi nyams dgu*).

The nine peaceful expressions are as follows: The body, face, arms, and so on of peaceful deities are not hard and unyielding as though made of wood or some other substance. They are soft and tender (*mnyen pa*).

Their bodies are well-proportioned and lithe (*lcug pa*). Their flesh is firm and not flaccid (*'khril bag chags pa*). The joints of their limbs are supple and shapely (*'phrul ldem dang ldan pa*). They are youthful and full-bodied with perfect skin (*gzhon tshul can*). The color of their bodies and the ornaments they wear are distinct and brilliant (*gsal ba*). They shine with innumerable rays of light (*'tsher ba*). They are truly magnificent (*lhun sdug pa*) with all the glory of the marks of the enlightenment of great beings, and they are overwhelming in their splendor (*gzi byin dang ldan pa*).

The nine demeanors of the wrathful deities are divided into three sets relating to body, speech, and mind. Regarding their bodily demeanor, wrathful deities have a great beauty in that they express their love and compassion for beings (*sgeg pa*). They are heroic in their wrath (splendid with a ferocious prowess) (*khro nyams kyi dpa' ba*). They are hideous with an expression of utter darkness (*mi sdug pa*). As to their three demeanors of speech, they utter sounds of laughter: "HA HA!" and "HUNG HUNG!" (*dgod pa*). They have terrible voices, menacing and roaring (*gshe ba*), which are unbearably loud and ferocious (*drag shul*). As for their mental demeanor, they have a compassion that reaches out to ignorant and foolish beings (*snying rje*). They have an anger that subdues evil beings with savage rage (*rngam pa*) (like a mother fighting to retrieve her child who has fallen into a ravine). Finally they remain in a state of serenity (*zhi ba*), pacifying both good and evil in the same taste of ultimate reality.

Peaceful sambhogakaya deities are arrayed in five silken garments and eight precious ornaments—thirteen items altogether. The five garments are: an iridescent silken sash that is blue and red in color; five-colored tassels that hang loosely from the headdress; a short-sleeved shirt (sometimes replaced by a long shawl); an upper garment made of white silk decorated with golden traceries; and a lower garment of many colors covering the legs. The eight ornaments are: a diadem of precious stones; earrings; a necklace hanging closely around the throat; precious armlets; a necklace hanging down to the level of the heart; a necklace hanging down to the level of the navel; bracelets; and anklets. Peaceful nirmanakaya deities wear the three kinds of Dharma (monastic) robe.[237]

Wrathful deities are arrayed in three garments: a human skin around the waist, an upper garment of elephant skin, and a kilt of tiger skin.

They have two kinds of ornament: those made of human skulls and those made of snakes. To begin with, they wear a crown of five dry skulls, and some deities wear a shoulder belt of rotting human heads. They have a necklace reaching to the level of their navel, composed of fifty freshly severed heads all dripping with blood. They have armlets, bracelets, and anklets made of fragments of skulls. They tie up their hair with the white snakes of the royal caste; they adorn their ears with the yellow snakes of the merchant caste, and their necks with the red snakes of the brahmin cast. They wear the green snakes of the menial caste around their wrists and ankles, and have a necklace reaching to the level of their hearts made of the black snakes of the outcastes. These five snake wreaths symbolize the intrinsic purity of the five poisons. Finally, wrathful deities are daubed with three substances: heaps of ashes of human corpses, drops of blood, and smearings of fat. The three kinds of garment, the two kinds of ornament, and the three kinds of daubing are known as the eight accoutrements of the charnel ground.

There are eight criteria [for measuring the quality] of the visualization—four of clarity (*gsal ba'i tshad*) and four of stability (*brtan pa'i tshad*)—which apply even to the stylistic details of the palace, such as the decoration of the roof and walls. The four criteria of clarity are as follows. First, the visualization should be bright (*sal le*): every detail, even to the white and black of the eyes, must be clear and distinct. Second, it should be limpid (*seng nge*), with everything clear, empty, and lucid. There should be a sharpness of awareness, without any dullness in which clarity and awareness are lacking. Third, it should be splendidly radiant (*lhag ge*). Every feature, even individual pores and hairs, should be pervaded by omniscient wisdom manifesting in innumerable qualities within the limpidity of the sense powers and consciousness. The visualization should be brilliant and vibrant, not like a rainbow or some other inanimate thing. Fourth, the visualization should be vivid and full of life (*lhang nge*). The deity should not be merely thought about ("It should be like this; it ought to have this or that"). It should arise in the mind as though visually perceived.

The four criteria of stability are as follows. First, the visualization should be free from the instability (*mi g.yo*) that comes from laziness or forgetfulness. Second, it should be unchanging (*mi 'gyur*)—it should not fade or become dim. Third, even when one meditates for a long time, the visualization should remain unaffected even by the subtle arising of the slightest thoughts—it should be completely unchanging (*mngon par mi 'gyur*). Fourth, in whichever way it is meditated upon—regarding color, feature of face, of limb, or posture (whether walking or sitting), and whatever lights may be radiated or absorbed—it is exactly thus that the deity should manifest (*ji ltar bsgom pa de ltar 'byung ba*).

When a visualization possesses these eight qualities, it is said to be "clearly manifest" (*rnam par gsal ba*). By repeatedly training oneself in this way, one will pass through the five experiences and come to their final conclusion.[238] The generation stage practice reaches its accomplishment when it is mastered in terms of the third of the three kinds of object. Regarding the latter, it is said in the *Instructions on the Great Glorious One:*[239]

> At the outset, the mudras (or forms) of the wisdom deities manifest as the imagined objects of the mind. Later, when the mind is well trained, they appear visibly as objects of sense. Finally, when the body and mind are perfectly trained, the deities manifest as tangible objects within the indivisibility of the two truths.[240]

It is also important to understand how the recollection of perfect purity and so forth is to be applied to the visualization.[241]

The nail of mantra, the essence of the deity

This refers to the recitation of the mantra, the essence and profound secret of the speech of all the Tathāgatas. It is on this basis that all sounds come to be perceived as having the nature of mantra. In the very moment they appear, they dissolve in the nature of ineffable emptiness.[242] The nail of mantra (*snying po sngags kyi gzer*) also refers to the training in the vajra recitation.[243]

The nail of unchanging ultimate wisdom

The nail of unchanging ultimate wisdom (*dgongs pa mi 'gyur ba'i gzer*) refers to the fact that skillful means are conjoined with extraordinary wisdom. Here, skillful means refers to the aspect of appearance (objects and sounds manifesting as deities and mantra); extraordinary wisdom[244] means the view of ultimate reality.

The nail of enlightened activity by means of the radiation and absorption of lights

The nail of the radiation and absorption of lights (*'phro 'du phrin las kyi gzer*), related to the deity, mantra, and ultimate nature, is the utterly pure path [by means of which supreme and ordinary enlightened activities are accomplished].[245]

A practice that is characterized by a strong clinging to the visualized forms is the complete opposite of the correct generation stage (endowed with the four nails); and it has been said that this kind of generation stage is practiced by non-Buddhists, and that certain kinds of demons that move in the air also possess it. As it is written in the tantra: "Without the nail of unchanging ultimate wisdom, even if one gains accomplishment as the Great Glorious One, the attainment will be ordinary. It will not be supreme. The one who goes astray in this way will become like the demon Rudra."

9. Progress through the grounds and paths of realization

59 For someone engaged in the Mantrayana, the generation stage is the unmistaken method for speedily realizing the thought-free primordial wisdom of the path of seeing, as this is set forth in the expository causal vehicle of the Bodhisattva path and celebrated in all the tantras of the old and new translations as the supreme accomplishment of Mahamudra. The path of Secret Mantra is a path replete with many skillful means and is without hardship. It is superior to the difficult path of the expository causal vehicle. Whatever kind of generation stage one practices, all appearing aspects are visualized as deities. For example, in the case of the six branches,[246] the (visualization of) the palace is the branch of Vairochana; passion is the branch of Vajradhara;[247] the bestowing of empowerment is the branch of Akshobhya; the making of offerings is Amoghasiddhi; the offering of praise is Ratnasambhava; and the tasting of amrita is Amitabha. It is in this way that one takes both rupakaya and enlightened activities as the path, and thus accumulates merit.

Through the understanding that all is entirely without intrinsic being, one takes the dharmakaya as the path and accumulates nonconceptual primordial wisdom.

Practitioners with sharp faculties—that is, those who take support of these two accumulations as the contributory cause, and who have gained clarity, purity, and stability in their practice of the generation stage (coordinated with the five paths of the causal vehicle)[248]—will progress thanks to their purification of the impure elements. They actualize the path of accumulation and also the stages of warmth, peak, and acceptance of the path of joining. At the stage of the supreme mundane level, they realize the state of a "Vidyādhara with a karmic body." This whole process is known as the "approach" phase (bsnyen pa). And it is with such a body that, on the path of seeing, they actualize the body of union associated, at the outset, with the path of learning, and attain the level of "Vidyādhara with power over life." Since such practitioners are now closer to the yidam-deity than before, this phase is referred to as "close approach" (nye bsnyen). On the path of meditation, the level of a "Vidyādhara of Mahamudra" is achieved. This is the same as accomplishing the yidam-deity. The practitioners' own benefit and the benefit of others are simultaneously achieved. This is the phase of "accomplishment" (sgrub pa). Finally, when all striving to achieve their own benefit is concluded, the practitioners' enlightened activities in postmeditation equal those of the Tathāgatas. When this happens, since the five kayas are spontaneously accomplished, these practitioners become similar to Vajradhara. All the qualities of elimination and realization are brought to perfection. This is the phase of "great accomplishment" (sgrub chen), the level of the "spontaneously accomplished Vidyādhara." The spiritual qualities of the four kinds of Vidyādhara relating to the realization of the purity and equality (of all phenomena) gradually increase as if one were climbing a stair. So it is that one achieves all the qualities of the five kayas, such as the five certainties (of place and so forth). And thanks to the extraordinary power of skillful means and wisdom, one comes, as if by magic and in the twinkling of an eye, to the highest pure field of Akanishtha.

7. The perfection stage
8. A brief explanation

61 In this section, an explanation is given of the perfection stage, where the predominant factor is wisdom.

In the father, or Mahayoga, tantras such as *Yamantaka* and *Guhyasamaja*, the thought-free primordial wisdom, profound and luminous (or, in the words of the root text, "luminous and empty") is cultivated by purifying the winds of the five elements. This is achieved by causing them to enter the central channel.

In the mother, or Anuyoga, tantras like *Vishuddha, Kila, Scripture of All-Inclusive Knowledge, Chakrasamvara,* and *Hevajra,* two methods are revealed, the chief purpose of which is to give mastery over the essential constituents (the bodhichitta or essence-drops), thereby engendering the primordial wisdom produced by their blissful melting. These methods are, first, the skillful means related to one's own body (namely, the practices of tummo, blazing and dripping, and so on) and, second, the skillful means related to the body of a partner, whereby one takes support of a karmamudra or consort in order to develop the primordial wisdom of the four joys.

62 In the nondual tantras, such as *Vajrasattva Mayajala, Kalachakra,* and *Sarvabuddhasamayoga,* one meditates principally on luminous, thought-free, inconceivable primordial wisdom, the luminosity of the great essence-drop, which is neither one nor many. By this means, there arises a perfect concentration marked by undefiled bliss.[249]

The first two classes, the father and mother tantras, teach the perfection stage mainly related to the wind and essence-drop. This perfection stage is a path that uses concepts and visual forms (*snang bcas dmigs pa'i lam*). The third class, that of the nondual tantras, principally sets forth the primordial wisdom of the union (of the dharmakaya and the rupakaya). The perfection stage of the nondual tantras is that of a luminosity that is free of forms.[250]

8. A detailed explanation

9. The perfection stage with visual forms

10. An explanation of the aggregate of the vajra body

11. An explanation of the aggregate of the vajra body according to the general tantra tradition[251]

12. A short explanation

To begin with, in the perfection stage that uses visual forms,[252] primordial wisdom must be generated by mastering the channels, winds, and essence-drops. In order to practice in this way, it is very important to understand what exactly these components are. The channels are referred to as "stationary" because, in being the nature of the deity, they do not move.[253] The wind contained within the channels is called "mobile" because it is [the vehicle of consciousness, and thus] the compounder of the three worlds. Supported, as it were, by both the channels and the winds, the essence-drop or bodhichitta[254] is said to be "positioned," in the sense that it is conveyed back and forth and is set in various positions by the winds. This bodhichitta[255] is by nature free from stain and is endowed with every perfect quality. A body that is endowed with the three coarse aspects of the channels, winds, and essence-drops is an extraordinary support[256] and is referred to as the city of the vajra aggregate. In this context, "vajra" refers to the inseparability of the enlightened body, speech, and mind—in other words, the inseparability of the three kayas.[257] Aggregate means a conglomeration of many things, referring, in this case, to the various displays of the perfectly pure nature: form and so on. And since it is the dwelling place of self-arisen, self-cognizing primordial wisdom, it is called a city.[258] If this support (the aggregate of the vajra body) is mastered, the wisdom of the three kayas, which is supported thereby, will be actualized in this present life. This method is indeed a great wonder.

12. A detailed explanation

13. The stationary channels[259]

The consciousness of a being in the bardo, which is in the process of gaining the support of a human body in one of the three cosmic continents, enters in the midst of the semen and ovum in the womb of its future mother. It is within this support (the mingled essences) that the channels first take shape. This begins at the navel, where the knot of channels contains two "eyes" and is shaped like the knot used to hobble the three legs of a horse together.[260] From this the body gradually takes shape. When the outer universe is formed, the quintessence of the elements becomes the central Mount Meru, and then by gradual degrees the golden mountains are formed, while the residue of the elements becomes the cosmic continents, the surrounding boundary, and so on. In parallel fashion, the quintessence of the male and female elements becomes the central channel or *uma* (Skt. *avadhuti*), together with the two lateral channels, *roma* (Skt. *rasanā*) and *kyangma* (Skt. *lalanā*), which are like pillars in the center of the body.

65   Within these channels are three seed-syllables. They are like the main figure and retinue (in a mandala), and act as the basis: outwardly, for the body, speech, and mind; inwardly, for the three poisons or defilements; and secretly, for the enlightened body, speech, and mind, as well as for "light," "increase of light," and "culmination of light." The various tantras and pith instructions describe the location of the syllables differently, but if the matter is discussed according to the function of the three channels, it seems sufficient to say that OM is in the roma, AH is in the kyangma, while HUNG is in the central uma.

66   The central channel is so called because, in terms of its position, it is situated between the two lateral channels and because, in terms of its ontological status, it is beyond the extremes of existence and nonexistence.[261] At the upper end of the central channel is located (in the form of the syllable HANG) the white essence-drop obtained from one's father. It has the nature of skillful means. At the lower end is the red essence-drop obtained from one's mother. This is in the form of the shortened A[262] and has the nature of wisdom. The upper end of the central channel penetrates the brahma aperture at the crown of the head, while the lower end enters the secret center below the navel. And between these two extremities, the central channel, which is of nondual nature, is the basis of the universal ground, which subsists in the form of the life-wind—the central channel being like space.

On the right of the central channel is the roma, the so-called corpse or taste channel.[263] This is so named to reflect its nature. Being unable to perform any function, it is like a corpse; but once brought under control, it is the channel that elicits the taste of bliss. On the left of the central channel is the kyangma, the so-called solitary channel. Its name reflects its character, for it is like an isolated rod that is not connected to anything else. When it is mastered by means of the pith instructions, the thought-free experience of ultimate reality occurs. It is thus the channel that elicits freedom from discursiveness.

The colors of the roma and kyangma are respectively white and red. In women, the position of the roma and kyangma is reversed, owing to their specific relationship with skillful means and wisdom. For them, therefore, the kyangma is on the right of the central channel. The three channels are the "mothers" of all the other channels—which is why their names all end in the syllable MA.[264]

The central channel is light blue in color. The roma and kyangma branch out from the uma at the level of the navel, but they loop around it and constrict it at the level of the kidneys and so on, up to the crown of the head. By being thus entwined with the uma, they form a series of twenty-one knots.

13. The chakras or channel-wheels

In order to purify the three poisons and the obscurations of the three doors,[265] and in order—as a result of such a purification—to actualize the qualities of the enlightened body, speech, and mind, it is said that one should, as the means of purification, meditate on three chakras: the chakras at the navel, throat, and heart. Similarly, for the purification of the three doors together with their activities, and for the actualization of the result of such a purification—namely, the four kayas or the enlightened body, speech, mind, and activities[266]—the means of purification is to meditate on the three chakras just mentioned, together with the fourth chakra at the crown of the head. In order to purify the five poisons and the five aggregates, and in order to obtain the five kayas and five primordial wisdoms, one must further add the chakra at the secret center. Finally, for the purification of the five poisons, together with the sixth poison of avaricious greed; for the purification of the five aggregates together with their habitual tendencies; and for the attain-

67

ment of the result of such purification—namely, the six wisdoms (that is, the previous five together with self-arisen primordial wisdom), the six paramitas, or again the five kayas accompanied by the sixth kaya of great bliss—one should also meditate on the space chakra of the ushnisha. The number of the radial (petallike) channels decreases and increases according to the sequence of chakras, three by three.[267] Moreover, there is a variation in the syllables positioned in them since the objects to be purified (defilements in the mind, channels, sense organs, and so on) as well as the means of purification (methods of meditation according to the essential instructions) also vary. The result, however, is the same.[268]

68   In the navel chakra of manifestation,[269] there are sixty-four radial channels; in the throat chakra of enjoyment, there are two sets of eight radial channels, making sixteen in all; and in the heart chakra, there are eight radial channels. The syllable HANG is located at the crown of the head in the chakra of great bliss, which possesses thirty-two radial channels. The bliss-preserving chakra of the secret center has seventy-two channels.[270] The ushnisha chakra is limpid and clear like space [it is free of all residual wind-mind and essence-drops]. For this reason, it does not consist of coarse channels. This chakra therefore has no numbering of channels and is referred to as the chakra of the realm of space.

69   In the center of each of the six chakras and in the intervening positions between them, there occur twelve transits or displacements of wind (*rlung gi 'pho ba*), which convey and position the white and red essence-drops in the channels. It is thanks to this that, in the outer world, the sun and moon [are seen to] move along the celestial belt of wind-energy and through the twelve mansions or houses.[271] Inwardly, these twelve transits of wind correspond to the twelve successive links of dependent arising, which are the ground or root of samsara, in which beings move and turn because of their karma and defilements. By binding the operations of the channels and winds,[272] the practitioner brings the essence-drops under control, thereby preventing their transit through the impure channels. Passing through the paths of the roma and kyangma, the essence-drops are reversed at the lower extremity of the uma, and propelled upward.[273] When they enter the primordial wisdom chakra at the secret center, the first transit of the wind and the

first dependent link are halted, and the qualities of the first ground of realization are achieved.

In the same way, the successive transits of the wind through each of the chakras and through the intervening positions between them (as far as the space chakra of the ushnisha) are brought to a halt, as also the corresponding dependent links. In this way, the twelve grounds of realization are gradually perfected. When the wind-mind, accompanied by the essence-drop, mingles with the realm of space [ushnisha chakra], all the outer and inner interdependent cycles of samsara are interrupted and the unchanging great bliss, actual buddhahood, is attained.[274] Such is the tradition of the Primordial Buddha, namely, the tradition of *Kalachakra*.[275]

Different tantras have different perfection-stage practices according to their presentation of the six chakras. The *Mayajala*, for example, says that the channels of the chakras mentioned above contain the seeds of the six realms. These harbor the propensities associated with those same realms, which are to be purified through the path of the perfection stage. They consist of impure winds and essence-drops. These arise from the two kinds of ignorance, and take the form of seed-syllables. By mastering the wind and essence-drop of pure wisdom, which have the nature of awareness and are the agents of purification, the habitual tendencies of the six classes of beings are annihilated—"purified," as the root text says—"by the six Munis or Sages."[276] Through such practice, avaricious greed and so on is purified, and the qualities of the six paramitas are naturally perfected. In this context, the expression "six paramitas" refers to the pure winds and essence-drops of the six chakras, as well as to the pith instructions on how to meditate on them. Once the six seed-syllables are purified, the result of this purification is accomplished, namely, the five distinct primordial wisdoms (mirrorlike wisdom and so on) together with the sixth, the self-arisen primordial wisdom, which is the inconceivable nature of the preceding five. It is thus that all the qualities of buddhahood are achieved.

Likewise, according to the tradition of the root tantra of the *Mayajala*, there is in the heart, and arising from the unobstructed creative power of the five primordial wisdoms, the wheel of peaceful deities: the channels and essence-drops, which are the basis on which thoughts are purified into deities. Then, in the crown of the head, there arises the profound radiance of these same peaceful deities, based on the channels and essence-drops. This is the wheel of the wrathful deities. In the heart, there are forty-two radial channels corresponding to the forty-two peaceful deities. In the skull, there are fifty-eight channels corresponding to the fifty-eight wrathful deities. It is thus that the number of channels corresponds to the hundred sacred families of the deities.[277] There are lesser channels in infinite number, but one speaks particularly of seventy-two thousand channels in which the winds and essence-drops circulate.[278]

When, according to this tantra (explained in the form of oral advice), pith instructions are given for the practice of the paths of liberation and skillful means, it is said that the path of liberation teaches mainly the generation stage according to the individual sadhanas of the peaceful and wrathful deities. As for the path of skillful means, there are two approaches or doors: the path that liberates through the upper door, and the path of enjoyment of the three worlds through the lower door.[279] It is said that, thanks to these two approaches, the wisdom of luminosity is instantly actualized. Such is the tradition of the *Vajrasattva Mayajala*, which is the ground from which all the [Mahayoga] tantras derive. It is the king of all pith instructions.

13. The mobile winds on the outer, inner, and secret levels[280]
14. The winds on the outer level

73   Regarding the mobile winds, a distinction is made between the major and minor winds of the earth, water, fire, and air elements.[281] In every healthy adult, in the course of a single day, there moves a complement of 21,600 major winds of the four elements.[282] As it is written in the *Word-Transcending Tantra*:

> One and twenty thousand
> And six hundred winds
> Are supported by the channels,
> And are referred to as the major mobile winds.

In elderly people, the number of winds declines: fifty-eight are missing; in children,[283] on the other hand, in whom the elements are not fully developed, thirty-two winds are absent. The minor winds of the elements refer mainly to the winds of mental processes.[284] These function continuously as the vehicles of the eighty-four thousand kinds of thoughts, corresponding to the eighty-four thousand kinds of defilement. It is in reference to these minor winds that the *Mayajala* declares: "The others number four and eighty thousand." Leaving aside the winds that pass through the mouth and nose [and are involved in the respiration process], it is said that if a count is made of the winds that are the bases of thought and primordial wisdom, and circulate through the pulsating channel[285] that branches out from the chakra of enjoyment, one will come to a total of one hundred and twenty-six thousand winds moving within the body.

There are five winds that act as the roots of all the other major and minor winds. These are: the life-supporting wind, the fire-accompanying wind, the all-pervading wind, the upward-moving wind, and the downward-voiding wind.[286] Their individual functions are as follows. The life-supporting wind dwells in the heart[287] and is the support of life; the fire-accompanying wind dwells in the stomach and produces warmth; the all-pervading wind is present throughout the body and is the source of physical strength; the upward-moving wind makes possible the respiratory functions; and the downward-voiding wind provides for the functions of walking, sitting, urination, and defecation.

The upward-moving wind is male in character and dwells in the upper part of the body. The downward-voiding wind is female in character and resides in the lower part. The three remaining winds are neutral and reside equally in the upper and lower parts of the body.[288] When the winds circulate through the nostrils, the male wind related to skillful means passes through the right nostril, the female wind related to wisdom passes through the left nostril, and the neutral wind passes through both nostrils equally. These are the coarse aspects of the winds, in other words, the outer winds.

74

75

14. The winds on the inner level

The inner winds have an inward function more subtle than the winds previously described.[289] They are colored in accordance with their corresponding element: the earth-wind is yellow; the water-wind is white; the fire-wind is red; the air-wind is green; the space-wind is deep blue. When one meditates on them, their respective shapes are as follows: the earth-wind is square; the water-wind is semicircular; the fire-wind is triangular; the air-wind has the shape of a bent bow; the space-wind is circular.[290] As to their function, these winds, which are by nature the karmic wind, are the support for the aggregates, elements, and sense-fields, which manifest and remain for as long as the winds do not dissolve.[291] They are the basis for the deluded perceptions of samsara.[292]

Coming now to a more detailed explanation, the winds constitute the support for both the ordinary mind and for primordial wisdom.[293] When the mind is in its impure state, and when circumstances that call forth the five poisons or defilements present themselves, it is on the basis of the five winds that these same defilements automatically proliferate.[294] When, however, the mind is in a state of pure primordial wisdom, the five winds are the foundations for the appearance of the five primordial wisdoms, which directly cognize all things both in their nature and in their multiplicity.[295] Thus the five winds are like the causes from which the ordinary mind and primordial wisdom both proliferate as though they were results. They are the basis for them.

[The manner in which these winds circulate is as follows. In the summer, it is the wind of fire that circulates; in the autumn, it is the wind of air; in winter, it is the wind of water; and in the spring, it is the wind of earth. Consequently, it is necessary to meditate specifically on the wind that counterbalances the one that is dominant in a given season. It is also possible to meditate on the wind of space, which is good in any season. Alternatively, if one is suffering from an illness, one can meditate on the wind that counteracts it and thus cure oneself of the complaint.][296]

76 In particular, if the five refined winds of the elements, bound together in the single wind-mind,[297] are made to enter the dhuti, or central channel, various phenomena will appear, and these are the signs that the five

winds have been refined. When the wind from the right side of the body enters the central channel, the appearance of smoke occurs. When the wind from the left side enters the central channel, mirages occur. When the wind in question is that of fire, one will see blazing lights; when the wind is that of water, one will see something like clouds and moonlight shining through a skylight; when the wind is that of earth, one will see a golden-colored radiance and flashes of lightning; when the wind is that of space, dark-blue circles will appear and disks of rainbow light.[298] When all the winds enter the central channel, they give rise to the vision of five-colored light, rainbows, disks of light, deities, and so forth. In particular, with the achievement of a perfect concentration connected with the limitless ayatanas of earth, air, fire, water, and space, miraculous powers are gained, such as the ability to change things into earth, air, fire, and so on.[299] The five defilements are also purified, five-colored lights are seen, and the power of traveling to buddhafields is gained. Every excellent quality is acquired, such as the five primordial wisdoms, and many wondrous powers. As it is said in the *Mayajala*:

> When the five winds gain in strength,
> Five lights are seen, five inner primal wisdoms.
> To the field of the five kayas one can go.
> The five unbounded ayatanas and the rest are gained.

14. The winds on the secret level

The secret winds are extremely difficult to realize, for their nature is the five aspects of ultimate primordial wisdom; they have nothing to do with gross phenomena endowed with shape, color, and other characteristics. When the inner winds previously explained enter the central channel and the outer, inner, and secret winds fuse together inseparably, thought-free vipashyana, the wisdom mind of luminosity, is perfected.[300]

13. The positioned bodhichitta

The bodhichitta, the quintessence of the elements—that is, the male and female essences—is the support of consciousness. It is positioned

77

in the channels by the wind, and flows in the following way. The root text says that there issues "from the upper end of the roma" (by which is meant the letter HANG in the crown of the head), a flow of white essence-drops, the lunar amrita, which pervades the entire body. Likewise it is said that "from the lower end of the kyangma"—by which is meant the "A-SHÉ" (Tib. *a shad*)[301] in the secret center—the red essence-drops, the solar blood, spread through the channels and fill them.

Owing to the interdependence of skillful means and wisdom, in the case of men, the end of the wisdom channel (kyangma) is tied, whereas in the case of women, the end of the channel of skillful means (roma) is tied. This is why the red essence contained in a man's body, and the white essence contained in a woman's body, are retained and cannot be emitted.

78   As well as flowing within the two [lateral] channels, the refined essential constituents—in other words, the refined white essence-drops of skillful means and the refined red essence-drops of wisdom—spread out to the radial channels of the chakras and channel knots, which are in the shape of letters, and in their nature are said to correspond to the twenty-four sacred lands. The white and red essence-drops dwell there in the form of dakas and yoginis. They are the radiant display of the mind: nondual appearance and emptiness, skillful means and wisdom inseparable. These dakas and yoginis, who are joined in union, receive from the practitioners who meditate on the yoga of blissful melting (of the white essence-drop) the offering of nondual bliss-emptiness.[302] It is thus that the practitioners of this yoga quickly complete the two accumulations.

12. Conclusion

79   In short, the stationary channels, which are the foundation of the physical body, are like conduits used for irrigation. The mobile wind, which is the foundation of speech, is like a steersman going to and fro, traveling to samsara or nirvana. The essence-drops (in other words, bodhichitta, which is based upon the wind and is the foundation of the mind) are like water that gathers in the places to which it is channeled.[303] The six chakras are arranged vertically along the central channel, which is

like a vital axis. This, the actual central channel,[304] is present, and yet it has no material substance. It is (like) Rahu. For just as in the outer world, Rahu can with his mouth and tail devour the sun and moon, so it is that, inwardly, through concentration on the blazing A-SHÉ and the dripping HANG (the expression respectively of the red and white essence-drops in the lower and upper ends of the central channel) the winds can be made to enter, remain, and dissolve in this same channel. If one is able to bind therein the [karmic] wind by meditating on the uninterrupted flow within the space of this channel of the white and red essence-drops, which have the nature of the sun and moon respectively, then in the outer world, Rahu will be powerless to cause solar and lunar eclipses. In other words, a yogi who is adept in this practice will have power over the movements of the sun and moon.

Just like the volcanic fire[305] that, at the end of time, consumes the oceans, the fire emerging from the A-SHÉ consumes all the aggregates and elements without exception. This is why it is called ferocious, or tummo.[306] According to the essential instructions, practitioners must bind "life" (the wind) and "exertion" (the mind) together inseparably in the expanse of Rahu, the central channel. By means of the mobile wind, this "chariot" is brought to each of the chakras in succession, and this results in the refinement of the wind-mind. Gradually, the knots on the central channel are loosed two by two.

When the refined wind and the refined essence-drops enter the "belly" of Rahu, the first ground of realization is actualized, together with all its qualities. From that point onward, up to the tenth ground of realization, excellent qualities increase. Finally, when the last knot (the twenty-first) is loosed, the refined wind-mind, accompanied by the essence-drops, ascends to the ushnisha. When this happens, the level of Vajradhara is attained.

11. An explanation of the aggregate of the vajra body according to the tradition of the *Mayajala*, as explained in the *Secret Heart-Essence*

There now follows a brief explanation of the relevant section of the *Mayajala*, the king of tantras for the old translation school, as given by the great master Vimalamitra[307] in his commentary the *Secret Heart-Essence*.

The universe, together with its living contents, is by nature complete within one's own body and mind. The center of the city of the aggregate of the vajra body is the place where the utterly pure nature, the dharmakaya, resides. This may be described as the sugatagarbha, the nature of the mind, which remains in a neutral state[308] throughout the three times, past, present, and future. In the *Manjushri Nama Sanghiti*, it is written: "He is the one who realizes the timelessness of the three times." All Buddhas—past, present, and to come—attain enlightenment solely through the actualization of this fundamental nature. It is said in the tradition of the *Mayajala* that this actualization is achieved through the perfection-stage practice that brings under control the seed-syllables dwelling in the heart, from which both samsara and nirvana emerge and into which they both dissolve.

82   Because the heart (that is, the chakra of ultimate reality) is indestructible—in other words, unchanging—it is called Vajrasana, the vajra-throne; and because its expanse is so profound, it is called the everlasting knot. Here, in the center of each of the eight refined channels are the seed-syllables, which are present there as objects to be purified,[309] together with the agents of purification, the wisdom syllables OM, AH, and HUNG. It is on these syllables that one should concentrate one's practice. When commenting in the *Secret Heart-Essence* on the root verse of the *Mayajala*—"One should know that there are eight"—Vimalamitra says:

> Within the hollow recess at the center of the heart, there are eight channels, threadlike and refined, each of which is like a chewed tendon. Of these, three are the channels of ultimate nature, one is the channel of primordial wisdom, three are the channels of the ordinary mind, and one is the channel of perfect qualities.

The three channels in the middle are the bases of the three kayas and the unchanging ultimate nature. In front of them is the channel that is the basis for the arising of the primordial wisdom, whereas behind them is the channel of perfect qualities, from which boundless pure appearances arise, such as buddhafields and measureless palaces. On the left are the three channels of the ordinary mind, which are the bases for all the deluded dualistic appearances of the three worlds, as well as for the three poisons. Categorized according to their function, these eight channels are reduced to four groups or kinds.

In the middle of each of the channels belonging to these four groups are found the seed-syllables of samsara, together with the eight consciousnesses, all of which are present as objects to be purified. They are accompanied by the seed-syllables of nirvana, which are agents of purification. In the center of the channels of ultimate nature, which are bright yellow and round in shape, are su and tre, the seed-syllables of the asuras and animals. Above them is the essence of the vajra body in the form of the syllable om, gleaming with light like a tent of glossy silk. Likewise in these channels, there is the consciousness of the universal ground. In the primordial-wisdom channel, which is dark blue and square in shape, are white a and red nri, the seed-syllables of gods and humans. Above them is the nature of the vajra mind in the form of a dark-blue hung. Here, too, is found the mental consciousness. In the center of the channels of the ordinary mind, which are red and semicircular in shape, are du and pre, the seed-syllables of hell beings and pretas. Above them is the nature of the vajra speech in the form of the syllable ah, shining like a ruby. Here, too, is the defiled consciousness. Finally, in the center of the channel of perfect qualities, which is dark red and triangular in shape, are the five sense consciousnesses.

The habitual tendencies, which propel beings into the six realms of samsaric existence, are stored in the seed-syllables of the six realms (which are objects to be purified) and generate the hallucinatory perception of these same realms. In general, positive actions of body, speech, and mind, which bring about the result of liberation, and in particular all the practices that employ the three vajras as the path, are stored in the seed-syllables of the enlightened body, speech, and mind, and produce the qualities of the path and its result. More specifically, through the visualization of the seed-syllables of both the objects and the agents of purification, through the perfection stage practice whereby the wind-mind is mastered, and through the recitation of the seed-syllables of the enlightened body, speech, and mind, these same syllables gain in strength and are able to purify the seed-syllables of the samsaric realms, together with the habitual tendencies that are lodged within them. It is by such means that the three vajras are accomplished.

84   At the center of the radial channels of the heart chakra, is the essence-drop that gathers within itself the five quintessences (of the elements). Now according to other classes of tantra, the middle channel (of the three in the center) is the authentic central channel. But even the refined wind of the central channel must enter the channel of primordial wisdom. Within this refined luminous channel, which is white like a crystal thread and ten times finer than a horse hair, is found the appearing aspect of the extremely subtle wind-mind, in other words, its unobstructed radiance based on the mingling of the quintessence of "female essence" (meaning "blood") and of "breath." It is the extremely subtle, luminous essence-drop endowed with the five-colored light of wisdom. This luminous essence-drop consists of the quintessences of the five elements. The quintessence of earth is like a white silken thread; the quintessence of water (which is the nature of blood) is like liquid vermilion; the quintessence of fire is like the warmth that makes a kind of haze on a mirror when it is left in the sun. The quintessence of the wind element is like the moist exhalation emitted by gold when it is in the earth. The quintessence of the space element is openness. This essence-drop is the basis for the naturally luminous nature of consciousness: uncompounded bodhichitta. It is for this reason that the chakra of ultimate reality at the level of the heart is referred to as the "palace of Samantabhadra and Samantabhadri," the inseparability of the appearance and emptiness of self-cognizing primordial wisdom. And the latter's unceasing radiance of the five wisdoms constitutes the Buddhas of the five families. In inconceivable ultimate reality, there is no place at all for support and supported. Yet, on the conventional level, there is the appearance of something supported, for which reason, one speaks of deities dwelling in their palaces. When the refined wind-mind gathers in the center of the chakra of ultimate reality at the heart, the spontaneous radiance of uncompounded primordial wisdom—the nirvanic perceptions of pure buddhafields, palaces, deities, rays of light, and the lights of primordial wisdom—arises even while one is still on the path.

85   When one is finally freed from the aggregates, the elements, and sense-fields—that is, all the impure phenomena that are but the display

of the five-colored lights (the appearance aspect) marred by the karmic wind—the dharmakaya (the emptiness aspect), the nature beyond all conceptual constructs, is actualized.

In truth, however, appearance and emptiness have never been separate. They are not two distinct realities to be blended into one. When deluded perceptions, together with the associated habitual patterns, are reabsorbed into the expanse of ultimate reality, appearance and emptiness mingle in a single taste. It is thus that the twofold accumulation of the path is effortlessly perfected, and buddhahood is attained. The place where enlightenment is accomplished is the utterly pure field of Akanishtha, which, on account of its infinite dimensions and configuration, is also called Dense Array. This is not a concrete location, different from the three worlds or the nature of the mind. When all the impure features of the wind-mind, the stains that conceal the expanse of ultimate reality, are removed, this buddhafield spontaneously manifests as the self-experience of primordial wisdom.

The physical body, therefore, is the support or basis of self-cognizing   86 primordial wisdom, the great and all-pervading ultimate nature of all phenomena, whether of samsara, nirvana, or the path. Even in the state of samsaric delusion, the mind in its ultimate condition is naturally and perfectly pure; and all the kayas and wisdoms are spontaneously and fully present in it. Its enlightened qualities are neither spoiled or reduced in number (and therefore incomplete), nor are they weakened or diminished. This can be illustrated by a drop of mercury which, though it falls into a pile of dust, remains unmixed with it. This unchanging nature, this ultimate bodhichitta or sugatagarbha, is present in every being that has a mind, down to a tiny insect on a blade of grass. As it is explained in all the tantras, commentaries, and essential instructions: "The sugatagarbha is present in all beings just as oil is present in all sesame seeds."

10. **An explanation of the actual perfection stage**
11. **The skillful path of one's own body**
It is taught that if one understands the constitution of the channels,   87 winds, and essence-drops of the aggregate of the supporting vajra body;

and if one understands what it supports, namely, the primordial ground, which is ultimate reality or the nature of the mind; and if in one's practice, one focuses on the vital points of this vajra body, following the essential instructions of the profound perfection stage, the wisdom that is based thereon will be swiftly actualized. It should be understood, furthermore, that all the essential instructions of the perfection stage of the tantras of both the old and new translations are included within the six yogas.

First of all, the root of all the paths of the perfection stage is the practice of tummo (*gtum mo*).[310] For all appearances, which are the aspect of skillful means, are to be purified in the expanse of unborn wisdom. Second, the foundation of the path is the practice of the illusory body (*sgyu lus*).[311] One must grow accustomed to the concentration in which one views all pure and impure phenomena as being without inherent existence, like illusions. It is impossible to free oneself as long as one believes that phenomena exist truly. Third, the sign of "warmth" or progress on the path is the dream yoga (*rmi lam*), whereby dreams (the state of delusion within delusion) are purified. It should be understood that the sign indicating that one is able to free oneself in the present life, at death, or in the bardo state, is that one can dissolve one's dreams into the state of luminosity, or else purify them through the recognition that they are illusions. For this reason, it is necessary to train in dream yoga. Fourth, the essence of the path is the practice of luminosity (*'od gsal*), which should be the main object of meditation. Fifth, the harbinger on the path, is the practice related to the bardo (*bar do*), which creates a link between the practice of the path and its result. Sixth, the practice that gives confident assurance while one is on the path is the transference of consciousness (*'pho ba*). If through laziness or untimely death and so on, practitioners have not won through to the ultimate point of the path, they must use the appropriate essential instructions, and forcefully and swiftly transfer their consciousness to a pure field.

Tummo, the root of the path[312]

There are three kinds of tummo: the tummo practice (*las kyi gtum mo*), the experiential tummo (*nyams kyi gtum mo*), and the supreme tummo (*mchog gi gtum mo*). In the tummo practice, one must restrict one's physical activity by keeping the body motionless in the seven-point posture; one must restrict one's speech by holding the vase breath; and one must restrict one's mind[313] by meditating on the tummo, the blazing and dripping, and so on.

Experiential tummo comprises all the experiences that arise indicating that, thanks to concentration on the wind-mind, the wind has gathered in the central channel. For example, there will be the perceptions of smoke, mirage, and fireflies, and the blissful experience of emptiness.

Supreme tummo, the freedom from discursive thought, occurs when the wind-mind dissolves in the central channel, and there manifests the experience of luminosity induced by the appearance of light, the increase of light, and the culmination of light.[314]

Illusory body, the foundation of the path

There are three kinds of illusory body: the impure illusory body,[315] the pure illusory body, and the hidden illusory body of wind-mind. The practice related to the impure illusory body is the meditation in which one sees all outer and inner phenomena as an illusion and dream. The practice related to the pure illusory body is the meditation in which one sees all appearances as illusion-like deities. When practicing the hidden illusory body of wind-mind, one first acquires the habit of meditating alternately on appearances as deities and on their dissolution into luminosity. When one has removed one's clinging to one's ordinary coarse body, one will, at the time of dissolution [into luminosity], arise again in the form of a deity, which is like an illusory apparition composed of wind-mind. At that point, one appears to oneself in the form of the deity, and one's earlier coarse body no longer appears in the perceptions of others. When this happens, it is called the accomplishment of the illusory body.

Dream yoga, the gauge of progress on the path

Dream yoga is part of the illusory body practice.[316] First of all, one should train oneself to recognize one's dreams as dreams, practicing the dream yoga either through the power of one's will and aspiration, or of the wind.[317] One should then train in transforming one's dreams. By means of one's dreams, one should travel to buddhafields or to different places in the world, going to frightening places, into fire, water, deep ravines, and so on. Finally, by perceiving all the visions of one's dreams as deities and palaces, one should purify them by understanding that they are illusory apparitions. One should then train in the process of dissolution, letting them melt into luminosity—the skillful method whereby dreams subside in the expanse of emptiness.

Luminosity, the essence of the path

The apparitional deity figuring in the previous practice of the illusory body should be made to melt into the state of luminosity through the process of dissolution, and one should train oneself in the coemergent wisdom of the four joys, by using any of the practices based either upon one's own body (tummo, for example) or upon the body of a consort. By such means, the state of luminosity will dawn in the mind, called forth by the four voids, or four joys.

The four voids (*stong pa*) are as follows. The first void occurs, when consciousness dissolves into "light" (*snang ba*), and thirty-three kinds of thoughts deriving from aversion are halted. As an outer sign of this, there manifests the "light of the path of whiteness," similar to the autumn sky suffused with moonlight. As an inner sign, there occurs the experience of clarity beyond all center and circumference. The name of this experience is "void."

The second void occurs when the "light" dissolves into "increase of light" (*mched pa*), and the forty kinds of thought deriving from desire are halted. As an external sign of this, there manifests the "path of redness," which is like the autumn sky suffused with sunlight. As an inner sign, there arises an unbounded bliss. This is called great void.

The third void occurs when the "increase of light " dissolves into the "culmination of light" (*thob pa*), and the seven kinds of thought deriving from ignorance are halted. As an outer sign of this, there occurs the path of blackness similar to the darkened autumn sky, and as an inner sign, there occurs the experience of an absence of thought that is devoid of center and circumference. This is called utter void.

It is then said that the "culmination of light dissolves into luminosity." In fact, however, when the thought-free experience of the foregoing "culmination of light" clears a little, there naturally arises ultimate, coemergent primordial wisdom, which is the luminosity immanent in the ground nature. This is like the autumn sky at dawn, free from the previously mentioned conditions (moon, sun, and darkness). This is called the luminosity of total void.

The thirty-three thoughts or mental states associated with aversion (for unwanted objects) are:

1. slight dislike (toward an unwanted object),
2. moderate dislike (toward an unwanted object),
3. intense dislike (toward an unwanted object),
4. mental movement (the mind is unsatisfied with mere reflection on inner mental images—of things, people, power, possessions, and so on—and moves out toward extramental things),
5. mental engagement (the mind pursues its object with specific interest),
6. slight regret (at the absence of a desired object),
7. moderate regret (at the absence of a desired object),
8. intense regret (at the absence of a desired object),
9. quietude (the mind's natural state, the experience of calm after the removal of the unwanted object),
10. mental disquiet (an agitated state of mind or manifest worry),
11. slight fear (or dread on encountering an unwanted object),
12. moderate fear (or dread on encountering an unwanted object),
13. intense fear (or dread on encountering an unwanted object),
14. slight craving (or attraction for an object),
15. moderate craving (or attraction for an object),
16. intense craving (or attraction for an object),
17. strong grasping (the seizing of desired objects through fighting or lawsuits),
18. nonvirtue (the state of mind that vacillates at, or is impatient with, the prospect of doing good),
19. hunger (the desire for food) and thirst (the desire for drink),
20. slight feelings (of pleasure at the discomfiture of enemies, and of displeasure or indifference at the contentment of enemies),
21. moderate feelings (of pleasure at the discomfiture of enemies, and of displeasure or indifference at the contentment of enemies),

22. intense feelings (of pleasure at the discomfiture of enemies, and of displeasure or indifference at the contentment of enemies),
23. cognition (the mental state of knowing),
24. cognitive basis (the thought of the object known),
25. discernment (distinguishing right from wrong),
26. a sense of shame (shrinking from negative action because of one's moral conscience or knowledge of the Dharma),
27. compassion (the desire to free others from suffering),
28. love (for those one likes and wants to protect from unwanted things),
29. moderate love (for those one likes and wants to protect from unwanted things),
30. intense love (for those one likes and wants to protect from unwanted things),
31. doubt (uncertainty concerning the actions of others, lack of certainty),
32. covetousness (the malicious wish to acquire the things of others, the so-called act of gathering), and
33. avarice (clinging to one's possessions; this is also understood as jealousy, a state of mind that is disturbed by the perfections of others).

The forty thoughts or mental states associated with desire are:

1. attachment (the clinging of the mind to an object that has been acquired),
2. desire (for an object not yet acquired),
3. joy (slight feeling of delight on seeing a pleasant object),
4. moderate joy (a more intense feeling of delight on seeing a pleasant object),
5. intense joy (an extremely intense delight on seeing a pleasant object),
6. rejoicing (the happiness that comes from achieving one's desired aim),
7. intense exhilaration (the repeated experience of happiness),
8. amazement (a state of astonished doubt regarding the various

things one hears, or astonishment on seeing something not encountered before),

9. excitement (a state in which the mind is carried away on seeing pleasant objects),
10. satisfaction (the experience of happiness or contentment produced by pleasant objects),
11. the desire to embrace,
12. the desire to kiss,
13. the desire to absorb,
14. stability (a mental disposition that cannot be changed),
15. diligence (striving in virtue),
16. pride (an attitude of self-importance),
17. sense of engagement (the wish to see something through to the end),
18. a thieving attitude (the wish to steal),
19. belligerence (the wish to vanquish the forces of others),
20. delight (interest felt in the practice of virtue),
21. determination free of doubt (an arrogant attitude of perseverance in nonvirtue or in the gaining of something),
22. moderate determination,
23. intense determination,
24. proud impertinence (the wish to engage holy beings in argument without reason),
25. flirtation (to assume an impressive or flirtatious demeanor in the presence of someone attractive),
26. hostility (a rancorous attitude),
27. virtuousness (the wish to strive in good actions),
28. the impulse to speak clearly (for the sake of correct understanding),
29. the desire to speak truth (without deceit),
30. the desire to speak untruth (the wish to conceal the truth),
31. certainty (stability of mind),
32. uninterest (not to want to possess something),
33. disposition of a donor (the wish to give one's possessions),
34. encouragement (the wish to stir the fainthearted),

35. fortitude (the wish to prevail over one's enemies, namely, the defilements),
36. shamelessness (not to avoid the ten nonvirtues but to indulge in them, either for one's own sake or on account of the teachings),
37. deceitfulness (the intention to mislead),
38. viciousness (skill in evil attitudes),
39. malice (to wish evil on others), and
40. dishonesty (a lack of probity).

The seven thoughts or mental states associated with ignorance are:

1. moderate desire (a state of wishing without knowing what one really wants),
2. forgetfulness (a low level of mindfulness),
3. confusion (for example, to take a mirage for real water),
4. taciturnity (a state of not wishing to speak),
5. weariness (a feeling of fatigue),
6. indolence (a lack of joy in virtue), and
7. doubt (hesitation with regard to what is true, or to be uncertain about the karmic principle and ultimate reality).[318]

Whether it is induced by the experience of "light," "increase of light," or "culmination of light," or indeed by the four joys, luminosity is always the same. It is simply luminosity. There is a distinction to be made, however, between "example luminosity" and "ultimate, actual luminosity." The example luminosity has several stages and occurs up to the point where one sees the truth of the path of seeing. This realization corresponds to ultimate luminosity, which, from this moment onward, is unchanging. The "ground-luminosity" is the luminosity that arises at the end of the dissolution process occurring at the moment of death, during sleep,[319] and so forth. Thanks to their training on the path, practitioners are able to recognize it and are thus able to mingle either with the example or the actual, ultimate luminosity.

The bardo, the harbinger on the path[320]

The bardo practice is the harbinger on the path because it forms a link between the practice and its result. When the ground-luminosity—

elicited by the three experiences of light, increase of light, and culmination of light—arises in the bardo of the moment of death, practitioners of superior capacity are able to recognize it, for they have previously become confidently familiar with it. They are thus able to gain liberation in the luminosity of the dharmakaya. A practitioner of moderate capacity will use the support of the practice of the illusory body, and will arise, while in the murky bardo of becoming, in the illusory form of a deity.[321] Practitioners of basic capacity, who are subject to both craving and grasping, will have the power either to select an excellent womb in the natural bardo of life and close the door of the less fortunate ones, or else to concentrate on going to the pure fields. They will thus be in a position to take birth as a being capable of practicing the Mantrayana and will be able to continue on the path.

The practice of transference, which gives confident assurance while one is on the path

Following the essential instructions, it might be necessary, at the end of one's life, to transfer one's consciousness forcefully and swiftly to a pure field.

A superior practitioner, who has realized the view of ultimate reality in this life and who has attained the full reach of accomplishment, has no need to practice transference. But for those whose practice is weak, transference will act as their guardian escort.[322] As it is said, when those of weak practice notice the signs of approaching death and are certain that they are about to die, they must, before the stages of inner dissolution occur, transfer their consciousness to a pure land. They do this by visualizing their consciousness in the form of a ball of light and by uttering the appropriate syllables.

Conclusion

Practitioners who endeavor on the path of these six yogas will gain accomplishment simply by mastery of the channels, winds, and essence-drops of their own bodies, without relying on the body of a consort. This path is therefore called the skillful path of one's own body (*rang lus thabs ldan*), or the path that liberates through the upper door.[323]

11. The skillful path of the consort's body

88 By means of the skillful path of their own body, practitioners straighten their channels, master the essence-drops, and purify the winds. When these three elements are brought completely under control, they are refined and become serviceable. It is then that practitioners can follow the skillful path of another's body (*gzhan lus thabs ldan*), in other words, the path of the lower door of enjoyment of the three worlds.[324] Such practitioners are introduced instantaneously to the coemergent primordial wisdom of blissful emptiness, thereby embarking on the path of Noble Beings.[325] This is an amazing skillful means whereby all the channels, winds, and essence-drops, the ground of all samsaric phenomena, become the path that liberates in the state of great luminosity. It is the instantaneous path of skillful means, otherwise known as the path of the consort's body.[326] Alternatively, it may be said that this is an extraordinary path of skillful means wherein the entire range of the generation and perfection stages is practiced in an authentic way.

9. The perfection stage that is without visual forms

89 The perfection stage that utilizes visual forms (*snang bcas rdzogs rim*) must be purified and refined into the perfection stage that is without forms (*snang med rdzogs rim*), in other words, the inconceivable primordial wisdom beyond all conceptual constructs. All the deities of the generation and perfection stages, with faces, arms, and so forth, finally come to rest in the state beyond all reference.

When practitioners have purified their clinging to impure reality, by meditating on phenomena (the inanimate universe and its living contents) as pure lands, palaces, and deities, these same pure appearances then melt into light. The pure land dissolves into the palace, and gradually the palace dissolves into the retinue, which in turn dissolves into the main deity. The main deity then dissolves into the wisdom deity, which then dissolves into the seed-syllable in the heart. The seed-syllable (for example, HUNG) then dissolves gradually, beginning with the shabkyu up to the anushvara, which then dissolves from below into the nada.[327] All is now empty and is like the limpid sky. The practitioner then rests in a state of natural spaciousness beyond conceptual constructs, the domain of self-cognizing primordial wisdom.[328]

7. Conclusion: The benefits of the generation and perfection stages

The generation-stage practice puts a stop to the habitual propensities 90 associated with the world, bodies, and minds. In other words, it eliminates the assumption of the true existence of the appearances associated with the three doors of body, speech, and mind. The perfection stage practice then removes all subtle clinging to the sublime excellence of the deities. In other words, it eliminates subtle clinging to appearance and activities, regarded as illusion-like deities. Bliss arises on the basis of the essence-drops; clarity occurs on the basis of the winds; and the compounded state of thought-free wisdom and the uncompounded, coemergent primordial wisdom arise on the basis of the channels.

The practices of the utterly profound perfection stage on the channels, essence-drops, and winds are therefore the supreme means of eliciting coemergent primordial wisdom. This is expounded only in the highest tantras. By contrast, in the three lower, outer tantras, only the dissolution of the deities at the end of the session and the resting in thought-free meditation are expounded. For those with sharp faculties and diligent endeavor, such practices constitute the short path to the attainment of the Vajradhara level in a single lifetime. This is an extremely profound path that should be concealed from those who are not ready to receive it. It should not be practiced by those who lack the requisite karmic fortune.

6. Samaya, the favorable condition for progress on the path
7. A brief explanation

Samaya is the friend that helps us to progress through the generation 91 and perfection stages, and to perfect the two accomplishments. People who receive empowerment, thereby entering the Secret Mantra, must, according to their promise, observe without fail all the crucial precepts of the Mantrayana, concerning what is to be done and what is to be avoided.[329]

The extraordinary method of the Mantrayana is to use defilement and the objects of sense as tools upon the path. The practitioners of Secret Mantra believe not only that what is to be adopted or abandoned is without real existence on the ultimate level (a view held in common with the adherents of the lower vehicles), but they also consider that it has no reality even on the conventional level. Indeed, given this special feature of the Secret Mantra, the view and meditation (as related to the capacity of the practitioner in question) harness the defilements, unfailingly counteracting the ordinary experience of them. The practitioners of Mantra must act like peacocks, which are able to swallow strong poison that is deadly to everyone else and extract its essence, so that their feathers grow ever more splendid. They must transform their defilements into helpful assistants, with the result that their view and meditation are even more enhanced.

7. **A detailed explanation**
8. **The categories of samaya**
9. **The general vows of the Anuttaratantras**
10. **The distinction between "samaya" and "vow"**

92 With regard to the promises that are to be kept in the Secret Mantra, there is a difference in the way the Tibetan words *dam tshig* ("pledge") and *sdom pa* ("vow") are used. As the translation of the Sanksrit word "samaya," *dam tshig* means a "burning pledge."[330] For it is explained that, if samaya is kept without being spoiled, it confers the benefit of burning away all one's faults.[331] It is said in the *Vajra Tent Tantra*:

> If from the wisdom minds of holy ones
> You have received empowerment and blessing,
> And if you act according to your pledge,
> All discordant faults are burned away.[332]

Samaya is also defined as a "word of pledge" (*dam bcas pa'i tshig*), a promise that is not to be transgressed.

With regard to *sdom pa* (a vow or a bond), on the other hand, it is said that, once the precepts, whether of injunction or prohibition, are understood, practitioners must make sure, in the case of injunctions, *to bind* their three doors of body, speech, and mind "in the three mandalas." In the case of prohibitions, they must make sure to bind (that is, restrain) themselves from all that is not to be done—as well as from dualistic thoughts.

As mantric vows, therefore, samaya and vow are different aspects of the same nature.[333]

10. The individual considered as the basis of samaya

The Mantrayana vows are the foundation of all tantric trainings. There- 93 fore, if these vows have not been received; if they have degenerated through a downfall that is accompanied by the full complement of "entangling attitudes"[334] and have not been restored; if they have been relinquished by being returned and so on; or if the person in question is mentally deranged and incapable of recognizing faults—in all such situations, downfalls cannot be committed and accomplishments cannot be gained. For there are no vows to act as their foundation. By contrast, those who have received the tantric vows, who do not violate them and do not give them up, and who, being in their right mind, are able to remember their commitments and distinguish right from wrong—all such people are vessels both for accomplishments and downfalls.

10. Factors productive of a complete downfall

The abandonment of bodhichitta, which is the fifth root downfall[335] of 94 the Mantrayana, constitutes a defeat in itself, irrespective of the previously mentioned entanglements.[336] In the case of the other thirteen or twelve downfalls, however, the presence or absence of entangling attitudes makes a difference, since they determine whether or not a complete downfall has occurred.

Take, for example, the act of showing disrespect to one's teacher. A great and complete downfall occurs when three entangling attitudes are fully and constantly present in the mind, from the second moment of one's evil intention until the act of disrespect is complete. These three attitudes are: first, the continued desire to censure one's teacher; second, the lack of regret for what one is doing and the failure to recognize one's fault; and third, the absence of an inner sense of guilt at having done something that damages the Mantrayana vow, as well as a shameless indifference to the opinions of others. In addition to these three, there is a fourth attitude, namely, a feeling of satisfaction in having shown disrespect. A downfall of this kind destroys the culprit's vow, and rules out the possibility of remedial forces.

95   If, on the other hand, an intention leading to a root downfall occurs, but one does not remain in it constantly until the completion of the action; or if any of the three entangling attitudes is absent (because, for example, one recognizes that the action is evil and does not wish to continue with it, or one is ashamed of oneself and feels disgraced in the eyes of others, or one is revolted by one's own behavior), the act does not constitute a genuine defeat or root downfall, because all the elements are not assembled. It does, however, constitute an infraction (*sbom po*).

10. How the samayas are to be observed

96   Taking the entangling attitudes into consideration, practitioners should have a sound understanding of what the downfalls are. They must observe in thought, word, and deed all the root and branch samayas, condensed as they are into fourteen root downfalls and eight complementary infractions. And throughout the three periods of the day and the three periods of the night, they should remain attentive, as though on guard against an enemy, and be ever mindful of the precepts that are to be observed. In each period, they should minutely examine themselves to see if they have committed any of the fourteen downfalls.

97   If they find that they are guilty, they should never lapse into indifference, but should confess their faults immediately and with remorse, thinking of ways to repair their fault. If, on the other hand, they find themselves without transgression, they should rejoice and dedicate their achievement to the benefit of others. And from that moment onward, whether downfalls have been committed or not, they should always, at cost of life and limb, maintain an attitude of steady self-control, so as never to be stained even by less important misdemeanors.

98   If, in any of the six periods, day or night, one forgets to check, with attention and vigilance, whether one is guilty of a downfall, one commits what is called a grave infraction.[337] If no examination is made in the six following periods, it is said that this infraction is multiplied by

six. Moreover, if the twenty-four-hour period in which these six infractions are committed is passed mindlessly and without vigilance, so that they are left unrepaired, it is said that, by the dawn of the following twenty-four-hour period, they become twelve infractions. With this in mind—namely, the fact that infractions increase on a daily basis—practitioners should be extremely careful. And they should be skilled in applying the same principle also to the branch samayas.

10. The violation of the samayas
11. An explanation of the fourteen root downfalls

It is useful to begin with a consideration of the fourteen root downfalls   99
since they adumbrate the general practice of Anuttaratantras like the
Kalachakra, the *Tantra of Red Yamari*, and the *Tantra of Black Yamari*.

The first downfall is to show disrespect to the vajra master.[338] Before and until enlightenment is gained, we are linked with three kinds of teacher who reveal the path of Dharma to us. First is the extraordinary teacher from whom empowerment is received (and whose importance it is hardly necessary to mention); second is the teacher who, motivated by an attitude of kindness, explains unerringly even a single line of the tantras; and third is the teacher who explains the important, essential points of meditation according to the profound pith instructions of the Vajrayana path. This being so, one must respect them sincerely and without guile, rendering them the three kinds of service.[339] If one fails to do this, and if out of anger or jealousy one abuses them and treats them with contempt, the fault is worse than the five sins of immediate effect. Moreover, if one fails to repair the fault with confession and a firm purpose of amendment, not only will one fail to gain liberation (to say nothing of accomplishment in the Mantrayana), but one will, at death, fall directly into hell.

The second downfall is to transgress the word of the Sugatas.[340] This   100
means the transgression of general and particular precepts regarding actions that are allowed or prohibited by the Buddha according to the three kinds of vow: the pratimoksha vow, the bodhisattva vow, and the mantrayana vow. This fault also includes the ignoring or repudiation of the words of an authentic teacher. True teachers act in consideration of

the needs of their disciples, of the time of the latters' training, of their abilities, and of their individual karmic dispositions. Therefore, it may well appear that they give teachings in the wrong order, that they act inappropriately or even contrary to the Dharma. But if one allows oneself to be guided by the words of such teachers, confident that their actions have an underlying meaning and purpose, one will eventually understand that their behavior is meaningful and justified. It is therefore a mistake to dismiss the teachers' instructions, telling oneself that their words are misplaced. If one ignores such teachers' words, the second downfall is committed.

101   The third downfall is to have a hostile attitude to the vajra kindred.[341] If one nurtures attitudes of anger, jealousy, or rancor, and criticizes, even in jest, one's vajra kindred with whom one has received empowerment (and who are therefore as intimate as brothers and sisters of the same parents); and if one fails to respect them but treats them with contempt and so forth, this (all the entangling attitudes being present) constitutes a root downfall. The venerable Buddhajnanapada[342] says in his *Presentation of the Stages:* "Those who belong to the same mandala and who have the same guru and spiritual consort become increasingly close as they progressively receive the four empowerments." And Shantipa[343] says: "Those who have the same master and who have received empowerment in the same mandala are kindred. They should not discuss each other's defects in a spirit of jealous rivalry." This is how the learned masters of the past and of more recent times have specified the meaning of this downfall. It is indeed a profoundly important and sensitive issue. In point of fact, one should not harbor negative feelings toward any being at all. Indeed, all beings, innumerable as they are, possess the same essence, the same sugatagarbha. In this sense, we all enjoy a general kinship (*spyi'i mched*). Moreover, all who follow the Buddha's teaching are distant relatives (*ring ba'i mched*) within the same Dharma lineage, while those who keep the same samayas within the vows of the Mantrayana are indeed close brothers and sisters (*nye ba'i mched*). Therefore, we must keep from ever entertaining a negative attitude toward anyone. It is said in the *Elucidation of Samaya:*

> Awareness is possessed by all, unnumbered, beings,
> And thus they are not different from myself.

We all are kindred in our shared sugatagarbha.
And since, by nature, all are future Buddhas,
We all enjoy a general kinship,
As though belonging to my father's clan.
All who have embraced the Buddhadharma are my distant kin,
While those are close who share my view and action,
And closest those who have the same samaya and a single father.

The fourth downfall is to abandon the attitude of loving-kindness.[344] This consists in being pleased to see that those who have harmed others willingly and with cruelty are tormented with physical and mental pain because of their former actions in this and previous lives. Given that for a Bodhisattva to relinquish affection for even a single being constitutes an extremely heavy fault, is there any need to add that the wish to deprive anyone of happiness constitutes a root downfall of the Mantrayana?

The fifth downfall is to lose one's bodhichitta.[345] As soon as either of the two aspects of bodhichitta[346] is damaged, and the promise to attain enlightenment for the sake of others is broken, aspiration bodhichitta is completely lost. And since in the Mahayana, bodhichitta is the root of both the sutra and the mantra paths, its loss entails a full defeat, irrespective of the presence or absence of the entangling attitudes. Moreover, to permit the emission of one's bodhichitta out of desire is inappropriate. Therefore, if it is lost, a downfall occurs.

The teachings state that there are seven circumstances in which semen may be released:

At the secret empowerment[347] and the third empowerment,[348]
When practicing "one taste"[349] and as an offering to the deity,
To spread the lineage and to make the nectar pill,[350]
To check the signs of death: these are the occasions.

The sixth downfall is to criticize generally other traditions.[351] Since the teachings say that one should not criticize even the doctrines of non-Buddhists, is there any need to mention the fault of denigrating the outer and inner Buddhist vehicles?[352] This downfall refers to the scornful derision of any of the Buddha's teachings, whether sutra or mantra, expounded in any of three vehicles: those of the Shravakas, the Pratyekabuddhas, and the Bodhisattvas. This includes criticism of the teachers who expound such doctrines, saying that the Buddha did not himself teach them, that they are not his teachings, and that they do not constitute an authentic path. Moreover, all teachings regarding the four main activities and the lesser activities, the pure vision teachings (which are able to produce the two kinds of accomplishment), the mantra rituals belonging to the kahma and terma lineages, the pith instructions, the guidelines for the practice and so forth, and all the commentaries on the sutra and tantra teachings given by the learned and accomplished masters of India and Tibet—all are in harmony with the teachings and wisdom of the Buddha. They can be classified either as teachings authorized by him or as teachings that are blessed by his body, speech, mind, qualities, and activities, and are therefore indistinguishable from his own words. Failure to consider them as the Buddha's teaching and to disparage them constitutes the sixth downfall.

105   The seventh downfall is to divulge the secret.[353] This consists in giving teachings on the generation stage to those who have not received the vase empowerment, or at least the authorization to meditate upon a deity,[354] and also in giving teachings on the perfection stage to those who have not received the higher empowerments. Similarly, teachings should not be given to those who have broken their samaya and who, careless of the benefits of keeping samaya and of the dangers of breaking it, have not repaired their downfalls. The teachings should not be given to unsuitable vessels: people who, even though they have received an empowerment, are fearful of the profound view and action of the Secret Mantra. Neither should they be given to those who are as yet unready to receive the profound teachings, or to those who have some special impediment. To instruct all such people directly in the extraordinary and profound teachings of the Vajrayana, the view associated with its practices, and its extraordinary conduct, is to divulge the secret, and is specified here as a root downfall. Furthermore, even to bestow the blessings of a deity,[355] to give authorizations for the practice, and to give reading transmissions, are regarded as divulgations of the secret. It is

therefore important to check the vessel—in other words, the disciple—before giving the teaching. Otherwise a downfall may occur.

The eighth downfall is to abuse and show contempt for one's psy-chophysical aggregates.[356] The five aggregates, the physical body, and so forth, are the Buddhas of the five families (Vairochana and the rest); the five elements are the five female Buddhas; the senses and their ob-jects are the male and female Bodhisattvas; and so on. If one fails to recognize them as being primordially deities, and instead understands them to be genuinely true sufferings, engendered by true origins—namely, karma and defilement (as assessed by the discursive intellect according to the lower vehicles)—one might, out of contempt for the body, cut one's limbs, drink poison, leap into precipices, or perform extreme austerities like excessive fasting, thereby inflicting great tor-ments on oneself. If one has a negative perception and contempt for one's body and the other aggregates, and if this is accompanied by the entangling attitudes, a root downfall is committed.

The ninth downfall is to harbor doubts about the fact that phenom-ena are utterly pure by nature.[357] The primordially pure nature of all phenomena, the union of inconceivable emptiness and the primordial wisdom of luminosity, is the sphere of the Buddhas alone, free as they are from all obscuration. This very nature is the sugatagarbha of each and every living being. It is therefore said that there is no difference between Buddhas and ordinary beings, except for adventitious defile-ments, which have been purified in the case of Buddhas, but not in the case of beings. Now if one understands this doctrine (of the sugatagar-bha) merely as an indirect kind of expedient teaching[358] and doubts it; if one thinks that the Buddha was referring simply to the lack of inher-ent existence and expounded the doctrine of the buddha-nature only so that immature beings would put aside their fear and rejoice in the path; and if one cultivates such a notion with the entangling attitudes present, the downfall of rejecting the authentic path is committed.[359]

The tenth root downfall is the failure to "liberate" the wicked.[360] This refers to the failure to "liberate" beings belonging to the following ten categories: those who abuse the Three Jewels and in particular one's own teacher; those who in different ways destroy the Dharma of trans-mission and realization, and so forth; those who violate their samaya, fail to repair it, and persist in their degenerate behavior; those who, having once engaged in the Mantrayana, abandon it out of contempt; those who are hostile to the Mantrayana teachings; those who intrude without authorization upon the gatherings of those engaged in secret practice—whether through the power of their authority or on the false pretense of being authorized; those who inflict harm on beings; the enemies of those who observe their samaya; those of evil character, whose actions are exclusively negative and the cause of future misery; and the wicked beings who are now suffering (as the result of their actions) in the three lower realms.

As it is said in the *Elucidation of Samaya:*

> The assailant of the Triple Gem,[361] the teacher's foe,[362]
> Those with spoiled samaya, those who turn away,
> Enemies, intruders, those who only harm,
> The foes of those who keep samaya,
> And those of evil life, and those in the three lower realms:
> These ten the yogi should indeed release.

All these beings are suitable candidates for "liberation" through the ferocious activities of powerfully accomplished practitioners. If, however, the latter fail to liberate them; if they complacently tolerate their behavior, and even aid and abet them with physical and verbal expressions of sympathy, they commit a downfall.[363]

109   The eleventh root downfall is to subject the ineffable, ultimate nature to logical assessment.[364] That to which the word "dharmadhatu" refers is beyond name, example, and indication; it is beyond all conventional labeling. And even though the discursive intellect can, in its ratiocinations, understand ultimate reality as being "emptiness" and "lack of self," in fact this "no-self" of phenomena is exclusively the field of self-cognizing primordial wisdom. It stands in clean contradiction to the conventional, dualistic mind. The sharp, investigating intellect may indeed point to what is a lesser kind of emptiness of phenomena,[365] such as the aggregates, and say that it is ultimate reality, thereby claiming a superior view. But to evaluate the unborn nature, namely, inconceivable

ultimate reality, according to the criteria of ordinary thought, constitutes the eleventh downfall.

The twelfth root downfall is to cause the faithful to lose heart.[366] This does not just refer to the failure (though laziness and so on on the part of those who are qualified) to instruct those who are proper vessels for the Mantrayana and the pith instructions, or who are spontaneously endowed with the three kinds of faith in the Dharma (vivid, yearning, and confident), refusing to instruct them in the teachings to which they are drawn. [For the downfall to occur] there must also be the intention to cheat people by telling them things that contradict their true interest. When, through such behavior, one causes people to lose heart, so that their faith and aspirations are spoiled and they turn from the teachings, and when all the entangling attitudes are present, a root downfall is committed.

The thirteenth root downfall is the failure to accept the samaya substances.[367] This refers to the samaya substances associated with the practices of the Secret Mantra at a specific moment in time.[368] The downfall consists, for instance, in regarding the five meats and five nectars, which are to be consumed, according to the way that they appear—rejecting some because of their bad smell and revolting taste, and craving others and enjoying them with pleasure. This also covers the fault of straying into two extreme positions. The first of these is to prize the attitude of the Shravakas and to refrain from consuming such substances through failure to assimilate (by view and meditation) the authentic mode of conduct (*brtul zhugs*) of the Mantrayana. For in the Mantrayana, one does not accept or reject the samaya substances on the basis of ordinary discrimination. Instead, one enjoys them as the adornment of primordial wisdom, because one has realized the ultimate nature, the equal status, of all phenomena. The second extreme position is to enjoy such substances carelessly and without the complete certainty of the Mantrayana view. When the entangling attitudes are present, this constitutes a root downfall.

The fourteenth root downfall is to have contempt for women, who have the nature of wisdom.[369] It is said that to have contempt for Vajrayogini and other wisdom dakinis who transcend the world constitutes a root downfall in both the Yogatantra and the Anuttaratantra.

Mamos,[370] dakinis, and so on, assuming a worldly guise, judge between good and evil. They search and examine the practitioner's samaya. Therefore the root verse says that the yoginis of the Mantrayana guard the frontier of samsara and nirvana. If one shows disrespect to the wisdom dakinis; if one scorns the worldly dakinis who are born in pure lands and sacred places; if one ignores the fact that the five elements are the five female Buddhas, considering them to be only what they appear to be, and dismissing them accordingly; and if one is a misogynist, scorning women in general (who are of the nature of wisdom), especially those who are the basis for the profound empowerment that gives birth to the coemergent wisdom of great bliss—and when the entangling attitudes are all complete—the fourteenth root downfall is committed.[371]

11. An explanation of the category of infractions
12. The eight infractions

113 The eight infractions (*sbom po*) complement the fourteen root downfalls. Although they are not complete defeats (*pham pa*) that totally annihilate the vow, they nevertheless impede the attainment of accomplishment. Nagarjuna has extracted from the tantras the following list.

114 The first infraction is to take as one's consort an ordinary person, whose mind has not been ripened by empowerment and who has not been purified through the observance of samaya and the vows.

The second is to extract through the power of wind, but without the correct practice that generates the wisdom of bliss and emptiness, the nectar or red essence that gives rise to bliss and is needed for the sacred pill, from the "well of awareness," the secret space of an unsuitable consort, who lacks the qualifications stipulated in the tantras.

115 The third is to exhibit unnecessarily to those who have not received empowerment, and especially to those who have no faith in the teachings of the Secret Mantra, the images of yidam-deities, the texts of tantras, elucidatory commentaries, and pith instructions, and ritual implements such as the vajra and bell, and to perform the lotus mudra, and so forth.

The fourth is to disturb the assembly of those who are performing the rituals of the Secret Mantra—such as the sacred feasts (ganachakra)—by quarreling with the teacher or the vajra kindred, and to distract their meditation by any sort of worthless and careless chatter, jokes, and such like, which are indicative of inattention and a lack of mindfulness.

The fifth is to fail to instruct, even though one is able, those who   116
have faith and who request the sacred Dharma and are ready to receive it—discussing other, meaningless, topics instead.

The sixth is to stay more than seven days among those who are genuine Shravakas, or else mere academics, who are devoid of respect and who criticize and pass judgment on the view and practice of the Secret Mantrayana.

The seventh is to mislead others by putting on an arrogant pretense   117
of upholding the teachings of the Vajrayana, even though one understands neither the meaning of the tantras, nor the tantric rituals and their outer, inner, and secret principles.

The eighth is to give secret teachings and pith instructions (normally imparted only to specific disciples),[372] to those who, though they have received empowerment, nevertheless harbor doubts and have no faith in the profound view and meditation of the Mantrayana, and who are thus fitted to receive no more than general explanations of the kind given before a large assembly.[373]

12. Other categories of infraction

Related to this catalog drawn up by Nagarjuna,[374] there is another list   118
ascribed to the master Shura[375] and the yogini Lakshminkara, who instead of the second and seventh (taking the nectar and masquerading as a mantra practitioner), mention two other infractions.

Of these, the first is to bestow an empowerment without having previously performed correctly the practice of the deity, together with the recitation of the mantra (according to number, time, or sign) and to engage in the activities related to the mandala, such as consecration, fire offering, and so on, and to acquire an entourage of disciples prematurely. The second is to eat in the afternoon (with the exception of the ganachakra feast) and to neglect other precepts, thus transgressing the pratimoksha discipline and the bodhisattva precepts. This applies even when one does not denigrate such precepts, but nevertheless fails to acknowledge their great purpose and makes light of them.

All these infractions are injurious to one's training. They are said to rob practitioners of accomplishment—meaning that they create obstacles to it. They should therefore be taken into careful consideration.

11. The textual sources describing the downfalls

119 The root downfalls common to all the Anuttaratantras were organized into the list of fourteen items, universally acknowledged in both the Old and New Traditions, by the master Shura, who is also known as Bhawilha. Moreover, each of the four classes of tantra (Kriya, Charya, Yoga, and Anuttara) has its own version of the fourteen downfalls. This is clearly shown in the *Kalachakra-tantra,* the *Secret Tantra of General Rites,* the *Tantra of the Enlightenment of Vairochana,* the *Illumination of Reality,* and so forth. It is important to be aware of them.[376]

10. How damaged samaya is repaired
11. Why it is necessary to restore samaya

120 People who endeavor in the practice must preserve the samaya as though their lives depended on it. It should be easier for them to accept death rather than break their samaya. For if they do not maintain the samaya constantly, sincerely, and without pretense, hell is their only possible destination. The practitioners of the tantric path are like snakes inside a bamboo cane [there is no way out for them apart from the top or the bottom]. If they fail to repair their damaged samaya, it is certain that they will go to hell. On the other hand, if their samaya is pure, buddhahood is accomplished in one life (in the best of cases) or, at the longest, in sixteen. Aside from these two eventualities (hell or buddhahood), there is no third alternative. Therefore, when a downfall occurs, one should experience intense regret and remorse for one's wrong attitude and behavior, and one should strive to repair it at once and without delay.

11. The repairing of damaged samaya

The first root downfall—namely, that of showing disrespect to the
teacher—is a particularly heavy fault. It is said in the *Mayajala-tantra:*

> To denigrate the teacher,
> To offend and grieve the teacher's heart
> Will lead to torments that will last as long
> As it would take to empty out the seas
> By scattering drops of water with a hair:
> These torments have been called the vajra hell.

If this downfall has been committed, one should, with strong and heartfelt regret, pay devoted homage to the teacher and offer him everything one possesses, imploring his forgiveness. Following this, one should again request empowerment and repair one's vow. If, however, the teacher is not present or lives in a distant place impossible to reach because of the dangers of the road, one should visualize the teacher, acknowledge him or her as sovereign of the mandala, and perform many times the self-empowerment (*bdag 'jug*), thereby restoring the samaya.

The same applies to other faults and infractions. If the teacher, in whose regard one might feel shame and a dread of censure, is not present, one should make one's confession to another practitioner whose Mantrayana vows are intact and pure. It is said in the *Tantra of the Ornament of the Vajra Essence:*

> If faults and downfalls are committed,
> First, feel strong regret
> And then before the proper object
> Bow down thrice and ask
> That you be heard.
> Confess your every violation of the threefold vow.

In addition, at the end of a celebration or meeting of practitioners, for example, the transgressor should prostrate and with a great sense of inner discipline invoke the Buddhas, Bodhisattvas, and great

Vidyā-dharas. The transgressor should then pronounce his or her secret name and say:

"From among the fourteen root downfalls and eight additional infractions, which violate the disciplinary precepts recorded in the scriptures of the Vidyādharas, the Vinaya of the Vajrayana, I am—through ignorance and defilement—guilty of such and such a fault. I confess sincerely, hiding nothing. For if, in the presence of the Buddhas, Bodhisattvas, and the great Vidyādharas, I were to cover it and keep it secret, there would be no way to reach the state of bliss where faults and downfalls are no more. Henceforward, I will perfectly restrain myself from wrong."

123   The person receiving the confession asks: "Do you acknowledge your actions as faults?"

The one confessing declares: "I do acknowledge them as faults."

The person receiving the confession asks: "Will you henceforth utterly refrain from repeating the transgression?"

The one confessing replies: "I pledge myself, with determination and a sense of self-control, to uphold the discipline in accordance with the Dharma [as carefully] as if it were a burden carried on my head."

This exchange is repeated three times, and finally the one receiving the confession says: "This is indeed the way!" (Thus indicating that this is the way to purify the downfalls and faults.)

To which the one confessing replies with conviction: "It is well."

124   If one delays in repairing one's faults and downfalls, their power increases from one day to the next. It is said in the *Tantra of the Ornament of the Vajra Essence:*

> If you live in constant carelessness,
> Your faults and errors may be small and trifling
> But they will strike you like a serpent's fang
> And sap your mind, and speech, and body's strength.

Therefore, in order to prevent them from increasing in strength, one should always confess one's faults six or three times by day and night, visualizing, above the crown of one's head, Vajrasattva, embodiment of the one family of the Great Secret. One should apply the four strengths and recite without distraction the hundred-syllable mantra twenty-one, a hundred, or a thousand times. One should also recite the confession composed by Shura (Bhawilha), in which each of the fourteen downfalls is mentioned.

The manner in which the hundred-syllable mantra is to be recited is described in the *Catalog of Infractions:* "Instead of the syllable MÉ," it says, "one should pronounce one's own name. Thus one should recite "SARVA SIDDHI (then insert one's name) prayatsa." This will prevent the effect of one's downfalls from increasing. The *Tantra of the Ornament of the Vajra Essence* declares:

> Meditate on Vajrasattva
> Saying one and twenty times
> The mantra of a hundred syllables.
> All downfalls will be blessed thereby
> And their effects will not increase.
> This is said by all accomplished ones.
> Cleanse them thus between your sessions.
> By doing this a hundred thousand times,
> You will be truly purified.

9. An explanation of the samayas according to the *General Scripture of Summarized Wisdom,* the *Mayajala-Tantra,* and the tradition of the Mind, the Great Perfection[377]

10. The samayas according to the *General Scripture of Summarized Wisdom*[378]

There are samayas to be observed belonging to the three classes of tantra of the old translation school. These are the Anuyoga tantra class represented by the *General Scripture of Summarized Wisdom,* the Mahayoga tantra class represented by the *Mayajala,* and the tantras of the Mind, namely, the Great Perfection. These samayas are not shared by the tantras of the new translation schools.

First comes the tradition of the *General Scripture of Summarized Wisdom.* In this tantra it is said that:

125

There are samayas that should be observed
Of vajra body, speech, and mind.
Then there are samayas that concern
The things to be performed,
The things to be regarded as attractive,
Those not to be spurned,
Those that should be known,
And those on which to meditate.

There are three root samayas to be observed, the main object of which concerns the inseparability of the deity from the teacher. The body is the principal ground or cause whereby benefit is procured and harm averted. Therefore, with regard to the body samaya, one must pay respect to the teacher and the deity, and one must abandon harmful behavior toward all beings, of whom the vajra kindred are but the symbol. For all beings are potential disciples of one's teacher. By practicing the generation stage, one should also purify one's clinging to one's own body, which is the ripened result of past karma.

Positive and negative actions are grounded in, and generated by, speech. Therefore, with regard to the speech samaya, one must not break the continuous stream of mantra and mudra. Moreover, in order to remove all faults of speech, one must do what the teacher says and not disregard the wishes of the vajra kindred.

The principal cause for birth in samsara is the mind. Therefore, with regard to the vajra-mind samaya, one must eliminate all mental faults, one must not divulge the secrets, and one must cultivate the twofold bodhichitta. One must blend one's mind with the teacher's mind, and practice the various kinds of concentration. The *Elucidation of Samaya* says:

Your form is the great mudra of the Conquerors.[379]
As such also cognize the bodies of all other beings:
The vajra form of undivided voidness and appearance.
Actions, sights, and sounds
Are all the mind's display.
All you do appears, yet is unreal.
But if you are not constantly aware

And do not watch your mind with vigilance and scrutiny,
How can you penetrate the Secret Mantra of the Mahayana?

In addition to the three root samayas, there are the five groups of branch samayas. These are, first, the five actions to be skillfully performed, namely, tana, or liberation; gana, or union; theft; lies; and worthless chatter. Second are the five defilements, which are to be harnessed and employed upon the path, considering them as attractive, as the root verse says—meaning that they are not to be rejected. Third are the five nectars that are not to be spurned as impurities: excrement, urine, mamsa (human flesh), rakta (blood), and "dew" or semen. Fourth are the five objects that, by means of the view, are to be known or recognized as deities. This is a reference to the five aggregates, the five elements, the five sense objects, the five sense organs, and the five colors.[380] Fifth are the five objects to be integrated through meditation as being inseparable from oneself, namely, the five enlightened families of tathāgata, vajra, jewel, lotus, and action. Taken with the three root samayas, the twenty-five branch samayas make a total of twenty-eight, as described in the *General Scripture of Summarized Wisdom*.

10. **The samayas according to the *Mayajala***

The tradition of the *Mayajala* speaks of five root samayas. It is said in   126
the *Guhyagarbha-tantra*:

> Do not spurn the unsurpassed; show reverence to the teacher;
> Do not cut the continuity of mudra and of mantra;
> Show love to those engaged upon the perfect path;
> And do not speak of secret things:
> These are the five root samayas,
> The supreme pledges of enactment
> And the pledges to be kept.[381]

In addition, ten branch samayas are taught:

> Ignorance, desire, and anger,
> Pride and envy: these do not reject!

The fluids white and red, with urine, flesh, and excrement:
These are five pure substances and must not be shunned!

First we will explain the root samayas. It is written in the *Elucidation of Samaya*:

The twofold bodhichitta, the six kinds of teacher,
Four of kindred, three of mantra, four of mudra,
Ten kinds of secret: all are known to be the roots.

The first injunction, "not to spurn the unsurpassed," refers to the twofold bodhichitta. Regarding ultimate bodhichitta, this means that one should remain in the great dharmakaya, the indivisibility of the two superior truths.[382] In the case of relative bodhichitta, it means that one should have the sublime intention to liberate beings that are without this realization. In this tradition, these two aspects of bodhichitta are included in the meditation upon the yidam-deity, and are not expounded separately from it. Indeed, the pledges of the general Mahayana (not to give up bodhichitta and not to lose respect for the Three Jewels) and the commitment of the outer Secret Mantras (to pay homage to, and meditate upon, one's yidam deity) are, according to the tradition of the *Mayajala*, all condensed in the meditation on the sign-mudra of the deity's body,[383] practiced within the union of emptiness and compassion. The Buddha and the Sangha are the particular aspects of bodhichitta, the nondual union of skillful means and wisdom. The Dharma, for its part, is the nature of bodhichitta. Therefore, on the relative level, precious bodhichitta shares the same nature as the Dharma (indeed, the latter is its very nature). On the ultimate level, the Three Jewels are totally beyond all conceptual construction. They are the primordial wisdom of union, which is symbolized by the sign-mudra of the deity's body. It is said in the *Precious Jewel Commentary*:[384] "The nature of the Three Jewels is bodhichitta. The teacher who imparts bodhichitta is the sign-mudra of the supreme deity."

Once one has understood how the Three Jewels are contained within bodhichitta, four other items remain to be explained.

The second injunction, "to show reverence to the teacher," applies to the six kinds of teacher. The *Elucidation of Samaya* specifies these six as: the universal teacher, the teacher who gives access to the Dharma, the teacher who bestows the empowerments and samayas, the teacher in respect of whom one is able to repair broken samayas, the teacher who opens one's mind, and the teacher who imparts the pith instructions. The universal teacher, in being an object of general respect, is the one who provides a small connection with the Dharma.[385] The teacher who provides access to the Dharma is, for instance, an abbot who imparts monastic vows. The teacher who confers empowerments is the teacher of samayas and initiation. The teacher who restores broken samaya is the teacher to whom one confesses one's downfalls. The teacher who opens one's mind is the teacher who explains the tantras and so forth, while the teacher who gives pith instructions is the one who imparts oral teachings and guidelines. Of these, the teacher by whose kindness one has received the teachings of the Secret Mantra is the vajra master. He or she is a person of the highest—indeed perilous—importance.[386] This is particularly true of teachers who give empowerments, expound the tantras, and give the pith instructions. One should never turn away from them, but treat them with the greatest respect. The progressive degrees of their kindness are illustrated in the *Elucidation of Samaya* by the following examples:

> Greater than the king who rules the land,
> Than uncle, father, mother, eyes, and heart—
> In this way should one's teachers be regarded.[387]

The third injunction, "not to cut the continuity of mantra and mudra," is explained in the *Elucidation of Samaya* as referring to "the root mantra, the generation mantra, and the activity mantra,[388] while the four mudras or seals are the samayamudra [enlightened mind], the karmamudra [enlightened activity], the dharmamudra [enlightened speech], and the mahamudra or enlightened body." For a person of superior faculties, the three kinds of mantra and the four types of mudra remain constant, day and night, like an ever-flowing stream. A person of moderate capacity keeps this continuity during six or four periods every month, while one of basic faculties maintains it on the special auspicious days occurring annually in certain months.[389]

The fourth injunction, "to show love to one's kindred," refers to the fourfold kindred mentioned previously[390] when discussing the third root downfall. Of these, it should be understood that the second, third, and fourth groups—namely, those who are engaged on the authentic path, and especially those with whom one is intimate [in belonging to the same mandala]—are the most important. But even given these different degrees, one should never allow oneself to feel distant from any of them. Instead, one should have an altruistic, loving, and benevolent attitude toward them. It is said in the *Terrifying Lightning Tantra*:

> For vajra kindred you should feel great love,
> For, close or far, they are your very kin.
> Regarding those with whom you entered on the perfect path,
> At all times you must leave aside
> The slightest thought that they might be at fault.
> With love and strong affection look on them—
> Each and every one—as though they were your very eyes.
> In short, at cost of life or limb,
> Fulfill your brothers' and your sisters' needs.
> And why? Because the vajra kindred,
> From this day and till enlightenment is reached,
> Will be your perfect, never-parting friends,
> As light and wick within the selfsame lamp.

The people to whom the fifth injunction, "not to speak of secret things," applies are described in the *Subtle and Extensive Samayas*:

> Those of spoiled samaya, those who have abandoned it,
> Those without samaya, those who have not seen the mandala,
> All these people, intimate or otherwise.

Indeed, the profound view should be kept hidden from those of lesser understanding, for instance the practitioners of the Hinayana. The extraordinary activities [such as tana and gana] should be kept secret from all those who are not intimately linked [that is, belonging to the same mandala]. If one reveals the name and form of one's yidam-deity and so on to those with whom one is not intimately linked, the samaya is impaired. And even if they are revealed to those who are intimate,[391] it is said that one's accomplishment will be damaged. For this reason, they should be kept secret. The secrets to be kept are stated in the *Subtle and Extensive Samayas* as:

> General secrets, intermittent secrets, four of each,
> Appropriate secrets and entrusted secrets: ten in all.

The ten secrets cover specific objects and periods of time, which should not be divulged to others. The *Elucidation of Samaya* defines the four general secrets as the "profound view, unconventional conduct, the name and form of the deity, and signs of one's accomplishment." The same text defines the intermittent secrets as the secrets concerning place, time, companions, and ritual implements connected with the practice. The category of things that are appropriate to be kept secret covers everything that should not be seen or heard, such as the activities pecu-liar to the Mantrayana, the substances of samaya, as well as the misde-meanors of one's vajra kindred. "Entrusted secrets" refers to everything that the teacher or the vajra kindred have entrusted to us in secrecy.[392]

Slightly different distinctions are made between root samayas of en-actment (*bsgrub*) and samayas to be kept (*bsrung*).[393] It may be said, how-ever, that the samaya of bodhichitta and the samayas of both mantra and mudra are "samayas of enactment," while all the others are "sa-mayas to be kept." With regard to the samayas of body, speech, and mind, those relating to the teacher and the vajra kindred constitute the samaya of body; those concerning mantra and mudra belong to the samaya of speech, while the ten secrets refer to the samaya of mind. The samaya of bodhichitta also belongs to the mind samaya. As the *Peaceful Tantra of the Eight Herukas, Embodiments of the Sugatas*[394] says: "Medita-tion on the three kinds of bodhichitta belongs to the samaya of the vajra mind." The subdivision of the root samayas results in one hundred and sixty samayas.[395]

127   The branch samayas are the means to ensure that the root samayas are observed. They are grouped in two categories: things that are not to be rejected and things that are not to be shunned.

Things not to be rejected

The things not to be rejected are the five defilements (ignorance, desire, hatred, pride, and envy). The defilements in fact have two aspects. On the one hand, there are the five poisons in the usual negative sense (*log pa'i dug*). On the other hand, according to the hidden meaning, there are the five poisons that are utterly pure (*yang dag pa'i dug*). The five poisons in the negative sense are the true defilements. How then are they not to be rejected? It is through recognizing the essence of defilements like desire that one sees that they are, by nature, natureless. Consequently, there is no need for antidotes to the defilements, just as there is no need to dam the mirage of a river. If defilement is dealt with skillfully, it becomes the friend of wisdom. In the same way that one uses water to wash out water caught in one's ears, and in the same way that a peacock can consume poison, the defilements themselves are the best antidotes for the defilements, and therefore they are not rejected.[396] As the *Ocean Tantra* says:

> The path of the defilements is immaculate.
> And objects of desire, through skillful means, are supreme
>   ornaments.
> By tasting each and every one of them,
> One speedily becomes a glorious heruka.

And it is further said in the *Heap of Jewels:*

> Just as filthy ordure from the town of Vaishali
> Is useful for the field of sugarcane,
> Manure of the defilements of a Bodhisattva
> Benefits the field of the enlightened qualities.

And the *Compendium of the Mahayana* adds:

Managed with the greatest skillful means,
Defilements are the branches of enlightenment.

Why is this so ? If one recognizes the primordial nature of the defilements as the five enlightened families, and harnesses them on the
path, the obscuration of ignorance will be dispelled and the defilements
will themselves transform into the five primordial wisdoms. It is like
pressing sesame seeds when one wants to obtain oil. The *Twenty-Eight
Samayas* says:

Primordially, the five defilements, envy and the rest,
Are by their very nature five enlightened families.

Stupidity or ignorance is thus the samaya of Vairochana, the primordial wisdom of the dharmadhatu. Desire is the samaya of Amitabha, the
all-discerning primordial wisdom. Anger is the samaya of Akshobhya,
the mirrorlike primordial wisdom. Pride is the samaya of Ratnasambhava, the primordial wisdom of equality. Jealousy is the samaya of
Amoghasiddhi, the all-accomplishing primordial wisdom.

According to the hidden meaning, one speaks of the five utterly pure
poisons. In the case of stupidity, this means that, when the equality of
samsara and nirvana is realized, one no longer has a biased, partial view,
and in one's conduct, one makes no discrimination, adopting this and
rejecting that. In the case of desire, this means that, out of compassion,
one has love for beings who do not have this understanding. Anger, for
its part, eliminates mistaken mental states. And when the equal status
of everything is realized, pride ensures that one's view is never narrow
and confined. Finally, jealousy does not allow any dualistic view and
conduct in the expanse of ultimate reality. These five utterly pure poisons are all present when one rests in the view. One should constantly
experience them.

Things not to be shunned

These are the five great nectars: the vajra dew (semen); rakta (blood);
excrement; mamsa (human flesh); and urine. They should be accepted

128

eagerly, both because of their "fourfold establishment" (*grub pa bzhi*), and because of their "three ways of being" (*yin pa gsum*).

Regarding the former, these substances are established (as nectars to be accepted eagerly), first, by reason of their ultimate nature. They are, from the point of view of the dharmatā, beyond all conceptual construction; by nature they are established as neither pure nor impure. Understanding this, one should accept them as the display of wisdom. Second, they are established as nectars by reason of their intrinsic character. Even though the five substances appear to be real phenomena, their nature is utterly pure; they have the nature of the five enlightened families. With this understanding, one should accept them. Third, they are established as nectars by reason of their efficient potency. These five nectars are samaya substances able to produce realization, because the supreme and ordinary accomplishments are gained by relying on them. Therefore they should be accepted. Fourth, they are established on account of their consecration. They are samaya substances that in the past were consecrated as such by, among others, the Great and Glorious One.[397] Consequently, all the mamos and dakinis will be drawn toward practitioners who use them correctly, and they will assist them in their practice. One should therefore accept the five nectars, because it is thanks to them that one will swiftly gain accomplishment.

The three ways of being are as follows. First, the five nectars are medicines against disease. Excrement cures illnesses caused by poison; urine cures swellings on the neck and throat; flesh is a remedy for contagious diseases such as leprosy; rakta cures rheumatism; and the white bodhichitta dispels fever. Second, the five nectars are the supports for the common accomplishments. By using excrement, one will gain great power; by using urine, one develops a melodious voice; flesh gives rise to longevity; rakta produces a bright complexion; and the white bodhichitta bestows an unfailing memory. Third, the five nectars are the supports of the five enlightened families and the five primordial wisdoms. Excrement corresponds to the tathāgata family and the wisdom of the dharmadhatu; urine corresponds to the action family and all-accomplishing wisdom; flesh corresponds to the jewel family and the wisdom of equality; rakta corresponds to the lotus family and all-discerning wisdom; and white bodhichitta corresponds to the vajra family and mirrorlike wisdom.

To realize that all phenomena [which are represented by the five nectars] are pure and equal, and to act without making any discrimination, adopting this and rejecting that, is the mode of conduct[398] of the Buddhas. One should act accordingly, and accept the five nectars with enthusiasm.

These ten branch samayas may be further subdivided. By distinguishing the aspects of skillful means and wisdom—in the five defilements not to be rejected and the five nectars not to be shunned—one arrives at ten samayas for each grouping. When these are again subdivided according to enlightened body, speech, mind, qualities, and activity, fifty samayas will result for each group, producing a total of a hundred samayas. By a further twofold distinction—distinguishing between wisdom taken as the main aspect endowed with skillful means, and skillful means taken as the main aspect endowed with wisdom—one arrives at two hundred samayas. However, these are distilled into twenty by distinguishing the aspects of skillful means and wisdom in the ten samayas, which form the basis for all such categorizations. As the root text says, this is "the teaching of the all-seeing Rongpa," and it is found in the *Precious Jewel Commentary* by Rongdzom Chökyi Zangpo. The textual source of this categorization is in fact the root tantra, namely, the *Guhyagarbha*, which says:

129

> Each of the five root samayas now split into two
> Gives rise to ten, which then are multiplied by three.[399]
> The branch samayas, in two groups of five,
> Are subdivided twentyfold.

10. The samayas according to the tradition of the Mind, the Great Perfection

11. The samayas of "nothing to keep"

Those who have been perfectly introduced to the nature of the mind, and are able to abide in it, realise that outer appearances are groundless and that inner awareness is object-free. Such people settle in the state

130

in which they do not discriminate between what is to be accepted and what is to be rejected. For in this fundamental nature of awareness, obscurations and faults (to be abandoned) are absent—indeed, they are wholly nonexistent. This is the so-called samaya of nonexistence (or absence) (*med pa'i dam tshig*). The *All-Illuminating Essence Tantra* says:

> In great primordial wisdom, self-aware,
> Samaya and its keeper are not two.
> And spoiled and unspoiled likewise are not separate.
> The teachings of the eight (preceding) vehicles are all concocted words.
> No observance do I have: it's called the [pledge of] "nonexistence."

Dualistic phenomena, such as vow and absence of vow, thing and nonthing, origination and cessation—and all thoughts and assumptions—share a single ultimate nature. If a name were to be given to the state of resting, without affirmation or denial, in this one nature, which cannot be seen by watching, and which is the one ineffable primordial wisdom—it could be called the samaya of the one [nature] (*gcig pu'i dam tshig*).

The *All-Illuminating Essence Tantra* says:

> The samaya of "nothing to keep" cannot be transgressed,
> For the manner of observing it
> Is the one primordial wisdom self-aware.
> This is called [samaya of] one [nature].

When one settles in the one ultimate nature, in the realization that outer and inner phenomena are without existence, when awareness of the five sense perceptions is left open and nondiscursive, all phenomena are decisively settled in the vast spaciousness of the ultimate nature. This is referred to as [the samaya of] all-embracing evenness (*phyal ba'i dam tshig*). The *Tantra of the All-Creating King* says:

The unceasing primal wisdom does not experience "things."
This is called [samaya of] an all-embracing evenness.

Furthermore, in the radiance of primordially pure awareness of ultimate reality, the qualities of knowledge are spontaneously present. [If one remains in this nature] one constantly experiences phenomena in terms of the "four visions." This is said to be the samaya of "spontaneous presence" (*lhun grub kyi dam tshig*). It is not the practice related to the four visions or experiences of thögal, and yet [if one preserves the one primordially pure awareness,] all appearances, free from origin and cessation, are spontaneously present in primordial wisdom itself. They should not be looked for elsewhere. And this is why one speaks of "spontaneous presence." The *Tantra of the All-Creating King* says:

> Since all appearing things without exception
> Are perfect and complete in bodhichitta, nature of the mind,
> I name them as spontaneously present.

In all, one speaks of four samayas of "nothing to keep" (*bsrung du med pa'i dam tshig*).[400] But this is simply to distinguish conceptually the different aspects of the state of abiding (free from distraction and "purposeful" meditation) in the state of primordially pure awareness. Essentially, these four samayas or aspects are not different. In ultimate reality, space-like and inconceivable, there is nothing to give up; there is nothing to implement; there are no samayas to keep. For those who continually abide in ultimate reality, there is nothing to transgress, not even slightly. Joined to the ultimate state of awareness through the mediation of the four great samayas, there is no stirring from the fundamental, natural state of things. This is the reason for teaching the four samayas as things to be realized. The *Mound of Gems Tantra* says:

> Then the samayas of "nothing to keep":
> Of "one [nature]," "nonexistence," "spontaneous presence,"
> "All-embracing evenness"—all of them will be your friends.

The samayas of "nothing to keep" refer to the way in which one remains in the fundamental nature of things, the vajra-like indestructible state, which is primordially free of defect, unsundered by duality. Mind and appearance are both overpowered by the primordial wisdom of the dharmakaya. This is what is called the kingly way. Nevertheless, one should not make the mistake of thinking that this is a disparagement of the lower samayas. The great master Padmasambhava, the second Buddha, said:

> Great King, in my teaching of Secret Mantra, the view is attuned to the dharmakaya, but the conduct is in harmony with the way of the Bodhisattva. Do not let your conduct get lost in the view. If it does, you will know neither virtue nor sin, and you will be unable to repair your negativities later on. On the other hand, if your view follows and keeps company with your conduct, you will be fettered by things and their attributes, and liberation will elude you. My Secret Mantra teaching is mostly focused on the mind; the view is the most important thing. In the future, many will have the certainty of words but will not have the certainty of the view. And to the lower realms will they go.

Therefore, if, before you have gained stability in the practice, you go around proclaiming in the lofty Dharma language of the Great Perfection, "There is no virtue, there is no sin; the karmic principle of cause and effect has no existence; there is no harm in distraction and the objects of the senses; there is nothing to meditate on and no one who meditates," you will remain in ordinariness. Trafficking thus the very life of the Doctrine, you will cut yourself off from it. It is therefore of the highest importance to persevere constantly in the practice, in harmony with the Dharma: physically, verbally, and mentally.

11. The samayas of "something to keep"
12. The root samayas

131 As we have already explained, with regard to their physical, verbal, and mental activities, practitioners of the Great Perfection do not intention-

ally persist in the discrimination between positive and negative, accepting the one and rejecting the other. On the other hand, since they abide in the great samaya of primordial observance (*ye bsrung chen po*), all negativities are overpowered and they are unstained by faults—just as space is unstained by dust. This approach, however, is possible only for highly realized beings. Beginners who are only just embarking on the path of the Natural Great Perfection must follow the instructions of their teachers and, without clinging to the true existence of faults and obscurations to be abandoned, together with their remedies, they must strive with mindfulness, vigilance, and carefulness in order to cleanse themselves of faults and to ensure the complete purity of their practice. If deteriorations do occur, methods exist whereby they can be repaired. Just as it is an easy matter to repair the damage done to a golden vessel, it is easy to amend the fault if one proceeds according to the teacher's instructions. It is extremely important to strive in keeping the samayas. As the explanatory *Tantra of Manjushri* says:

> Empowerments are based upon samayas.
> They vanish when the latter are impaired,
> Like paintings on collapsing walls.

As it was said, realization cannot grow in the mind if the foundation, one's samaya, is impure.

With regard to the various categories of the samayas of "something to keep" (*bsrung du yod pa'i dam tshig*), the *Tantra of Awareness Self-Arisen* says:

> As shown in brief, keep well within your mind
> The hundred thousand pledges that have been explained.
> According to their shortened exposition,
> First is the samaya of the view, whereby one understands;
> Second is samaya of continuous activity;
> Third is the samaya linked to general practice;
> Fourth is common, general samaya;
> Fifth is the samaya of the body, speech, and mind;

Sixth are the samayas considered complementary;
Seventh are samayas important for particular occasions.

These seven categories of samaya are further condensed into three:
general, special, and additional samayas.

As regards the first category, that of the general samayas, it is said in
the *Peaceful Tantra*:

In the pratimoksha and the bodhisattva vows,
In Kriya, Charya, and the Yoga tantras,
Whatever has been taught as something to be kept
Is counted as the common, general samaya.

With regard to the second category, that of the special samayas,[401]
those of the Great Perfection are, as similarly explained in the *General
Scripture of Summarized Wisdom*, subdivided into the three samayas of body,
speech, and mind. The *Arrangement of Samayas* says:

Body, speech, and mind:
For each of these, nine sections are explained
According to observance and activity.[402]

As it was said, there are twenty-seven categories of samaya. The root
samayas are the samayas of the teacher's body, speech, and mind, because it is on the teacher that the birth of the genuine view and meditation of the Natural Great Perfection depends. It is the teacher who first
introduces the disciples to the state of realization, and who then dispels
their obstacles and improves the quality of their meditation. Finally, it
is the teacher who brings the disciples to the realization wherein all
phenomena subside in ultimate reality. The teacher is thus the embodiment of the Buddhas of the three times, the sovereign of all the enlightened families and of an ocean-like infinity of mandalas. The teacher is
the essence of the three vajras themselves. Each of the three root samayas of the teacher's body, speech, and mind is divided into outer,
inner, and secret sections, which are again divided into outer, inner, and

secret. This comes to a total of twenty-seven samayas, which may be described as follows.

The samayas associated with the body

The secret aspect of the outer body samaya is not to kill any sentient being. The inner aspect of the outer body samaya is to abstain from sexual impurity. The outer aspect of the outer body samaya is not to steal.

The outer aspect of the inner body samaya is never to have contempt for one's father, mother, brothers, and sisters, or for one's own body. The inner aspect of the inner body samaya is never to have contempt for those who wish to engage in, who have engaged in, or who display the external signs of having engaged in, the teachings of the Hinayana and the Mahayana. The secret aspect of the inner body samaya is not to injure with poison, weapons, and so on the mandala of the deities—in other words, one's own body. "One's own body" occurs in the root verse, and therefore it appears necessary to include it here in the list.[403]

The secret aspect of the secret body samaya is to guard oneself from all disrespectful actions, such as stepping over one's teacher's shadow, or holding weapons, stretching oneself or making an exhibition of oneself in the teacher's presence. The inner aspect of the secret samaya is to do no harm to the teacher's consort. The outer aspect of the secret samaya is not to mock one's vajra brothers or sisters because of their physical appearance, apparel, and so on—and never to inflict physical violence on them, or to induce someone else to do so.

The samayas connected with speech

The outer, inner, and secret categories of the speech samaya are as follows. The outer aspect of the outer speech samaya is never to lie, even to ordinary beings, with a view to furthering one's own purposes. The inner aspect of the outer speech samaya is to avoid divisive speech. The secret aspect of the outer speech samaya is to avoid words that are harsh and wounding to others.

The outer aspect of the inner speech samaya is never to be disrespectful, and never to criticize or use abusive words with those who teach the Dharma. The inner aspect of the inner speech samaya is never to be disrespectful, and never to criticize, or abuse, those who reflect on and practice the Dharma. The secret aspect of the inner speech samaya is never to be disrespectful, and never to criticize or abuse those who meditate on the profound fundamental nature of phenomena.

The secret aspect of the secret speech samaya is never to disparage, disobey, or abuse one's teacher. The inner aspect of the secret samaya is to refrain from doing the same toward his consort. The outer aspect of the secret speech samaya is to refrain from the same toward the vajra kindred.

The samayas connected with the mind

134 The outer, inner, and secret aspects of the mind samaya are as follows. The outer aspect of the outer mind samaya is to refrain from covetousness. The inner aspect of the outer mind samaya is never to think malevolently of others, including ordinary beings. The secret aspect of the outer mind samaya is to refrain from wrong views in respect of all [Buddhist] tenets.

The outer aspect of the inner mind samaya is to refrain from wrong, careless, and foolish conduct. The inner aspect of the inner mind samaya is to preserve oneself from faulty meditation, whether through torpor, agitation, and any kind of obscuring deviation. The secret aspect of the inner mind samaya is to avoid the mistaken views of eternalism, nihilism, and all extreme positions.

The secret aspect of the secret mind samaya is to keep one's teacher constantly and devotedly in mind (for example, six times by day and night). The inner aspect of the secret mind samaya is to remember constantly the yidam-deity, the vajra kindred, and so forth. The outer aspect of the secret mind samaya is to keep constantly in mind the view, meditation, and conduct of the Great Perfection.

The sense of these samayas has been explained according to the tantras. Since, however, one's teacher is the guide who liberates from samsara, the essence of all the samayas can be condensed into a single point: One should never do anything to violate [the samayas] of the teacher's body, speech, and mind. It is said in the *Supreme Samaya Tantra:*

Those who by the power of body, speech, and mind
Attend and reverence their teachers as they may
Will mightily perfect the two accumulations.
Blessings will arise without impediment.

12. The branch samayas

Practitioners on the path of the unsurpassable Mantras, who have un-   135
derstood that all phenomena are by nature the three mandalas,[404] place
the seal of Samantabhadra[405] upon all their perceptions and activities.
If they do not break this seal, not only will they not be stained by
karma and defilements, whereby ordinary beings are bound in samsara,
but they will perfect the two accumulations and be of immense benefit
to others. Those who have mastered such a wonderful and extraordinary
method observe the twenty-five branch samayas.

First are the five samayas of actions to be performed physically or
verbally. These are tana ("liberation"); gana ("union"); taking what is
not given; lying; and worthless chatter. It is important to know when
these actions are allowed and when they are forbidden. They are permitted when one has the confidence that comes from realization, and when
one is certain that the outcome will be for the benefit of others. Otherwise one must refrain.

Second are the five samayas of defilements not to be abandoned.
These are desire, hatred, ignorance, jealousy, and pride. They are instead
to be experienced divested of their (seemingly) autonomous real existence, for it is this that fetters us.[406]

The third group of five is that of the samayas of things to be readily   136
accepted, namely: excrement, urine, mamsa, rakta, and dew or semen.
One should make use of them in a manner free from the dualistic
concepts of purity and impurity.

The fourth group of five is that of the samayas of things to be
known. This refers to the fact that the five aggregates are the five Buddhas; the five elements are the five female Buddhas; the five sense objects
are the five female Bodhisattvas; the five sense organs are the five male
Bodhisattvas; and the five colors are the five wisdoms. The wisdom that
realizes the purity and equality of everything enables one in this way to
experience phenomena as deities.

In addition, there are the five samayas of things to be meditated upon and assimilated. This refers to the families of vajra, jewel, lotus, action, and tathāgata. These will be assimilated by habituation to the view of universal purity and equality, by means of the five procedures,[407] the three concentrations, and so forth.

This exposition of the five groups of branch samayas is the teaching of the *Elucidation of Samaya*. This same text declares:

> The five to be performed, the five not to be shunned,
> The five to be accepted gladly, and the five to be assimilated,
> The five that should be known—
> All these have been described as five uncommon pledges.

The additional samayas form the third category.[408] The *Tantra of the Great Nirvana of Kila* says:

1. Do not slay the lion, king of beasts.
2. Pour no vials of poison in the vessel.
3. Do not cut the precious sapling's root.
4. Do not drink boiled water come from melting ice.
5. Do not part the anthers of the lotus bloom.
6. Do not pour the essence in a perforated cup.
7. Do not garner wealth and sustenance without examination.
8. Do not cast white crystal in the mud.
9. Do not place the milk of lions in an evil vessel.
10. Do not burn the wishing-jewel upon the hearth.
11. Do not break the wings of the garuda, king of birds.
12. Do not strike the ground with sky-iron claws.
13. Do not eat the leavings of the tiger and the leopard's feast.
14. Do not break the rock replete with vajras.
15. Do not tear the armor of the vajra-fence.
16. Do not douse the dark-dispelling lamp.
17. Do not block the vajra river's stream.
18. Do not give away the royal seal.
19. Do not throw away the foundation stone of the vajra fortress.
20. Do not, through desire, dislodge the precious crest jewel of the victory banner.

These are the twenty samyas, expressed in indirect language, which are to be observed in addition to the general and special samayas when practicing in large gatherings.[409] The twenty samayas mean, respectively:

1. Do not sneer at the teacher.
2. Do no harm to the teacher's consort.
3. Do nothing to interrupt the accumulation of merit by the faithful.
4. Do not misuse or misappropriate religious patrimony, the wealth of offerings; do not drink alcohol to intoxication, which is the cause of ruin.
5. Do not have sexual relations with the consorts of vajra brothers or sisters.
6. Do not have sexual relations with an improper consort.
7. Do not use the possessions of people influenced by evil forces, or possessions that are subject to quarrels or disputes; do not eat unblessed food.
8. Do not damage your bodhichitta.
9. Do not teach to unsuitable hearers.
10. Do not reject a suitable disciple.
11. The male and female should not separate; bliss should be united with emptiness.
12. Do not quarrel with your vajra kin.
13. Do not take the soiled leftovers of others.
14. Do not covet the teacher's residence or seat.
15. Do not break retreat limits, either of oneself or others.
16. Do not forsake the practice of concentration and vipashyana.
17. Do not interrupt with ordinary speech the continuity of recitation and of rituals.
18. Do not depart from the sign-mudra of empowerment; do not speak to others about the symbols taught in the tantras.
19. Do not disturb the mandala of practitioners; do not perform repelling rites with those who have broken samaya.
20. Do not forsake the teacher, lord of all the enlightened families.

9. An explanation of the twenty-five modes of conduct and of the vows of the five enlightened families

10. The twenty-five modes of conduct

137 The twenty-five modes of conduct,[410] arranged in five sections each of five parts, are taught in the *Elucidation of Samaya*. In the same vein, the *Kalachakra* also specifies that "the twenty-five modes of conduct refer to the avoidance of the five negative actions (this is the foundation of the training), the five lesser negative actions, the five kinds of killing, the five kinds of hostility, and the five kinds of desire."

The avoidance of five negative actions is as follows. First, one must not injure beings, even the tiniest insects; indeed, one should not have the slightest malevolence toward them. Second, one must not lie with the intention to deceive. Third, one must not steal or appropriate the possessions of others, even things that animals possess. Fourth, one must abstain from lustful sexual misconduct. Fifth, one must not intoxicate oneself with alcohol, a cause of ruin. These five negative actions are like ropes that bind beings in samsara. If one is unable to refrain from them, the remaining modes of conduct will not be imparted. They are consequently called five foundations of the training.

The five lesser negative actions are: first, to lay bets, as when gambling with dice or playing chess; second, to consume wrong kinds of sustenance, such as eating meat from animals killed for food or money; third, all kinds of unworthy chatter, such as talk about wars and commerce; fourth, to take pleasure in evil religious traditions in which cattle and other animals are sacrificed to propitiate ancestral spirits or to cure diseases; and fifth, to follow barbaric religious practices that are outlandish and uncouth, such as eating the meat only of animals that one has slain oneself, to wear only white clothes, or to drink only the water consumed by certain kinds of bird. One should refrain from such activities.

The five kinds of killing are: first, to sacrifice cows on the expectation of gaining a higher rebirth; second, to kill children as offerings to the mamos; third, to kill a man for the sake of another; fourth, to kill a woman for the sake of another; and fifth, to slay the teacher of gods and humankind, in other words, to abuse and to destroy the images of the Buddhas and Bodhisattvas, and to destroy books and stupas. People with barbarous ideas consider harmful and destructive behavior as a religious practice, and regard such heinous deeds as virtuous. For that reason, these actions are set apart from the five previous negative actions and are explained separately from them. It is also said that to slaughter yaks, cattle, and sheep, while at the same time claiming to revere the Three Jewels, is no different from such barbaric conduct—even if one does not profess such beliefs.

The five kinds of hostility are anger and animosity expressed toward five kinds of people: virtuous friends; superiors and elders (whether by age or seniority in the Dharma, and so on); Buddhas; the Sangha; teachers and abbots. One should turn one's mind from these four groups of five kinds of negativity, and abstain from them in practice.

The five kinds of attachment and desire are linked with the five sense objects, in relation with which they arise through the interdependence of sense organ and consciousness. This is illustrated by the words of the *Mahayana Pitaka:* "Because of eye contact there is feeling," (and so on up to) "because of bodily contact there is feeling." Desire is consummated in an action that has the power to set in motion a new existence. One should therefore abandon the five kinds of desire. This is done in two ways. In the generation stage, the sense organ, its object, their contact, and the consciousness arising from this contact and so on are purified, and thus assume the status of a deity. In the yoga of withdrawal practiced in the perfection stage,[411] one severs the constant engagement of the five senses in their objects.

These are the twenty-five modes of conduct of Vajrasattva described in the commentary on the *Kalachakra-tantra.* They are referred to as "samayas" because they are not to be transgressed, and as modes of conduct because it is through them that one's body, speech, and mind become the enlightened body, speech, and mind of Vajrasattva.

10. **The vows connected with the five enlightened families**
11. **General vows**
The general vows of the five enlightened families[412] are common to the tantras of both the old and the new translation traditions. The transla-

tions of the *Guhyasamaja, Union with the Buddhas, Secret Moon Essence* tantras, and so on,[413] made by Vairotsana, Kawa Peltsek, Chokro Lui Gyaltsen, and others, until the time of Rinchen Zangpo, are considered the old translations. With Rinchen Zangpo, the period of the new translations begins.

138   The vow or samaya[414] of the tathāgata family of Vairochana (which the root verse calls Buddha yoga) consists in a particular aspect of the vow of bodhichitta, both in aspiration and action. First, one takes the vow of aspiration bodhichitta with the thought that, when the state of Vajrasattva has been attained, one will establish all beings in his level. Then, as a matter of course, one takes the vow of active bodhichitta, firmly observing the three disciplines, which, in the present context, have the following special features. To refrain from negativity means to turn away from ordinary perceptions; to gather virtue means to "gather" (or dissolve) delusions into the state of wisdom; and to benefit beings means to engage in the four activities.

The vow or samaya of the vajra family of Akshobhya consists in possessing a vajra and a bell, and in upholding the mudra (or form of the deity) and the teacher.[415]

The vow or samaya of the jewel family of Ratnasambhava consists in the generous giving of Dharma, wealth, protection from fear, and love.

The vow or samaya of the lotus family of Amitabha consists in upholding and expounding the teachings of the three vehicles of the Pratimoksha, Bodhichitta, and Secret Mantra.

The vow or samaya of the action family of Amoghasiddhi consists in "revering," or earnestly engaging in, every kind of activity, such as offering and praise to the Buddhas and Bodhisattvas, and the performance of the fire offering and so on.

11. The special vows of the five enlightened families

139   The special vows of the five enlightened families[416] are explicit teachings to be taken literally only in the case of exceptional practitioners who abide in the view, meditation, and conduct of the Anuttarayoga, and who have gained certainty therein. The vows of the five enlightened families are as follows.

It is taught that practitioners belonging to the vajra family should kill. On the outer level, this means to "liberate" the ten fields or the seven degenerate objects.[417] On the inner level, this is explained as referring to the "killing" of the karmic wind and thoughts in the central channel. On the secret level, it means "killing" all thoughts in the unborn nature.

Practitioners of the jewel family should steal. On the inner level, this means that skillfully, one should bring within one's power a qualified consort.[418] On the outer level, it means to take the possessions of those who do nothing to accumulate merit, and to use them without attachment in order to make offerings. On the secret level, this refers to the fact that one must appropriate, by one's own strength and power, the qualities of perfect buddhahood, which cannot be bestowed by anyone else.

The vow of those who belong to the lotus family is to venerate, that is, to take support of a woman (described in the root verse as one with the lovely eyes of a deer). On the secret level, this means to enjoy the "lady of emptiness," who has the nature of wisdom and is endowed with the supreme attribute [of bliss]. It means to enjoy the mudra of self-cognizing primordial wisdom (mahamudra). On the inner level, this means to meditate on the mental consort (the dharmamudra), and on the tummo (the samayamudra). On the outer level, it means that one should rely on an actual consort, a karmamudra. In so doing, one is also relying on the three other mudras (the dharmamudra, the samayamudra, and the mahamudra). In other words, by meditating with the three specific attitudes, by adopting skillful conduct, and by having certainty in the view (as associated respectively with these three mudras), one will generate the example wisdom, which is itself induced by the bliss that comes from the melting of the essence-drop. By this means, the ultimate truth, the unchanging coemergent primordial wisdom, is actualized.

The vow of the action family is to tell lies. On the outer level, this means that one must tell illusion-like lies in order to save the property of the teacher, the life of beings, and to preserve one's samaya, and so forth. On the inner level, this means that, when the life-wind dissolves in the heart, all the teachings will, for the practitioner, manifest in a boundless way. He or she will then be able to give teachings that are illusion-like and adapted to the capacity of every being. On the secret level, it means that one will utter illusion-like falsehoods about liberating beings from samsara—beings who, though they appear, have no real existence.

The vow of the wheel family of the tathāgata is, on the outer level, to enjoy as mere illusions the five nectars, the five meats, and so on, together with the sensual pleasures that result from form and the other of the five sense objects. This means to be without any belief in their real existence. On the inner level, the reference to (the consumption of) the five meats means that by binding the quintessence of the five senses, the seed of discursive thoughts is devoured by nonconceptual, ultimate reality. When drinking alcohol, it is as if one is drinking the coemergent primordial wisdom generated from the blissful melting of the essence-drop, falling from above and borne up from below. On the secret level, appearances and mental states are effortlessly cleansed in the state of purity and equality.

The branches of the vows of the five enlightened families, which are taken after the vows of bodhichitta in aspiration and action, are not explicitly expounded [in the root text]. They consist in pledges associated with various referents and attitudes of bodhichitta, such as the promise to free (from conceptual obscurations) those who, like the Shravakas, are not yet free; to "take to the other shore" those who have not yet crossed over; to rouse those who are not yet roused, and so on. They are the same as the ones described in the *Bodhisattva Grounds of Realization,* and have already been explained in the eighth chapter of the present work.

141   Furthermore, as the root text says (adapting the *Vajra Peak Tantra*):

> Do not scorn the devas and asuras,
> And for the hidden ones have no contempt.
> Do not despise the mudras or the mount,
> The weapons or symbolic attributes.

It is thus explicitly taught that the devas and asuras are not to be despised. Neither should one scorn the "hidden ones," that is, the yakshas who protect the Buddha's teachings. One should not be disrespectful to the four mudras and especially, one should never revile the perfect body of the yidam-deity. One should not despise the teacher's mount or conveyance (meaning the teacher's possessions, such as his seat, chariot, horse, and so forth).

"Arms" or "weapons" here refer to the special kinds of weapons that are the attributes of the yidam-deities: swords, wooden clubs, and so on. The symbolic attributes are the articles that the yidam-deities of the five families hold in their hands. None of these should be treated with disrespect. It is, in addition, forbidden to step on or walk over the shadows cast by representations of the enlightened body, speech, and mind—statues of the deities, for example, or the body of one's teacher, stupas, and so forth. If this is unavoidable, one should repeat the mantra VAJRAVEGA AKRAMA HUNG considering that by the power of the mantra and mudra of vajra strength, the shadow is lifted up into the air so that one can walk under it.

In the same way, one should not walk over the old, stale remnant of offerings made to the Buddha and the deities. One should not consume them oneself, nor put them in a place where people might tread on them. Finally, one should not consume butter or foodstuffs that have been modeled into the shape of a deity's attributes. It is forbidden.

Of the special vows of the five families of the Vajrayana, actions such as killing, stealing, sexual activity, lying, divisive speech, harsh words, and worthless chatter are to be taken literally by practitioners whose realization is certain. They are to be understood indirectly or metaphorically by those whose practice is still on the level of aspiration.[419] For instance, "killing" means the killing or dissolution of the wind in the central channel; "stealing" means assimilating by one's own efforts the meaning of the Mahayana teachings, and so on. If beginners in the practice of the Mantrayana do not distinguish these two levels of the teaching and take these vows literally, they will fall down to the hell of Torment Unsurpassed or the other lower realms. It is therefore important to act with the greatest circumspection.

In short, the nature of the mind, which dwells within from the very beginning, is not visible to us, just as the whiteness of a conch is not visible to a person suffering from a bile disorder. Obscured from beginningless time by the thoughts of the eight consciousnesses, it is invisible and as if concealed. This is why it is described as "secret." The *Guhyagarbha-tantra* declares:

> EMAHO! This nature, secret from the start,
> Appears in many forms, yet secret is its character.
> It is completely secret by its very nature;
> It is not other than extremely secret.

As long as those of inferior fortune or merit do not realize directly this profound fourfold secret nature, the teachings about secret activities should be hidden in symbolic language. Such people should refrain from attempting actions that are beyond them, such as union, "liberation," and so on. They should be instructed only indirectly, according to their capacity and as appropriate to the level of their understanding at a given time.

8. The repairing of damaged samaya
9. The individual considered as the basis of the vow

144 Even extremely vicious beings, who kill brahmins every day and commit negative actions of immediate effect, like murdering their fathers and mothers, can take the Mantrayana vows. Obviously, there is no need therefore to emphasize the fact that, compared with the lower vehicles, the Secret Mantra or Vajrayana is superior and extraordinary in its skillful means.

9. The causes of damaged samaya and the connected antidotes

145 There are four sources of downfalls. The first is to be ignorant of the boundary line between what is to be done and what is to be avoided in respect of each of the downfalls. The second is a lack of respect for the teacher who gives instructions on this crucial subject. The third is to be careless of the precepts, thus committing faults through sheer caprice. The fourth is to have such strong defilements that, however carefully one may act, one is powerless to curb them by applying antidotes. Furthermore, however well one knows what the downfalls are, forgetfulness will always lead to the deterioration of one's samaya. And if mindfulness is not clear and sharp—in other words, if one is slack and without

vigilance in examining whether downfalls have been committed—one's samaya will be damaged. When these two factors are added to the previous four, one arrives at six factors that lead to the deterioration of samaya.

The antidote to one's strongest defilement should be cultivated with mindfulness and vigilance. For instance, an expert surgeon operating with a scalpel on a blind eye will work with extreme care and concentration. In exactly the same way, one must observe the samayas. As we have said, one must be constantly focused, throughout the six periods of the day and night, on the crucial points of what is to be adopted and what is to be rejected, examining one's mind with narrow scrutiny.

9. The repairing of damaged samaya
10. Why it is easy to repair damaged samaya

The repairing of damaged samaya is easier than the repairing of faults in the lower vehicles. If the Shravakayana discipline is damaged through any one of the four defeats, provided there is no intention to conceal one's fault, one receives a penance as laid down in the precepts[420] and can thereby repair one's mistake. This is allowed for as many as seven times. Generally speaking, it is said that if a monk incurs a defeat and, being without any intention to conceal his fault, receives a penitential precept, and if such a monk gives back his vow, he may at a later stage take the full ordination vow. It is said in the commentary on the Karmashataka that a man can be ordained as many as seven times. A monk who conceals his defeat, however, is unable to repair the fault even once. It is just as when an earthenware pot is shattered: it cannot be mended again.

To damage the Bodhisattva vow can be compared to breaking a vessel made of precious metal—which can be repaired by a skillful smith. The Bodhisattva vow can be repaired through confession by relying on the spiritual master as the external condition. By contrast, the impairing of the vows of the Secret Mantra is like slightly denting a precious vessel. Without having to depend on external conditions, one can repair the fault oneself, through the generation and perfection stage practices and so forth. This is a much better way of repairing faults.

10. The methods of repairing broken samayas
11. Repairing the broken samayas of body, speech, and mind

149 Regarding the body samaya, if one behaves insultingly, even in one's dreams, toward the vajra teacher and the vajra kindred, one should immediately pay respect to them in thought, word, and deed, and make them pleasing offerings of ganachakra and other gifts, thus restoring one's spoiled samaya. This should be done quickly. For it is said in the *Tantra of the Great Array of Ati*:

> To the teacher and the teacher's close companions,
> To the vajra kindred, to one's brothers and one's sisters,
> Words of censure, open or concealed
> Or even indirect, should never be addressed.
> And if this happens, even in one's dreams,
> One should confess them in one's heart.
> For if what one has done in thought or very deed
> Is not confessed through lack of mindfulness,
> One falls headfirst into the realms of hell.

If the speech samaya connected with the teacher and the vajra kindred is impaired, one should visualize one's teacher in the form of the Buddha Vajradharma, red in color, the embodiment of the vajra speech of all the Tathāgatas, either above the crown of one's head or as inseparable from oneself, and one should recite his hundred-syllable mantra (i.e., OM PADMASATTVA SAMAYA MANUPALAYA, etc.) one hundred thousand times. And one should devote oneself exclusively to praising the teacher's qualities.

If the mind samaya is damaged through ill will, through the divulging of secrets to the unprepared, and so forth, one should visualize oneself in the form of Vajrasattva, the embodiment of the vajra mind of all the Tathāgatas, and meditate upon one's teacher above one's head, offering the prayer of seven branches. One should consider that the teacher grants the four empowerments and then melts into oneself. Observing silence for three years, one should abide one-pointedly in meditation, mingling inseparably one's mind with the teacher's mind. This, it is said, is how to repair the mind samaya when it has deteriorated.

11. Repairing deteriorated samayas that have exceeded the time period for confession

The twenty-four-hour day is divided into six periods. If in any of these periods one begins an action that results in a downfall,[421] and if one fails to remedy this by applying antidotes in the same time period, the downfall is said to exceed its time limit for confession. This is what is termed a *downfall exceeding the time period for confession* (*thun 'das gyi ltung ba*). If the downfall is not confessed on the same day, one speaks of it as a *transgression* (*'gal ba*). If it is not confessed within a month, one speaks of a *deterioration* (*nyams pa*). If it is not confessed within a year, one says that there is a *breach of limit* (*'das pa*); and if two or three years are allowed to elapse without confession, the samaya is said to be *torn apart* (*ral pa*). If the downfall is confessed in the same period as it was committed, it can be repaired. But the more the confession is delayed, the heavier the fault becomes. After three years have gone by, the samaya cannot be repaired, even if the downfall is confessed.

If a transgression is committed, it can be repaired by the ganachakra offering. If a deterioration is committed, it can be restored by making pleasing offerings to the teacher and the deity. A breach of limit can be rectified by offering all one's treasured possessions—all that one cherishes most, such as one's child, spouse, wealth, and so forth. If a tearing apart has occurred, it can be repaired if one follows the teacher's instructions with great endeavor and without a thought for life or limb. All these remedies are described in the *Vajra Sun Array Tantra*.

11. Other ways of repairing deteriorated samayas

Other reparatory methods exist in addition to the ones just mentioned. One may take the four empowerments repeatedly from one's teacher. One may take self-empowerment by means of one's own visualization. When in solitude, one can meditate upon the generation and perfection stages. Likewise, according to the *General Scripture of Summarized Wisdom*, there exist reparatory methods related to the five ways of deterioration.[422] These are categorized as reparations through action, the offering

150

151

152

of material objects, willingness, concentration, and suchness. The restoration of samaya through action (*las kyis skang ba*) is achieved by means of the fire-offering ritual, torma offering, and the recitation of the hundred-syllable mantra. In order to repair a great deterioration, one must recite the mantra one hundred and thirty thousand times; to purify a root deterioration, one must recite the mantra fifty-three thousand times; to purify a branch deterioration, one must recite the mantra five thousand three hundred times; to purify a deterioration through association with samaya-breakers, one must recite the mantra three hundred times; to purify an incidental deterioration (such as a deterioration committed not for self-centered reasons but in order to please others),[423] one must recite the mantra fifty-three times.

It is also possible to restore deteriorated samaya by taking support of material objects (*rdzas kyis skang ba*),[424] of keen willingness (*'dun pas skang ba*),[425] and of concentration (*ting nge 'dzin gyis skang ba*). "Concentration" here means that the faults are restored by meditating on the common yoga of the perfection stage, such as the skillful path of one's own body, specified in the root verse as the "discipline of non-emission,"[426] and the yoga of the essence-drop, the so-called blazing and dripping. It is also possible to perform a fire offering related to the activity of pacifying. Also, one can visualize the whole of samsara and nirvana as the deity, to whom one then offers a torma. One can also repair a downfall through the mantra and mudra, as explained in the Yogatantra.[427] It is through the various stages of such a practice that one summons [the consciousness] and separates it from the lower realms.[428]

It is also said in the *Vajra Pinnacle Tantra:*

> With the mantra of the seed-syllables, purify as follows:
> Imagine on the soles of your two feet the letter YAM,
> And RAM upon your secret door.
> Within your navel are the seeds of the six realms,
> And in your heart, upon a throne of PHAT,
> Are the quintessences of body, speech, and mind.
> The wisdom wind appears from YAM,
> From RAM, the wisdom fires burn up
> Consuming all the tendencies that lead to the six realms.

Your three doors turn into enlightened body, speech, and mind.
With PHAT you are propelled into the dharmadhatu.

This is an extremely profound pith instruction. One should, in addition, perform rituals of purification, such as cleansing oneself with the water contained in a vase and that has been consecrated with the dharani of Vajravidarana and Bhurkumkuta,[429] and so on. With a great yearning to be purified, one should take the empowerments of the Buddhas of the five families from empowerment deities manifesting from the ultimate expanse. One should perform cleansing rituals, such as washing one's body as a mode of practice, considering that the river and so forth (in which one does it) is by nature Mamaki, arisen from the syllable BAM. The fire of tummo burns the syllable KAM visualized in one's navel, and consumes all one's negative actions visualized in the form of a scorpion in the heart. Purification by using the wind element refers to the hoisting of banners and flags over shrines, temples, and so forth.

It is also possible to declare one's misdemeanors in the midst of a large assembly or in the presence of a blessed support. One should perform the ganachakra offering and so on, and exert oneself by every means to ransom the lives of animals. One should also read the scriptures (the sutras and tantras), and in particular the *Sutra of Liberation* and the *Stainless Confession Tantra.* One should recite dharanis and mantras, and especially the mantra of a hundred syllables, which is the quintessence of the mind of all the Tathāgatas. One should offer mandalas, as well as the prayer of seven branches. One should erect stupas representing the qualities of realization and elimination of the Tathāgatas. If one is unable to do this, one should make tsatsas instead. There are yet other ways of purifying broken and deteriorated samayas. The practices of purification are indeed limitless. Those just mentioned are the general ways of purification. In particular, [for a practitioner engaged in the three yogas: Maha, Anu, Ati], there is a general cleansing ritual, which is the confession prayer called *Churning the Depths of Hell* (*na rag dong sprugs*), which purifies everything.[430] It is said that:

> Whoever makes prostrations to the deities of the peaceful and
> wrathful mandalas of the *Mayajala* will purify all breaches and
> deteriorations of samaya. Even the five sins of immediate effect

will be purified. Even if one were in hell, its depth would be churned, and one would go instantly to the buddhafields of the Vidyādharas.

In all ritual confessions, it is extremely important to generate feelings of remorse.[431]

8. The defects resulting from the degeneration of samaya

154 However much of one's life is spent in practice, if one fails to confess one's wrongdoings, there will be no accomplishment, and in fact the effects of one's practice will be reversed.[432] All joy and prosperity will diminish, one's life will be short, and sickness will abound. And in the next life, one will fall into the unequaled vajra hell.

8. The benefits resulting from a pure observance of the samayas

Those who observe the samayas purely will gain in sixteen lifetimes, or at the swiftest in this present life, at the moment of death, or in the bardo, the supreme accomplishment and spiritual qualities, such as the eight common accomplishments. As it is said:

> Enjoyment of the sky, the sword, and pill,
> Fleet-footedness, the vase, and power over demons,
> Extraction of the essence and the balm of magic sight.[433]

One will also obtain the ten powers as these were explained on the sutra path.[434] These ten powers have several aspects. In an outer sense, they are connected with the seven impure Bodhisattva grounds, while in an inner sense, they are associated with the three pure grounds. The extremely pure ten powers arise when the level of buddhahood is attained.

Likewise the eight qualities of mastery will be gained.[435] These are:

> Fineness, lightness, subtle power,
> Power to enjoy, and lordship, graciousness,
> Universal sway, and the capacity to show forth things

According to the wish of beings:
These are the eight great qualities of mastery.

Fineness refers to the realization that phenomena are beyond all conceptual constructs. Lightness indicates the wisdom wind, by which one is able to travel to any world system. Subtle power means the fading of all duality. Power to enjoy refers to the enjoyment of the five sense objects as the display of ultimate reality. Lordship indicates the assumption of great strength in the subduing of the four demons. Graciousness refers to the ability to satisfy the wishes of beings. Universal sway means the ability to establish beings in the perfection of the twofold accumulation so that there is no moment when one is not of benefit to others. The capacity to show forth things according to the wishes of beings refers to the miraculous powers deployed as a means to gain the twofold goal.

Those who possess these qualities are the Vidyādharas on the four levels, as has been explained above.[436]

When the path of learning has been completely traversed, supreme accomplishment is gained—the enlightened body endowed with seven qualities of union[437] is accomplished. This means that first, all aspects of the enlightened body arise as the manifold illusory appearance of phenomena—this is referred to as *union.* Second, all aspects of enlightened speech, free from the obscuration of sounds and words, are *perfect enjoyment.* Third, all aspects of the enlightened mind are free from dualistic thoughts and enjoy immutable *great bliss.* Fourth, the enlightened mind subsists *without inherent existence.* It is not a mere nonaffirmative negation established by analysis, but is characterized by self-cognizing awareness. These first four aspects perfect one's own aim. Continuing with the seven qualities of union, there is, fifth, the effortless accomplishment of the aims of others through *nonconceptual great compassion.* Sixth is the *unceasing constancy* of this compassion. And seventh is the *unobstructed arising* of form bodies and infinite methods of Dharma according to the aspirations and faculties of beings. With these last three aspects, the aim of others is automatically accomplished. With the qualities of the five kayas thus perfected, one departs for the field of Akanishtha. The spontaneous accomplishment of this twofold aim is known as buddhahood.

The Ground of the Great Perfection

1. A brief explanation of the ground of the Great Perfection

In his first turning of the wheel of the Dharma, the Buddha, skilled in means and endowed with compassion, gave instructions for those who are embarking on the path by discoursing upon impermanence and the rest of the sixteen aspects of the four noble truths. For disciples of medium capacity, he set forth the three doors of perfect liberation: the cause as absence of attributes, the result as absence of expectancy, and the nature as emptiness.[438] These instructions belong to the second turning of the wheel of Dharma. The essence of these instructions, the meaning that is to be implemented, is great, self-cognizing primordial wisdom (*so so rang rig pa'i ye shes*), and this forms the subject of the final turning of the wheel of Dharma.

In the *Sutra Requested by King Dharanishvara* and in the *Mahaparinirvana-sutra*, the Buddha taught in extensive detail that the ultimate nature, as set forth in the second turning of the Dharma wheel, dwells naturally in all beings as the sugatagarbha.[439] In this way, he expounded for those of sharp capacity the exact nature of knowledge objects. The essence of the teachings of the second and third turnings is the fundamental nature of all phenomena: profound, peaceful, beyond conceptual construction, and endowed with the character of luminosity. And after distinguishing the ordinary mind (that is, ordinary states of consciousness) from primordial wisdom, this fundamental nature is set forth as the naked condition of this same primordial wisdom. This teaching is known as the Great Perfection, and is ultimately identical with the Great Madhyamaka of union (the subtle inner Madhyamaka).[440] The only difference between them lies in the manner of their exposition.

In the term "Great Perfection," "perfection" refers to the fact that all phenomena, of both samsara and nirvana, are perfectly (totally, completely) contained within self-cognizing awareness,[441] whereas "great" indicates that this same awareness is primordial wisdom, by which samsara and nirvana are both pervaded. The Great Perfection relates to the ground, the path, and the result.[442]

2   In accordance with the aspirations of beings, the Buddha gave vast and manifold teachings, and these constitute the excellent path that leads beyond suffering. The sublime doctrines of the different vehicles (from the Shravakayana till Anuyoga) were set forth solely for the cleansing of the defiled ordinary mind. Consequently, all the different practices of the lower paths—the three vows, the six paramitas, the generation and perfection stages of the common path of the Secret Mantra—are steps and stages leading to the path of the Great Perfection.

1. A detailed explanation of the ground of the Great Perfection
2. An explanation of the common ground of samsara and nirvana
3. An explanation of the ground itself
4. A general explanation of the fundamental nature of the ground[443]

3   Regarding the indivisibility of samsara and nirvana, when the ground of the Natural Great Perfection[444] is established, it is understood that the phenomena of samsara and nirvana do not stir from the ultimate expanse. Therefore, even when delusory appearances manifest (which they do as long as ultimate reality remains unrealized), these same appearances have never been other than the utterly pure nature of awareness. They are as nonexistent as the horns of a rabbit. Consequently, the ground for what appears as samsara and nirvana (nonexistent as these are)[445] is the nature of awareness (*rig pa'i chos nyid*), and this is primordially and perfectly endowed with the three kayas. Its pure nature (*ngo bo dag pa*) is dharmakaya; its luminous character (*rang bzhin gsal ba*) is sambhogakaya; and its cognitive potency endowed with the essence of awareness (*thugs rje rig pa'i snying po can*) is nirmanakaya.[446]

4   When the appearances of the ground arise from the ground, [two things may occur]. If these appearances (which, rising like a cloud, are the cause of the eight consciousnesses) dissolve back into the ground,[447] the utterly pure kayas and wisdoms manifest, and this is buddhahood. If, on the other hand, the appearances of the ground are veiled by

coemergent ignorance, and if conceptual ignorance further apprehends this self-experience of awareness (*rang snang*) as outer objects, there unfolds the duality of apprehended object and apprehending subject;[448] impure samsara manifests in the manner of a dream, and consequently one is an ordinary being. But although the appearances of the ground manifest in these two aspects of samsara and nirvana, the latter never part from the state of the ground, just as when good and bad dreams occur during sleep, they never separate from the sleeping state. The phenomena of samsara and nirvana are not "new occurrences" arising from some other source. Neither will they stir from the ground and go elsewhere at some future point.

4. An explanation of the various assertions made about the ground

Reflecting about the nature of the ground, certain practitioners of the Great Perfection have, from their own limited point of view, formulated seven positions. Some have said that the ground is primordial purity (*ka dag*), others that it is spontaneous presence (*lhun grub*). Some have said that it is indeterminate (*ma nges pa*); others have claimed that it is determinate (*nges pa'i don*). Some have said that it can transform into anything (*cir yang bsgyur du btub pa*), while others have said that it may be defined as anything at all (*cir yang khas blang du btub pa*). And there are others who have asserted that the ground manifests as a manifold variety (*sna tshogs su 'char ba*).[449]

The advocates of these seven opinions establish the ground, which is by nature the union of primordial purity and spontaneous presence, conceptually. And in so doing, they define it unilaterally in terms of one or other of its aspects. They understand the ground only in part, and do not grasp it fully as it really is. This shortcoming is illustrated by a story found in the *Sutra of the Quintessence of Primordial Wisdom*:

> Once upon a time, a king summoned a group of blind men. He placed an elephant in front of them and asked them to describe it. Those who touched the elephant's trunk said that the elephant was like a hook; those who touched its eyes said that it was like a bowl; those who touched its ears said that it was like a winnowing fan; those who touched its hindquarters said that

it was like a sedan chair; while those who touched its tail declared that it was like a rope. Without perceiving it fully, the blind men were all describing the same elephant. In just the same way, Buddhahood has been defined in terms of one or other of its aspects. Some have said that it is emptiness, others that it is illusoriness, others that it is luminosity, and so on. But they all fail to understand it fully.

The same scripture contains another example illustrating how the Shravakas, Pratyekabuddhas, and Bodhisattvas fail to see or realize the essence of buddhahood as it is:

> A man blind from birth asked someone to tell him the color of ghee. He received the answer that it was like snow. On touching snow, the blind man thought that the color of ghee was cold. He then inquired about the color of snow and was told that it was like a swan's wing. When he heard a swan's wings flapping, he thought that the color of snow was like the sound of wings. Then, when he asked about the color of a swan's wing, he heard that it was like a conch. He touched a conch and concluded that the color of a swan's wing was smooth.

It is thus that those who hold the seven partial positions just referred to do not have an adequate understanding of ultimate reality. They describe it in the same way that the men blind from birth described the shape of an elephant or the color of a swan.

4. A detailed explanation of the ground according to our own unmistaken tradition

7   Our tradition teaches that the nature of awareness—which is primordially pure in being beyond conceptual construction—contains within it a luminosity, an unceasing and natural radiance, that is the essence of the kayas and wisdoms. It is like the sun and its rays. The qualities (of this luminosity) are primordially and spontaneously present. These aspects of appearance and emptiness, being distinct, are not identical. And yet their nature is one and the same. They are as inseparable as a

pot and its own emptiness. They are not two separate substances, but are like water and its wetness.

Considered from the point of view of its emptiness, one cannot say of this nature that it is of such a shape and color. It is beyond all conceptual construction, all the characteristics by which things are identified. While it is possible for all such conceptual constructions regarding the nature of awareness to be discarded through a process of "exclusion" (*rnam bcad*), it is impossible to identify awareness in the manner of a "detection" (*yongs gcod*).[450] This is why one speaks of "primordial purity." This does not mean, however, that awareness is simply a nonentity, like space. For considered from the point of view of its appearance, within the unceasing natural radiance of the profoundly indwelling luminosity (*gting gsal*), there is the creative power (*rtsal*) of cognitive potency (*thugs rje*), which can manifest in any form. And this is why one speaks of "spontaneous presence" (*lhun grub*). As it is written in the *Pearl Necklace Tantra:* "The ultimate nature is primordially pure and indescribable. Its character is spontaneous, and whatever appears is perfect." This implies, moreover, that the ground does not fall into the extremes of permanence or annihilation.

Now if it is shown that it is incorrect to say that the ground is exclusively primordial purity, and that it is incorrect to say that it is exclusively spontaneous presence, does it not follow that it is incorrect to say that it is both? But existence and nonexistence—or, in other words, spontaneous presence from the standpoint of appearance, and primordial purity from the standpoint of emptiness—are simply aspects differentiated within the one ground, which is the mind's nature. They are not two different substances, and therefore there is no contradiction. For example, when one is falling asleep, thoughts, both gross and subtle, come gradually to a halt, and in the state of deep sleep, the eighty kinds of thought[451] are arrested, and one does not dream. Dreams occur when the mind's radiance, mounted on the winds, begins to unfold. During sleep, in other words, there are two states of mind which are, however, indissociable from the sleeping state. Likewise, in the primordially pure nature, no delusions exist. There has never been a wandering in samsara in the past, there is no wandering now, and there will never be any wandering in the future. Yet, because of the unceasing radiance of the

8

ground, or its spontaneous creative power, a variegated display unfolds, and this may appear either as samsara or as nirvana.[452]

9   As an illustration of this, one could say that the natural (blue) light of a sapphire and the natural rainbow light of a clean rainbow-crystal subsist within their respective jewels as a profoundly indwelling luminosity. And except when prompted by circumstances like the sun's rays and so on, this luminosity is not outwardly manifest in a manner perceptible to the senses. Now in accordance with this illustration of the ground and the appearance of the ground, when one remains in the state of ground-luminosity (for example, at the moment of death), primordially pure awareness is free from all adulterating conditions. It is like an immaculate autumn sky. At that time, there is no perception of entities endowed with characteristics, whether in terms of impure phenomena like form and the other sense objects (together with the six types of consciousness that apprehend them) or in terms of pure phenomena like deities and lights.[453] And yet, the natural radiance of the ground[454] is present as an "inner luminosity." As long as conditions are not encountered that could cause the appearances of spontaneous presence to arise outwardly, "the seal," as the root verse says, "is not broken." In other words, there is no outward manifestation. This state is referred to as the *ever youthful vase body,* or rather, *the ever youthful body [enclosed] with a vase.*[455]

10   The nature (*ngo bo*) of awareness is free from thoughts, gross and subtle. Being beyond thought and expression, it is empty; it is unoriginate. But because of its natural radiance, which is the aspect of spontaneous presence, the display of the three kayas can unobstructedly arise. Therefore the ground from which all appearances of both samsara and nirvana manifest is the ground-awareness (*gzhi'i rig pa*). But since primordial purity and spontaneous presence have a single nature, these appearances of the ground do not stir from the ground of empty luminosity. Since this fundamental nature (*gnas lugs*) has never been stained by the impure five aggregates, it is primordially immaculate. Therefore it is "pure" (*byang*). Since it is intrinsically endowed with the qualities of the three kayas, it is perfectly "accomplished" (*chub*). And since it is able to manifest unceasingly in any way, it is "mind" (*sems*). This pure, accomplished mind[456]—namely, primordial wisdom, which is subtle and dif-

ficult to realize—is the ground's inner luminosity. It does not radiate outwardly (*phyir mi gsal ba*), either as pure or impure phenomena such as colors, "self and other," and so on—all of which fall to one side or other, either of delusion in samsara or freedom in nirvana.

From the standpoint of primordial purity, the fundamental nature, 11 the common ground of samsara and nirvana, has no intrinsic existence as the kayas and wisdoms, and therefore it is not buddhahood. Neither does it exist as the aggregates, elements, sense-fields, and so on, with the result that it is not the state of ordinary beings either. Although it is referred to as the "one and only sphere" (*thig le nyag gcig*), it does not exist as a single causal entity; and even though it may be labeled as the three kayas and so on, the one ultimate expanse is beyond differentiation. This nature is beyond all conceptual construction, and thus it does not dwell either in the extremes or in the middle position. On the other hand, if it is assessed from the point of view of spontaneous presence, it is not an empty void. It is the ground from which the kayas and wisdoms arise,[457] and yet it does not exist as a material entity.

[Finally, this fundamental nature, the common ground of samsara and nirvana, may be considered from the point of view of both primordial purity and spontaneous presence taken together.] Devoid of the conditions[458] conducive either to delusion or to freedom, the nature of the ground (*ngo bo*) is dharmatā (the ultimate nature of all things), beyond all conceptual extremes of existence, nonexistence, and so on. It is primordial purity, which cannot be established, or defined in one way or another. Since its character (*rang bzhin*) is unceasing and unobstructed, primordial purity is inseparable from the spontaneous presence of kayas and wisdoms. And since its cognitive potency (*thugs rje*) is unceasing and unobstructed, enlightened activities pervade the fields of both samsara and nirvana. These three aspects are inseparable, and this inseparability is posited as the one fundamental ground.

3. An explanation of the appearances of the ground
4. A general explanation of the manner of their arising

From the state of the natural radiance of the fundamental nature of the 12 ground (the "vase-body"), the appearances of the ground arise, in other words, the entire dimension of spontaneous presence. The luminosity of the ground, which is the union [of primordial purity and spontaneous presence], is said to be an empty luminosity in which there is awareness, self-cognizing primordial wisdom. And this, being the union of appearance and emptiness, does not fall to one side or the other [existence or nonexistence]. Awareness has the character of the "life or essential [wind]," and from this the other winds derive. There is the upward moving wind, which is the "horse" or vehicle of the wisdom that recognizes the nature of the mind; the downward-voiding wind, which is the shining light of the wisdom that apprehends the nature of apparent sense objects; the fire-accompanying wind, which has the power to ripen or burn; and the all-pervading wind, which has the power to perfect and accomplish. The nature of these five winds is unceasing radiance, which is the basis, or essential factor, for the arising of the appearances of spontaneous presence. Thanks to the five winds, [inner luminosity] is poised, ready to be projected outward.

Thus, the kayas, wisdoms, and cognitive potency of the inner luminosity cannot be dissociated from the five winds. They are all of one taste. They are not manifest, but are present in the manner of "an ever youthful body [enclosed] within a vase." As soon as the seal is broken, the luminous dimension of primordial wisdom (*ye shes 'od kyi sbubs*), or the appearance of the ground, arises in the manner of an outwardly radiating luminosity—without ever separating from the primordially pure ground. This is called the appearance of the spontaneously present nature (*rang bzhin lhun grub kyi snang ba*).

4. The eight ways in which the appearances of the ground arise

13 When the appearances of spontaneous presence are on the point of arising, there emerges, in the space-like openness of the radiance of the ultimate nature (*ngo bo'i gdangs*), the radiance of the character of the ground (*rang bzhin gyi gdangs*), in the form of five lights. When this occurs, the radiance of the awareness of cognitive potency (*thugs rje'i rig gdangs*) arises in the form of cognition (*shes pa*), which detects and examines the objects that appear. At that point, there is no "ignorance" in the nature of the ground, for this is primordially pure like the unclouded sky. Nevertheless, since this cognition fails to recognize these spontaneous appearances as the self-experience of awareness (*rang snang*), this cogni-

tion assumes—by comparison with the awareness (*rig pa*) that arose as the radiance of cognitive potency—the guise of ignorance, an absence of awareness (*ma rig pa*). Spontaneous appearances stir from limpid primordial purity, which is as clear as a cloudless sky, and they do so in the form of outwardly radiating luminosity. They manifest or arise in eight ways: the six ways and the two doors.

The appearances [of the ground] arise spontaneously. (1) They arise as cognitive potency (*thugs rje*), and beings are benefited. But when (as in certain texts) this spontaneous arising is not mentioned, appearances are said (2) to arise as light: all-pervading rays of light. (3) They arise as primordial wisdom. And since this is an unceasing enjoyment, the natural light of primordial wisdom manifests in the form of pure buddhafields. (4) They arise as the [peaceful and wrathful] deities. Since the ultimate nature is unobstructed, awareness "ripens" into deities: all phenomena manifest as the groupings of the five enlightened families. (5) Beyond all dualistic apprehension of subject and object, appearances arise in a nondual way. In other words, they cannot be individually determined, and consequently have neither a singular nor a plural nature; they abide in thought-free concentration. (6) Finally, they arise in a manner free from all extreme ontological positions. Thanks to unobstructed skillful means, they do not abide in ordinary deluded perception, and remain for an instant in the ultimate nature.

The two doors are as follows. The recognition of the spontaneous appearance of the ground as being the self-experience of primordial wisdom is the door of total enlightenment in the primordial ground, after the manner of Samantabhadra. Failure to recognize this constitutes the door of delusion of ordinary beings. In this context, it has been said that since, with regard to the ground's appearance, there are two kinds of delusion, higher and lower, it is necessary to understand what Samantabhadra's ground of freedom is.[459]

At the stage of the ground, and owing to the strength of delusion, all the appearances of the ground are in a state of dissolution, and these appearances subsist as inner luminosity. And since this radiance is able to arise as the appearances of both samsara and nirvana, it is called the dimension of precious spontaneous presence of the ground. At the stage of the path, the appearances of the ground manifest [from the dimension just mentioned] as the four visions of luminosity and so on. This is the ground of both delusion and freedom; it is the dimension of the precious spontaneous presence of the path. At the stage of the result, the appearances of the ground dissolve because they are recognized as the self-experience of awareness itself. This is the ground from which the infinite qualities of buddhahood manifest; it is the dimension of the precious spontaneous presence of the result. These eight doors of arising, or the three dimensions of precious spontaneous presence (*lhun grub rin po che'i sbubs*), are the point where samsara and nirvana meet and are seamlessly connected.[460]

14   All this is very difficult to understand. It is set forth in the tantras of Atiyoga, the summit of all vehicles, as well as in the essential commentaries made on them by the Vidyādharas of India: instructions that are like keys for opening the tantras' meaning. Here in Tibet, the land of snowcapped mountains, this matter was perfectly examined in the *Precious Treasury of the Supreme Vehicle* composed by Longchen Rabjam, the all-knowing king of Dharma and only eye of beings, the stainless light of whose wisdom sends forth a myriad rays of knowledge.[461]

2. The freedom of Samantabhadra
3. The way Samantabhadra is free in the dharmakaya

15   When the luminosity of the ground, the natural radiance of primordial purity, arises, and when the nature of the appearances of the ground is seen,[462] in that very instant a freedom marked by six special features is attained. It is thus that, prior to the enlightenment of any Buddha, the primordial Buddha Samantabhadra abides from the very first in the recognition of the nature of the mind, the self-arisen primordial wisdom. Free from the mistaken belief that the apprehending mind and the apprehended object have real existence, his experience is utterly pure.

Samantabhadra's realization and freedom are characterized by the following six features. First, the appearance of the ground is his self-experience, in other words, the self-experience of awareness (*rang ngor snang ba*). Second, this appearance is superior to the ground itself (*gzhi las 'phags pa*). Third, the particular qualities [of the ultimate expanse] are discerned (*bye brag phyed pa*) and, fourth, on the basis of this discernment, freedom occurs (*phyed thog tu grol ba*). Fifth, this freedom does not arise through the intervention of extraneous factors (*gzhan las ma byung ba*). And sixth, this freedom dwells in its own place (*rang sar gnas pa*).

Taking these points in order, we can say that, first [in the case of Samantabhadra,] when the appearances of the ground arise, no unfolding of delusion occurs through the turning of the mind outward in the belief that the appearances of the ground are an extramental reality. [For Samantabhadra recognizes them as] his self-experience, that is, as the self-experience of self-cognizing awareness (*rang rig pa'i ngor snang ba*).

Second, once they are recognized as the self-experience of awareness itself (*rang snang*), these appearances are superior to the ground, which is by nature indeterminate (being neither freedom nor delusion). They are also superior to the spontaneous appearances of the ground. And since they have become the ground of freedom, they cannot, at a later stage, become the ground of delusion.

Third, [primordial wisdom] is not something new that, previously absent, suddenly arises. Therefore, the recognition of awareness within the appearances of the ground is called a "*ripening* of the ground into the fruit of primordial wisdom." In the very instant that the nature of awareness is recognized—by means of wisdom free from all obscuring veils—all the qualities that are naturally present in the ultimate expanse become spontaneously apparent. For in the self-experience of awareness, the obscurations related to the universal ground of different habitual tendencies are cleansed away. And this is so primordially. Just like the sun emerging from behind the clouds, the qualities that are especially superior to the ground of samsara are discerned.

Fourth, as soon as these qualities are discerned, wisdom (*shes rab*) ripens into the svabhavikakaya, which, inseparable from the primordial wisdom of the dharmakaya, captures the citadel of the primordial purity of the ground, and dwells there constantly and unchangingly.

Fifth, without depending on outer conditions, such as instructions given by others, Samantabhadra attains buddhahood through his own strength, by recognizing his own nature in a direct act of self-cognizing awareness.

Sixth, the ground of freedom dwells now in its own place[463] within the primordial state, with the result that it is impossible for delusion to gain entry.

In the very instant that Samantabhadra sees, by virtue of these six special features, that the appearances of the ground have the nature of the inconceivable ocean of kayas and wisdoms (this is the resultant aspect of the vase body), he is perfectly enlightened: the primordial Buddha Samantabhadra. This is thanks to his accumulations, which are complete primordially, and his equally primordial freedom from obscuration.[464]

3. How the sambhogakaya buddhafields manifest

16 Without stirring from the ultimate expanse of the dharmakaya (the ground of primordial purity, the expanse of purity and equality beyond all conceptual construction), the qualities of this same expanse, which are the unfolding creative power of inner luminosity and are utterly free from obscuring propensities, arise naturally through the six doors of the ground's spontaneous presence. These qualities manifest as the sambhogakaya buddhafields and the buddhas of the five families, which are the exclusive self-experience of the sambhogakaya (*rang snang longs sku*). Through the creative power of each of the five enlightened families, and based upon the mandala of the inexhaustible ornaments of the body, speech, and mind of Buddha Mahasagara in five families,[465] there appear the infinite and inconceivable buddhafields, vast as space itself, which are called the Aeon of Great Brahma.[466]

3. How the nirmanakaya accomplishes the benefit of beings

17 For Bodhisattvas on the grounds of realization, whose obscurations are mostly purified, the sambhogakaya buddhafields and Buddhas appear as "nirmanakaya buddhafields and teachers of luminous character" (*rang bzhin sprul sku*). By contrast, for unenlightened beings, who arise "through the impure door of samsara," the nirmanakaya teachers appear according to the different perceptions, dispositions, and aspirations of these same beings—ranging from the supreme nirmanakaya down to the "diversified nirmanakaya" (*sna tshogs sprul sku*). Their enlightened activities, which remove the delusions of samsara, are as limitless as the boundless reaches of space.

18 Through the recognition of the primordially and naturally pure dharmadhatu—in other words, the immaculate primordial wisdom

or tathāgatagarbha—adventitious obscurations together with habitual tendencies are purified; and the result (namely, the twofold purity) is actualized. The two accumulations are effortlessly completed. Primordial wisdom (*ye shes*) is accumulated through the wisdom (*shes rab*) that perfectly cognizes the utterly pure nature. Merit is accumulated through the actualization of the qualities that are spontaneously present in the ultimate expanse. The supreme Teachers perfectly master and enjoy the qualities of these two virtuous accumulations. They, their buddhafields, and the display of their activities for the sake of others appear in accordance with each and every being, and are as all-pervasive as the dharmadhatu. Such is the unlimited display of the wisdom of the Buddhas. This cannot be fathomed even by their offspring, the Bodhisattvas, still less by the minds of ordinary beings.

The Buddhas are untouched by any kind of dualistic perception be- 19 cause all the habitual tendencies related to the mind and mental factors have been exhausted. They therefore have no thought of appearing in the form of a specific teacher, or of displaying specific activities for the benefit of specific beings. They act effortlessly like the wish-fulfilling jewel and the tree of miracles, which satisfy all desires. From within the expanse of the dharmakaya, beyond all conceptual construction, the unobstructed radiance of cognitive potency (*thugs rje*) manifests, in the perception of beings, as enlightened activity.

The *Precious Treasury of the Supreme Vehicle* states that, for the Prasangika Madhyamikas, the true Buddha is the dharmakaya, utterly pure and empty. For such a Buddha, all conceptual constructs of existence and nonexistence have subsided, and there are neither even kayas nor wisdoms. But in the perception of beings, thanks to their prayers and the compassion of the Buddhas, the latter appear in bodily form and seem to act. They are considered to be like the shrine of the garuda, the wish-fulfilling jewel, or the tree of miracles. As we find in the *Introduction to the Middle Way:*

> This peaceful kaya, radiant like the wish-fulfilling tree,
> Is like the wishing-jewel that without forethought lavishes
> The riches of the world on beings till they gain enlightenment.

It is perceived by those who are beyond conceptual construction.
(9:18)

2. How beings become deluded
3. The causes and conditions of their delusion

20   It is through the failure to understand that the appearances emerging
from the ground (the dimension of precious spontaneous presence) are
the self-experience of awareness that beings arise in the three worlds. In
the formless realms, the mind, resting one-pointedly in the state of calm
abiding, is supported by the four "name" aggregates (feeling, perception, conditioning factors, and consciousness). In the form realm, the
mind, abiding in a state of concentration that is without the true profound insight of vipashyana, is supported by a refined body of light. In
the desire realm, the coarse mind, characterized by various movements
of thought, is supported by a material body of flesh and blood.[467]

The root text says that in the original ground of primordial purity
and spontaneous presence, there are no delusory appearances nor
any cause for them—which means that in the ground, there is no ignorance. Nevertheless, it is not denied that there is a radiance ever liable
to manifest as the ground's appearances. Where therefore does the
basis for delusion lie? It lies in the failure to recognize that the radiance
of the ground, naturally arising through the eight doors, is the self-
experience of awareness. There is no ignorance in the ground itself.
Neither is there any ignorance later on, when freedom in the ground is
won. And from this it follows that the ignorance just mentioned is an
adventitious condition. The natural creative power (*rtsal*) of awareness
has actually created a veil[468] whereby awareness is obscured—on account of which, one speaks of an "ignorance that has the same nature
(as awareness)" (*bdag nyid gcig pa'i ma rig pa*).[469]

21   As this ignorance increases in power, the subtle ability of the examining cognition comes welling up. This is coemergent ignorance (*lhan cig
skyes pa'i ma rig pa*). Once there is a failure to recognize this examining
cognition as the natural radiance of awareness, then even when coarse
thoughts related to names, meanings, and the self do not arise, they are
always apt and ready to do so. This is called conceptual ignorance (*kun*

tu brtags pa'i ma rig pa). From these three kinds of ignorance,[470] four conditions of delusion evolve in the following manner.

The ground has three aspects: nature, character, and cognitive potency. The radiance of the nature is a space-like openness. Within it, the radiance of the character arises and remains as the "abode of light." This is the causal condition that gives rise to the deluded subject [namely, consciousness]. It is like the face that is naturally present when there is a person with a body and limbs. Now in relation to what appears as the causal condition, there arises a subtle state of thought, which is the radiance of the awareness of cognitive potency, thanks to which all subsequent delusions arise. This is the dominant condition. It is like the reflection of a face in a mirror. When these two conditions, causal and dominant, join together, the outer object and the inner subject are construed as distinct objects of reference, though they are not so. This is the object condition of the duality of subject and object. It is as if the mirror and the reflection in it were apprehended as two separate things, whereas this is not the case. The simultaneous occurrence of these three conditions forms the immediately preceding condition, whence delusion seamlessly manifests. From the four conditions, there manifests the delusion of a variety of causes, effects, names, and appearances. The way in which this happens is described in the *Tantra of Auspicious Beauty:*

> Delusion derives from four conditions, and from these same
> four conditions the end of delusion also derives. From the causal
> condition, apprehended as endowed with reference points, there
> arises the delusion that effects have various causes. The dominant
> condition, apprehended as consciousness, produces the delusion
> of a variety of names. From the object condition, apprehended as
> a person, arises the delusion of an infinity of effects. From the
> immediately preceding condition, the apprehension of the [pre-
> ceding three conditions], there arises the delusion of a variety of
> appearances.[471]

So it is that one is deluded. And yet, if one were to recognize the nature of delusion, one would find freedom within it.

23   For those who are not free, it is through the coming together of causes and conditions that false appearances, together with the deluded perception of them, gradually strengthen. As a result, defective mental processes, defilements, and habitual tendencies with regard to material environment, minds, and bodies (*gnas don lus gsum*) proliferate, and the apparition of the higher and lower states of samsara and all the different kinds of beings occurs.

In the state of samsara, the twelve factors of dependent arising, from ignorance onward, revolve constantly like the wheels of a chariot. *Ignorance* corresponds to the three kinds of ignorance that are the failure to recognize the nature of spontaneous radiance of cognitive potency. Because of ignorance, *conditioning factors* appear, in other words, the four conditions (of delusion) that produce samsara. Thanks to these, there arises a rough kind of cognition that examines objects, and this is *consciousness.* Through consciousness, *name and form* come into being, with form arising as elements and colors. Thence arise the *sense organs* and, thanks to these, *contact*, the experience of objects. From this there arises *feeling* (pleasant, unpleasant, and neither), and because of this, *craving* occurs: the state of mind that wants pleasure and recoils from pain. Thence comes *grasping*, the powerful seizing of objects. And from this comes karmic action and defilement, which project the mind into the next existence, and this is *becoming.* Thence one takes *birth* as a specific individual. Then one must experience childhood and youth, one grows old and one dies, and this is *aging-and-death.*

Taking one's present life as an example, the links of dependent arising unfold as follows. In the previous life, the ground-luminosity of the moment of death subsided because it was not recognized. The first moment of this failure (which makes possible the appearance of the bardo of becoming) corresponds to ignorance. The period beginning at that moment and lasting until the cessation of the outer breath at the moment of death in the next life, is covered by the twelve links of dependent arising as they unfold in their forward order. One then passes through the stages of dissolution, traversing the twelve links in reverse order, until one reaches the ground-luminosity. This is to say that there is no ignorance either in the ground or the appearances of the ground. If there is a failure to recognize these appearances for what they are, samsara unfolds. But when they *are* recognized, liberation occurs. This is what we call straying into samsara and being liberated in nirvana.

3. The manner in which delusion occurs

Through the power of believing that the ground's appearance is inher- 24
ently existent, the innumerable phenomena of samsara arise: the universe and its inhabitants who belong to the six realms, three higher and three lower, taking birth there in four possible ways. All this appears without existing truly, like the black lines seen by people suffering from an ocular disorder. It is like a magical illusion: not a single atom exists in truth. From the very moment that it appears, it is devoid of inherent existence. Regarding the delusion that is occurring now and that is based simply and solely on empty forms that have never truly existed, [we can say that] at the outset, there is ignorance, and through the display of such ignorance, ordinary mind manifests. Through the ornament of the mind (apprehension and clinging), the examining cognition (*dpyod byed kyi yid*) arises. And from the examining cognition, the defilements derive. This is the nature of our delusion.

The mind gives rise to six kinds of examining cognition. First is the cognition that is concomitant with ignorance. This is the coemergent or innate sense of self, the thought "I." Second is the cognition of mental consciousness: the imputed self and so on. Third is the determining cognition, which distinguishes good from bad. Fourth is the "ever-searching cognition," which looks for enjoyment of pleasure and avoidance of pain. Fifth is the coarse cognition, which earnestly involves itself in action, for example the act of killing. And sixth is the definitely settled cognition, which repeatedly affirms something in the mind without forgetting it.

There then arise the extremely coarse [kinds of] thought belonging to the six types of consciousness. Thought, which habitually apprehends as real what in fact has no true existence, reifies phenomena that are purely imaginary (*chos btags pa ba*) through its apprehension of, and clinging to, the personal and phenomenal self. This is an extremely powerful fetter. The nature of the mind is like space. It is without intrinsic being and is beyond all conceptual construction. It transcends both bondage and freedom. Nevertheless, it is completely bound by the dualistic apprehension of things, thanks to which the personal self and the phenomenal self appear to be really existent. Taking for real what appears but does not exist, and clinging to it, is like being deceived by the illusion created by a whirling firebrand. As it is written in the *Sutra of the Questions of Rashtrapala:*

> Like mirages, illusions, and the moon in water,
> All things lack intrinsic being.
> Taking them for real, the ignorant are bound by them
> And thus they go in circles like a potter's wheel.

25   Phenomena are not extramental things that exist inherently. They are the ripening of the mind's propensities. And so it is that, in the realm of samsaric existence, the one and the same daytime is for some (such as human beings) a time of light, while for others (like owls) it is a time of dark. Likewise, since it appears to the gods as amrita, to humans as water, and to beings in hell as fire, one and the same river is productive of both pleasure and pain.[472] Such perceptions, mutually incompatible as they are, follow the patterning of our propensities. From the standpoint of the objects perceived, there is nothing definite in them (they do not actually exist as "this" or "that"). As it is written in Longchenpa's *Precious Treasury That Fulfills All Wishes:*

> The mind compounds, the mind produces, every act.
> Things appear to mind, which mind then reifies.
> Strive therefore to tame your erring mind.

3. Distinguishing between mind and appearance

26   Outer phenomena are nothing but the ripening of the mind's propensities. The appearing objects of perception (*snang yul*) are not, however, the mind itself. For example, when the reflection of one's face appears in a looking glass, this reflection is produced interdependently. But there is no mixing together of the (actual) face with the mirror. As it is said in the *King of Concentration Sutra:*

When a woman with her face adorned
Gazes in a looking glass or oil-filled plate,
Although her face appears thereon,
It is not there and yet it is not absent.
All things are like this, you should understand.

Through the power of the mind's habitual tendencies, phenomena, 27
which do not truly exist, nevertheless appear; and adventitious deluded
thought clings to them as real. One may take, for example, a material
form. When, on seeing a striped rope, one has, on account of defective
vision, the impression of a snake, the apprehended aspect (*gzung rnam*)
is the skandha of form. The first moment of consciousness (produced
by the skandha of nonconceptual feeling), which mistakenly apprehends
the rope as a snake, is the "apprehended phenomenon." This is not as
described by the Sautrantikas, according to whom it is the aspect of the
[outer] object that arises [in the mind], with the apprehended aspect
and the apprehending aspect relating to each other as object and subject.[473] Subsequently [after the first moment of consciousness], there
comes the evaluation of the apprehended object by the mental factor of
perception, and the mind mistakes the rope for a snake. This is the
apprehending mind that has the character of the skandha of perception.[474]

If this were not so, if one asserts that an *appearing object* in the extra- 28
mental world (in other words, an actual snake) is the same as the *apprehended object* (*gzung ba*)—namely, the mere impression of a snake—while
the mere consciousness of the person to whom the snake appears, is the
apprehending subject (*'dzin pa*)—it would follow that for the Noble
Ones, who are free from the duality of apprehending subject and apprehended object, illusion-like appearances would vanish. And the consequence of this would be that the Buddha could not know (with the
wisdom that knows phenomena in their multiplicity) the aggregates and
other objects of knowledge. This and many other difficulties would
follow. In particular, it is an important mistake simply to declare that
"all appearances are the mind," while failing to distinguish between the
perception of an object and the appearing object of perception. As it is
said in the *Precious Treasury That Fulfills All Wishes:*

The ignorant declare that all is mind,
Yet greatly do they err regarding the three ways that things
    appear.[475]
Many faults and great confusion follow.
Give up the false tradition of these cowherds!

Many logical inconsistencies ensue from such a position. It would mean, for instance, that when one person attained buddhahood, all beings would become Buddhas, too. Likewise it would follow that the mind coexists with phenomena. Consequently, when such phenomena ceased to exist, the mind would also cease to exist; and when one died, phenomena would also cease. These and other difficulties would follow.

29   Consequently, the way to pass beyond sorrow is to sever the root: the act of straying into the duality of apprehending subject and apprehended object. Because of ignorance, the ultimate nature of things (which is not established in any way) is falsely construed in terms of a duality of subject and object. And it is through this circumstance, which is adventitious, that innate ego-clinging occurs. The ruler of existence is the self: the thought of "I" and the clinging to "mine." As it is said in the *Introduction to the Middle Way:*

Beings think "I" at first, and cling to self;
They think of "mine" and are attached to things.
They thus turn helplessly as buckets on a waterwheel,
And to compassion for such beings I bow down! (1:3)

If therefore one cuts the root of duality, which is the basis of samsaric delusion (the belief in the real existence of what does not exist), all adventitious stains, the phenomena of samsara—which, like waves emerging from the ocean, have arisen from the expanse of awareness, the "all-creating king"—will dissolve back into it. And this is buddhahood.

CHAPTER 12

The Extraordinary Path of Practice of the Great Perfection

1. A brief explanation

The six paramitas or transcendent perfections, the great highway of the
sutra and mantra teachings of the Victorious Ones of the three times,
bring fortunate beings to the ultimate result, which is the actualization
of the state beyond all learning: the union of the dharmakaya and rupakaya. The paramitas have the power to effect the completion of the two
accumulations, while one is on the path, and the attainment of the two
kayas, which is the ultimate result. This power in fact depends upon the
paramita of wisdom, the unmistaken understanding of the fundamental
nature of phenomena. This is the nature of the mind, which is luminous
in character and free from conceptual construction.[476] As it is said in
the *Verses that Summarize the Prajnaparamita-sutra*:

> Blind from birth, without a guide,
> The teeming multitudes know not which path to take.
> How can they reach the town?
> When wisdom is not there, the five perfections are deprived of
>   sight.
> Unguided, they are powerless to reach enlightenment.
> Yet when they are caught up and seized by wisdom,
> They gain their sight and thus assume their name.

This path whereby one sees ultimate reality as it truly is, the union
of skillful means and wisdom, can never lead either to the state of
samsaric existence or to the peace of the Shravakas and Pratyekabuddhas.

2   Does this mean that the Great Perfection and the Middle Way (Madhyamaka) are identical? In answer to this question it must be said that the primordially perfect nature of the mind—the "great perfection," or tathāgatagarbha endowed with every quality—is the ground that dwells primordially within us. And it is a great primordial secret, for it lies unrecognized. This secret of the mind, known to the Buddhas, is extremely difficult to see for those who lack the proper skillful means. It is the fundamental nature of emptiness (in other words, the ultimate stage of perfection); it is the ultimate truth devoid of all characteristics whether pure, impure, or anything at all, and it is freedom from all conceptual extremes. In this ultimate expanse, all mental activity subsides, and for this reason, this same nature cannot be found or understood even as the Middle Way. It is without intrinsic being; it is empty. But from the standpoint of its spontaneous presence, it is the limpid and radiant uncompounded luminosity, the unceasing, illusory display of primordial wisdom. This is the Great Perfection.

1. A detailed explanation
2. The distinctive features of the path of the great perfection
3. The superiority of the Great Perfection as compared with other paths

3   However much ordinary scholars may debate, proving their positions and disputing with their adversaries; and however much they examine the profound truth with the keen intelligence that is the fruit of their reflection, they can only understand it through inference, and in either exaggerated or understated terms. The profound truth in itself is utterly beyond their reach. Borne along by the destructive gale of thought, they are completely at variance with inconceivable ultimate reality, the domain of actual primordial wisdom. As it is said in the *Way of the Bodhisattva:*

> The ultimate is not within the reach of intellect,
> For intellect is said to be the relative. (6:2)

And in the *Lankavatara-sutra* we find:

> These naughty children, common scholars,
> Like dead men do they study it.

In the meditative equipoise of the Noble Ones too, ultimate reality—self-cognizing primordial wisdom beyond all conceptual construction—cannot be known in the manner of a "detection" (*yongs gcod*); and it is beyond conceptual and verbal expression.

All exponents of the Doctrine, up to and including the Chittamatrins, fail to realize ultimate reality as it truly is. The self-arisen primordial wisdom of the Victorious Ones is beyond the concepts and analysis of substantialist thinkers, and indeed it surpasses the reflection of all ordinary beings, up to and including those on the path of joining, who are on a lower level of realization.[477] This primordial wisdom is the ultimate reality of things. And since it is *primordially* a state of openness and freedom (*ye grol*), it does not become free at some later point thanks to extraneous factors.[478] It is this very state that is directly shown, "nakedly," on the path of the Natural Great Perfection.

Awareness or ultimate reality—the fundamental nature of knowledge objects—does not fall to the side of appearance, the extreme of existence. It is not "fettered" by appearance, for it has the nature of emptiness, which is the ground of phenomena. Neither does it fall to the side of emptiness, the extreme of nonexistence, for it is endowed with the essence of natural, unceasing luminosity. The two aspects, appearance and emptiness, are united. Awareness, self-arisen primordial wisdom, transcends freedom as well as bondage, and is the state of the dharmakaya Buddha. Now the natural creative power of this ultimate reality (the infinite qualities, ocean-vast, of the kayas and wisdoms) is primordially inseparable from this same nature, just as the rays of the sun are inseparable from the sun itself. In the state of awareness, objects of perception, forms and so on, arise unceasingly, and yet they do not "cover" or impair awareness, for awareness is empty. And since awareness does not stray into objects but keeps to its genuine condition, there is no "covering" or apprehension by the ordinary mind of appearing objects. For awareness is empty of ordinary mind.

Because it cannot be established in any way, awareness is empty; it is primordially pure. Nevertheless, the creative power of its spontaneous presence is unceasing. Awareness, which is the union of these two aspects and is free from any point of reference, is a seamless, wakeful state of openness. It is one with ultimate reality from which there is nothing

4

5

to remove and to which there is nothing to add, and in which there is neither increase nor decrease. As it is said in the *Tantra of the Vast Expanse of Space:*

> Not rejecting anything, and yet transcending all,
> Awareness is impartial, has no target, it is free and open wide.
> You cannot say that "it is this," for it exceeds all thought.
> It is nondual; 'tis one with an immense expanse.

3. The particular features of the three inner classes of the Great Perfection

6 Ultimate reality, the fundamental state of the Great Perfection, which is beyond all deliberate and active effort, and transcends the intellect, cannot be described qualitatively and is beyond categorization. Nevertheless, according to the mental capacities of beings, the Great Perfection is set forth in three classes. As the *Tantra of the Great Array of Ati* says:

> For those inclined to mind,
> The mind class is set forth.
> For those inclined to space,
> The space class is set forth.
> For those who do not strive in stages,
> There's the pith instruction class.

Practitioners of the mind class consider that phenomena are not different from the nature of the mind, and therefore they have nothing to reject.[479] The ground from which the varied display of phenomena unceasingly arises is the creative power of awareness,[480] which is like the brilliant sheen of a limpid mirror. As the *Tantra of the All-Creating King* says:

> Phenomenal existence, the universe and contents,
> Buddhas and beings: all are made by mind,
> Are one within the mind's expanse.

Practitioners of the space class say that phenomena are neither existent nor nonexistent; they are rather the "arrayed ornaments of self-experiencing awareness" (*rang snang bkod pa'i rgyan*).[481] Unlike the practitioners of the mind class, they do not speak about the creative power of awareness but of the great and infinite expanse, primordially empty, which does not fall into any ontological extreme.[482] In the mind class, "creative power" is assimilated to the display, whereas in the space class, "ornament" is assimilated to inner awareness.

According to the pith instruction class,[483] phenomena appear although they are without existence. When their ultimate nature is established, it is understood that they are simply empty reflections beyond the need either of rejection or the application of antidotes. There is not even the slightest effort made to induce the subsiding of thoughts or to settle in the ultimate expanse. Consequently, the pith instruction class is eminently superior.

2. An explanation of the actual path of the great perfection
3. The ways of subsiding or freedom
4. How one is to understand that there is nothing to be freed

The three classes of the Great Perfection unanimously teach that there is nothing to be freed. For though one may consider that the nature of the mind is what is to be freed, the truth is that this nature has neither beginning nor ending, neither origin nor cessation.[484] Therefore it is primordially nonexistent. There is no need for a dam to keep back water that is just a mirage. In the same way, since there is nothing by which bodhichitta—the groundless, pure, and accomplished mind—is obscured, there is nothing to free it from, and no method for doing so. On the other hand, since the radiance of its natural luminosity is unceasing (sense objects appear without reprieve), bodhichitta, the pure and accomplished mind, is not a blank void. It is primordially unceasing, ever present. One must see that it is empty, but this simply means that the natural radiance of awareness is groundless, devoid of any root whereby it might have real existence. This radiance manifests spontaneously in the expanse of primordial purity and is characterized by five modes of subsiding or "states of openness and freedom."[485]

4. A specific explanation of the individual modes of subsiding or "states of openness and freedom"

8　There are five kinds of subsiding, the first of which is "primordial subsiding," the primordial state of openness and freedom (*ye grol*). In the very midst of the eight kinds of consciousness, which are like clouds, there is awareness, which is like space. Awareness is unstained by the defects of samsara and is free of conceptual construction. Consequently, whatever thoughts arise, there is no need for awareness to be subsequently freed by extraneous factors that might contrive this freedom. Awareness is already free from the very first.[486]

The second kind of subsiding is "self-subsiding" (*rang grol*). This means that one has nothing to do but remain relaxed in the mind's natural condition, to which one has been introduced by one's teacher— though when there is a continuous stream of powerful thoughts, one does need to make some slight use of an appropriate antidote. All phenomena, which have arisen through the creative power of awareness, "self-subside." They subside by themselves, and their subsiding does not depend on extraneous factors, just as running water has no need of anything to drive it on.[487]

The third kind of subsiding is "naked or direct subsiding" (*gcer grol*). When thoughts spread out in delusion, they subside when one watches the face or nature of awareness. Instead of running after thoughts like a dog chasing after a stone that someone throws, one should watch directly, "nakedly," the nature of awareness, and be like a lion that chases the stone-thrower. If one does so, thoughts subside. For in both [the nature of awareness and the thoughts], there is no basis on which they might depend.[488]

The fourth kind of subsiding is the "subsiding of extremes" (*mtha' grol*). Being unborn, the nature of awareness is free from the extreme of existence, but it does not remain in the extreme of nonexistence because it is unceasing. Being uninterrupted, it is free from the extreme of nonexistence, but it does not remain in the extreme of existence because it is not a truly existing permanent entity. Since its creative power arises in a variety of appearances, it does not exist as a single thing. Since it is beyond all conceptual construction, it cannot be designated as plural. Awareness is Samantabhadra free from all extremes.[489]

The fifth kind of subsiding is "subsiding into the one [awareness]" (*gcig grol*). Awareness, in which the two truths are inseparable, and which is free of conceptual construction, does not exist either as singular or plural. Conventionally, however, this all-penetrating primordial wisdom (*zang thal gyi ye shes*) is referred to as the one and only sphere of the dharmakaya (*chos sku thig le nyag gcig*). Within this single expanse of awareness, all thoughts subside, and therefore there are no phenomena. Devoid of all characteristics, everything is like limpid, pure space.[490]

3. An explanation of the ten distinctions
4. Distinguishing awareness from the ordinary mind

As will be explained later, the word "those" (*gang dag*) in the third line   9
of the root stanza refers to all people, whether they have realization or
not. The introduction to naked awareness, lying immanent in the
ground and transcending the ordinary mind and its ignorance, is an
extraordinary feature of the Natural Great Perfection. Those who accurately realize the nature of awareness recognize the appearances that
manifest from within the ground for what they are, and they find freedom in the state of awareness, which is devoid of intrinsic being. Arriv-
ing at the state of the exhaustion of phenomena in ultimate reality, they
come to the buddhafield of Samantabhadra, and take possession of the
kingdom of the dharmakaya. Beings who do not realize the nature of
awareness perceive these appearances in a dualistic way, and though they
do not move from the expanse of awareness, they nevertheless circle in
samsara, moving from delusion to delusion in the state of the universal
ground of habitual tendencies.

In brief, the ordinary mind can be distinguished from awareness with   10
the help of examples.

In its genuine condition, awareness is undisturbed by the eight consciousnesses. It is like the water of an immense and waveless ocean. The
ordinary mind, on the other hand, is agitated by thoughts, like foaming
water filled with bubbles.[491] Even so, a mind that is simply still and
without thoughts is not awareness. Although the ordinary mind without
thoughts[492] and thought-free awareness[493] may resemble each other
from the point of view of their being simply still, they are in fact completely different.

Awareness is the perfect knowledge of ultimate reality: the absence of intrinsic being in all phenomena. It is completely free of any clinging to the true existence of things. It is an all-penetrating clarity (*zang thal gyis gsal*). By contrast, the ordinary mind may be compared to a pool of stagnant water. The subject-object dualism, concomitant with ignorance, veils or darkens the lamp of self-arisen awareness. The ordinary mind is a state of dullness and confusion.

11   Awareness does not engage with objects of the ordinary mind. It is "self-cognizing primordial wisdom." This can be illustrated by the "light" of the new moon: a profoundly indwelling luminosity, which does not radiate outward. Therefore, despite the fact that the five primordial wisdoms are spontaneously present in awareness, the latter is without thoughts related to sense objects. By contrast, even when it is still, the ordinary mind nevertheless "moves" and follows after different objects. It is like the light of the moon on the fifteenth of the month, which radiates outward and engulfs everything.

Awareness, which is the union of appearance and emptiness, has two properties: the limpid clarity of penetrating insight unstained by ignorance, and the absence of impairing objects.[494] There is no nirvana, no "state beyond suffering," other than this. By contrast, the ordinary mind is characterized by a complete merging with the objects of the six consciousnesses. As it is said in the *Tantra of the All-Creating King*:

> Since the self-arisen primal wisdom has no thought of objects,
> It is not stained by habits of discursive thought.

4. Distinguishing awareness from the ordinary mind in relation to stillness

12   To remain in the recognition of all-penetrating awareness means to rest in vipashyana, the wisdom (*shes rab*) that is primordially present in ultimate reality, the fundamental nature of phenomena. Awareness is totally beyond the need to add or remove anything. It does not depend on methods for achieving concentration, and since sharpness and clarity are intrinsic to it, it is free from both agitation and torpor.

In the kind of concentration where the ordinary mind is used as the path, the practitioner settles one-pointedly, fixing on an object of focus, a deity and so on. This meditative concentration and the view that has been previously established are related respectively as something that is supported and something that supports. The view to be meditated upon is the object, and the meditative concentration is the subject. It is by such factors as these, however, that awareness, free from the duality of subject and object, is obscured. The aforementioned concentration therefore is no more than a state of repose in which one can take a momentary rest from thoughts. It is of no great value.[495] As it is said in the Great Perfection tantra, the *Primordial Wisdom Similar to Space:*

> Concentration free from objects and from action,
> Insight of the awareness of the Great Perfection:
> Consider them as equal and you err and deviate.

4. Distinguishing awareness from the ordinary mind with reference to unfolding creative power

The words of the root verse, "Awareness manifests in objects of the senses" (*rig pa yul la shar*) means that the creative power of cognitive potency (*thugs rje 'i rtsal*) manifests unceasingly. However, because the nature of awareness and the manifestation of its creative power are not distinct and separate entities, and because, in the state of awareness, thoughts do not chase after sense objects (for their root or basis has been recognized), there is no examination or scrutiny either of the outer objects of the six consciousnesses or of the inner mind. There is not even any fixated settling in the unborn ultimate nature. When stripped to its naked state [when, in other words, it is divested of all concepts], mind-transcending awareness, the ultimate nature of things, is beyond change. It cannot be overwhelmed by appearances. It is like mercury, which does not mix with the dust when it falls on the ground.

By contrast, the ordinary mind fails to recognize the actual nature of the apprehended objects, and thus it clings to them. It merges with the various dualistic thoughts of subject and object that follow each other continually, and thus it perpetuates phenomenal existence, and karma is accumulated. As it is said in the *Tantra of the Six Expanses:*

Awareness, self-cognizing, free from thoughts,
Perceptions of the ordinary mind: these two are different things!
How wrong it is to think they are the same!
The perfect creativity of wisdom
And the cogitations of the mind: these two are different things!
How wrong it is to think they are the same![496]

When one settles in the nature of awareness, the ordinary mind dissipates naturally and is left behind. The settling of the mind in its natural state (*rang bzhag*) is said to be an extremely important point.

4. Distinguishing awareness from the ordinary mind with reference to the mode of subsiding or freedom[497]

14   Awareness is the nature of the mind. Therefore even in the case of ordinary beings, "awareness does not push the mind aside," for the mind is pervaded by it. On the other hand, "with awareness, mind does not keep company";[498] they are like light and dark. If one is able to prolong the time during which one remains in the natural flow of awareness (to which one has been introduced), apprehended objects and the apprehending consciousness (which has the nature of a conceptual obscuration concomitant with ignorance), together with defilements like attachment (which are of the same substance as this same consciousness), all flee from awareness as if they had warned each other. The dualistic interplay of subject and object spontaneously vanishes, like clouds that melt away in the sky. And when they are gone, one is released from the prison of dualistic thought and defilement from which it is extremely difficult to escape. The special teaching of the pith instruction class of the Great Perfection effects this liberation without difficulty.

15   No other path possesses such instructions as these. The Shravakas and the Pratyekabuddhas discard defilements. The Bodhisattvas tame them with the help of antidotes like emptiness. And the practitioners of the general Mantrayana, up to and including Anuyoga, adopt skillful methods, such as the inner tummo fire, that use defilements as the path. It is thus that the union of bliss and emptiness, the primordial wisdom of the four joys, is cultivated, and defilements are brought onto the

path. On the other hand, the defilements that are to be discarded and the antidotes whereby they are discarded cannot occur simultaneously in a single mind stream. And if they are not simultaneous, defilements cannot actually be used as the path. According to the mind class, it is considered that by recognizing the nature of all arising thoughts, the latter subside in their true condition [of awareness]. But since the recognizer is necessarily the mind, and since the mind cannot see itself, it cannot be in this way that thoughts subside. According to the space class, the mind and phenomena are viewed as the ornament of awareness itself. And it is believed that they are purified by abiding in meditative equipoise in the one ultimate reality. But since awareness is the nature of primordial wisdom, and since, when one settles in this state, the ignorant mind is not present, it follows that primordial wisdom does not see it. Therefore it is pointless to strive in the purification (of phenomena and mind) by means of resting in the ultimate expanse and so forth.

In the expanse of the nature of awareness, all tenets—such as the assertions that phenomena are empty of themselves or that their nature is empty of what is extraneous to it—fall apart. Whatever is to be discarded, as well as the antidotes, vanish by themselves (rang grol) without leaving any trace. This path—the path of the pith instructions—is a great wonder and is superior to every other way.

4. Distinguishing the universal ground from the dharmakaya

In the primordially pure expanse of emptiness, the universal ground (which is the basis of the impure mind) and the dharmakaya (which is the basis of primordial wisdom) are one. Now the dharmakaya is awareness, vast and deep like a waveless ocean, whereas the consciousness of the universal ground is a veil whereby this same awareness is obscured. The so-called universal ground is the support both of negative propensities and of the positive propensities that purify or consume them, like rust consuming iron. They both veil the dharmakaya. The universal ground is none other than this. And depending on action, whether positive or negative, this same ground is like a sailor voyaging either toward nirvana or toward samsara.[499]

16

4. Distinguishing the state of delusion from the state of freedom[500]

17 Delusion consists in the failure to recognize the true status [of appearance arising] from the fundamental nature of the ground, the state of luminosity. To recognize it is freedom. These two states may be illustrated, in the first case, by sleep, on the basis of which every kind of dream manifests and, in the second case, by the waking state where the continuum of one's dreams is interrupted. To be deluded while one is in the condition of the universal ground, when the knowledge of primordial wisdom is obscured by ignorance, is like being in a state of deep sleep when the five sense faculties are withdrawn and gathered within. The experience of phenomena, which do not exist in reality, is similar to the dreaming state. When one gains freedom from obscurations, and recognizes the nature of the dharmakaya in reality, this is like being roused from sleep and perceiving the objects of the five senses.

4. Distinguishing the ground from the result with reference to spontaneous presence

18 The awareness of the primordial ground belongs neither to samsara nor to nirvana. It is indeterminate in that it can be the cause either of delusion or of freedom. Now in this state of primordial purity, there is an unceasing radiance spontaneously present. This spontaneous radiance is one in substance with the "primordial purity of the place of freedom,"[501] which is attained on completion of the path,[501] and which, being endowed with the twofold purity, is free from adventitious stains. They are the same in the sense that the ultimate expanse endowed with the three aspects of nature, character, and cognitive potency (*ngo bo rang bzhin thugs rje*) is unchanging. On the other hand, the spontaneous radiance of the ground and the primordial purity of the place of freedom are different in that the former is the [possible] ground of subsequent delusion, while the latter is not. The spontaneous presence of the primordial ground is the ground from which both samsara and nirvana arise. This spontaneous presence therefore also constitutes the ground of delusion. The place of freedom, on the other hand, in being utterly without ignorance, cannot be the ground of delusion.[502] It is extremely important to distinguish between these two.[503]

4. Distinguishing the path from the result with reference to primordial purity

Similarly, there is, on the one hand, the primordial purity of the place 19
of freedom (the primal wisdom of inner luminosity), experienced when
the qualities of the ultimate expanse are brought to perfection. On the
other hand, there is the primordial purity of awareness in which practitioners remain in meditative equipoise in a state of ineffable realization while still on the path. Because, in both cases, dualistic appearances
subside in the ultimate expanse, and there is a freedom from conceptual
construction, these two states are equal in that they are unconfined and
do not fall into the extremes of appearance, emptiness, and so on. However, since the place of freedom, the primordially pure expanse, is completely cleansed of the impure wind-mind together with its tendencies
(through the power of meditation performed while one is still on the
path), it is devoid of the deluded perceptions of samsara. What is
more, even the perceptions of nirvana are absent, for the aspects of
outwardly radiating primordial wisdom have dissolved into the ultimate
expanse.[504] Primordially pure awareness does not depart from the state
of dharmakaya. It dwells neither in samsara nor in nirvana. While one
is on the path, however, the impure aspect of the wind-mind is not
completely extinguished. It is associated with the circumstantial cause
of delusion, the subject-object duality implicit in the senses and their
objects. And this adulterates and "burdens" the creative power of awareness with the stains of both mind and mental factors, which cast a veil
over uncontrived awareness. Only occasionally does one abide truly in
the expanse of primordial purity, where all dualistic appearances subside. Nevertheless, if one trains oneself, leaving the mind in its natural
state, one will be able, in due course, to realize awareness free from all
fixation and clinging.

4. Distinguishing the deities appearing in the bardo

For those who engage in this path and who persevere in the practice, but 20
who fail to gain freedom in the first bardo [the bardo of the moment of
death], the radiance of awareness, spontaneously present in the ground,
will gradually manifest in the course of the bardo of ultimate reality.

This is particularly true for seasoned meditators who have gained proficiency in thögal, the yoga of spontaneous presence. This great spontaneous presence will gradually appear, within a certain number of "days of concentration," as deities, buddhafields, and so on.

Those who have trained in uniting the conceptual generation and perfection stages as well as in the transference of consciousness, are able to arise as illusion-like deities, while they are in the bardo of becoming.

These two kinds of illusory form are similar in being the mere appearance of deities in the bardo. And yet it should be understood that they are different, depending on whether the practitioners concerned gain freedom or not. In the first case, when deities arise in a buddhafield, they are the effortless, spontaneous radiance of uncompounded primordial wisdom. Simply by recognizing them as the vast self-experience of primordial wisdom, practitioners gain freedom in the inner ultimate expanse. In the second case, these luminous appearances manifest from the creative power of the wind-mind that has been imbued with positive tendencies. Compared with the situation previously described, this is but a limited display. The practitioners in question are not liberated; they must still traverse the rest of the path.

4. Distinguishing the buddhafields that give release

21 Those who, in particular, are engaged in the practice of the path of the Great Perfection, who keep a pure samaya but have yet to accomplish their practice fully, are extremely fortunate. It does not take them long to behold the sambhogakaya Buddhas, complete with all the major and minor marks of enlightenment, which are perceptible (like reflections in a mirror) to the Bodhisattvas on the ten grounds of realization. After death, when in the bardo of becoming, they reach, through the power of the truth of ultimate reality, one of the five nirmanakaya buddhafields of luminous character, displayed by the cognitive potency (*thugs rje*) of the state of awakening through the doors of spontaneous presence.[505] There they traverse the rest of the path and swiftly attain the primordial expanse, as if they were waking from a dream. It is said in the *Tantra of the Great Array of Ati:*

In the final period of "five hundred phases" of the age of dregs,[506]
The Secret Essence will appear within the human realm.
Beings who follow it are fortunate.
Those who have experience of this Essence
Come to the unchanging ground.
But beings in this age of dregs have shortened lives and many ills.
They therefore fail to have assurance of the view of Secret Essence.
Yet by simply seeing it they gain release
And go to the eleventh ground of Universal Light.
They take miraculous pure birth in nirmanakaya buddhafields,
Rescued from the trammels of a womb.

3. An explanation of the key points of the practice
4. The practice of those who perceive everything as the self-experience of awareness[507]
5. Trekchö, the path of primordial purity[508]
6. The view that severs the continuum of the city (of samsara)

Thanks to its particular character, the path of the Natural Great Perfection is the highest and shortest of all Vajrayana paths. Its view consists in the direct realization of the fundamental state of phenomena as it truly is.[509] This fundamental state is untainted by adventitious impurity, and is therefore beyond bondage and liberation. From the very beginning, it is free from all conceptual construction. It is primordially pure awareness, which has the nature of the three doors of perfect liberation. Its nature is free of all concepts. It is *empty from the very beginning*. For in emptiness, there is not even nonexistence, let alone existence. This awareness is inconceivable and inexpressible, and transcends all such features as size, shape, duality, and so forth. It is consequently *beyond all characteristics* that the mind can ascribe, and the ordinary mind cannot reach it. Yet by its very nature, it possesses—like the sun its rays—the qualities of the resultant fruit: the kayas and primordial wisdoms. Therefore it is *beyond any expectancy of a result* that could issue from a deliberate effort of adopting and rejecting. For when one settles in the natural uncontrived state, all the qualities of awareness are completely present.

Awareness is not found on the dualistic path of "apprehender and apprehended." It is not an object of knowledge. It is beyond the ontological extremes of existence and nonexistence, of phenomena conceived of in terms of "I" and "mine." And since the realization of all-penetrating awareness, which has the nature of the three doors of perfect liberation, severs the continuum of the "city of samsara," which is the mind's creation, this view (of the Great Perfection) is called the severing of the continuum of the city.[510]

6. Meditation is the self-subsiding (of thoughts) through the absence of all clinging

23 To remain in the view to which one has been introduced is conventionally called "meditation" but, in truth, the meditating mind and the view meditated upon are not two different things. If the mind remains in the view, in the natural and uncontrived state, the fundamental nature of awareness will be seen directly in its nakedness. And since that which is seen is free from good and bad thoughts and does not change according to circumstances, one cannot (while in that state) accumulate actions that, through ignorance and dualistic thoughts of subject and object, lead to samsaric existence.[511]

6. Conduct that overpowers appearances

24 Outer objects of the senses (form and so forth) and the ignorant minds that cling to them in terms of a personal and phenomenal self, together with all the thoughts that are the result of this ignorance, are not the handiwork of a creator god like Ishvara. As though they were a picture being drawn, they are the products of adventitious thought accompanied by the fully developed propensity to perceive both outer objects and the inner mind as really existent things. It is like the old woman who meditated on herself as a tiger.[512] All appearances, which are thus based on the mind, manifest as the empty forms of the unceasing natural radiance that arises from the ground, the nature of the mind, which, like space, has no reality in any way. Although they have no root in the nature of the mind, it is through the distorting effects of ignorance that the appearances of samsara and nirvana seem to have an origin. But in

the very moment that they arise, they subside in the unborn nature of awareness. As the *Pearl Necklace Tantra* says:

> The dharmakaya similar to space
> Is covered by the clouds of adventitious thought.
> And so the undeluded ultimate reality
> Appears like a delusion in the mind.[513]

6. The result is the actual nature (the dharmakaya) beyond all exertion

Other than the familiarization of oneself with the state wherein view, meditation, and conduct are united, there is no further "result" to be realized. There is consequently no need for any other practice. When one has gained proficiency therein, apprehended phenomena are completely purified thanks to one's understanding that outer things have no existence; and the apprehending mind is simultaneously revealed as groundless and rootless, for it is not found in the manner of an inner subject. Groundless awareness is not something that the intellect can indicate. For all these reasons, one can never again be caught in delusion.

At that time, it is pointless to depend on the devices of the mind, all the conventional processes fabricated by the intellect, such as reading the scriptures, memorizing words and meanings, and meditating one-pointedly, concentrating on objects of focus, and reflecting on, and analyzing, the meaning of texts. And since there is no distinction made between practice sessions and the period between these sessions, the ordered structure of view, meditation, and conduct falls apart. When thoughts are cleared away in ultimate reality, the use of antidotes through intentional meditation becomes redundant. Knowing that awareness is the dharmakaya, one develops a confident certainty that both Buddhas and beings are primordially without existence. There is no result to be looked for or hoped for, other than self-cognizing awareness free from the duality of apprehender and apprehended. It is in this ultimate reality that the realization of all the Buddhas of the three times comes to perfection. Thus the result is actual, self-cognizing awareness.[514]

5. The particularity of thögal,[515] the practice of spontaneous presence

26   The unexcelled path of thögal is higher than the path of trekchö.[516] When, through meditation, one gains certainty in the view of trekchö, and when one has mastered the essential points of the thögal practice through the different ways of sitting and gazing at the sky and so on, rough, well-defined thoughts cease, and subtle (difficult to notice) thoughts naturally vanish. From the very first, the appearances of the ultimate expanse—from the five-colored lights and vajra chains (the radiance of awareness) up to and including the deities—are directly detected by the visual sense. It is therefore unlikely that one will stray from the fundamental nature into the state of mere emptiness. And if there is no clinging to these appearances [one will not fall into the extreme of real existence, either]. The impure materiality of the outer elements (earth, stones, mountains, cliffs, and so on), which is the product of our beginningless tendency to perceive outer objects in the ordinary manner, will be naturally worn away, and all the phenomena of the outer environment and one's own body will be released into an insubstantiality that is open and unobstructing. Phenomena composed of outer elements are refined into the great luminosity of primordial wisdom, and the three kayas are made perfectly manifest while one is still on this path.

   Now the full accomplishment of trekchö only results in the simple dissolution of the inner elements of one's body into infinitesimal particles. It does not lead to the refinement of these elements into the body of light, with the result that the body of great transformation is not achieved. On the path of thögal, however, one's impure elements *do* transform into the vajra body of great transformation free from birth, aging, and death: the wisdom body of union. The ordinary body, speech, and mind transform into the enlightened body, speech, and mind. And as with the mighty Conquerors—Padmasambhava, Vimalamitra, and Jnanasutra—it is in such a body that one will labor for the welfare of beings until the very emptying of samsara.

27   Thögal transcends the analytical paths of the other Buddhist schools in the lower vehicles. It is superior even to the mind and space classes and so on[517] of the Great Perfection, where the view is established as the nature of the mind, free from ontological extremes, and where medi-

tation means settling in this view, leaving everything just as it is. There is no need for meditation on a deity and so on. As for conduct, since whatever arises subsides of its own accord, there is no need for the practices of adopting and rejecting. Finally, the result is not expected to come from elsewhere because the resultant qualities of the kayas and wisdoms are primordially, spontaneously, and perfectly contained in the creative power of awareness.

The path of thögal is distinguished from all lower teachings by seven salient features. First, practitioners on this path are not distinguished by the sharpness or dullness of their faculties, but rather by the intensity of their endeavor, greater or lesser as this may be. Second, practitioners do not rely on mental analysis because they can see ultimate reality directly. Third, because they have a direct realization of awareness as it truly is, they do not rely on mere words. Fourth, since the natural luminosity (of primordial wisdom) is actually present, the ground, path, and result are not chronologically related to each other. Fifth, since it does not depend on karmic sequences, good or bad, this path is free from the strenuous and discriminative practices of adopting and rejecting. Sixth, since the self-arisen luminosity manifests from within, there is no difference between young and old practitioners. Seventh, practitioners enjoy a perfect experience of the three kayas even while they are still on the path. They capture the everlasting kingdom of spontaneously present awareness in the expanse of primordial purity.

To meet with the pith instructions of a path like this is of the highest significance, and we are urged to strive in the practice of them.

4. The practice of those who perceive appearances in the manner of sense objects
5. Sustaining meditative equipoise with shamatha and vipashyana
6. A brief explanation

It is indeed true that those who perceive appearances as the self-experience of awareness (*rig pa rang snang gi blo can*) are able to preserve the state of awareness to which they have been directly introduced. And by mastering the crucial points of the thögal practice, they gain freedom by directly beholding the radiance of awareness and so on.[518] By contrast, those who perceive appearances as sense objects (*snang ba yul gyi blo can*) are unable to effect the dissolution, in the primordially pure expanse of the dharmadhatu, of the inner adventitious factors of delusion, namely, the eight consciousnesses that are associated with the apprehension of "I" and "mine." They glimpse the face of awareness, but are led astray by good or bad adventitious circumstances: illness, evil influences, wealth, power, and so on. They must strive therefore in methods that overcome this distortion of the mind: the dualistic appearance of discursive thought in terms of apprehending subject and apprehended object. For this is the way of ordinary beings, and it cannot but propel them further into samsara. To be sure, the duality of apprehender and apprehended is indeed samsara's root and lord, and it is that which, for beginners, obscures the nature of their awareness.

29   As in the common vehicle, however, there are remedies for this predicament: the skillful methods of shamatha or calm abiding, whereby mental stillness is achieved, and of vipashyana or profound insight. In this regard, there are two instructions. The first is based on the understanding that shamatha and vipashyana share the same nature. The second presupposes that they are different.

6. A more detailed explanation

In the first case, which is according to the teaching of the *Sutra on the Wisdom of the Moment of Death*, when one meditates with focused mindfulness on a support, the stillness aspect of the mind (namely, its one-pointed concentration) constitutes shamatha, while the clarity aspect, the all-discerning wisdom that understands the support to be without inherent existence, is vipashyana. These two aspects are in union. They are not two distinct things, subject and object. It is thus that one rests in meditative equipoise, in the state of ultimate reality free from ontological extremes. And one integrates emptiness found in meditation with compassion arising in postmeditation. All the key points of meditation are summerized in this.

30   The guiding instruction in which shamatha and vipashyana are considered to be distinct has two approaches. In the first, shamatha and vipashyana are considered to arise mainly on the basis of the wisdom resulting from hearing and reflecting on the teachings. In the second approach, shamatha and vipashyana are considered to arise thanks to

oral instruction on the techniques of meditation. This distinction is also made in the sutras. According to the first approach, when shamatha and vipashyana arise from the wisdom just mentioned, they accord with the letter of the teachings. When, through hearing and reflection, one eliminates all misconceptions regarding the teaching of a specific text, this is analytical meditation. Achieving certainty in the absence of inherent existence, one settles in that very state. This is resting or placement meditation. This is similar to the way in which Madhyamikas proceed. The mind that dwells one-pointedly (according to the nine ways)[519] on the meaning that has been learned and reflected upon is placed in a state of stillness (shamatha)—meaning that it is freed from discursive thought. It is thanks to this that one realizes the absence of self (both of the object of focus and of the mind that focuses) and a state beyond all conceptual construction. One is free from the apprehension of, and clinging to, the object of focus, and this is authentic vipashyana. According to this method, it is through exertion that shamatha and vipashyana are accomplished.

Shamatha and vipashyana deriving from oral instruction do not depend on the reading and analysis of texts. Instead, they follow the spirit of the teachings. And they are accomplished by meditating according to a teacher's instructions. Meditation focused on outer objects, such as the form of a deity or a seed-syllable; concentration on inner objects, such as the winds and essence-drops; and mastery of the key points of physical posture, the channels and winds, all give rise to the experience of bliss, clarity, and no-thought. A mind that remains one-pointedly therein, untroubled by mental movement, is in a state of shamatha. To recognize that the appearing object is primordially beyond all conceptual construction and has the nature of luminosity, and to dwell in a state that is free from all clinging are the twin constituents of authentic vipashyana.

6. A short account of the union of shamatha and vipashyana

When shamatha and vipashyana are practiced, there are three ways in which dualistic thoughts subside. In the case of practitioners of highest capacity, in whom realization has unfolded, unwholesome discursive thoughts subside in the moment of their arising and do not proliferate further: all that arises is settled in the state of dharmakaya (*chos skur lhongs*).[520] All thoughts, good and bad, are thus on a level, and there is no need for such practitioners to rely on antidotes. For them, sleeping and sitting are the display of the mandala. Their footprints are its dots of colored sand. Their movements are the deity's display.

Practitioners of medium capacity, on the other hand, need to meditate and grow used to the path of the union of shamatha and vipashyana without losing the clear state of the view that they have previously established. As they meditate in this way, all thoughts, both good and bad, subside in the expanse of primordial purity, like clouds that melt away in the abyss of space.

33 As presented in the sutras, practitioners of basic capacity begin by striving to accomplish shamatha. When they have achieved a good stability in a given concentration—whether on a deity, a seed-syllable, or a square design and so on —they go on to cultivate the all-perceiving wisdom of vipashyana. They then train in the union of shamatha and vipashyana, and gradually come to the point that is called the time when thoughts subside in their natural condition (*rnam rtog rang sar grol ba'i dus*). And just as one cannot find ordinary earth and rocks in a land of gold, however much one may search for them, in just the same way, whatever main minds and thoughts or mental factors arise, they arise as the great expanse, the free openness of the ground (*gzhi grol*), wherein mind and appearances are inseparable, blended into a single taste. At that point, one is usually able to display signs of accomplishment, such as the ability to pass through objects and so on.

5. Bringing thoughts onto the path

34 Those who are on this supreme path of skillful means by which thoughts are purified should not push away bad thoughts or encourage good ones, as and when they arise. They should not run after them as ordinary people do. However strong one's fixation on thoughts may be, it is extremely important, in the early stages, to take support of mindfulness without losing it. As one trains in such mindfulness, the mind becomes increasingly calm so that, when it is completely still, one may feel, for example, that dualistic appearance has dissolved. And various kinds of preternatural knowledge will arise. But when this happens, it is

important not to cling to such experiences as though they were true. All clinging to experience is an obstacle, the work of demonic forces. In all such situations, the single taste of all things must be preserved. This is a matter of crucial importance. If one manages to refrain from following and clinging to anything at all—maintaining an even taste—one will not deviate. If one understands that all is without origin; if one does not stir from the true state of awareness; and if one leaves the six consciousnesses in a state of relaxation without closing the doors of the senses, one will gain all the qualities of the path even without striving for them. The five kinds of vision will be attained (the eye of flesh, the divine eye, the wisdom eye, and so on), as well as the six kinds of preternatural knowledge, such as the recollection of past lives:[521] all the qualities of the refined sense powers and their associated consciousnesses, which are pure by their very nature. As it is written in the *Guhyagarbha-tantra*:

> Wonderful displays and marvelous qualities
> From nowhere else derive
> But from the wisdom that relies on skillful means.
> From here indeed do they arise.

For such practitioners, thoughts arise in just the same way as for ordinary people. But it is not the mere thought, in the moment that it arises, that accumulates karma. It is through the continuous profusion of thoughts, and the clinging to them, that beings are fettered in samsara. If one's thoughts are linked with the objects of the six consciousnesses, one is but an ordinary being, and one is propelled into samsara. The situation is different, however, when the duality of apprehending mind and apprehended object is eliminated. Objects of perception— forms, sounds, and so on—unceasingly arise, appearing like reflections in the stainless mirror of limpid consciousness. They are like stars reflected on the surface of the sea. They are the manifold display of all the bright qualities of the unceasing radiance of the senses. And yet, in the very instant of their arising, they are, by their very nature, empty. If the mind does not cling to, and examine, the sense objects, thinking of them as existing in a concrete manner (thus straying into the side of appearances)—in other words, if the mind is not attached to them as being "this or that"—the link between apprehending mind and apprehended phenomena, mutually related as subject and object, is severed in the state of object-free awareness. And as the state of thought-free, self-cognizing, primordial wisdom is preserved with a natural, uncontrived mindfulness, all the impure elements (earth, water, and so on), both outer and inner, are spontaneously cleansed. And the level at which phenomena are exhausted in ultimate reality is reached. Such practitioners need not wait long—for many lives—to attain the ground of unsurpassed primordial wisdom, following in the footsteps of the Victorious Ones. They attain it here and now.

1. Conclusion of the chapter

36 In short, the path of the Great Perfection may be summarized in five extraordinary paths.

The first is the path of the ultimate expanse of the utterly pure nature. It is the unmistaken realization that phenomena have but one nature in the ground of primal purity. They have the nature of the ultimate expanse.

The second is the path of awareness, which is an extraordinary wisdom.[522] These first two paths are in truth the union of the ultimate expanse and awareness.

The third path is that of luminosity, which consists of the two lamps. The first is the *lamp of the far-catching water lasso*,[523] which perceives the phenomena of samsara and nirvana, and consists of the channels that link the heart with the eyes. The second is the *lamp of the empty disks of light*, which is the radiance of primordial purity appearing in the form of disks of light. On the basis of these two lamps, the appearances of luminosity arise and increase. The conditions for their arising are, first, the outer expanse, which is free from obscuring conditions and similar to the limpid sky, and, second, the inner expanse of awareness,[524] which is unborn and therefore unchanging.

The fourth path is that of trekchö: the clear conviction that thoughts are primordially pure. One therefore understands that appearances are groundless, consciousness is objectless, awareness is without support, and the exhaustion of phenomena is ineffable.[525] The arising and subsiding of thoughts occur simultaneously. As it is said in the *Testament:* "Phenomenal existence arises within the dharmakaya buddhafield and subsides there."[526]

The fifth path is that of thögal, and is essentially the path of the ultimate expanse and of awareness. On the path of the two lamps, there arises the lamp of self-arisen wisdom, which possesses the three aspects: nature, creative power, and radiance.

Jigme Lingpa asks us to understand that these are the five supreme, extraordinary paths of the Natural Great Perfection. In the case of practitioners of the highest capacity, it is here that the three kayas are perfectly perceived while one is still on the path, and the ground endowed with the six special features of the result is attained in a single lifetime. Practitioners of medium and basic capacity gain liberation in the bardo. Thanks to our old friend ignorance (the failure to understand that the adventitious appearances of phenomena have no real existence) and thanks to the delusions by which we are deceived, we have been bound until now in the dreadful and unending wasteland of samsara by the iron-strong shackles of karma and defilements, the motives of our every act. Jigme Lingpa advises us to be weary of all this. And in order to capture the everlasting kingdom of the primordial ground so as to be able to work effortlessly for the benefit of beings, he instructs us to rely upon trekchö and thögal and the rest of the five supreme paths,[527] passing swiftly beyond suffering into the city of the three spontaneously present kayas, which are supreme peace.

CHAPTER 13

The Great Result That Is Spontaneously Present

1. The result is not produced by extraneous causes

We have already seen how the freedom that derives from the recognition 1
of the true nature of the appearance of the ground constitutes a superior
kind of freedom, for it is endowed with the six special features associated
with Samantabhadra.[528] Here, the only explanation given of the result is
a detailed description of the principal ways in which the array of the
sambhogakaya buddhafields appears to beings who are to be guided.

When the fundamental nature of the ground of the Natural Great
Perfection has been established, and when its extraordinary path, characterized as this is by a total absence of deliberate action and effort, has
been understood, one comes, through training, to the primordial ground
as it truly is. Thus one attains the level of the result: the kayas (the
supports) and the primordial wisdoms (the supported). This does not
mean, however, that the kayas and wisdoms were previously absent from
the ground and that, thanks to meditative practice, they arise newly
through extraneous causes. Self-cognizing primordial wisdom (*rig pa'i ye
shes*) is obscured by adventitious stains, namely, the samsaric propensities that are rooted in the universal ground. In the expository causal
vehicle, this impure universal ground is purified by being transmuted.
In the Mahayoga of the inner tantras, it is purified through the perception of phenomena as deities, not through the recognition of the nature
of the ground's appearance. Nevertheless, when the impure universal
ground is purified, the mind and mental factors together with their
objects (which are all based on the universal ground) sink back into the
dharmadhatu [and all the qualities spontaneously present in the ground
are actualized]. As it is said in the *Sublime Continuum*:

Since faults are adventitious to it,
While perfect qualities inhere within its nature,
Ultimate reality is unchanging:
As it was before, so after it will be.

2   Take, for instance, the following example. The clouds that hide the sun are in fact produced by the power of the sun itself. For when the sun's rays strike the surface of the sea, a warm vapor rises and causes a mist to gather in the sky, leading to the formation of clouds whereby the sun is overcast. In like manner, when from the ground-awareness, endowed as it is with the nature of the three kayas, appearance (the spontaneous creative power) of the ground stirs, this same appearance is not recognized as the self-experience of the ground-awareness. Instead, it is through the power of the delusion suffered throughout our beginningless series of lives that the ingrained tendency to grasp at self and other gives rise to a display of knowledge objects (illusory phenomena, animate and inanimate, the universe and its inhabitants), together with their apprehending subjects (the thoughts belonging to the eight consciousnesses, which are the cause of samsaric existence). Self-cognizing primordial wisdom is thus concealed as if by adventitious clouds. But when obscurations are cleansed away in the dharmadhatu, self-arisen primordial wisdom appears like the sun shining naturally in a cloudless sky. In other words, when self-arisen primordial wisdom is freed from the obscurations (whether conceptual or deriving from defilement) associated with objects of knowledge, it shines, naturally luminous, in the sky-like dharmadhatu.

1. A detailed explanation of the five kayas[529]
2. The three kayas of inner luminosity of the ultimate expanse
3. An explanation of the three kayas
4. The vajrakaya, the unchanging and indestructible body

3   The nature of the dharmakaya, in which the three kayas are undivided, is emptiness and is indicated by the word "vajra." From the standpoint of the dharmadhatu endowed with twofold purity, this dharmakaya is called the unchanging vajra, while from the standpoint of the appearance of its distinct qualities, it is called manifest enlightenment. The

unceasing natural radiance, the union of appearance and emptiness, is free from all dualistic appearance. This is the primordial wisdom of the dharmadhatu, of which, if one were to distinguish them, the three kayas of inner luminosity are no more than subdivisions.

The original ultimate universal ground (*ye don kyi kun gzhi*)[530]—the stainless dharmadhatu, the very nature of awareness—is obscured by the twofold veil of the universal ground that is the support of various propensities. When this is dispelled by the two accumulations, the primordially pure nature (*ngo bo ye dag*) is cleansed of the two kinds of adventitious obscuration (*glo bur 'phral dag*). The ultimate result is thus attained. It is supreme enlightenment endowed with twofold purity, and it has the character of an entire ocean of kayas and primordial wisdoms. Buddhahood is the actualization of ultimate reality, the primordial, ultimate expanse. As the state of great purity and equality, it is itself an "expanse beyond all expectation."[531] Just as the light that radiates outward at the full moon is present but not visible at the time of the new moon (for then it is withdrawn into its own depths), in the same way, changeless ultimate reality, free from any thought of subject and object, and devoid of intrinsic being, is ever present as the ultimate expanse, the emptiness aspect, of the kayas and wisdoms. This is the unchanging vajrakaya (*mi 'gyur rdo rje sku*) endowed with the essence of uncompounded primordial wisdom.

4. The abhisambodhikaya, the body of manifest enlightenment

The state of emptiness endowed with the most sublime of all attri-
butes,[532] as realized in the meditative equipoise of Noble Beings, is the inseparable union of appearance and emptiness. It is the ultimate expanse, in which all conceptual construction subsides. It is here that adventitious stains are naturally cleansed away, and the infinite qualities of the ten strengths and so on are fully deployed. Buddhahood is attained in the very moment that this occurs. [In their ultimate nature, these qualities are not differentiated.] From the standpoint of their appearance, however, each quality is distinct. There are thus ten strengths, four fearlessnesses, eighteen distinctive qualities, great compassion, thirty-seven factors leading to enlightenment, and so on.[533] If the ultimate expanse is assessed from the standpoint of the qualities of enlight-

enment resulting from both realization and elimination, it constitutes the abhisambodhikaya, the body of manifest enlightenment (*mngon par byang chub pa'i sku*), the unceasing knowledge of mirrorlike primordial wisdom.[534]

4. The dharmakaya, the body of peaceful ultimate reality

5   As the mind's engagement with outer objects of knowledge (forms and so on) subsides, all grasping at the inner cognizing mind as something truly existent dissolves into the ultimate expanse, and the illusions of the relative level disappear. By contrast, the self-cognizing awareness immanent in the ground of suchness remains. It abides free from all extremes, falling neither into permanence nor annihilation. The outwardly radiating luminosity of primordial wisdom is withdrawn into the ultimate expanse. Although it is thus stilled, or "absorbed," as the root verse says, it is not a state of dullness or obscurity. For its knowing aspect is not lost—there remains the primordial wisdom of extremely subtle inner luminosity. This is an unceasing state of knowing, and forms the basis for an ocean of kayas and primordial wisdoms. It is the exclusive domain of the Buddhas. It is beheld by them alone, who are beyond the state of resting, and of not resting, in meditative equipoise. It is seen by no one else. This foundation or ground for the arising (of outwardly radiating luminosity) is called the peaceful dharmakaya, the body of peaceful ultimate reality (*zhi ba chos sku*).

3. From the standpoint of ultimate reality, the three kayas of inner luminosity cannot be differentiated
4. The three kayas of inner luminosity are not objects of the ordinary mind

6   The three kayas of inner luminosity, which are knowable only to self-cognizing primordial wisdom, are referred to as the buddha-nature (*rgyal ba'i khams*). In truth, since the buddha-nature exists neither in the singular nor the plural, it is not an entity. On the other hand, since the primordial wisdom that knows things in their multiplicity is present in the manner of inner luminosity,[535] buddha-nature cannot be said not to exist. Since, like space, it is utterly pure by nature, it cannot be thought of in terms of the kayas and wisdoms (of outward luminosity). Neither

is it stained by impure attributes. The radiance whereby it manifests—in other words, the outwardly radiating luminosity—is stilled in
the ultimate expanse. The buddha-nature is beyond the power of words
to describe, for it is dharmatā, the ultimate truth. Concepts, investiga-
tions, metaphors, arguments—none can indicate it, for it is incompatible with the ordinary mind, mental factors, comparisons, and so forth.
The full array of a Buddha's qualities is beyond the scope even of the
great Bodhisattvas on the tenth ground of realization.

4. The manner in which the three kayas of inner luminosity dwell in the dharmadhatu

The dharmadhatu is a state that lies open and manifest only to the
Buddhas, our guides. It is a state of emptiness, beyond all conceptual
construction. Being inconceivable, it is profound. Being naturally pure,
unstained by the mind and mental factors or thoughts, it is peaceful.
Since its knowing aspect is ceaseless or unchanging, it is "ever youthful."
Since it dwells as inner luminosity and does not manifest as the sambhogakaya of outwardly radiating luminosity—or in other words, since
its inner radiance, which manifests as the endless qualities of buddhahood, is unceasing—Jigme Lingpa refers to it as the "fair interior of
the mansion of the vase." As we find in the tantra (the *Guhyagarbha*):
"There is no outside and no inside, all is contained within."

The wisdom minds of the Buddhas of the three times remain evenly
and constantly within the expanse of the dharmadhatu. But when this
state is considered from the point of view of appearance, it follows that
the Buddhas "do not see each other," because the self-experience of
awareness has dissolved into the ultimate expanse. As the *Tantra of the
Wondrous King* says: "All the Buddhas, past, present, and to come, dwell
in the palace of the dharmadhatu without seeing each other."

Furthermore, the nature of phenomena is beyond the concepts of singular and plural. Those who have perfectly realized this nature as being
the ultimate expanse of emptiness have "gone to suchness." They are
tathāgatas. Therefore, since in ultimate reality, all Buddhas constitute a
single expanse of wisdom of one taste, there is no seeing of Buddhas by
Buddhas. There is no Buddha-who-sees and no Buddha-who-is-seen—in

the same way that the azure sky cannot look back at itself and say, "I am like this."

2. An explanation of the two kayas of outwardly radiating luminosity
3. An explanation of the sambhogakaya[536]
4. The sambhogakaya in which the ground and result are not separate
5. A brief explanation

8   When, in the beginning, one fails to recognize the nature of appearances as they arise from the ground, these appearances manifest as samsara. Finally, when one attains freedom, these same appearances subside, becoming of a single taste with the ultimate expanse, and for this reason the self-arising of the ground is said to sink back into the ground itself (*rang byung rang la thim*). Primordial wisdom (the unceasing knowing aspect of luminosity) never stirs from the inner ultimate expanse beyond all conceptual construction. But, thanks to its natural radiance, and through the eight doors of spontaneous presence, the outwardly radiating luminosity of cognitive potency (*thugs rje*) appears as the sambhogakaya, the "body of perfect enjoyment"—the body that "perfectly enjoys" the teachings of the Mahayana.[537] This sambhogakaya is endowed with the five certainties. The *place* is the field of Densely Arrayed Luminosity; the *time*, being "exhausted in the ground" (*dus gzhir rdzogs*), is inconceivable; the *Teachers* are the Buddhas of the five families; the *teaching* is the Natural Great Perfection; and the *retinues* of the Buddhas are not different from the Buddhas themselves. The Teachers, retinues, and so on are all distinctly manifest. Their bodies and buddhafields are endowed with the major and minor marks together with an ocean of perfect qualities.

5. A detailed explanation of the five perfections of the sambhogakaya
6. The perfection of the place

9   The place is the spontaneous and perfect display of the effortless creative power of self-cognizing wisdom. It is "inferior to nothing" (*'og min*) and is thus the highest field of Akanishtha.[538] It is adorned with the

perfect and abundant array—namely, the self-experience of primordial wisdom—and therefore it is called "Dense Array." It is there that the natural creative power of the five primordial wisdoms unceasingly appears. Lights and radiant beams shine, sparkle, and glow. They are like rainbows that arch across and fill the vault of heaven. As a symbol of emptiness and compassion, the jeweled ground is soft and yielding to the tread, springing back when the feet are raised. There are other inconceivable qualities of this perfect array. They are by nature the five primordial wisdoms of the union [of appearance and emptiness]. As symbols of all the perfect qualities in full flower, there are immeasurable palaces, square in form and of surpassing beauty. They have four doors, three of which symbolize the three doors of perfect liberation, while the fourth symbolizes uncompounded luminosity. These four doors also symbolize the four unbounded qualities. As an indication of the eight perfect freedoms,[539] there are, above the porticoes, eight ornamental cornices (*rta babs*) in the form of lotus, coffer, ledge, tassels, frieze, jeweled traceries, spouts, and garuda heads made of diamond or other precious substances.[540]

As a symbol of the fulfillment of all wishes, there are five concentric walls, which are the display of the five wisdoms. There are the four buttress blocks, which symbolize the four sublime wisdom aspects of each of the five wisdoms. As the symbol of unchanging ultimate reality, the walls are surmounted by yellow ledges. Then there are pendent strings of jewels adorned with suns and moons that move in the wind. There is a covered terrace to show that beings are protected by compassion. As a sign of inconceivable ultimate reality, there is a balustrade with three stupas. To show that the objects of the senses are not rejected but enjoyed as ornaments of the self-experience of wisdom, there are offering goddesses upon a surrounding plinth. There is the "Fair-Eyed" vajra goddess of form and so forth, dancing gracefully and joyfully, emanating offering clouds of empty bliss. Signs of different qualities and activities are placed aloft: tail-fans, banners, parasols, victory banners topped with wish-fulfilling jewels, and a canopy contrived of various silks and precious stones. On a lotus, there is a precious Dharmawheel with thirteen tassels. There is a shrine room adorned with flat victory banners. As an indication that the dharmadhatu is impossible to quantify, the palace cannot be measured in the ordinary manner, as having a certain surface and height. Wherever one looks, there is the fathomless palace of the limpid, five-hued lights of primordial wisdom. And to show that the qualities of wisdom are incalculable, the dimensions of the palace are beyond computation. It appears to fill the entire extent of space itself.

10   In every one of these space-pervading palaces, there is a throne for the main Buddha of each of the five families. The throne is upheld by lions to symbolize fearlessness of mind and subjugation of the four demons; by elephants to indicate the taming of the ten negativities; by all-knowing horses to indicate the mastery of miraculous powers; by peacocks to indicate the attainment of the ten powers; and by shang shang birds to indicate the accomplishment of the four activities. As a symbol of purity unstained by the defects of samsara, the thrones are surmounted by lotus seats. On them, as a symbol of the union of skillful means and wisdom, there are the disks of sun and moon, whereon the Buddhas sit.

6. The perfection of the time
This time transcends past, present, and future, for the latter are exhausted in the ground, the unchanging ultimate reality.

6. The perfection of the Teacher
In this uncompounded time of Samantabhadra, there appear, without ever stirring from the ultimate nature, changeless wisdom-bodies endowed with all the thirty-two major and eighty minor marks of buddhahood. Theirs is a great spontaneous presence beyond birth and death. They are stable and everlasting, not subject to decay or decline. They are the five Teachers of the mind transmission of the Buddhas: dark blue Sarvavid-Vairochana [of the tathāgata family], the primordial wisdom of the dharmadhatu; white Akshobhya of the vajra family, mirror-like primordial wisdom; yellow Ratnasambhava [of the jewel family], the primordial wisdom of equality; red Amitabha of the lotus family of enlightened speech, all-perceiving primordial wisdom; and green Amoghasiddhi of the action family, all-accomplishing primordial wis-

dom. These five Teachers have three faces and six arms, and their attributes are as described in the *Vajra Mirror Tantra*:

> Vajra, wheel and flaming blade,
> Bell and lotus-blossom, gem.
> The implements change places, turn by turn.
> The first hand at the heart, the left embracing round.[541]

The indivisibility of skillful means and wisdom is indicated by the union of the Teachers with the consorts belonging to their respective families, namely, Dhatvishvari, Buddhalochana, Mamaki, Pandaravasini, and Samayatara. They have the same colors as the respective Buddhas, and have one face and two arms. In their right hands they hold the attribute of their family, and in their left they hold a bell. The Teachers and their consorts are endowed with all the perfections of the seven qualities of union.[542]

6. The perfection of the retinue

The minds of the Teachers—in other words, their great primordial wisdoms—manifest as their retinues. These consist of the eight male and female Bodhisattvas[543] and the four doorkeepers and their consorts.[544] They are not different from the Buddhas whom they surround.

6. The perfection of the teaching

The wheel of Dharma of the Natural Great Perfection is ineffable, inconceivable, and indescribable. Indeed, the term "wheel of Dharma" is simply a name given to the realization of the naturally luminous character of the mind's nature, the union of appearance and emptiness. It is free from the twofold veil and does not stir from the state of luminosity. The wheel of Dharma, beyond sound and word (in the ordinary sense of these terms), "turns" within the perception of the Buddhas' retinues. As it is said in the sutra:

> Nothing did the Victor's Son set forth.
> Not teaching, he has taught extensively.

4. The sambhogakaya of the spontaneously present result
5. The peaceful mandala of the upper palace

When the karmic wind is purified, the sambhogakaya, endowed with the seven qualities of the three kayas,[545] manifests spontaneously as the Vajradhatu mandala of Akanishtha.

In the upper peaceful palace,[546] the place of the essence of enlightenment—in other words, the field of Akanishtha, the sambhogakaya's exclusive self-experience—forty-two peaceful deities dwell and reign. The union of the ultimate expanse and primordial wisdom, referred to in the root verse as the "sublime coition,"[547] is Samantabhadra with his consort. This constitutes the ground from which the sambhogakaya and the nirmanakaya emanate, and it pervades all the principal deities and their retinues. It is the nature of the enlightened mind, which is itself without face or arms. It is all-encompassing and is thus the dharmakaya. For this reason, Samantabhadra and his consort are not located within the mandala. They manifest as the six Munis, the "sages of awareness" (rig pa'i skyes bu), who labor for the benefit of the beings in the six realms of existence. Consequently, in the ultimate, actual Akanishtha, the buddhafield that is the sambhogakaya's exclusive self-experience, there are thirty-four Victorious Ones, appearing in bodily form. They are the ten male and female Buddhas of the five families, together with the twenty-four deities of the retinue, namely, the sixteen outer and inner Bodhisattvas, male and female, together with the eight male and female doorkeepers.

These deities represent the intrinsically pure aggregates, elements, and so forth spoken of in the lower tantras,[548] or the aspect of appearance (phenomena) and the aspect of emptiness (the nature of phenomena) as delineated specifically in the cycle of the *Shri Vajrasattva Mayajalatantra*—all of which constitute the natural aggregate of the vajra body, the components of which are as follows. First, there are the five aggregates, which have, from the very beginning, the nature of the five Buddhas. Second, there are the five elements, which have the nature of the Buddhas' consorts. Third, there are the twelve outer and inner ayatanas (namely, the six sense powers and their objects) and the six consciousnesses, which are, altogether, the eighteen dhatus or constituents,[549] and which have the nature of the outer and inner male and female Bodhisattvas, together with the wrathful male and female doorkeepers. Thus the three worlds constitute a single buddhafield, the great, primordial, and utterly pure mandala of the deities of the three seats all complete (*gdan gsum tshang ba'i dkyil 'khor*).

The above mentioned (peaceful) mandala, and all the mandalas that are "present in the body" (*lus grub*), as taught in the majority of the Anuttaratantras of the old and new translation traditions (for example, the *Mayajala*, the *Buddhasamayoga*, and the *Guhyasamaja*) are buddhafields that are the exclusive self-experience of the sambhogakaya.[550] Because of this, they are all equal in their purity.

5. The wrathful mandala of the lower palace

It is generally thought that, at the time of the ground, the sambhogakaya mandala, the mandala that is exclusively the sambhogakaya's self-experience (*rang snang*), is not wrathful. But since, at the time of the ground, skillful means and wisdom are never separate, the radiance of awareness *does* manifest as a wrathful mandala. Here, however, the wrathful mandala is explained as being related to the time of the result, for it is considered that, at the time of the ground, there is no thought or recollection of its purity. The wrathful mandala is located below the peaceful palace as the self-arisen mansion, the spontaneously present palace of the Gathering of the Great Assembly (*tshogs chen 'dus pa*).

Upon the superimposed strata of the elements, which are themselves by nature the utterly pure expanse of the five female Buddhas, above a Mount Meru composed of bones, upon a ground of jeweled rock, and in the center of a blazing mass of fire (the natural light of wisdom), there is a dreadful, terrifying palace. It is a fortress made of skulls with nine concentric walls. These are separated by nine courts. The first three innermost courts are successively colored yellow, white, and red. The next three are colored yellow, red, and white, while, of the last three, the first is colored black, the second has four colors according to the directions, and the final court is green. Each of the outer doors (of the last court) is equipped with two cornices below and above, symbolizing karmic cause and effect. The first (the lower one) is a raised pediment. The second is the ornamental cornice above the portico.

In the center of the palace, upon a square platform adorned with four ornamental buttress-like steps,[551] there is an eight-spoked wheel, the hub of which is filled by a great rock composed of three- and five-pointed vajras. Above this, there is a white, thousand-petaled lotus, on which are disposed twenty-four sun and twenty-four moon disks arranged in pairs, and respectively symbolizing means and wisdom. Upon these are twenty-four pairs of powerful and arrogant spirits in close embrace. The males are facing down, the females facing up. Eight large animals are standing on them, trampling the male spirits on their backs and the females on their chests. These beasts are the ferocious tiger, the frightful lion, the cruel leopard, the savage bear, the mighty elephant, the majestic buffalo, the grasping crocodile, and the aggressive snake.

14   Upon them all stands the Lord, the glorious embodiment of samsara and nirvana. He is the Supreme Heruka Mahottara (*che mchog*), and is so-called either because he is greater even than Mahadeva, who is highest in the three worlds, or because in him all the sublime qualities of the deities of the mandala are embodied. He is dark blue with a gleam of sapphire, and his splendor blazes like the light of a million suns. He has twenty-one faces. The main central face is the same color as his body; the three faces to the right are colored yellow, red, and green; and the three faces to the left are red, blue, and green. Above them, the central face is yellow; the two faces to the right are red and green; and the two faces to the left are dark blue and white. Above them, the central face is dark blue; the two right faces are yellow and green; the two left faces are white and red. Above them the central face is dark purple, the right face is white, and the left face is green. Finally, on the summit the face is red and utters the screaming cry of a horse. His eight legs are spread apart and he has forty-two arms. His two main hands hold Samantabhadra and his consort, while the twenty hands on the right hold the Buddhas of the five families, the eight male Bodhisattvas, the four male wrathful doorkeepers, and the three Munis of the higher realms. The twenty hands on the left hold the five female Buddhas, the eight female Bodhisattvas, the four female wrathful doorkeepers, and the three Munis of the lower realms. This comes, altogether, to the forty-two peaceful deities. Mahottara is adorned with the six bone ornaments, the eight trappings of the charnel ground,[552] and the eight glorious attributes.[553] Above each of his heads, there sits a Buddha whose

head is adorned with a stupa formed of seven jewels. And on the summit of each stupa, there is a crest jewel ablaze with a thousand lights.

His supreme consort, Dhatvishvari (the Sky-Faced Queen), is blue. [15] She has nine heads and eighteen arms. Her eight legs are spread apart and her two principal hands hold a vajra and a skull-cup filled with blood. The eight hands on the right hold the mamos (Skt. *matarah*) of the sacred lands and regions, while the eight hands on the left hold the animal-headed goddesses (Tib. *phra man;* Skt. *pishachi*).

The father-mother deities may be arranged one on top of the other in tiers, just as for instance in the ritual for the preparation of the amrita medicine. In the center of the mandala is the Heruka of Supreme Power (*dbang mchog heruka*). On his head is Dhatvishvari. On Dhatvishvari's head is Mahottara. Alternatively, they may be in union. That is, the consort Dhatvishvari is standing on the shoulders of the Heruka of Supreme Power, and the head of Mahottara is sunk halfway into her secret space. This is the "head union" (*dbu sbyor*). Or again, the eight legs of Mahottara are standing on the eight lateral heads of the Sky-Faced Queen, while the eyes of her central face are joined with the secret of Mahottara. In this and other ways, the father-mother deities are in union.

All the phenomena of both samsara (the three worlds) and nirvana (the paths of the nine vehicles, together with their resultant qualities) are naturally and perfectly contained in the great and glorious Lord, from the throne beneath his feet to the wheel that crowns his head. The world of desire is perfectly contained in the ocean of blood, the world of form in the ground of corpses, and the formless world in the Mount Meru composed of skeletons. The Shravakas, Pratyekabuddhas, and Bodhisattvas are the rock of jewels. The three outer tantras are the vajra rock; the yoga of the generation stage is the white lotus, while the yoga of the perfection stage corresponds to the Buddhas of the diadem and the victory banners. The yoga of the Great Perfection is perfectly contained in the crest jewel that radiates a thousand lights. All the teachings up to and including Mahayoga are perfectly contained within the throne, while the Anuyoga is the body of the deity, and the Atiyoga is the crest jewel of the victory banner above his head.

In front of the Great Glorious One is the Heruka of Supreme Power. [16] He is dark blue with nine heads, eighteen arms, and four legs. He is in union with the wrathful consort Dhatvishvari. Then there are the nine glorious herukas. These represent the purified aspect of the nine degrees of clinging to body, speech, and mind as a self, and the pure aspect of the nine levels of the three worlds. In front of the Heruka of Supreme Power, there is the heruka of the vajra family; and on the four main spokes of the eight-spoked wheel, there are the herukas of the buddha, lotus, jewel, and action families. On the four intermediary spokes are Raksha and the remaining three herukas. These nine glorious herukas have three heads and six arms, and are in union with their consorts. On the four corners of the central platform and on the four buttress-like steps are Gauri and the rest of her kind, the eight gaurimas. They are the pure aspect of the eight consciousnesses.

In the first court of the mandala are the eight animal-headed goddesses: the Lion-Faced one and so on. They symbolize the intrinsic purity of the objects of the eight consciousnesses. In the second court are the eight goddesses who "draw up from the lower states" (*spor byed ma*), such as the goddess "Endowed with the Rays of the Sun," who represent the intrinsic purity of the main and intermediary directions. At the four doors are the four female doorkeepers, such as the "Lady Who Seals," who represent the purity of the elements. In the third court are the twenty-eight powerful goddesses, who represent the intrinsic purity of the twenty-eight vertebrae in the backbone. Each of the courts has its four respective doorkeepers. All the deities are resplendent with the glorious major and minor marks of the enlightened body; their speech is glorious with stirring melody; their minds are glorious and ablaze with compassion. They are resplendent with the display of all the nine demeanors of wrath.

The area from the center and as far as the third court is the mandala of the sambhogakaya's exclusive self-experience. This is the primordially and spontaneously present appearance of the outwardly radiating luminosity of the primordially pure ground. Now whereas this appearance of the ground arises, from the standpoint of skillful means, as the peaceful mandala, it manifests, from the standpoint of wisdom, as the wrathful mandala. For this reason, it is also said in our tradition that the wrathful mandala is the exclusive self-experience of the sambhogakaya. It is the mandala of the spontaneously present, ultimate Akanishtha.

Outside this mandala is the mandala perceived by other beings (*gzhan snang*). This comprises (concentrically) the mandala of swift action, the mandala of the ocean of samaya, the mandala of the "liberating" gings, and the mandala of the emissaries.[554] In the fourth courtyard (the mandala of swift action), there are groups of seven dakinis in each of the four directions. In the east, there is the Dakini of Charm and her companions; in the south, there is the Subduer and her companions; in the west, there is Yakshini and her companions; and in the north, there is the Sow-Faced dakini and her companions. Moreover, there is one dakini in each of the four doors, the Flower-Vase dakini and so on. In this court, therefore, there are thirty-two dakinis. In the fifth court (the mandala of the ocean of samaya), there are seven mamos, Famous Vajra and so on. In the four doors are the four sisters, the Swift Lady of the Four Continents and others. In the sixth court [the mandala of the "liberating" gings], there are eighteen gings, Vajrabhuta and so on, six classes of three. There is a group of three gings in each of the four directions. There is one ging in each of the four doors and a further two gings, one to the east and one to the west, each ready to receive commands.

There then follows the mandala of the emissaries, which is threefold. These are, concentrically, the mandala of the display of wrathful deities, the mandala of the swift mind, and the mandala of the ocean of samaya.[555] In the seventh court (the mandala of the display of wrathful deities), there are, beginning with Vijaya and Vajratopa, sixty wrathful deities (male and female in union). There are three pairs in each of the main and intermediary directions, one pair in each of the four doors, and a further two pairs, one in the east and one in the west. In the eighth court [the mandala of the swift mind], there are, in each of the four directions, sixty emissaries of the enlightened body, speech, and mind (two hundred and forty in all). Their color corresponds to the direction in which they are standing. In the ninth court [the mandala of the ocean of samaya], there are sixty mamo-emissaries, fifteen in each direction. All the deities located in the courts, from the fourth till the ninth, subdue negative and misleading forces. Thus they are included in the manifestations that are perceived by other beings (*gzhan snang*). Just as the six Munis appear to the beings of the six realms, they appear in the perception of the obstacle-making spirits and so on. For this reason, they do not belong to the mandala of Akanishtha, which is the exclusive self-experience of the sambhogakaya.

4. A summary of the sambhogakaya in which the ground and result are not separate, together with the sambhogakaya of the spontaneously present result

18   Regarding the manner in which these two mandalas, peaceful and wrathful, are the exclusive self-experience of the sambhogakaya, it may be said that from within the expanse of the uncompounded primordial wisdom of the dharmakaya, which is permanent by nature (*ngo bo nyid kyis rtag pa*), a natural, outwardly glowing radiance is spontaneously present as the sambhogakaya buddhafields endowed with the five perfections. These buddhafields are permanent on account of the constant and sustained continuity [of this radiance] (*rgyun gyis rtag pa*). The sambhogakaya is in turn the ground for the arising of the nirmanakaya, which is also permanent in being an unbroken sequence (*rgyun mi 'chad par rtag pa*). When the end of the path of learning is reached and all the veils that obscure the buddha-nature are removed, the display of primordial wisdom, encompassed by the Buddha's mind alone, appears as the place, Teacher, retinue, and so forth. Thus, although this display appears as buddhafields and palaces, and the principal deities with their retinues contained therein, there is no qualitative difference between them in that some are outer, some inner, some higher, and some lower. They are all equal as the display of Samantabhadra, the one, self-arisen primordial wisdom.

Since the minds of all the sambhogakayas, which are experienced exclusively by themselves (*rang snang longs sku*), never move from the expanse of the dharmakaya, they are not discursive. Since their speech transcends ordinary sound and word, it is ineffable. Since their bodies appear in great splendor and majesty, they display all the major and minor marks complete. With the perfectly pure eyes of primordial wisdom, which beholds all phenomena as its own self-experience, the sambhogakaya Buddhas behold each other at all times and without hindrance.

The sambhogakaya fields and the qualities of enlightenment, which 19 lie within the experience of all the Buddhas of the three times, are space-like and unimaginable. There is nothing superior to them, nothing higher. They do not fall into the extremes either of permanent existence or annihilation. And since they are encompassed by neither samsaric existence nor the peace of a one-sided nirvana, even the noble Bodhisatt-vas, the great and pure beings who dwell on the grounds of realization from the first till the tenth, are unable to perceive them. For the Bodhi-sattvas have not yet discarded all the obscurations that veil the buddha-nature. These obscuring veils are incompatible with the inconceivable twofold knowledge of the Victorious Ones: the knowledge of the na-ture of things just as it is, and the knowledge of phenomena in their multiplicity. In the ultimate Akanishtha, the sambhogakaya's exclusive self-experience, the Buddhas dwell in the wheel of everlasting continu-ity, which has the nature of the fourth inconceivable time, and tran-scends the specific and relative duration of the three "compounded" times: past, present, and future. Since the principal sambhogakaya Bud-dhas and their retinues are of the same wisdom mind, they are one and the same in their nature, and cannot be distinguished qualitatively. They perceive themselves and each other exclusively as part of their own self-experience (*rang snang*).

3. An explanation of the nirmanakaya
4. A brief explanation
From within the expanse of the sambhogakaya's exclusive self-experience, 20 and in order to guide beings, pure and impure, the cognitive potency (*thugs rje*) of the Buddhas effortlessly displays three kinds of Teacher or Guide. These are first, the nirmanakaya of luminous character (*rang bzhin sprul pa*), which is in harmony with the sambhogakaya; second, the nir-manakaya that is the guide of beings (*'gro 'dul sprul pa*), which manifests as the Teachers of the six classes of beings; and third, the diversified nirmanakaya (*sna tshogs sprul pa*), which manifests as both animate beings and inanimate things.

4. A detailed explanation
5. The nirmanakaya of luminous character
6. The nirmanakaya of luminous character that is counted as the sambhogakaya (in the vehicle of the paramitas)[556]
7. A brief explanation

The luminosity of the primordial wisdom of the dharmakaya of the Victorious Ones radiates outwardly and manifests in the field of Akanishtha as the sambhogakaya endowed with the major and minor marks, the display of the ultimate expanse. In the experience of the noble Bodhisattvas, the superior beings to be guided, it appears as if "transferred" into, or reflected in, a clear mirror. Since this reflection is similar to the Teacher as he appears in his own self-experience, it is counted as sambhogakaya. And since it is perceived by beings to be guided, it is counted also as nirmanakaya. Thus it has a status that is half nirmanakaya and half sambhogakaya (*phyed sprul longs sku'i gnas*). It is as when the autumn moon rises in the clear sky. Its reflection in a vessel appears in accordance with the water contained therein, whether clean or muddy.[557]

7. A detailed explanation in six points
8. The place

21   The place of this nirmanakaya appears as the five buddhafields. In the center, the creative power of the primordial wisdom of the dharmadhatu, corresponding to the enlightened body, displays the Akanishtha field of the Great Powerful One. In the east, the creative power of mirrorlike primordial wisdom, corresponding to the enlightened mind, displays Abhirati, the field of Manifest Joy. In the south, the creative power of the primordial wisdom of equality, corresponding to enlightened qualities, displays Shrimat, the field of Glory. In the west, the creative power of all-perceiving primordial wisdom, corresponding to enlightened speech, displays Padmakuta, the field of Heaped Lotuses. In the north, the creative power of all-accomplishing primordial wisdom, corresponding to enlightened activities, displays Sukarmasiddhi, the field of the Accomplishment of Highest Action.

8. The Teachers

In the five buddhafields, there dwell respectively: Vairochana, king of form; Akshobhya, king of consciousness; Ratnasambhava, king of feeling; Amitabha, king of perception; and Amoghasiddhi, king of conditioning factors. These five supreme Teachers, endowed with endless qualities of enlightenment such as the major and minor marks, appear, according to the dispositions of beings, as an infinity of peaceful and wrathful deities that are similar to the deities of the sambhogakaya's exclusive self-experience.

8. The primordial wisdoms

Though the Teachers appear differently in the five buddhafields, their minds are not separate from each other. The one primordial wisdom of buddhahood arises as the enlightened minds of the Buddhas of the five families, namely, the five primordial wisdoms. Each of the five wisdoms has four attendant wisdoms, thus making twenty-five primordial wisdoms altogether. For example, the primordial wisdom of the dharmadhatu, the enlightened mind of Vairochana, is endowed with four attendant wisdoms: the mirrorlike wisdom of the dharmadhatu wisdom and so on. The mirrorlike primordial wisdom has also four attendant wisdoms: the dharmadhatu wisdom of the mirrorlike wisdom and so on.

The first of the five wisdoms is the primordial wisdom of the dharmadhatu. This wisdom, the wisdom of knowing that phenomena are not distinct in their ultimate nature, is unshaken by the perception of phenomenal characteristics. It pervades the entire universe, animate and inanimate, and is inexpressible. Just as one cannot speak about, or describe, the shape of space, so too, the wisdom of the dharmadhatu, which embraces all phenomena, is ineffable. Although this wisdom knows the nature of phenomena, it transcends the boundary of knowable things, for it is of one taste with the dharmadhatu.

The second wisdom is mirrorlike primordial wisdom. The clear surface of a mirror is able to reflect images without effort. In the same way, the primordial wisdom of unceasing knowledge, free of the "dust" of the concepts of apprehended object and apprehending subject, and free of all exertion, is the ground from which arise the three subsequent wisdoms, which are in fact the conceptual classification of the manner in which phenomena are known.

The third wisdom is the primordial wisdom of equality. The phenomena of samsara and nirvana have the same taste. They are equal, neither good nor bad. The wisdom of equality knows that phenomena cannot be defined (in themselves) as good or bad, as things to be adopted or rejected, and so on. It knows, by dwelling in the expanse where all conceptual construction subsides, that samsara and nirvana are indivisible.

The fourth wisdom is all-discerning primordial wisdom. This wisdom detects all interdependently produced phenomena separately, as the distinct appearances of causes and effects. It has the constant and unimpeded knowledge of the nature of phenomena (the absence of both the personal and phenomenal self), together with the knowledge of all phenomena in their multiplicity, from the five aggregates up to omniscience.

The fifth wisdom is all-accomplishing primordial wisdom, which operates effortlessly for the benefit of others. This wisdom accomplishes great waves of benefit for the sake of others, by means of the activities of body, speech, and mind, free from any obscuring "attachment and impediment." Its activities are spontaneous until the very emptying of samsara.

These primordial wisdoms may be summarized as follows. The primordial wisdom of the dharmadhatu refers to the knowledge of the nature of things. The remaining four wisdoms refer to the knowledge of phenomena in all their multiplicity.

8. The retinue

23 The enlightened Teachers are accompanied by retinues that are different from themselves, and these are composed solely of Bodhisattvas dwelling on the grounds of realization, from the first till the tenth. Rays of light emanate from the Teachers' bodies, and imbue the minds of their disciples with the perfect doctrine of the Mahayana. Just as the dirt on one's face (which one cannot see) becomes evident when one looks in a mirror—with the result that one can wash it away—so too, the Bodhisattvas dwelling on the grounds of realization can, when they behold

the "half-nirmanakaya half-sambhogakaya Teachers" (*sprul pa'i longs sku*) recognize their own obscurations. They see that there is still a difference between themselves and the sambhogakaya Teachers. And by degrees they are able to rid themselves completely of the most subtle conceptual obscurations that veil the great enlightenment: obscurations the depth of which is difficult to fathom and which are extremely hard to recognize. On the first ground, they completely purify greed; on the second ground, they purify distorted discipline; on the third, they purify anger; on the fourth, they purify laziness; on the fifth, they purify distraction; on the sixth, they purify distorted intelligence; on the seventh, they purify ineptitude in skillful means; on the eighth, they purify obscurations with respect to courage and determination regarding the benefit of others; on the ninth, they purify lethargy with regard to the goal that they aspire to; on the tenth, they purify the subtle conceptual obscurations that veil primordial wisdom.

When all these have been purified, the Bodhisattvas progress to the eleventh ground of Universal Light and achieve perfect enlightenment. As it is said in the *Guhyagarbha-tantra*:

> In the supreme place of Akanishtha unsurpassed,
> The Teacher takes the form of Vairochana.
> To the Bodhisattvas that encircle him
> No word of supreme teachings does he speak
> But with his body shows them forth.
> The blemishes upon one's face may be removed
> According as one sees them in a mirror.
> Likewise, when the retinues behold the Buddha's form,
> They see, as though reflected in a glass,
> The deep and boundless stains obstructing their enlightenment.
> And therefore they can cleanse them on the ten grounds step-by-
>   step,
> Attaining perfect, unsurpassed enlightenment.

8. The time

24 As long as the mighty Bodhisattvas on the ten grounds have not attained to their level of realization, the sambhogakaya Teachers, the lords of the world, continue to appear within the wheel of inexhaustible ornaments of the enlightened body, speech, and mind of the dharmakaya's expanse, devoid of intrinsic being. These Teachers have overcome the demon of death and therefore do not display a departure into nirvana. They abide in the wheel of everlasting continuity, so that pure worldly beings (the Bodhisattvas) may gain the special riches of the qualities of the Mahayana.

8. The defilements to be purified

25 The five dormant defilements (still to be purified) of the Bodhisattvas (who are therefore still to be guided) are transmuted by their corresponding antidotes. These antidotes are the five buddhafields and the five enlightened Teachers who expound therein the five supreme teachings, deriving from the [five] primordial wisdoms and transcending conventional expression. For example, as the antidote to ignorance, the teacher Vairochana expounds, in the buddhafield of Akanishtha, the supreme teaching of the primordial wisdom of the dharmadhatu. And the wisdom attained is that of the dharmadhatu. The same applies respectively for the other defilements, with the result that all five wisdoms are attained.

As it is said in the *Eighty-Chapter Mayajala*:

> The five defilements, craving and the rest,
> Are said to be the five authentic primal wisdoms.

In this regard, it has been said that, when ignorance is being purified, the Bhagavan king of form expounds the supreme teaching of the primordial wisdom of the dharmadhatu. Similarly, in the case of anger, the king of consciousness expounds the teaching of mirrorlike wisdom. In the case of pride, the king of feeling expounds the teaching of the wisdom of equality. In the case of desire, the king of perception expounds the teaching of all-discerning wisdom. And in the case of jealousy, the king of conditioning factors expounds the teaching of all-accomplishing wisdom. It is thus that the defilements are transmuted (into their corresponding wisdoms).

These five groups of five (defilements, wisdoms, buddhafields, Teachers, and teachings) can also be applied to the ten grounds of realization. On the path of seeing, the ignorance that consists in conceptual imputation is transmuted. The universal ground subsides in the ultimate expanse, and Perfect Joy, the first ground of realization, which has the nature of the primordial wisdom of the dharmadhatu, is attained, along with the vision of Vairochana. Following this, in the course of the three lesser grounds of the path of meditation (the second, third, and fourth grounds of the ten), pride is gradually transmuted. The mental consciousness subsides in the ultimate expanse, the primordial wisdom of equality is gained and the three grounds of realization—namely, Immaculate, Luminous, and Radiant—are attained, along with the vision of Ratnasambhava. In the three middle grounds of the path of meditation (the fifth, sixth, and seventh), thoughts of desire are transmuted. The defiled consciousness subsides in the ultimate expanse, all-discerning wisdom is gained, and the grounds Hard to Uphold, Clearly Manifest, and Far Progressed are attained, along with the vision of Amitabha. In the three great grounds of the path of meditation, thoughts of anger subside. The consciousness of the universal ground is transmuted, mirror-like wisdom is gained, and the eighth ground, the Immovable, is attained, along with the vision of Akshobhya. On the ninth and tenth grounds—namely, Perfect Intellect and Cloud of Dharma—the seed of jealousy is purified, the five sensory consciousnesses subside in the ultimate expanse, the four perfect knowledges[558] are gained, and all-accomplishing wisdom is attained, along with the vision of Amoghasiddhi. Consequently, beginning with the path of seeing and until the end of the tenth ground, the nine grounds of the path of meditation are gradually perfected, while at the end of the tenth ground, the empowerment of great rays of light is received and the essence of perfect enlightenment is reached.

7. Conclusion

Although it is permissible to refer to the five buddhafields just mentioned as "half-nirmanakaya fields" (*phyed sprul*), they in fact appear only to the Bodhisattvas on the ten grounds of realization, and do not figure in the experience of the Shravakas, Pratyekabuddhas, and others. Similarly, even though the five Teachers appear as sambhogakayas, they, their retinues, their buddhafields, and so on, are not exclusively the self-experience of their primordial wisdom, unavailable to beings other than themselves. For they are indeed perceived by the pure minds of the Bodhisattvas dwelling on the grounds of realization. For this reason, they are called semi-apparent sambhogakaya buddhafields, or nirmanakaya buddhafields of luminous character.[559] This is explained in the tantra the *Conjunction of the Sun and Moon.*

6. **The nirmanakaya of indwelling luminous character**[560]
7. **The actual nirmanakaya of indwelling luminous character**
8. **A brief explanation of the nirmanakaya fields of the ten directions**

27 In general, according to all other, more common, teachings, practitioners must progress gradually upon the grounds and paths. By contrast, those who have received the instructions of the extraordinary path of the Natural Great Perfection—even those of only basic capacity—have no need to depend on the attainment of the grounds of realization. For them, all the grounds and paths may be covered in a single stroke. They can directly experience, in this very moment, the radiance of awareness that is in the depths of their hearts: the supreme mandala of primordial wisdom's self-experience, which is utterly beyond all intellectual analysis. A perfect teacher, who has realized within this mandala the sublime truth of fundamental nature, mastering it with the assistance of the key methods, such as the three ways of sitting and the three ways of gazing, can grant the empowerment of the creative power of awareness that is proper to thögal, thereby blessing and introducing practitioners to the nature of their minds. Those practitioners who do not spoil their samaya (the very life force of this empowerment) but observe it purely; who, by adopting the three ways of sitting and gazing, train, during the day, in manifest luminosity (the radiant light rays that are the self-experience of awareness); and who, during the night, train according to the pith instructions in the practice of bringing phenomena into the vase of the heart's luminous radiance—such practitioners may not perhaps achieve a great development in their meditative experi-

ence, and they may fail to reach the full scope of realization (the recognition of the wisdom state of primordial purity in which all phenomena are exhausted), and therefore they may fail to gain freedom in this very life. Nevertheless, the involvement of such fortunate persons in negative actions will be very slight, and their dreams will be positive. Thanks to their former training and the blessings of the truth of ultimate reality and of their teacher, they will find that, when the seal of their bodily support is broken, there will be no further tendency, in the bardo of becoming, to take rebirth. And they will have a karmic fortune equal to those who reach the grounds of realization, for whom the nirmanakaya fields of luminous character appear. These practitioners will go to the pure nirmanakaya fields of the ten directions. These fields are the appearance of the ground. This appearance is present within such practitioners, and manifests, through the doors of spontaneous presence, as an array of beams of light, thanks to the cognitive potency (*thugs rje*) of buddhahood.

8. The five buddhafields that grant release and freedom[561]

There are, generally speaking, ten buddhafields, to which is added the buddhafield of the Mount of Flaming Fire, thus making eleven altogether. The teachings specify that these are gathered into the five buddhafields that bring one to great release in the primordial state, thus granting complete freedom from both samsara and nirvana. Starting from the east, there is the buddhafield of Manifest Joy, where the ground, palace, and so on are of crystal. In the south, there is the field of Glory, where everything is gold. In the west, there is the field of Heaped Lotuses, where all is made of rubies. And in the north, there is the field of the Precious Array, also called the Accomplishment of Highest Action, where the ground and palace are of emerald.

All the palaces have four porticoes surmounted by various ornamental cornices. In the four directions, there are windows through which, after the rising of the sun, five-colored lights fill the palaces, green light appearing in the north. At the four corners of the palaces, there are four stupas made of pearl, and between them are hanging garlands of bells, great and small. They tinkle sweetly in the breeze with the sound of the teachings on the three doors of perfect liberation. The four directions are filled with different scents stirred up by the wind. Clouds of perfume fan the four banners with their varied silken ribbons.

29   Outside the palaces are pools of water endowed with the eight excellent qualities. On their banks grow sweet-scented palm trees, their leaves and branches adorned with swaying lattices and pendent ornaments of different jewels. At a greater distance are eight small lakes with different kinds of birds: shang shang, peacocks, katari, parrots that can speak with human words, goslings, grouse, hoopoes, warblers, kangkari, divine birds with bell-like calls, cuckoos, and kritipa birds, which are like golden vajras. They are all of different colors. Some are turquoise blue, some are coral red, some are emerald green, and some have the whiteness of conch. The lovely, sweetly tuned song from the lyres of their throats resounds constantly on all sides, a joy to all who hear it.

30   The Bodhisattvas dwelling there are but one lifetime away from enlightenment. The merest recollection of food and drink is enough to satisfy them. They are untroubled by defilement and therefore know no illness. Thus they are perfectly at ease. Even if sickness were to arise, they would only need to drink from the streams, or bathe themselves therein, for the waters have the power to soothe all ailments, which depart never to return. All clothing and jewels appear as soon as the Bodhisattvas think of them. In short, the first three buddhafields possess the amenities equal to those of the gods of the Heaven of the Thirty-Three. And the buddhafield called the Accomplishment of Highest Action affords enjoyments equal to those found among the gods of the form realm.

All around is a fence contrived of seven precious substances and ornamented with a cornice. In the center are teaching thrones contrived of precious gems. In these same buddhafields are the Teachers of the four families: Vajrasattva, Ratnasambhava, Amitabha, and Amoghasiddhi who, at all four periods of the day and night, expound the sacred Dharma without interruption. In the evening, Vajrasattva, Ratnasambhava, and Amitabha expound the teachings of the expository causal vehicle. At midnight, they set forth the outer Mantrayana. At dawn, they teach the inner Mantrayana, and at midday, the unsurpassable teachings of the result, namely, the Great Perfection. Amoghasiddhi, for his part, sets forth the guiding instructions in the evening. At midnight, he gives teachings of empowerment. At dawn, he gives teachings on conduct and, at midday, on the view and meditation.

In the central position in the midst of these buddhafields, there is, suspended in the air, the buddhafield of the Glorious Heruka, the great charnel ground known as the Mount of Flaming Fire. Its palace is a square fortress contrived of skulls. Its bricks are skulls and of these, superimposed, its walls are made. The ends of the roof beams are adorned with skulls with hair. The height and surface of the fortress is immeasurable. Everything in the fortress is held together with nails of meteoric iron. All is drenched in a gentle rain of blood. The bases of the pillars are the sun and moon; the capitals of the pillars are in the form of sea monsters. The main beams are the eight Mahadevas all stretched out, while the lesser crossbeams are made of human corpses. By day, there is a storm of wind; by night, a blazing fire rages. In the four corners are hoisted parasols contrived of human skin. Five goddesses tread their dance. The entire ground is but a turbulent lake of blood. Within the palace, there appears the Lord Kumaravirabalin, the "Powerful Youthful Hero." He is the secret form of him who inwardly is Vajradhara and, outwardly, none other than the Buddha Shakyamuni.

He has a form of wrath though his mind never parts from the state of peace. From this Teacher emanate Vajrapani and the other dakas, together with the peaceful dakini Purna, the Conch-Throated Brahma, and the Youthful Moonlight Sage, as well as the secondary retinues: the dakini Ekajati, together with the six sisters, their fourteen female attendants, fifty-eight maid servants with their attendants—thousands upon thousands of dakinis in measureless clouds. The Teacher is surrounded by a countless retinue of human teachers, Garab Dorje and so on, for whom he turns the wheel of Dharma of the unsurpassable Secret Mantrayana of the resultant level, whereby their minds are liberated.

Innumerable Bodhisattvas take miraculous birth from lotuses in those buddhafields and have the form of youthful gods and goddesses. They have perfected the unsurpassable yoga of the Secret Mantrayana and have become accomplished sages, endowed with twofold siddhi. They are free of dualistic thoughts of apprehended object and apprehending subject, and they are without any of the three aspects of the ordinary mind: the universal ground that contains all habitual tendencies, the defiled mind, and the five associated, functioning sense consciousnesses. They are also free of the six kinds of examining cognition that engenders delusion, as well as of the six root defilements. They are without the three kinds of ignorance and its four conditions. They are free of the main mind and mental factors concomitant with ignorance.

33   These buddhafields appear through the empowering strength of the Teacher, the Bhagavan Vajradhara, as the very character of luminosity (*rang bzhin nyid du bkod pa*). They are therefore known to the Bodhisattva Vidyādharas as the nirmanakaya buddhafields of luminous character. As for what causes the perception of these buddhafields, since they are the display of the spontaneous radiance of the precious, naturally luminous primordial wisdoms (mirrorlike wisdom and so forth) that dwell in the heart, and of the luminosity of the wrathful mandala that dwells primordially in the mansion of the skull, they appear on the secret path of the Natural Great Perfection for those who train themselves in manifest luminosity. This is explained in the *Tantra of Awareness Self-Arisen.*

7. The highest celestial pure lands[562]

34   Related to the nirmanakaya buddhafields of indwelling luminous character are the well-known pure lands of the Copper-Colored Mountain, Shambhala, Alakavati, and so forth. They appear in the pure perception of mantra practitioners, the practitioners of great bliss, and they are, as it were, symbolized by the twenty-four sacred lands. Eight of these are in the possession of the gods and gandharvas that live in the sky, and are therefore known as celestial pure lands (*mkha' spyod*). Eight are held by yakshas and rakshasas, who live on the earth, and are therefore called terrestrial pure lands (*sa spyod*). Finally, eight are held by nagas and by asuras who dwell inside Mount Meru, and others. They are consequently called subterranean pure lands (*sa 'og spyod*). These fields are the home of wisdom dakinis who have mastery of ultimate coemergent luminosity (*lhan cig skyes ma*). They are also inhabited by dakinis who were born there (*zhing skyes ma*) and also by the female practitioners of mantra (*sngags skyes ma*), who, thanks to their practice of the meditation and conduct of the Mantrayana, are able to go there, together with all the other awareness-holding dakas and yoginis. Through the practice of the Vajrayana path, they have awakened the power of their accumula-

tions of merit and wisdom. Endowed with the same fortune as those who belong to the retinue of Jetsun Mahaguru (Guru Rinpoche), the Lord of Secrets (Vajrapani), and so on, they join the ranks of the Vidyādharas, wherever they happen to be. There they train themselves in the remaining portions of the generation and perfection stages.

Regarding the vajra teachers, holders of awareness, who set forth these different paths, it cannot be said that they dwell in one sacred place or field, and not in another. For practitioners with devotion and pure perception, they truly dwell wherever the practitioners are. In their presence, the practitioners progress in the profound view of the Mantrayana, and are thus able to display powerful yogic activities. The Vidyādhara teachers perform various enlightened activities in different world-systems, working for beings and benefiting them according to their aspirations. They care for the faithful, and uproot deceptive, evil forces.

These pure lands appear for those whose devotion, pure perception, and other seeds of virtue are fully developed, and also for those who have purified their perception through the practice of the generation stage, and whose channels, essence-drops, and wind-mind have been refined through the accomplishment of the profound yogic practice of the perfection stage. They appear for those who have gained accomplishment and have mastery of the Secret Mantra. One should not think that these pure lands are specific, geographic locations in the common perception of all, to which ordinary individuals with impure thoughts can travel if they so wish. It should be understood that they appear only for those whose perception is pure.

5. The nirmanakaya guides of beings
6. The explanation of the guides themselves

From the dharmakaya, the state beyond conception, there appear spontaneously the sambhogakaya Buddhas from whose six centers stream forth luminous garlands of clouds of syllables, manifesting as the supreme nirmanakaya guides of beings in the six realms of every world system. This process is described in the *Heart-Essence of the Dakini:*

> From the tongues of the father-mother sambhogakaya deities emanate wheels of six syllables. These are (low) A, the sound of

ultimate reality beyond conceptual construction; (high) A, the sound of the purity that is the freedom from duality of the apprehended and apprehender; HA, the sound of self-arisen ultimate reality; SHA, the sound of unceasing wisdom (*shes rab*); SA, the sound of unchanging ultimate reality; and MA, the sound of the state of equality of ultimate reality. The wheels of six syllables link the main and intermediary directions of the six realms of billions of Jambudvipas. They emanate, in unbounded quantity, the "semi-nirmanakayas," which appear in the sambhogakaya mandala (that is, the nirmanakayas of luminous character), the six Munis (namely, the nirmanakaya guides of beings), as well as, in accordance with the perceptions of beings, the impure nirmanakayas, whether animate or "contrived." All of them work for the benefit of beings.

According to what has just been said, the nirmanakayas are displayed in accordance with the various perceptions of beings in the six realms, three higher and three lower. And according to the karmic fortune of the beings of these six realms, they manifest under different names, appearing for example as their kings, such as Indra, lord of the gods. These are the six guides or "sages of awareness," who have accomplished the Secret Mantra and are endowed with the major and minor marks. For example, Dharmaraja, with his fire and water, does not indeed dwell in the hell realm. It is only because of the specific perceptions of hell beings that he appears there. Although he and his retinue inflict torment, their purpose is to bring the suffering of beings to an end. It is therefore certain that they embody the enlightened activity of the Buddhas.[563] This is said in the auto-commentary.

36   The six Munis, manifesting [in different forms, such] as the great drum of the gods and so forth, according to the disposition of beings, appear equal in number to the countless beings who are found in infinite worlds of the great billionfold universal systems of the ten directions—which are arranged vertically like a flight of steps, or horizontally like an unfurled brocade of interconnected colors. The Munis strive in inconceivable ways for the benefit of beings, guiding them in the four ways, until the emptying of samsara.[564]

First, beings are guided by the supreme nirmanakaya through the great merit of his enlightened body. For he displays, among other things, the twelve great deeds whereby beings are benefited, such as his descent from Tushita.

Second, beings are guided by the supreme nirmanakaya by means of his enlightened speech. For with well-turned sentences and the sixty melodies of Brahma's voice, he constantly sets forth, for all to hear, the teachings either of the three vehicles of the Shravakas, Pratyekabuddhas, and Bodhisattvas, or the teachings of the sole and unsurpassed vehicle. The methods of entry into the Dharma accord with the varying dispositions of beings. Mindful of the remedies for the three defilements or poisons, the supreme nirmanakaya sets forth the Tripitaka. And mindful of the "fourth poison," which is the indiscriminate mingling of the previous three, he teaches the fourth pitaka of the Secret Mantra. Each of these four poisons has twenty-one thousand subdivisions. Consequently, each of the four pitakas taught by the supreme nirmanakayas comprises twenty-one thousand sections, so that there are, in all, eighty-four thousand means of entering the Dharma. These teachings are seemingly expounded, yet they are not the product of discursive thought, nor are they set forth in ordinary words pronounced by tongue or lip. Indeed, such teachings manifest in the realms of beings through the compassionate power of the Victorious One. For he declared, "No teachings have I given, yet teachings do appear for beings everywhere." As it is said, the enlightened speech appears in various guises for beings in accordance with their varying states of mind.

The third way in which the supreme nirmanakaya guides beings is by means of his enlightened mind. Free from attachment and impediment, and constantly throughout the three times, he knows and perceives beings who are to be helped, and also the best method and moment for doing so. The supreme nirmanakaya has the preternatural knowledge of the previous lives of beings. And yet, although the Buddha has a distinct knowledge of all phenomena—past, present, and to come—he does not reflect in an ordinary way, saying for instance, "This has happened in the past." For he knows primordial time, the fourth time, which has the nature of equality. This is the timeless, ultimate expanse, wherein the three times do not come into being and where the two kinds of obscuration and all habitual tendencies are no more. In other words, he has a perfect knowledge of the "wheel of inexhaustible ornaments of Samantabhadra's body, speech, and mind," and has the preternatural knowledge of the exhaustion of all stains. He has the preternatural knowledge of the states of others' minds, whether virtuous, sinful, or morally neutral, knowing them distinctly. He has the preternatural knowledge and ability of wondrous display, whereby he acts meaningfully according to beings' aspirations. He has the preternatural knowledge of the divine eyes, seeing with divine sight where the beings of all the worlds will be reborn when they die. He possesses the preternatural knowledge of the divine ears, whereby he perceives the sounds of all the universe. Altogether, he possesses six kinds of preternatural knowledge. Furthermore, he possesses the endless qualities of enlightened body, speech, and mind, such as the ten strengths of knowledge and so on— all of which can be summarized in these six kinds of preternatural knowledge, which are themselves the qualities of his enlightened mind. Thus Buddha's work for beings is ever timely, neither too late nor too soon by even a single moment.

39   The fourth way in which beings are helped refers to the inconceivable enlightened activities whereby the supreme nirmanakayas guide beings. According to the dispositions of those to be guided, they cause to appear, at all times, various enlightened bodies and buddhafields, such as the twenty-five buddhafields [located on the lotus in the hands of Buddha Vairochana Mahasagara]. And through the inconceivable secret of their minds, they have at all times mastery of the qualities of elimination and realization. Likewise, at all times, they show themselves with peaceful or wrathful countenances, and so forth. And at all times, they teach the Dharma with the infinite symbolic means of the inconceivable secret of their speech.

In this way, they secure the benefit of others by means of four methods of guiding. Through their enlightened body, speech, and mind, they bring about the benefit of beings directly, whereas through their enlightened activities, they achieve the benefit of beings both directly and indirectly. In short, their enlightened exploits are at all times spontaneous and unceasing.[565]

Thus, from within the expanse of the dharmakaya, there appears the 40
sambhogakaya, and from this there manifest the supreme nirmanakayas,
which free the minds of beings by means of their two primordial wisdoms. These two wisdoms are, first, the wisdom that, in relation to the
nature of phenomena, knows the nature as it is of everything. It is the
wisdom that knows profound and ultimate truth. Second is the wisdom
that in relation to phenomena sees all things in their multiplicity. It is
the wisdom that knows distinctly each and every phenomenon of the
relative truth. The supreme nirmanakayas reveal infinite ways of teaching endowed with four special features. They are meaningful; their
words are stainless; they eliminate the defilements; and they reveal the
benefits of ensuing peace. It is thus that the teachings of the Dharma are
not mixed—that is, they have nothing in common—with non-Buddhist
teachings.

6. The secondary emanations of the nirmanakaya guides of beings

The secondary emanations of the nirmanakaya guides are beyond 41
counting. Just as the number of beings is inconceivable, so too is the
number of these emanations. They manifest in all the states of existence
of the six classes of beings. In the various realms of the gods, they
appear as their respective Lords (Brahma, Indra, Vishnu, and so on),
guiding their attendant gods and removing their suffering. Likewise, in
the human realm, they appear as the Shravakas and Pratyekabuddhas
for those who are disposed to the Hinayana, as Bodhisattvas for those
who are drawn to the Mahayana, and as Chakravartin lords, kings, ministers, and so on, when it is appropriate for beings to be coerced by law
in the practice of the ten positive deeds. In the realm of the asuras, they
appear as Vemachitra and so on. Among the races of the birds, they
appear as the Woodpecker,[566] as the golden king of peacocks, as the
partridge, and others. For the animals of the wild, they appear as the
lion king Dridhasamadana,[567] as the Sharabha,[568] Kunda, and so on.
The display of their different emanations is inconceivable, including
even rocks and trees.

In short, they appear in whatever forms are suitable for the guiding 42
of beings, hell beings, pretas, and so forth; and their work for them is
always timely. Their assistance never fails through indolence or distraction.

Such appearances of the nirmanakaya occur in the countless fields of the six worlds of the ten directions. Referring to the six worlds, the *Guhyagarbha* says: "Because of karma there are six worlds where beings walk with heads upright, horizontal, or downward turned." The six worlds of these beings are square in shape, round, semicircular, triangular, flat, and without an upper covering. Speaking of the manner in which beings move, the *Avatamsaka* says: "The different kinds of karma are inconceivable. Hell beings walk with their heads down. The beings of the world of the Lord of Death [the world of the pretas] walk with their heads horizontal, while in the realms of animals, gods, and humans, they walk either upright or with their heads downward turned."

The various actions of beings of the six worlds—positive, negative, or a mixture of these two (together with the associated habits)—result in the various states of existence. In the heavens, the gods experience only pleasure, while the denizens of hell know only suffering. Other beings, such as humans, experience sometimes pleasure and sometimes pain. According to the perceptions of the deluded mind, the dwelling places of the gods, humankind, and so on, are found in the upper spheres, while the abodes of suffering are down below.

43   It is there that boundless emanations are displayed through the compassion of the Victorious Ones and in accordance with the varying perceptions of beings, whose benefit they contrive. The teaching of these emanations also varies, according to the disposition of beings to be guided. Generally, the Buddha's teachings are of three kinds: the teachings spoken by himself, the teachings blessed by him, and the teachings that he authorized. The teachings blessed by the Buddha are again said to be of three kinds, those blessed by his body, speech, and mind. Likewise, the agencies and means whereby such teachings are given are also different. As it is said in the *Compendium of Explanations*:

> By the blessing of this teacher,
> Teachings come from birds or bushes, tiny stones,
> From spotless lotuses or wishing trees, or drums.
> And since these have the Buddha's blessing,
> They are called the Buddha's words.

The *Verses that Summarize the Prajnaparamita Sutra* says:

> Whatever doctrines that the Hearers of the Conqueror
> Revealed, explained, set forth with reasoned argument,
> And which these high and noble ones
> Performed with ease, their fruit attaining,
> All came through the Tathāgata's power.
> For all the teachings that the Conqueror explained,
> His followers, these supreme beings, trained in them.
> They realized them and set them forth as they had learned—
> Not by their own, but by the Buddha's power.

The manner in which the teachings are given is also inconceivable. For this may be through neither sound nor word. For example, in the buddhafield Incense-All-Amassed, the Bodhisattvas dwell in the vicinity of a great frankincense tree. And as they inhale the fragrance of this tree, the concentration of "perfect freedom" arises in their minds. In other worlds, the Buddha's teaching is also transmitted through the ingestion of food; in others, it is through the wearing of the Dharma robe, by gazing at the Buddha's form, or by dreaming of him, and so forth. All this is inconceivable, as the *Ratnakuta* describes. The time when beings are guided is also indefinite. For it depends on the fortune—that is, the merit—of each and every being. Such are the ways in which the nirmanakayas appear to beings in the impure realms.

6. The illusion-like appearance of the nirmanakaya guides of beings

The appearances of different nirmanakaya guides arise for the sake of beings, thanks to the conjunction of the power of the Buddhas (who have recognized their own immaculate nature) and the aspirations and virtuous conduct of beings. The cognitive potency (*thugs rje*) of the three kayas of the expanse of inner luminosity arises as outward luminosity that manifests as the two form bodies of primordial wisdom and pure enlightened action, and especially, in the perception of ordinary beings, as the supreme nirmanakayas (the Lion of the Shakyas and so forth). These manifestations are no more than the mind's own self-experience,

44

as when one sleeps and perceives the Buddha in a dream. Their Dharma is like a teaching heard in a dream. And in such cases, both the Buddha (who is dreamed of) and the mind (that dreams) are without intrinsic being. The so-called Buddha has no other nature. The mind to which the Buddha appears is by nature luminosity devoid of self. And what appears as the Buddha is an empty form devoid of intrinsic being. One should understand that they are hollow and unreal, as the profound sutras say. The *Ratnakuta* declares:

> To dreamlike beings, dreamlike I appeared.
> The dharma I set forth, yet this too lacks reality;
> No other nature does it have.
> Understand that all is hollow, empty, and devoid of self.

Everything in samsara and nirvana is a dreamlike display. Even though the nirmanakaya Buddhas do appear to beings who may be guided, from the very beginning they have never stirred from the state of the dharmakaya endowed with twofold purity. They manifest in the manner of reflected forms, which appear appropriately to beings and within the framework of the truth of suffering. They have no intrinsic being. Samsara and nirvana are likewise without inherent existence: they are like illusions and dreams. And as such, the nirmanakayas, the display of compassion (*thugs rje*), appear to impure beings and in accordance with their disposition. And they do so uninterruptedly until the very emptying of samsara.

Neither Buddhas nor beings move from the sole ultimate expanse, which appears as nirvana or samsara to minds that are, respectively, pure and impure. Those who attain this fundamental nature are said to be great beings who behold suchness. The *Sutra of the Non-Arising of All Things* declares:

> Buddha, Dharma, Sangha: none of these exists.
> Wise are those who thus have understood.
> Beings are by nature the Enlightened, it is said;
> And the Enlightened are by nature beings.

Beings and the Enlightened are not different.
Supreme are those who thus have understood.

5. **The diversified nirmanakaya**
6. **The diversified nirmanakaya itself**
7. **The nirmanakaya that appears as inanimate objects**

The nirmanakaya of luminous character, as explained above, is regarded   45
in the sutra context as the sambhogakaya. The nirmanakaya of luminous
character gives rise to appearances that are not different from it in
nature, namely, the six Munis together with the diversified nirmanakaya,
animate and inanimate. The inanimate diversified nirmanakaya consists
of the supports of the enlightened body, speech, and mind that occur
naturally (without intentional contrivance) as mountains, rocks, valleys,
and so on. This also includes the array of the twenty-four sacred lands
and so on, as well as images and paintings of the body, speech, and
mind of the Tathāgatas, made by smiths, artists, the weavers of tapes-
tries, and so forth. All these are the activity of the Buddhas.[569] As it is
said in the sutra:

> Many forms are bodied forth,
> Bringing beings to virtuous deeds.

And as our compassionate teacher has specifically declared:

> When the final period of five hundred has arrived,
> I will come in form of scriptures.
> Show respect for them, considering them as me.

As it is said here, there is not the slightest difference between the
Buddha and the scriptures. Moreover, for those who wander in the
desert, where there are no viharas or monastic dwellings, no houses, no
gardens, or the necessities of life, the nirmanakaya manifests as cities,
lotus gardens with different flowers, wishing-trees and jewels that grant
all their needs and wants. When there is water to be crossed, it appears
in the form of rafts, ships, river-spanning bridges. And likewise, it appears as carriages for travel, food, clothing, and the rest. This nirmana-

kaya manifests according to need as any kind of inanimate object, dispelling sorrow and inviting happiness. And this is true even when, on account of one's obscurations, one fails to perceive that they are the nirmanakaya itself.

7. The animate nirmanakaya

46 The animate, or "born," nirmanakaya (*skye ba sprul sku*) brings benefit to beings both directly and indirectly. During a period of famine, it manifested as King Padma, who took birth as a great fish in order to satisfy his hungry subjects with his own flesh. When beings were suffering from incurable disease, it manifested as a certain kind creature that cured the sufferers with its own flesh. Once, when many people were in fear of their lives in the land of flesh-eating demonesses, it manifested as the wise horse Balaha, who saved them all from danger. For worms living in a filthy swamp, it appeared as a golden bee that taught them the Dharma with its buzzing. When the worms died, they were reborn in Sukhavati as Bodhisattvas with sweet breath. All such various manifestations bring about the immediate and ultimate happiness of beings, and they do so effortlessly and unintentionally. Such nirmanakayas are glorious, as has been explained. They bring great benefit and happiness to beings, whether directly on indirectly. As it is written in the *Sutra of the Hundred Actions*:

> The tides of serpent-crowded seas
> May fluctuate and change.
> Yet for his children, those whom he might train,
> The Buddha's acts are always timely.

6. Conclusion: the dissolution of the rupakaya's appearance
7. The dissolution of the nirmanakaya into the sambhogakaya

47 Enlightened activity arises from the ultimate expanse, and at length sinks back into that same expanse. When the time for guiding beings is passed—that is, when the work for beings of a specific Buddha is complete, and no beings remain, whether generally or in particular, that he or she might benefit—the form body of such a teacher dissolves into the ultimate expanse. The way this happens may be illus-

trated as follows. When there are no more vessels of water present on the ground, the reflection of the moon that appeared in them, as the root text says, "melts back," or is withdrawn into the basis from which it came, namely, the moon that is aloft in the sky. This means that, although the reflection does not actually merge with the moon, it vanishes without trace. In the same way, all the appearances of the nirmanakaya—from those perceived by beings, purely or impurely, right up to the nirmanakaya of luminous character—dissolve back into the actual, ultimate Akanishtha, the expanse of the sambhoga-kaya's exclusive self-experience. They become inseparable from it and are no longer perceptible.

7. The dissolution of the sambhogakaya into the dharmakaya

The following example illustrates the dissolution of the sambhogakaya's own field of experience into the dharmakaya. Beginning with the six-teenth day of the lunar month until the night of the new moon, as the moon reduces in size, it is not that the phase of one night is absorbed into the residual phase of the following night or that the sections simply disappear into nothing. Rather, the moon's outwardly glowing radiance is gathered back into a profoundly indwelling luminosity from which no light is outwardly projected. In the same way, the self-experienced sambhogakaya with its buddhafield are gathered back into the primordial wisdom of the dharmakaya, the inner, ultimate expanse that is utterly free of conceptual movement. As it is said in the *Illuminating Lamp:*

> The primal wisdom of the dharmakaya dwells within the ground.
> Inasmuch as it is knowing, it is illuminating,
> But here there is no coarse and apprehending thought.
> It is cognitive potency both natural and spontaneous.
> This state of knowing, luminous, aware,
> Subsists and does not merge with objects.

This state in which the wisdoms of the three kayas mingle in a single taste is considered (in the view of the Prasangika Madhyamaka) to be the supreme and ultimate cessation of the Buddhas where all the operations of the mind and mental factors, and even the extremely subtle dualistic appearance, subside into the dharmadhatu free from all conceptual construction—just as a fire dies out when the fuel is all consumed. This is not just the lesser and temporary cessation of the Arhats of the Hinayana, in which the subtle tendencies still remain. As it is written in the *Introduction to the Middle Way:*

> The tinder of phenomena is all consumed
> And this is peace, the dharmakaya of the Conquerors.
> There is no origin and no cessation.
> The mind is stopped, the kaya manifests. (9:17)

7. The abiding of the dharmakaya in the dharmadhatu

49   According to the teaching of the Natural Great Perfection, when adventitious obscurations and the eight consciousnesses (the mind and mental factors occurring within the three worlds) cease, self-cognizing primordial wisdom does not come to an end. All enlightened qualities remain unceasing, just as the rays of the sun. At the time of the ground,[570] they are concealed by veils of delusion. As the *All-Illuminating Essence Tantra* says:

> In the nighttime of the new moon,
> Though the moon is fully present,
> It is not seen because of the sun's power.
> From the first until the fifteenth day,
> It grows to fullness and then grows no more.
> Likewise, beings are never parted
> From the precious sphere,
> And yet, because of their delusions' strength,
> It cannot manifest.

As it has been said, practitioners on the path of learning gradually remove their obscurations and attain buddhahood. It is then that they actualize the inner luminosity, the state of the ever youthful vase body. This means that the form bodies, the aspects of outward luminosity, are absorbed into the dharmadhatu, which is indivisible from the subtle (in the sense of "hard to realize") primordial wisdom of inner luminosity. Yet the nature of this state is not, in itself, dull or obscured (*rmugs*). All the qualities of elimination and realization are fully perfect within it, just as when the moon is full. This is the highest achievement. There is nowhere to go beyond this. And in the very instant that beings to be guided appear (in whichever place or time), the kayas and enlightened activities of primordial wisdom of outwardly radiating luminosity endlessly and effortlessly unfold, the basis for this being provided by the unceasing radiance of the cognitive potency of inner luminosity.

This inconceivable, ultimate reality is set in a state of utter evenness, for all dualistic appearance has subsided into its expanse. This is the result possessed only by Buddhas, whose distinctive quality is to be always in a state of meditative equipoise; it is the state of the great spontaneous presence of all enlightened qualities. In the unborn, ultimate, sky-like expanse, the kayas and wisdoms are spontaneously present. They are unchanging, neither decreasing nor increasing. They are like the sun and its rays.

The manner in which, on completion of the teaching of the *Guhyagarbha-tantra*, the wisdom mind of the Buddha Samantabhadra remained poised in the dharmatā is described by Longchenpa in his commentary on that same tantra:[571]

> In this way he expounded the *Guhyagarbha*. The Tathāgatas of the five families (the sambhogakaya's exclusive self-experience) are displayed within the state of luminosity. They are as numerous as the seeds in a sesame pod and pervade the whole of space. Samantabhadra does not consider them, in a dualistic manner, to be different from himself; he rests content in their indivisibility. He dwells in a state that is unchanging throughout the three times. For these times are exhausted; they have expired in the ground, the spontaneously present nature. He dwells in the fourth time, the wheel of ultimate reality. This ultimate expanse of equality appears as a buddhafield that is devoid of both center and circumference. Its array is by nature the wheel of the inexhaustible ornaments of the body, speech, and mind of the Teacher, Samantabhadra. This "Densely Adorned Array" will be in the future what it was already in the

past. Its nature is as unchanging as space, free from both increase and decrease.

1. **The virtuous conclusion**
2. **The circumstances that make possible the composition
of shastras**

The composition of shastras and commentaries on the Buddha's words, written through the power of one's own wisdom, requires, generally speaking, the presence of three factors. Jigme Lingpa, the composer of this text, declares that he made a full examination of himself regarding his qualities of mind, his attainment of the noble grounds of realization, and so on. And none of the requisite qualities just mentioned was found to be lacking.

All the learned and accomplished masters of India and Tibet, themselves the authors of commentaries, were Bodhisattvas and disciples of the Buddha. Their spiritual attainments rendered them the Buddha's regents and holders of the treasury of his teachings. They were thus equipped to compose treatises on the utterances and intended meaning of the Enlightened One.

This is true also in the present case. When Jigme Lingpa was striving in the practice at Samye Chimpu, he received the blessing of the body of the omniscient Drimé Özer, the lord of the three worlds and the future Buddha Sumerudhipadhvaja. In other words, he beheld the face of the wisdom body of Gyalwa Longchenpa like a reflection appearing in a limpid pool. He received the blessing of Longchenpa's speech and was thereby authorized to compose this treatise. And he received the mind blessing whereby his mind and the mind of Longchenpa mingled inseparably. When he was thus blessed in body, speech, and mind, Jigme Lingpa was inspired with Longchenpa's compassion so that the courage to compose this treatise arose in him. Had he not received in this way the transmission of such extraordinary qualities, his actions would have caused him to wander from the path of freedom into the abyss of samsara, thus wasting his precious human existence, that excellent support endowed with freedoms.

Jigme Lingpa indeed possessed all three qualifications required for the composition of treatises, and therefore his explanations are faultless and unerring. Thanks to his Guru's blessing and the wisdom arising from his meditation, he directly beheld the truth of the dharmatā. Having seen it, he was united inseparably with his yidam deity, and there arose quite naturally within him the wisdom that distinguishes the two truths within objects of knowledge. It was on the basis of all these qualifications that Jigme Lingpa composed his work, and he was free of any sense of proud superiority that might derive from a work of ordinary intelligence founded on study and reflection, relying on inferential reasoning and without a direct vision of ultimate reality. His treatise is therefore without a flaw. Even so he declares that, if his work seems to contradict the scriptural traditions upheld by the holders of the various tenet systems, he confesses all such faults and begs for forgiveness.

The meaning of the expedient and definitive teachings, ocean-vast, of the Victorious One, the profundity of which is hard to sound, can be understood only by resting evenly in the state of ultimate reality. It is realized only by the primordial wisdom that knows suchness as it truly is and the wisdom that comprehends without error all phenomena in their multiplicity. Without these two wisdoms, any understanding will be partial and inexact. But Jigme Lingpa says of himself that he has actualized the primordial wisdom of the twofold knowledge and has perfectly beheld the deep meaning of the sacred texts. This therefore is a guarantee that if one approaches his book with the three kinds of wisdom [deriving from hearing, reflection, and meditation], and if one puts its teaching into practice, one will never be misled.

2. The dedication of the merit of composition

By the power of the merit resulting from his composition, Jigme Lingpa expresses the wish that he and all beings might board the great ship, the excellent path of the great vehicle of both the sutras and tantras of the faultless tradition of the Victorious One, which cleanses away the impurity of the two obscurations. And he prays that he and all beings might come swiftly to the sacred island of the jewellike qualities of the dharmakaya and rupakaya: the state of the final result, the state of great enlightenment in which the stains of the two extremes completely disappear.

And until this is attained, he makes the wish that he, and indeed all of us, might dwell in lovely forest glades, valleys of healing plants, where all kinds of wild animals disport and play. May we live in places where, with the passage of the seasons, the trees clothe themselves with a raiment ever new, and utter never a sound to upset the wise yogis dwelling there. May we live in places where birds delight the heart with their different voices, and with their soft, sweet calls urge the minds of yogis to liberation—driven on by the power of their weariness with samsara (coiling like a venomous serpent in the roots of a tree) and by their determination to leave it. Amid such sweet incitations, and thanks to all the other excellent qualities of forest dwellings, may the distractions of our senses be completely stilled, and may we attain the perfect glory of that meditative concentration that is the union of calm abiding and profound insight.

In brief, may our view (the realization of the fundamental nature of all things) be firm like a lion, unshaken by the hurricane of thoughts that hold to ontological extremes. And may the actions of our body, speech, and mind follow like a fox in the footsteps of the guardians of beings, the children of the Conqueror's heart, the Bodhisattvas who are mighty in the world. From this time onward, therefore, in all our lives to come, may we never be a burden for other beings. May we never harm even a single pore of their flesh. With skillful and powerful activities, and in fitting ways, direct and indirect, may we become a glory of happiness and benefit for all beings without end—for all of them without exception.

At the request of Chöje Drakpuk-pa of Latö in Tsang, this *Rain of Joy*, this *Treasury of Precious Qualities*, was composed by a Dzogchen yogi who touched with the crown of his head the dust of the feet of the second Buddha, Padmasambhava, the great and glorious master of Oddiyana. This same yogi realized the fundamental nature of the ultimate and *self-arisen vajra* (*rang byung rdo rje*), the primordial wisdom of the space-like dharmakaya. The mandala of his *knowledge and love* (*mkhyen brtse*), the primordial wisdom of the sambhogakaya, has come to full flower. And the myriad beaming rays of light (*'od zer*) of his enlightened activities, the work of the nirmanakaya, show forth the path to beings in accordance with their needs. This same Rangjung Dorje Khyentse

Özer, also known as Jigme Lingpa, holder of the vidya-mantras and yogi of the vast expanse, composed this text in the lonely place of Tsering Jong, in the uncontrived palace of luminosity, Pelden Pema Öling.

2. Colophon

Great expanse and self-arisen vajra, primal purity,
Lotus grove of qualities of spontaneous luminosity,
Great upholder of awareness-creativity,
The play of great primordial wisdom,
Inseparable three kayas, Jigme Lingpa, care for us!

The deeds of your compassion take on perfect form,
The image of the dharmakaya you have realized,
Within this *Treasury of Precious Qualities,*
This perfect shrine of Buddha's teaching.
Its path you have explained,
Unfolding it in joyful glory for the fortunate.

For those of confused mind
Who enter in the grove of perfect Dharma,
Who journey on the pathways of the three inerrant vehicles,
It is an unmistaken guide that easily and swiftly
Leads us to the land of supreme primal wisdom,
And with its perfect explanations
Has restored the youthful strength and beauty
Of the children of the gods.

This jewellike looking glass where words and sense are clarified
Will set on us the mark of hearing, thought, and meditation,
And be a joyful feast for all like-minded spiritual friends.

With thoughts like these, I make the wish
That this book be the eyes of all who journey on the road to
    freedom!

May there be an increase in the three activities,
Whereby the doctrine of the supreme vehicle
Is both taught and realized!
May all the beings of this age of dregs be rich with glorious bliss!
And through the following of this good and perfect text,
Through explanation, study, and assimilation,
May I and others gain the twofold goal!

The vajra master Ngawang Drakpa Tendzin, Longchen Yeshe Dorje (Kangyur Rinpoche), who was a powerful lord of learning and accomplishment endowed with the highest qualities of elimination and realization, composed a series of commentarial notes inserted into the root text of the *Treasury of Precious Qualities.* These were copied out and arranged into a single text that, in the process of its redaction, was supplemented by certain additional notes that seemed appropriate. Finally, as the text was going to press, and at the repeated request of the sons of my Lord's body, speech, and mind, as well as of his consort and daughters, and also of his faithful disciple Konchok Tendzin, I, Mangala Shribhuti, who am numbered also among this master's disciples, composed the introductory and concluding verses, in the monastery of Kunzang Chökhorling, Darjeeling. May this be for the service and furtherance of the Supreme Vehicle.

APPENDIX 1 ⌇

The Three Transmissions of Kahma, the Orally Transmitted Teachings

The kahma, the long lineage of orally transmitted teachings, consists of three kinds of transmission:[572] first, the mind transmission
of the Buddhas (*rgyal ba dgongs pa'i brgyud pa*);[573] second, the knowledge
transmission of the Vidyādharas (*rig 'dzin rig pa'i brgyud pa*);[574] and third,
the hearing transmission of spiritual masters (*gang zag rna bar brgyud pa*).[575]

1. The mind transmission of the Buddhas

The Teacher Samantabhadra is primordially enlightened. The infinite
display of his cognitive potency (*thugs rje*)[576] manifests as the pure fields
of all the Buddhas, the sacred places, and the Teachers appearing in
the four kayas.[577] Samantabhadra's retinue, which is not different from
himself, is composed of the spontaneously accomplished Vidyādharas
endowed with the five kayas, and of inconceivably infinite hosts of Victorious Ones. To them, Samantabhadra does not teach the Dharma by
means of word and symbol. He expounds without expounding, within
the natural, effortless luminosity of great cognitive potency, the radiance
of self-cognizing primordial wisdom. And the retinue unerringly actualizes ultimate wisdom, with qualities of elimination and realization that
are inseparable from Samantabhadra himself. Thus without stirring
from the state in which the mind of the Teacher and the minds of his
retinue are indistinguishable, he causes three great manifestations to
appear within the realms of those to be guided.

The first of these is *the manifestation appearing in the manner of bodily emanations*, which benefit beings in ways appropriate to their karmic fortune.
These emanations are the nirmanakaya of luminous character (*rang bzhin
sprul pa*),[578] the nirmanakaya guide of beings (*'gro 'dul sprul pa*),[579] and the
diversified nirmanakaya (*sna tshogs sprul pa*).[580]

The second is *the manifestation appearing in the manner of speech emanations.*
Within the expanse of the three indivisible secrets of emptiness,[581] the

syllable A spontaneously manifests. It is the symbol of the Unborn,[582] and from it all the vowels and consonants unfold. It is thus that ultimate wisdom (*don gyi dgongs pa*), wherein the signifying and the signified are one and the same, appears as a "host of syllables,"[583] which are its indications and are the means whereby the welfare of beings is spontaneously accomplished. Apt to appear in verbal form,[584] this ultimate wisdom, spontaneously luminous in the vast expanse of the mind of [Samantabhadra] the Teacher of the sixth family, and made to arise in the minds of the Buddhas of the five families, is communicated[585] in words by Vajrapani and others,[586] Teachers perceptible to other beings. These teachings were set down in writing by [the rakshasa] Matyaupayika and others, and have been gradually passed down to us. And similarly, even now at the present time, teachers expound the meaning contained in these ancient scriptures and that appears in their minds in the form of "term-universals" (*sgra phyi*), so that, through the medium of language, this same meaning appears in the minds of us, their hearers. This is the emanation of the Tathāgatas' speech, the wondrous activity of the "wheel of syllables."[587]

The third *manifestation* is that which appears in the *manner of mind emanations.* Samantabhadra's undeluded wisdom, the fundamental nature that is apt to be expressed in verbal form, empowers his retinue, which is not different from himself, so that this wisdom is perfectly assimilated thereby. Ordinary beings, however, cannot realize the ultimate in this way. But so that they might remain in suchness, finding rest from the stream of their thoughts, Samantabhadra reveals, in the vast expanse of his wisdom, the teachings of the unsurpassable vehicle of the Great Secret. For those who are without the karmic fortune to realize the ultimate state directly, this vehicle appears rather as a system of vehicles arranged in stages, which gradually introduce and indicate the profound meaning.

1. The knowledge transmission of the Vidyādharas

This lineage of transmission has descended gradually to fortunate beings, both divine and human. The nonhuman transmission of the Vidyādharas has descended from the Lords of the three families, who bestowed teachings in the realms of gods, nagas, and yakshas. Manjushri Kumara instructed the god Yashasvi Varapala (*grags ldan phyogs skyong*); Avalokiteshvara instructed the naga-king Takshaka (*mgrin pa nag po*); and Vajrapani instructed the yaksha Samantabhadra (*kun tu bzang po*). And these teachings gradually spread.

The following history applies to both the human and nonhuman transmission lineages of the Vidyādharas. In the Fortunate Kalpa, this present age, our Teacher Shakyamuni, the fourth of the thousand Buddhas to come (and who is identical with the Buddha of the sixth family),[588] expounded the teachings of the Tripitaka. To some extremely fortunate beings[589] he also bestowed the teachings of the Secret Mantra, although he did not give such teachings openly. Shortly before he passed beyond sorrow, he said: "My disciples! You who have great miraculous powers and who practice the Dharma in the ten directions of the six worlds, come! For I have something to give you." And those who had miraculous powers heard and understood these words:

> Wherever you might be within the six realms—
> Fields of the Victorious Ones,
> Turn to me and lend your ears.
> This day the Conqueror will grant a threefold nectar.
> All you who wish to vanquish the three poisons
> Should assemble here.

And all, with the exception of the five noble beings of sublime lineage,[590] came into the presence of the Buddha, who declared that for those who still had doubts, the time had come to ask their questions; for his nirvana was at hand. Then Kujara, king of Vidyādharas, rose from his seat, assumed the posture of a gazing lion,[591] looked upon the Teacher's countenance and said:

> You have the nature of the sky itself
> And are beyond "to die" and "not to die."
> In keeping with the world you now intend
> To lay your life aside, thus teaching us.
> Full well you have expounded, stage by stage,

Three vehicles of teaching that will lead
To the attainment of enlightenment
Through gaining of the grounds and perfect freedoms.[592]
Yet your final teaching you have not set forth:
The great, unbounded skillful means
Whereby all things are seen as equal,
Neither to be taken nor rejected.
Nowhere else should buddhahood be sought.

In answer to this and other requests, the Buddha said:

After I have passed away and in this world am no more seen,
When eight and twenty years have run their course,
The sacred essence of those teachings
That in three celestial realms are now proclaimed,[593]
Will be revealed, foreshadowed by auspicious signs,
To Ja, the king, most high and fortunate of men,
Who reigns upon the eastern marches of this land.
And on the mountain known as Hill of Terror,
Vajrapani will expound it to the Lord of Lanka
And to his fellows, those of lesser rank.

"To be sure," the Buddha continued, "the great vehicle of ultimate suchness appears on twelve occasions.[594] (1) It arises to dispel the suffering of not knowing.[595] (2) It arises when the lamp of the world is kindled.[596] (3) It appears when ultimate certainty is attained.[597] (4) It appears for beings who are on the point of enlightenment. (5) It appears when the ultimate view [of great purity and equality] is accurately expounded.[598] (6) It appears when beings are ready to receive it.[599] (7) It appears as a result of blessings.[600] (8) It appears when the transmission lineage is skillfully propagated.[601] (9) It appears for the sake of certain persons.[602] (10) It appears following a prediction.[603] (11) It appears in order to sever a stream of powerful karma.[604] (12) It appears when the meaning of the tantras is expounded."[605]

The knowledge transmission of the Vidyādharas is composed of three streams of transmission: Mahayoga, Anuyoga, and Atiyoga.

2. The transmission lineage of Mahayoga, the system of tantra[606]

As the Buddha prophesied in the above quotation with the words "When eight and twenty years have run their course" and "The great vehicle of ultimate suchness arises to dispel the suffering of not knowing," the tantras of the Mahayoga were propagated in the following way.

Twenty-eight years after the Buddha's passing, King Ja beheld in his dreams seven omens. Later, on the roof of his palace, he discovered an image, one cubit high, of Vajrapani, together with a great number of precious volumes of the tantras of the Secret Mantra. The pages of the books were of precious gold, with letters written in melted lapis lazuli. King Ja prayed, and as a result was able to understand the chapter known as the *Vision of Vajrasattva*. He meditated on this text for six months, using the stanzas and the image of Vajrapani as a support for his practice. At length, he beheld Vajrasattva in a vision and received his blessing; and the meaning of the tantras appeared perfectly to his understanding.

King Ja expounded them to the master Kukkuraja, who transmitted them to Simharaja. The latter taught them to Uparaja, who in turn expounded them to his daughter Gomadevi. Until that point, all these lineage holders became Vidyādharas, together with all the beings in their vicinity.[607] This transmission of extraordinary knowledge was unbroken, and it inaugurated the knowledge transmission of the Vidyādharas.

2. The transmission lineage of Anuyoga, the system of explanatory teaching[608]

It was at that time also that, on the summit of Mount Malaya, five noble beings of sublime lineage[609] invoked the Buddhas of the ten directions, chanting a devotional hymn of twenty-three lines that began:

> Alas, alas, sorrow and grief,
> Now that the Teacher's shining lamp has set,
> Who will drive away the darkness of the world?

The Tathāgatas therefore invoked Guhyapati, Lord of Secrets,[610] who, on the peak of Mount Malaya, set forth for the five noble beings the *Scripture of Summarized Wisdom* and other texts. Thanks to the blessing of this teaching, all the tantras of the Anuyoga, the system of explanatory teaching, appeared and were subsequently practiced in the forests of Simhala, the land of Lanka. A transmission lineage from King Ja also exists. At Dhanakosha also, in the western land of Oddiyana, Vajrapani expounded the glorious secret tantra, the *Guhyagarbha,* with its pith instructions, together with the tantras of *Kila, Matarah (Mamo),* and others, to the nirmanakaya Garab Dorje. All these transmissions came down to Padma Thödrengtsel of Oddiyana, and it was from him that they gradually spread.

2. The transmission lineage of Atiyoga, the system of pith instructions[611]

Atiyoga was first propagated in the celestial realms in the following manner. At the urging of all the Buddhas, there appeared from the heart of glorious Vajrasattva a shining wheel of jewels, and this he gave to Sattvavajra,[612] saying:

> The hidden sense of nondual primal wisdom,
> Primordial buddhahood beyond all action and exertion,
> This path renowned as the Great Middle Way
> Reveal to the assembly gathered here.

And Sattvavajra pledged himself to teach, saying:

> Vajrasattva, vastness of the sky!
> Hard it is for me to speak
> Of what exceeds the range of words.
> And yet for those who have not grasped the sense
> I shall use words as signs, wherewith to point it out,
> That they may understand
> And, by well-suited practice, be set free.

Thus he spoke. Then, in consultation with the Buddhas of the five families, he removed all misconceptions regarding every aspect of the Atiyoga: the marvelous essence of the teachings, the ultimate wisdom beyond exertion, which arises spontaneously and transcends the law of cause and effect. He thus distilled the essence of the wisdom of the Conquerors. In the Heaven of the Thirty-Three, on the pinnacle of the palace called All-Victorious, he then transmitted, through the use of symbols, this same wisdom, entirely and in an instant, through direct empowerment granted in the manner of a king,[613] to Adhichitta, the son of the god Devabhadrapala. He taught him, completely and in the shortest possible instant of time, a large number of tantras and pith instructions, and empowered him as the foremost regent of the Buddhas. He then proclaimed:

> May this marvelous essence of the teachings,
> Now expounded in the three realms of the gods
> Be propagated in the central land of Jambu
> By my heart son, emanation of an emanation.[614]

It was thus that the doctrine spread throughout the three realms of the gods.

The Atiyoga teachings appeared in the human world in the following manner. To the west of India, in Oddiyana, the land of dakinis, there dwelt a king called Uparaja and his queen Alokabhashvati. Their daughter, Bright Flower, had been ordained and, living in community with five hundred nuns, she perfectly observed her vows. Now Adhichitta (the god's son) was transformed into the syllable HUNG by Vajrapani (who had taken the form of a swan, the king of birds), and he melted into the princess's heart. And at length, when the princess had reached her time (although there had been no visible signs of pregnancy), there sprang from her breast a gleaming nine-pronged vajra, which disappeared, leaving in its place a child, whose body displayed the major and minor marks of buddhahood. He held a vajra in his right hand and a wand of precious substances in his left, and recited the verse that begins "Vajrasattva, vastness of the sky." And since all were happy to see him and he was holding a vajra, they named him Garab Dorje, the Vajra of Supreme Joy. Since everyone was delighted, they called him Gyépa Dorje, Vajra of Delight, and as he was laughing, they named him Shepa Dorje, Laughing Vajra. When at length, Garab Dorje ascended the throne, Vajrapani appeared in person and bestowed on him, completely and in a single instant, the empowerment in the manner of a king. In one moment, he transmitted to him all the tantras and pith instructions, such as the twenty-thousand volumes of the Nine Expanses,[615] empowering him as the holder of the Doctrine. And oath-bound protectors were set as guardians of the teachings.

Then the nirmanakaya Garab Dorje transmitted the ultimate wisdom, simply by a symbolic indication, to Jampel Shenyen (Manjushrimitra), who completely and immediately assimilated it. He then bestowed on him the complete range of tantras and pith instructions. Jampel Shenyen transmitted these in turn to Shri Simha, who also attained the highest realization. When requested, Shri Simha transmitted the same teachings to the Second Buddha of Oddiyana, the scholar Jnanasutra, and the great pandita Vimalamitra. All these masters obtained complete realization simply by means of symbolic indications, and they all attained the supreme level of Vidyādhara. This is why this lineage is renowned as the Vidyādhara transmission through symbols.

i. The hearing transmission of spiritual masters

Princess Gomadevi transmitted all the Mahayoga tantras to the later Kukkuraja, to Lilavajra, and to Buddhaguhya. The latter two transmitted them to Vimalamitra, and from him they gradually spread. The Anuyoga transmission that passed through King Ja is slightly different from the one previously stated. As far as concerns Tibet, it is recorded that Nubchen Sangye Yeshe journeyed to India, where he requested and received from the master Prakashalamkara the empowerments and instructions of the Anuyoga tantras, while from Dhanarakshita and others he principally requested the textual explanation of the tantras. He then returned to Tibet, where he transmitted them to Nub Yönten Gyamtso. This constitutes one lineage. There also exists a second lineage descending from Su Legpa'i Drönme, which was handed down generation by generation in the Zur clan. This transmission resembles that of the Mahayoga tantras.

The propagation of the sutras and tantras generally in Tibet occurred in the following way. The first king of Tibet was the son of the Indian king Shatanika. He came to Tibet, where he was known as the Lord Nyatri Tsenpo. He was an emanation of the Bodhisattva Sarvanivara-navishkambhin (*sgrib pa rnam sel*). The sacred Dharma first came to Tibet many generations later, in the reign of Lhathothori Nyentsen, who was himself an emanation of the Bodhisattva Samantabhadra. Five generations later, in the reign of Songtsen Gampo, an emanation of Avalo-kiteshvara, the precious tradition of the Buddhadharma was implanted in Tibet. Again after five generations, King Trisong Detsen, an emanation of Noble Manjushri, invited a hundred and eight panditas from India. Under his aegis also, these same panditas, assisted by a body of Tibetan translators, who were themselves emanations, rendered into Tibetan the teachings of the sutras and tantras. The abbot Shantarakshita set forth the doctrines of the Vinaya and the sutras, while the masters Padmasambhava and Vimalamitra established the teachings of the Secret Mantra. It was thus that the precious Doctrine of the Buddha, of the sutras and the tantras, spread and filled Tibet like the light of the rising sun.

At that time also, Padmasambhava, the Second Buddha of Oddiyana, and the great pandita Vimalamitra gave instructions to their closest disciples: the King, the Subject, and the Companion (namely, Trisong Detsen, Vairotsana, and Yeshe Tsogyal), together with Nyangwen Tingdzin Zangpo and other fortunate disciples—all of them ready vessels for the teaching. They turned the Dharma-wheel of the three inner classes of tantra, in particular the Great Perfection or Atiyoga, clearly indicating the three key aspects of differentiation (*shan 'byed*), clear certainty (*la bzla*), and spontaneous freedom or self-subsiding (*rang grol*).[616] These teachings have gradually come down to our own teachers, and constitute the hearing transmission of spiritual masters.

[*Taken from the commentary of Yönten Gyamtso, YG III, 9–21*]

APPENDIX 2 ≈

The Manner in Which the Tantras Are Expounded

1. How the teacher is to teach

Aparticular feature of the Secret Mantra is the use of six exegetical perspectives (*mtha' drug*) and four expository methods (*tshul bzhi*) in order to determine the meaning of the teachings. When the latter have been correctly understood by means of such methods, they can be expounded to others in accordance with their aspirations. The six exegetical perspectives and the four ways of exposition in fact correspond to the third and fourth of the seven "ornaments" specified as methods for expounding the Mahayoga.[617] However, all the general inner tantras of the Secret Mantra, as well as the treatises of essential instructions appertaining to them,[618] should be set forth without contradicting the six perspectives and four ways just mentioned.

2. The six exegetical perspectives

The *Heruka Galpo Tantra* says:

> These are the six perspectives of extensive explanation:
> The expedient sense and the definitive,
> The meanings indirect and direct,
> And explicit statement and the metaphorical.

The sense is said to be expedient (*drang don*) or definitive (*nges don*) in relation to the text's intended meaning. The meaning is said to be direct (*dgongs min*) or indirect (*dgongs pa*), depending on the words used. Finally, a statement is regarded as explicit (*sgra ji bzhin pa*) or metaphorical (*sgra ji bzhin ma yin pa*) on the basis of the meanings and the words together.

According to the first pair of perspectives (expedient and definitive), it is possible—depending on whether or not the disciple has the proper karmic fortune—to use a single vajra statement to teach two distinct things. If one uses it to expound the generation stage with all its subsections, it constitutes an expedient teaching, whereas if one uses it to explain, for example, the causal continuum (or tantra) and the perfection stage, it expresses the definitive meaning. Thus a single tantric text may be expounded on two different levels, outer and inner.[619]

With regard to the second two perspectives, when a single vajra statement expresses two different meanings referring to the generation or perfection stage, with words that seem in contradiction, so that one is forced to interpret it according to an underlying sense, the teaching in question is said to be indirect. For example, we find in the *Guhyagarbhatantra:*

> As very subtle, uttermost samaya,
> Trace upon the palm of Mahamudra
> The sacred mandala of Mind
> And make of it a span four-fingers wide.

This is to be understood as a reference to the expanse of the mother and the four joys.[620] If, on the other hand, the sense is clearly intelligible by means of formulations that express it openly, with the result that one is not obliged to search for an underlying meaning, then the teaching in question is direct.

As for the last two perspectives, explicit statements describe, for instance, the external mandala and rituals like the fire offering, with words used according to their generally accepted sense, both in common parlance and in the language of the commentaries. By contrast, metaphorical statements describe extraordinary, powerful activities in words that are not employed according to their usual sense, whether in ordinary language or technical language. For example, "union" and "liberation" are referred to as "vowels and consonants," whereas the process of reversing the red constituent by skillful means is indicated in the *Word-Transcending Tantra* with the words:

> The nature of the distilled flower
> Is said to melt into the mouth of the Lord.

2. The four ways of exposition

The *Heruka Galpo* speaks of four senses: the literal (*tshig gi don*), the general (*spyi'i don*), the hidden (*sbas don*), and the ultimate (*mthar thug gi don*).

The first way of exposition, that of the literal sense, evaluates the meaning of the words expounded according to the conventions of grammar and logic.

The second way of exposition, that of the general sense, covers the teachings common to the sutras and the tantras. For example, to a disciple who is put off by the practice of the slow and arduous path of the sutras (as compared with the swift and easy path of Mantra), it will be pointed out that the sutra path is a step toward the mantra path. By contrast, it may happen that someone is put off by the mantra path, thinking that it makes no distinction between clean and unclean in the manner of dogs and swine. Such a person might also consider that "union" and "liberation" and so forth are the practices of heathens, for harmful actions are advocated as part of the spiritual path. In such cases, it must be pointed out that, on the sutra path also, if one fails to give up clinging to the concepts of "pure" and "impure," the realization of the equality of all phenomena will never be attained. And it can be further said that anything done with a truly positive attitude, devoid of all clinging, results in the accumulation of merit, as when Captain Goodheart increased his merit by slaying the Black Spearman. Thus, since these teachings are common to both the sutras and tantras, they belong to the general way of exposition. Likewise, since the teachings on the meditation on celestial palaces, deities, and so forth are common to the generation and perfection stages, they are also of a general meaning.

The third way of exposition, that of the hidden sense, concerns yogas such as union with a mudra (that is, the body of a partner), or the harnessing of the channels, winds, and essence-drops of one's own body. All this is explained on the level of the hidden meaning. These teachings are also referred to as "hidden" because they are situated midway between the general meaning and the ultimate meaning, and are like the heart within the body.[621]

The fourth way of exposition, that of the ultimate sense, sets forth the ultimate wisdom of luminosity and the fundamental nature, the union of the two truths—the realization of which expresses the final point of the path and the result. All the meanings mentioned previously find their consummation in the ultimate teachings, which is another reason for their being so called.

Explicit statements, the commonly direct explanation, the expedient sense, the literal sense, and the general meaning, all concern the generation stage and may be taught to a large assembly of people (*tshogs bshad*). Metaphorical expressions, the definitive sense, the indirect meaning, the hidden sense, and the ultimate sense concern the perfection stage and are teachings to be given only to specific disciples (*slob bshad*). The extraordinary direct explanation is included in the hidden and final teachings. The teachings must be given in the manner thus described and in accordance with the capacity of the disciples. The teachers must not expound simply according to the ideas that arise in their own minds and according to their predilections, for this would not be helpful for the disciple, and the secret of the teachings would thus be violated.

1. **How disciples are to receive the teaching**
2. **Mental attitude**

Disciples must adopt the vast attitude of bodhichitta, together with the vast and skillful attitude of the Secret Mantra.

All beings who wander in samsara have buddhahood as their nature from the very beginning, and yet this is veiled by adventitious, delusory thoughts. As a result, they suffer, being tormented by their karma. One must come to the sincere and heartfelt decision that, in order to liberate beings within the primordial place of freedom, one will act on a vast scale so that not even the name of samsara will be left. It is with this objective that, having entered the profound and swift path of the vajra vehicle of the Secret Mantra, one must resolve to remove all misconceptions through hearing and reflecting on the teachings. One must resolve to rely on the profound key points of the generation and perfection stages, and to train oneself in the six transcendent perfections of the Mantrayana, implementing them by means of meditative training.

Moreover, the Mantrayana is a swift path, for it is rich in profound and skillful means. It is based on the transformation of perception that results from bringing the mind into harmony with its fundamental nature. This is why disciples must remind themselves that the place where the teachings are given and received is not an impure location. It is the perfect realm of Akanishtha, the palace of the dharmadhatu. The teacher is in turn regarded as the perfect Teacher, the dharmakaya Samantabhadra. The disciples are the perfect retinue: the male and female Tathāgatas belonging to the mind transmission lineage of the Victorious Ones, and the male and female Bodhisattvas[622] of the Vidyādhara lineage of transmission through symbolic indication. The teaching is the perfect doctrine of the unsurpassable vehicle, the ultimate wisdom of natural luminosity. The time is perfect also; it is the revolving wheel of everlasting continuity. It is important to bear all this in mind. To consider things in this way is not a species of make-believe, a mental fabrication of something that is not there. On the contrary, it is to see things as they really are.

The teacher is indeed the embodiment of the three kayas, the essence of the Three Jewels and the Three Roots. He or she is the emanation of the Buddhas of the past, the source and wellspring of the Buddhas of the future, and the representative of the Buddhas of the present. It is the teacher who cares for the beings of this decadent age, untamed even by the thousand Buddhas of this Fortunate Kalpa—thereby excelling them all in kindness and compassion, while being their very equal in the qualities of enlightenment. As for the disciples, they possess the sugatagarbha as their ground. They possess the support of a precious human body. They have a favorable situation, in other words, the proximity of a spiritual teacher. And finally, they have skillful means: the reception of the teachings and instructions. There is no doubt therefore that they are the Buddhas of the future. Furthermore, the place, time, and teachings are perfectly pure by their nature. For as it is said in the tantra:

> The universes, thousand-thousandfold, in all the ten directions,
> Are from the first devoid of being.
> The three dimensions of existence are a buddhafield.
> The present fivefold decadence is a greatly blissful situation—

Everything and everyone is pure essentially.
No need to look for buddhahood in some other place.

2. Conduct

With regard to their behavior, disciples should adopt a perfect mode of conduct as concerns what is to be done and what is to be avoided, as has been explained at the beginning of the sutra section. It is said in the *Jatakamala:*

> Take your place upon a lowly seat,
> With dignity and self-control.
> Look upon the teacher with a joyful gaze.
> Imbibe the nectar of his teaching.
> And, with perfect concentration, listen!

This is how one should listen with a respectful attitude and conduct.

1. The method of explanation and study

Whenever the teachings of the Vajrayana are concerned, it is essential to receive empowerment and to observe perfectly the root and branch samayas; and, if mistakes occur, to correct them. If the minds of the master and students are not completely pure, these teachings will have no effect. Therefore, in accordance with our tradition, at the beginning of the explanation of the tantra section of the *Treasury of Precious Qualities,* disciples should recite the prayer called the Jubilant Confession taken from the sixteenth chapter of the *Stainless Confession Tantra,* otherwise known as the General Confession to the Sugatas, and the teacher should give a commentary on it. Both teacher and students should make confession every day and, in addition, recite the hundred-syllable mantra as much as they can in order to purify their minds. The explanation and study should then be done in terms of the five-or three-element structure.[623] Throughout that time, both teacher and students must avoid eleven faults relating to body, speech, and mind. They should avoid all incorrect physical behavior (such as drowsiness, and the stretching of their limbs). They should not tell jokes, laugh or chatter, argue angrily, or engage in purely academic debate. No teaching should be given in the absence of adequate pith instructions, or if the instructions are false. No one should listen to the teachings unless they are truly ready. No teachings should be given, or received, with the intention of gaining a good reputation or material advantage. Neither should there be any spirit of competition. As we have just said, the teacher should teach in a beautiful, clear way, while the students should listen attentively and with a perfect attitude and deportment, and with a great sense of gratitude. And both teacher and students should dedicate the merit of their labors.

[Taken from the commentary of Yönten Gyamtso, YG III, 24–31]

APPENDIX 3 ⬡∼

The View Expounded in the Guhyagarbha, *the Root Tantra of the* Mayajala Cycle

Clear certainty with regard to the great purity and equality of all existent phenomena is the pinnacle of all views, the ultimate point of all doctrinal systems, and the final destination to which all paths tend. Basing myself on the instructions of my teachers,[624] I will now give a brief explanation of how, in the Nyingma school, this is established by means of the view of the unsurpassed tradition (of the *Guhyagarbha-tantra*).

In general, all (Buddhist) views are accounted for within three principal views: (1) the view that considers phenomena and is the subject on the conventional level (*tha snyad kyi yul can chos can lta ba'i lta ba*); (2) the view that considers the nature of phenomena and is the subject on the ultimate level (*don dam pa'i yul can chos nyid lta ba'i lta ba*); and (3) the view that considers self-cognizing awareness and is the subject that ascertains the two truths as inseparable (*bden gnyis dbyer med par nges pa'i yul can rang rig lta ba'i lta ba*).[625]

According to the uncommon view (of the *Guhyagarbha*), these three views establish that all phenomena have the nature of the great dharmakaya, the indivisibility of the two superior truths. The superior relative truth is established on the basis of the view of relative phenomena just mentioned. It is the view that all appearances are pure in being the mandala of the kayas and wisdoms. The superior ultimate truth is established on the basis of the view of the ultimate nature of phenomena. Here, the ultimate nature of phenomena is understood as the seven riches (the five resultant qualities together with the ultimate expanse and primordial wisdom) of the secret treasure-house of all the Tathāgatas.[626] These seven riches are devoid of intrinsic being, and are all equal in the ultimate expanse. By means of the view of self-cognizing awareness, these two superior truths are experienced (by way of an objectless self-illumination)[627] as being inseparable and equal.[628]

Although the views of the sutras and tantras do not differ, in simply establishing what is to be evaluated (the dharmadhatu) as beyond conceptual construction, they do differ from the standpoint of the knowing subject, the way in which the dharmadhatu is perceived. And since all views are necessarily posited from the standpoint of the knowing subject, we are taught that the difference between the sutra and tantra views is very great.[629]

Practitioners on the path of Secret Mantra are superior to those on the path of the sutras because they see the inseparability of the two truths with greater clarity while they are in meditative equipoise and because they have a greater certainty of it in their postmeditative experience. On the mantra path, moreover, from the very beginning and thanks to their hearing and reflection on the teachings, practitioners rid themselves of misconceptions concerning the view. They consider all phenomena, of both samsara and nirvana, to be perfectly pure and equal.[630] Since their view is thus unclouded, the truth of origin manifests for them as the truth of the path, and the truth of suffering appears as the truth of cessation. Defilements dissolve into primordial wisdom, and suffering melts away into great bliss.[631] The path of Secret Mantra thus shows that the cause and fruit are indistinguishable, on which account it is called the resultant vehicle and the Vajrayana, both in name and truth.[632]

The view of phenomena

The first of the three views just mentioned establishes the purity of phenomena. It teaches that all appearances are pure in being deities, and that all defilements are pure in being primordial wisdom. For practitioners who believe in the existence of an outer, extramental, world,[633] the purity of phenomena is established in the following way. All phenomena, which we now perceive impurely, are, according to their fundamental nature, pure deities, palaces, and so on. The element water, for example, is perceived by pretas as pus and blood, whereas it is perceived in an increasingly pure manner by humans, gods, and Vidyādharas. In the case of enlightened beings, however, all latent propensities have been exhausted. It follows therefore that, from the standpoint of their wisdom that sees the nature of all phenomena, all concepts of purity and impurity are stilled, with the result that Buddhas see nothing at all. On the other hand, from the standpoint of their wisdom that perceives phenomena in all their multiplicity, they experience water in an utterly pure way: as the boundless mandala of the self-display or self-experience of primordial wisdom (*rang snang ye shes kyi dkyil 'khor*). Primordial wisdom (the knowing subject), wherein all defilements are purified, is ultimate valid cognition, and whatever ultimate valid cognition sees is established as the actual nature of its object. Consequently, all appearances are, according to their fundamental nature, the mandala of kayas and wisdoms. This is because the Noble Ones, free from error, perceive appearances as pure, just as for example a person with healthy and undamaged eyes sees a white conch as white.[634]

It could, however, be objected that since the perceptions of the Noble Ones are their own subjective experience (*rang snang*), they are not the same thing as the impure appearances that we experience now.[635] The answer to this is that, in general, the "thing" that is observed by all has no reality as an extramental object.[636] This being so, what the ordinary mind perceives are *impure appearances*, and what primordial wisdom perceives are *pure appearances*. They are no more than dependently arising appearances. And qua dependent appearances, they are on a level: there is no difference between them.

This is illustrated by the following story. When Shariputra perceived the field of Buddha Shakyamuni impurely, as our world, and when Tsangpa Ralpachen perceived it, more purely, as being like the divine realm called Mastery over the Magical Emanations of Others,[637] the Buddha himself revealed the true nature of his buddhafield to his disciples so that they perceived it as utterly pure, like the eastern buddhafield of the Buddha Ratnalankara, "Jewel-Adorned." The Buddha told them, moreover, that this was how his buddhafield had always been, though they had not seen it so. Consequently, even though the deluded mind perceives phenomenal appearance impurely (just as jaundiced people see a white conch as yellow), phenomena are, nevertheless, according to their fundamental nature, pure (like the actual white color of the conch shell).[638]

Through this kind of reasoning about phenomena, one is able to realize the equality of all phenomena, for one understands that all things without exception are equal in their natural purity. The purity of all phenomena can also be proved by the application of reasoning directed at the ultimate truth.[639] All impure appearances included within the truths of suffering and origin are by nature completely and primordially pure. For if one analyzes phenomena in order to reach their ultimate status, they are all found to be without origin. Inseparable from emptiness, phenomenal appearance is established as pure, for there is no impurity within the nature of emptiness.[640]

It may be objected that since in emptiness there is neither purity nor impurity, it cannot be used to establish appearances as pure.[641] Once again, since emptiness endowed with supreme attributes is established as the indivisibility of the two truths, appearances are, by the same token, shown to be pure.[642]

For those who say that whatever is commonly perceived is simply the mind's subjective perception or experience, and does not constitute an outer, extramental world, defilements are shown to be pure in being primordial wisdom. The argument runs as follows. Phenomena, defined as being no more than the mind's subjective perception, appear to ordinary beings as impure, to practitioners on the path as pure, and to the Buddhas as utterly pure. Thus defilements and their effects occur when one's mind is darkened by obscuration. All such appearances, together with the minds that entertain them, are illusory, hallucinatory appearances. But when obscuration is removed, there is only the perception, or rather self-experience, of primordial wisdom. This primordial wisdom is necessarily the fundamental nature of the mind, and thus it is proved that (even) the ordinary mind and defilements are, in their essential nature, pure.

For example, a sphere made of an alloy of gold and mercury has the color of fresh butter, and people who do not know what it is might in fact take it for butter. But those who see this object for what it is know that gold assumes a pale color due to the admixture of mercury. If, however, the alloy is slightly exposed to heat, it will become red (like copper), and again, if the heat is increased it will once more assume the appearance of gold, at which point its color will stabilize and will no longer be susceptible to change. In a similar way, the nature of the mind, the sugatagarbha, assumes an impure appearance when it is distorted by dualistic perception. And ignorant beings take this impure appearance as reality. By contrast, those who have gained certainty with regard to the purity and equality of phenomena know and tell themselves that what appears impurely through the distorting effect of dualistic perception is in reality entirely pure.

In the case of practitioners whose obscurations are removed to some degree, perceptions and appearances are correspondingly more pure. In the case of Buddhas, in whom all obscurations have been completely removed, primordial wisdom appears and is perceived in a manner that is completely pure; it is just as it really is. And this pure perception can suffer no further change. Thus, appearances are established as pure, as deities,[643] and the ultimate deity is dharmatā. This ultimate deity, which is self-arisen primordial wisdom, manifests as the relative, symbolic deity, in the form (or mudra) of the measureless palace and the deities contained therein.[644]

If the perceptions of enlightened beings are without impurity, it may be asked whether the Buddhas are aware of the impure, deluded perceptions of ordinary beings. If they are aware of them, this means that they have impure perception. On the other hand, if they are not aware of them, they are not omniscient. To this we could ask a further question: Can the Buddhas perceive the objects that appear as true, as well as the subjective apprehension and clinging to such objects—as it were, from the point of view of those who cling to true existence? If they perceive them, it follows that the Buddhas have a perception of true existence and see truly existent phenomena. Alternatively, if they fail to see them, they are not omniscient. What is the answer to this conundrum? If it is answered that, although the Buddhas are aware of the way things appear to beings, true existence does not appear to them, and that they do not see truly existent phenomena because, within the very nature of phenomena, true existence is impossible, by the same token, we may also argue that although they are aware of the impure and deluded perceptions of beings, the Buddhas are themselves without impure perception. They do not perceive impure phenomena for the simple reason that such phenomena are in fact impossible.

The view of the ultimate nature of phenomena

The view of the ultimate nature establishes the equality of all phenomena. People who are able to gain full accomplishment at a single stroke realize this equality through the skillful means of the pith instructions and so on.[645] It is unnecessary for them to make lengthy investigation. But for those whose certainty in the great equality of all phenomena comes gradually, it is necessary to pass through four successive stages: emptiness (*stong pa*), union (*zung 'jug*), absence of conceptual constructs (*spros bral*), and equality (*mnyam pa nyid*). Each stage arises on the basis of the understanding of the stage preceding it.

The process is as follows. To begin with, by means of an investigation of phenomena using the great arguments of Madhyamaka (the reasoning of "neither one nor many" and so on), one comes to the conclusion that the aggregates and other phenomena have no existence as such. This lack of inherent existence is their "emptiness." On the other hand, even their lack of existence is without intrinsic being. Phenomena are like the reflection of the moon on the water: they appear, and yet are empty.

These two aspects (of appearance and emptiness) are "in union." Indeed, to speak of two separate aspects is simply for the purposes of explanation. In reality they are of one taste. When the thought that apprehends the union of these two aspects (appearance as the thing to be negated and emptiness that is the negation of it) dissolves by itself, and when one is able to settle without negating or asserting anything, this is the stage called the absence of conceptual constructs. And as one becomes habituated to this, the mental states whereby one apprehends separately the nature of every phenomenon subside in the sphere of the one ultimate reality, and here, the stage of "equality" is perfected.[646]

The fact that phenomena are all equal in the emptiness of ultimate reality is likewise shown by the analytical investigation of Madhyamaka. The similarity is, however, confined to the demonstration of the equality of phenomena, in the sense of their being beyond conceptual construction. By contrast, in the present context (that of the *Guhyagarbha*), it is taught that phenomena are an infinite purity (*dag pa rab 'byams*), the mandala of deities. This is why there is reason to think that it is necessary to establish phenomena as being equal in the ground of appearance, emptiness endowed with supreme attributes, that is, the seven spontaneously present riches of the ultimate truth.[647]

The view of self-cognizing awareness

The indivisibility of purity and equality is established and perceived directly as the supreme dharmakaya by means of the view of self-cognizing awareness. The aspect of purity, established from the standpoint of appearance, and the aspect of equality, established from the standpoint of emptiness, are indivisibly united in a single taste within all phenomena. This is the natural conclusion of the previous two views. Everything that appears is empty of all ontological extremes. And what is equal in the sphere of emptiness arises as the pure kayas and wisdoms. The indivisibility of these two factors, which coalesce within the single sphere of the dharmakaya, is the domain of the direct perception of self-cognizing awareness.[648]

Thus far, purity, equality, and their indivisibility have been established separately. But now the root tantra of the *Vajrasattva Mayajala*, which demonstrates that phenomena (the display either of the ordinary mind or of primordial wisdom) subsist within the indivisibility of the two truths, establishes these three factors in unison, by using the arguments of the four understandings.[649]

As the root tantra says:

> A single cause, the way of syllables,
> The empowering strength, direct perception:
> With these four understandings, all is perfect.
> All things are the great king, truly perfect.[650]

Accordingly, by using these four arguments to evaluate the object to be assessed—namely, phenomena assumed to be real—one comes to their ultimate conclusion, the understanding to which each of the arguments leads. When we refer to the object of assessment—namely, phenomena assumed to be real—we are referring to samsara and nirvana: the object examined by means of the "argument of a single cause."[651] However, samsara and nirvana are not to be assessed as autonomously existing entities possessed of specific characteristics.[652] For samsara consists of appearances that have no reality and therefore cannot be established as an object of assessment. And nirvana completely transcends the scope of the ordinary mind and therefore cannot be regarded as an object of assessment either. Neither is it necessary to do so, since it is not nirvana that is entangling us. This is why the *Array of the Path of the Mayajala* says that we should assess the two spheres of our "imputation or reification." And it is said in the *Stages of the Path*[653] that we should investigate our belief in the reality of samsara and nirvana. As has been said, so-called nirvana and so-called samsara appear to the mind as pure and impure in the manner of object-universals (*don spyi*), and it is these that are to be assessed by the four kinds of argument.

According to the argument based on the notion of a single cause, the subjects of discussion, namely, samsara and nirvana (which appear to be, and are taken to be, two distinct realities, though they do not exist in this way) have but a single cause: the unoriginated expanse of the mind's nature. For this appears as either nirvana or samsara, depending on whether it is realized or not realized. It is like the orphaned prince who was either mistaken as an ordinary man or recognized as a prince. On both occasions he had a single princely nature. The *Ocean Tantra* says:

> Because they have a single cause within the space of dharmatā,
> All things without exception that appear to us
> Are understood as bodhichitta, the enlightened mind.

The final conclusion of this argument points to the unoriginated nature of phenomena.

Each of the following arguments takes as its subject the conviction induced by the conclusion of the argument that went before.

According to the argument related to the manner in which speech sounds manifest, the unoriginated nature, far from being an empty void, possesses an unobstructed radiance, from which the enlightened body, speech, and mind manifest. For it is like the sound A,[654] which is itself beyond all indication but which, owing to the movements and articulations of the mouth, appears unhindered in the variety of speech-sounds, which consequently are pointers to it, just as a finger can point at the moon.

The *Ocean Tantra* says:

> All that now appears as enlightened body, speech, and mind
> Is understood to be the ornament of speech.[655]
> All is the sound of speech,
> And by skillful means is sealed (as an unhindered play).

The conclusion of this reasoning is the unceasing, unobstructed display [of the unoriginated nature].

According to the argument of empowering strength, the unobstructed display is inseparable from the unoriginated nature because it is by the empowering strength (*byin rlabs sam stobs*) of this unobstructed display that the nature of phenomena is established as unoriginated. Conversely, it is through the empowering strength of the unoriginated nature that its display manifests unobstructedly. The example given here is that of the reflection of the moon in water.[656] Alternatively, from a direct realization of both the unoriginated nature and its unobstructed display, there automatically arises an empowering strength whereby it may be understood that the two are indivisible. The reason why this is so is that, since the seven riches of the superior ultimate truth are spontaneously present as the cause (the nature of phenomena), their appearing aspect (the universe and beings) is perceived as the mandala of the kayas and wisdoms. For example, the unoriginated nature and its unobstructed display can be compared with a piece of gold and its color.[657] The *Ocean Tantra* says:

> By the empowering strength of their inseparability,
> By the empowering strength of that very thing,
> All spontaneously appears thus, undivided.
> This empowering strength is marvelous, unimagined.

This then points to the indivisible nature.[658]

According to the argument of direct perception, the indivisible nature of the two truths is beyond the scope of intellect, for it is understood through the direct perception of self-cognizing awareness, by way of an objectless self-illumination. The self-cognizing awareness referred to here indicates self-cognizing primordial wisdom. The inseparability of the two superior truths is the fundamental nature of all phenomena, for the Noble Ones have perceived it so, just as a healthy person sees the whiteness of a white conch shell. The *Ocean Tantra* says:

> Within the self-born, self-arising mind,
> These two are not divided.
> Clearly perceived, this cannot be denied
> Within awareness, unborn, self-cognizing.
> This is said to be the highest of all realizations.

This points to the final conclusion: the indivisibility of the two truths is by definition beyond the ordinary intellect.[659]

To practice the Mantrayana path after one has, by means of these four arguments, attained certainty in the inseparability of the two superior truths, is of the highest moment. The inseparability of the two truths, just as it is, cannot be assimilated through intellectual analysis alone. Nevertheless, it is through inferential investigation that one can come to a perfect certainty that such must be the case. Then, by dint of pursuing the path of meditation, it is possible to come to a direct realization of the fundamental nature of things.

[Taken from the commentary of Yönten Gyamtso, YG III, 76–89]

APPENDIX 4 ⌒
The Ten Elements of the Tantric Path

The path of Secret Mantra may be divided into ten elements.[660]

> The view, the conduct, mandala, empowerment, and samaya,
> Offerings, mantra, concentration, activities, accomplishment:
> The tantras of the Secret Mantra should be thus divided.

Let us consider these in order. The view concerns ultimate reality; conduct is the abandonment of constraints; mandala is the array of appearance; empowerment indicates gradual progression; samaya is what is not to be transgressed; offerings are the things presented to the different senses; mudras bind while mantras are recited; concentration is unwavering; enlightened activity is displayed; accomplishment is what is striven for. These are the so-called ten elements of the tantras (or eleven, if the mudra and mantra are counted separately).

These same elements should be understood in the following way. The view is the unmistaken realization of the fundamental nature of knowledge objects or phenomena. Correct conduct regarding the activities specific to the Secret Mantra consists in the abandoning of the limitations of dualistic clinging (*gzung 'dzin gyi la dor ba*). The phenomena of the stages of ground, path, and result, and the array of all appearances, are perfect as the (mandala of the) deity. Empowerment gives the ability to progress gradually to the levels of ordinary and ultimate attainment. Samaya consists in not transgressing the specific precepts. The whole of phenomenal existence arises as the mudra of offering made to the different sense faculties of the deity and to the state of ultimate reality. For one who recognizes the true nature of phenomena, their three ways of being (*yin pa gsum*) and their fourfold establishment (*grub pa bzhi*),[661] every movement of the breath is mantra. All appearances and activities are perfectly sealed by awareness; they do not stir from the four mudras. Concentration does not wander from the profound stages of generation and perfection. The deployment of activities that are inseparable from the view of ultimate reality and have the nature of the four boundless attitudes is of benefit both to oneself and others. Finally, accomplishment refers to the authentic attainment of the desired siddhi.

These ten elements may be summarized as follows. Empowerment is the entrance to the path of Mantrayana. For although, in their causal or ground aspect, we already possess the four vajras of body, speech, mind, and primordial wisdom, they have not yet ripened into their final resultant state. The attendant cooperative condition for this ripening or actualization is empowerment. Empowerment enables one to meditate upon the four paths and to attain the four resultant kayas. As Vimalamitra says in his *Fundamental Text:*

> Just as sharpening gives power to a blade,
> Empowerment, when truly gained, gives power.

And yet it is not enough just to receive an empowerment. With the exception of those who have the supreme good fortune to achieve liberation at the very moment of initiation, everyone else must strenuously meditate on the generation and perfection stages. These are the skillful means whereby it is possible to free oneself from one's ordinary body, speech, and mind, together with their habitual tendencies, which shroud the face of one's own, indwelling, primordial wisdom. And even if one meditates on these two stages, if one fails to keep the samaya, the two accomplishments will not be achieved. Therefore in one's conduct, and as the favorable condition for the path of practice, the samaya must be perfectly observed, as the tantras explain. If these three elements (empowerment, practice, and samaya) are maintained together, the path of the Mantrayana is far superior to that of the paramitas. It is without doubt the authentic supreme path. On the other hand, if one tries to practice the stages of generation and perfection without receiving empowerment, or if one practices but neglects the samaya, one's path is but a dim reflection of the Mantrayana path; it is neither unmistaken nor supreme.

[Taken from the commentary of Yönten Gyamtso, YG III, 94–96]

APPENDIX 5 ❧
The Mandala

It is generally said that the granting of empowerment is based on one of four mandalas, according to the capacity of both master and disciple. These mandalas are: first, the natural mandala of primordial wisdom (*rang bzhin ye shes kyi dkyil 'khor*); second, the mandala of superior concentration (*lhag pa ting nge 'dzin gyi dkyil 'khor*); third, the mandala of the experience of awareness (*rig pa nyams kyi dkyil 'khor*); and fourth, the mandala of superior representation (*lhag pa gzugs brnyan gyi dkyil 'khor*).

In the first case, the master, who is a perfect buddha, bestows empowerment on a disciple on the ultimate path [the final moment of the tenth ground][662] by relying on the natural mandala of the display of primordial wisdom and on the goddess of primordial wisdom [namely, the dharmadhatu, emptiness]. The *Vajra Mayajala* says:

> The embodiment of all the Conquerors
> Bestows upon his retinue, the ocean of primordial wisdom,
> Empowerment through his great primordial wisdom,
> Based upon the natural mandala
> Together with the goddess of primordial wisdom.
> The disciples thus become great Vajradhara, Lord of Secrets.

In the second case, a master who is close to attaining buddhahood bestows empowerment on a disciple who is a Vidyādhara on the path of seeing or meditation, by relying on the mandala of superior concentration [the appearance aspect] as well as on the goddess of awareness [the emptiness aspect]. The *Vajra Mayajala* says:

> To those upon the grounds of realization, first to tenth,
> Is granted the empowerment by the stream of concentration,
> Within the mandala of blazing concentration,

Relying on the goddess of awareness.
And therefore they progress from ground to ground,
Acquiring greater wisdom
And the power to show forth buddhafields and miracles.

This is as when master Buddhaguhya displayed the vajradhatu mandala, tracing its design on Lake Manasarovar, and granted empowerment to Wé Manjushri[663] and others. Likewise, the great master Padma conferred the initiation of Kila on Yeshe Tsogyal in the Lion Cave of Taktsang, showing her the mandala of Kila as vast as the sky. Such mandalas are also referred to as emanated mandalas (*sprul pa'i dkyil 'khor*), or as mandalas that are the image of superior concentration (*lhag pa ting nge 'dzin gyi gzugs brnyan*). The *Sequence for the Vajra Mayajala* says:

A master who is on the path but close to its conclusion
Emanates threefold[664] the two and forty deities.
He merely draws, with vajra lines,
The mandalas of a thousand Buddhas and the rest:
Mandalas a league in length, and deities, he manifests.
These are the images of superior concentration.

In the third case, a master who is on the path of seeing bestows on a disciple who is on the path of joining and is a suitable candidate for the practice of the yogas of one or many deities [as described in the *Guhyagarbha-tantra*] an empowerment based upon the mandala of the experience of awareness and upon the consort dakini, the creative power of awareness. As it is said in the *Vajra Mayajala:*

A master who has gained
The vajra body of the path of seeing
Unites the yogi who has gained experience
On the path of joining
With the vajra body that is free from stain.
He does this based upon the consort dakini,

Awareness's creative power,
Within the mandala of the experience of awareness.

In these three cases, empowerments are bestowed using only the three mandalas mentioned. There is no need for the fourth kind of mandala (the mandala of superior representation). And this is thanks to the extraordinary abilities of the disciples concerned.

In the fourth case, a master who has gained stability in concentration bestows empowerment on faithful and fortunate disciples using the mandala of superior representation and a qualified karmamudra. The *Vajra Mayajala* says:

> The yogi who has gained stability of awareness
> Bestows upon the yogi who is fortunate,
> In the mandala of superior reflection,
> And based upon the lovely karmamudra consort,
> Empowerment and blessings.
> He grants it with the help of skillful ritual
> And with the pith instructions of the empowerment's lineage.
> The disciple who has gained experience of union
> Attains the fundamental nature.

It is said that, in such a situation, and regardless of whether the master is a noble or ordinary being, the disciples are, for their part, ordinary beings and cannot therefore enter any of the first three mandalas. For this reason, it is necessary to take support of the mandala of superior representation, as well as of the karmamudra. The mandala in question need not be made of colored powders. For even in the case of beginners, if the latter are of a superior capacity of mind—in other words, above the usual threefold distinction of sharp, medium, and ordinary faculties—and if they have devotion to the mandala of the master's body, they can, at the very outset, take support of such a mandala. If they are skilled in perceiving the body of the teacher as a mandala, they have no need for the support of an outer mandala.

The master Ghantapa (Drilbupa) has said:

The two constructed mandalas
Are said to match the student's powers.
They are not for the achievement of the wise.

It is also said that disciples of superior capacity may use a mandala made of small heaps (of rice and so on). The root empowerment of the *Eight Herukas, Embodiments of the Sugatas* says:

When empowerment is bestowed,
According to disciples' strength
High, medium, or low,
Empowerment is granted in three mandalas—
Of flowers, painted images, or powders.

For disciples of medium capacity, a mandala of painted cloth is used. In the *Compendium of Ritual Geometry,* Vimalamitra speaks of frescoes and paintings:

When the body of the deity
Is drawn complete upon a temple's even wall,
Upon a cloth or white birch skin,
On bark of trees or leaves of palm,
On winding sheet or human skin,
From these, the signs of your accomplishment may come.

In particular, the master Gyalwa'i De has said:

If you cannot work with colored sand,
Draw the mandala upon a cloth,
Together with the image of the mudra,
The body of the Lord Heruka.

For disciples of basic capacity, however, the use of a mandala made of colored powders is mandatory. This is said in many tantras, and many accomplished and learned teachers of the past and of more recent times have adopted this practice.[665] Consequently, if for no valid reason, without giving thought to the sharpness or dullness of the disciples' faculties, all empowerments are given in the most unelaborate and easy manner, the result will be that not only will such empowerments fail in their intended purpose, but the heavy fault of granting the empowerment in an unauthorized manner will be incurred.

[*Taken from the commentary of Yönten Gyamtso III, 159–164*]

APPENDIX 6 ⊘⟿
The Winds

Consciousness in itself is powerless to move from one place to another. It is only through the operation of the winds that it spreads into different parts of the body. If, by working with the physical body and the channels, one is able to bring the winds under control, consciousness can be harnessed. Control of the wind-energy is therefore extremely important.

The teachings speak of many kinds of wind, but here we will explain only the four characteristics of stillness (*gnas*), movement (*rgyu*), rising (exhaling, *ldang*), and entering (inhaling, *'jug*). At first, when taking birth in a new existence, the consciousness mounted on the wind enters the womb. Taking support of the mingled essences of the father and mother, the wind remains there in a condition of *stillness,* and the consciousness faints into a state of oblivion. At this time, the wind has the nature of the wisdom wind. Then by degrees, the ten kinds of wind manifest, beginning with the life-wind, and the physical body develops. For as long as the being in question is alive, the body does not rot, and this is due to the *moving* winds. The winds that *rise*[666] and *enter* generate different thoughts and feelings. It is these last two winds that are used on the path in the practice of yoga. When death occurs, these rising and entering winds cease, and this, by definition, marks the end of life. Although, generally speaking, the ten winds, which perform their functions in their respective domains, are all *moving* winds, nevertheless, the moving life-wind (*srog rtsol*) may be said to have the aspects of entering, remaining still, and rising. The life-wind only transits through the nostrils.

The winds related to consciousness have the nature of the wisdom wind. This is ultimately devoid of movement and is therefore said to remain in a condition of stillness. On the other hand, the *Kalachakra* states that "The wisdom wind moves once for every thirty-two and a half respirations."[667] And in the *Vajra Garland Tantra,* it is said that the wisdom wind moves at the end of each of the four periods of the day. The wind related with the element of space pervades the body, circulating within and throughout it. But it actually moves only at death when it leaves the body.

The wind of primordial wisdom dwells in the shortened A.[668] Because this is located at the point where the two channels of duality, roma and kyangma, are joined to the central channel, the wind of primordial wisdom manifests as "life" (*srog*) and "exertion" (*rtsol*).[669] It is thanks to this that the twenty-four inner sacred lands manifest in the radial channels of the four chakras and that, by virtue of interdependence, the full array of sacred lands and places appears in the outer world.

In harmony with the movement of the inner winds, there occurs the outward manifestation of years and months, the three kinds of day (solar days, lunar days, and zodiacal days), the hours, and so on. As long as the impure wind is in motion, the innumerable movements and transformations of this life will occur.

Although I (Yönten Gyamtso) lack the good fortune to be able to practice and gain experience in any of the vehicles, high or low, I wished to commit this to writing as a help for beginners. Nowadays one finds only fragmentary instructions on the profound perfection stage endowed with characteristics, and consequently it is rarely practiced. However, I believe that it is important to mention briefly the interdependent correspondence between the outer world and the inner world, as described in the commentaries. For in the expository causal vehicle, the root of existence is said to be the apprehension of, and clinging to, the self; and the root of this is the movement of the karmic wind. Now because the wind and the mind function together, they must be purified together. And thus we come to the essential point of this entire teaching: Subtle, deluded perceptions cannot be averted without relying on the Secret Mantra.

The movement of the wind-mind may be arrested in various ways. It may be halted indirectly [by realizing the wisdom of no-self], and it may be halted suddenly and forcefully by binding its movement [as in the Anuyoga]. In addition, without having to rely on such efforts, there is the path of the supreme pith instructions [of the Atiyoga], whereby the wind-mind is spontaneously purified. In the final analysis, however, all three ways are geared to the same objective.

Therefore, if one thinks that there can be no true vipashyana without the sharp reasoning of the Madhyamaka (with the result that other paths are imperfect); if one thinks that, without the skillful methods that directly halt the working of the winds in the channels, there is no way to arrest the movements of the karmic wind (and that therefore these practices are the only ones required); or again, if one thinks that, compared with the effortless practice, in which everything is left just as it is, all other practices with effort are inferior—all such clinging to one's preferred path, considering it better than any other, is a great obstacle.

One should refrain from such reflections, and one should strive as much as possible to practice the teaching that one finds inspiring and beneficial. One should by all manner of means try to understand how all the other practices of the pith instructions are included, directly or indirectly, in one's own practice, and are in harmony with it. It should be clearly understood that just as all kinds of treacle have a sweet taste, all the Buddha's teachings likewise are one and the same on the path of liberation. And even if one does not practice them all, one should nevertheless respect them all. This is a vital point and should be kept in mind.

I myself am destitute of the experience that is the essence of the practice. Yet I do hope to benefit others with the thunderous reverberation of my verbal explanations! For though I myself have been unable to accomplish anything at all, these words, written down here, derive from the instructions of my holy teacher [Patrul Rinpoche].

[Taken from the commentary of Yönten Gyamtso III, 174–78]

APPENDIX 7 ⟨⟩

A Brief Summary of the Stages of Generation and Perfection

On the path of Secret Mantra, when the mind stream has been well ripened by empowerment, all the constantly revolving delusions [the twelve links of dependent arising] produced by thought, proliferating adventitiously within the sphere of primordially pure ultimate reality, are made to dissolve in the inconceivable, secret expanse of the body, speech, and mind of the Tathāgatas. The Secret Mantra is a path far greater than any other.

There are many kinds of practice within the three inner tantras, but they may be condensed into the two stages of generation (kyerim) and perfection (dzogrim). These correspond to the two key aspects of the Mahayana path, namely, skillful means and wisdom, which are, in turn, the two accumulations. Being well versed in the profound view and skillful means, and in order to dispel their clinging to impure appearances, practitioners meditate on these same appearances as being the mandala of the deities of the three seats. In other words, they practice the generation stage, which is endowed with four special features. And in order to eliminate the impurities of body, speech, and mind, and to penetrate the quintessential nature, they practice on the perfection stage endowed with three special features, meditating on coemergent primordial wisdom.

The four special features of kyerim are as follows. The first is the feature of the ritual: the complete ritual, or sadhana, of the generation stage, as taught in the tantras. The second is the feature of the result: the ability to develop the power of the mantra.[670] The third is the feature of the nature: the emptiness and bliss that results from "melting."[671] The fourth is the feature of the function: the fact that the generation stage ripens into the stage of perfection.

The three special features of dzogrim are as follows. The first is the feature of the cause: the practice focused on the aggregate of the vajra body. The second is the feature of the function: the purification of the channels, winds, and essence-drops in the central channel. The third is the feature of the result: the union of bliss and emptiness, which is identical with coemergent bliss and empty form.

A person of sharp faculties can, from the very beginning, practice the kyerim and dzogrim together in union. Those who are unable to do this must first gain stability in the kyerim and then train in the dzogrim. Nagarjuna has said:

> For those who, well established in the generation stage,
> Wish to practice the perfection stage,
> The perfect Buddha has set forth
> This method, which is like a ladder's rungs.

Kyerim and dzogrim are superior to the causal vehicle and, in brief, this is due to the way in which they generate the qualities of elimination and realization.

As for the way in which the practitioners of kyerim abandon the factors to be eliminated, it may be said that, of the two kinds of obscuration (conceptual and deriving from defilement), they principally take defilement as their path. They cultivate the stable pride or confidence of being a deity, they consider sense objects as the display of the ultimate nature, and they behave in a manner that is free from accepting and rejecting. Since, however, they associate all such practices with the view of ultimate reality,[672] it follows that they do not fail to eliminate the conceptual obscurations as well.

With regard to the truths of suffering and origin, kyerim practitioners take the truth of origin (defilement) as their path, thus transforming into a pure path every action that would normally propel them into samsaric existence. Finally, with regard to the two main factors belonging to the truth of suffering—namely, birth and death—these same practitioners take birth as their path.

The [nonconceptual] dzogrim causes all the subtle or gross thoughts related to the duality of subject and object to dissolve, altogether and at once, into the ultimate expanse. It therefore constitutes the principal antidote to conceptual obscuration. On the other hand, the [conceptual] dzogrim, which is endowed with characteristics, takes the support of skillful means (a consort) and uses the taste of pleasure as the path, transforming it into the wisdom of the four joys and so on. It therefore also acts as an antidote to the obscurations deriving from defilement, and therefore eliminates the truth of origin. Of the two factors associated with the truth of suffering—namely, birth and death—it uses death as the path.

Regarding their respective paths, the practice of kyerim brings to completion the accumulation of merit, whereas that of dzogrim fulfills the accumulation of wisdom. It is thus that one journeys to the final point of the five paths. Regarding the result, kyerim (which uses the rupakaya as the path) and dzogrim (which uses the dharmakaya as the path) rapidly actualize the rupakaya and dharmakaya.

[Taken from the commentary of Yönten Gyamtso, YG III, 204–207]

APPENDIX 8 〜

Transmission Lineages of the Treasury of Precious Qualities

There are two principal transmission lineages of the *Treasury of Precious Qualities* leading to Kangyur Rinpoche:

1. Jigme Lingpa

   Dodrup Jigme Trinlé Özer
   Gyalsé Shenphen Thayé
   Orgyen Jigme Chökyi Wangpo (Patrul Rinpoche)
   Orgyen Tendzin Norbu
   Gemang Khenpo Yönten Gyamtso
   Khenpo Samten Gyamtso
   Khenpo Dawö Shönnu
   Kangyur Rinpoche, Longchen Yeshe Dorje

2. Jigme Lingpa

   Jigme Gyalwa'i Nyugu
   Dzogchen Khenpo Pema Dorje
   Jamyang Khyentse Wangpo
   Jedrung Trinlé Jampa Jungne
   Kangyur Rinpoche, Longchen Yeshe Dorje

There are two principal transmission lineages of the *Treasury of Precious Qualities* leading to Dilgo Khyentse Rinpoche:

1. Jigme Lingpa

   Dodrup Jigme Trinlé Özer
   Gyalsé Shenphen Thayé
   Orgyen Jigme Chökyi Wangpo (Patrul Rinpoche)
   Orgyen Tendzin Norbu
   Gemang Khenpo Yönten Gyamtso

Benchen Khenpo Zöpa Tharchin
Dilgo Khyentse Rinpoche, Tashi Peljor

2. Jigme Lingpa

Jigme Gyalwa'i Nyugu
Gyalsé Shenphen Thayé
Dzogchen Khenpo Pema Dorje
Shechen Gyaltsap Pema Namgyal
Dilgo Khyentse Rinpoche, Tashi Peljor

Notes 🌀

ABBREVIATIONS USED IN THE NOTES

DKR   Additional notes added by Dilgo Khyentse
Rinpoche to Kangyur Rinpoche's commentary (see
colophon)

DKR/OC   Oral commentary by Dilgo Khyentse Rinpoche,
given in Bumthang, Bhutan, 1983

KPS   Khenchen Pema Sherab

YG III   Yönten Gyamtso (*nyi ma'i 'od zer*), vol. 3 of the
Commentary on the Treasury of Precious Qualities

1   See appendix 1.

2   This corresponds to the dharmakaya level. [DKR]

3   This corresponds to the sambhogakaya level of the five enlightened families.
[DKR]

4   This corresponds to the nirmanakaya level. [DKR]

5   A full explanation of the terma tradition may be found in Tulku Thondup,
Hidden Teachings of Tibet (London: Wisdom Publications, 1986).

6   *mkha' 'gro gtad rgya'i brgyud pa.* Guardians of the teachings were entrusted with
the Dharma-treasures, and they were instructed to bestow them on beings
with the proper karmic fortune. [DKR]

    [DKR/OC] Guru Rinpoche entrusted certain teachings to the dakinis,
with instructions to deliver them to particular emanations, either of himself
or of one or other of his disciples, who would appear at some later time.
When, therefore, these beings appear in the world, the dakinis confer on
them the empowerments and instructions related to the teachings concerned.

7   *smon lam dbang bskur gyi brgyud pa.* [DKR/OC] Thanks to Guru Rinpoche's
special prayers, tertöns (or revealers of treasure teachings) appear at key mo-
ments in times marked by unrest, misfortune, famine, wars, epidemics, and
so forth. They have the power to avert these calamities and to strengthen the
teachings and promote general prosperity. It is thanks to Guru Rinpoche's
prayers that such emanations awaken to their nature as tertöns, and recover
the teachings that Guru Rinpoche bestowed on them in person. They gain
accomplishment through these treasure teachings, and then reveal and propa-
gate them for the benefit of others.

8   *shog ser tshig gi brgyud pa.* The treasure teaching appears in the form of script on scrolls of yellow paper, which were concealed as the treasure. This kind of transmission is said to be the vehicle of the greatest blessing. [DKR]

[DKR/OC] A distinction is made in the termas between outer, inner, and secret teachings. These are "earth-termas," "mind-termas," and "pure visions," respectively. In the case of earth-termas, the teachings are transcribed in various symbolic scripts (that of the dakinis and so on) on five different kinds of yellow scrolls, which are then concealed in rocks, in lakes, or in the earth. Only those disciples who have received these teachings from Guru Rinpoche and who have fully realized them (with the result that their minds are one with the mind of the Guru) are able to discover these scrolls. It is to them that the terma protectors entrust the treasures. When the tertön sees the symbolic script, he or she recalls the moment when Guru Rinpoche bestowed the empowerment, expounded the tantra, and revealed the pith instructions. The tertön is thus able to unfold the teachings written on the yellow scroll in a more or less expanded way. The tertön then practices these teachings before revealing them to others. Since the teachings are revealed in the way just described, one speaks of the "written transmission on yellow scrolls." These scrolls, moreover, can be seen by ordinary people, who as a result are inspired with faith and confidence.

9   *bka' bab lung bstan gyi brgyud pa.* [DKR/OC] For example, Guru Rinpoche entrusted to Nub Sangye Yeshe the tantras, the commentaries on them, and the pith instructions related to Manjushri; and predicted that, at a certain time subsequently, Nub Sangye Yeshe would take birth and reveal the teachings.

10 *nyams len byin rlabs kyi brgyud pa.* [DKR/OC] In this case, the tertön receives the teaching by reading the yellow scrolls, or he receives them directly from Guru Rinpoche (whether in a vision or in a face-to-face encounter). The tertön then practices the teachings and attains the supreme and ordinary siddhis. At that point, the link between Guru Rinpoche and the tertön is like the relationship between a man and his own hand. The tertön is able to bestow empowerment and transmit teachings to worthy disciples.

11 *snyan brgyud dmar khrid kyi brgyud pa.* [DKR/OC] The tertön receives the terma from the mouth of Guru Rinpoche or Yeshe Tsogyal. This is in the form of secret pith instructions that are inaccessible to the narrow minds of mere scholars. The tertön practices accordingly, gains confidence in the generation and perfection stages of the Secret Mantra, and finally discloses the pith instructions, which, based on direct experience, are as precious as the blood of his or her heart. This is called a hearing transmission, since the tertön receives it from the very mouth of Guru Rinpoche or Yeshe Tsogyal.

12 *phrin las phyag bzhes kyi brgyud pa.* [DKR/OC] In the course of a vision, the tertön receives instructions on how to perform various activities related to the practice, such as the performance of rituals, and the making of tormas.

13   [DKR/OC] These three kinds of transmission do not exclude each other. When Jigme Lingpa achieved the same realization as Longchenpa—when their minds mingled and became one, so that in view and meditation they were as similar as a statue and its mold—this constituted the mind transmission of the Buddhas. When Jigme Lingpa beheld the wisdom body of Longchenpa in three visions, and received the blessings of his body, speech, and mind, thus becoming the heir and holder of the teachings of the Great Perfection, this was the transmission through symbols of the Vidyādharas. When Jigme Lingpa heard Longchenpa say: "Let the realization be transferred into your mind. Let it be transferred into your mind. Let the verbal transmission be complete. Let it be complete," this constituted the hearing transmission of spiritual masters.

14   *'jigs med phrin las 'od zer*, the first Dodrupchen Rinpoche (1745–1821). He was one of the main disciples of Jigme Lingpa and a lineage holder of the Longchen Nyingthig teachings. See Tulku Thondup, *Masters of Meditation and Miracles* (Boston: Shambhala Publications, 1996), pp. 136–62.

15   *rgyal sras gzhan phan mtha' yas* (1800–?). According to a prediction, he was an incarnation of Minling Terchen Gyurme Dorje. A scholar of great accomplishment, he was a disciple of Jigme Trinlé Özer, Jigme Gyalwa'i Nyugu, Dola Jigme Kelzang, and the fourth Dzogchen Rinpoche. He founded the Shri Singha College of Dzogchen Monastery and taught there. See *Masters of Meditation and Miracles*, pp. 198–99.

16   *o rgyan 'jigs med chos kyi dbang po*, otherwise known as Patrul Rinpoche (1808–87). He studied with many masters and became a great teacher, famous for his uncompromising simplicity of life. He eschewed any kind of honor or position in the monastic hierarchy, and spent his life wandering from place to place in the guise of a beggar. Among his numerous literary compositions are *The Words of My Perfect Teacher*, a *Structural Outline of the Treasury of Precious Qualities*, and an *Explanation of the Difficult Points of the Treasury of Precious Qualities*. See *Masters of Meditation and Miracles*, pp. 201–10.

17   *o rgyan bstan 'dzin nor bu*, known as Onpo Khenpo Tenli or Khenpo Tenga, was a nephew of Gyalsé Shenphen Thayé. He was the heir to, and main holder of, Patrul Rinpoche's exegetical teachings (*bshad khrid*), which he then transmitted to Khenpo Shenpen Chökyi Nangwa (Khenpo Shenga) and Khenpo Yönten Gyamtso (Khenpo Yonga) of Dzogchen Monastery. See *Masters of Meditation and Miracles*, pp. 226–27.

18   *yon tan rgya mtsho*. He was an abbot and teacher of Gemang Monastery (a daughter house of Dzogchen Monastery) in eastern Tibet, who composed a two-part commentary on the root text of the *Treasury of Precious Qualities*, on the basis of the *Structural Outline* and the *Explanation of Difficult Points* by Patrul Rinpoche.

19   Abbot of Kathog Monastery and uncle of Kangyur Rinpoche.

20 Another lineage of transmission exists, passing from Jigme Lingpa's disciple Jigme Gyalwa'i Nyugu through Jamyang Khyentse Wangpo and so on, to Kangyur Rinpoche. See appendix 8.

21 For a description of how the tantras are taught and received, see appendix 2.

22 [DKR/OC] Just as the sesame seed is saturated with oil, and just as the sun's light is ever present in the sun.

23 The word used here for mind is *yid shes.* According to Dilgo Khyentse Rinpoche, *yid shes* ("mental consciousness") normally refers to the ordinary ground of delusion, the mind that operates within the dualistic framework of subject and object. In the present context, however, it refers to the mind's pure aspect: the simple clarity and knowing of awareness.

24 In other words, the result is already present, fully accomplished. The buddha-nature is not merely a seed, or potential to be developed, as it is said in the causal vehicle.

25 [DKR/OC] There is no need to establish the emptiness of phenomena; the result (the kayas and wisdoms) is used immediately as the path itself.

26 [DKR/OC] For example, the dissolution of the suffering and deprivation of beings through the visualized projection of light.

27 *ma rmongs.* Literally, nonstupidity, nonconfusion.

28 [DKR/OC] That is, view and meditation.

29 Phenomena are pure on the relative level, and equal on the ultimate level.

30 [DKR/OC] The indivisibility of the two truths.

31 The cause refers to the ground and the means to the path. [DKR]

32 *log pa'i zhen snang yul dang bcas pa.* [DKR/OC] That is, as truly existent. This is the deluded clinging to the world in general, to the beings who inhabit it, and to defilements.

33 There is no delusion in the ground. It is through failure to recognize the ground that delusion arises. In other words, the way things appear does not accord with their fundamental way of being (*gnas snang mi mthun*). Thus ground and delusion are causally unrelated. [KPS]

34 [DKR/OC] In the uncontrived dharmatā, within the indivisible union of the two truths, the universe, its inhabitants, and their mindstreams are the mandala of the three seats

35 This refers to samaya. [DKR]

36 The word "traveling" refers to the path, while "attributes" refers to the qualities gained. [DKR]

37 The path of the outer tantras is long compared with that of the inner tantras, thanks to which buddhahood can be attained in a single lifetime. On the

other hand, since it can lead to enlightenment in six, seven, or sixteen lives, the path of the outer tantras is short compared with that of the expository causal vehicle. [DKR]

38 [DKR/OC] This means that the dharmatā is used as the path.

39 [DKR/OC] Even when the nature is veiled by obscurations, great primordial purity is still present, however impure it may seem. But when the ever-present ground is actualized, there is no longer any discrepancy between the way it is and the way it appears. There is only the great primordial purity.

40 That is, the stages of generation and perfection. [DKR]

41 That is, the great yoga of the spontaneously present result. [DKR]

42 *ngo bo bdag gcig gi 'brel ba.* In other words, the relationship between the ground and the result is not a causal one.

43 [DKR/OC] Such as the production of gold by alchemical process, or the creation of a vetala (*ro langs,* reanimated corpse).

44 The primordial wisdom of the paths of seeing and meditation. [DKR]

45 For example, in the cycle of the *Vajrasattva Mayajala,* the *Guhyagarbha* is the root tantra, while the other tantras are the "branches" that furnish detailed explanations of the main topics, for example the samayas, which are only briefly mentioned in the root tantra. See Jamgön Kongtrul, *Systems of Buddhist Tantra* (Ithaca, N.Y.: Snow Lion Publications, 2005), p. 519n3–4.

46 See appendix 1, p. 323.

47 Depending on how the ultimate nature is introduced. [KPS]

48 Defilements and sense objects. [DKR]

49 [DKR/OC] In other words, such a person will be able to purify negativities much more swiftly through the practice of the Secret Mantra.

50 The teachings of the sambhogakaya Buddhas are beyond all verbal expression. [DKR]

51 Such as the *Guhyasamaja-tantra* (which was taught by the historical Buddha). [DKR] See Jigme Lingpa and Kangyur Rinpoche, *Treasury of Precious Qualities,* bk. 1 (Boston: Shambhala Publications, 2005), p. 468n158.

52 [DKR/OC] "Secret mantra" corresponds to Kriya, Ubhaya, and Yoga; "greatly secret" corresponds to Maha, Anu, Ati; and "extremely secret" refers to the innermost, unsurpassable section of Ati (*yang gsang bla med*).

53 See *Treasury of Precious Qualities,* bk. 1, p. 484n257.

54 For a detailed exposition, see Jamgön Kongtrul, *Myriad Words* (Ithaca, N.Y.: Snow Lion Publications, 2003), pp. 133–34.

55 [DKR/OC] This refers to strict dietary regulations such as eating only the three sweet substances, etc.

56 Beings of this type act in a balanced manner. Mentally they intend their own benefit, but in body and speech, they act skillfully and in a manner that also benefits others. [DKR]

57 The Anuttaratantra is intended for ordinary, common people, those of lowest social rank. [DKR]

58 The empty luminosity of the nature of the mind can manifest in any form. [DKR]

59 This does not mean that they are unnecessary. They are not, however, set forth as the principal concern. [DKR]

60 These gods may be manifestations of the Buddha's activities. [DKR]

61 This corresponds to the cleanliness of the Kriyatantra. [DKR]

62 This corresponds to the Charyatantra. [DKR]

63 This corresponds to the Yogatantra with its confident pride of being the deity. [DKR]

64 This corresponds to the Anuttaratantra, which uses desire as the path. [DKR]

65 "The five meats are the flesh of humans, and the meat of dogs, horses, cows, and elephants (animals that were not killed for consumption in India, the central land)." [YG III, 481:1–2]

66 The five nectars are excrement, urine, human flesh, blood, and semen. See also Jamgön Kongtrul, *Buddhist Ethics* (Ithaca: Snow Lion Publications, 2003), p. 472n145.

67 "In the outer tantras, skillful means and wisdom are meditated upon successively. This refers to the elementary generation stage and the elementary perfection stage. Some say that these practices are simply the yoga of skillful means and the yoga of wisdom, and affirm that they cannot be called the authentic stages of generation and perfection." [YG III, 51:6]

68 For example, Manjughosha for the male Bodhisattvas, Sarasvati and Prajnaparamita for the female Bodhisattvas. [DKR]

69 For a detailed discussion of the Kriyatantra, see *Systems of Buddhist Tantra*, pp. 100–114.

70 *rigs gsum gyi lha.* These are Manjushri of the body family, Avalokiteshvara of the speech family, and Vajrapani of the mind family.

71 *mkha' spyod rig 'dzin.* This kind of Vidyādhara is a mundane being (i.e., still in samsara). For a detailed explanation of such Vidyādharas, see *Systems of Buddhist Tantra*, p. 377n124.

72 *bya rgyud tsam po pa'am rang rgyud pa.*

73 This means that, even though one visualizes oneself as a deity, one considers this as the meditational deity (Tib. *dam tshig sems pa*; Skt. *samayasattva*), and it

is still necessary to generate a visualization in front of oneself, and invite the wisdom deity to enter it. The wisdom deity thus visualized in front is regarded as superior to oneself, and it is from this deity that one requests empowerment and blessing.

Sakya Pandita says, in the *Analysis of the Three Vows*, that there is no self-visualization in authentic Kriyatantra and that, if self-visualization occurs, the tantra in question is not a pure Kriyatantra. This view is contradicted, however, by the *Tantra of the Empowerment of Vajrapani* and others. See YG III, 53:3–6.

74 [DKR/OC] The view of the Prajnaparamita, emptiness.

75 Compare this point with the more extensive account given in Dalai Lama, *The World of Tibetan Buddhism* (Boston: Wisdom Publications, 1995), pp. 115–17.

76 Buddhaguhya (*sangs rgyas gsang ba*) was a disciple of Buddhajnanapada and Lilavajra, among others. A master of great accomplishment, he became particularly adept at the *Mayajala-tantras*, for which he composed many commentaries. See Dudjom Rinpoche, Jikdrel Yeshe Dorje, *The Nyingma School of Tibetan Buddhism* (Boston: Wisdom Publications, 1991), pp. 464–66.

77 "The first deity is the view of emptiness: one meditates on the principle of one's own nature. The second is the deity as letter: one meditates on the moon disk. The third is the deity as sound: one meditates on the resounding mantra appearing on the moon disk. The fourth is the deity as form: one meditates on the moon disk and the mantra, which radiate and reabsorb rays of light that perform the enlightened activities. The moon disk and the mantra then transform into one of the deities of the three families. The fifth is the deity as mudra, whereby the visualization is sealed with the mudra according to the family of the deity concerned. The sixth is the deity as symbol, which means that in all one's activities, one never separates from the support of the deity [in other words, one constantly maintains the visualization of the deity]." [YG III, 54:5–55:2]

78 *khrus.* "Outer purification consists in actual ablution. Inner purification means to cleanse away one's root downfalls. Secret purification is to rid oneself of dualistic thought." [YG III, 56:6–57:1]

79 "The cleanliness of one's raiment means, outwardly, that one's clothes should be new and clean; inwardly that the vows should be kept; and secretly, that one should meditate on the deity." [YG III, 57:1–2]

80 "The outer ascetic practices are aids to the maintenance of inner cleanliness, in other words, concentration. With regard to the self-visualization practiced in the course of the fasting ritual (*smyung gnas*), Sakya Pandita specifies in the *Analysis of the Three Vows* as follows:

> If thus you practice, this is not the fasting ritual.
> When as a deity you visualize yourself,
> To make offerings to this deity is meritorious.

To fail to do so is a fault.
If you wish to undertake the ritual of fasting,
You should do so in your common form.

"My [i.e., Yönten Gyamtso's] teachers, however, question this. They say that visualization of oneself as a deity is not an obstacle to the performance of the fasting ritual. If the fast is not wrongly motivated (through an actual wish to deny offerings to the deity), there is no conflict. If there were, this would also imply that it is incorrect for practitioners of the generation stage to confess their wrongdoings. However, all the teachings of great beings have an underlying wisdom intention. It is unimaginable that they should contain something incorrect. Nevertheless, since there are many fasting rituals of both the Old and New Traditions in which one does visualize oneself as a deity, I have written this in order to dispel the doubts that certain people may have." [YG III, 57:2–6]

81   For a detailed discussion of the Charyatantra, see *Systems of Buddhist Tantra*, pp. 115–25.

82   "The Ubhayatantra path is condensed into three topics: (1) the first is the bipartite introductory practice (*'jug pa'i spyod pa*), which is (i) the outer section consisting of the empowerment, and (ii) the inner section, which is subdivided into the conceptual (*mtshan bcas*) and the nonconceptual (*mtshan med*) practices; (2) the second topic is the practice of application (*sbyor ba'i spyod pa*); and (3) the third topic is the practice of proficiency (*grub pa'i spyod pa*)." [YG III, 59:1–2]

83   The preceding paragraph describes the inner introductory practice, which is conceptual. "Nonconceptual yoga consists of meditation on ultimate bodhichitta, endowed with three distinctive features: (1) adoption of the view (through analysis of phenomena, whereby one gains a direct understanding that they are devoid of origin); (2) preservation of the view (by actualizing a state that is free from thoughts); and (3) when one arises from such meditation, a great compassion and concern for those who lack this realization." [YG III, 60:2–3]

84   These are the four families of body, speech, mind, and qualities, corresponding to the families of tathāgata, lotus, vajra, and jewel.

85   For a detailed discussion of the Yogatantra, see also *Systems of Buddhist Tantra*, pp. 127–40.

86   This is probably a reference to the *Stages of the Path of the Mayajala* by Buddhaguhya (*sgyu 'phrul drva ba'i lam rim*).

87   [DKR/OC] That is, with regard to the view, meditation, and conduct of the Mantrayana.

88   This refers to a group of factors of "awakening to total purity and accomplishment," modeled on the group of the "awakenings of the Buddha," and

constituting the procedure for the practice. See *Systems of Buddhist Tantra*, p. 414n45.

89 That is, in contrast with the Mahayoga, where one meditates on the deity in connection with the process of samsaric birth.

90 *mngon byang lnga.* "First, one meditates on thought-free emptiness. Second, one meditates on a crescent moon that appears from this emptiness. Third, one concentrates on the full moon. Fourth, one meditates on a five-pronged vajra standing on the moon. Fifth, beams of lights radiate from, and reabsorb into, the vajra, which then transforms into the deity.

"The five factors of awakening may alternatively be understood as: (1) visualization of a seat consisting of a lotus and a moon, whereby every place becomes a perfect buddhafield; (2) concentration on the seed-syllable, whereby all sounds become a perfect teaching; (3) concentration on the attribute or symbol of the mind, whereby the time is perfected as everlasting continuity, i.e., the inconceivable time beyond past, present, and future; (4) concentration on the complete body of the deity and the mandala, whereby the perfection of teacher and retinue is accomplished; and (5) concentration on the jnanasattva (wisdom being), whereby perfect primordial wisdom, or the nature of the deity, is accomplished." [YG III, 64:3–65:2]

91 "Concentration means the visualization of the principal deity and the retinue. They are blessed by the Lords of their families, and empowered by the strength of the mantra and concentration. One then pays homage and makes offerings and praise." [YG III, 65:3–4]

92 "There are two stages in this training: the practice of the supreme victorious mandala as the foundation (*gzhi dkyil 'khor rgyal mchog*) and, based on this, the practice of the supreme victorious activity (*las rgyal mchog*). One concentrates on them until one gains the desired accomplishment. As for the subtle aspect of the practice, one concentrates on a small attribute such as a vajra, from the size of an inch down to a grain, and finally one rests in the thought-free state." [YG III, 66:2–4] See also *Buddhist Ethics*, p. 503n315.

93 "With regard to the yoga of wisdom, one settles in the expanse of primordial wisdom wherein there is no duality between the ultimate nonconceptual wisdom and the relative appearance of the deities of the Vajradhatu." [YG III, 66:4–5]

94 [DKR/OC] If, for example, the main deity of the mandala is Vajrasattva in union with his consort, and if it was found that one belongs rather to the lotus family (according to the place on which one's flower fell), one will attain realization much more quickly if one meditates on Amitabha. Amitabha will therefore replace Vajrasattva in the center of the mandala. The consort of Vajrasattva will not change, however, but will now be in union with Amitabha.

95 Sakya Pandita asserts in the *Analysis of the Three Vows* that there is no difference between the view of the sutras and the tantras. (He says that something superior to the "absence of all conceptual constructs" is necessarily a "conceptual construct.") According to Gyalwa Longchenpa and Mipham Rinpoche, however, the views of the sutras and tantras are different. This is due to the fact that, in the case of the Madhyamaka, the view is related to the ultimate nature as the *object* (*yul*), whereas in the tantra, the view is related to primordial wisdom, which is the *subject* (*yul can*). And since the scope of this primordial wisdom gradually increases, there is a difference between the various views. [KPS]

96 *rnal 'byor chen po*, or great yoga. Jamgön Kongtrul explains that this yoga is so called because it is far superior to the systems of the three outer tantras. See *Systems of Buddhist Tantras*, p. 312.

97 [DKR/OC] In the Hinayana, the truth of suffering is to be known, and the truth of origin is to be rejected. In the Mahayoga, the five major elements and five aggregates (regarded in the sutra context as "sufferings") are perceived as the five female and five male Buddhas respectively. The eight consciousnesses and their objects are perceived as the eight male and female Bodhisattvas. The four limbs of the body are perceived as the four door-keepers, etc. Finally, karma and defilements are perceived as having the nature of wisdom. One recognizes that the universe, beings, and defilements are primordially the display of the kayas and wisdoms.

98 The perfection stage, here, is an aspect of Mahayoga, and is not to be confused with the Anuyoga. In fact, the generation stage practice of Mahayoga also has a corrective effect on the channels, etc. It is said that meditation on the lotus and the disks of the moon and sun has an effect similar to meditation on the channels, and on the white and the red essence-drops respectively. See also *The Nyingma School of Tibetan Buddhism*, pp. 362–63.

99 "Aggregate of their vajra body" is a rendering of *rdo rje lus* in contrast with *rdo rje sku*, which is translated simply as "vajra body." The former is the subtle aspect of the physical body and is composed of the channels, winds, and essence-drops. The latter is the indestructible wisdom body, which utterly transcends these categories.

100 [DKR/OC] That is, thoughts that are under the power of karma and defilement.

101 *shin tu rnal 'byor* [Skt. *Atiyoga*]. As Jamgön Kongtrul explains, this yoga is so called because it is the supreme training, the summit of all vehicles. See *Systems of Buddhist Tantra*, p. 337.

102 [DKR/OC] Primordial wisdom "as it is" is the naked content of the meditative equipoise of the Buddhas.

103 [DKR/OC] The primordial purity of phenomena is *recognized* and is not merely contrived as in the visualizations of the generation stage.

104 [DKR/OC] This refers specifically to human beings living in the cosmic continent of Jambudvipa, not in the other continents.

105 The five physical elements are earth, air, water, fire, and space. It should be noted that, according to Dilgo Khyentse Rinpoche, "consciousness" in this context refers not merely to gross, ordinary, consciousness, but to primordial wisdom.

106 See the section on luminosity in the perfection stage, p. 172.

107 See p. 172 and also *Systems of Buddhist Tantra*, p. 421n5.

108 For a detailed presentation of the symbol ÉWAM, see *Systems of Buddhist Tantra*, p. 188–97.

109 The anushvara and visarga are features of the Devanagari script in which Sanskrit is written. The anushvara is a dot (a small circle when copied in Tibetan) indicating the nasalization of the vowel thus marked. It is often rendered by an *m* or *ṃ* in English transliteration (e.g., saṃsara). The visarga consists of two dots (or circles) written vertically. It indicates an unvoiced breathing at the end of a syllable and is transliterated in English as an *h* or *ḥ* (e.g., naraḥ).

110 [DKR/OC] The anushvara (the dot above the WAM) is the symbol of the white lunar essence-drop produced by the melting of the syllable HANG. When purified, it is the vajra body. The visarga, the two dots following the WAM, symbolizes emptiness, the red solar essence-drop. When purified, it is the vajra speech. The syllable A is the central channel free from attachment, hatred, and ignorance. It is indeterminate, leaning neither to samsara nor nirvana. It is the great Middle Way or great darkness, and refers to the vajra mind. The expanse of the mother and the two kinds of essence dwell in É. The syllable É refers to the emptiness aspect, the syllable WAM refers to the appearance aspect.

111 "In some contexts, the dharmakaya is called the universal ground, the common foundation of both samsara and nirvana. It is not the same as the universal ground of habitual tendencies." [YG III, 639:5]

[DKR/OC] It is necessary to distinguish the universal ground referred to in the Sutrayana (the ground of accumulated tendencies and karma) from the universal ground as understood (in certain specific contexts) in the Mantrayana. Here, the universal ground (*kun gzhi*) is the tathāgatagarbha, the nature of all phenomena, and is the ultimate foundation of samsara and nirvana. If one gains experience of it and trains in it, it forms the basis of all the qualities of the ground, path, and result, and is therefore called the cause continuum, or tantra (*rgyu'i rgyud*). It is within this cause tantra that the distinction is made between view, meditation, conduct, and result, and it is through the practice related to these that the cause tantra of the universal ground (*kun gzhi rgyu'i rgyud*) is established and understood with certainty.

The view is the recognition of ultimate reality; meditation is the experience of it; conduct is a behavior that is constantly informed by a mindfulness of both view and meditation; and the result is the purification of all deluded perceptions in the ultimate expanse—meaning the actualization of the nature of all things. Although differentiated, these four aspects are not different things. They are one and the same. In order to actualize the qualities of the view, meditation, conduct, and result, one must tread a path consisting of the conceptual generation stage, the nonconceptual perfection stage, and their nondual union. These three methods bring the mind to maturity. First the mind is ripened by empowerment and then it is liberated from the fetters of defilement through the two stages of generation and perfection.

In this context, "mind" (*sems*) is to be understood as the ordinary mind associated with dualistic clinging, whereas the nature of the mind is the tathāgatagarbha, which is recognized when the mind is seen to be free from all duality of subject and object, and to be naturally beyond origin, dwelling, and cessation. Anyone wishing to actualize the qualities of the tathāgatagarbha must realize this self-arisen primordial wisdom. When this is done, one arises in a wisdom body, and one's mind itself stands revealed as primordial wisdom. The kayas and primordial wisdoms are inseparable; they are primordially and spontaneously present. The wisdoms are the main figures in the mandalas, and the kayas are their retinues. These two, the kayas and wisdoms inseparable, constitute the primordial, ultimate mandala.

Ultimate reality is realized, just as it is, thanks to the teacher's pith instructions. One will not have just a glimpse of this ultimate nature; one will truly experience it through the practice related to the view, meditation, and conduct. In the best case, one considers the teacher who introduces one to the dharmakaya wisdom as having the same qualities as the Buddha, and indeed as being of even greater kindness. If one has such confidence and devotion, then, as Nagarjuna says in the *Five Stages:* "When one falls from the summit of Meru, like it or not, one falls. When one has received the teachings from a kind teacher, like it or not, one gains liberation." Devotion is thus the universal panacea. When one sees the teacher as the Buddha in truth, one realizes ultimate reality even if one never even thinks about it. When the teacher, manifesting as the main figure of the mandala, bestows empowerment on a disciple who has such devotion, the disciple is introduced to the wisdom of empowerment, just as a heap of dry grass is set alight by the rays of the sun passing through a magnifying glass. Moreover, if one has meditated for a long time on the generation and perfection stages, then the qualities of the kayas and wisdoms inherent in the tathāgatagarbha will become manifest spontaneously and increasingly—whether one wants it or not! It is like a crop that automatically develops from the seeds when all the conditions of warmth, manure, and water are present.

By contrast, mere scholars, even those of great erudition, are powerless to realize ultimate wisdom as it truly is, simply through the manipulation of ideas about relative and ultimate, appearance and emptiness. On the other hand, if one has no idea of the way to get to Bodhgaya, it is useless simply to want to go there. Likewise, if one has no clear knowledge of the view of the Mantrayana (through study and meditation), no advantage is gained. Therefore, as it is said, the view is of the first importance. If one has realized the view of the ultimate nature, there is no question that one will realize the supreme siddhi. If, by contrast, one fails to realize the view, then even if one meditates for years on the generation and perfection stages and recites millions of mantras, no siddhi will be forthcoming. The realization of the view of great purity and equality is like the universal monarch who can effortlessly gather all beings under his sway simply by showing them his golden wheel.

112 See appendix 3.

113 [DKR/OC] This means that one must not fall under the power of dualistic thoughts.

114 [DKR/OC] They are the display of deities, mantras, and wisdom.

115 [DKR/OC] If one possesses the ultimate view beyond intellect, one will be like Guru Rinpoche who, having received the empowerment of the creative power of awareness (*rig pa'i rtsal dbang*), could transform the entire universe and beings, samsara and nirvana, according to his wish. The ability to do this derives from an absolute confidence and mastery of the view. Such a view is not an object of ordinary discursive reasoning, and it is not something that can be merely learned. To possess such a view is like taking possession of an invincible fortress that is completely impregnable. Those who remain constantly in such a citadel (namely, in the state of equality) experience a kind of meditation that is free from the "dangerous paths" of torpor and agitation. For such practitioners, all perceptions of the six consciousnesses arise as the manifestation of primordial wisdom. Since all thoughts are purified in the dharmatā, all phenomena (the universe, its inhabitants, and their defilements) act as an enhancement to the meditation of such practitioners.

When meditation and postmeditation become indivisible, all distinctions between nonvirtue and the path to liberation (which are to be rejected and undertaken respectively) will vanish by themselves. Every physical, verbal, or mental action performed by beings who possess such a view and meditation will be the display of wisdom, total purity. At that point there is no notion of keeping or breaking samaya. Everything is the display of deities, mantras, and wisdom. The stage of perfection is to maintain the realization that the forms visualized in the stage of generation are not gross forms concerning which one may have thoughts of attachment or aversion, but the expression of wisdom. This corresponds to the "nail of unchanging ultimate wisdom" implemented in the generation-stage practice (see p. 151).

116 [DKR/OC] On the relative level, one speaks of view, meditation, and conduct. In truth, however, these are not isolated entities but the display of a single nature. If the fortress of the view is taken, meditation and conduct will

arise. If meditation does not deviate, the view and conduct will naturally be present. If one sets up the life-tree of conduct, one will at the same time be practicing the view and meditation.

117 Here "the view" refers to the inseparability of the two superior truths of the Mantrayana (*lhag pa'i bden pa dbyer med*). See appendix 3.

118 [DKR/OC] A mandala, whether painted or constructed of colored powders, is no more than a symbol. In fact, everything that appears is the naturally present mandala. The mandala is not something newly and artificially produced by the practice. The path is not meant to fabricate something that is in fact unreal. Instead, it makes manifest what is already naturally present. If the stage of generation is secured by the nail of unchanging ultimate wisdom (see note 115), there is no need for subsequent meditation on the perfection stage. Moreover, meditation on the generation stage confers stability in the perfection stage. Conversely, when the latter attains its goal, progress also occurs in the former. Those who practice thus will be beyond ordinary action, and whatever they do will benefit others.

119 See appendix 4 for the ten elements of the tantra path.

120 [DKR/OC] If people repeatedly ask a master to be allowed to enter the Vajrayana, even though they lack the diligence and unfailing devotion necessary for entering the Mantra path, the master may, in the best of cases, confer on them the outer, "beneficial empowerments." This will make them happy and will benefit them, allowing them to meditate on the deity and recite the mantra, thus traversing the path the long way round. In ancient times, the four empowerments were granted one by one, according to the disciple's progress in the practice. In the present age, however, out of fear that the transmissions may die out, a qualified teacher grants to a suitable disciple the four empowerments all together on one occasion. Empowerments are mostly given on the basis of a painted mandala. But in fact, the mandala ought to be constructed in three dimensions, and should be the size of an actual house. This was the practice in ancient India. The disciples, after making prostrations outside, should then enter the mandala through the eastern gate. And sitting in front of the guru, the lord of the mandala, they should receive empowerment from him.

121 [DKR/OC] This means to recognize the natural presence of the tathāgatagarbha in all beings—in other words, that they are all, by their very nature, pure deities. The expression "yoga of the vajra" refers to meditation on a vajra standing on a moon disk—the vajra being a symbol of ultimate bodhichitta, and the moon a symbol of relative bodhichitta.

122 [DKR/OC] Receiving an empowerment in the terma tradition is the same as meeting Guru Rinpoche in person. And as Guru Rinpoche himself said, those who receive such empowerments will not fall into the lower realms but will instead be born of kingly lineage. Receiving one empowerment every year

means that, after a hundred years, one has received a hundred empowerments; and even if one's karma is such that one must be reborn as an animal, one will become a peacock or a lion, sovereigns among the animals. Keeping the samaya ensures an improved situation in one's subsequent existences.

123 *sbyangs rtogs sbar gsum.* [DKR/OC] This refers respectively to the dissolution or *purification* of one's ordinary perception of the torma into the expanse of emptiness. This is followed by an *understanding* of its nature as being wisdom amrita (i.e., the five nectars and five meats, corresponding to the five enlightened families), and then to its *increase* (each particle of the torma symbolizing infinite offerings of things pleasing to the senses).

124 See *Treasury of Precious Qualities,* bk. 1, pp. 198–201.

125 [DKR/OC] In accordance with the Mahayoga tradition, the teacher should, in a gradual manner, give to disciples who have faith, the ten outer "benefiting empowerments" (*phan pa'i dbang*). To diligent disciples, he should give the five inner "enabling empowerments" (*nus pa'i dbang*). To disciples who are able to engage in the profound yogic practice, he should bestow the three secret empowerments. And with great compassion, he should take great care of all his disciples, not allowing their potential to be wasted.

126 This is done by requesting the owners of the land and the spirits who preside over it for permission to use their territory.

127 See also *Systems of Buddhist Tantra,* pp. 218–23.

128 [DKR/OC] The disciples must purify themselves outside the mandala with water from the vase of activity (*las bum*). They must then cover their eyes with a red ribbon and hold a flower in their hands. The teacher asks them: "What do you desire?" The disciples reply: "I desire great bliss, supreme good fortune." The disciples offer their bodies to all the Buddhas, whereupon the teacher, visualizing himself in the form of a heruka, emanates wrathful forms and drives away all obstacle-makers. He then visualizes the five male and five female Buddhas on his ten fingers. From their hearts emanate rays of light, which dispel the defilements of the disciples. The teacher then visualizes the disciples as deities. The three centers of the disciples' bodies are protected by the armor of the three vajras. The teacher then bestows on the disciples the samayas of the three vajras. He explains all the root and branch samayas. He gives to the disciples the "water of commitment" from a small conch, saying that if they keep the samaya, buddhahood will be reached in one life, but that if they fail to keep it, they will fall into the vajra hell. The master then admonishes the disciples to practice the yogic activities without any hesitation or fear, according to their samaya. The disciples throw their flowers into the mandala in order to determine their connection with the deity. They then place their flowers on the crowns of their heads as the diadem of their enlightened family, in connection with which, they each receive a secret name.

129 In other words, if he or she has not yet reached the path of seeing.

130 This refers to the families of enlightened body, speech, and mind; in other words, to the mandalas of Manjushri, Avalokiteshvara, and Vajrapani respectively.

131 *cod pan.* In the lower tantras, the crown is merely jeweled; it does not carry the symbols of the five Buddhas. [KPS]

132 *mtha' rten gyi dbang.*

133 This is done by exhibiting the mudra of the teachings. [KPS]

134 The former give permission to hear the tantras, and the latter give permission to explain them. [KPS]

135 *rig pa'i dbang lnga.* "These are so called because they cause one to recognize the nature of the five aggregates, the five defilements, and all other samsaric phenomena, as being the five Buddhas, the five wisdoms, and so on—thus purifying them in the expanse beyond suffering, and causing one to awaken to ultimate reality." [YG III, 166:5–6]. See also *Systems of Buddhist Tantra*, p. 227.

136 These five empowerments correspond respectively to Akshobhya, Ratnasambhava, Amitabha, Amoghasiddhi, and Vairochana. [KPS]

137 "The Yogatantra empowerments correspond, by and large, to the vase initiation of the Anuttaratantras. However, since the latter have many extraordinary qualities, their empowerments are superior to those of the Yogatantra." [YG III, 145:4–5] For a discussion of the sevenfold vase empowerment, see *Systems of Buddhist Tantra*, pp. 225–26.

138 [DKR/OC] The class of tantra (*rgyud sde*) and the class of sadhana (*sgrub sde*) refer respectively to the kahma and the majority of the terma teachings.

139 The enumeration given here differs slightly from other accounts in which the "permission" is added after "name." See *Systems of Buddhist Tantra*, p. 229, where the list (water, crown, silk ribbons, vajra and bell, conduct, name, and permission) is in agreement with *Kalachakra Tantra: Rite of Initiation* (London: Wisdom Publications, 1985), pp. 109–17.

140 The last four lines of this quotation are particularly obscure, and this is only a very tentative rendering. The Tibetan text reads: *'gyur dang mi 'gyur bar chad can / bar ched med pa de las bzhan / zhes bcu bdun dang.*

141 *rgyud lung man ngag.* This classification refers respectively to the Mahayoga, Anuyoga, and Atiyoga.

142 According to Longchenpa, this may refer to the attributes or to the seed-syllables of the five families. [KPS]

143 *rdo rje rgyal po bka' rab 'byams.* This empowers the disciple to become a vajra master with the knowledge of all the teachings of the sutra and tantra. The empowerment is granted by showing the throne, chariot, canopy, parasol, etc. [KPS]

144 There are various interpretations concerning the root and explanatory tantras of the elucidatory system of Anuyoga. The *Scripture of All-Inclusive Knowledge* (*kun 'dus rig pa'i mdo*) is regarded by some authorities as the root tantra, while the *Scripture of Summarized Wisdom* (*mdo dgongs pa 'dus pa*) is taken as the explanatory tantra. Others say, however, that the first chapter of the *mdo dgongs pa 'dus pa* is the root tantra, and that the remaining chapters constitute the explanatory tantra. The *mdo dgongs pa 'dus pa* has as its principal mandala the (Anuyoga) mandala of *Gathering of the Great Assembly* (*tshogs chen 'dus pa*), accompanied by many secondary mandalas corresponding to the vehicle of "the gods and humankind," and the vehicles of the Shravakas, Pratyekabuddhas, and Bodhisattvas, and of Kriyatantra, Ubhayatantra, and Yogatantra. [KPS]

145 That is, the physical body (the residue of the five impure elements), which "ripens" into the deity. [DKR]

146 That is, the deities belonging to the Anuyoga mandala of the *Gathering of the Great Assembly* (*tshogs chen 'dus pa*).

147 Renowned, that is, in the Anuyoga tradition. [DKR]

148 The plow breaks up and renders workable the hard ground, a metaphor for the rough, untrained mind. [KPS]

149 "Those who have the karmic fortune enabling them to enter immediately into the mandala of ultimate bodhichitta may receive the empowerment of the creative power of awareness, which does not depend on the example wisdom of the third initiation." [YG III, 147:6]

150 "According to the class of pith instructions of the Atiyoga, these four empowerments purify the defilements of body, speech, mind, and conceptual obscurations. They establish the potential for the enlightened body, speech, mind, and self-arisen luminosity. They respectively empower the practitioner to meditate, in accordance with Atiyoga, on the uncommon generation stage, on the tummo-fire, on the union of bliss and emptiness, and finally to realize the primordial wisdom of primal purity (*ka dag*)—and experience directly the spontaneously present luminosity (*lhun grub*). . . . It should be understood that, though this classification of empowerments resembles the fourfold classification according to the common Anuttaratantras, the meaning is not the same." [YG III, 148:3–6]

151 *zab khyad sgrub dbang.* This is an empowerment given in a special situation, when the teacher as well as the disciples practice the sadhana for a certain period in a closed situation, at the end of which the empowerment is given. [KPS]

152 This text is usually ascribed to the master Shura (Ashvaghosha).

153 See appendix 1.

154 *gzhi'i dbang.* [DKR/OC] These are called "empowerments," because they empower the sugatagarbha to manifest fully. This happens instantaneously or gradually, according to the capacity of the being concerned.

155 The use of "empowerment" indifferently in these three contexts is somewhat awkward. It is worth remembering that the English term, which works well enough in the case of the "path empowerment," is a translation of the Tibetan *dbang*, which simply means "power."

156 Earth, water, fire, air, space, and consciousness.

157 In other words, only beings in the desire realm are appropriate vessels for empowerment. "Of these, however, the gods, the asuras, the inhabitants of Uttarakuru, and beings caught in the lower realms are not in possession of the *perfect* support for empowerment. Only the inhabitants of the other three cosmic continents are referred to as extraordinary vessels for empowerment. In our world, where karma ripens very quickly, they are referred to as supreme vessels for empowerment. This, however, is not a clear-cut definition, because, for example, four of the five noble beings (i.e., a naga, a yaksha, a rakshasa, and a celestial being) and also certain Arhats (who while dwelling in the state of nirvana without residue, engaged in the path of mantra in their mental bodies) *were* extraordinary vessels for the initiation." [YG III, 153:1–2] See also appendix 1.

158 For a discussion of the essence-drop (*thig le*), or essential constituent (*khams*) and its different categories, see note 254 and *Systems of Buddhist Tantra*, p. 181–84 and notes.

159 For a discussion of the various kinds of causes and conditions, see *Myriad Worlds*, pp. 188–93.

160 "In fact, this is not an inflexible rule. If a person's mind has been ripened by empowerments received in previous existences, it is possible to aspire to the higher empowerments and to receive them. A person with sharp faculties who is able to gain accomplishment at a single stroke (*cig char pa*), who receives the empowerment of the creative power of awareness right in the beginning of the path, may gain immediate realization." [YG III, 155:1–2] This is illustrated in the story of King Indrabodhi. See *Treasury of Precious Qualities*, bk. 1, p. 468n158.

161 These syllables are A SU NRI TRE PRE DU (respectively, the syllables of gods, asuras, humans, animals, pretas, and hell beings).

162 Respectively, OM AH HUNG and É WAM.

163 That is, primordial wisdom in its veiled condition, as it occurs in the case of ordinary beings.

164 "For craving is the root of all the fetters that enslave beings in the state of samsaric existence." [YG III, 158:4]

165 "Each of the four empowerments is considered in relation to nine topics: (1) that to which it is the main antidote; (2) the mandala on which it is based; (3) the empowerment bestowed; (4) the defilements purified; (5) the view realized; (6) the path of practice for which it empowers; (7) its highest attain-

ment; (8) the instruction for the moment of death (transference); and (9) the result obtained." [YG III, 158:6–159:1]

166 For a description of the various kinds of mandala, see appendix 5.

167 "Such as those accruing from the act of killing." [YG III, 169:2]

168 The four states are the waking state, dream, deep sleep, and sexual climax.

169 *lus kyi thig le,* the essence-drop located in the center of the chakra at the crown of the head. See *Systems of Buddhist Tantra,* p. 449n89.

170 "The first two essential features are associated with a view that is adulterated with a certain clinging (present while one is on the path) to appearance and emptiness as separate realities. The third feature is free of such clinging and is the view related to the time of result. However, if this last view is compared with the view of the perfection stage, it, too, is found to be contaminated [by some degree of clinging]." [YG III, 170:5–6]

171 "In this context, the so-called highest attainment (*grub mtha' snyogs*) is the gaining of a ground of realization or the accomplishment of a Vidyādhara level through the direct realization of the given view." [YG III, 171:3–4]

For Longchenpa, the first Vidyādhara level corresponds to the path of joining. In the commentary on the *Guhyagarbha* by Zur Shakya Senge, it is said to correspond to the first ground of realization. [KPS]

172 This refers either to the transference of the consciousness to a pure field or to birth in a family of tantric practitioners. There also exists a method of transference of consciousness called transference through the transfiguration of perception and appearance (*snang ba bsgyur ba'i 'pho ba*), in which one's consciousness is transferred to the yidam-deity and the corresponding buddha-field as visualized in the generation stage. [KPS]

173 [DKR/OC] The disappearance of this pulsation indicates that the twenty-one knots that obstructed the central channel have been loosed.

174 "This empowerment is called 'secret' not only because it should be kept hidden from those who lack the proper karmic fortune, but also because the latter should not even hear about it." [YG III, 172:6]

175 When the wind agitates the essence-drop associated with speech (*ngag gi thig le*), located in the chakra at the throat, the person concerned has the ability—and also the tendency—to speak a great deal. [KPS]

176 For a detailed explanation of the winds, see appendix 6 and *Systems of Buddhist Tantra,* p. 176–80.

177 "When the associated set of yogic exercises (*'khrul 'khor*) is performed, the wind is used to undo the knots on the channels. With the help of the tummo fire, the bodhichitta melts; and thanks to the exercises of physical yoga, all the channels are filled with bodhichitta, as a result of which, dualistic thoughts are brought to a halt. Many kinds of concentration are mastered thereby,

such as that of the ten limitless ayatanas. In the same way, mastery is gained in the four activities, and many qualities of the path increase like a summer stream in spate." [YG III, 179:1–3]

178 This explanation of the four degrees has been rendered following the text of Yönten Gyamtso. [YG III, 179:3–6]

179 *rlung sems.* This expression makes explicit the fact that mind and wind are constant companions.

180 [DKR/OC] When the wind-mind deviates in the eight channels of the heart chakra, a learned and intelligent person will become completely stupid.

181 "The first three wisdoms are contaminated by dualistic clinging. The fourth is not." [YG III, 179:6]

182 Before the path of seeing is reached, one is unable to realize actual, ultimate luminosity (*don gyi 'od gsal*). Only the "example luminosity" (a kind of fore-taste) is attained.

183 "The syllables are of three kinds. First, there is the unfabricated, spontaneously present syllable (*rang bzhin lhun grub kyi yi ge*), namely, the luminous nature of the mind. Second, there are the syllables or speech-sounds dwelling in the channels of the body (*rtsa yi yi ge*), namely, the vowels and consonants, which are the seeds of the deities. Third, there are the sign-syllables of words and the objects to which they refer (*sgra don rtags kyi yi ge*), in other words, term-universals and object-universals. Their primary written form is Lentsa, Devanagari, Tibetan script, and so forth." [YG III, 298:5–6] The Tibetan term *yi ge* primarily means a syllable or speech-sound (*skad kyi gdangs*) as distinct from a mere noise.

184 *gsung dbyangs kyi yan lag drug bcu.* For the sixty aspects of melodious speech, see Jamgön Kongtrul, *The Light of Wisdom* (Boston: Shambhala Publications, 1995), pp. 195–96.

185 "It is extremely difficult to impart (and also to receive) openly and in public the third empowerment as it is literally described. It is nowadays granted using an image of the consort, etc., whereby disciples endowed with both sharp faculties and faith are greatly benefited." [YG III, 187:1]

186 "It is said that those who receive the third empowerment based literally on the secret mandala of the consort must have previously trained their own body on the path of skillful means. Their channels must be perfectly straight, their winds must be purified, and their essence-drops must have been brought under control. Trained in the view of the two previous empowerments, such disciples must be able to employ this method on the path, according to the extraordinary view and meditation, and without clinging to the bliss of 'dripping.'

"If beginners, who lack this capacity, claim to be practitioners of Mantra and become enmeshed in ordinary desire, they are destined for the lower realms. One may lack the karmic disposition enabling one to take the ordination vow and keep its precepts, but if one practices to the extent of one's ability and with as much faith in the karmic law, and as much faith in the Three Jewels as one can, all will be well. If one fails to do this, and instead claims to be a mantrika; and if, with proud feelings of superiority, one tries to acquire wealth and renown, this is what is called wrong pride. And to gain one's livelihood by such means is wrong livelihood. Those who act in this way use the profound teachings only to bring ruin to themselves and others.

"I think that it is far better to be ordinary, humble laypeople who try to practice virtue and shun evil as much as they can. Those who are able to observe correctly the Pratimoksha vows, as explained in the Vinaya, by binding the doors of their senses, but are unable to practice correctly the path of skillful means of the Mantrayana, should, with faith and confidence in the Secret Mantras, exert themselves mainly on the 'path of liberation' (grol lam). For if they train on the path of skillful means (thabs lam) literally as it is taught (relying on the secret mandala of the consort), this will become an obstacle on their path, and their discipline will be distorted. It was with such practitioners in mind that Atisha wrote in his Lamp for the Path:

> As for the secret empowerment of wisdom—
> Because it is forbidden in the strongest terms,
> In the great tantra of the Primordial Buddha,
> Those who practice chastity should not receive it.

"However, those who are able to use such skillful means may indeed take the support of the mudra of the path of the third empowerment. For them it is not forbidden. For it is well-known that one who is a supreme vajra-holder is indeed a renunciate who maintains the vow of chastity. On this the tantras of Kila and Kalachakra concur:

> Of the three, the bhikshus are supreme,
> And then the shramaneras come,
> And then, in final place, the laity.

". . . As it is said, one should cultivate a sincere devotion to the vajra-holders who possess the three vows (like the majority of the Indian and Tibetan siddhas). And it is important to think how excellent it would be to live, in one's future lives, according to the view and action of the general Mahayana as vast as space, and the extraordinary view and conduct of the Vajrayana—and not merely adhering to the teachings of the Hinayana in the opinion that the latter are superior. How marvelous it would be to recognize that phenomena are not truly existent, and to understand the one taste of samsara and nirvana. And how splendid it would be to be capable of correctly implementing the skillful means whereby the defilements arise as primordial wisdom and whereby all phenomena (aggregates, etc.) are seen to be the mandala of the deities, pure from the very beginning. How excellent to take respectful support of a mudra, whose nature is wisdom, and who is a helpful friend who can reveal in truth the wisdom mind of the Buddha! One should never scorn or criticize such a consort, for this does violence to the path of skillful means and is utterly wrong." [YG III, 181:5–184:4]

187 That is, covetousness, evil intent, and wrong views.

188 *yid 'dzin pa'i thig le.* This is the essence-drop situated at the center of the chakra at the heart.

189 *snang mched thob gsum.* For a detailed discussion of the various meanings of these three lights, see *Systems of Buddhist Tantra,* pp. 251–60, and p. 420n5.

190 "Gross bodhichitta" is the name given in the tantras to the male and female essential substances. It has a coarse and a fine component. The coarse component corresponds to the actual generative fluids, whereas the fine component is that which gives radiance and strength to the body.

191 "Furthermore, signs appear indicating that the essence-drops are purified. The essential fluid becomes clear like water. The practitioner has neither white hair nor wrinkles, experiences no need either for food or clothing, is able to pass through rocks and mountains, and has power over the outer and inner sacred places, lands, the dakas and dakinis, etc." [YG III, 189:6–190:2]

192 *'pho ba'i bag chags.* [DKR/OC] The expression "utterly subtle conceptual obscurations" refers to the obscurations that are implied, and actually produced, by the progression of the three lights: "appearance of light," "increase of light," and "full culmination of light" (*snang gsum 'pho ba'i sgrib pa*). First, there is the "light" that allows the perception of phenomena (*snang ba*). This is followed by "increase of light" (*mched pa*), in other words, the discrimination between good and bad, and so on. It is on this basis that attachment or revulsion occurs. This is "full culmination" (*nyer thob*). This process disappears only when dualistic apprehension ceases.

193 This is a translation of the Tibetan *thugs rje.* This word, which is usually regarded as the honorific equivalent of *snying rje* (literally, "lord or power of the mind or heart"), is in ordinary Mahayana contexts translated as "compassion." And in such contexts, this very approximate rendering works well enough. In other contexts, however, the word has other connotations that are perfectly in line with the literal Tibetan meaning but which cannot, by any stretch of the imagination, be covered by the English word "compassion." In the terminology of the Great Perfection, *thugs rje* is defined by Khenpo Yönten Gyamtso as "unadulterated awareness that has not yet stirred from its original state." See note 496.

194 "As with any practice for the transference of consciousness, this transference has three stages: training, familiarization, and implementation. It is said that if one familiarizes oneself with this practice, when the moment of death comes, one will have the power to implement it. This can be done all by

oneself, or with the help of another person who is able to refresh one's memory. One confesses all one's faults and shortcomings, and prays to the teacher with great intensity. Then with the thought: 'Now, for the sake of beings, and by using my own death, I must recognize my own mind as Buddha,' one should remain in a state of meditative equipoise, thus performing the transference." [YG III, 194:3–6]

195 "All the views mentioned are referred to as 'views of experience and concentration.' They are different from the views of the causal vehicle, which are established through hearing and reflecting on the teachings. The fading away of the pulsation of the channels (*rtsa'i 'gros thim*) and so forth refers to the fact that the impure channels, winds, and essence-drops melt into the state of pure primordial wisdom. The granting of these empowerments does no more than sow the seed in one's mind of the possible attainment of the ultimate goal. It does not mean that the result is actually achieved. It is said that if one receives an empowerment from a qualified teacher but fails to keep the samaya, one will be reborn immediately after death in the lower realms. However, without having to wait for a long time, one will meet the Mantrayana teachings again and practice this path. If one keeps the samaya but omits to practice the stages of generation and perfection in the same life that the empowerments were received, one will be reborn for seven times in a family of 'pure' lineage, and will gradually reach the ultimate extent of the path, thus gaining liberation. If one receives an empowerment, keeps the samaya, and strives in the practice, one will actualize, in this very lifetime, at the moment of death, or in the bardo, all the qualities of the four kayas (the resultant effects as these have been previously explained).

"Now the result of a given empowerment cannot be attained in isolation—that is, by relying solely on the practice related to that empowerment alone. It must be associated with other practices. It is only by meditating on all of them together that the qualities of the four kayas are realized simultaneously. They are not actualized gradually, one after the other. This is similar to the causal vehicle, where it is said that the two accumulations bring forth the two kayas. However, the mere accumulation of merit without wisdom will not in itself result in the attainment of the rupakaya. It is through the simultaneous accumulation of both wisdom and merit that, when buddhahood occurs, the two kayas are achieved together and at once." [YG III, 195:3–196:5]

196 "Shimcha" means to "cast" or "sprinkle." "Shekata," or rather "shikta" (from "abhishikta"), means to "pour into a mold." See *Systems of Buddhist Tantra*, p. 205.

197 "This refers only to those of superior karmic fortune. Normally, impurities are truly eliminated by the practice of the path corresponding to the empowerment granted." [YG III, 197:2]

198 "The empowerments of cause (ground), path, and result are not arranged in

chronological sequence in the way that cause and result are related in the causal vehicle. They are in fact inseparable and are so called only according to the circumstances of the practitioner. The first three empowerments (vase, secret, and wisdom) are compounded and relative because the manner of introduction and the ensuing practice are both associated with the ordinary mind. The fourth empowerment shares the nature of the uncompounded ultimate truth, because both the way of introduction and the practice linked with this are associated with primordial wisdom, which transcends the ordinary intellect." [YG III, 199:5–200:2]

199 See note 156.

200 Literally, "four names." A reference to the first element in the expression "name and form" (Skt. *namarupa;* Tib. *ming gzugs*), which is the fourth of the twelve interdependent links, and corresponds to the five aggregates. In addition to the form aggregate (the body), the four "name-aggregates" are the four mental aggregates: feeling, perception, conditioning factors, and consciousness.

201 *mtshungs ldan gyi rgyu.* Concomitant causes are said to be concordant and simultaneous by virtue of sharing certain factors, like fellow travelers on a journey, who do everything together and in the same way.

202 "It is also said that when the sambhogakaya Buddha, appearing as the illusory display of primordial wisdom, bestows the three profound empowerments on a disciple on the final path (i.e., at the end of the tenth bhumi), by means of which the propensity to experience successively the three stages of light, increase of light, and culmination of light (*snang gsum 'pho ba'i bag chags*) is purified, the minds of the teacher and disciple mingle inseparably." [YG III, 199:3–4]

Considering such quotations, one should bear in mind that the sambhogakaya Buddha is not an external entity that empowers the disciples from outside. The sambhogakaya Buddha is the actualization of the inner qualities of the tathāgatagarbha by the Bodhisattvas themselves. The Bodhisattvas are in fact empowered by their own primordial wisdom. [KPS]

203 [DKR/OC] The criterion that determines whether or not the empowerment is truly received is the presence or absence of total confidence that the master giving the empowerment is one with the deity of the mandala. Even if, in a given situation, the disciples do not follow exactly all the details of the empowerment, if they have faith in the master and have fervent devotion, the empowerment is received.

204 "According to the Anuttaratantras, once the vase empowerment has been granted, the Mantrayana vows relating to the generation stage are explained. And at the conclusion of each of the three higher empowerments, one receives the vows relating to the perfection stage associated with that empowerment. These vows share the same nature as the vows of the generation stage. It is thus that, by gradual degrees, the lower vows are enhanced while the specific

aspects or characteristics of the vows (*ldog pa*) remain distinct. It is therefore on the basis of the vows that excellent qualities are cultivated or downfalls occur." [YG III, 200:4–6]

205 For a brief explanation of the stages of generation (kyerim) and perfection (dzogrim), see appendix 7.

206 "In contrast with those who are karmically fortunate (who have trained in the profound path of the generation stage in their previous lives) and those who are possessed of very sharp faculties (and are able to gain accomplishment in the 'sudden' manner), if ordinary beings (who progress by stages) enter this path without proper preliminary training on the common path, they will only waste their potential. In brief, the key points of the training are revulsion for samsara, gained by means of Hinayana practice, and the sincere altruistic attitude of the general Mahayana. All the main principles of the path are complete, and all the secondary elements of the path are naturally included, within these two factors. Anyone who possesses these two factors and who enters the Mantrayana, by relying on a fully qualified teacher, will become a true practitioner of the Mantrayana path.

"On the other hand, if one's mind has not been turned away from samsara in general, and especially from the ordinary appearances of this life; if one is without a good and altruistic heart; and if one enters the Secret Mantra nonetheless, by receiving empowerment and training in the generation and perfection stages—one may indeed succeed in giving an excellent impression of oneself. But however high the view that one talks about may be, and however great one's skill in the practice, and though indeed one may gain such common accomplishments as flying in the sky like a bird, or passing through mountains and cliffs and so on, one's path will be a mistaken path. It will result in no more than the continuation of samsaric existence. It is therefore of the highest moment not to deviate from these crucial points of the path." [YG III, 208:4–209:5]

207 This is a reference to the modes of birth occurring in the different ages of the world. The traditional account of the evolution, or rather devolution, of beings in the universe is given in the second chapter of the *Treasury of Precious Qualities*, bk. 1, pp. 360–62.

208 "Some of the pretas that move in space, some demons, yakshas, and rakshasas are born from eggs. Birth from warmth and moisture means birth from earth, stones, water, trees, and so on." [YG III, 208:2]

209 The concentration on great emptiness corresponds to the empty nature (*ngo bo stong pa*), the dharmakaya; the concentration on compassion corresponds to the luminous character (*rang bzhin gsal ba*), the sambhogakaya; and the concentration on the cause or seed-syllable corresponds to the unceasing cognitive potency (*thugs rje ma 'gags pa*), the nirmanakaya of inner luminosity.

210 [DKR/OC] The words "ripens into" refer to the beneficial preparation for the perfection stage, which is like the clearing and plowing of a field.

211 "The term 'beginner' is understood to apply to all practitioners up to and including those who are able to visualize the mandala roughly for only a brief moment. However, following the explanation given by Nagarjuna in the *Five Stages* and by Aryadeva in the *Lamp That Integrates the Practices*, if a distinction is made between the generation and the perfection stages, all the aspects of the generation stage are classified as being for 'beginners,' while the opposite is said of practitioners of the perfection stage. Concerning the 'two-step generation stage,' there are two traditions: the tradition of the sadhana class (*sgrub sde*) and the tradition of the tantra class (*rgyud sde*). The following explanation comes from the sadhana tradition of the Vidyādhara Padmasambhava, as set forth in the *Plenitude of Secrets of the Eight Mandalas* (*bka' brgyad gsang ba yongs rdzogs*)." [YG III, 224:5–225:2]

This is a terma text in six volumes revealed by Guru Chöwang (1212–70). It is one of the three major termas on the Eight Great Mandalas, and has Chemchok (Mahottara) as its main deity. Since the present explanation is given in terms of this terma, when allusions are made to the principal deity, the reference is to Chemchok.

212 [DKR/OC] The other tathāgatas, summoned by the sound of the deities in union, enter the father's mouth and, through the fire of pleasure, melt into his heart. They then emerge from the secret space of the mother, appearing as the mandala of the eight herukas. Consequently, to generate "others as one's children" means to summon the other tathāgatas, and cause them to emerge and appear as the deities of the mandala. They are the children of "oneself," i.e., the tathāgatagarbha.

213 [DKR/OC] According to the terminology used in the *Mayajala*, the three concentrations are "great emptiness," "mirage-like compassion," and "the single mudra or deity" (*stong pa chen po, snying rje sgyu ma, phyag rgya gcig pa*).

214 [DKR/OC] The practitioner meditates on the eight herukas positioned on the eight spokes of the iron wheel: in the east, there is Yangdak Heruka (Tib. *yang dag*; Skt. *Vishuddha*); in the south is Shinjeshe (Tib. *gshin rje gshed*; Skt. *Yamantaka*); in the west is Tamdin (Tib. *rta mgrin*; Skt. *Hayagriva*); in the north is Phurba (Tib. *phur ba*; Skt. *Kila*); in the southeast Mamo Pötong (Tib. *ma mo rbod gtong*; Skt. *Matarah*); in the southwest is Rigdzin Lama (Tib. *rig 'dzin bla ma*; Skt. *Vidyādhara guru*); in the northwest is Möpa Trangag (Tib. *dmod pa drag sngags*; Skt. *Vajramantrabhiru*); in the northeast, Jigten Chötö (Tib. *'jig rten mchod bstod*; Skt. *Lokastotrapuja*). And on the main (central) seat is oneself in the form of Chemchok Heruka (Tib. *che mchog he ru ka*; Skt. *Mahottara*) in union with his consort.

215 [DKR/OC] They are the display of the eightfold wisdom of oneself in the form of the cause heruka (Chemchok).

216 That is, the seed-syllables of the forty-two peaceful deities, etc.

217 [DKR/OC] This is, as it were, a state of no-thought.

218 [DKR/OC] They emerge like newborn children (*sras*) and are always in peaceful form.

219 [DKR/OC] The goddess with the hook touches the lotus upon which are the deities that dwell in Akanishtha, the self-arisen wisdom.

220 The samayasattva (*dam tshig sems dpa'*) is the visualized deity; the jnanasattva (*ye shes sems dpa'*) is the wisdom deity invited from the ultimate expanse.

221 *gnyug ma'i lha.* In other words, Samantabhadra, with one head, two arms, etc.

222 The notions of purification, perfection, and ripening may be applied to the generation stage that purifies birth from an egg as follows. "The melting into light of the principal and surrounding deities ('one's own children'—as described in the detailed kyerim), and the resting of these same deities in the state of emptiness (as described in the short kyerim) *purify* the moment of death, when all outer and inner appearances and thoughts momentarily cease. Since one's habitual tendencies are thus purified in the ultimate expanse, these meditations *perfect* the dharmakaya present in the ground [see note 223]. Finally, by arresting all dualistic concepts, these same meditations *ripen* into the perfection stage of luminosity, which has the nature of primordial wisdom. Furthermore, the visualization of the main and surrounding deities (oneself as 'the child of others,' as described in the detailed kyerim), together with the meditation on the sadhana according to a given text (as described in the short kyerim), *purify* the vast array of perceptions occuring both in the bardo (after death when the wind-mind gradually increases in strength) and during life. These meditations *perfect* countless rupakayas (the bodies of the deities of the level of union on the path of no more learning), which arise from the dharmakaya and are as infinite as the dharmadhatu. And they *ripen* into the ability of the dzogrim practitioner to manifest in the body of the level of union on the path of learning." [YG III, 237 :3–238 :2]

223 *gzhi la rdzogs.* It should be remembered that when a quality is said to be perfected, this means that an already perfect quality, primordially present in the fundamental nature of the mind, has been uncovered and actualized.

224 In other words, these meditations are beneficial for the practice of the perfection stage.

225 *gzhi 'bras lto sbyar.* [DKR/OC] In other words, the equality of the ground (the tathāgatagarbha) and the result (buddhahood). In the Mantrayana, both ground and result are pure; the enlightened qualities are all complete in the ground. This is in contrast with the path of the sutras, where one considers the ground as impure, the path as both pure and impure, and the result as pure.

"First of all, that which is to be purified, is samsara. Second, thanks to diligence in the practice of the path, the agents of purification develop in the mind. Third, the fruit of this purification is the actualization of the final result. According to this threefold classification, there are factors of awakening (*mngon byang*) related to the ground, path, and result." [YG III, 243:6–244:2]

226 These factors of awakening of the ground are the five primordial wisdoms, which are the nature of the five factors to be purified.

227 The body of union of the nirmanakaya refers to the nirmanakaya of luminous character. See chapter 13, p. 294.

228 From this point onward, it is impossible to fall into the lower realms, and it is certain that one will attain the path of seeing. Here, the expression *rigs nges thob pa,* the literal meaning of which is "attainment of the definitive lineage," refers to the attainment of the level of acceptance (*bzod pa thob pa*) on the path of joining.

229 This fourth method is not specifically mentioned, but is nevertheless implied, in the description of the remaining four factors of awakening.

230 That is, an egg, warmth and moisture, and miraculous birth.

231 "Generally speaking, it is [only] practitioners who are well trained in the previous two, elaborate, generation stages who are able to practice this genera- tion stage (of the Anuyoga level), which purifies birth from warmth and moisture." [YG III, 255:1]

232 [DKR/OC] Just by uttering the seed-syllable AH, the whole mandala of the peaceful and wrathful deities appears. One does not meditate on the three concentrations, the stages of visualization, the invitation of the wisdom dei- ties, and so on. One should not think, however, that this kind of generation stage practice is incomplete. On the other hand, it is suitable only for prac- titioners who have achieved stability in the three earlier kinds of generation stage. In other words, it corresponds, broadly speaking, to practitioners who are on the path of joining.

233 One may meditate in an aspirational manner (*mos sgom*) or in a truly perfect manner (*lam nges rdzogs*). In the second case, one trains gradually in the three concentrations until they are perfect and firm, and then one meditates gradu- ally and systematically on the rays of light, the palace, and the deities, until the visualization is perfectly achieved.

234 This is the specific exegetical tradition of the Nyingma school. Concentration on suchness or emptiness purifies one's clinging to appearances. Concentra- tion on compassion for mirage-like beings purifies one's clinging to empti- ness. Concentration on the seed-syllable purifies one's clinging to the previous two aspects as being two separate realities. [KPS]

235 "At the start of all one's meditation sessions, even when one's meditation is only aspirational (*mos sgom*), one should complete all the foregoing sections of the ritual and, with a relaxed mind, rest evenly in the concentration on suchness and the all-illuminating concentration until one's mind is perfectly focused on them. One should not be satisfied with the mere recitation of

words. Then one should concentrate systematically on the seed-syllable and the rest of the visualization. This should be the principal feature of the practice. Until one has achieved stability in the generation stage, in which emptiness and appearance are not separate, one should not emphasize the mantra recitation and the radiation and absorption of lights. It is thus that, at every step of the generation stage—whether one is practicing aspirationally, or even meditating in a truly perfect manner (*lam nges rdzogs*)—one should make sure that, in one's practice, the three concentrations are maintained inseparably.

"It is not enough to practice in a sporadic, haphazard way. When a fresco is painted on a wall, the wall serves as the basis for the painting. Without a wall, where could the fresco be placed? On the other hand, even if there is a wall, as long as this is unplastered, the painting of the fresco remains impossible. The plastered surface is the cooperative condition that brings the wall and fresco together. When the fresco is made, wall, plaster, and painting all coexist. In the same way, since the deity is the display of emptiness and compassion, when one meditates on the complete mandala arisen from the concentration on the seed-syllable, these three elements (deity, emptiness, and compassion) are necessarily inseparable. For if ordinary appearances are not purified into emptiness, where can the mandala be visualized? Since all phenomena are empty, and since samsara and nirvana are inseparable, if the mandala of the enlightened body, speech, and mind is meditated upon, it is indeed possible to actualize it. Emptiness, therefore, is the foundation of the generation stage. As it is said [in the *Mulamadhyamaka-karika*, 24:14]:

> Where emptiness is granted
> Everything is likewise granted.
> Where emptiness is unacceptable
> All is likewise unacceptable.

"If phenomena were not empty and ordinary appearances really existed (as they seem), meditation on the generation stage would serve no purpose. As the saying goes, 'Buckwheat will not turn into rice, however much you may empower it!' On the other hand, even if you do know that all is emptiness, if you lack the impulse of compassion, you will never be able to manifest in the rupakaya for the benefit of beings—you will only be like the Shravakas and Pratyekabuddhas, who pass into cessation and who do not assume form bodies in order to work for the good of others.

"Again, you may think that meditation on emptiness and compassion is enough and that there is no need for meditation on the generation stage. But thanks to the path of Secret Mantra, the realization comes swiftly that appearances—illusion-like and arising through interdependence—are primordially pure: they are the wheel of inexhaustible ornaments of the enlightened body, speech, and mind. The generation stage in conjunction with these two elements (of emptiness and compassion) is indeed the supreme method for the attainment of this realization." [YG III, 265:1–266:6]

"Meditation on suchness corresponds to the diamond-like concentration (*rdo rje lta bu'i ting nge 'dzin*). Meditation on compassion corresponds to the mirage-like concentration (*sgyu ma lta bu'i ting nge 'dzin*). Within the practice of both these meditations, the meditation on the seed-syllable—which is the cause of the generation of the deity—corresponds to the fearless or heroic concentration (*dpa' bar 'gro ba'i ting nge 'dzin*)." [YG III, 267:6–268:1] For the diamond-like concentration, etc., see *Treasury of Precious Qualities*, bk. 1, p. 479n222.

236 *srog sdom gzer bzhi*. "Grounded in the three concentrations, all the sections of the generation stage are practiced according to the pith instructions on the *four life-fastening nails*, which rivet the body, speech, and mind (together with their activities) to the three secrets and enlightened activities of the Tathāgatas." [YG III, 268:1–2]

237 The three Dharma robes are: the upper robe (*bla gos* or *chos gos*), the lower robe (*mthang gos*), and the mantle worn by bhikshus (*nam byar*).

238 These five experiences were described by Nyoshul Khen Rinpoche as features of the path of the practice. (1) To begin with, one experiences strong mental movement like a waterfall crashing down a mountain side (*g.yo ba'i nyams ri gzar gyi chu lta bu*). There is a swift movement of the mind, with many thoughts arising and subsiding in quick succession. (2) One then has an experience (which is itself a kind of achievement) that may be likened to a torrent in a ravine (*thob pa'i nyams gcong rong gi klung lta bu*). The splashing movement of the waterfall is somewhat contained, since it is passing through a narrow channel. Moreover, the movement of the water slows down so that one can see the stones on the bed of the stream. In other words, one begins to detect signs of progress (seen in one's dreams, meditation, or even in the outer world). At this point, it is important to take one's mind firmly in hand and to refrain from clinging to such experiences. (3) There follows the stage of habituation, which is like the slow current of a wide river (*goms pa'i nyams chu chen dal 'bab lta bu*). The mountain stream running pell-mell through the ravine then transforms into a slow-running river. The mind is free from major movements of thought. Nevertheless, others remain that are more difficult to detect, and it is important to check with one's teacher and to avoid any kind of conceitedness. (4) After this, one experiences an almost complete absence of movement, like a still lake moved only by the breeze (*mi g.yo ba'i nyams mtsho chung rlung gis bskyod pa lta bu*). At this point, the river has merged with a lake. If there is a wind, ripples form on the surface; but otherwise the lake is calm. At this point in the meditation, practitioners have many experiences of clarity, visions of deities, seed-syllables, and so on. It is most important to avoid any sense of pride. (5) Finally, there comes the ultimate, perfect experience similar to a great and waveless ocean (*mthar phyin pa'i nyams rgya mtsho chen po rlabs dang bral ba lta bu*). The lake turns into a vast ocean untroubled by any waves. The mind of the practitioner is without distraction of any kind. These same five experiences are concisely described in YG III, 705:5–707:3.

239 *dpal chen zhal lung.* An instruction on the *Gathering of the Great Glorious One* (*dpal chen 'dus pa*). Both are termas of Jigme Lingpa.

240 "In the early stages, while one is unused to self-visualization as a deity, when one thinks or tells oneself, 'I am the deity,' and 'The deity is like this and like that,' the deity appears in the mind in a conceptual manner. This experience is referred to as the deity manifesting as a mental object. As one trains in this way, the appearance of the deity eventually becomes stable, and there is no further need for the intentional conceptualization of the deity's form. It manifests clearly and distinctly within a thought-free state of shamatha, as though one were watching an object with normal eyesight. This is called the deity manifesting as a visual object. Finally, when one is truly expert (*gyad du gyur*) in the generation stage practice, and the level of Vidyādhara with a karmic body (*rnam smin rig' dzin*) is attained, all the aspects of one's own appearance (aggregates, elements, and senses) are blended with the mandala of the deity. Appearances are no longer perceived as ordinary. This is the stage in which the illusory body of the deity is actualized, in other words, the body of the union (of the dharmakaya and rupakaya). This is also referred to as the deity manifesting as a bodily or tangible object." [YG III, 273:4–274:3]

241 "During the first stage, when the mandala manifests as a mental object, one should preserve *the recollection of perfect purity* (*rnam dag dran pa*) of all the aspects of the mandala. The buddhafield and the palace should not be regarded as ordinary material things, nor should the deities be thought of as ordinary persons. One should consider that they are all expressions of the one primordial wisdom manifesting as the symbolic mudra (deity) endowed with attributes. Every element of the mandala is perfectly pure, from the wheel, which lies below the palace and signifies the five primordial wisdoms that cut through defilement, until the jewel ornament on the highest pinnacle. The three faces of the principal deity signify either the three doors of perfect liberation or the three kayas. Its six arms signify either the five wisdoms together with the sixth (namely, the self-arisen primordial wisdom), or the six paramitas. The four legs signify either the four boundless attitudes or the four bases of miraculous powers (of the path of accumulation), and so on. In such a way, one should call to mind the purity of all the aspects of the principal and surrounding deities—their faces, arms, posture, ornaments, garments, and so forth.

"One should also have a *firm pride or self-assurance* (*nga rgyal brtan pa*) that one is indeed the deity. One should not think that one is not really the deity and that one is only visualizing it, or that this deity is not genuine but just a representation, an imagined mental object. On the contrary, one should be aware that one's self-cognizing awareness (the nature of which is the union of appearance and emptiness, of one taste with the primordial wisdom of all the Tathāgatas) is the primordial, true, and authentic deity of ultimate reality, the unceasing creative power of which arises as the display of the mandala of the palace and the deities. One should be mindfully focused on this. When the visualization becomes very stable, there is no need for the two aspects of perfect purity and firm self-assurance of being the deity to be intentionally contrived. They are self-evidently present.

"The nail of concentration on the deity has three functions. First, from the lower point of view, that of samsara, it *purifies* the propensities for the formation of the body through the four kinds of birth. Second, from the higher point of view, that of buddhahood, it *perfects* the result [already present] in the ground. This is the inconceivable secret of the enlightened body, which transcends all physical characteristics such as face and arms, and manifests in form bodies according to the needs of beings. Third, from the intermediate point of view, that of the path, since the entire network of channels is purified as a pure deity, this practice *ripens* into the perfection stage, which brings the aggregate of the vajra body under control." [YG III, 274:3–276:1]

242 "In the heart of all the deities, there are 'wisdom beings' (Skt. *jnanasattva*). These resemble the deities themselves but are without ornaments and implements. In the heart of the wisdom beings, there are 'concentration beings' (Skt. *samadhisattva*) in the form of the seed-syllables corresponding to the life force of the deities in question. Placed in front of this letter is the beginning of the encircling mantra. Concentrating one-pointedly on this, one should perform the recitation, either accumulating a specific number of recitations, practicing for a fixed period of time, or until the signs of accomplishment appear. In particular, one should strive in the vajra recitation, recognizing as mantra the exhalation, inhalation, and retention of the breath.

"From the lower point of view, that of samsara, the mantra recitation *purifies* all the speech propensities of beings. From the higher point of view, that of buddhahood, it *perfects* the result [already present] in the ground. This is the inconceivable secret of enlightened speech beyond words: the arising of countless systems of teaching, which are themselves no more than the forms and aspects of enlightened speech. From the intermediate point of view, that of the practice on the path, since the recitation of mantra purifies speech (which is of the nature of wind) so that it becomes the display of mantra, it *ripens* into the practice of the perfection stage, which takes the wind as its support." [YG III, 276:3–277:1]

243 [DKR/OC] This coordinates the inhalation, retention, and exhalation of breath with the recitation of OM AH HUNG.

244 "Visible objects and sounds, the world and its inhabitants, appear— spontaneously and of themselves—as deities, mantras, and palaces. This, however, is not compounded, a contrivance imagined by the mind. In their purity and equality, phenomena *are* the spontaneous display of great emptiness, ultimate reality. Phenomenal existence is the mandala arising within the ground nature (*snang srid gzhir bzhengs kyi dkyil 'khor*). When one abides in this mandala, there is not the slightest dualistic apprehension of self and other,

samayasattva and jnanasattva, things to be accomplished and agents of accomplishment, purity and impurity, and so forth. Within the expanse of nondual great equality—in other words, in the mandala of the primordial buddhahood of samsara and nirvana—it is impossible to perceive a difference between the 'deity' and oneself. One's utterly pure nature is inseparable from the nature of the deity. It is in this understanding of great equality, the Vajradhatu mandala, that one must train oneself." [YG III, 277:3–6]

"From the lower point of view, that of samsara, this aspect of practice *purifies* all the propensities of the mind, which have mere clarity for their nature, and all the thoughts that radiate from them. From the higher point of view, that of buddhahood, it *perfects* the result (already present) in the ground. This is the inconceivable secret of the enlightened mind (ultimate reality devoid of all conceptual elaboration) and of all its forms, namely, the countless kinds of preternatural knowledge. From the intermediate point of view, that of the path, one's training in ultimate reality, which is the indivisibility of appearance and emptiness, *ripens* into the meditation on the bliss, clarity, and emptiness of the perfection stage, which takes relative and ultimate bodhichitta as its support." [YG III, 278:4–279:1]]

245 "The universe and its inhabitants are visualized as the mandala of deities. The minds of the latter do not stir from the realization of ultimate reality. Their speech is the indestructible resonance of the mantra that is their essence, and it is endowed with sixty melodious qualities. Their bodies display the nine expressions of peaceful deities or the nine demeanors of wrathful deities. From the mantra garland in their hearts, there emanate countless rays of light: shining white, brilliant yellow, intense red, dark green, and dazzling blue. These make offerings to the mandala of the Buddhas and Bodhisattvas of the three times and ten directions, in the manner of the gods that dwell in the heaven of the Enjoyment of Magical Creations (where the one who offers and the one who receives the offering are not separate). These offerings satisfy the Buddhas and Bodhisattvas with the savor of the great primordial wisdom of bliss and emptiness.

"Although within the perceptual field of primordial wisdom, not even the name of samsara is found, nevertheless, in the field of the ordinary mind's dualistic perception, there is a strong clinging to an environment, mental states, and to the physical forms of beings (*gnas don lus*). The rays of light of skillful means touch all illusory beings (which appear without truly existing), together with their unimaginably numerous environments in the six realms, instantaneously cleansing their ignorance and deluded perceptions. Their bodies transform into the bodies of deities, their speech becomes mantra, and their minds become the unchanging wisdom of the dharmakaya. They are indeed Buddhas. One comes to the understanding that the world does not have even a nominal existence. This aspect of the practice, referred to as the yoga of the spontaneous accomplishment of the twofold goal, is the main factor that brings about supreme accomplishment.

"Furthermore, the rays of white light perform the act of pacifying; the yellow rays perform the act of increasing; the red rays perform the act of attracting; and the green rays perform the act of subjugating through ferocious means. And it is through alternating the visualization of the radiation and reabsorption of lights (and the different focus of activities) that one achieves the eight common accomplishments.

"From the lower point of view, that of samsara, it is through this practice that all physical, verbal, and mental activities are *purified*. From the higher point of view, that of buddhahood, this practice *perfects* the result (already present) in the ground: the inconceivable activities of the enlightened body, speech, and mind. From the intermediate point of view, that of the path, this training, which is free from all active effort, and through which the twofold goal is spontaneously accomplished, *ripens* (in the perfection stage) into the common conceptual path (*dmigs bcas*) related to the activities of body, speech, and mind, and into the nonconceptual path (*dmigs med*) of primordial wisdom, the yoga of manifest luminosity, whereby phenomenal existence is purified into a body of light.

"In this respect, it is said:

> The ground, path, and result are not different. Their union is the path of buddhahood. They are one from the very outset, and the result is perfect in their one taste. Let us be more specific about this teaching. The view is the changeless, ultimate wisdom. This is the *ground*. Meditation is the *path* and refers to the deity, mantra, and, implicitly, conduct. Enlightened activity refers to the supreme and common *result*. This is referred to as the "primordial path of union."

"In this same spirit, since the nail of unchanging ultimate wisdom refers to the *view*, it is the *ground*. By contrast, the nail of concentration on the deity refers to *meditation*. The nail of the mantra also refers to the *meditation* and, by implication, also to *conduct*. The second and third of the nails just mentioned constitute the *path*. The (fourth) nail of radiating and absorbing lights, which secures the common and supreme accomplishments, and effects the enlightened activities here and now, in the present moment, refers to the *result*. We should therefore refrain from considering that the four life-fastening nails—or the view, meditation, conduct, and result; or again, the ground, path, and result—are distinct or separate, random or successive. We must understand that from the very outset, they are neither one nor many; they are an indivisible union." [YG III, 279:2–282:1]

246 This is a reference to the six branches of visualization (*mngon rtogs yan lag drug*) decribed in the *Vajra Tent Tantra*. See *Buddhist Ethics*, p. 503n317.

247 Passion or great bliss keeps all the qualities of the result in the state of nonduality. [KPS]

248 "The teachings explain that, in the (causal) expository vehicle, a great length of time is required for the gradual attainment of the qualities of the ten

grounds and five paths, whereas through the mantra path, they are achieved swiftly. Other than this simple difference of speed, however, progress and the acquisition of the resulting qualities are actually quite similar on both paths.

"The manner in which one progresses on the grounds and paths of the Secret Mantra may be briefly explained as follows. From the standpoint of the actual path, one speaks about the generation stage, but from the standpoint of the way in which it is implemented, one speaks of the path of liberation through wisdom. If, through hearing and reflecting on the teaching, practitioners of the path of liberation acquire certainty in the view of the Mantrayana, and if they apply this in their practice, they will—through the path of the generation stage alone—gain worldly accomplishment, the level of the Vidyādharas of the desire and form realms, who have the same karmic fortune as the gods of these same realms (up to the heaven of Akanishtha). Then, thanks to the skillful means associated with the perfection stage, they will achieve liberation.

"In itself, the generation stage is not a path that leads beyond the world. However, when certain fortunate beings of superior capacity receive the appropriate empowerments and instructions, they will, from the very first, practice both the generation and the perfection stages together, and consequently attain realization and liberation at the same time. Beings of this kind are called practitioners of the path of liberation who gain accomplishment at a single stroke (cig char pa), because for them, the qualities of the result arise all together and at once. Those practitioners who progress gradually (rim gyis pa) on the path of liberation train in the concentrations of the five "contaminated" (zag bcas) yogas—a path that is nevertheless in harmony with the view of purity and equality. Thanks to these yogas, practiced in both the meditation and postmeditation phases, the ordinary deluded thoughts of such practitioners will gradually disappear by themselves (rang grol), just as when an ordinary stone, placed next to the kostubha gem, gradually turns into gold. And when thoughts disappear, the movements of the wind (which are indissociable from them) cannot but disappear also. When a vital organ ceases to function, all the other organs also cease to function. In like manner, when dualistic, deluded thought processes (together with the circumstances that trigger them) subside and vanish of their own accord—like ice melting into water—the primordial wisdom of the path of seeing (in other words, the ultimate truth) is actualized. And this brings the practitioner to the result, namely, the path of no more learning. As it is said in the Guhyagarbha:

> Within the mandala of perfect primal wisdom,
> Through the even unity of hearing, of reflection, and of meditation,
> The self-arisen primal wisdom is swiftly and spontaneously achieved.

"The perfection stage (so called from the standpoint of the actual path) is, from the point of view of its implementation, referred to as the definitive path of skillful means. It is mainly thanks to the amazing practice of skillful means that immanent primordial wisdom arises swiftly, just as when mak-shika is applied to iron and transforms it instantaneously into gold. 'Gradual practitioners' of the path of skillful means pursue the trainings related to the *upper door*, by taking support of the six chakras, and they perform the practice of 'blazing and dripping' whereby the primordial wisdom of bliss is gener-ated. Practitioners who are capable of 'sudden accomplishment' on the path of skillful means take support of the *lower door*. And through the practice of dripping, holding, and retaining [the essence-drop], reverting it upward and spreading it, they actualize coemergent wisdom." [YG III, 292:2–294:4]

"The path of liberation (*grol lam*) and the path of skillful means (*thabs lam*) are described as methods of practice related to the generation stage and perfection stage respectively. This is according to whether emphasis is placed on skillful means or wisdom. This does not mean, however, that the genera-tion stage is lacking in skillful means or that the perfection stage is lacking in wisdom. The generation stage also naturally purifies the channels, winds, and essence-drops. It does so because it possesses the skillful means that elicit the wisdom of the perfection stage. Likewise in the perfection stage, by means of skillful means, the extraordinary view of wisdom manifests as a deity, as do all thoughts. It should be understood therefore that both these stages are practices wherein the two aspects are united. If this were not the case, it would be impossible to make progress on the path. There is moreover no difference between them in that they both result in the vision of the funda-mental nature.

"Based on such methods, the stages of progress constitute a general outline of the Vajrayana path, every step of which, from the construction of the mandala up to the path of no more learning, can be subsumed in the four mudras. The ground of the practice is the karmamudra. The practitioners themselves are the samayamudra. The actual practice is the dharmamudra. And the result is the mahamudra. The karmamudra consists of all the stages of constructing the mandala related to the expanse of the mother, the source of phenomena. The samayamudra is the mind of the person engaged in these stages of practice, and is related to his or her samaya-bound conduct. The dharmamudra is based upon the six paramitas and is related to the four levels of Vidyādhara. The mahamudra is related to the level of mahamudra natu-rally endowed with the three kayas and seven qualities (of union)." [YG III, 295:5–296:6]

249 "When the refined essence-drops enter the central channel, there arises a concentration marked by undefiled bliss, the luminosity of bliss (*bde ba'i 'od gsal*). Clear luminosity (*gsal ba'i 'od gsal*) occurs when the five refined winds gain in strength and enter the central channel. Inwardly, there then arises a sama-dhi of unobscured lucid clarity. Outwardly, the five winds passing through the nostrils become colored, and the light display of the five primordial wisdoms arises as deities and luminous disks of light. Thought-free luminos-ity (*mi rtog pa'i 'od gsal*) refers to the state of abiding in this luminosity without

clinging to it, and without conceptualizing its bliss or clarity. And this dissolves into the fundamental nature, the ultimate mode of being, great inconceivable luminosity." [YG III, 315:2–6]

250 *snang med 'od gsal.* "Luminosity devoid of form is a luminosity in which the appearance of subject and object is not dualistic. The two kinds of perfection stage practice mentioned here are also referred to respectively as dzogrim with characteristics (*mtshan bcas rdzogs rim*) and dzogrim without characteristics (*mtshan med rdzogs rim*). The various kinds of dzogrim practice are all grouped under these two headings." [YG III, 318:1–2]

251 [DKR/OC] In the terminology of the causal vehicle, the body of an ordinary being, marred as this is by affliction, is defined as a "true suffering" and is the basis for karma and defilement. Conversely, it is through defilement that beings perform the negative, positive, and neutral actions that give rise to their bodies. The body is consequently regarded as something undesirable. In the Vajrayana, however, the body is viewed according to its true status: the channels constitute the nirmanakaya; the wind is the sambhogakaya; and the essence-drop of the union of bliss and emptiness is the dharmakaya. When this is correctly grasped, a body endowed with the six elements becomes a suitable vessel for the Vajrayana. One speaks, accordingly, of the aggregate of the vajra body. If this is not understood and if the body is regarded as something ordinary, it becomes impossible to implement the crucial methods of the path.

252 *snangs bcas rdzogs rim.* [DKR/OC] This means that one takes into account the fact that one's body appears in a particular form. When the channels, winds, and essence-drops (which are by nature pure) are cleansed of their adventitious stains, the wisdom of clarity, bliss, and no-thought arises, and subsequently the ultimate primordial wisdom manifests.

253 [DKR/OC] The channels are also called "stationary" because they are the location, or "station" (*gnas*), of the deities.

254 "Bodhichitta (in this context) may be classified as: (1) the essence-drop beyond all conceptual construction, the self-cognizing primordial wisdom; (2) the essence-drop of delusion and ignorance, in other words, the ordinary mind; and (3) the substantial essence-drop of the five elements, the white and red essential constituents (*khams dkar dmar*)." [YG III, 319:5–6]

[DKR/OC] The essence-drop beyond all conceptual construction (self-cognizing primordial wisdom) is introduced during the fourth empowerment. With regard to the essence-drop of delusion and ignorance (that is, the ordinary mind), when the luminosity of primordial wisdom manifests outwardly but is not recognized for what it is, it becomes the cause of delusion in the three worlds of samsara. The substantial essence-drop formed from the quintessence of the five elements (the white essence-drop in the crown of the head and the red essence-drop located just below the navel center) is the support for both the essence-drop of primordial wisdom and the essence-drop of ignorance. All three are aspects of one and the same thing, and the latter two are based on the first (the substantial essence-drop).

Practitioners who meditate on the essence-drop will come to recognize the latter's threefold character and, by using the substantial essence-drop as the path, will purify the essence-drop of ignorance, cleansing it of stains, whereupon it becomes the essence-drop of self-cognizing primordial wisdom. The untying of the first two knots on the central channel, which effects the attainment of the first ground of realization, rests upon the experiential recognition of the essence-drop of primordial wisdom. Since the essence-drop of primordial wisdom is veiled by the essence-drop of ignorance, and since both are based on the substantial essence-drop of the five elements, it is through the practice upon the latter that the veils of ignorance are dissipated and enlightened qualities revealed. This is the full extent of the practice of the perfection stage, the cause of the birth of ultimate wisdom.

Simply to practice on the substantial essence-drop, allowing the essence-drops to flow downward and then reversing them upward, is a technique known even to non-Buddhists and constitutes only a minor attainment. The vajra body, speech, and mind are primordially pervasive and dwell in the ordinary body, speech, and mind. The ordinary body derives from the blending of the essences of one's father and mother. It grows and ages, while the primordial, naturally present wisdom body, speech, and mind dwell in the buddha-nature, the nature of the mind, and remain unchanging. The wisdom body, speech, and mind and the ordinary body, speech, and mind are different in that the former is subtle and the latter is gross. And in this context, "subtle" does not indicate something fine or tenuous like a thin thread; it means profound and hard to realize.

255   [DKR/OC] On the basis of the essence-drops, there arise the experiences of bliss, clarity, and no-thought, which lead to the ultimate bodhichitta. It is for this reason that the essence-drop is referred to as bodhichitta—the name of the result being given to its cause.

256   "All beings endowed with the tathāgatagarbha are inseparable from the uncontrived, enlightened body, speech, and mind (gnyug ma'i sgo gsum). However, beings who are without the six coarse elements (for instance, those belonging to realms of existence higher than the human condition), are inferior supports for the Mantrayana path." [YG III, 319:6–320:1]

[DKR/OC] Beings in the form and formless realms have bodies that are composed of subtle elements, not of the six coarse elements. Consequently, they cannot experience bliss, clarity, and absence of thought. And since they are without the substantial white and red essences, they can have no experience of the nondual union of bliss and emptiness. They are therefore unsuitable vessels for the secret and wisdom empowerments. The inhabitants of Jambudvipa, by contrast, are particularly suitable vessels for the generation and perfection stages of the Mantrayana.

257 [DKR/OC] "Vajra" indicates nonduality, indestructibility. It is through the practice based on the coarse aspects of the channels, winds, and essence-drops, that the vajra body, speech, and mind (which are already present from the very beginning) are revealed. Because the bodies of Buddhas are wisdom bodies (space-pervading vajra bodies), even a single pore of their skin or one of their hairs is able to perform the same actions as the Buddhas themselves.

258 [DKR/OC] A city is a dwelling place where many people live and meet together. In the same way, the self-arisen primordial wisdom dwells in the three vajras, ever present and uncontrived, and these in turn dwell in the city of the coarse channels, winds, and essence-drops—in other words, a body composed of the six elements. According to the causal vehicle, the aggregates, elements, sense-organs and their objects are ordinary. In other words, they are stained with impurity and involved in suffering. By using the skillful means of the Vajrayana, practitioners regard them as the vajra-city of the three seats of the deities—in other words, as something to be realized and not rejected. It is through meditating on them in this way that samsara is gradually purified. And when the wisdom of great bliss takes birth, the universe and the beings who inhabit it will be perceived as pure.

259 [DKR/OC] Located on the central channel are five chakras or channel-wheels, from which seventy-two thousand channels spread out, fine like threads of silk. The karmic wind, which serves as the vehicle, or conveyance, of the mind, causes the channels to pulsate. When the channels and the winds circulating in them are impure, then ignorance, attachment, and hatred ensue; and from these are formed the three worlds of samsara. When, on the other hand, the channels and winds are pure, the result is clairvoyance, the ability to perform miracles, and so forth.

260 On the formation of the "eyes," see note 523 and *Myriad Worlds*, p. 216.

261 "The uma or central channel (*dbu ma*) is a sort of axis or 'life-tree' along which all the chakras are located. It is not wholly inexistent as a causally efficient entity, for otherwise the qualities that arise when it is brought under control would be impossible to explain. It is neither the life-channel (*srog rtsa*) nor the spinal cord (*rgyungs pa*), for these are coarse channels, and it is said that if the wind enters the life-channel, madness and unconsciousness ensue, and this is contrary to the way the [real] uma is defined. Nevertheless, there is no such thing as an uma that is independent from, or unsupported by, these two channels. As Saraha says, 'Wind and mind are supported by the life-channel. Therefore, when it (the *srog rtsa*) is brought under control, the ordinary mind is naturally halted.' And as the *Heart-Essence of the Dakini* also says, 'The *uma of skillful means*, the so-called avadhuti, is what ordinary people call the spinal cord; and the *uma of wisdom*, the *ever-trembling* (*kun 'dar ma*), is commonly identified with the life-channel. The *uma in which skillful means and wisdom are united* lies in front of the backbone and behind the life-channel, and it is without blood and lymph.'

"There are three umas: the *localized uma* (*gnas pa'i dbu ma*), the *actual uma* (*chos nyid kyi dbu ma*), and the *ultimate uma* (*don dam pa'i dbu ma*). The first of these is, from the point of view of its actual condition, the channel that supports life. The second [which is the channel employed in the perfection stage practices] is the genuine central channel (*mtshan nyid kyi rtsa*) and is marked by four features. It has a luminous nature, it is unobstructed and intangible, and as long as the body, mind, and breath remain together, it is present. To that extent, it is not nonexistent. When, however, the body, mind, and breath go their separate ways, it disappears, and to that extent it is not existent. It is like a rainbow, which appears when the proper conditions are present, and disappears when they disperse. When one is meditating, one should consider that this uma is in the middle of the life-channel. This is because both the universal ground (*kun gzhi*) and the life-wind (*srog rlung*) are supported by it, and thus they are in fact all of the same taste. Finally, the *ultimate uma* refers to the actual condition of the result: the absence of intrinsic being (*ngo bo med pa*)." [YG III, 325:4–327:1] See also *Systems of Buddhist Tantra*, pp. 172–76.

262 *a thung.* This is the so-called *a-shad,* the vertical line of the Tibetan letter A, which is pointed at the lower extremity and widens toward the top. It is, however, visualized upside down, i.e., with the pointed end uppermost.

263 This is a play on words. The Tibetan word *ro* means both "corpse" and "taste."

264 "The three channels may be evaluated according to their function. Blood, lymph, and the bodhichitta all circulate in the roma. Therefore, if one is skillful in working with the essence-drops, one's karma related to physical action will be exhausted. All craving for food will end, and one will be able to subsist on the food of samadhi. By contrast, the quintessence of the elements, as well as the wisdom wind, all circulate in the kyangma. Therefore, if one is skilled in working with this channel, the karma related to speech will be exhausted, and the need for clothing will be brought to an end. The ultimate uma has the nature of light. It is an empty, all-penetrating openness (*zang thal*). Therefore, if one is skillful at working with the wind [bringing it into the central channel], the karma of mental actions will be purified, together with all craving for drink. Dreams will end, and finally one will realize ultimate reality beyond the two extremes: the primordial wisdom of luminosity." [YG III, 322:6–323:3]

265 [DKR/OC] If the three doors are purified of their defilements and the wind-mind is refined so as to be able to express its qualities, power is gained over material form, and one is able to pass one's body through the eye of a needle or sit in vajra posture on the tip of a blade of kusha grass, and one gains the accomplishment of tummo-fire. This is the result of a purified wind-mind, as described in the *Kalachakra-tantra.* The rainbow body of great transformation, attained by Guru Rinpoche and Vimalamitra, is something different. It is a body of light, where the qualities of the path of no more learning have been

actualized, and buddhahood achieved. On the other hand, the refinement of the wind-mind is something that even non-Buddhists can achieve. It is an ordinary accomplishment.

266 [DKR/OC] In the present context, only four families are envisaged. The reason for this is that the quality aspect is included in the enlightened body, speech, mind, and activity. The result accomplished can also be described as the vajra body, speech, mind, and wisdom.

267 This means that from the chakra at the crown of the head until the chakra of the heart, there is a diminution in the number of channels. By contrast, from the chakra in the heart until the chakra in the secret center, there is an increase in the number of channels.

268 [DKR/OC] The various descriptions found in different tantras are not in contradiction. The stationary channels, the mobile winds, and the bodhichitta positioned thereon, as well as the five chakras, are common to all [human] beings. The way in which they are formed, however, may vary according to particular individuals. For this reason, the omniscient Buddha has described different formations, patterns, and numbers of channels, corresponding to the different kinds of beings. However, the result of meditating on them is the same. In any case, when all dissolves into the central channel, there is no difference in the buddhahood that is achieved. It is as when people travel to the same place: some may journey by road or by air, but their destination is the same.

269 "The navel chakra is referred to as the chakra of manifestation (*sprul pa'i 'khor lo*) because it is from here that the body develops. When the wind-mind enters it, infinite visions of Buddhas and buddhafields arise. . . . The chakra at the throat is called the chakra of enjoyment (*longs spyod kyi 'khor lo*) because, by implementing the pith instructions related to this chakra, one is able to enjoy sense objects without impediment. . . . The chakra at the heart is called the chakra of ultimate reality (*chos kyi 'khor lo*) because, when the wind-mind enters it, the inconceivable dharmatā is actualized. The chakra at the crown of the head is called the chakra of great bliss (*bde chen gyi 'khor lo*) because the syllable HANG located there is the source of great bliss. The chakra at the secret center is called the bliss-preserving chakra (*bde skyong gi 'khor lo*) because it is here that coemergent bliss is preserved. When the wind-mind and essence-drop dissolve into the ushnisha, all residues become limpid, like space, which is why the ushnisha is called the chakra of the realm of space (*nam mkha'i khams kyi 'khor lo*). This name also reflects the fact that the ushnisha does not consist of coarse channels—which is why the number of channels is not specified for it. Some authorities say, on the other hand, that the space chakra of the ushnisha has four radial channels. Others declare that it has the same number of channels as the chakra of the secret center." [YG III, 328:3–329:3]

270 [DKR/OC] The commentaries state that in each of the chakras there are, to begin with, four channels, each of which divides into two. These subdivide into two, and the process continues until the number of channels appropriate to the chakra in question is reached. When one meditates on the chakras, however, it is important to visualize all the channels as stemming directly from the center of the chakra. The effect of this is to reduce the number of obstacles on the path. In some tantras, the chakras are described as having an umbrella-like appearance. For example, the chakra located at the crown of the head has its concave side turned downward, while the concave side of the throat chakra is turned upward. Likewise, the heart chakra is turned downward while the navel chakra is turned upward. However, unless it is specifically mentioned, one should not meditate on them in this way. Instead they should be visualized as flat disks. Again, some tantras speak of the chakra channels not as being straight and sticklike, but as loosely entwined loops, like knots on a snake. But once again, when meditating on them, one should visualize them as straight.

271 [DKR/OC] According to the *Kalachakra*, the first twelve of the sixty-four channels of the navel chakra correspond to the twelve astrological houses (*khyim*) through which the sun, moon, and the other planets transit, propelled and supported by the celestial belt of wind-energy. The time period (*dus 'byor*) needed for the transit (*'pho ba*) of the wind through each of the twelve channels corresponds to 1,800 respirations, or 120 minutes. Each of these periods corresponds to the outer transit of the sun and moon through one of the twelve astrological houses. A person with a stable accomplishment of the inner yoga of channels and winds is aware of the moment that the sun and moon pass from one house to another. When these twelve transits of the wind occur without being obstructed, this constitutes (by virtue of the twelve interdependent links associated with them) the point at which samsara is set in motion. If these twelve transits are dominated by the purified wind-mind, the twelve interdependent links will be reversed and brought to a halt. These two trajectories, one deluded and one undeluded, correspond to the forward and reverse order of the twelve interdependent links, as expounded in the teachings belonging generally to both the sutras and the tantras. In the reverse order, the wind-mind dissolves into the space of the central channel, thanks to which no further delusion can arise. See also *Systems of Buddhist Tantra*, p. 438n24.

272 [DKR/OC] In the case of ordinary people, the wind-mind flows in the impure channels, thereby creating an increase of defilement. By contrast, practitioners are able to close the doors of the impure channels and to open the doors of the wisdom channels, thereby causing all perfect qualities to arise. Air is inhaled through the nostrils, travels through the roma and kyangma, and arrives at their point of junction with the uma, which looks like the lower part of the Tibetan letter CHA. And when the wind passes through it, the effect is like using a pair of bellows to revive a fire.

273 [DKR/OC] When the white essence-drops enter the central channel, one experiences an extraordinary bliss. When the red essence-drops enter the central channel, an extraordinary experience of clarity arises. When both essence-drops enter the central channel, the experience of no-thought manifests.

274 This entire process is described in vivid detail in the fourth chapter of the *ye shes mtsho rgyal rnam thar,* the life story of Yeshe Tsogyal. See Gyalwa Changchub and Namkha'i Nyingpo, *Lady of the Lotus-Born* (Boston: Shambhala Publications, 1999), pp. 42–44.

275 [DKR/OC] There are several tantras of *Kalachakra.* One of these is the *Abridged Kalachakra (Laghutantra),* which is divided into five chapters: (1) Cosmogony; (2) The Channels, Winds, Essence-Drops and Connected Matters; (3) Empowerment; (4) The Sadhana; and (5) Wisdom. While everything derives from the root tantra, it is from the *Laghutantra* nowadays that the empowerment is given. The Lord Buddha himself expounded numerous versions or aspects of the *Kalachakra,* while the abridgement in five chapters was expounded by Kalki Manjushriyashas (Rigden Jampal Trakpa), the lineage king of Shambhala, who was an emanation of Manjushri. Subsequently, his son, Kalki Pundarika (Rigden Pema Karpo), an embodiment of Avalokiteshvara, wrote a commentary on the abridgement entitled *Stainless Light: The Great Commentary on Kalachakra.* See also Lhundup Sopa, Roger Jackson, and John Newman, *Wheel of Time* (Madison, Wisc.: Deer Park Books, 1985), pp. 59–65.

276 *thub pa drug.* These are the so-called nirmanakaya guides of beings (*'gro 'dul sprul pa*)—one for each of the six realms. They are discussed later, in chapter 13.

277 [DKR/OC] There are variations of detail according to the different tantras. The forty-two peaceful deities dwell within the channels of the heart chakra in the form of the refined white and red essence-drops. The self-radiance of the forty-two peaceful deities arises in the crown chakra as the fifty-eight wrathful deities. It is just like a palace located on the ground that would be reflected in a crystal mirror hanging in the sky above it. The deities reside in the channels of the crown chakra in the form of white and red essence-drops. According to the root tantra of the *Mayajala,* when the refined wind-mind dissolves into the indestructible essence-drop of the heart chakra, buddhahood is attained.

278 [DKR/OC] The white and red essence-drops positioned in the channels are of an inconceivable quantity. The seventy-two thousand channels are mentioned as the location in which they are found, in much the same way that one gives a name to a town or city where people dwell, whereas one does not name an empty place.

279 [DKR/OC] The path of the upper door concerns the upper opening of the central channel at the level of the chakra of great bliss, the place where the

syllable HANG is located. When the letter HANG is melted by the fire of tummo, the bodhichitta drips down from it. Of the three lower channels that serve for the passage of excrement, urine, and essential fluids, the path of the lower door works with the third. It involves the method of union of the vajra and the lotus and is called the path of the enjoyment of the three worlds. The three worlds are the desire realm (corresponding to the physical body, the "fully manifest city"); the form realm (corresponding to speech, the "half-manifest city"); and the formless realm (corresponding to the mind, the "un-manifest city"). These three worlds correspond to the three chakras of the crown of the head, the throat, and the heart. They are purified by the ascent and descent of the red and white essence-drops respectively, and by the experience of the four joys.

280 See also appendix 7 and *Systems of Buddhist Tantra*, pp. 176–80.

281 [DKR/OC] Wind has the character of being in constant motion. The major winds are associated with the elements. The wind of the earth element predominates in the spring, when the earth is ready to make the plants and trees grow. The wind of the water element predominates in the winter, when everything is pure and clean. The wind of the fire element predominates in the summer, which is a time of heat and heaviness. Finally, the wind of the air element predominates in autumn, which is characterized by a lighter atmosphere.

282 These winds have the "characteristics of inhalation and exhalation." In other words, they correspond to respirations or breaths. See *Systems of Buddhist Tantra*, p. 178–79.

283 [DKR/OC] From birth until the age of six or seven years.

284 [DKR/OC] The minor winds, which correspond to the eighty-four thousand defilements, are like vehicles that carry the mind into delusion.

285 [DKR/OC] This is the pulsating carotid artery (*'phar rtsa*) in the neck. Colloquially, it is known as the great channel (*rtsa chen*).

286 [DKR/OC] When the life-supporting wind (*srog 'dzin gyi rlung*) departs from the life-channel (*srog rtsa*), death occurs. The fire-accompanying wind (*me mnyam gyi rlung*) engenders warmth. It is this that extracts and assimilates the essential component of food, leaving aside the residue. The all-pervading wind (*khyab byed kyi rlung*) fills the whole body from the top of the head down to the soles of the feet. This wind makes possible the extension and contraction of limbs, as well as the growth of hair and nails and so on. This is the wind that maintains the body in its functioning condition. The upward-moving wind (*gyen rgyu'i rlung*) is the force residing in the upper part of the body and is responsible for the functions of the throat: the swallowing of food and the activity of speech. Finally, the downward voiding wind (*thur sel gyi rlung*) circulates in the lower part of the body and makes possible the voiding of excrement, urine, and so on.

287 [DKR/OC] Without going into exhaustive detail, it may be said roughly that the tathāgatagarbha dwells in the heart, which, in the terminology of thögal, is the "lamp of the heart of flesh" (*tsitta sha'i sgron ma*). According to the *Guhyagarbha-tantra*, when the refined wind-mind dissolves into the expanse of the tathāgatagarbha in the heart center, this same tathāgatagarbha stands revealed, and enlightenment occurs. Therefore, the outer Vajrasana (the place in the physical world where the thousand Buddhas of the present kalpa attain enlightenment) corresponds to the inner Vajrasana, the heart center where the luminous primordial wisdom is actualized when the refined wind-mind dissolves into the indestructible essence-drop. When, subsequently, the wisdom wind moves, the eighty-four thousand sections of the Dharma arise.

Some teachings say that the bardo consciousness cannot go to Vajrasana, understood as the physical location in India. But for the omniscient father and son, Longchenpa and Jigme Lingpa, when, in this context, one speaks of the place of enlightenment of all the Buddhas, the reference is not to Bodhgaya in India, but to the heart center and the primordial wisdom dwelling there. Moreover, those who have realized the ultimate primordial wisdom of the indestructible essence-drop are able to seize the consciousness of beings in the bardo and transfer it at will, so that it no longer wanders in the bardo state. The outer Vajrasana is thus a symbol of the inner Vajrasana.

The statement in the *Kalachakra* to the effect that enlightenment is attained when the wind-mind dissolves into the chakra of the ushnisha, should not be considered a contradiction of the above statement. For when the stainless qualities—namely, the major and minor marks of buddhahood—are perfected, the ultimate manifestation of merit is the ushnisha. Chakravartins also have a sort of ushnisha, but this is not like the one possessed by Buddhas. The ushnisha of Lord Buddha extended into the sky beyond the possibility of measurement. Even Maudgalyaputra, for all his magical powers, was unable to see where it ended. The reason for this is that the Buddha's ushnisha has no size, but pervades the ultimate expanse. When the wind-mind dissolves into the chakra of the ushnisha, buddhahood is attained. In the teachings of the Great Perfection, the essence-drops are described as rising up, being piled vertically above the head. And when the wind-mind dissolves into the chakra of the ushnisha, the "exhaustion" of phenomena in suchness (*chos nyid zad sa*), buddhahood, is achieved. These two accounts, while displaying slight differences, express the same truth.

288 [DKR/OC] When one holds the "vase breath" (*bum chen*), one holds the neutral winds.

289 These winds do not differ from the ones just described; they are simply their subtler aspects.

290 "There are various explanations as to their location. Some authorities say that the inner winds are in the heart chakra; others say that they are present in the middle of all five chakras." [YG III, 337:4–5]

291 "At the moment of death, these winds dissolve—that is, they lose their strength—and for a time, the five aggregates, etc., disappear. Since these inner winds have not been purified into the wisdom wind, they will arise again and, simultaneously with them, the bardo of becoming will manifest, followed by the next life." [YG III, 337:6–338:1]

292 [DKR/OC] The "clinging to subject and object" mentioned in the Sutrayana is referred to in the Mantrayana as the "coursing of the wind in roma and kyangma." The wind moving in these channels is necessarily a karmic wind. When it enters the central channel, it becomes a wisdom wind.

293 [DKR/OC] In fact, the wisdom wind and the karmic wind are the same thing. If this wind is brought under control, it engenders wisdom; if it is not controlled, it gives rise to the ordinary mind, together with its poisons. Thus the most important thing, at the perfection stage, is to work effectively on the wind, since it is by such a means that one will also be able to work with the essence-drop, which the wind conveys. If, as a result, one attains mastery of the essence-drop, the mind, which is supported by it, will also cease to move, thereby giving rise to the experiences of bliss, clarity, and no-thought.

294 [DKR/OC] Anger proliferates through the male wind, desire and attachment through the female wind, and stupidity through the neutral wind.

295 [DKR/OC] When the winds have been purified and transmuted into the wisdom wind, the eighty-four thousand sections of the Dharma will arise effortlessly, just as they did in the case of the omniscient Jigme Lingpa.

296 This excerpt is taken from YG III, 338:4–6.
    [DKR/OC] In the summer, one should meditate on the wind of water, and in the autumn on the wind of earth. If one fails to meditate on the wind of water in the summer, one's heat may become excessive, and fever and liver complaints will ensue. If in the autumn one does not meditate on the wind of earth, one will be excessively tired, with a wild and agitated mind. If in winter one does not meditate on the wind of fire, diseases connected with cold will ensue. And since in spring the earth wind brings heaviness, one should counterbalance it with the wind of air. According to the Great Perfection teachings, if one meditates simply on the wind of space, which is blue in color and pervades all the other elements, no obstacles will be encountered, and one's progress will be swift. The five winds move with the breath, and their strength may vary. As we have said, if one has an illness provoked by the cold, one should meditate on the wind of fire; if one is suffering from fever or a bile imbalance, one should meditate on the wind of water; if one is troubled by a preponderance of phlegm, one should meditate on the wind of air.

297 [DKR/OC] What does it mean to say that the five winds are "bound together" in the single wind-mind (*rlung sems*)? It means that, when the breath is held below the navel, compressed between the upper and lower winds, one

concentrates one's attention one-pointedly on that place. Wherever the wind goes, the mind will follow.

298 [DKR/OC] These lights and disks of light correspond to the "empty forms" (*stong gzugs*) mentioned in the *Kalachakra*. When lights and disks of light filling the channels are set in motion by the wind, they will appear in one's waking perceptions.

299 *zad par gyi skye mched bcu.* When perfect concentration on the limitless ayatanas is achieved, it is possible to take the specific quality of one element and give it to the others. The solidity of earth, for example, can be transferred to water, so that one can walk on it. See *Treasury of Precious Qualities*, bk. 1, p. 432.

300 [DKR/OC] The channels, winds, and essence-drops exist on three levels: outer, inner, and secret. When the outer winds are mastered, using the appropriate methods, one comes to the inner winds, and these, when mastered, give way to the secret winds. Wisdom grows until one reaches ultimate wisdom, which represents the final extent of the tummo practice. All teachings—outer, inner, and secret—aim at the realization of primordial wisdom. The outer aspect of the teachings belongs to the generation stage. The inner teachings are concerned with the tummo fire, the illusory body, the dripping of the essence-drops, and so on, and correspond to the conceptual perfection stage of Anuyoga. This (according to the *Kalachakra*) is related to the external structure of the world (the continents, the movements of the sun and moon, and so on). The secret aspect corresponds to the Great Perfection. References to the outer aspect of the channels, winds, and essence-drops can also be found in the sutras, and even in the scriptures of certain non-Buddhist traditions. Proceeding gradually from the outer to the secret levels, the teachings become progressively more profound, and the path swifter to accomplish. And yet there is no contradiction between any of these levels.

301 See note 262.

302 [DKR/OC] This is the secret ganachakra offering.

303 "If the body is straight, the wind will also be straight, thanks to which one will behold the ultimate nature of the mind. One should therefore adopt the proper bodily posture (either the seven-point posture of Vairochana or any other posture described in the pith instructions relating to the meditation on the channels and winds). If the posture is correct, the wind will not move and thoughts will subside, thereby facilitating the birth of primordial wisdom." [YG III, 343:6–344:2]

[DKR/OC] If one straightens the channels, it is as though one were creating a smooth road on which many people can travel with ease. This is the purpose of the seven-point posture. The movement of the impure karmic wind will be halted, the doors of the impure channels will be closed, and the doors of the pure channels will open. When the Arhats were meditating in the forest sitting in such a posture, the monkeys would imitate them, and as a result they too had some experience of mental calm. This was due solely to their physical posture.

304 See note 261.

305 See *Treasury of Precious Qualities*, bk. 1, p. 134, and *Myriad Worlds*, p. 111.

306 [DKR/OC] "Tum" (*gtum*) means "wild," "hot tempered." This refers to the fact that the tummo fire consumes all the impurities of the essence-drop. The feminine particle "mo" (*mo*) indicates the fact that this fire has the nature of wisdom, which is the feminine aspect.

307 Vimalamitra (*dri med bshes gnyen*) was a disciple of Shri Simha and Jnanasutra. The teachings of the Great Perfection that this great master brought to Tibet are known as the *Heart Essence of Vimalamitra* (*bi ma'i snying thig*). They were transmitted in a secret lineage of transmission from one master to a single disciple, and the texts themselves were concealed. This lineage of transmission came down to Longchen Rabjam.

308 [DKR/OC] That is, tending neither to virtue nor nonvirtue.

309 [DKR/OC] These are the seed-syllables of the six realms.

310 [DKR/OC] When practicing the generation stage, one considers all phenomena—the universe, beings, and their minds—as the display of the wisdom deity. This wisdom deity must in turn be dissolved into the stainless space of ultimate nature. The union of skillful means and wisdom is a feature of all Mahayana teaching. Consequently, as we have seen, when one practices correctly on the channels, winds, and essence-drops (which are the aspect of skillful means), the primordial wisdom, which is the tathāgatagarbha, is actualized. And this is the quintessence of all paths.

In the practice of tummo, the aspect of skillful means is the primordial wisdom of great bliss dwelling in the form of the white letter HANG at the top of the central channel, whereas the wisdom aspect is the blazing red A-SHÉ located at the bottom of the same channel. The appellation "tummo" is normally used to mean a wild, hot-tempered woman. It is applied metaphorically to this practice because, when the blazing fire of tummo consumes the defiled aggregates and elements, the stainless wisdom of great bliss is revealed, and deluded clinging to real existence collapses all by itself. When one performs the visualization of the tummo practice, one imagines that the tummo fire penetrates the defiled aggregates and sense organs, cleansing the impure channels, winds, and essence-drops. At the same time, one imagines that the pure essence-drops drip from the HANG and fill one's entire body. When this happens, all phenomena of both samsara and nirvana are established as constituting the three doors of perfect liberation, and one gains a direct realization of emptiness. This is the genuine or ultimate, inner tummo.

For the visualization of this procedure, one concentrates on the red A-SHÉ, four finger-widths below the navel. This is not the complete (Tibetan) letter A, but its final vertical stroke, which is somewhat broad at the top and tapers to a point at the bottom, thus forming an elongated triangle (which, in the present context, is visualized upside down, that is, with the point uppermost). This symbolizes the three doors of perfect liberation: the ground, which is the emptiness nature; the path, which is devoid of characteristics; and the result, regarding which one has no expectation. The A-SHÉ is composed of very hot fire. Any part of the body that this fire touches is bathed in great bliss. The flames, as they mount up, are fine and curling. Outwardly, they consume all the propensities for birth in the three worlds. Inwardly, they burn away the stains of body, speech, and mind.

As the fire burns, it crackles and makes the sound "PHEM, PHEM," which is the root syllable for invoking the dakas and dakinis, for inviting the real presence of the primordial wisdom of great bliss. The white essence-drops drip from the top of the head, and unite with the red essence-drop of the tummo fire, whereby the white essence is melted. This elicits the experience of the four joys in the four chakras. The white essence, now melted, has the nature of the vajra body, the primordial wisdom of great bliss. The arousing of the four joys is the vajra speech, while the fact that the experience of bliss brings a halt to all discursive thought is the vajra mind. Consequently, "melting" (*zhu*) means "body"; "joy or bliss" (*bde ba*) means "speech"; and "no-thought" (*mi rtog pa*) means "mind." The ultimate expanse, endowed with the three doors of perfect liberation, is thus realized.

This practice is called tummo (Skt. *chandali*) because it has the power to burn away all defilements and to develop wisdom. It can also be interpreted as referring to the nature of bliss, since its effect is nondual, empty bliss. When one has practiced tummo—which is the appearing aspect of empty and blissful primordial wisdom—one must go on to practice its emptiness aspect. This refers to the practice of the illusory body.

311 [DKR/OC] The practice of the illusory body has two aspects: pure and impure. First, with the help of the eight similes of illusion [a dream, an illusion, trompe l'oeil, a mirage, the moon in water, an echo, a city in the clouds, and an apparition], one must realize the illusory nature of relative phenomena, which appear through the interplay of dependent arising. Then one must realize that the body and mind, to which one clings as if they were one's own self, are illusory and dreamlike.

When the practices of tummo and the illusory body are conjoined, then it is as the saying goes: "When there are no differences between day and night, the view is fully recognized. When there are no differences between this and future lives, meditation has been perfected." According to the Mantrayana, "daytime appearances" correspond to this present life, while "nighttime appearances" (dreams) refer to the next life. If one manages to blend daytime experiences with one's nighttime dreams; if one is able to recognize and transform one's dreams; and if one gains experience in dream yoga also in (the waking experiences of) the daytime, one will be able to transform and emanate phenomena. It is by means of dream yoga, too, that one can gauge one's progress in the practice of the illusory body. When dreams dissolve into the state of luminosity and cease (i.e., when one does not dream anymore), one is able to attain liberation in the present life. Before this happens, however, it is necessary to become adept in transforming dreams at will. This means transforming them from pure to impure (for example, changing a deity who is foretelling the future into a frightful lion or bear) and from impure to pure (like changing a pit of venomous snakes into a multitude of wisdom deities). It also means that one should be able to develop one's dreams as one wishes. If one has this capacity, it means that a certain stability in the practice has been achieved.

The final objective of the tummo, illusory body, and dream yoga practices is the recognition of luminosity. If one fails to achieve this goal in the present life, then in order to create a "bridge" to one's next life, it is necessary to engage in the bardo practice. For example, if one has reached the level called the intensification of meditative experience (*nyams snang gong 'phel*), then in one's next life (like piping water from one place to another) one will meet with a qualified Dzogchen master, so that one can progress to the next stage called reaching the culmination of awareness (*rig pa tshad phebs*). Finally, if one faces an untimely death, one can practice phowa, or the transference of consciousness.

312 The following presentations of tummo, the illusory body, and dream yoga are taken from YG III, 361:2–362:6.

313 [DKR/OC] If the mind is not attentive (with the concentration of someone threading a needle) and if, as a result of this, the wind goes into the wrong channels, obstacles will arise—even mental and emotional disturbance.

314 [DKR/OC] This is the actualization of emptiness endowed with supreme qualities.

315 [DKR/OC] In the tantras it is written that, attired and adorned as a deity, one should sit surrounded by four mirrors. When offerings are made to oneself as the deity, are the reflections in any way benefited? Likewise, when one is reviled, are the reflections in any way harmed? By meditating that the image and oneself are one, one is working on one's feelings of attachment and animosity.

316 [DKR/OC] In some measure, the practice of the illusory body corresponds to meditation, while the practice of dream yoga corresponds to postmeditation. In one's daily activities, one should cultivate the thought that everything is a dream. During the night, when one is actually dreaming, one should be able to recognize one's dreams as dreams, thanks to the habit one has acquired in one's waking hours. When the practice of tummo goes well, and the wind-mind enters the central channel, one recognizes one's dreams quite spontaneously. If one has good dreams (such as meeting one's teacher, seeing a deity, and so on), or if one has bad dreams (for example, being attacked by a wild

animal), one recognizes the dreams simply as dreams, neither beneficial nor harmful. One can then transform good dreams into bad dreams, and bad dreams into good ones. One can cause them to develop, and one can visit the buddhafields and hell realms at will. For example, one can overcome the burning fire into which one has fallen, knowing that it is no more than a dream and that there is nothing to fear.

If one is able to blend the phenomena of the waking state in the daytime with the experiences of the dream state at night, it will also be possible to use the visions experienced in the bardo as the path. As it is said, "If there is no difference between the appearances of the waking state in the daytime and the dream state at night, realization expands like space." One should blend the yoga of the daytime with the yoga of the night as though one were preparing a field in which to grow crops. The channels are like watercourses that bring water to the plantations. One must close the doors of the karmic wind, and open those of the wisdom wind. If the watercourses are in good condition, the water (meaning the white and red bodhichitta) can be transferred, up and down, at will. The "water" is propelled by air pressure (in other words, the wind), which works like the pump in a pond, forcefully projecting the water into the channel. The pump itself should be in good working order and should be able to propel the water. If one has managed to straighten the channels, purify the wind, and position the essence-drops correctly, it is then that one can take the support of a consort. This is not in the manner of ordinary desire but of the bliss that brings liberation. This is the "great bliss" that leads to ultimate, primordial wisdom. It is a great bliss that fills the whole of space.

317 This refers to the practice related to the channels and winds.

318 See also *Systems of Buddhist Tantra*, p. 260–64, and Tsele Natsok Rangdrol, *The Mirror of Mindfulness* (Boston: Shambhala Publications, 1989), pp. 32–33.

319 [DKR/OC] Practitioners can catch a glimpse of luminosity while in the state of deep sleep. On the basis of the example luminosity, they can be guided to ultimate, authentic luminosity in much the same way that by looking at a picture of the moon they can form an idea of how it really looks in the sky, or can gain an idea of the bliss and perfection of the field of Sukhavati by gazing at a painting of it.

320 The following presentations of the bardo and the practice of transference are taken from YG III, 368:5–369:4.

321 [DKR/OC] Once the experiences of light, increase of light, and culmination of light have arisen, the ground-luminosity will arise. If, during one's life, one has meditated a great deal on the example luminosity, one will be able to recognize the ground-luminosity. If actual, ultimate luminosity is recognized, this is in fact the accomplishment of the bardo practice, and no subsequent practice is needed. For a practitioner of medium capacity, however, the lumi-

nous appearances of the ground will once again arise out of the ground-luminosity, and this is the bardo of ultimate reality (*chos nyid bar do*). There then follows the bardo of becoming (*srid pa'i bar do*). For when the luminosity aspect (*snang ba*) is obscured (*mun pa*) and not recognized, one must wander in the darkness of the bardo of becoming. At that time, by using the support of the practice of the illusory body, one will be able to arise in the form of the yidam-deity that one has meditated on, and one will be able to lead to the pure lands many beings who have a similar karma.

322 [DKR/OC] While traveling through a forest filled with wild and dangerous beasts, one is happy to be accompanied by an escort. In just the same way, if, in this present life, one fails to attain the goal, one should take support of the transference of consciousness in order to ensure a birth in the next life that is favorable to the practice of Dharma. Without fear or apprehension, one should make the resolution: "Now, by following the Guru's instructions, I will go to a buddhafield."

323 *steng sgo rnam grol gyi lam.* [DKR/OC] This name derives from the fact that the practice in question places emphasis on the letter HANG located at the upper extremity of the central channel.

324 *'og sgo khams gsum rol pa'i lam.* [DKR/OC] The expressions "lower door" and "enjoyment of the three worlds" are used to indicate the fact that, in the first case, the essence-drops are held in the secret center and, in the second case, the stains of the three worlds are thereby purified and the experiences of bliss, clarity, and no-thought are revealed. See also note 279.

325 "In the Tripitaka of the causal vehicle, woman is described as the source of defilement. In the Mantrayana, however, she is regarded as the wellspring of emptiness, and Prajnaparamita herself, the mother of all the Buddhas. If a practitioner takes skillful support of her, he will quickly reach supreme accomplishment. If the consort is a woman belonging to one of the five families and has all the characteristics described in the tantras; if she is a woman who has achieved ultimate coemergent luminosity (*lhan skyes ma*) [if, in other words, she is a wisdom dakini like Yeshe Tsogyal]; if she is a woman "mantra-born" (*sngags skyes ma*), that is, one who has purified her mind through empowerment and the generation stage; or if, finally, she was born in any one of the twenty-four sacred lands and so on (*zhing skyes ma*), accomplishment will be swift to manifest.

"By simply taking support of such a consort—joining skillful means and wisdom, and arresting respiration (the seed of obscuration) by holding one cycle of the vase breath—the practitioner achieves unchanging bliss. Gradually, if the practitioner is able to gather the movement of the 21,600 respirations in a single breath (*'pho ba gcig*), all the qualities of the grounds and paths of realization will manifest quickly and powerfully. If the practitioner takes support of a qualified consort with the help of the three perceptions [DKR/OC: That is, thinking of himself and his consort as deities, of their secret parts as the lotus and vajra, and of the union as the practice aimed at achieving the supreme siddhi]; if he is adept in the four pith instructions concerning the 'dripping, holding, reversing, and spreading,' all the qualities of the path will be brought to perfection.

"As the essence-drops gradually drip from the crown of the head to the chakras at the throat, heart, navel, and secret center, the practitioner experiences the four joys, which are in fact the wisdoms of the four empowerments. The four states of wakefulness, sleep, dream, and orgasm are purified. The essence-drops, which are the support of the body, speech, mind, and habitual tendencies, together with the obscurations of the three doors, both individually and altogether without differentiation, are purified. The practitioner then experiences the wisdom of luminosity free and naked of any (mitigating) experience. He holds the essence-drops in the vajra vase without emitting them. Subsequently, by implementing the pith instruction on 'reversing,' he holds the essence-drops in the crown of the head. Then, with the help of the wind and the yogic exercises ('khrul 'khor), and especially through the Dzogchen view of the indivisibility of the ultimate expanse and awareness, the practitioner is able to spread the essence-drops throughout his body, thereby attaining to the great bliss that is utterly unchanging." [YG III, 370:3–371:6]

326 [DKR/OC] Some (certain non-Buddhists, for example) say that the ordinary bliss of union is the great bliss itself. This is not so. When actual great bliss arises, it is the supreme and unchanging primordial wisdom. And it is not impermanent but constant. The pleasure of ordinary sexual intercourse, which is no more than the result of mere friction, is not great bliss.

327 "The nada symbolizes the extremely subtle wind, which is the nature of the three worlds. And it is said that this subtle wind subsists till the attainment of buddhahood. This is meditated upon, visualized as having three curves, which symbolizes that it holds the habitual tendencies of the three worlds. When this is purified, it transforms into utterly unchanging great bliss, the nature of the three kayas." [YG III, 373:5–6]

328 "This dissolution stage is extremely important. For it purifies the habitual tendency of death, it creates the causal link for the attainment of the dharmakaya, and it ripens into the "dissolution of the illusory body of the perfection stage into the state of luminosity." [YG III, 374:1–2]

329 [DKR/OC] Beginning with the precepts of refuge and bodhichitta.

330 The Sanskrit word "samaya" generally means a "coming together," an agreement, pact, or covenant, and in the present context it is usually understood in the sense of a sacred pledge. The second element of the Tibetan translation (dam tshig) has two possible meanings. It can be understood either as part of the verb 'tshig pa ("to burn") or else as a noun meaning simply "word." The commentary addresses both acceptations.

331 [DKR/OC] In other words, if one perceives all appearances, sounds, and thoughts as deities, mantra, and wisdom (this being the root of all samayas), all faults will be consumed. See YG III, 380:5.

332 "The same tantra says that if one fails to keep the pledge, one will be burned in flames of hell." [YG III, 380:6]

333 *ngo bo gcig pa ldog chas dbye ba.* It has been said that the line referred to in these two sentences has been removed from Jigme Lingpa's text, and that therefore its inclusion is not essential. [DKR]

334 "The so-called entangling attitudes (*kun dkris*) are generally defined as those factors that produce a root downfall of bodhichitta. These same factors also produce a complete downfall in the Mantrayana." [YG III, 383:6]

335 "The expression 'root downfalls' is used for the following reason. When the roots of a tree are torn away, this marks the end of the trunk, branches, leaves, and fruit. In the same way, the vows are the roots from which all positive qualities develop. And if the roots are cut, no qualities will grow. Thus one speaks of 'root.' And since the breaking of the vows causes one to sink into the lower realms, one speaks of 'downfalls.'" [YG III, 390:3–5]

336 "According to some authorities, the fourth downfall, the abandonment of loving-kindness, also constitutes a defeat in itself, whether the entanglements are present or not." [YG III, 384:1–2]

337 *kha na ma tho ba'i sbom po.*

338 *slob dpon smod pa.*

339 For the three kinds of service (*zhabs tog rnam pa gsum*), see *Treasury of Precious Qualities*, bk. 1, p. 201.

340 *bde gshegs bka' 'das.*

341 *mched la 'khu ba.*

342 Buddhajnanapada (*sangs rgyas ye shes zhabs*) was a disciple of Manjushrimitra from whom he received the mind class teachings of the Great Perfection. Some authorities equate this master with Shri Simha. See *The Nyingma School of Tibetan Buddhism*, p. 494–96.

343 Shantipa, also known as Ratnakarashanti, was the keeper of the eastern gate of Vikramashila. He was a celebrated exponent of the Prajnaparamita, Madhyamaka, logic, and grammar. He taught Madhyamaka as the foundation for the Vajrayana, and he attained the level of Vidyādhara through the practice of *Guhyasamaja.* He was one of Atisha's teachers, and his lineage was brought to Tibet by Drogmi Shakya Yeshe.

344 *byams pa 'dor ba.*

345 *byang sems 'dor ba*

346 That is, compassion focusing on beings, and wisdom focusing on enlightenment.

347 [DKR/OC] That is, when giving the empowerment.

348 [DKR/OC] That is, when receiving the empowerment.

349 [DKR/OC] That is, of suffering and happiness.

350 This is a pill containing the five nectars.

351 *grub mtha' smod pa.*

352 [DKR/OC] To criticize Buddhist doctrines and the beliefs of non-Buddhists is permissible only when it is necessary for the clarification of mistaken understanding, and in order to bring beings on to the Buddhist path.

353 *gsang ba sgrog pa.*

354 *rjes gnang.* [DKR/OC] This is a ritual authorizing disciples to meditate on the deity, recite the mantra, and cultivate concentration. It does not have the same maturing power as the empowerment.

355 *rigs gtad.* This means to bestow the blessings of the deities of the body, speech, and mind families, namely, Manjushri, Avalokiteshvara, and Vajrapani. It does not require the presence of the mandala.

356 *phung po smod pa.*

357 *rang bzhin dag pa'i chos la the tshom za ba.*

358 *ldem dgongs.* See *Treasury of Precious Qualities,* bk. 1, chap. 9, p. 338–41.

359 The doctrine of the tathāgatagarbha is expounded and supported by many arguments in ten profound sutras, such as the *Sandhinirmochana-sutra,* together with texts like the *Sublime Continuum.* Some teachers of the new translation tradition appear to have asserted that this teaching is expedient. [KPS]

360 *gdug pa can mi sgrol ba.*

361 This includes those who harm the images of the Buddha, the Dharma of transmission and realization, and the yellow-clad Sangha. [DKR]

362 Those who harm a teacher who has mastery of all the Buddha's teachings. [DKR]

363 "On the other hand, if practitioners abandon the attitude of love (repudiating the people in question and mentally turning away from them), they commit the fourth downfall." [YG III, 409:3]

364 *ming bral chos la tshad mas gzhal ba.*

365 *stong pa nyi tshe ba,* the emptiness of phenomena asserted in conceptual terms.

366 *dad ldan sems sun 'byin pa.*

367 *dam rdzas ji bzhin mi bsten pa.*

368 For example, at the ganachakra or sacred feast offering.

369 *shes rab ma la smod pa.*

370 For example, the Dharma-protectors Ekajati or Tseringma.

371 "When, in the common sutras, the Buddha spoke of the defects of women, he did so with a certain underlying intention and pedagogical purpose [i.e., to aid the monks in the practice of chastity]. And when, in accordance with the Buddha's words, some teachers have expressed a certain critique of women, they have done so likewise with a view to (the same) particular purpose. Barring this specific circumstance, no one should ever gratuitously scorn or show contempt for women." [YG III, 415:5–416:1]

372 *slob bshad.* This concerns teaching on the perfection stage.

373 *tshogs bshad.* In the case of Anuttaratantras, this refers to the teachings on the generation stage.

374 Nagarjuna (*klu grub*), the second-century founder of the Madhyamaka system, is credited, in Tibetan tradition, with works on the tantra, such as the commentary on the *Guhyasamaja-tantra* called the *Five Stages* (*rim lnga*).

375 Shura (*dpa'bo*), alias Ashvaghosha (*rta dbyangs*), was a Hindu scholar who, influenced by Aryadeva, converted to Mahayana Buddhism. The author of the *Buddhacharita* (a biography of the Buddha), he is an important figure in the Sanskrit poetic tradition.

376 For a detailed exposition of the samayas and downfalls of the different tantra classes, see *Buddhist Ethics*, pp. 231–42.

377 That is, *mdo sgyu sems gsum.* The literal meaning of this expression is "scripture, illusion, and mind." It is an abbreviated reference to three items: the *mdo dgongs pa 'dus pa,* the *sgyu 'phrul drva ba,* and the *sems sde.* This is the terminology used in the kahma teachings to refer respectively to Anuyoga, Mahayoga, and Atiyoga.

378 This is one of the principal tantras of the Anuyoga class. It consists of seventy-five chapters divided into ten sections, and was translated into Tibetan from the Gilgit language of *bru sha* by Chetsenkyé (*che btsan kyes*). See note 144.

379 The seal or mudra of the Conquerors refers here to the vivid, yet empty, body of the deity. [KPS]

380 These must be recognized as being, respectively, the five Buddhas, the five female Buddhas, the five female Bodhisattvas, the five male Bodhisattvas, and the five wisdoms. [DKR]

381 *bsgrub dang bsrung ba'i dam tshig.* See p. 201 for an explanation of this distinction.

382 The truths of purity and equality (*dag* and *mnyam*). See appendix 3.

383 *rtags kyi lha sku phyag rgya.* "Sign" in the term "sign-mudra" is no doubt a reference to emptiness and compassion, of which the body of the deity is the sign. However, it may also refer to the deity's family, on the symbol of which the flower fell during the empowerment. [KPS]

384 This is Rongdzom Pandita's commentary on the *Guhyagarbha.*

385 This means a teacher who commands universal respect, such as the present Dalai Lama. For a detailed discussion of the six kinds of teacher, see *Buddhist Ethics,* p. 497n261.

386 The vajra master is described as a "perilous object" (*yul gnyan po*) because any action, positive or negative, performed in respect of such a master, produces extreme results for good or ill.

387 These comparisons refer respectively to: (1) the teacher worthy of respect; (2) the teacher who brings beings onto the path; (3) the teacher who gives empowerment; (4) the teacher to whom one confesses faults and downfalls; (5) the teacher who explains the tantras; and (6) the teacher who gives pith instructions. [DKR]

388 The root mantra, for example HUNG, is the unmistaken cause; the generation mantra is the cooperative condition; the activity mantra is for recitation. [DKR]
   "Unmistaken cause" means the cause of the deity; "cooperative" refers to the seed-syllables of the elements, the palace, and so on; the "activity mantra" is the main mantra of the deity used in the recitation. [KPS] For an alternative explanation, see *Buddhist Ethics,* p. 497n265.

389 For example, the four major Dharma feasts, such as the celebration of the Buddha's descent from the Heaven of the Thirty-Three.

390 See p. 184.

391 That is, those who are intimate but have not yet perfected their practice. [DKR]

392 See also *Buddhist Ethics,* p. 281.

393 This distinction is made by Longchenpa in *Dispelling Darkness in the Ten Directions,* his commentary on the *Guhyagarbha-tantra.* [KPS]

394 *bka' brgyad bde gshegs 'dus pa'i zhi ba'i rgyud,* a terma discovered by Nyangrel Nyima Özer (1124–92).

395 "In contrast with the practitioners of the lower vehicles, adepts of the Mantrayana are without acceptance or rejection. For they do not ascribe reality to the vows or to the observance of them. The object of observance, the person who observes, and the attitude and action of observing, are all regarded as the display of self-cognizing primordial wisdom: the ultimate deity of dharmatā. And even though, [by way of skillful means] on the relative level, these practitioners do accept some things and reject others, nevertheless, thanks to their wisdom, they know that all such things are beyond the categories of good and ill, adoption and rejection.
   "Thus an individual samaya (for example, 'not to spurn the unsurpassed') has the twin aspects of skillful means and wisdom, each of which is subdivided according to three features. The 'unobstructed feature' refers to the enlightened body, the 'unborn feature' refers to enlightened speech, and the

third feature—the union of the previous two—is the enlightened mind. Six samayas are thus obtained. Each of these six can once again be subdivided into five: the body (the aspect of support); speech (the aspect of experience); the mind (the aspect of absence of conceptual constructs); qualities (the aspect of individually appearing attributes); and activities (the aspect of their effectiveness). This results in thirty samayas. When skillful means and wisdom are added, this comes to thirty-two samayas. It is thus that a single samaya in fact comprises thirty-two samayas. If one subdivides the remaining four samayas in the same way, one will arrive at a grand total of one hundred and sixty samayas." [YG III, 440:5–441:5]

396 "If one fails to deal skillfully with defilements, but instead eliminates them by using other antidotes, only the uncompounded result [the cessation of the Shravakas] will be actualized. The qualities of buddhahood will not manifest. It is just as when a seed is roasted (no plant can grow). But if one recognizes that the defilements are without inherent existence, and if one is able to handle them skillfully, neither arresting them nor indulging in them, then the great courage of the general Mahayana, the two accumulations included within the practice of the six paramitas, and all the wisdoms and accomplishments of the Mantrayana, will arise according to one's wish. It is just as when the seed and all the necessary circumstances of water, manure, and warmth are assembled: the fruit grows effortlessly to maturity." [YG III, 442:3–6]

397 For example, the herukas Mahottara or Hayagrīva.

398 Mode of conduct (*brtul zhugs*) is here defined as the taming (*brtul*) of ordinary thought and action and the entry (*zhugs*) into the ultimate reality.

399 See note 395.

400 [DKR/OC] One gives the name "samaya" to the unmoving primordial wisdom of the ultimate expanse. Since everything is the display of this wisdom, this samaya cannot be transgressed.

401 "These are the root and branch samayas of the *mdo sgyu sems gsum* (Mahayoga, Anuyoga, and Atiyoga), which encompass all the common Anuttaratantras." [YG III, 453:4–5]

402 It is important to know what is to be avoided and also what is to be undertaken—and how. The meaning of the last line (*'jug dang las kyis rnam pas bshad*) is difficult to construe. This is an approximate rendering. [KPS]

403 That is, as referring to the outer aspect of the inner body samaya.

404 Appearances, sounds, and thoughts are by nature the three mandalas of the enlightened body, speech, and mind; in other words, the deity, mantra, and wisdom. [KPS]

405 That is, the view of the purity and equality of all phenomena. [KPS]

406 "The manner of not rejecting the five poisons in the usual, negative, sense

(*log pa'i dug*) has already been explained above, as also the five poisons that are utterly pure (*yang dag pa'i dug*). To be more specific, it might be thought that to examine the five poisons (in their negative sense) using the arguments of Madhyamaka, constitutes the path. But sealing the poisons with a mere understanding (of their nature) without bringing them under control is of no help whatsoever. And even if they were to be brought under control in this way, this would amount merely to the general Mahayana purification of defilement into its ultimate nature. It would not constitute the special approach of the mantra path. For if one meditates on love and so forth as a remedy to the defilements, one is using the antidotes as the path, not the defilements themselves. This approach is common also to the Hinayana path.

"Moreover, one may block the defilements, settling in a state that is like a feeling of exhaustion, but if one does this on purpose, the state achieved goes no further than the universal ground, or a mental state of no-thought. And if one remains in a state of nonclinging to the defilements, one is using primordial wisdom as the path, not the defilements themselves. Therefore, when defilements occur, if one leaves them as they are, in the knowledge that they are themselves primordial wisdom by their nature; and if one has no clinging to them and does not do anything to block them, one will not fall victim to such defilements, and one will accumulate neither the karma nor the habitual tendencies associated with them. Defilement itself becomes a favorable condition for the path. Indeed, it becomes the path itself. The *Vajra* (*Mayajala*) says: 'Defilements are like illusions. By their nature they are empty. By their nature they are impermanent. When their nature is known, they subside.' If one is without such an understanding, one may, with the self-assurance of being the deity, practice the perfection stage with characteristics, which uses desire as the path. In this way, defilements are used skillfully as the path itself, with the result that these same defilements are gradually transformed into primordial wisdom, just as iron is alchemically transmuted into gold." [YG III, 461:4–462:6]

407 "The five procedures (*cho ga*) are: to be accepted by a teacher who infallibly reveals the path; to receive an empowerment from such a teacher; to keep the samayas and vows; to know the pith instructions with regard to the practice; and to be able to practice with great endeavor." [YG III, 465:3–4]

408 These additional samayas (*lhag pa'i dam tshig*) are related to specific times, for example, the performing of drupchens or retreats.

409 For it is mainly at those times that such breaches of the samaya occur.

410 See note 398 and *Buddhist Ethics*, pp. 246–48.

411 *so sor sdud pa'i rnal 'byor*. This is the first branch of the sixfold yoga (*sbyor ba yan lag drug*) practiced in the perfection stage of the *Kalachakra-tantra*. For a detailed discussion of this subject, see *Buddhist Ethics*, p. 477n165.

412 See also *Buddhist Ethics*, pp. 246–53.

413 This line in the root verse is perhaps a footnote; it does not appear in Jigme Lingpa's autocommentary *rnam mkhyen shing rta*. [DKR]

414 "Generally speaking, to be of a particular family does not mean that one is absolved from observing the vows of the other four families. It indicates that special care must be taken to observe the vows of one's own family. This is why the vow of each of the five families is referred to as a 'samaya.'" [YG III, 472:1–2]

415 The vajra is the symbol of enlightened mind; the bell is the symbol of enlightened speech; and the deity's form is the symbol of enlightened body. This vow consists therefore in recognizing that one's body, speech, and mind are the three vajras, and in maintaining this recognition in one's meditation. To "uphold the teacher" means to accept the teacher as one's master, to be approached with faith and devotion. [KPS] See *Buddhist Ethics*, p. 250.

416 See also *Buddhist Ethics*, pp. 253–56.

417 See tenth root downfall, pp. 187–88, and *Buddhist Ethics*, p. 476n162. The seven degenerate objects are sometimes defined as: (1) those who are degenerate in their approach to the holy beings (despising their teachers and their vajra kin); (2) those who are degenerate in regard to the Buddha's teachings (ignoring and despising the karmic principle of cause and effect); (3) those who are degenerate in their view (understanding the two truths in a nihilistic sense); (4) those who are degenerate in their action (bringing suffering to the innocent); (5) those who are degenerate in their clinging to distinctions (approaching the Dharma in a sectarian spirit); (6) those who are degenerate in their greed (robbing and destroying without shame); and (7) those who are degenerate in wickedly inflicting suffering on beings.

418 "One should take her red essential element through the control of one's wind." [YG III, 478:5]

419 This passage has been rendered according to YG III, 485:4.

420 For example, one of the penitential precepts (*chad pa las kyi bslab pa*) states that the repentant monk must assume the lowest rank for the rest of his life, and that he is unfit to act as the leader in the ritual of purification and restoration (*gso sbyong*). [KPS]

421 "Generally speaking, for the majority of downfalls to be complete, four elements must be present: (1) an object with regard to which the downfall is committed; (2) the intention; (3) the perpetration of the physical or verbal act (if the downfall is one of body or speech); and (4) the completion of the act (whether physical, verbal, or mental). If these four elements are present, a "defeat" is said to occur, and the mantra vow is lost. If one oscillates between the mental commission of any of the root downfalls (i.e., the wish to commit them) and the application of antidotes to the same, it is true that the four elements are not complete. However, if one fails to confess [this wish] imme-

diately, and the time period for confession is exceeded, it is still called a downfall exceeding the time period for confession. Barring an actual defeat, this is the next most serious negative action. . . . With regard to the nature of the breaking of samaya transgression, one speaks of root downfalls, infractions, and faults, in decreasing order of gravity." [YG III, 496:2–497:1]

422 "The five deteriorations are as follows. First there is 'great deterioration' (*kun tu nyams pa chen po*), namely, defiled behavior with strong entangling attitudes, or frequent defiled behavior in respect of highly important objects (one's teacher, etc.). The second and third are the 'root' and 'branch deteriorations' (*rtsa ba'i nyams pa* and *yan lag gi nyams pa*) as commonly explained. The fourth is deterioration occurring 'through association' (*zlas nyams*), that is, through associating with those who have broken their samayas and who are not engaged in repairing them. One should not meet or speak to such people even for a moment. . . . The fifth refers to 'incidental deterioration' (*zhar nyams*), a deterioration incurred in order to please others, not just for self-centered reasons." [YG III, 500:2–501:3]

423 An example of this would be to explain the meaning of the symbols of the Mantrayana in an inappropriate situation.

424 That is, the offering of jewels, etc.

425 That is, uttering a loud confession with a yearning melody.

426 *'pho med tshul khrims.* That is, of the white bodhichitta.

427 That is, the visualization of the deity (mudra) and the recitation of the deity's mantra.

428 *ngan 'gro dgug dral.* This is a reference to the practice of *gnas lung* (the rite of purification for guiding the consciousness of beings in the bardo), etc. [KPS]

429 *rnam par 'joms pa* and *sme ba brtsegs pa.*

430 "One should visualize all the deities of the peaceful and wrathful mandalas and cultivate strong devotion toward them. Without straying from the meditation by losing the view, one should, on the outer level, make expiatory offerings (*skang ba*) to the deities just mentioned. For this, one should use pure substances of the best quality, such as a 108 offerings of amrita medicine, 108 offerings of rakta, and 108 tormas, in which not a single ingredient is lacking. One should also make 108 lamp offerings. If this quantity is beyond one's means, one should prepare as many offerings as one can. On the inner level, one should also make expiatory offering of one's own body. This implies amrita to represent the white essential constituent, rakta to represent the red essential constituent, together with a torma and lamps to symbolize respectively the channels and the wind-mind. On the secret level, one should make expiatory offerings of bodhichitta.

"In this context, amrita-medicine (*bdud rtsi'i sman*) represents great bliss, the nature of spontaneously arising awareness; rakta represents the nature of emptiness; torma their union; and the lamps the character of luminosity; etc. If, on an auspicious day (the full or new moon, the eighth day of the month, and so on), one makes confession, performing the visualization according to the words of the prayer, together with such outer, inner, and secret offerings of amrita and rakta, it is said that everything will be purified. And even if one is not able to do so, if one constantly bears in mind the first part of this confession, which ends with the recitation of the hundred-syllable mantra, accompanying it with prostrations, all breaches and degenerations of the samaya will be purified." [YG III, 505:3–506:2]

431 "If one does not feel remorse, it is impossible to reject one's fault, and one is in effect deceiving the object of confession. One's ability to amend one's negative behavior will be meager, and the strength of one's remedial practice will be feeble." [YG III, 506:4–5]

432 "The practice of pacifying activities will result in an increase of disease and evil forces. The practice of increase will lead to a lessening of one's life span and merit, etc." [YG III, 507:5]

433 "The 'enjoyment of the sky' (*mkha' spyod*) refers to the ability to remain in celestial fields without dying. The 'power of the sword' brings victory over one's enemies. If one holds in one's hand the pill made of special medicinal substances and blessed by the mantra, one becomes invisible. By wearing special sandals, one can traverse the oceans in a moment. The vase brings forth inexhaustible treasure. To have mastery over demons or yakshas means that the eight classes of spirits are at one's beck and call. By extracting the essence [of the elements], one gains longevity, great strength, and a lotus-like radiance, becoming lighter than flax. Finally, if one applies the magic balm to one's eyes, one gains the power to detect buried treasures." [YG III, 511:3–512:1]

434 See *Treasury of Precious Qualities,* bk. 1, p. 387.

435 "The eight qualities of mastery (*dbang phyugs kyi don brgyad*) are explained in other texts as related to the common accomplishments. The latter are obtained through a mundane path or the rudimentary stage of generation. In the present text, however, they are explained as corresponding to the eightfold noble path on the path of learning. They cause one to attain the path of no more learning, namely, the actualization of the three vajras. This occurs at the last moment of the path of learning when the extremely subtle pulsation of the channels and the movement of the wind and essence-drops (the support of duality) are, together with the propensity for the thoughts of the eight kinds of consciousness, completely purified." [YG III, 512:5–513:2]

436 See p. 153. "Etymologically, a 'Vidyādhara' is one who, by relying on the pith instructions of the Mantrayana, *upholds,* or unerringly maintains *awareness,* the sugatagarbha." [YG III, 514:5]

437 *kha sbyor yan lag bdun.* Union (*kha sbyor*), here, means equality, evenness (*mnyam pa nyid*). [KPS]

438 "It is said that three approaches to ultimate reality are implicit in all phenomena. They are known as the three doors of perfect liberation (*rnam thar sgo gsum*) and are: emptiness, absence of (truly existing) attributes, and absence of expectancy.

"1. Emptiness is defined as the 'absence of reference' or 'unfindability,' in other words, the absence of inherent existence. Phenomena, from form to omniscience, are totally devoid of even the slightest degree of intrinsic being. Their true status lies outside the range of discursive cognition, and consequently it is precisely mental construction that veils it. Phenomena, the objects of thought, appear only as long as thoughts occur (namely, the ordinary mind and its mental factors). For in themselves, phenomena are without true existence, not only on the ultimate level but even on the conventional level.

"2. Absence of attributes or featurelessness is defined as 'pacification' or 'subsiding.' Phenomena arise in interdependence as the natural display of emptiness. Thus, from the very outset, conceptual ascriptions like existent or nonexistent, good or bad, and definitions in terms of productive causes and conditions (beneficial or otherwise) cannot properly be applied to them. To divide the phenomenal field into self and other, clean and unclean, and so on, is the very antithesis of the absence of attributes. For the truth is that, within the nature of emptiness, the dharmadhatu, the domain of nonconceptual primordial wisdom, phenomena do not exist in this way.

"3. Absence of expectancy is defined as 'absence of suffering and ignorance.' The phenomena included within the categories of true sufferings and true origins ('true sufferings' means the universe and its inhabitants, and their 'true origins' means karma and defilement born of ignorance) have never existed [as such]. Therefore they are no different from 'nirvana,' the state beyond suffering. As the *Way of the Bodhisattva* (9:103) says:

> Something such as this does not exist, not even slightly.
> Beings by their nature are beyond the reach of suffering.

"The antithesis of this is our tendency to consider samsara and nirvana as distinct realities, and to imagine that nirvana is a goal to be attained—whereas in the nature of the mind itself, there is no distinguishing between samsara and nirvana. As the *Introduction to the Middle Way* (6:208–9) affirms:

> The character of emptiness
> Is absence of a real, existent referent.
>
> The absence of all attributes is peace.
> And third, (the absence of expectancy) has been defined as
>   nonexistence
> Of all suffering and ignorance.

"The three doors of perfect liberation are also associated with the ground, path, and result. Emptiness refers to the ground because it lies beyond the extreme ontological positions of existence and nonexistence. Absence of attributes refers to the path because, even at the present moment, phenomena are without real existence. Absence of expectancy refers to the result, because no hope or reliance is placed in the future. The *Introduction to the Middle Way* (6:216) says:

> The present instant does not stay;
> The past and future have no being.
> Because these three cannot be pointed out,
> They are referred to as the unobservable.

[YG III, 517:6–520:1]

439 "The naturally pure dharmadhatu, the nature of the mind, luminous primordial wisdom, is ever present and unchanging. Its appearance aspect is the source of the rupakaya's major and minor marks. Its emptiness aspect is present primordially and spontaneously, the dharmakaya beyond all mental constructs. It is like a jewel because its qualities are present naturally. Like space, it is unchanging, and all beings are pervaded by it in the same way that water is pervaded by its wetness. The *Sublime Continuum* says:

> Like a jewel, like space, like pure and limpid water,
> Such is the nature of the mind.
> At all times it is free from the defilements.

"Therefore, of the second and third turnings of the Dharma wheel, it is in the third that the final, definitive teaching is expressed. In the *Mahaparinirvana-sutra*, the second and third turnings of the wheel of Dharma were explained with the following example. A certain doctor gave medicine to a sick baby and told its mother not to feed it until it had digested the medicine. Accordingly, the woman smeared her breast with bile, telling her child that she could not feed it because there was poison on her breast. Although the baby wanted to drink its mother's milk, it could not because her breast had a bitter taste. When, however, the medicine had been digested, the woman washed her breast and wanted to feed her child. The latter, however, was wary of the bitter taste and would not suckle. When the woman explained why her breast had tasted bitter, the baby gradually came to drink her milk again.

"Now in the same way that the woman had put bile upon her breast, the Tathāgata taught that all phenomena are devoid of self (they are without inherent existence). He did this so that his disciples would meditate on emptiness. But later, just as the woman washed her breast and suckled again, the Buddha said that all beings are pervaded by the tathāgatagarbha. And after speaking in this way, the Buddha declared: 'O monks, you too must distinguish these two instances. The tathāgatagarbha is not nonexistent. In the past (in the *Prajnaparamita-sutras*), I spoke of emptiness, but you should know that I intended only the absence of inherent existence. Indeed, meditation on an emptiness that is just nothingness would not give rise to the kayas and wisdoms of buddhahood. For as the cause is, so is its fruit.'" [YG III, 521:5–523:5] [DKR/OC] Emptiness compared to a bitter taste refers to "mere emptiness." But there are two aspects in the tathāgatagarbha: emptiness and luminosity. The second turning of the wheel expounds only the emptiness aspect, while the third turning of the wheel expounds emptiness and luminosity inseparably united.

440 In his *Fundamentals of the Nyingma School* (*rnying ma'i rnam gzhag*), Dudjom Rinpoche says on several occasions that, in the context of "rough and outer" Madhyamaka (*rags pa phyi'i dbu ma*)—namely, the texts and arguments of the Svatantrikas and Prasangikas—it is shown that there is no contradiction in the fact that, though phenomena are without intrinsic being on the ultimate level, they nonetheless arise through interdependence on the relative level. In addition, in the subtle, inner Madhyamaka (*phra ba nang gi dbu ma*), otherwise known as the resultant Madhyamaka of union (*zung 'jug 'bras bu'i dbu ma*), based on the third turning of the Dharma-wheel, it is established that the dharmadhatu is the ultimate expanse indivisible from the kayas and wisdoms. It is not mere voidness, a nonaffirmative negation.

441 It should be noted that the terms "awareness," "self-cognizing awareness" (*rig pa* or *rang rig*), and "self-cognizing primordial wisdom" (*rig pa'i ye shes* or *so so rang rig pa'i ye shes*), as these occur in the Great Perfection teachings, do not have the same meaning as in the context of Chittamatra. In the *Treasury of Teachings*, the auto-commentary on the *Precious Treasury of the Dharmadhatu*, Longchenpa says: "Awareness, which sees that there is no duality of apprehended object and apprehending mind, is called self-arisen primordial wisdom. However, this is not the self-cognizing, self-illuminating awareness asserted in the Yogachara Chittamatra. For since [according to the Great Perfection] there is neither outside nor inside, awareness does not exist as the 'inner mind.' Since there is neither self nor other, it does not exist as 'self-cognizing awareness.' Since there has never been an apprehending mind and apprehended object, it does not exist as 'that which is free of them.' Since there is no object of feeling and knowledge, it does not exist as 'nondual experience.' Since there is neither mind nor mental factors, it does not exist as 'one's mind.' Since there is neither luminosity nor nonluminosity, it does not exist as 'natural luminosity.' And since it transcends awareness and lack of awareness, it cannot even be called 'mere awareness.' This is what we mean by the 'Great Perfection beyond all extremes.' Although awareness is referred to as 'self-arisen primordial wisdom,' 'bodhichitta (pure, accomplished mind),' 'dharmakaya,' 'great spontaneous presence of the ultimate expanse,' and 'naked self-illuminating awareness,' one should understand that these are mere ascriptions that simply point to it. For if one were to grasp at these

names as being awareness itself, the latter would not be at all different from the self-cognizing, self-illuminating mind free from the duality of the object and subject of the Chittamatra school." [*Treasury of Teachings (lung gi gter mdzod)*, p. 76:1–6].

442 "Regarding the Great Perfection of the ground, one speaks of 'perfection' because the phenomena of both samsara and nirvana are all perfectly contained in the nature of awareness (*rig pa'i ngo bo*). The phenomena of samsara are like appearances in a dream: they appear without having true existence. They are but the creative power of awareness—considered (wrongly) to have a real existence of its own. The phenomena of nirvana are spontaneously present in awareness, in the same way that rays of light are present in the sun. It is thus that the phenomena of both samsara and nirvana are perfectly contained in awareness. This perfection is qualified as 'great' because the ground (the nature of awareness) is primordial wisdom, which pervades samsara and nirvana.

"The Great Perfection of the path is the method whereby adventitious obscurations (which are themselves the manifestation of the creative power of awareness (*rtsal snang glo bur ba'i dri ma*) vanish of their own accord. This happens when one remains without any mental contrivance, without any manipulation, in a state free from all conceptual construction, in a state where (the main) mind and mental factors subside in the ultimate expanse, the sphere of self-arisen primordial wisdom, which is free of all deliberate action and is beyond ordinary mental states. Since all the qualities of both path and result are spontaneously present in this state, it is called perfection. And because it is the final point of all vehicles and paths, it is called great.

"The Great Perfection of the result is self-cognizing primordial wisdom (*rig pa'i ye shes*), which is free from all obscuring stains and habitual tendencies. Because it is the ground whence the kayas and primordial wisdoms arise, it is called perfection. And since by nature it constitutes the qualities of elimination, realization, and enlightened activity, it is called great." [YG III, 524:6–525:6]

443 [DKR/OC] What we call the "ground" is the union of emptiness and luminosity. It is the dharmatā: motionless, ultimate reality, the tathāgatagarbha. At the slightest arising of the creative power of awareness (and there is no question of its not arising), there occurs what is called the appearance of the ground (*gzhi snang*). The appearance of the ground and the creative power of awareness are the same thing. This creative power moves, whereas awareness itself is always motionless. It is as when the sun rises. The sun's rays cover the earth, but the sun does not move out from itself. Its rays are like the creative power of awareness. The appearance of the ground is said to "move," in the sense that it is the ground's radiance, not because it is drawn out by something extraneous.

It is true that, of necessity, the doors of freedom and delusion arise from within the ground. The ground alone, however, does not give rise to them. Their occurrence depends on the appearance, or rather the appearances, of the ground emerging from the ground. If, in the moment of their arising, the appearances of the ground are recognized as the self-experience of awareness (*rang snang*), one is not deluded, and freedom occurs. Otherwise, if one looks outwardly, thinking that the appearances of the ground are something outside awareness, one is in delusion. Therefore the door of both samsara and nirvana (of freedom and delusion) is the *appearance* of the ground, not the ground itself.

As for the ground itself, this is none other than the tathāgatagarbha. What is the difference between awareness and the ground? "Awareness" is the name given to the *actualization* of the fundamental nature of the ground. Therefore, while awareness is necessarily the ground, the ground is not necessarily awareness.

444 *rang bzhin rdzogs pa chen po.* [DKR/OC] In the expression "Natural Great Perfection," the term "natural" (*rang bzhin*) refers to the fact that the "face" or likeness (*bzhin*) of ultimate reality or dharmatā is shown exactly as it is, without modification or elaboration.

445 "In the vehicle of the paramitas, it is said that although samsara and nirvana are not different (in that neither the one nor the other has real existence), they do seem different on the conventional level. But now, when the ground of the Natural Great Perfection is established, it is taught that, also on the conventional level, the aggregates (and the other phenomena of samsara) and the kayas and wisdoms (the phenomena of nirvana) are the same in the state of awareness. And so, when the nature of all phenomena is realized just as it is, the qualities of buddhahood, the kayas and wisdoms, do not arise as something new. For they dwell already in awareness, the self-arisen primordial wisdom endowed with the nature of the trikaya—an expanse from which they have never departed. And likewise, when one is deluded, through failure to recognize the fundamental nature, the various appearances of the outer and inner things of samsara do not arise anew, either. For throughout the entire time that one is deluded, these same appearances are none other than the primordially pure nature of awareness. The phenomena of samsara are like a rabbit's horns. In themselves, they are completely nonexistent." [YG III, 528:2–529:1]

446 It is important to note that in this account of the trikaya, the sambhogakaya and the nirmanakaya are aspects of inner luminosity, as will be explained. They are distinct from the sambhogakaya and nirmanakaya of outwardly radiating luminosity (the rupakaya in the usually accepted sense).

447 Through their being recognized for what they are: the self-experience of awareness (*rang snang*).

448 For an explanation of what is meant by the duality of apprehended and

apprehender (or percept and perceiver), see chapter 11, commentary to stanzas 27–28, p. 249.

449 "The defects of these opinions are described in tantras such as the *Six Expanses*." [YG III, 530:5]

450 That is, it can be described negatively (apophatically) by removing extraneous characteristics, but it cannot be described in positive terms (kataphatically) as this or that. See Shantarakshita and Mipham, *Adornment of the Middle Way* (Boston: Shambhala Publications, 2005), pp. 269 and 275.

451 See chapter 10, pp. 173–76.

452 "The recognition or nonrecognition of the nature of the appearance of the ground is the criterion for the occurrence either of nirvana or samsara." [YG III, 542:3]

453 Jamgön Kongtrul comments that "Awareness that dwells in the ground is present as the inner expanse (*nang dbying*). At the beginning and the end [i.e., at the time when ultimate reality stands spontaneously revealed during the final stage of the death process—which is an end in relation to the past life and a beginning in relation to the future life], it is only present as a profoundly indwelling luminosity and does not appear as deities and lights [of outwardly radiating luminosity]. But when awareness rises from the ground, it reveals its natural luminous radiance. When dwelling in the heart, awareness is called the awareness that dwells in the temporary ground. Because it has already arisen from the ultimate expanse as samsara and has not yet reached the place of freedom, it is still considered to be the appearance of the ground. To be more specific, 'unripe' awareness (*rig pa ma smin pa*) dwells in the expanse of the naturally radiant five lights—like an unhatched peacock within its egg. When the four visions are experienced on the path, awareness is, at that time, manifesting like a rainbow in the sky. And when the material body is purified, awareness is perfected and 'ripens' into the kaya—like the peacock emerging from the egg. Consequently, the ground of the ultimate expanse differs from the 'temporary ground' in that it is not within the visible abode of light, whereas the latter is." See Jamgön Kongtrul, *Treasury of Knowledge* (*shes bya kun khyab*), p. 133.

454 *rang bzhin lhun gyis grub pa'i rang gdangs.* "Various names are used to indicate the ground. The *Precious Treasury That Fulfills All Wishes* says: 'The ground has many names. Since samsara and nirvana arise from it, it is called the ultimate expanse (*dbyings*). Since it has been present from the beginning, it is called the spontaneously present nature (*rang bzhin lhun grub*). Since it is concealed by obscurations, it is called the essential element (*snying po'i khams*). Since it is the fundamental nature, it is called the ultimate truth. Since it is primordially pure, it is named immaculate luminosity. Since it dwells in neither of the two extreme positions, it is said to be the nature of the Middle Way. Since it transcends all conceptual constructs, it is transcendent wisdom. Since it is

empty and immaculately luminous, it is the indivisibility of the two truths. Since it is unchanging, it is suchness, the ultimate nature, etc. All this is said by those who are wise and learned.'

"Here a question may be raised. If Madhyamaka, Prajnaparamita, and the Great Perfection are only different names for the same thing, how is it that the Great Perfection is superior to the vehicle of the paramitas? The answer is that whereas they are all the same (as we have said) on the ultimate level, they differ considerably both in the way they establish the ground, and also in their associated meditative practices. According to the vehicle of the paramitas, it is believed that the sugatagarbha is present in the mind like a seed, which, thanks to the two accumulations (acting as cooperative conditions), develops 'newly' into the qualities of the result (enlightenment). Therefore it is with effort that the path is traversed. According to the Great Perfection, on the other hand, it is believed that in the sugatagarbha all the qualities of enlightenment are naturally present already, and therefore the path does not require any exertion. Therefore, the way of establishing and implementing the union of emptiness and dependent arising—in other words, the way of establishing the indivisibility of the two truths according to Madhyamaka, and the so-called indivisibility of the two superior truths of the general Mantrayana, and also the indivisibility of primordial purity and spontaneous presence in the Great Perfection—are all different. Nevertheless, it is important to understand that, in their essential meaning, they are in fact the same." [YG III, 545:1–546:3]

455 "The words 'ever youthful' (gzhon nu) is used because the nature of awareness, being uncompounded, does not decay and disintegrate as a compounded phenomenon does. In the expression 'vase body' (bum pa'i sku), the term 'body' (kaya) refers to the fact that the inner luminosity just mentioned is the ground of arising of the three kayas, which is unceasing and unobstructed within the ultimate expanse." [YG III, 542:1–2]

"In the same way that a statue with a head, arms, etc., when placed inside a vase, is concealed by that very vase and is not visible, likewise, even though the inner luminosity is endowed with all the qualities, the latter are not externally manifest." [YG III, 543:3–4]

"In a similar way, the sutras of definitive meaning, together with the commentaries upon their intended meaning, illustrate the fact that the tathāgatagarbha dwells concealed within the obscurations. In the sutra Holding the Root of Virtue, we find: 'The tathāgatagarbha is like a flame inside a vase. When the vase breaks, the flame becomes visible.' And Nagarjuna says in his Praise of the Dharmadhatu: 'Just as a flame within a vase cannot be seen outside, so too the light of the dharmadhatu in samsara is not seen. When the vase is broken, the flame sheds light on everything. So too, when obscurations are destroyed by diamond-like concentration, the radiance of the dharmadhatu fills the whole of space with light.'" [YG III, 544:1–4]

456 Here, as elsewhere in the three chapters on the Great Perfection, the Tibetan translation of "bodhichitta" (*byang chub kyi sems*) is understood, and literally translated, according to its strict (Tibetan) etymology: pure and accomplished mind.

457 "This ground for the arising of the kayas and wisdoms is the inner luminosity which, though absorbed within, is not obscured (*nang gsal thim la ma rmugs*)." [YG III, 548:2]

458 In some editions of the root text, *skye med* ("unoriginate") is found here instead of *rkyen med* ("unconditioned"). Khenpo Yönten Gyamtso mentions both these alternative readings, but shows a preference for the reading *skye med*.

459 "'Higher delusion' (*yar 'khrul*) refers to the appearances of the kayas and wisdoms that arise (for beings who are not yet free) through the door of perfect purity at the time of initial delusion, in the bardo of reality (after the moment of death), and on the path of the practitioner. Whatever arises assumes, from the very first moment, an aspect of ignorance [the subject-object duality]. This is because the outwardly arising radiance is impaired by the karmic wind and ordinary mind. These appearances (deities, lights, and so on) are in fact no more than a delusion, albeit a good one. They are not what the Buddhas—who are completely free from habitual propensities—perceive. The very nature of these appearances must be recognized, and they too must return to the ultimate expanse. This is a crucial point.

"'Lower delusion' (*mar 'khrul*) refers to the appearances of the six realms of existence, which arise through the gate of impure samsara. For the Buddhas, who have gained complete freedom and who possess great and non-conceptual compassion, beings who believe in the true existence of such appearances are the object of enlightened action, and this is in accordance with the varying aspirations of the beings in question. And whereas the Buddhas have no deluded perception of the six realms of existence, the beings who believe in the true existence of the appearances of those same six realms are indeed mistaken in what they perceive. They are false, on the other hand, for those who believe in the true existence of the appearances of the six realms as perceived by the different classes of beings. But in the very instant that these appearances are recognized as the self-experience of awareness (*rang snang*), they dissolve of their own accord, and the everlasting kingdom of primordial purity is captured. This is why the arising of pure appearance is not, in itself, beneficial, and the arising of impure appearance is not, in itself, harmful. On the contrary, the root of freedom is the absence of belief in the true existence of these appearances—once they have been recognized as the self-experience of awareness (*rang snang*). The root of delusion is the belief in the true existence of these appearances when they have not been so recognized. For this reason, and in any situation, one must not judge what arises or manifests as either good or bad. Instead, one should leave one's awareness free and open. It is important to understand this crucial point regarding the way that the appearances of the ground arise." [YG III, 552:2–553:3]

460 "In itself, camphor is neither good nor bad. It is good for hot kinds of disease and bad for cold ones. Similarly, for those who lack realization, the ground's spontaneous presence appears as defects, whereas for those with realization, it appears as excellent qualities. The spontaneous presence is therefore the door of both delusion and freedom. Furthermore, if one does not know the fundamental nature of the ground, one does not know the ultimate view of the Great Perfection.

"The key point of this is as follows. Although from the standpoint of the primordial purity of the ground, neither samsara nor nirvana exist, the following three dimensions of spontaneous presence are the juncture at which samsara and nirvana are seamlessly joined. Since in the dimension of the spontaneous presence of the ground, there is an unceasing radiance that is able to manifest as the appearances of samsara and nirvana, it follows that samsara and nirvana are connected in this single ground. The arising of the appearance of the ground constitutes the dimension of the spontaneous presence of the path. Since this provides the condition for both freedom and delusion, it is the meeting place of samsara and nirvana, the point at which they are linked. Thanks to the qualities of the eight ways of arising as explained above, one can, even when one is deluded, be the object of a Buddha's activities and become a Buddha. In the dimension of the spontaneous presence of the result, the kayas, buddhafields, and so forth, are ready to arise. And when they do arise, there is an ability to display activities for the sake of beings to be guided. This renders possible the relationship between the guides and those to be guided." [YG III, 558:6–559:6]

461 This eulogy is based on the etymology of Longchenpa's personal name Drimé Özer (*dri med 'od zer*), Stainless Rays of Light.

462 That is, their lack of intrinsic being.

463 That is, the place of freedom. See note 502.

464 "Practitioners who, thanks to meditating on the path, attain enlightenment endowed with six special features, are also referred to as the primordial Buddha Samantabhadra, for their enlightenment is primordial enlightenment. These six special features are also referred to in the following way: (1) when the appearances of the ground first arise, they are spontaneous (*snang ba lhun grub*); (2) these spontaneous appearances are the self-experience of awareness itself (*lhun grub rang snang*); (3) the self-experience of awareness is primordial wisdom (*rang snang ye shes*); (4) primordial wisdom is primordial freedom (*ye shes ye grol*); (5) primordial freedom is self-cognizing awareness (*ye grol rang rig*); and (6) self-cognizing awareness is the dharmakaya (*rang rig chos sku*); it is said that, as the awareness of cognitive potency (*thugs rje*) arises outwardly to a slight degree, the practitioner instantly actualizes the six features and gains awakening." [YG III, 563:1–3]

465 The full name of this sambhogakaya is Vairochana Mahasagara, who, in the aspects of the five families, is referred to as Vairochana-Vairochana, Vairochana-Akshobhya, Vairochana-Amitabha, etc. "Mahasagara" means "great ocean" and was systematically rendered by the Tibetan translators as "Gangchentso" (great snow mountain lake). This translation was perhaps devised as a means to convey the idea of vastness for the Tibetans, who for the most part had never seen the ocean and had little idea of its immensity.

466 This is probably a reference to the nirmanakaya buddhafields. See Dudjom Rinpoche, *Fundamentals of the Nyingma School* (*rnying ma pa'i bstan pa'i rnam bzhag*), p. 112: "The threefold arrangement of buddhafields corresponds to the three kayas of the Buddhas. The dharmakaya fields are called the Fields of the Indestructible Essence of Luminosity. The sambhogakaya fields are the Fields of the Drumbeat of Brahma. The nirmanakaya fields are called the Fields of Great Brahma's Aeon." See also *The Nyingma School of Tibetan Buddhism*, p. 118.

467 See *Myriads Worlds*, pp. 215–16.

468 That is, examining cognition.

469 *bdag nyid gcig pa'i ma rig pa.* "The ignorance that has the same nature as awareness is actually the reverse of awareness. It is the failure [of the examining cognition] to recognize its own nature of awareness. As such, it becomes the cause, so to speak, of the other two kinds of ignorance." [YG 569:6] In other words, ignorance is a "cognition" that proceeds from awareness and does not differ from it by nature; this natural identity, however, is not recognized.

470 According to Longchenpa: "When the appearance of the ground arises from the ground, and the creative power of cognitive potency (*thugs rje*) arises naturally as a state of clarity and knowing that is able to examine things, there occur, through a failure to recognize the nature of this appearance, three aspects of ignorance that are concomitant with this appearance. The first is the ignorance that has the same nature as awareness. It is the cause of the two other kinds of ignorance. It is the failure of the arisen cognition to recognize its own nature as the nature of awareness. The second is coemergent ignorance, and is the simultaneous arising of the cognition and its failure to recognize the nature of the appearance of the ground. The third is conceptual ignorance. This is the thought that the self-experience of awareness is something 'other,' something extraneous to it [in the sense of subject and object]. These three kinds of ignorance are different aspects of a single nature of a single cognition (*shes pa gcig*)." See *tshig don rin po che'i mdzod* (*Precious Treasury of Words and Meanings*), pp. 40:5–41:1.

471 This is a tentative translation of a particularly obscure passage.

472 This is not intended to imply that there is a river existing objectively, independent of all perception. It means only that where humans might see a river of water, hell beings would see a river of fire, etc. The common denominator

of the two experiences is not an extramental object, but simply a commonly occurring "mere appearance" (*snang tsam*). See note 636.

473 See *Adornment of the Middle Way*, pp. 194–97.

474 "At that moment, all the other mental factors (concerning the snake) constitute the skandha of conditioning factors. Thus the appearing object of perception arises in the apprehended and apprehending aspects that appropriate the five skandhas." [YG III, 585:1]

475 *snang ba rnam gsum*. This refers to the material environment, mental states, and beings (*gnas don lus gsum*).

476 "The Great Perfection and the Perfection of Wisdom are distinct only in name. For while the practice and the way of establishing the ground in the Great Perfection differ from the way they are explained in the vehicle of the paramitas, the Great Perfection and the Perfection of Wisdom are the same in meaning." [YG III, 590:5]

477 That is, they have not yet reached the first ground of realization, the path of seeing.

478 "It could be objected that if ultimate reality—namely, self-cognizing wisdom—is primordially a state of openness and freedom (*ye grol*), it ought to follow that beings are naturally free without needing to follow the path. The truth is, however, that (most) beings do not have recourse to authentic teachers. They are not ripened by empowerment and they do not strive to gain freedom by means of the liberating practice. They are ignorant of the different methods of practice. They do not, by relying on the preliminary practices, train to remove their obscurations and complete the two accumulations: the skillful means though which suchness is realized. They fail to grasp the key points of 'self-subsiding' (*rang grol*) and of 'leaving as it is' (*cog bzhag*) by depending on the main practice. And they do not, through devotion, receive a teacher's blessing. How can beings be free without making an effort? As the *General Scripture of Summarized Wisdom* declares:

> What a marvelous, wondrous thing it is:
> This secret mystery of all the perfect Buddhas!
> Each and every being is Buddha,
> Yet, obscured by thoughts, they do not know!

"Others may object that, if the wisdom of analysis is absent from the main practice, there will be no vipashyana, and this is a defect. The answer to this is that, for beginners in the practice, the wisdom of analytical investigation consists in a diligent searching for the mind. As it is said in the *Ratnakuta*: 'What, O Kashyapa, is the wisdom that analyzes each and every phenomenon? It is a sustained and thorough searching for the mind.' The objects of thought, and the wisdom that analyzes them, gradually disappear, just as a fire goes out when its fuel has been consumed. And a powerful wisdom, true vipashyana, supervenes. The *General Scripture of Summarized Wisdom* also says:

From two sticks rubbed together and a breath of air
Comes fire by which the sticks themselves are burned.
Just so when powerful wisdom has been born,
It burns away discursive thought.

"In the present case, meditative equipoise in the inconceivable ultimate nature, the primordial wisdom of the Natural Great Perfection, is devoid of all thoughts concerning past, present, and future. But this is not in contradiction with the great and well-known collections of teachings that the Buddha himself set forth. As it is said in the *Ratnakuta*: 'What, O Kashyapa, is the remedy that leads beyond the world? It is a sustained and thorough searching for the mind. The mind *in itself*, O Kashyapa, is not something that can be analyzed; it is not something that can be shown. It is not something that appears and it is not something that can be perceived. It has no dwelling place. O Kashyapa, the Buddhas have not seen it, they do not see it, and they never shall. O Kashyapa, when the mind is searched for, it is not discovered. Not discovered, it is not observed. And what is not observed has no past, no future, and no present. What did not exist in the past, will not exist in the future, and is not occurring now. It perfectly transcends the three times.'" [YG III, 597:1–599:3]

479 "It is said in the *Treasury of Teachings*, Longchenpa's auto-commentary on the *Treasury of the Dharmadhatu*: 'Bodhichitta, the pure and accomplished mind, cannot be established in any way as this or that, and yet, like space itself, it is the ground of all things. It has an unceasing creative power, which is like the reflecting surface of a stainless mirror. Its display consists of phenomena, which arise in their various forms but are all unreal in the manner of the eight examples of illusion.' Accordingly, the ground whence this varied display manifests—as the whole phenomenal array of samsara, nirvana, and the path—is the unceasing creative power of awareness. The nature of this creative power and its manifold display is bodhichitta: the pure, accomplished mind.

"When one has come to a decisive understanding of this bodhichitta, of its creative power, and display, one does not intentionally put a stop to thoughts (good or bad, the defilements and so on), which arise in the manner of a display. Moreover, since there is neither sameness nor difference in ultimate reality beyond all conceptual construction (the primordial wisdom of the expanse of purity and equality), bodhichitta, its creative power, and its display are not considered to be really existent categories, even though they are distinguished. It is thus that phenomena are beyond the reach of the assertions of mistaken thought—for example, that phenomena are the mind, and that the mind exists. And knowing that thoughts have no inherent existence, one does not place the 'seal of conceptualization' on phenomena, denying, for example, their real existence—saying things like 'Everything is empty' or 'All ordinary cogitations (such as *This is an object of perception, This is the mind in movement, This is unforgetting mindfulness*) are empty.'

"It is said in the *Tantra of the All-Creating King*:

> In ultimate reality, which is unborn and completely pure,
> Unreal forms arise that seem like things that have an origin.
> However they be born, they are not other than this nature.
> Stay therefore in great bliss, free of effort.

[YG III, 601:3–602:3]

480 This principally refers to the aspect of luminosity. [DKR]

481 The aspect of emptiness is predominant. [DKR]

482 "Outer and inner phenomena have nowhere to go (no place of subsiding) other than unborn ultimate reality, the expanse of Samantabhadri. Consequently, practitioners of the space class are free from the limitations implied by antidotes. They are free of all deliberate action. For them, the wisdom mind, which is neither existent nor nonexistent, is neither fettered nor free. In whatever way that outer phenomena and the inner movements of the mind appear, arising and subsiding in one's perception, they are, from the standpoint of emptiness, primordially 'subsided' or free (they are a state of openness primordially, *ye grol*).

"Therefore the practitioners of the space class do not say that phenomena are 'awareness manifesting outwardly' (*rig pa phyi ru shar ba*). The mind and mental factors are simply awareness experiencing itself (*rang snang ba*). They are neither the agent of manifestation nor the thing manifested. Consequently, all the circumstances of sense objects and thoughts belonging to the side of appearance cannot compromise the ultimate state of emptiness. Manifold appearances are all empty in themselves; they vanish on their own! However they may appear, they are but awareness experiencing itself, an array of ornaments like the stars and planets spread out in the sky.

"So it is that the practitioners of the space class do not consider (as in the mind class) that phenomena are the creative power (*rtsal*) and display (*rol pa*) of outwardly manifesting awareness. They do not consider that the three (awareness, its creative power, and display) exist in a relationship of mutual dependence, and that they fall into different categories. They speak instead of the great, primordially free expanse of openness (*ye grol klong 'byams chen po*). As it is said in the *Tantra of the Six Expanses*:

> Beyond elaboration of many words and signs,
> Not born from mantra, from the outset perfect in itself,
> Utterly bereft of causes and conditions,
> It is free from all the stains of "view and meditation."
> Free from all extremes, yet in the middle not observed:

No aspects does it have,
No objects does it have.

[YG III, 602:6–603:6]

483 "Settling in the fundamental nature without considering awareness as either luminosity or the empty ultimate expanse, practitioners of the profound pith-instruction class are free from the limitations implied by the idea that there is something to abandon and that there are methods for doing so. For them, the radiance of great ineffable primordial purity, which transcends the ordinary mind, manifests of its own accord, through the 'doors of spontaneous presence,' as the self-experience of awareness (*rang snang*). Therefore, in displayed appearances (*rtsal snang*), there is nothing that can cause obscuration, and there is no room for delusion. Phenomenal appearances are equal to ultimate reality beyond conceptual constructs. It is because of this crucial point that the pith instruction class is superior to the previous two.

"The practitioners of the mind class implement the luminosity aspect of the mind and also the greater part of the aspect of profound emptiness. But since (in their case) the creative power of luminosity is not 'settled' in the ultimate nature, these practitioners are quite close to a deliberate fixation on the creative power and its display. The practitioners of the space class practice both profound emptiness and luminosity in equal measure. But because they fix deliberately on the ultimate nature, they are close to deviating into the side of emptiness. Since the practitioners of these two classes do not go to the crucial point by being convinced of the 'oneness,' the equal taste, of the appearing object and the cognition of it [that is, of the fact that they are neither existent nor nonexistent, that they are a groundless, all-pervading space beyond all reference (*spyi 'byams*)], this occasions an obscuration, a deviation from the fundamental nature of things (*gshis shor gyi gol sgrib che ba*). The *Tantra of the Great Array of Ati* says:

If it is not established thus,
There's no difference from the clinging
Of the analytic mind.
Thus this essence, truly secret,
Is superior to them all.

"And it is said in the *Tantra of the Vast Expanse of Space:*

Because these ordinary appearances are indeed delusions,
Deluded visions grow apace for those who hold to them.
And so for those who follow as their path delusive thoughts
A time of freedom from delusive cause and fruit will never come.
Therefore, it is crucial to adopt as path unerring luminous appearance
And primordial wisdom where discursive mind has ceased
And when one stays in unmoved equipoise,
The limpid pure awareness is revealed through focusing on luminosity.

Within this single fundamental nature,
Three experiences of its appearing mode occur.
From the radiance of nature
Comes a state of no-thought, freedom from elaboration;
From the radiance of character,
Comes the limpid brilliance of a natural luminosity;
From the radiance of cognitive potency
Comes bliss-awareness in an endless stream.
The experience of the three kayas is as vast as space.

"Although thögal is said to be the extraordinary and supreme teaching of the pith instruction class, it is also true, nevertheless, that the view and meditation of the primordial purity (of trekchö) is also superior to the other classes. Here, all the adventitious occurrences of the mind and phenomena—considered respectively in the mind and space classes as a display (*rol pa*) or as an ornament (*rgyan*)—appear but are without real existence. They are just empty reflections. They are not even regarded as a mere display or as an ornament, as they are when the luminosity and emptiness aspects are practiced separately. Understanding that not even the names of luminosity and emptiness exist in the ineffable, ultimate nature beyond the intellect, one is completely free of any kind of deliberate fixation. As it is said in the *Vast Expanse of Space:*

"Whatever may appear, whatever may arise:
All is but the play of dharmakaya."
The trap of such good thoughts as these—
Even this has no reality!
The state that's free from willful spurning and adoption
Does not come by spurning all such thoughts.
It comes instead by leaving them to melt away in their own place.

"It has been said that the mind class mainly teaches the ways in which thoughts subside, while the space class mainly teaches the method of settling in the expanse of emptiness. In the pith instruction class, however, there is not even the slightest effort made to induce the subsiding of thoughts or to settle in the expanse of emptiness. This class therefore is supreme." [YG III, 604:1–606:4]

484 "What is to be freed" (*dgrol bar bya ba'i gzhi*) can be understood in two senses: either as the nature of the mind, which is to be freed from what obscures it, or as the adventitious stains themselves, which are to be removed from the mind that they obscure. As Yönten Gyamtso says, "'That which is to be freed' (*dgrol bar bya ba'i gzhi*) may also be understood in the sense of 'that which is made to subside,' referring in other words to obscuring stains [or thoughts]. On the other hand, since, on account of their all-pervading nature, there are no thoughts that do not subside in the very moment of their arising, these so-called thoughts have no existence." [YG III, 608:1–3]

485 "If one settles, free of all contrivance, in the state of natural luminosity within the expanse of primordially pure awareness, thoughts subside all by themselves, and a natural mental concentration is spontaneously accomplished. . . .

"The self-subsiding of thoughts occurs either with or without effort according to the different mental capacities of practitioners. In the first case (self-subsiding with effort), practitioners remain without stirring from the fundamental nature and, thanks to their profound insight (vipashyana), recognize the nature of whatever thoughts and defilements arise. They settle in this state of recognition without moving from it; they do not follow after thoughts and they are free from the fetters of antidotes. And since these defilements and thoughts have no existence in the ground of awareness, their illusory movement, devoid of inherent existence, fades away, just as when troubled water clarifies when it is left to stand.

"In the second case (self-subsiding without effort), since the 'place of arising' and 'that which arises' have the same taste, it follows that the dharmatā and the thoughts—in other words, the ultimate nature and the display of its creative power—are not two separate things. All subsides even as it arises. Whatever emerges is powerless to stand firm." [YG III, 608:4–609:4]

486 "The freedom of awareness is not contrived or brought about by extraneous factors. Awareness is primordially free, primordially 'subsided.' It is a state of openness and freedom. As it is said in the *Pearl Necklace Tantra:*

> By effort it is not made free;
> It abides in freedom from the very start.

"And in the *Tantra of Meaningful Effort:*

> The nature of the mind is from the outset free.
> What outer factors for its freedom can there be?

"Ordinary beings, who are attached to 'I' and 'mine,' cling to adventitious, delusory appearances, which have never truly existed. Thus they are deceived. Practitioners, on the other hand, should consider that, in whichever way these appearances unfold, they do so within the state of awareness. And this awareness is primordially empty, rootless, and beyond all dependence. It is like space wherein the karmic relation of cause and effect can leave no trace.

"Those who practice should, without partiality, allow such apparent but nonexistent empty forms to subside as soon as they arise. They should come to the clear conviction that there is nothing else for them to do. For it is as when a mirage of water appears. Since from the very first, there is no water present, the 'subsiding' (the disappearance) of the water is already achieved. One should understand this, and be convinced of the truth of it. It is unnecessary to cause such water to subside or disappear. As it is said in the *Precious Treasury of the Dharmadhatu:*

In awareness, changeless, free from all construction,
Arising is primordial arising, remaining is primordial remaining,
Subsiding is primordial subsiding. They have the character of space.

[YG III, 610:1–611:1]

487 "'Self-subsiding' implies that the use of antidotes is unnecessary. In the teachings belonging to the mind class, it is said that 'Subsiding occurs all by itself; it is not brought about by extraneous factors.' All sights and sounds manifest spontaneously through the creative power of awareness. In the very moment that they appear, they are already possessed of a nature that transcends both existence and nonexistence, permanence and annihilation. They are not made to subside by extraneous factors, neither do they do it to themselves. They subside quite naturally, like the flowing of a gentle stream that 'subsides' (never remains the same) by its very nature.

"Ordinary childish beings are fettered by their clinging to the supposed inherent existence of their personal selves and phenomena generally. And, like water frozen into ice, even the contrived view (the belief in the emptiness of the five aggregates and so on), meditation, and conduct are defective notions that mar and veil the process of self-subsiding. Indeed, the conventional path of view, meditation, and conduct—which has the compounded nature of the relative truth—has been set forth for those who do not at once realize this key point of self-subsiding. In the end, however, even this path necessarily subsides naturally into the expanse of dharmakaya. Self-subsiding therefore is by nature simply the absence of intrinsic being. All the other aspects of the path, like the notions of skillful means and wisdom, stray in the direction of ontological exaggeration—and it is not thanks to them that self-subsiding occurs. If those fortunate beings who have entered upon this path recognize that the genuine state of awareness dwells naked and primordially pure in the expanse of the dharmakaya, and if they can remain in this nature of awareness, then all thoughts, which arise for them through the creative power of awareness, vanish naturally and are cleared away without leaving any trace, just like knots tied on a snake, which come loose all by themselves. It is said in the *Precious Treasury of the Dharmadhatu*:

In awareness, even and unmoving,
When thoughts arise, they "self-arise"
    and keep their true condition;
When they abide, they "self-abide"
    and keep their true condition;
When they subside, they "self-subside"
    and keep their true condition.

[YG III, 611:2–612:4]

488 "Awareness is constant and uninterrupted like a river. When, through the unceasing creative power of awareness, the eye sees any kind of object,

whether of attachment, aversion, or anything else, thoughts of desire or revulsion begin to proliferate. If in that very instant and with lightning speed (*thog
babs chen po*), one focuses on them directly, 'nakedly,' and stares at them, and if
one settles nakedly in the state of awareness, all mental constructs in relation to
visible form [as an object of attachment and so on], are instantly cut. The mind
does not cling to the object, and the appearing object does not stain the mind.
Although the object of perception does not depart, the mental state [of being
attached, etc.] completely vanishes and subsides. This is the so-called nonreferential feeling (or perception) arising through the conjunction of eye, object, and
consciousness. The same is true when one hears sounds with the ears, smells
odors with the nose, tastes savors with the tongue, and feels objects of touch
with the body, or when one focuses on the objects of the five senses or on
object-universals and so on with the mental faculty.

"If one acquires the habit of causing these distinct and separate phenomenal perceptions to subside directly—instantaneously, with lightning speed—
then at length, all perceptions will be cleansed away in a 'naked subsiding.'
This will put an end to the entire foundation for the karmic law of cause and
effect—a mechanism that is contrived in terms of subject and object, mutually dependent and linked together as apprehender and apprehended, which
accumulates the habitual tendencies of samsara. And the process of simultaneous arising and subsiding will naturally and uninterruptedly unfold. As it is
said in the *Tantra of the Six Expanses:*

> In the nature of the mind, perceptions are
> With lightning speed, and in their very place, directly cleansed.

[YG III, 612:4–613:5]

489 "Awareness is Samantabhadra: all-penetrating, empty, luminosity (*stong gsal
zang thal*), the vast expanse of Vajrasattva. If one recognizes this state and
remains in it without fluctuation or movement—not thinking either of outer
objects or of the inner mind, nor even setting oneself (intentionally) in the
unborn nature—awareness is stripped to its nakedness, and buddhahood is
found within oneself. As the *Tantra of the Lion's Perfect Power* says: 'Since it is
the absence of extremes, we call it the subsiding of extremes.' The *Precious
Treasury of the Dharmadhatu* also says:

> Samantabhadra's vast expanse is from the outset changeless.
> Since it does not change, it is the vast abyss of Vajrasattva.
> "Buddhahood" is no more than the name ascribed
> To simple recognition of this nature.

[YG III, 614:3–5]

490 "Awareness, in which the two truths are not separated, and from which all
conceptual construction is absent, does not exist either in the singular or the
plural [i.e., it is not a really existing thing]. In the language of conventional

truth, however, it is referred to as the one and only sphere of the dharmakaya (*chos sku thig le nyag gcig*). Without depending on the skillful means and wisdom of the lower paths, all phenomena subside in the state of naked awareness, the one all-penetrating primordial wisdom. If this state is not lost, all movements of the body, all expressions of speech, and all thoughts and states of mind are [experienced simply as] clear appearances of unreal things. Since they have no reality in the nature of awareness, they are devoid of all characteristics in themselves. They manifest naturally as the enlightened body, speech, and mind of the Victorious Ones. As it is said in the *Unwritten Tantra*:

> The one and only sphere is free of all conceptual constructs;
> It transcends the different states of mind and all expression.

"And in the *Precious Treasury of the Dharmadhatu*, it is said:

> Howsoever one may sit,
> One sits in the awareness state;
> Howsoever one may dwell,
> One dwells in the awareness state;
> Howsoever one may go,
> One goes in the awareness state.
> By nature there's no going and no coming
> In enlightenment's expanse.
> No going and no coming
> Is the body of the Conquerors.
>
> Howsoever one may speak,
> One speaks in the awareness state;
> Howsoever one expresses,
> One expresses in the awareness state;
> By nature there's no speaking, no expressing
> In the enlightened mind.
> No speaking, no expressing
> Is the speech of all the Conquerors
> Past, present, and to come.
>
> Howsoever one may think,
> One thinks in the awareness state;
> Howsoever one may ponder,
> One ponders in the awareness state;
> Primordially there's no pondering, no thinking
> In the enlightened mind.
> No pondering, no thinking
> Is the mind of all the Conquerors
> Past, present, and to come.

"In other words, if there is no movement from the awareness state, awareness transcends all going, coming, speaking, expressing, and the objects of all thoughts. Therefore if there is no stirring from the expanse of the one, sole awareness, this constitutes the realization of the three kayas. The realization of the trikaya is nowhere else. As the *Unwritten Tantra* says of awareness:

> Not existing yet arising in whatever form, it is nirmanakaya.
> Delighting in itself, it is sambhogakaya.
> Without substantial ground, it is the dharmakaya.
> Such is the result: expanse of the trikaya spontaneously present.

"If therefore one recognizes that the previous four ways of subsiding (according to the different capacities of beings) share the single characteristic of subsiding in the single ultimate nature of self-cognizing awareness, one will come to the conviction that all phenomena of both samsara and nirvana subside within primordial, all-pervading emptiness." [YG III, 614:6–616:4]

491 "The practitioners of Atiyoga, the peak of all vehicles, know how to preserve quite straightforwardly the state of awareness. For them, thoughts subside like figures drawn on water, and there is no need for various antidotes. Such practitioners do not stir from the wisdom of the dharmakaya. By contrast, from the path of the Shravakas (who consider nirvana and samsara in terms of good and bad and who strive, with regard to the four truths, in methods of adopting and forsaking) until the path of Anuyoga (where one practices the perfection stage of empty bliss), the eight vehicles take as their path adventitious thoughts, which have never existed in the state of the dharmakaya. These thoughts are like bubbles on water; they are transient and changing. And it is believed that when the mind is freed from the stains of such thoughts, the primordial wisdom of the dharmakaya is actualized." [YG III, 619:3–6]

492 As during meditation, when all manifest mental movements are brought to a halt and the mind is one-pointedly concentrated. [DKR]

493 Thought-free awareness perceives in an "objectless manner." [DKR]

494 To dwell one-pointedly in the absence of impairing objects corresponds to shamatha.

495 That is, in the present context.

496 "Here there is a possible objection. Is it not the case that, in the practice of the Great Perfection, one uses the ceaseless arisings of the ordinary mind as the path? Or, to put it differently—is it not the simultaneous arising and subsiding of thought, the aspect of cognitive potency (*thugs rje*), that is used as the path? In answer to this it must be said that [far from referring to ordinary thought] the 'aspect of cognitive potency' refers to the true and unadulterated awareness of the ground of arising, which has not yet stirred from its original state. It is *this* that is used as the path. Thoughts that, through the creative power of cognitive potency, have arisen *as the ordinary mind*, are never used as the path. When one settles in awareness, the ordinary mind dissipates naturally and is left behind." [YG III, 625:3–5]

497 "The ordinary mind, which subsides, and awareness, into which it subsides, may be distinguished according to their function and name. The mind, which is cohesive like water, is the basis of thoughts. Supportive, like the earth, it accommodates the various 'gatherings' [i.e., consciousnesses]. Proliferating, like fire, it experiences the objects of the senses. Weightless, like the wind, it bears and carries beings [from life to life]. It is thus that the so-called mind is said to have the character of ignorance.

"By contrast, the so-called nature of the mind is said to have the character of awareness because it involves the realization of the unborn, fundamental nature, because it is a mindfulness that neither ceases nor diminishes, because it exemplifies actual immutability, and because it cannot be identified as a circumscribed object. And since, on this path, awareness is realized directly and nakedly (i.e., free from concepts), no distinctions can be made in terms of sharp and dull faculties. Since the continuity of awareness is preserved unbroken, the wisdom of the natural state of the mind is uninterrupted. Since the radiance of awareness is manifest to sense perception, there is no dependence on conceptual analysis. And since the awareness that transcends intellect and thought is realized directly (*zang thal du*), it does not depend on the wisdom that results from hearing and reflection. Simply by preserving awareness alone, one comes to the understanding that the view, meditation, conduct, and result are contrived phenomena.

"Now there are two kinds of people who are able to realize awareness as it truly is in its great spontaneous presence. The first kind of person is in harmony with the nature of things, he or she is free of deliberate action and effort, with a mind that is slow moving and placid, a 'simple soul,' carefree and relaxed. The second kind of person is one who has an extremely keen intelligence and who first brings to completion the wisdom of hearing and reflection. He or she is then able to acquire a deep-seated certainty in the path that is beyond all fabrication." [YG III, 630:1–631:3]

498 "The ordinary mind, having the nature of ignorance, is not concomitant with awareness. For it cannot be concomitant with buddhahood in which the latent tendencies of ignorance have been exhausted. Moreover, when one rests in awareness at the time of the path, the ordinary mind stops." [YG III, 632:1–2]

499 "Just as there is a distinction between the ordinary mind and awareness, there is an analogous distinction between the universal ground and the dharmakaya. When the displayed appearances of spontaneous presence fail to sink back into awareness but fall beneath the power of ignorance, the ground of these manifold appearances (all of which have the nature of the mind and mental factors) is called the universal ground or alaya. This ground is the support within which all the propensities of the three worlds are first deposited; it is the path on which they are then held; and it is the vessel in which these propensities finally ripen into their effects.

"By contrast, the dharmakaya is the support of primordial wisdom, which does not fall beneath the power of ignorance. It has the nature of the dharmadhatu and is devoid of the duality of apprehending subject and apprehended object, and is unstained by karma and habitual tendencies. As is it said in the *Six Expanses:* 'O Great Being! The abode of the mind is the universal ground. Why so? Because, containing all objects of thought, the universal ground is known as mind. The abode of primordial wisdom is the dharmakaya. Why so? Because in the dharmakaya, devoid of thought, there is no mind that apprehends things as different from itself.'

"The dharmakaya and the universal ground may be distinguished by means of examples. The *All-Penetrating Wisdom Tantra* says:

The ground of all phenomena is uncompounded.

> It is an expanse, self-arisen, vast, ineffable,
> Beyond denominations of samsara and nirvana.
> To recognize that very ground is to be enlightened.
> Beings fail to do so and they wander in samsara.

"Within the uncompounded expanse of awareness, the dharmakaya and the universal ground are not separate, and therefore they are 'one.' Now the dharmakaya is primordially pure awareness free from all conceptual construction, and devoid of intrinsic being. But although within it there is room (unobstructed and unceasing) for all manner of arising, the dharmakaya is not adulterated by adventitious stains. It is beyond all dimension and measure like a limpid ocean.

"The consciousness of the universal ground, on the other hand, has the nature of ignorance. It manifests owing to the failure to recognize spontaneously displayed appearance for what it is, and it is that which veils the dharmakaya. This universal ground is the place or support from which manifest all the compounded phenomena that are included within the categories of mind and mental factors. It pervades the mind and mental factors and is their indwelling nature. Like a ship full of people, it is a vessel that contains the seven active consciousnesses, which manifest based on the body and one's habitual tendencies. Samsaric propensities ripen into the varied display of the six classes of beings. By contrast, and thanks to the ingrained habits that they have cultivated in the course of their path, the Shravakas and Pratyekabuddhas obtain the peace of a one-sided nirvana, which however does not take them beyond the universal ground. So it is that the consciousness of the universal ground can move either toward samsara or toward nirvana. Alternatively, the word 'nirvana' in the root text may be taken as a reference to the removal of adventitious ignorance together with the universal ground, as a result of which, like a ship reaching dry land, the dharmakaya is cleansed of that which veils it so that its twofold purity becomes manifest.

"The universal ground may be divided into four categories: (1) the original ultimate universal ground (*ye don gyi kun gzhi*); (2) the ultimate universal ground of joining (*sbyor ba don gyi kun gzhi*); (3) the universal ground of the propensities leading to the assumption of a bodily form (*bag chags lus kyi kun gzhi*); and (4) the universal ground of various propensities (*bag chags sna tshogs pa'i kun gzhi*). These are explained respectively as follows: (1) the ultimate expanse is referred to as the 'original ultimate universal ground,' in the sense that it provides the occasion for the unfolding of samsara, owing to the initial movement of cognition occuring within it, which, by comparison with awareness, is a state concomitant with ignorance; (2) cognition (by which things are examined) either fails to recognize its own nature and, turning outward, joins one to samsara, or, it recognizes its nature and joins one to nirvana; (3) this universal ground [of bodily propensities] is so called because, in harboring the tendencies to manifest in bodily form, it provides the support for the appearance of gross bodies formed of the four elements, of mental bodies, and so on; and (4) the universal ground of various propensities is a term used in reference to the various mental propensities contained within the ground. For this reason it is said that:

> The universal ground is ground of all,
> Of nirvana too it is the ground.

"As it has been said, the universal ground is not regarded as the dharmakaya. Nevertheless, there are some contexts where the dharmakaya *is* referred to as the universal ground, but in this case, the reference is to the common ground of all, that is, of both samsara and nirvana. This 'common ground of all,' however, is not to be identified with the universal ground that is the receptacle of the various propensities.

"The nature of the dharmakaya is empty, endowed with the essence of primordial wisdom. Its character is luminous, endowed with the essence of light. Its cognitive potency (*thugs rje*) is unceasing and is endowed with the essence of awareness. In itself, it is never stained by mental obscuration. The dharmakaya is also referred to as the pure and accomplished mind or bodhichitta, as self-arisen primordial wisdom, and as the ultimate expanse, the great spontaneous presence, and so on. These names are merely conceptual labels. For the dharmakaya in its fundamental nature is said to be inexpressible, to transcend the intellect, and to be wholly beyond all mental construction. This is the 'Great Perfection.' It is not the same thing as 'luminosity and knowing' (*gsal rig*), 'emptiness' and so on, as posited in various other tenet systems. If one holds to the conclusion that the Great Perfection is 'luminosity and emptiness' and so forth, one has strayed into error." [YG III, 636:5–640:4]

500 "It may be said generally that, in the very nature of the mind (in other words, luminous primordial wisdom, the awareness that is free from all mental construction), delusion and freedom are both absent. For if there is no delusion, there can be no freedom contingent on delusion. And, as it has been

explained, there is no delusion because the eight consciousnesses together with their objects merely appear; they do not truly exist.

"It might be argued that, if the eight consciousnesses do not exist, the mind has no existence at all, so that when enlightenment is gained, one will be reduced to an inert object. The answer is that although [at the time of enlightenment] there is no [ordinary] mind, there is the fundamental nature of the ground, the nature of the mind. There is luminous primordial wisdom. As it is said in the noble *Prajnaparamita in Eight Thousand Lines:* 'The mind is not mind, the nature of the mind is luminosity.' And the *Sublime Continuum* says: 'Since the nature of the mind is luminous, they see that the defilements have no essence.'

"How then does this semblance of delusion and freedom occur? The appearances of the creative power of spontaneous presence are like clouds that appear and disappear within the sky-like, primordially pure awareness, free of mental construction, from which they never stir. If one fails to recognize the nature of these appearances and if one clings to them, one does not see what is really there, namely, ultimate reality. And instead there appears uninterruptedly what is not there: the illusory phenomena of samsara. As it is said:

> Those who do not see what's there
> But see what is not there
> Are in the deepest darkness.

"If one recognizes the appearances of the ground for what they are and does not cling to them, all these illusory appearances are reabsorbed into the ultimate expanse, and the fundamental nature is realized as it truly is. This is freedom or nirvana." [YG III, 641:4–642:6]

501 That is, when the appearances of the ground, the aspect of outwardly radiating luminosity, return to the ultimate expanse, like clouds vanishing in the sky. See YG III, 643:6.

502 "Here, the qualities of the ultimate expanse are perfected and the display of the three kayas is unceasing and unobstructed. But since it is free of ignorance, [the place of freedom] cannot be the ground of delusion." [YG III, 644:2–3]

503 "It has been said (by Patrul Rinpoche) that if one has no understanding of what is actually meant by the 'ground' but says things like 'When the fruit is gained, one is liberated in the ground,' this is no more than a pale reflection of the Great Perfection." [YG III, 644:2–3]

504 "This is the state of the ever youthful vase body, the extremely subtle primordial wisdom of inner luminosity." [YG III, 645:2]

505 Here a distinction is made between the nirmanakaya buddhafields of luminous character, which are counted as the sambhogakaya, and the nirmanakaya buddhafields of indwelling luminous character. See chapter 13, pp. 294–300 and pp. 300–304.

506 For an explanation of this term, see Patrul Rinpoche, *The Words of My Perfect Teacher* (Boston: Shambhala Publications, 1998), p. 27.

507 *rig pa rang snang gi blo can.* These are practitioners of very sharp faculties who gain realization at a single stroke (*cig char pa*). They realize immediately the view to which they were introduced, and meditate on the basis of this view.

508 *khregs chod.* Cutting through the seeming solidity of the mind's conceptual display.

509 In other words, the view of the Great Perfection is not an idea about, or a conceptual estimate of, the nature of phenomena, as is the case with other views. It consists in a direct experience and realization.

510 See YG III, 655:3.

511 "For even though the display of appearances occurs unceasingly just as before, ordinary, solidly appearing thoughts are no more. They are like the trail of ashes left when a rope of grass has been completely burned. If, when one is meditating in this way, all-penetrating awareness is not recognized, and one is unable to bring about the dissolution of the thoughts that arise through awareness's creative power, the proliferation of thoughts, and even the state of resting without movement, are but fetters that bind one in samsara.

"As it is said in the auto-commentary: 'Some people belonging to our own school are mistaken in their view and meditation. With regard to the latter, they say that any thoughts that occur are the spontaneously arisen primordial wisdom. But the truth is that, through a failure to recognize the nature of awareness within these thoughts, the creative power and display of awareness themselves drift into the state of being "true origins" (*kun 'byung*). Thoughts arise thanks to habitual tendencies, they are "other-arisen," which is why they follow after the objects of the senses. Because they appear as objects and are liable to dissolution and destruction, they are apprehended as *form*. In the guise of *feeling*, thoughts cling to objects and experience them. As *perception*, thoughts move out and examine the features of objects, and in the manner of *conditioning factors*, they constantly give rise to contaminated mental events. Finally, thoughts are taken as objects, and this is the aspect of [mental] *consciousness*. It is thus that self-arisen primordial wisdom is veiled, and the mind and mental factors continue in their courses. And although these people think that they are undistracted in the flow of mindfulness, what is actually happening is that they are using their minds to examine their minds, and are thus not in the slightest degree superior to ordinary beings in samsara.'

"Consequently, the shamatha and vipashyana of the unmistaken view of the sutras and tantras refer to meditative equipoise in thought-free primordial wisdom, in which all thoughts—the causes of the aggregates, elements, and sense-fields—completely subside. It is said in the *Mulamadhyamaka-karika* (18:7):

All that can be said is halted,
For all that can be thought is halted:

Not arisen and not ceased,
The nature of phenomena is like nirvana.

"And the *Avatamsaka* says:

All those who wish to enter the domain of the Victorious Ones
Must cleanse their thoughts away till they become like space.
They should abandon thoughts, reflections, grasping at ideas,
And they should enter with a space-like mind.

"If one settles in this primordial wisdom, the two form bodies will manifest naturally, without depending on compounded causes. The *Tantra of
Awareness Self-Arisen* says:

Since the sun of one's awareness rises from the state of emptiness,
It never sets. From this most precious mandala
The five unchanging Bodies straight away appear.
Nondually they are savoured in the throught-free state.

"If one meditates in this way and settles, without any clinging, in the
space-like state of spontaneously arisen awareness, all adventitious thoughts
naturally subside, like clouds that melt away in the sky. This is called meditation that is the self-subsiding of thoughts through the absence of all clinging."
[YG III, 657:1–659:2]

512 And eventually was seen as one.

513 "The *Avatamsaka* says:

The mind is like an artist.
Contrived by mental aggregates,
All the many regions of the world
Are like paintings that the mind has made.

"This is what phenomena are like. Therefore in the case of practitioners
who have realized the unborn nature, no matter how the unceasing creative
power moves within the space-like nature [of awareness], it is just as if one
were drawing something on water: it immediately vanishes back into the
water. Whatever arises sinks back into the unborn nature in the very moment
of its arising. These practitioners never take the activities of body, speech,
and mind as really existing things, no matter how they appear. They over-
power them with awareness. This is called the conduct that overpowers appearances." [YG III, 660:1–4]

514 "For those who gain a stable proficiency in primordially pure, space-like
awareness, external appearances, the material objects of perception—which
are understood to be like the reflection of the moon on water—subside. The
bodies of such practitioners are able to pass through mountains, rocks, and
walls. And their minds dwell in supreme truth. They obtain the five kinds of
vision, the preternatural knowledges, and so on; and they are freed from

rebirth. And even the infinitesimal particles of the four elements of which their bodies are composed are purified by the fires of wisdom.

"Like a vanishing mist, such beings depart into the expanse of space, accompanied by miraculous signs. Their awareness is gathered in the expanse of the dharmakaya, and they work for the sake of beings through an uninterrupted stream of emanations until the emptying of samsara. There are also some who dissolve their bodies into infinitesimal particles and, if it is of benefit to beings, they bless them as pearl-like relics (*ring bsrel*) and leave them behind. And there are some who have refined their wind-mind into its natural condition by achieving the full extent of realization. But if, on account of their undistracted work for the sake of others, their bodies do not dissolve completely into atoms, they become very small and light. This happens because these practitioners have mastered all-penetrating awareness and have dissolved into primordial purity. The *Pearl Necklace* says:

> Pure from the beginning, free from stain;
> Manifesting from the outset, free of lineage.

"As they remain without alteration or effort in primordially pure awareness, there manifests the indwelling primordial wisdom, the fundamental state of the sublime, actual nature (*yongs grub chen po'i gnas lugs*). This is called the result that is the actual nature beyond all exertion (*'bras bu rtsol med yongs grub*)." [YG III, 662:3–663:4]

515   *thod rgal*, literally "leap over," in the sense that, thanks to this practice, the objective is reached directly and immediately, leaping over the intermediary stages.

516   [DKR/OC] Without the certainty of the view of trekchö with its emphasis on the emptiness aspect, which here means the recognition of the nature of awareness (a recognition that severs the root of karma and defilement), the experiences of thögal, where the aspect of luminosity is predominant, will not bring progress on the path. It is possible to attain enlightenment through the practice of trekchö alone, but if trekchö is associated with thögal, the goal will be achieved more swiftly. Moreover, it is only through the practice of thögal that the great rainbow body of transformation can be attained.

517   That is, the three lower sections (outer, inner, and secret) of the pith instruction class.

518   This and the preceding sentence are taken from YG III, 692:4–5.

519   That is, the nine methods or rather stages of accomplishing shamatha. See Maitreya's *Ornament of the Sutras*, 14:11–14, and the Dalai Lama, *Opening the Eye of New Awareness* (London: Wisdom Publications, 1985), p. 66.

520   "In such a situation, there is no need for the assistance of positive thoughts like faith, because the result that virtue is normally considered to accomplish dwells (already) in the state of the dharmakaya. And even if negative thoughts

(defilements) arise, they are not harmful, since they are settled in the state of unobstructed openness (*zang thal*) of the dharmakaya, and will not accumulate karma that projects one into samsara." [YG 701:4–6]

521 See *Treasury of Precious Qualities*, bk. 1, app. 5, p. 387.

522 "If the wisdom that knows the nature of the ultimate expanse is lacking, there is a danger that the all-penetrating, empty, inner space will be mistaken for a mere nothingness." [YG III, 714:5–6]

523 "In reality, primordial wisdom is supported by four lamps. When the body begins to take shape in the womb, it is on the basis of the humidity there, which has the nature of the water element, that two pairs of eyes are formed within the knot of (three) channels located at the navel. These are the eyes of the elements (*'byung ba'i spyan*) and the eyes of the lamp (*sgron ma'i spyan*).

"From the eyes of the elements, the body itself develops. The eyes of the lamp, on the other hand, correspond to the two channels [of the three already mentioned] that are found in the pupils of the physical eyes—fine at their root and broad at the other extremity, like the horns of the *men* antelope. These channels are the foundation for the ultimate state beyond suffering— expressed in the appearances of primordial wisdom in the form of lights, circles of light, deities, and so forth. These channels are referred to as the *lamp of the far-catching water lasso* (*rgyang zhag chu'i sgron ma*). Furthermore, there is a middle channel (the third of the three mentioned). This penetrates the brahma aperture, and it is here, in this channel, that there manifest the vajra chains of thought-free awareness, and the many disks of light arranged in fivefold patterns.

"These (three) channels contain the various aspects of all the four lamps. The tips of the two channels correspond to the *water lamp*; the disks of light correspond to the *lamp of the empty disk of light* (*thig le stong pa'i sgron ma*); the five-colored lights correspond to the *lamp of the utterly pure ultimate expanse* (*dag pa dbyings kyi sgron ma*); and the thought-free mind corresponds to the *lamp of self-arisen wisdom* (*shes rab rang byung gi sgron ma*).

"The eyes of the elements perceive all ordinary appearances, and they are the support for the water lamp, through which luminous appearances arise. Consequently, the water lamp perceives, not the appearances of delusion, but the appearances of primordial wisdom.

"The lamp of the empty disk of light is a circular disk of light endowed with a rim of five colors. It acts as the support for the arising of all the aspects of luminosity.

"The lamp of the utterly pure ultimate expanse is the outwardly projected radiance of the inner ultimate expanse of the ground of arising. For indeed there is both an outer expanse and an inner expanse. The outer expanse is the blue-colored radiance that first appears within immaculate space. This outer expanse is no more than the condition of open space. It is not the actual ultimate expanse. The inner expanse arises, as if unfolding from within the outer expanse just mentioned, and manifests as a five-colored radiance. The expressions 'outer expanse' and 'inner expanse' indicate only that the latter arises from within the former. It does not mean that one space is inside, and one space is outside. In other words, despite this terminological distinction, they are not different. It is just that the tent of rainbow light has moved ('pho ba) from the state of invisibility and is now visible.

"The nature of the lamp of self-arisen wisdom is the inner awareness, limpid and clear, which arises, objectless and self-illuminating, when, by means of the special manner of gazing on the part of the lamp of the far-catching water lasso, one focuses on the lamp of the empty disk of light. It is said that it is of the greatest importance not to stray from this. The creative power (rtsal) of the lamp of self-arisen wisdom is the wisdom, sharp and rapid, that arises, manifesting outwardly—in words and teachings welling up from within. The radiance (gdangs) of the lamp of self-arisen wisdom appears as the vajra chains, which are like floating threads of gold." [YG III, 665:6–667:5]

See also Sogpo Tendar, legs bshad gser gyi thur ma (The Golden Scalpel Commentary), p. 551.

524 The creative power of awareness is the wisdom resulting from meditation; the radiance of awareness consists of the vajra chains. [DKR]

525 See YG III, 716:2.

526 'das rjes. This citation is from Garab Dorje's testament called The Three Words That Penetrate the Essence (tshig gsum gnad brdeg).

[DKR/OC] These instructions belong to the kind of teachings that arise in the minds of greatly realized beings just as they are leaving this world, and which they transmit to their disciples. The Heart-Essence of Vimalamitra (bi ma'i snying thig) contains similar instructions, previously bestowed by Garab Dorje, Manjushrimitra, Shri Simha, and Jnanasutra.

527 "For practitioners of the highest capacity and through the implementation of this secret and profound path, the impurity of the aggregates melts away, and freedom is gained through the methods of either trekchö or thögal. In the case of trekchö, the body of the practitioner dissolves into infinitesimal particles—in a 'space-like death' or a death that is 'in the manner of the dakinis.' In the case of those who gain freedom through the practice of thögal, the body vanishes in a mass of light. This is death in the 'manner of a mass of fire' or 'in the manner of the Vidyādharas.' Those who attain complete realization but for whom, on account of their work for the sake of the doctrine and beings, the karmic wind is not exhausted, leave behind their bodily remains, or pearl-like relics, for the benefit of beings.

"When those who have no more clinging to the true existence of sense objects fall ill, they do not count on medicines and divinations. And at death, they do not place their hopes in the weekly ceremonies for the dead. They are happy to be in the wilderness like the creatures of the wild. Like lions, they have no fear of death; and though they perish like beggars in the street, they do not despair. Like little babies, they do not care whether they live or die." [YG III, 720:5–721:3]. See also Sogpo Tendar, *legs bshad gser gyi thur ma*, p. 539–40.

528 See chapter 11, commentary to stanza 15, p. 240.

529 "In the state of buddhahood, there is no inanimate materiality. Therefore the term "kaya" ("body") means that all the appearances of the form bodies of outwardly radiating luminosity have the nature exclusively of primordial wisdom." [YG III, 731:4–5]

530 Here, the original ultimate universal ground refers to the ultimate expanse itself, the common ground of samsara and nirvana. In contrast with the ground described in note 499, it is not a state concomitant with ignorance.

531 "For from its own side, it does not exist as distinct kayas and wisdoms." [YG III, 725:6]

532 *yon tan gyi rnam pa kun gyi mchog*, i.e., self-arisen primordial wisdom of luminosity (*rang byung 'od gsal ba'i ye shes*). [YG III, 727:4]

533 "Since the reference here is to the kaya of inner luminosity of the ultimate expanse, these qualities are probably not to be understood in the manner of the qualities realized by the kind of wisdom that engages in objects, in other words, by the nirmanakaya wisdom that sees the nature of phenomena and the wisdom that sees phenomena in their multiplicity [as understood in the vehicle of causality]. In general, when the three kayas are explained, the three kayas of inner luminosity are considered to be part of the dharmakaya. And if the latter is considered in terms of the primordial wisdoms with which these three kayas are endowed, this same dharmakaya is said to possess three wisdoms: the wisdom of primordially pure nature (*ngo bo ka dag gi ye shes*), the wisdom of spontaneously present luminous character (*rang bzhin lhun grub kyi ye shes*), and the wisdom of all-pervading cognitive potency (*thugs rje kun khyab kyi ye shes*). These three wisdoms are not actually separate in terms of their characteristics. They are facets of the luminosity of awareness, and as such provide the ground for the natural occurrence of all knowing. "The sambhogakaya [of inner luminosity] is endowed with five wisdoms, such as the wisdom of the dharmadhatu, mirrorlike wisdom, etc. These five primordial wisdoms do not imply a relationship of subject and object. They know the sambhogakaya's self-experience in the manner of a direct self-illumination (*thad ka'i snang ba rang gsal*). The nirmanakaya [of inner luminosity] has two wisdoms: the wisdom that knows the nature of things, and the wisdom that knows things in their multiplicity. But even these two wisdoms know effortlessly without the interaction of a subject and object [of knowing].

"Given that this is how these wisdoms are explained, it occurs to me (Yönten Gyamtso) that, in the context of the abhisambodhikaya, it might be appropriate to consider that these ten strengths and the other qualities or wisdoms constitute the primordial wisdom of spontaneously present luminous character (*rang bzhin lhun grub kyi ye shes*). On the other hand, it is not appropriate for someone with merely rational understanding to pronounce upon a Buddha's qualities, describing them in one way or another. But my estimate is made only in broad strokes based upon the explanations of my teacher, and after pondering the teaching of the omniscient Lord of Dharma [Longchenpa]." [YG III, 728:3–729:4]

534 That is, the mirrorlike wisdom of the sambhogakaya of inner luminosity, as explained in the previous note.

535 "It should be understood that when the inner luminosity is discussed in terms of the three kayas (dharmakaya, sambhogakaya, and nirmanakaya), in terms of the two wisdoms (the knowledge of both the nature and the multiplicity of phenomena), and in terms of the five wisdoms (dharmadhatu, mirrorlike, and so on), this refers to the genuine or actual three kayas and wisdoms. By contrast, the kayas and wisdoms of the *outwardly radiating* luminosity are but the display of the creative power of inner luminosity." [YG III, 738:3–5]

   This makes clear the importance of distinguishing the sambhogakaya and nirmanakaya of inner luminosity (where they refer, respectively, to the aspects of luminous character and cognitive potency—in the trio *ngo bo, rang bzhin, thugs rje*) from the sambhogakaya and nirmanakaya of outwardly radiating luminosity (the rupakaya in the usual sense).

536 Generally speaking, there are four kinds of sambhogakaya: (1) '*byung chen ngo bo'i sku,* the genuine sambhogakaya of the great elements; this is the kaya endowed with fivefold luminosity, which arises spontaneously from the dharmakaya; (2) *gnas pa khyab tshul gyi sku,* the abiding sambhogakaya, the light that embraces both Buddhas and beings; (3) *snang ba lam gyi sku,* the sambhogakaya that appears to beings on the path, that is, while they are in the bardo; and (4) *gdul byar snang tshul gyi sku,* the sambhogakaya that appears to beings to be guided (i.e., in the different families and mandalas, according to the various categories of beings). In the present context, only the fourth group is specifically mentioned. See YG III, 741:1–742:3.

537 In the common vehicle, the expression "body of enjoyment" refers to the "enjoyment" of the teachings of the Mahayana. In the Secret Mantra (and the Great Perfection), it refers to the fact that awareness is said to enjoy its own creative power.

538 "Parallel with the three kayas, there are three kinds of Akanishtha, the highest field. The dharmakaya Akanishtha is beyond any spatial category; it has neither center nor circumference. It is the ultimate nature beyond all conceptual construction, the sublime and ultimate destination of all the Buddhas. It is called the utterly pure and ultimate Akanishtha (*yang dag don gyi 'og min*). . . .

   "The sambhogakaya Akanishtha is the manifestation of great primordial wisdom, self-arisen from within the dharmadhatu. It appears in the form of palaces of light, with deities and retinues (all of which are spontaneously present as the five kinds of primordial wisdom) and it remains unchanging at all times. . . . The sambhogakaya Akanishtha is not the Akanishtha that is located above the pure levels of the form realm (see *Treasury of Precious Qualities*, bk. 1, p. 441n14 and p. 504), for it completely transcends it. It is the dwelling place of the Buddhas that only the Buddhas themselves can perceive. It does not belong to any spatial dimension; it is equal to the dharmadhatu. . . .

"The nirmanakaya Akanishtha is divided twofold. First, there is the nirmanakaya Akanishtha of luminous character, which appears to those who are on the grounds of realization . . . and manifests as the buddhafields of the five families. Second, there is the Akanishtha that is situated above the pure levels of the form realm, which appears as a blend of the worldly and transcendent Akanishthas." [YG III, 743:6–745:5]

"Master Buddhaguhya speaks of six kinds of Akanishtha, listing them as follows. First, the 'actual, ultimate Akanishtha' (*don gyi 'og min*) is the dharmadhatu, the abode of all the Buddhas. It is so called because there is nothing higher than it, nothing more profound. Second, the 'sign Akanishtha' (*rtags kyi 'og min*) appears as the shapes and colors of the measureless palaces, which signify the inseparable union of the ultimate expanse and primordial wisdom. It is the abode of the sambhogakaya Buddhas. It is so called because there are no higher indications of the dharmadhatu. Third, the 'knowledge Akanishtha' (*rig pa'i 'og min*) is the self-cognizing primordial wisdom that realizes the nature of phenomena as it truly is. It is the abode of the dharmakaya endowed with the two purities, and is so called because there is no higher knowledge than this. Fourth, the 'secret Akanishtha' (*gsang ba'i 'og min*) is the expanse of the mother. It is the secret abode of the enlightened body, and is so called because there is no path, place, or quality superior to this. Fifth, the 'conceptual Akanishtha' (*rtog pa'i 'og min*) is the palace of Akanishtha as meditated on by the beginner. It is the abode of the 'mandala of superior concentration,' and is so called because there is no higher concept or object-universal (*don spyi*) than this. Sixth, the 'worldly Akanishtha' (*'jig rten gnas kyi 'og min*) is located above the five pure celestial levels and is the abode of the Noble Ones. It is so called because there is no higher place in the form realm.

"These six Akanishthas may be condensed into the Akanishthas of the three kayas. The 'actual, ultimate Akanishtha' and the 'knowledge Akanishtha' are contained in the dharmakaya Akanishtha. By contrast, the 'sign Akanishtha' is contained in the sambhogakaya Akanishtha, while the last three are contained in the nirmanakaya Akanishtha." [YG III, 746:2–747:3]

539 For the eight perfect freedoms, see *Treasury of Precious Qualities*, bk. 1, p. 431.

540 These are tentative renderings.

541 This is a tentative translation. The third and fourth lines are particularly obscure.

542 *kha sbyor yan lag bdun.* "The first group of three qualities of union belongs to

the nirmanakaya as follows. First, the minds of the Buddhas, which are divested of all points of reference, are filled with great compassion. Second, their compassionate activity is uninterruptedly operative in the realms of beings. Third, their activities manifest unceasingly when the moment arrives for beings to be guided. [The second group of three qualities belongs to the sambhogakaya.] The fourth quality of union consists in the fact that the Buddhas are inseparably united with their consorts, who are but the natural light of their primordial wisdom. The fifth quality is that the undefiled bliss resulting from their union is unceasing. The sixth is that they constantly enjoy the wheel of Dharma of the mind transmission of the Buddhas, which is beyond words and phrases. And the seventh is that, even though all these branches are possessed by the Buddhas, the latter, being by nature beyond conceptual construction, are without intrinsic being. This last quality belongs to the dharmakaya." [YG III, 758:2–5]

See also Jamgön Kongtrul, *The Elements of Tantric Practice* (Ithaca, N.Y.: Snow Lion Publications, 2008), p. 292n62.

543 "The retinues of the Teachers (the Buddhas of the five families) are not composed of Bodhisattvas dwelling on the grounds of realization, who, starting out as ordinary beings, have trained themselves and purified their minds. The retinues in this case are composed of Bodhisattvas and wrathful subduing deities, who manifest through the creative power of the self-cognizing primordial wisdom of the Teachers themselves. Thus they are not different from the Teachers: their minds are not distinct (minds), and there is no hierarchical difference between them. The retinues of the Buddhas consist of the eight male Bodhisattvas (four outer and four inner) together with their eight consorts, thus making sixteen Bodhisattvas altogether. Of the eight inner Bodhisattvas, male and female, the males are: Kshitigarbha, Vajrapani, Akashagarbha, and Avalokiteshvara.

"In whichever of the five sense objects the stainless primordial wisdom of the Tathāgata's eyes is engaged, it beholds its object—in contrast with the function of ordinary visual consciousness—as being one with ultimate reality. This wisdom takes the form of Kshitigarbha (*sa yi snying po*). Similarly, in whichever of the five sense objects the primordial wisdom of their ears is engaged, it hears it as being one with suchness. This wisdom appears in the form of Vajrapani (*phyag na rdo rje*). In whichever of the five sense objects, the primordial wisdom of the Tathāgata's nose engages, it smells it as being one with the unoriginated nature. This wisdom appears as Akashagarbha (*nam mkha'i snying po*). In whichever of the five sense objects the primordial wisdom of their tongue engages, it tastes it as being one with nonduality. This wisdom appears as Avalokiteshvara (*spyan ras gzigs*). . . .

"The four consorts of the Bodhisattvas are Lasya (*sgeg mo*), Gita (*glu ma*), Mala (*phreng ma*), and Narti (*gar ma*). The objects perceived by these four primal wisdoms are greatly superior to the sense objects that appear to ordinary people. And since they are of the same taste with the primordial wisdoms themselves, it follows that each primordial wisdom perceives sense objects of all kinds. However, according to the sense object principally associated with a given consciousness, we can say that form appears as Lasya, sound as Gita, smell as Mala, and taste as Narti.

"Regarding the outer male and female Bodhisattvas, the sense organ of the Buddhas' vajra eye (which is superior to the ordinary visual sense and provides the support for the primordial wisdom that sees any of the five sense objects) appears as Maitreya (byams pa). Similarly, the faultless organ of hearing appears as Sarvanivaranavishkambhin (sgrib pa rnam sel); the olfactory organ appears as Samantabhadra (kun tu bzang po); and the organ of taste appears as Manjushri ('jam dpal).

"Regarding the four consorts, the manner in which the objects of sense are known using the support of the Tathāgata's eyes and so on, is again far superior to the way in which the ordinary senses perceive their objects. The ordinary senses, which are limited by attachment and impediment, know only forms and the other sense-objects as they exist in the present. By contrast, the knowledge supplied by the Buddhas' senses is greater. For they simultaneously see or know—without attachment or impediment—all the phenomena of the four times. This way of knowing the past appears as Dhupa (bdug spos ma). The knowledge of the present time appears as Pushpa (me rtog ma). The knowledge of the future appears as Aloka (snang gsal ma). And their way of knowing the fourth time (the primordial wisdom of equality, the unchanging ultimate reality in the sphere of self-arisen appearances) appears as Gandha (dri chab ma). Whether the consorts are understood to correspond to the objects (of the four times) or to the subjects (the primordial wisdoms), the meaning is the same. For they know that the subject and the object are of the same taste or nature." [YG III, 758:6–761:2]

544 "The wrathful subduing deities surrounding the Buddhas are the inconceivable manifestations of their skillful means and wisdom. They appear as the four doorkeepers, male and female, in order to indicate that no ordinary thought can cause harm to the mandala of the self-experience of primordial wisdom." [YG III, 761:5–6]

545 See note 542.

546 "Generally speaking, thanks to the radiance of unborn ultimate reality, the unceasing display may appear in any fashion. Consequently, different tantras describe different arrays of the spontaneously manifested mandalas, along with varying numbers of deities. It is a mistake to claim, out of partiality, that one of the mandalas is the only authentic one, while the others are not." [YG III, 764:3–4]

According to the Mayajala-tantra, the radiance of the peaceful deities dwelling in the heart gives rise to the appearance of the wrathful deities in the palace of the brain. In other words, the lower palace (in the heart) is peaceful, while the upper palace (in the brain) is wrathful. (See commentary to stanza

72 on pp. 159–60.) In the present context, however, the disposition of the deities is described according to the *Scripture of Summarized Wisdom* (*mdo dgongs pa 'dus pa*), i.e., in contrary fashion.

547 That is, of appearance and emptiness, or skillful means and wisdom.

548 The "lower tantras" here refers to the Mahayoga tantras, the principal subject of which is the generation stage. The *Vajrasattva Mayajala-tantra* also belongs to the Mahayoga class, but has special characteristics of its own. The tantras are described as lower because the explanation of the mandala is being given here in terms of Anuyoga, which is the higher tantra in the framework of Maha, Anu, and Ati. Moreover, according to the *Vajrasattva Mayajala-tantra*, the aspects of appearance and emptiness are symbolized by Samantabhadra and Samantabhadri respectively. [KPS]

549 That is, the twelve dhatus of the senses and their objects, together with the six dhatus of consciousness.

550 "The peaceful and wrathful mandalas that manifest in the perception of other beings (*gzhan snang*) are different from the buddhafield of Akanishtha. Three examples of these 'other-perceived' mandalas are found in the *Eight Sadhanas* (*bka' brgyad*). In order to subdue obstacle-creating spirits, the dreamlike manifestations of the worldly deities (which usually appear only as the retinue) transform into main deities." [YG III, 768:4–6]

The three mandalas referred to here are of *Matarah* (*ma mo rbod gtong*), *Vajramantrabhiru* (*dmod pa drag sngags*), and *Lokastotrapuja* (*'jig rten mchod bstod*).

551 Half the height of the central platform, and colored according to direction.

552 For the eight trappings of the charnel ground, see chapter 10, pp. 149–50.

553 The eight glorious attributes of the Heruka are as follows. First, his hair bristles and is standing on end, a sign of his disgust with samsara. Second, he has the vajra wings of a garuda, the sign of skillful means and wisdom. Third, his headdress is adorned with blue-red streamers, the sign that he overwhelms with splendor both samsara and nirvana. Fourth, he has a vajra on the crown of the head, the sign of his enlightened family. Fifth, he has the powerful armor of a rhinoceros, the sign of supreme and confident dignity. Sixth, he is in inseparable union with his consort, the sign of wisdom. Seventh, he has a double vajra of iron, the sign that he repels all negative forces. Eighth, his wings are the sign that he subdues with splendor and majesty.

554 These two sentences are supplied from YG III, 774:6.

555 These two sentences are supplied from YG III, 775:6.

556 *bgrangs pa'i rang bzhin sprul pa.*

557 "For close disciples, those with pure minds, it is the sambhogakaya appearing in the perception of others (*gzhan snang longs sku*). For more distant disciples, those who have not yet attained the grounds of realization but whose minds

are pure to a certain degree, it is the supreme nirmanakaya (*mchog gi sprul sku*)." [YG III, 782:5–6]

558 *so so yang dag par rig pa bzhi.* See *Treasury of Precious Qualities*, bk. 1, p. 389.

559 *phyed snang longs sku 'am rang bzhin sprul pa'i zhing.* This rendering is in accordance with the interpretation of Sogpo Tendar in his *legs bshad gser gyi thur ma* (*The Golden Scalpel Commentary*), p. 588.

560 *gnas pa'i rang bzhin sprul pa.*

561 *rnam grol dbugs chen 'byin pa lnga.*

562 *'og min mkha' spyod kyi gnas.*

563 "In the human realm, the nirmanakaya guide of beings appears in the form of the Sage, the supreme nirmanakaya, attired as a monk and adorned with the major and minor marks of enlightenment. For the gods, and the other realms, this same nirmanakaya guide of beings appears as the respective ruler of the class of beings concerned, appearing in the form best able to help them. Thus they are called Munis, or Sages. It is not to be understood that these Munis are different forms of our supreme nirmanakaya. The representation of the Muni or Sage of the god realm, depicted as white in color and holding a lute, was contrived, as a form for meditation, by those who are learned in the Secret Mantra and is a symbol of the various nirmanakaya guides of beings that might appear in the god realms." [YG III, 811:1–3]

564 "The field to be guided by one supreme nirmanakaya is one three-thousandfold universe. In this universe, there are a billion Jambudvipas in which a billion supreme nirmanakayas appear and display their deeds. And in the other realms, such as the realm of gods, there appears a similar quantity of guides in various forms. One cannot say definitely that a given three-thousandfold universe has such and such a dimension. This is so, first, because the karmic experience of beings is inconceivably various; second, because the manner in which dependent arising unfolds is inconceivable; and, third, because the manifestations of the Buddhas are also inconceivable. The *King of Concentration Sutra* says:

> On a hair tip, there are five abodes of beings:
> Hells-realms and the realms of stooping beasts,
> The realms of Yama, gods and humankind.
> They do not mingle; they do not transform.

"And:

> In their abodes are Buddhas born.
> The doctrine of these Knowers of the World shines forth.
> Yet, in these realms, the Dharma also wanes
> And tidings that these Guides have "gone beyond all pain" are also heard.
> And humans in their homes are similar to dreams.

"This three-thousandfold universe in which we dwell is contained in one infinitesimal particle in the begging bowl in the hands of Vairochana Mahasagara. And likewise, in one particle of the four elements, and in the space of a single needle-eye, there appear countless beings who have accumulated the same karma, together with their worlds. The wisdom of the Victorious Ones sees them all, and works for their sake." [YG III, 811:6–813:1]

565 "The three ways of guiding beings by means of the enlightened body, speech, and mind, are principally connected with the deeds of the Muni present in the human realm (in other words, Buddha Shakyamuni). By contrast, the Munis of the other five realms guide beings mainly through their enlightened activities." [YG III, 820:6]

566 "The Tale of the Woodpecker" is related by Shura in the *Jatakamala*, chapter 34.

567 For the tale of Dridhasamadana, see *Sutra of the Wise and Foolish*, chapter 49.

568 A fabulous eight-legged animal of great strength, able to combat lions and elephants. See *Jatakamala*, chapter 25.

569 "They are therefore fit to be regarded as the supreme nirmanakaya." [YG III, 833:3]

570 That is, in the condition of ordinary sentient beings.

571 That is, *phyogs bcu'i mun sel* (*Dispelling Darkness in the Ten Directions*), p. 619.

572 "The explanatory *Ocean Tantra* says: 'There is the mind transmission of the Buddhas, the knowledge transmission of the Vidyādharas, the hearing transmission of the yogis—down to our own teachers.' As it is stated, the continuity of the three kinds of transmission, from the sixth Buddha, Samantabhadra until the holy teachers of the present, is not severed [see note 17], and the blessings of the teachers' minds are not weakened." [YG III, 9:1–4]

573 [DKR/OC] This lineage of transmission passes from Samantabhadra to Garab Dorje.

574 [DKR/OC] This transmission is also known as *rig 'dzin brda' yi brgyud pa*, the transmission through the symbolic indication of the Vidyādharas. Its lineage passes from Garab Dorje to Guru Padmasambhava. Though these teachers assume the form of Vidyādharas, they have all in fact attained buddhahood.

575 This lineage, also known as *gang zag snyan brgyud*, consists of all the spiritual masters from Guru Padmasambhava to the teachers of the present time.

576 See notes 193 and 496.

577 That is, the dharmakaya, the svabhavikakaya, the abhisambodhikaya (the kaya of manifest enlightenment), and the sambhogakaya. These are the kayas appearing only to themselves; they are not perceived by others. Thus the nirmanakaya, which is apparent to others, is not included here. [KPS]

578 This refers to the sambhogakaya perceived only by Bodhisattvas on the ten grounds. See chapter 13, p. 294.

579 According to the Nyingma tradition, these are the six Munis or Teachers that manifest for the benefit of beings in the six realms of samsara. See chapter 13, pp. 305–8.

580 [DKR/OC] When, in a preceding existence, Buddha Shakyamuni took birth as a huge fish, this was an example of the diversified nirmanakaya. From the Mahayana point of view, the Buddha had attained perfect enlightenment many kalpas before the appearance of the supreme nirmanakaya Shakyamuni. Accordingly, the previous existences of Shakyamuni, usually regarded as revealing his progress on the bodhisattva path, were in fact manifestations of the diversified nirmanakaya. See also chapter 13, p. 314.

581 [DKR/OC] This refers to the fact that the Buddha's body, speech, and mind are not three distinct entities.

582 That is, emptiness.

583 *yi ge'i tshogs.* The first meaning of *yi ge* is a syllable or speech-sound (*skad kyi gdangs*), as distinct from mere noise. For the three different kinds of *yi ge*, see note 183.

584 *sgrar snang rung.* [DKR/OC] In answer to the need for the Doctrine to be communicated to beings, the eighty-four thousand sections of the Dharma, ever present in the wisdom mind of Samantabhadra, manifest unceasingly and effortlessly, in the form of the sixty aspects of the Buddha's speech, the spontaneous resonance of the Dharma emitted by the stirring of the leaves of the wish-fulfilling tree, etc.

585 [DKR/OC] Insofar as it remains in the minds of the Buddhas, the wisdom does not yet accomplish the benefit of ordinary beings.

586 For example, the dakini Mahakarmendrani (*las kyi dbang mo*).

587 *yi ge'i 'khor lo.* This refers to the luminous nondual wisdom, which is itself beyond words and is ever present in the vajra body. [KPS] See also note 183.

588 Samantabhadra is regarded as the Buddha of the sixth family in relation to the Buddhas of the five families, of whom he represents the union.

589 For example, the Buddha taught the *Guhyasamaja-tantra* to King Indrabodhi and the *Kalachakra-tantra* to to Chandrabhadra (or Suchandra), the dharma-king of Shambhala.

590 *dam pa'i rigs can drva ma lnga.* [DKR/OC] These were the god Yashasvi Varapala, and his four companions of lesser rank: the naga Takshaka, the yaksha Ulkamukha, the rakshasa Matyaupayika, and the man Licchavi Vimalakirti, all of whom were in deep meditation at that time.

591 [DKR/OC] This is an indication that Kujara was one in realization with the Buddha.

592 The eight perfect freedoms are understood as the absence of obstructions to certain levels of accomplishment. They are gradually acquired on the path and, taken together, they constitute one of the twenty-one qualities of dharmakaya wisdom. See *Treasury of Precious Qualities,* bk. 1, app. 9.

593 [DKR/OC] The Heaven of the Thirty-Three, Tushita, and Akanishtha.

594 Of the seventy-five chapters of the *General Scripture of Summarized Wisdom,* twelve begin with a discussion of one of these twelve "occasions." [KPS]
   [DKR/OC] It is, however, possible that the Mantrayana teachings appear even on other occasions. Even in a dark kalpa (when the light of the Dharma has not been kindled), when the karma of an extraordinary disciple belonging to the mantra lineage is awakened, the mantra teachings will manifest.

595 [DKR/OC] As when one realizes the insufficiency of the causal vehicle.

596 [DKR/OC] As when the Buddha Shakyamuni appeared.

597 [DKR/OC] As when realization is gained (the complete certainty of the wisdom of the fourth initiation) as a result of hearing, reflection, and meditation on, for example, the *Guhyagarbha-tantra.*

598 [DKR/OC] As, for example, by Rongdzom Chökyi Zangpo in his *Precious Jewel Commentary,* or by Gyalwa Longchenpa in the *Dispelling Darkness in the Ten Directions,* or by Lochen Dharma Shri in his *Wisdom Ornament of the Lord of Secrets* (These are all commentaries on the *Guhyagarbha.*) The teachings of the Mantrayana can arise even at the present time for those who realize the meaning of the *Guhyagarbha* in the way that Rongdzom Pandita and Longchenpa did. Such people are able to say that they received the teaching from Vajrasattva, and not from their teachers.

599 [DKR/OC] As when Guru Rinpoche came to Tibet and taught his twenty-five disciples.

600 [DKR/OC] As when the minds of guru and disciple mingle and become one in wisdom, as happened to Jigme Lingpa in the course of his visions of Longchenpa.

601 [DKR/OC] As when a tertön prophesied by Guru Rinpoche discovers treasure teachings and propagates them.

602 [DKR/OC] As when Vajrasattva appeared and taught the tantra entitled *Churning the Depths of Hell* to a brahmin suffering in hell for having killed his father, but whose time to be trained had nevertheless arrived.

603 [DKR/OC] As in the case of the Buddha's prophecy about King Ja.

604 [DKR/OC] As in the case of the brahmin mentioned in note 602.

605 [DKR/OC] As when Vajrapani expounded the *Guhyagarbha-tantra* to the five noble beings.

606 *rgyud mahayoga.* Mahayoga is called the "tantra system" because all ten elements

of the tantric path are contained in it: view, practice, mandala, empowerment, samaya, offering, mantra, concentration, activities, and accomplishment. See *Systems of Buddhist Tantra*, p. 505n22.

607 [DKR/OC] The material bodies of them all, down to the smallest insects, disappeared without trace and they went to celestial fields (*mkha' spyod*) in bodies of rainbow light.

608 *lung anu yoga.* Anuyoga is known as the "system of explanatory teachings" because, in addition to the ten elements of the tantric path, it supplies their full explanation.

609 See note 590.

610 Vajrapani.

611 *man ngag ati yoga.* Atiyoga is known as the "system of pith instructions" because it mainly consists of essential instructions for the actualization of primordial buddhahood, the state of pure awareness.

612 "Sattvavajra" is a name of Vajrapani.

613 *rgyal thabs spyi blugs.* [DKR/OC] When the Chakravartin, or universal ruler, wishes to appoint a successor among his five hundred sons, he places their names in a golden vessel. He prays to the Three Jewels, makes vast offerings, and then takes at random one of the names. When the heir apparent is duly enthroned, an elephant places a golden vase (tied to its trunk by means of a silken scarf) upon the prince's head. This is rather like the granting of empowerment whereby the guru's wisdom is transferred to the mind of the disciple, who then becomes the holder of the Dzogchen teachings. The wisdom of the Buddhas is transmitted, like the contents of one vase poured into another, filling it to the brim.

614 Garab Dorje is an emanation of Vajrasattva, who is himself an emanation of Samantabhadra.

615 These are the nine sections of the space-class teachings of the Great Perfection.

616 These key aspects are explained in chapter 12.

617 For a discussion of the seven ornaments, see *Systems of Buddhist Tantra*, pp. 283–91.

618 The *Treasury of Precious Qualities* is such a text.

619 [DKR/OC] The teaching on the generation stage is an expedient teaching because it uses the relative truth as the path. But all tantras, such as the *Guhyagarbha*, may be expounded on outer and inner levels, according to the sense of the generation or perfection stages.

620 [DKR/OC] The same statement could be understood, however, as referring to the generation stage.

621 [DKR/OC] In a similar way, the stage of perfection is the hidden meaning of the generation stage.

622 [DKR/OC] These are Bodhisattvas on the level of the result, belonging to the three families. They are fully enlightened and are Bodhisattvas only in name.

623 *chings chen po lnga*. These are the purpose, the proper arrangement of the subject, a word-for-word explanation, the overall meaning, and answers to possible objection. See *Treasury of Precious Qualities*, bk. 1, p. 439n4.

624 Patrul Rinpoche and others.

625 [DKR/OC] The "subject" of this experience is self-cognizing awareness, and the "object" of this experience is the dharmadhatu. When these two (subject and object) are experientially realized as one, there occurs the view of self-cognizing awareness (*rang rig gi lta ba*), or the view of the union of ultimate space and awareness (*dbyings rig zung 'jug gi lta ba*).

626 *skor bdun*. [DKR/OC] The five resultant qualities (*'bras chos lnga*) are the enlightened body, speech, mind, qualities, and activities, followed by the ultimate expanse (the aspect of emptiness) and primordial wisdom (the aspect of appearance). These are not compounded, concretely existent phenomena. They are aspects of the "emptiness endowed with supreme attributes" (*rnam kun mchog ldan stong pa nyid*).

627 *yul med rang gsal gyi tshul du*. [DKR/OC] In this experience, both that which sees and that which is seen are the same primordial wisdom. There is no duality of distinct subject and object.

628 *mnyam pa chen po*. [DKR/OC] Samsara is not something to be rejected; nirvana is not something to be desired. From the point of view of the causal vehicle of the sutras, the view of great equality occurs on the eighth Bodhisattva ground. In the present context, it is being discussed according to the view, meditation, and conduct of the *Mayajala-tantra*.

629 According to Mipham Rinpoche, a view is defined as the mind's certainty with regard to its object (in this case, the dharmadhatu), wherein all associated misconceptions are removed by the clarity of discernment. The view therefore relates to the knowing subject, not to the object itself. It relates to the discerning intellect. (Note that no reference is being made here to the view of the Great Perfection.) This kind of view, which is confined to the intellect, is held by practitioners on the paths of accumulation and joining, as well as by yogis on the grounds of realization (up to and including the seventh ground) when they are in the postmeditation state. By contrast, in the postmeditation state of beings on the eighth ground and beyond (as also in the meditative equipoise of beings on all the grounds of realization), it is impossible to speak of someone "holding a view." [KPS]

630 [DKR/OC] According to the view of the sutras, the relative truth is to be

laid aside, and the ultimate truth is to be realized. But in the Vajrayana, relative phenomena are in themselves the display of the kayas and wisdoms, whereas the ultimate truth is the nondual union of awareness and the dharmadhatu. The two truths posited in the Vajrayana are thus superior to the two truths propounded on the sutra level. They are indivisible, and this indivisibility constitutes the great dharmakaya beyond all ontological positions, profound, peaceful, luminous, and uncompounded. Phenomena are *primordially* pure. They are like gold, which, from its very origin, is precious. There is nothing impure in phenomena that needs to be cleansed at a later stage.

631 [DKR/OC] There is no need for antidotes, such as reflecting on ugliness as a remedy for desire, or on patience in order to counteract anger. Neither is it necessary to superimpose an idea of emptiness. In truth, desire has the nature of all-perceiving wisdom *from the very beginning*. If one realizes the true nature of suffering, the result of defilement, it dissolves into the wisdom of great bliss.

632 [DKR/OC] Usually buddhahood and the buddhafields are considered as the result of the path, but in the Vajrayana, the universe itself is considered as a buddhafield. Beings are the pure mandala of the three seats; and defilements (*rgyud*) have the nature of the five wisdoms and are thus used as the path. Consequently, there is nothing to be discarded, and thus we talk about the "vehicle of result" or "resultant vehicle." We speak of a "vajra vehicle" or Vajrayana because, just as a vajra cannot be destroyed by other substances such as iron, in the same way, when the view, meditation, and conduct of this vehicle are realized, one is invulnerable to thoughts that apprehend phenomena as autonomously existing within the dualistic interplay of subject and object.

633 Rongzom Pandita says that the purity of all phenomena is established in two ways, depending on whether one believes (like the Vaibhashikas and Sautrantikas) in the existence of an extramental world, or whether one considers (like the Chittamatrins) that outer objects are merely the mind's subjective perception. [KPS]

634 [DKR/OC] The universe, beings, and the latters' mindstreams appear in an impure manner to the ordinary perception of beings caught in delusion—in just the same way that a white conch appears yellow to someone sick with jaundice. In truth, however, the conch is white and is seen as such when the sickness is cured. Nothing happens to the conch, when this change in perception occurs, since white has always been its natural color. In the same way, phenomena, which we now perceive impurely, have never been other than deities, palaces, and wisdoms.

The element of water appears to beings in hell as molten bronze, and to pretas as pus and blood. To human beings it seems to be something that is drunk or used for washing. It is perceived by the gods as nectar, and by the

Vidyādharas as having the nature of Mamaki. This last case corresponds to the perception of the Buddhas; they have no perception of blood, pus, etc. The wisdom of the Buddhas is naturally pure of all conceptual formation, and they have no perception of compounded objects according to the dualistic interplay of subject and object. Since the Vidyādharas perceive water as Mamaki, when they make use of it for washing and so on, they experience the wisdom of great bliss. Similarly, the water of Sukhavati is endowed with eight qualities, and gives to the Bodhisattvas who bathe in it perfect memory and samadhi. Of course, this "water" is the same element that we have on earth; the difference is that, in Sukhavati, it is perceived as pure by the Bodhisattvas who live there. And if these same Bodhisattvas were to visit our world, they would perceive everything as pure in the same way.

Conversely, a preta finding himself in Sukhavati would experience the water there (though endowed with eight qualities) as blood and pus. It is thus that all appearances are dreamlike, and similar to illusions. The ordinary idea of water as something that is wet and flows downward does not resist investigation, and is found to be nothing but emptiness. And it is thanks to positive and negative action that the various appearances of water, as pure or impure, are perceived. Beings in hell, who have the most dense obscurations, experience water as molten bronze. Gradually, however, as obscurations become lighter, water is perceived as pus, then as a habitat or as something to drink, or as something that cleanses. Later it is seen as a health-bestowing drink or (by the gods and asuras) as amrita.

Buddhas are totally beyond the duality implied in something that is seen and someone who sees. They dwell permanently in a state of equality, the ultimate nature of things. Akanishtha, for instance, as seen by the Buddhas, is also referred to as the mandala of primordial wisdom's self-experience (*rang snang ye shes kyi dkyil 'khor*). The truth is that our own universe, the beings who inhabit it, together with their mind streams, are in fact Akanishtha itself. They are the same; and they are seen as such by the Buddhas, whose vision is completely healthy and totally devoid of error. They are like people with healthy eyes who see the white conch as white.

635 This objection is made by those who consider pure and impure to be two completely different realities. [KPS]

636 *blta bya thun mong ba.* This is a complex issue. The question is: Does there exist an objective, commonly present substrate for the different perceptions of beings, whether in or beyond samsara? To answer in the affirmative implies a belief in the existence of something that is in itself independent of, and unrelated to, perception. But there is no such thing. It is obvious, however, that something must be *posited*, even though nothing exists as such, otherwise there is no subject for discussion. Gyalwa Longchenpa (in his *Precious Treasury That Fulfills All Wishes*) and Mipham Rinpoche (in his *Lamp of Certainty*) define this "something" as "mere appearance" (*snang tsam*, the opposite of nonappear-

ance or absence)—the common undifferentiated basis for the contrasting perceptions of the six classes of beings. Other than mere appearance, there is nothing. [KPS]

637 The sixth and highest of the divine abodes of the desire realm.

638 [DKR/OC] The truth is that of all the different perceptions of "water," there is none that is somehow basic and definitive, such as being wet and downward flowing. Madhyamaka analysis shows that such a thing is wholly impossible. Impure appearances and perceptions are the products of hatred, selfishness, and so on; they are just the subjective experience of our minds. "Who made the fires of hell?" asked Shantideva; and he concluded that it is the outcome of the evil orientations of the mind.

It is according to a similar logic that the Buddhas and the Vidyādharas experience all appearances as pure. For them, both the object and the subject of the experience is primordial wisdom. In such wisdom, subject and object are one. In our present state, we consider the object as "outside" us, and the subject as "inside," the two being connected via the organs of sense. We assume the true existence of both, and this deluded perception causes the three worlds of samsara to arise. But for a Buddha, there is no division between subject and object; both are the same primordial wisdom. Forms seen, sounds heard, smells, tastes, and contact are all the display of a single wisdom.

The *Guhyagarbha* declares that all impure samsaric phenomena are the display, or subjective experience, of the ordinary mind (*sems kyi rang snang*), whereas all the phenomena of nirvana, the buddhafields, etc., are the display or self-experience of primordial wisdom (*ye shes kyi rang snang*). It follows that they (samsara and nirvana) are not basically different, for both are grounded in the principle of dependent arising. For example, the fires of hell are the natural display of anger. This is not, however, a dependent phenomenon commonly perceived by all beings, for if an enlightened being were to go to hell, he or she would find there only a pure land.

639 *don dam dpyod pa'i tshad ma*, such as the Madhyamaka argument of "neither one nor many."

640 [DKR/OC] Once the emptiness of all phenomena has been realized, no impurity is found, even if one searches for it. Similarly, someone with healthy eyes will never see a white conch shell as yellow, even if he wants to.

641 This kind of objection is made by those who consider that appearance and emptiness are mutually exclusive. Such people do not understand the union of appearance and emptiness, and think that emptiness is a mere nonexistence. [KPS]

642 [DKR/OC] We can talk about purity here because the nature of all things is emptiness, and within emptiness, there is no impurity. Emptiness can only be pure. Space is not soiled if one throws a handful of dust into it; neither is

it embellished if one does the same with flowers. The union of appearance and emptiness can only be, by nature, pure. The vast expanse embraces both the impure perceptions created by anger, and also the pure perceptions of buddhafields that are the result of pure aspirations. All these perceptions are grounded in the expanse (of emptiness), although this does not of course constitute a concrete foundation for them. Emptiness that is all-pervasive and endowed with supreme attributes is not "emptiness" conceived of as the opposite of appearance. Neither is it the opposite of "non-emptiness." It is the great primordial emptiness, which is neither voidness nor appearance, neither existence nor nonexistence. Its nature is utterly beyond all ontological positions. Just as rays of light issue from the sun, the kayas and wisdoms are the outflow of great primordial emptiness. They are totally pure and not even a trace of "true sufferings," such as the five aggregates, can be found in them.

643 "Deity" here means an appearance that is the union of clarity and emptiness.

644 [DKR/OC] Whereas ordinary beings experience impure perception, Bodhi-sattvas who are on the path experience perceptions that are partially pure. On certain occasions, the Bodhisattvas have visions and see everything as perfectly pure buddhafields, while at other times they perceive phenomena as ordinary and impure. Totally pure perception is the unique preserve of Buddhas, who never experience anything as impure. Now the fundamental nature of the mind is wholly unstained by delusion and defilements, but at the moment, this is something we cannot perceive. Nevertheless, impure perception has no effect on the actual purity of the mind's nature. It is just as when someone perceives a white conch as yellow: the fault is in the perception, not in the conch. When the pure is perceived as impure, that is how it *appears*. As long as one is apt to apprehend suffering, suffering appears. The ultimate deity is not a figure with a face and limbs. It is the view: ultimate, self-arisen primordial wisdom. This self-arisen wisdom, the dharmadhatu—namely, emptiness endowed with supreme attributes—cannot be perceived by ordinary beings. As a method to make this possible, one meditates on the form of deities, palaces, and so forth.

645 This is a reference to empowerment and the introduction to the nature of the mind.

646 There is no further notion that samsara is something to be rejected and that nirvana is something excellent to be desired.

647 [DKR/OC] From the ultimate point of view, the enlightened body, speech, mind, qualities, activities, ultimate expanse, and primordial wisdom (the seven riches of the ultimate truth) are all spontaneously present. They do not need to be *revealed* through an effort of one's intelligence, or by means of the blessings of the guru.

648 [DKR/OC] Emptiness is not a mere blank, for the kayas and wisdoms mani-fest in it. Emptiness is the source of everything, for appearance itself is the

radiance of emptiness. This can only be known through self-cognizing awareness; it is not a knowledge that comes through mere study and reflection. The deluded perceptions of samsara are the natural display of the ordinary mind. Pure appearances, by contrast, are the natural display of primordial wisdom. The "indivisibility" referred to here is the ultimate, fundamental nature of the mind. The display of the deluded mind dissolves into the pure expanse of primordial wisdom.

649 *rtogs pa bzhi'i gtan tshigs.* See also *Systems of Buddhist Tantra*, p. 317–18.

650 *mngon rdzogs rgyal po che.* [DKR/OC] This expression (a name of Samantabhadra) indicates that all is the perfect display of Samantabhadra himself.

651 *rgyu gcig.* [DKR/OC] The phenomena of both samsara and nirvana have a single cause or source (the nature of the mind).

652 *rang mtshan la bzhal du med pa.* [DKR/OC] Phenomena cannot be assessed according to characteristics perceived in the state of delusion (according to which samsara is to be rejected, and nirvana to be striven for).

653 This probably refers to the *Stages of the Path of the Mayajala* by Buddhaguhya. [KPS]

654 [DKR/OC] All the vowels and consonants, and the words that consist of them, are infinite expressions of A, the unoriginated nature, which is thus a symbol of emptiness.

655 "Speech" here being understood as the sound A.

656 [DKR/OC] The appearing aspect of phenomena (*snang cha*) and their emptiness aspect (*stong cha*) are not different in nature. The unceasing manifestation of phenomena, perceived as pure or impure, is but the self-display or self-experience of primordial wisdom. Fire "expresses" itself naturally by being hot. In the same way, the unborn nature expresses itself in limitless manifestation. If the nature were not unborn, an infinite display would be impossible. But even though this display seems solid and real, it is just like the reflection of the moon on the surface of the water.

657 [DKR/OC] If one realizes that the unborn nature and the display of phenomena are not separate, one will perceive nothing other than the complete purity of all things. This perception is the naturally arising power of a Buddha. The body, speech, mind, qualities, activities, ultimate space, and primordial wisdom of the superior ultimate truth express themselves in the ocean-like infinity of pure phenomena that a Buddha perceives. By contrast, the failure to understand this (the ultimate reality of the three worlds of samsara) is the cause of delusion. The term *lhun grub* ("spontaneously present") used in the text points to the fact that the delusions of samsara and the undeluded character of nirvana have not been purposely fabricated.

658 That is, the indivisible nature of relative truth and ultimate truth, appearance and emptiness, primordial wisdom and the ultimate expanse.

659 [DKR/OC] Undeluded, ultimate reality is the great purity, the union of the relative and ultimate truths, beyond the reach of the minds of ordinary beings. Self-cognizing awareness is not a thing, an object of perception. But on the other hand, neither is it an amorphous, indeterminate state, or blank torpor. It is not so because it possesses the aspect of clarity. It is the true nature of things because the Enlightened Ones have seen it so. It lies, by definition, beyond the intellect. Yet its realization may be approached through the exercise of the intellect.

660 *rgyud kyi dngos po bcu.* [DKR/OC] These ten elements are common to all the tantras of the Mantrayana. All objects of knowledge, from material things up to the state of omniscience, are unerringly known by the Buddha's wisdom. If one correctly understands the ultimate reality of all phenomena and acts accordingly, all dualistic perception and clinging to subject and object, which arise under the influence of delusion, will disappear like clouds melting away in the sky. This process is as natural as the burning effect of fire. One will no longer fall under the power of dualistic perception. One will gain an authentic realization of the unchanging nature of the ground (the union of the two truths), of the path (the union of the generation and perfection stages), and of the result (the union of the dharmakaya and rupakaya).

According to the view, meditation, and conduct of the Mantrayana, all phenomena are perfect in that they partake of the buddha-nature. To be able to explain, practice, or even hear this teaching, empowerment is an absolute prerequisite. Without empowerment, the guru is not permitted to explain that the universe and beings all have the nature of the mandala, and the disciple is not even allowed to look at the scriptures of the Secret Mantra: the tantras (*rgyud*), the elucidatory scriptures (*lung*), and the pith instructions (*man ngag*). When in ordinary life, someone is empowered to perform certain tasks, this means that he or she has the right to act. In just the same way, if one has received an empowerment of the Secret Mantra in a truly authentic manner, one has the right to study, practice, and eventually transmit, the teachings associated with that empowerment.

When he was at Samye, Guru Rinpoche bestowed the empowerments of the Secret Mantra on the king and his other close disciples; and in order to preserve the secret and withhold it from the vindictive queen Margyen Za and the evil ministers, he employed an archaic expression, using the term *rim pa* instead of *dbang*, or empowerment. Thus when Guru Rinpoche announced that he would give an empowerment, he said: "*rim pa byed kyi yod.*" The word *rim pa* was used because it means "stages" in the sense of "gradual steps," the implication being that, after the vase empowerment, one is allowed to practice the generation stage; after the secret and wisdom empowerments, one may practice the two aspects of the perfection stage; and after the fourth empowerment, one may implement the practice related to primordial wisdom.

When one has received the empowerment, one must keep and preserve its power by observing the root and branch samayas. Samaya, it is said, keeps the strength of the empowerment alive within one's being. If the samaya is damaged, the vital force of the empowerment is cut, and it is robbed of its power. Therefore, the samaya should never be transgressed. After receiving the vase empowerment, one should regard all the appearances of the universe and beings as the mandala of the three seats; it is henceforth improper to consider things in an impure way. Once one has received the secret initiation, one should meditate on one's body as the city of the vajra aggregate endowed with the channels, winds, and essence-drops. Henceforth, it is no longer acceptable to allow them to continue in the ordinary way. When the third empowerment is received, the example wisdom should take birth within oneself, and when the fourth empowerment is received, this should give rise to the birth of authentic primordial wisdom.

On the level of the causal vehicle and the three outer tantras, a distinction is made between offering substances that are appropriate and those that are inappropriate. In the inner tantras, by contrast, all forms perceived by the eye are vajra forms; all sounds are vajra sound; all thoughts are vajra mind. Whichever of the five kinds of experience occurs to the five senses, all are offerings that cannot but be pleasing to the deities of the mandala. This is why, in the highest tantras, one enjoys the five meats and the five nectars. Offerings such as these need no preparation on the part of the practitioner. All phenomenal existence, the entire universe, is one vast offering, for it is nothing but a display of the primordial wisdom of great bliss. All is the pleasing substance of samaya.

In addition, offerings of mudras and praises are made. "Mudra" means "seal." When a magistrate issues a license or permission, he or she stamps it with a seal, after which one may proceed with the work. If no seal is forthcoming, this amounts to a veto that cannot be ignored. In much the same way, since the seal of Samantabhadra has been placed upon phenomena, the latter receive a ratification of infinite purity. No impurity remains. The mudras performed during the rituals of the Mantrayana are intended to reveal this ultimate condition of phenomena, and to call the deity to mind. When, on presenting the offerings and mudras, one snaps one's fingers or clasps one's hands, it is at that moment that the physical offering of form dissolves into the deity's eyes, the offering of sound dissolves into the deity's ears, the offering of taste dissolves into the deity's tongue—and are found pleasing. When the wisdom mind of the deity is actualized, there is neither an object nor a subject of offering. Nevertheless, on the level of appearance, when such objects that are pleasing to the senses are offered to the deity as the display of great bliss, the deity accepts them with delight, as a result of which, the siddhis are granted. In short, the offerings are made and received within the ultimate nature, wherein there is no distinction between subject and object.

All phenomena, in their appearing aspect, have the nature of the male deity or "father" (*yab*). In their aspect of emptiness, they have the nature of the female deity or "mother" (*yum*). Therefore because these aspects are inseparable, phenomena have the nature of *yab-yum,* that is, deities in union. This is the primordial state of affairs—true from the beginning. It is not contrived anew. These three aspects (appearance, emptiness, and their union) are simply so, and it is just a question of recognizing what is already the case now and forever. It is not something that formerly did not exist and that one wishes to bring into being. Neither is it something that is not the case now, but might become so at some future time. It is simply the nature of things now and primordially. Even if one fails, for the moment, to realize it through one's meditation, it is still true that all phenomena are, now and forever, the mandala of infinite purity.

For practitioners who have extraordinary realization of the view and meditation, every breath that issues from their mouths has the nature of mantra. Even if they are not actually reciting mantras, whenever they breathe or speak, it is as if they were. Even when they speak of apparently ordinary things, the fact is that every sound that comes from their mouths is mantra—leading to the accomplishment of the deities. When one recites mantras, one should be clearly aware that such mantras are the display of the wisdom of the deities of the mandala. They are not mere words written in black ink on white paper. If one were to meditate on the 108 supreme peaceful and wrathful deities without reciting their mantras, one would be unable to have the vision of them or to hear their speech. Just as a torma that has remained for a long time in the mandala of an accomplished practitioner is known as a *druptor* (*grub gtor*), a torma of accomplishment, and brings liberation when it is tasted (for it has become one with the deity, and thus has this power), the same is true of the mantra. It is permeated with the wisdom, compassion, and power of the deity. It has become one with the deity. It is just like a man who cannot but answer when one calls him repeatedly by his name.

When one inscribes or recites a mantra, which contains the name of a deity and is blessed thereby, it has the power to dissipate one's obscurations and bring about the supreme and ordinary siddhis. Consequently, by performing a recitation, whether determined by numbers, or length of time, or the appearance of signs, it is possible to accomplish the deity (Manjushri or Avalokita, for example). This is the reason why, in all the Mantrayana scriptures, the mantras are extolled as possessing infinite and inconceivable qualities. For they are the expression of the wisdom of all the Buddhas. When practiced, they are like wish-fulfilling gems, which when held in the hand are able to grant every wish, calling into existence riches, food, and raiment of all kinds, curing illness and driving away famine. If one gains the conviction that the deity and mantra are one and the same, it is impossible not to achieve the supreme and ordinary siddhis.

And by performing the mudras, such as that of Vairochana, one will necessarily gain the accomplishment of the deity. When practitioners perform the mudras, they are not merely making beautiful movements with their hands. They perceive all appearances as the display of the deity, and have the vajra pride of perceiving that they themselves are the deity from the very first. Gathered within such an awareness are the *dharmamudra* of speech, the *samayamudra* of body, the *karmamudra* of activity, and the *mahamudra* of the mind. These are the seals that are utterly imprinted on phenomena. Mantras and mudras are like fire and wind that, working together, immediately consume and burn away the dry wood of ordinary perception. They collaborate in the attainment of the supreme and ordinary siddhis. They are not like dancing and singing, in the vulgar, ordinary sense of the word.

It is essential to realize that everything is the display of the deity, mantra, and primordial wisdom, and to meditate upon this unwaveringly. Otherwise, no benefit will be gained. Although there are many deities, peaceful or wrathful, and although the deity may be either the main figure in a mandala or part of the surrounding retinue, the situation is not as it is in the world, where the principal figure is superior to the others. All the deities are the single display of wisdom. By meditating on the deity, by reciting the deity's mantra and so forth, one will gain the ordinary accomplishments of longevity and health, and also the supreme accomplishment or realization, which appears as the wish-fulfilling jewel on the tip of the victory banner—effortlessly fulfilling every wish, and transmuting the entire earth into silver and gold.

The ten elements of the tantras must be known one by one, step-by-step. Once they are mastered, they have the power to bestow the supreme and ordinary accomplishments. They are just like the five elements, which, when combined in a certain way, can produce a machine that can fly through the sky or do the work of a thousand people.

In brief, the gateway to the practice are the four empowerments. These rest upon the four mandalas of body, speech, mind, and primordial wisdom, which in turn have the nature of the four vajras. Even ordinary people, who have not realized infinite purity, possess the supports necessary for the reception of the four empowerments: namely, the channels, winds, essence-drops, and primal wisdom. On the other hand, if the empowerment is not received, it is as if one has a great heap of grain but neglects to plant it. Nothing will grow, and there will be no harvest. The primordial wisdom implicit in the channels, winds, and essence-drops cannot be actualized. But if the empowerments *are* received, the corresponding paths and results—namely, the four kayas—may be gained. If the disciple is a superior being like King Indrabodhi, he or she will realize the result in the very moment of empowerment, and in that instant, the master and disciple will be united in a single wisdom. But even when this is not the case, if a guru endowed with perfect concentration confers the empowerment, the disciple will, at some point in the future, be able to bring the four kayas to maturity. And in the immediate term, he or she is empowered to perform the recitation and meditation, together with the other activities of the Mantrayana.

Just as the act of sharpening confers efficacy on the knife, the four empowerments sown within the soil of the channels, winds, and essence-drops, create the power necessary for the disclosure of their wisdom nature. The realization attained in the course of the empowerment varies from person to person. Only exceptional beings, like King Indrabodhi, who received the *Guhyasamaja* from the Lord Buddha, or the Dharma king Chandrabhadra, who received the *Kalachakra*, experience full realization of the Mahamudra at the very moment of receiving the empowerment. In the case of ordinary people, the abhisheka, or empowerment, both "cleanses and fills." It removes the veils that cover and obscure one's wisdom, and fills the mind with the seeds of the four kayas. Thus it causes to appear clearly what has always been present but has been concealed from time without beginning.

It is hard for ordinary people to gain liberation right away. Nevertheless, if one receives the seeds of the four kayas by means of the empowerments, and if one gradually implements the stages of the practice, these seeds will start to burgeon (just as happens when the farmer plows and plants his fields, tending and fertilizing them). And by and by, the power of the empowerment will make itself felt—though for this to happen, one must practice the stages of generation and perfection. Even so, one should have no expectations of achieving supreme accomplishment in a few months or even years. We should be like venerable Milarepa, who said: "Have no hope of swift attainment; practice till your dying day."

On the other hand, even if one perseveres in the yogas of the generation and perfection stages but fails to keep the samaya, not only will one not achieve accomplishment but one will instead experience the contrary effect. For example, if one practices a long-life sadhana, it will actually shorten one's life. If one tries to make rain, the sun will shine. One should consequently keep the samaya as carefully as one protects one' eyes. It is thus that one will be a true practitioner of the Mantrayana.

If one has not received the empowerment, then no matter how much one practices the generation and perfection stages, nothing will come of it. For there is no seed present. Until he had received empowerment from Marpa, Milarepa was unable to attain any meditative experience or realization. If the samaya between master and disciple is not preserved, the empowerment and the practice that follows will be just a show, no different from a film at the cinema. They will in no way constitute the path of Mantrayana.

661 See chapter 10, commentary to stanza 128, pp. 204–5.

662 [DKR/OC] This was the case when the Lord Buddha granted the empowerment of *Guhyasamaja* to Indrabodhi, and the empowerment of *Kalachakra* to Chandrabhadra, the king of Shambhala.

663 [DKR/OC] Probably a disciple of Buddhaguhya, though his identity is uncertain. His name does not figure in the biographies of the lineage masters.

664 That is, the triple manifestation of body, speech, and mind.

665 As in the case of the *Kalachakra* empowerment.

666 The rising (exhalation) of the wind activates, in the channels, the vowels and consonants (*yi ge*), which are clear in human beings but unclear in the case of animals. This is responsible for the degree of intelligence possessed by the beings in question. [KPS]

667 [DKR/OC] It is said that in one day, a healthy adult experiences 21,600 complete respirations, which means that the average length of a single breath is four seconds. For every 32 1/2 respirations, there is one movement of the wisdom wind. Given that, in the present age, it is said that the limit of human life is one hundred years, the duration of the wisdom breaths taken in a single lifetime, when added together, comes to a total of three years and three months. This is the reason for the duration of the traditional three-year retreat.

668 That is, the downward stroke of the Tibetan letter A; see note 262.

669 [DKR/OC] When the wind of primordial wisdom enters and circulates in these two channels, it becomes an impure karmic wind or wind-mind. See also chapter 10, commentary to stanza 79, p. 165. "Life" here refers to the life-wind, and "exertion" to the essence-drop, and thus to the mind.

670 The practice related to the four activities combined with the recitation of the appropriate mantra. [KPS]

671 This description of the special features of kyerim and dzogrim resembles the analysis made by Lochen Dharma Shri in his commentary on the *Guhyagarbha-tantra.* According to this account, Mahayoga contains features of the perfection stage that are not classified as Anuyoga. See note 98.

672 This refers to the concentration on suchness and the nail of unchanging ultimate wisdom, which the kyerim of the three inner tantras possesses.

Bibliography ⌘

ABBREVIATIONS

T   Tōhoku catalogue (of Kangyur and Tengyur texts)

PT   Peking Tengyur (Otani catalogue)

Ng   Nyingma Gyubum, as catalogued in "THL Master Edition of the Collected Tantras of the Ancients," www.thlib.org/encyclopedias/literary/canons/ngb/catalog.php#cat=ng

NL   Not located

WORKS CITED IN THE TEXT AND NOTES

Abridged Kalachakra-tantra, Laghutantra, *bsdus rgyud* (T 362)

Accomplishment of Wisdom Tantra, *dgongs pa grub pa'i rgyud*

All-Illuminating Essence Tantra, *thig le kun gsal gyi rgyud* (Ng 84)

All-Penetrating Wisdom Tantra, *dgongs pa zang thal*, terma of Rigdzin Godem

Analysis of the Three Vows by Sakya Pandita, *sdom gsum rab dbye*

Arrangement of Samayas, *dam tshig rnam par bkod pa*. See Ng 80 (*dam tshig bkod pa sa gzhi'i rgyud rin po che spungs pa'i rgyan*) or Ng 200 (*dam tshig chen po'i rgyal po dam tshig bkod pa'i rgyud*)

Array of the Path of the Mayajala by Indrabhuti, Māyāpathavyayasthāpana, *sgyu' 'phrul lam rnam par bkod pa* (PT 4737)

Avataṃsaka Sūtra, *mdo phal po che* (T 44)

Bodhisattva Grounds of Realization by Asanga, Bodhisattvabhūmi, *byang sa* (T 4037)

Catalog of Infractions by Ashvaghosha, Sthūlāpatti, *ltung ba sbom po* (T 2479)

Chakrasamvara-tantra, Cakrasaṃvaratantra, *'khor lo sdom pa'i rgyud* (T 385)

Chakrasamvara, Churning Samsara's Depth Tantra, *'khor ba dong sprugs* See Ng 93 (*rgyud thams cad kyi snying po 'khor ba dong sprugs chen po'i rgyud*) or Ng 840 (*thug rje chen po mngon po 'khor ba dong sprugs chen po'i rgyud*)

Churning the Depths of Hell, *na rag dong sprugs*

Compendium of Explanations, *bshad sbyar* (NL)

Compendium of Ritual Geometry by Vimalamitra, *thig gi pindhartha*

Compendium of the Mahayana by Asanga, Mahāyānasaṃgraha, *theg bsdus / theg chen bsdus pa* (T 4048)

Compendium of the Scripture's Secret Meaning by Dharmabodhi, Guhyasūtra-piṇḍārtha, *gsang ba'i mdo don bsdus pa* (T 4663)

Conjunction of the Sun and Moon Tantra, *nyi zla kha sbyor gyi rgyud* (Ng 214)

Dispelling Darkness in the Ten Directions by Longchenpa, *phyogs bcu'i mun sel*

Eighty-Chapter Mayajala, *sgyu 'phrul brgyad bcu pa* (Ng 526)

Elucidation of Samaya by Lilavajra, Samayavivyakti / Samayacitraprakāśa, *dam tshig gsal bkra* (Beijing Tg 4744)

Embodiments of the Sugatas by Nyangral Nyima Özer, *bde 'dus*

Essence of Primordial Wisdom Tantra, Jñānatilakatantra, *ye shes thig le'i rgyud* (T 422)

Established Secrets by Saroruha (Padmavajra), *gsang ba grub pa*

Exposition of the Specific Aspects of the Mayajala, *sgyu 'phrul bye brag bstan pa*

Extensive Mayajala, *sgyu 'phrul rgyas pa* (Ng 527)

Five Stages by Nagarjuna, Pañcakrama, *rim lnga* (T 1802)

Fundamental Text: The Lamp that Clarifies the Meaning of the Names, a commentary on the Namasamgiti by Vimalamitra, Nāmasaṃgīti-vṛtti-nāmārtha-prakāśa-karaṇadīpa, *mtshan yang dag par brjod pa'i 'grel pa mtshan don gsal bar byed pa'i sgron ma / gsal sgron (khog gzhung)* (T 2092)

Garland of the Teachings of the Aural Lineage, *rna brgyud lung gi phreng ba*

Gathering of the Great Glorious One, terma by Jigme Lingpa, *dpal chen 'dus pa*

General Scripture of Summarized Wisdom, Samājasarvavidyāsūtra, *spyi mdo dgongs pa 'dus pa* (T 829)

Guhyagarbha-tantra, Tantra of the Secret Essence, *gsang ba snying po* (T 832, Ng 524 et seq.)

Guhyasamaja, Union of Secrets Tantra, Guhyasamājatantra, *gsang 'dus* (T 442)

Heap of Jewels, Ratnakūṭa, *dkon mchog brtsegs pa* (T 45–93)

Heart Essence of the Dakini, *mkha' 'gro snying thig*

Heart Essence of Vimalamitra, *bi ma'i snying thig*

Heart Essence, *thugs thig*

Heruka Galpo Tantra, *he ru ka gal po'i rgyud* (Ng 646)

Hevajra Tantra, *kye rdo rje'i rgyud* (T 417)

Holding the Root of Virtue Sutra, Kuśalamūlasamparigraha, *dge rtsa yongs su 'dzin pa'i mdo* (T 101)

Illuminating Lamp, *sgron ma snang byed* (*alternative title for Great Perfection endowed with Conch Syllables*) (In *bi ma'i snying thig*)

Illumination of Reality by Anandagarbha, Tattvālokakarīvyākhyā, *de nyid snang byed* (T 2510)

Instructions on the Great Glorious One by Jigme Lingpa, *dpal chen zhal lung*

Introduction to the Middle Way by Chandrakirti, Madhyamakāvatāra, *dbu ma la 'jug pa* (T 3861)

Jataka, Life Stories of the Buddha, *skye rabs* (T 4150–4157)

Kalachakra-tantra, Wheel of the Time Tantra, Kālacakratantra, *dus 'khor gyi rgyud* (T 362)

Kila Tantra, Kīlatantra, *phur pa'i rgyud* (Ng 671 et seq.)

King of Concentration Sutra, Samādhirājasūtra, *ting 'dzin rgyal po'i mdo* (T 127)

King of Supreme Empowerment Tantra, *dbang mchog rgyal po'i rgyud* (Ng 141)

Lamp for the Path of Enlightenment by Atisha, Bodhipathapradīpa, *byang chub lam gyi sgron me* (T 3947)

Lamp of Certainty by Mipham Rinpoche, *nges shes sgron me*

Lamp of the Three Modes by Tripitakamala, Nayatrayapradīpa, *tshul gsum sgron me* (T 3707)

Lamp that Integrates the Practices by Aryadeva, Caryāmelāpakapradīpa, *spyod pa bsdus pa'i sgron ma* (T 1803)

Lankavatara-sutra, Laṅkāvatārasūtra, *lang kar gshegs pa'i mdo* (T 107)

Later Meditation Tantra, Dhyānottarapaṭalakramatantra, *bsam gtan phyi ma'i rgyud* (T 808)

Luminous Expanse Tantra, *klong gsal gyi rgyud* (Ng 139)

Mahaparinirvana-sutra, Mahāparinirvāṇasutra, *mya ngan las 'das pa chen po'i mdo* (T 120–121)

Mahayana Pitaka, Mahāyānapiṭaka, *theg chen sde snod*. See Bodhisattvapiṭaka, *byang chub sems dpa'i sde snod* (T 56)

Manjushri Nama Sanghiti, Litany of the Names of Manjushri, Mañjuśrīnāma-saṃghīti, *'jam dpal mtshan brjod* (T 360)

Mayajala-tantra, Tantra of the Net of Illusory Manifestations, Māyājālatantra, *sgyu 'phrul drva ba'i rgyud* (T 466)

Mound of Gems Tantra, *rin po che spungs pa'i rgyud* (See Ng 55, 110, 118, 203, 421)

Mūlamadhyamaka-kārikā by Nāgārjuna, Root Stanzas on the Middle Way, *dbu ma rtsa ba shes rab* (T 3824)

Net of Illusory Manifestations Tantra, Māyājālatantra, *sgyu 'phrul drva ba'i rgyud* (T 466)

Ocean Tantra, from the cycle of the *Māyājāla*, *(sgyu 'phrul) rgya mtsho'i rgyud* (Ng 534)

Peaceful Tantra of the Eight Herukas, Embodiments of the Sugatas, terma by Nyangral Nyima Özer, *bka' brgyad bde gshegs 'dus pa'i rgyud*

Pearl Necklace Tantra, Muktikāvalī, *mu tig 'phreng ba'i rgyud* (T 1189, Ng 100)

Plenitude of Secrets of the Eight Mandalas by Guru Chöwang, *bka' brgyad gsang ba yongs rdzogs*

Praise of the Dharmadhatu by Nagarjuna, Dharmadhātustava, *chos dbyings bstod pa* (T 1118)

Prajnaparamita in Eight Thousand Lines, Aṣṭasāhasrikā, *brgyad stong pa* (T 12)

Precious Jewel Commentary by Rongdzom Pandita, *dkon mchog 'grel pa*

Precious Treasury of the Dharmadhatu by Longchenpa, *chos dbyings rin po che'i mdzod*

Precious Treasury of the Supreme Vehicle by Longchenpa, *theg mchog rin po che'i mdzod*

Precious Treasury of Words and Meanings by Longchenpa, *tshig don rin po che'i mdzod*

Precious Treasury that Fulfills All Wishes by Longchenpa, *yid bzhin rin po che'i mdzod*

Presentation of the Stages by Buddhajnanapada, probably Herukasādhanavṛtti (T 1858), *rim pa rnam par bzhag pa*

Primordial Wisdom Similar to Space Tantra, *ye shes nam mkha' dang mnyam pa'i rgyud* (Ng 150)

Proofs of the Mahayana, *theg chen tshul grub* (Ng 764?)

Ratnakuta, Heap of Jewels, Ratnakūṭa, *dkon mchog brtsegs pa* (T 45–93)

Sambhuti, Perfect Union, explanatory tantra of Hevajra, Samputa?, *yang dag par sbyor ba'i rgyud* (T 381)

Sarvabuddhasamayoga, Union with the Buddhas Tantra, Sarvabuddhasamāyogadāki-nījalaśaṃvaratantra, *sangs rgyas thams cad dang mnyam sbyor ba mkha' 'gro ma sgyu ma bde ba'i mchog gi rgyud* (T 366)

Scripture of All-Inclusive Knowledge, *kun 'dus rig pa'i mdo* (Ng 479)

Scripture of Summarized Wisdom, Samājasarvavidyāsūtra, *mdo dgongs pa 'dus pa* (T 829)

Secret Heart-Essence by Vimalamitra, *gsang ba snying thig*

Secret Moon Essence Tantra, Candraguhyatilakatantra, *zla gsang thig le'i rgyud* (T 477)

Secret Tantra of General Rites, *gsang ba spyi rgyud* (Ng 56)

Secret Treasury, *gsang mdzod* (T830, Ng 481)

Sequence for the Vajra Mayajala by Buddhaguhya, Māyājālavajrakarmakrama, *sgyu 'phrul rdo rje las rim* (PT 4731)

Stages of the Path of the Mayajala, by Buddhaguhya, Māyājālapathakrama, *sgyu 'phrul drva ba'i lam rim*

Stainless Confession Tantra, *dri med gshags rgyud* (Ng 557)

Stanzas on the Middle Way by Nagarjuna, Mūlamadhyamakakārikā, *dbu ma rtsa ba shes rab* (T 3824)

Sublime Continuum by Maitreya/Asanga, Uttaratantraśāstra, *rgyud bla ma* (T 4024)

Subsequent Tantra (from the Guhyagarbha cycle), *rgyud phyi ma* (Ng 536)

Subtle and Extensive Samayas by Lilavajra, Samayānuśayanirdeśa, *dam tshig phra rgyas* (PT 4745)

Summary of Samayas by Atisha, Sarvasamayasaṃgraha, *dam tshig bsdus pa* (T 3725)

Supreme Samaya Tantra, *dam tshig mchog gi rgyud* (NL)

Sutra of Liberation, Pratimokṣasūtra, *so sor thar pa'i mdo* (T 2)

Sutra of the Hundred Actions, Karmaśataka, *las brgya pa* (T 340)

Sutra of the Questions of King Dharanishvara, Dhāraṇīśvararājaparipṛcchāsūtra, *gzungs kyi dbang phyug rgyal pos zhus pa'i mdo*, an alternative name for the Sutra of the Elucidation of the Great Compassion of the Tathagata, Tathāgatamahā-karunānirdeśasūtra, *de bzhin gshegs pa'i snying rje chen po nges par bstan pa'i mdo* (T 147)

Sutra of the Questions of Rashtrapala, Rāṣṭrapālaparipṛcchāsūtra, *yul 'khor skyong gis zhus pa'i mdo* (T 62 / 166)

Sutra of the Quintessence of Primordial Wisdom, *ye shes snying po'i mdo*, see Jñāna-garbhatantra, *ye shes snying po rgyud* (T 421) or Jñānasārasammucaya, *ye shes snying po kun las btus pa* (T 3851)

Sutra of the Teaching on the Non-Arising of All Things, Sarvadharmāpravṛtti-nirdeśa, *chos thams cad 'byung ba med par bstan pa* (T 180)

Sutra on the Wisdom of the Moment of Death, Atyayajñānasūtra, 'da' ka ye shes kyi mdo (T 122)

Tantra of Auspicious Beauty, bkra shis mdzes ldan gyi rgyud (Ng 106)

Tantra of Awareness Self-Arisen, rig pa rang shar gyi rgyud (Ng 96)

Tantra of Black Yamari, Yamārikrṣṇatantra, dgra nag po'i rgyud (T 473)

Tantra of Mahamaya, sgyu 'phrul chen po'i rgyud (T 425)

Tantra of Manjushri (explanatory tantra), 'jam dpal bshad rgyud (Ng 74)

Tantra of Meaningful Effort, brtson pa don ldan gyi rgyud (Ng 489)

Tantra of Red Yamari, Raktayamāritantra, gshed dmar rgyud (T 474)

Tantra of the All-Creating King, kun byed rgyal po'i rgyud (Ng 10, T 828)

Tantra of the Empowerment of Vajrapani, Vajrapāṇyabhiṣekatantra, phyag na rdo rje mngon par dbang bskur ba'i rgyud (T 496)

Tantra of the Enlightenment of Vairochana, Vairocanābhisaṃbodhitantra, rnam snang mngon byang gi rgyud (T 494)

Tantra of the Four Seats, Catuḥpīṭhatantra, gdan bzhi pa' rgyud (T 428)

Tantra of the Glorious and Supreme Primordial Buddha, Śrīparamādyatantra, dpal mchog dang po'i rgyud, see Kalachakra

Tantra of the Great Array of Ati, a ti bkod pa chen po'i rgyud (Ng 277)

Tantra of the Great Nirvana of Kila, phur pa myang 'das chen po'i rgyud (Ng 679)

Tantra of the Lion's Perfect Power, seng ge rtsal rdzogs kyi rgyud (Ng 101)

Tantra of the Ornament of the Vajra Essence, Vajrahṛdayālaṃkāratantra, rdo rje snying po rgyan gyi rgyud (T 451)

Tantra of the Play of Chakrasamvara, bde mchog rol pa'i rgyud (NL)

Tantra of the Questions of Subahu, Subāhuparipṛcchātantra, dpung bzang gis zhus pa'i rgyud (T 805)

Tantra of the Sacred Primordial Buddha, dam pa dang po'i rgyud, see Kalachakra

Tantra of the Six Expanses, klong drug gi rgyud (Ng 99)

Tantra of the Vast Expanse of Space, nam mkha' klong yangs kyi rgyud (Ng 121/146)

Tantra of the Wondrous King, rmad byung rgyal po'i rgyud (T 413 or 422)

Terrifying Lightning Tantra, rngam glog gi rgyud (T 830, Ng 481–482)

Testament, 'das rjes, by Garab Dorje (Ng 331?)

Three Stages by Vimalamitra, Māyājālopadeśakramatraya, *rim gsum* (PT 4742)

Treasury of Teachings by Longchenpa, *lung gi gter mdzod*, (auto-commentary on the Precious Treasury of the Dharmadhātu)

Twenty-Eight Samayas (by Ngari Pandita?), *dam tshig nyer brgyad pa*

Two Segments (condensed version of Hevajra Tantra), *brtag gnyis*

Union with the Buddhas Tantra, Sarvabuddhasamāyoga, *sangs rgyas mnyam sbyor* (T 366)

Unwritten Tantra, *yi ge med pa'i rgyud* (Ng 108)

Vajra Garland Tantra, Vajramālā, *rdo rje phreng ba'i rgyud* (T 445 or Ng 693)

Vajra Mayajala, Vajra of the Net of Illusory Manifestations, *sgyu 'phrul rdo rje* (explanatory tantra of the Māyājāla) (Ng 534)

Vajra Mirror Tantra, *rdo rje me long* (explanatory tantra from Māyājāla cycle) (Ng 533)

Vajra Peak Tantra, Vajraśekharatantra, *rdo rje rtse mo'i rgyud* (T 480)

Vajra Pinnacle Tantra, *rdo rje yang tog gi rgyud* (Ng 78)

Vajra Sun Array Tantra, *rdo rje nyi ma rnam par bkod pa'i rgyud* (NL)

Vajra Tent Tantra, Vajrapañjaratantra, *rdo rje gur gyi rgyud* (T 419)

Vajra Ushnisha Tantra, Vajroṣṇīṣatantra, *rdo rje gtsug tor gyi rgyud*

Vajrasattva Mayajala-tantra, Net of Illusory Manifestations of Vajrasattva, *rdo rje sems dpa' sgyu 'phrul drva ba'i rgyud* (T 833, Ng 527)

Verses that Summarize the Prajnaparamita-sutra, Prajñāpāramitāsaṃcāyagāthā, *mdo sdud pa (sher phyin sdud pa tshigs su bcad pa)*

Vishuddha Tantra, *yang dag gi rgyud* (Ng 851)

Vision of Vajrasattva, *rdor sems zhal mthong gi le'u* (Eighty-chapter Māyājāla) (Ng 526)

Way of the Bodhisattva by Shantideva, Bodhicāryāvatāra, *spyod 'jug* (T 3871)

Wheel of Wisdom Tantra, *ye shes 'khor lo'i rgyud* (Ng 157)

Wisdom Ornament of the Lord of Secrets by Dharmashri, *gsang bdag dgongs rgyan* (Ng 562)

Word-Transcending Tantra, *sgra thal 'gyur gyi rgyud* (Ng 95)

Yamantaka Tantra, *gshin rje'i rgyud* (Ng 594–629, 768 et seq.)

Tibetan Sources

Dodrup Jigme Trinle Özer (*rdo grub 'jigs med phrin las 'od zer*). The Precious Key (*yon tan rin po che'i mdzod kyi sgo lcags 'byed byed bsdus 'grel rgya mtsho'i chu thigs rin chen lde mig*). Chengdu: Sichuan edition, 1998.

Dudjom Rinpoche Jigdrel Yeshe Dorje (*'jigs bral ye shes rdo rje*). Fundamentals of the Nyingma School (*gsang sngags snga 'gyur rnying ma pa'i bstan pa'i rnam bzhag mdo tsam brjod pa legs bshad snang ba'i dga' ston*). In Collected Writings and Revelations of His Holiness Bdud-'joms Rin-po-che 'Jigs-bral-ye-śes-rdo-rje. Kalimpong: Dupjung Lama, 1979, vol. 2 (kha).

Jamgön Kongtrul (*'jam mgon kong sprul*). Treasury of Knowledge (*shes bya kun khyab*). Beijing: mi rigs dpe skrun khang (Minorities Publishing House), 2002.

Longchen Rabjam (*klong chen rab 'byams*). Precious Treasury of Words and Meanings (*gsang ba bla na med pa'i 'od gsal rdo rje snying po'i gnas gsum gsal bar byed pa'i tshig don rinpoche'i mdzod*). Dodrupchen Rinpoche, Sikkim National Press, Gangtok, [1975?].

Longchen Rabjam (*klong chen rab 'byams*). Treasury of Teachings (*chos dbyings rin po che'i mdzod kyi 'grel pa lung gi gter mdzod*). Dodrupchen Rinpoche, Sikkim National Press, Gangtok, [1975?].

Sogpo Tendar (*sog po ngag dbang bstan dar*). The Golden Scalpel (*yon tan rin po che'i mdzod kyi dka' gnad rdo rje'i rgya mdud 'grol byed legs bshad gser gyi thur ma*). Kyichu Monastery, Bhutan, 1978.

Yönten Gyamtso (*yon tan rgya mtsho*). Refulgence of the Sun (*yon tan rin po che'i mdzod kyi 'grel pa zab don snang byed nyi ma'i 'od zer*). In Bdud-'Joms 'Jigs-bral-ye-śes-rdo-rje (ed.), Rñiṇ ma Bka' ma rgyas pa (expanded edition of the Nyingma Kahma in 58 volumes). Kalimpong: Dupjung Lama, 1982–1987, volume 40 (thi).

Yönten Gyamtso (*yon tan rgya mtsho*). The Lamp of the Moon (*yon tan rin po che'i mdzod kyi 'grel pa bden gnyis gsal byed zla ba'i sgron me*). In Bdud-'Joms 'Jigs-bral-ye-śes-rdo-rje (ed.), Rñiṇ ma Bka' ma rgyas pa (expanded edition of the Nyingma Kahma in 58 volumes). Kalimpong: Dupjung Lama, 1982–1987, volumes 38, 39 (nyi, ti).

Western Sources

Dalai Lama. *The Kalachakra Tantra: Rite of Initiation.* London: Wisdom Publications, 1985.

———. *Opening the Eye of New Awareness.* London: Wisdom Publications, 1985.

———. *The World of Tibetan Buddhism.* Boston: Wisdom Publications, 1995.

Dudjom Rinpoche, Jikdrel Yeshe Dorje. *The Nyingma School of Tibetan Buddhism.* Boston: Wisdom Publications, 1991.

Gyalwa Changchub and Namkha'i Nyingpo. *Lady of the Lotus-Born.* Translated by the Padmakara Translation Group. Boston: Shambhala Publications, 1999.

Jamgön Kongtrul. *Buddhist Ethics.* Ithaca, N.Y.: Snow Lion Publications, 2003.

————. *The Elements of Tantric Practice.* Ithaca, N.Y.: Snow Lion Publications, 2008.

————. *The Light of Wisdom.* Boston: Shambhala Publications, 1995.

————. *Myriad Worlds.* Ithaca, N.Y.: Snow Lion Publications, 2003.

————. *Systems of Buddhist Tantra.* Ithaca, N.Y.: Snow Lion Publications, 2005.

Jigme Lingpa and Kangyur Rinpoche. *Treasury of Precious Qualities.* Book 1. Translated by the Padmakara Translation Group. Boston: Shambhala Publications, 2010.

Lhundup Sopa, Roger Jackson, and John Newman. *Wheel of Time.* Madison, Wisc.: Deer Park Books, 1985.

Patrul Rinpoche. *The Words of My Perfect Teacher.* Translated by the Padmakara Translation Group. Boston: Shambhala Publications, 1998.

Shantarakshita and Mipham. *Adornment of the Middle Way (Madhyamalankara).* Translated by the Padmakara Translation Group. Boston: Shambhala Publications, 2005.

Tsele Natsok Rangdrol. *The Mirror of Mindfulness.* Boston: Shambhala Publications, 1989.

Tulku Thondup. *Buddha Mind.* Ithaca, N.Y.: Snow Lion Publications, 1989.

————. *Hidden Teachings of Tibet.* London: Wisdom Publications, 1986.

————. *Masters of Meditation and Miracles.* Boston: Shambhala Publications, 1996.

Index

Ashvaghosha. *See* Shura
Atisha, xxi, 122, 422n343
    on third empowerment, 389
atiyoga, 7, 45, 108, 240, 384n141,
        424n377
    defined, 378n101, 470n611
    empowerments of, 122, 385n149,
        385n150
    practice of, 450n491
    transmission lineage of, 328–31
avadhuti. *See* central channel (*uma*)

bardo
    deities appearing in, 263–64
    practice of, 170, 176–77, 419n316,
        419n321
    purification of. *See* perfection stage:
        six yogas
bhaga, mandala of, 128
Bhawilha. *See* Shura
birth
    four ways of being born, 135,
        393n208. *See also* generation stage
    process analogous to the path, 15,
        135, 142
blazing and dripping, 416n310
bodhichitta
    abandonment of, 26, 181
    essence-drop, 155, 164, 405n254,
        406n255
        gross, 130–31, 390n190
        loss (emission) of, 29, 185
        positioned, 19, 22, 163–64
    pure and accomplished mind, 236,
        433n441, 438n456
    ultimate (nature of mind), 126, 131,
        376n83, 406n255
bodhisattvas, male and female
    outer and inner, 286, 463n543
    retinues of Buddhas, 64, 288,
        296–97, 337
    their seats: sense organs and objects,
        127, 378n97

body
    of manifest enlightenment. *See* abhi-
        sambodhikaya
    of peaceful ultimate reality. *See* dhar-
        makaya
    of perfect enjoyment. *See* sambhoga-
        kaya
    unchanging and indestructible. *See*
        vajra body (vajrakaya)
brahma aperture, 19, 156, 458n523
Buddha(s)
    male and female (aggregates and
        elements), 88, 127, 213, 387n97
    mind transmission of. *See* transmis-
        sion
    perceptions of, 438n459, 474n638,
        475n644
    their knowledge of perceptions of
        beings, 342–43, 345, 473n634
    their retinues, 463n543
    of the sixth family, 325, 468n588
buddhafield(s)
    five, that grant release and freedom,
        264, 301–4
    nirmanakaya, 70
    of luminous character, 242, 264,
        294–95, 300, 304
    sambhogakaya, 242, 286–87, 292, 315
    of Shakyamuni, 343
    in vajrayana, 472n632
    See also pure lands
Buddhaguhya, 101, 330, 354, 375n76
    on six kinds of Akanishtha, 462n538
Buddhajnanapada, 375n76, 422n342
    on vajra kinship, 184
buddha-nature, 28, 187, 281
    ground of purification, 86
    in Mantrayana, 86, 89, 109, 477n660
    nature of the mind, 89, 406n254
    not an expedient teaching, 30, 187
    in Sutrayana, 86
    three kayas of inner luminosity and,
        280

calm abiding, 57–58, 244, 270–72. *See also* shamatha

central channel
description of, 19, 156–58, 165, 168, 407n261
entry of essence-drops, 131, 404n249, 411n273
entry of winds into, 22, 129, 162–63, 404n249
expanse of Rahu, 165
killing of thoughts in, 219, 221
knots on, 22, 165, 406n254
location, 156
threefold classification of, 408n261, 408n264
See also blazing and dripping; channels

chakra(s)
bliss-preserving (secret), 158
different accounts of, 409n268, 410n270
in *Kalachakra*, 410n271, 413n287
in *Mayajala tantra*, 159, 411n277
of enjoyment (throat), 161, 387n175, 409n269
four joys and, 421n325
of great bliss (crown of head), 158, 409n269, 411n279
meditation on, 157, 410n270
position of, 157–58
of space (ushnisha), 158–59, 409n269, 413n287
of ultimate reality (heart), 166, 168, 388n180, 409n269

channel wheels. *See* chakra(s)

channels, 155–57, 166
of the eyes, 274, 458n523
generation stage and, 378n98, 404n248
in *Kalachakra*, 410n271
knots on, 12, 19, 131, 156–57, 387n177
like watercourses, 22, 419n316
pulsation of, 11, 128, 391n195, 407n259, 430n435

radial, 158, 160, 168, 407n259
division of, 410n270
sacred lands and, 164, 360
support for elements and life-wind, 133
for thought-free and coemergent wisdom, 179
for vase empowerment, 124
visualization of, 410n270
See also roma and kyangma

charnel ground, eight accoutrements of, 149–50

Charyatantra (conduct tantra), 6, 9, 95–97, 99, 103, 118. *See also* Ubhaya Charya vs Kriya, 100

Chemchok, 138, 394n211, 394n214, 394n215. *See also* Mahottara heruka

Churning the Depths of Hell, 227, 429n430

cognitive potency, 43, 45, 132, 237
appearances of the ground and, 239
vs compassion, xxix, 390n193
creative power of (*rtsal*), 235, 259, 450n496
as nirmanakaya, 232, 393n209
radiance of, 238–39, 243, 245–46, 317
source of nirmanakaya, 293
source of sambhogakaya, 62, 282
state of clarity and knowing, 440n470
See also ground

concentration
conceptual and nonconceptual, 104, 129
days of, 264
diamond-like, 398n235, 437n455
fearless or heroic, 398n235
mandala of superior, 353–54, 462n538
mirage-like, 398n235
in restoration of samaya, 226

concentration beings (samadhisattva), 400n242

consort(s), skillful path of, 38, 126, 154, 177–78, 419n316

consort(s) (*continued*)
  outer, inner, and secret, 219
  qualified, 420n325
  secret mandala of, 130, 388n185, 388–89n186
  unsuitable, 31, 190, 215
creative power of awareness. *See* ground

dakinis, 72, 189, 190
  drawn by samaya substances, 34, 204
  transmission entrusted to, 84, 369n6
death
  bardo at moment of, 177, 263, 438n459
  ground-luminosity at, 11, 12, 236, 246
  instructions for moment of (related to four empowerments), 128–32
  purification of death moment, 139, 395n222
  transference of consciousness, 170, 177, 390n194
defeats, 181, 185, 422n336, 428n421
  vs infractions, 31, 190
  of Shravakayana, 223
  See also downfalls; infractions, eight
defilements (five)
  in different vehicles, 260–61, 426n396, 427n406
  dissolve into primordial wisdom, 342–44, 446n485, 472n631
  five winds and, 162–63
  impure channels and, 410n272
  intrinsic purity of, 145, 342, 384n135
  purified by four empowerments, 385n150
  source of downfalls, 222
  used on the path, 34, 36, 126, 179, 197, 427n406
deity (deities)
  aggregates as, 187, 197
  appearing as three kinds of object, 399n240
  appearing in the bardo, 263–64
  change position in mandala, 106–170, 377n94

concentration on. *See under* four life-fastening nails
depiction of in outer tantras, 5–7, 13–14, 97–99
depiction of male and female in inner tantras, 106–7
peaceful, 21, 286, 411n277, 464n546
  eight ornaments, 149
  five garments of, 149
  forty-two, 64, 65, 160, 286, 288, 411n277
  nine peaceful expressions, 148, 401n245
phenomena as, 18, 92, 187, 213, 277, 342, 475n643, 478n660
pride of the deity, 399n241
principle of "six deities," 101, 375n77
status of deity and meditator in outer tantras, 100–105
of the three seats, 37, 64, 145, 148, 363, 407n258
ultimate deity, 345, 425n395, 475n644
wheels of peaceful and wrathful, 21, 159–60, 411n277, 464n546
wisdom beings and, 400n244
wrathful, 411n277, 464n544, 464n546
  nine wrathful demeanors, 66, 149, 401n245
  eight accoutrements, 149–50
  in wrathful mandala of lower palace, 287–91
delusion
  cause of, 244, 250, 263, 405n254, 476n657
  door of, 239, 242, 439n460
  essence-drop of, 405n254
  four conditions of, 47, 71, 245–46, 304
  vs freedom, 262, 434n443, 439n460, 454n500
  ground of, 262, 372n23
  higher vs lower, 239, 438n459
  manner of arising, 247, 454n500

no delusion in ground, 47, 235, 237, 372n33, 453n500

no potential for in place of freedom, 262, 454n502

Dense Array. *See* Akanishtha

dependent arising, twelvefold chain of, 47, 246, 363, 392n200, 417n311
corresponding to twelve wind transits, 20, 158, 410n271
in the Great Perfection, 246

detection (*yongs gcod*), 235, 253

deteriorations, five, 225, 429n422

Dharma, wheel of, 231, 432n439

dharmadhatu, wisdom of. *See* five primordial wisdoms

dharmakaya, 12, 24, 208, 262, 278, 280
awareness, 262, 267, 433n441, 448n490
emptiness, 169, 261, 393n209, 453n499
essence-drop of bliss and emptiness, 405n251
fields, 440n466
great, 88, 341, 351, 372n30, 424n382, 471n630
ground of rupakaya, 305, 309, 312
sambhogakaya gathered into, 76, 315
vs universal ground, 54, 261, 379n111, 395n222, 451n499, 453n499

dharmatā, 61, 87
buddha-nature, 281
ground, 237, 434n443
mandala of the three seats, 372n34
nature of the mind, 101, 126
ultimate deity, 345, 425n395

disciples
correct attitude and conduct of, 336–39
qualities of authentic, 8, 116

downfalls
abandonment of bodhichitta, 29, 181, 185
abandonment of loving attitude, 185, 200, 422n336, 423n363

complete, 181–82, 428n421

conditions for, 26

degenerate objects (in relation to tenth downfall), 428n417

entangling attitudes, 181–82, 422n334

four sources of, 40, 222–23

fourteen, 27–33, 182, 183–90, repairing of, 32–33, 41, 192–95, 226

root, 422n335

scriptural sources describing, 192

downward-voiding wind. *See* winds: five main

dream yoga. *See* perfection stage: six yogas

Drogmi Shakya Yeshe, 422n343

É WAM, meaning of, 109, 379n108, 379n110

eight common accomplishments, 228, 401n245, 430n433

eight qualities of mastery, 42, 228, 430n435

eight similes of illusion, 417n311

elements, 109, 133, 156, 379n105
basis of empowerment, 121, 385n145, 406n256
dissolution of (in trekchö), 268
eyes of, 156, 458n523
five female Buddhas, 127, 187, 190
quintessence(s) of, 168, 405n254
refined into light (thögal), 57, 268
winds of, 108, 154, 160–62, 414n296

embryo
development analogous to five paths, 142–43
purification of its development, 140–42

empowerment(s), 8–13, 112
according to classes of tantra
Anuttara, 118–23
Anuyoga, 121
Atiyoga, 122
Charya, 118

empowerment(s) (*continued*)
    Kriya, 117
    Mahayoga, 120
    Yoga, 118
    causes and conditions of, 123–25
    benefits of, 113, 114, 134, 382n122
    four, 125
        of atiyoga, 122, 385n150
        secret, 126, 128
        vase, 125, 127
        wisdom, 126, 130
        word ("fourth"), 126, 131, 385n149,
           385n150
    given compassionately to the
        unsuitable, 382n120
    granted in the manner of a king, 329,
        330, 470n613
    meaning of term, 132
    preparatory stages of, 116–17,
        383n128
    related to ground (cause), path, and
        result, 123, 133, 391n198
    through great rays of light, 134
emptiness
    endowed with supreme attributes,
        348, 351, 474n642, 475n644
    known only by self-cognizing
        awareness, 476n648
entangling attitudes. *See under* downfalls
equality, wisdom of. *See* five primordial
    wisdoms
essence-drops
    attainment of grounds and, 23, 159,
        165
    bliss, clarity, no-thought, 179,
        406n255, 411n273, 414n293
    classification of, 405n254
    control of, 158–59, 165, 404n249,
        421n325
    in Great Perfection, 413n287
    linked with body, 127, 387n169
    linked with mind, 130, 390n188
    linked with speech, 128, 387n175
    melting of, 12, 130, 219

    non-emission of (in both sexes), 164,
        421n325
    purified by empowerment, 126–33
    purified by tummo, 416n306, 416n310
    signs of purification of, 390n191
    substantial, meditation on, 405n254
    support of mind, 126, 168
    support of ultimate bodhichitta, 131
example wisdom, 12, 131, 219
    of third initiation, 385n149, 478n660

fire-accompanying wind. *See* wind(s):
    five main
five certainties (of sambhogakaya), 18,
    62, 153, 282
five "contaminated" yogas, 403n248
five deteriorations, 225, 429n422
five factors of awakening. *See under*
    generation stage
five meats and five nectars, 189, 220,
    374n65
    not used in outer tantras, 5, 100
five nectars, fourfold establishment and
    three ways of being, 204, 351
five primordial wisdoms, 203–5,
    294–96, 298–99
    attendant wisdoms, 295–96
    correlated with ten grounds, 299
    five winds foundation for, 162
five utterly pure poisons, 204
four doors of practice. *See under* Kriya-
    tantra
four expository methods. *See* four ways
    of exposition
four factors of awakening. *See under*
    generation stage
four kayas, 13, 133, 134, 391n195
    result of empowerment, 114, 134
    "result empowerments," 123, 386n155
four lamps (*sgron ma*)
    of the empty disks of light, 274
    of the far-catching water lasso, 274,
        458n523
    of self-arisen wisdom, 258, 275,
        458n523

of the utterly pure ultimate expanse, 458n523

four life-fastening nails, 148, 398n236

nail of concentration on the deity, 148, 399n241, 402n245

three functions of, 400n241

nail of enlightened activity, 152, 401n245

nail of mantra, 151, 400n242, 400n243

nail of unchanging ultimate wisdom, 151–52, 381n115, 402n245

related to view, meditation, conduct and result, 401n245

four lights (*snang ba*), 109, 172

four mudras (or seals), 199, 221, 351, 404n248

and deities, 14, 138

four states (waking, deep sleep, dream, orgasm), 127–31, 134, 421n325

four vajras, 112, 133, 134, 352, 480n660

four voids, 109, 172

four ways of exposition (*tshul bzhi*), 333, 335–36

fourth time, 67, 293, 307, 317, 464n543. *See also* wheel of everlasting continuity

Gangchentso, Buddha, 440n465. *See also* Mahasagara

Garab Dorje, 303, 328–30, 467n573, 467n574, 470n614

Testament of, 275, 459n526

Gathering of the Great Assembly (*tshogs chen 'dus pa*), 64, 287, 385n144, 385n146

generation stage, 106, 111, 125, 135, 147

five factors of awakening, 142–45

four factors of awakening, 139–41

four phases of, related to five paths and four Vidyādharas, 152–53

four special features of, 363

generating oneself as the child of others, 137

generating others as one's children, 136

practiced inseparably with perfection-stage, 106

purification of four kinds of birth

egg, 17, 135, 136, 139, 395n222

miraculous, 17, 135, 146, 147, 396n23

warmth and moisture, 16–17, 146–47

womb, 135, 139, 146

purification, perfection, and ripening, 135, 395n222, 401n244

three concentrations, 147–48, 393n209, 396n234, 396n235

in *Mayajala*, 394n213

three vajra methods, 15, 139, 141

great bliss

chakra of, 158, 409n269, 411n279

empowerment of, 121, 131

vs sexual pleasure, 421n326

unchanging, 159, 229, 421n325, 421n327

wisdom of, 416n310, 419n316

Great Perfection

five extraordinary paths of, 274

mind class, 52, 54, 254, 261, 444n483, 447n487

pith instruction class, 52, 54, 255, 385n150, 444n483, 460

vs prajnaparamita (madhyamaka), 231, 252, 436n454, 441n476

self-cognizing awareness in, 433n441

space class, 52, 255, 261, 443n482, 444n483

ten distinctions of awareness from ordinary mind, 257–65

two kinds of person able to realize, 451n497

view of, 265, 455n509

way of dying of practitioners of, 456n514, 459n527

See also thögal, trekchö

ground (in the Great Perfection)

appearance of, 236, 238, 241–42, 434n443

lower door, the path of. *See under* perfection stage

luminosity
empty, 236, 238, 374n58, 448n489
example (child), 129, 176, 419n319, 419n320
ground, 131, 176, 236, 419n321
inner, 77, 236–39, 438n457
three kayas of, 279–81, 435n446, 437n455, 460n533, 461n535
manifest, 69, 300, 304, 402n245
meeting of mother and child, 131
outwardly radiating, 280–81, 435n446, 461n535
two kayas of, 282, 460n529
three lights and, 176–77, 419n321
ultimate (mother), 140, 176, 388n182

madhyamaka (middle way)
great madhyamaka of union, 231, 433n440
Great Perfection and, 231, 252, 436n454
vs tantra, 107, 378n95, 427n406
Mahasagara (Gangchentso), 242, 308, 440n465, 467n564
Mahayoga, 107, 277, 333, 378n97, 469n606
eighteen empowerments of, 121, 383n125
perfection stage of, 107, 378n98, 482n671
transmission lineage of, 327, 330
See also tantra: father
Mahottara heruka, 65, 288, 289, 394n211, 394n214. *See also* Chemchok
mandala, 7, 8, 10, 148, 382n118
fourfold classification of, 353–57
of the experience of awareness, 354
natural mandala of primordial wisdom, 353

of superior concentration, 353
of superior representation, 355
peaceful (upper palace), 64, 286–87, 464n546
of the secret space, 11, 31, 14, 128, 130
of the self-display of primordial wisdom, 343, 473n634
of the three seats, 64, 127, 145, 407n258
wrathful (lower palace), 64, 287–92, 464n546
Manjushrimitra (Jampel Shenyen), 330, 422n342, 459n526
mantras, threefold classification, 100
Mantrayana
approach of, 87, 88, 93, 372n25
compared with Sutrayana, 86, 92, 352
etymology, 86
six paramitas in, 92
supports for, 406n256
synonyms for, 87
twelve occasions for appearance of, 326, 469n594
vows of. *See* samaya
woman in, 420n325
See also tantra; Vajrayana transmission lineages
meditation
analytical vs resting or placement, 271
in aspirational manner, 396n233
in truly perfect manner of (*lam nges rdzogs*), 396n233, 396n235
mind class. *See under* Great Perfection
mind transmission of the Buddhas. *See under* transmission
mirrorlike wisdom. *See* five primordial wisdoms
mother tantras. *See under* tantra
Mount of Flaming Fire (buddhafield), 71, 301, 303
Munis, six, 72, 159, 313, 467n565, 468n579

Munis, six (*continued*)
 nirmanakaya guides of beings, 293,
  306–7, 466n563
 See also sages of awareness

na rag dong sprugs (confession prayer),
  227, 429n430
nada, and symbolism of, 178, 412n327
Nagarjuna, 122, 190–91, 424n374,
  437n455
nirmanakaya
 their buddhafields, 264, 294, 299,
  300, 303
 diversified, 323, 468n580
  animate (born), 293, 306, 314
  inanimate, 75, 293, 313
 guides of beings, 67, 305–7, 309, 311,
  466n563. *See also under* Munis, six
 half-nirmanakaya, half-sambhogakaya, 294, 297, 299
 of indwelling luminous character,
  300, 454n505
 of inner luminosity, 393n209,
  461n535
 of luminous character, 46, 67,
  293–94, 313, 454n505
 counted as sambhogakaya, 294
 of outwardly radiating luminosity,
  435n446, 461n535

object commonly perceived, 343–44,
  473n636
offerings (in Secret Mantra), 351,
  477n660

pith instruction class. *See* Great Perfection
perception of beings in six realms,
  342–43, 472n634, 473n636
perfection stage, 108, 109, 128
 expounded only in highest tantra,
  179
 of Mahayoga, 107
 path of the lower door, 160, 178,
  412n279, 420n324

path of the upper door, 160, 177,
  404n248, 411n279
 six yogas, 170, 177
 bardo practice, 170, 176–77,
  418n311, 419n321
 dream yoga, 170–72, 418n311,
  418n316
 illusory body practice, 170–71, 177,
  417n311, 420n321
 luminosity, 24, 140, 170, 172, 176
 tummo, 11, 165, 170, 416n306,
  417n311, 418n316
 transference of consciousness, 11,
  128, 177, 387n172, 390n194,
  420n322
 united with generation stage, 106,
  110, 111, 128, 364
 with visual forms (conceptual),
  154–78, 405n250
 without visual forms (nonconceptual), 154, 178, 405n250
pure lands, 72
 three kinds of, 304
purity, twofold, 243, 262, 452n499
purity and equality, 153, 279
 two superior truths, 198, 341
 view of, 107, 326, 341–42, 345–47,
  381n111

rainbow body of great transformation,
  268, 408n265, 457n516
roma and kyangma, 19, 22, 156–57, 164,
  408n264
 in men and women, 19, 22, 157, 164
Rongdzom Chökyi Zangpo (Pandita),
  205, 469n598, 472n633

sacred lands, twenty-four, 164, 304, 313,
  360
sages of awareness, 21, 64, 72, 286, 306.
  See also Munis, six
Sakya Pandita, 375n73, 375n80, 378n95
samadhisattva, 400n242. *See also* jnanasattva; samayasattva

Samantabhadra (and Samantabhadri), 24, 86, 317
awareness, 256, 448n489
freedom of, 239, 240
ground of emanation of deities, 64, 286, 292
practice of, 111
primordially free, 46, 240
seal of, 213, 426n405, 478n660
six features of, 240–42, 277
sixth Buddha, 468n584
time of, 63, 73, 284, 307–8
way of teaching of, 323–24, 468n588
Samaya, 112, 114, 179
five deteriorations of, 225, 429n422
of five enlightened families, 217–22
general samayas of anuttaratantra, 180–94
conditions for, 181
fourteen root downfalls, 183–90
infractions, 190–92
observance of, 182
vs vow, 180–81
of General Scripture of Summarized Wisdom, 195–97
of Mayajala, 34, 197–205
five root samayas, 208–210
ten branch samayas: things not to be rejected, 202–3; things not to be shunned, 203–5
of Mind (Great Perfection), 35–36
of "nothing to keep," 205–8
reparation of, 192–95, 222–28
of "something to keep," 208–215
twenty-five modes of conduct, 216
samayasattva, 6, 100
sambhogakaya, 282, 461n537
buddhafields, 69, 242, 286–87, 440n466
semi-apparent, 300
five perfections, 282, 337. See also five certainties
four kinds of, 461n536
of inner luminosity, 460n533, 461n534

of outwardly radiating luminosity, 281
seven riches of superior ultimate, 341, 349, 471n626
wrathful mandala of, 287–92
Scripture of All-Inclusive Knowledge (kun 'dus rig pa'i mdo), 121, 154, 385n144
Scripture of Summarized Wisdom (mdo dgongs pa 'dus pa), 195, 197, 210, 225, 385n144, 469n594
seven degenerate objects, 219, 428n417
seven qualities of union, 229, 285, 462n542
shamatha, 269–72, 399n240, 455n511. *See also* calm abiding
Shambhala, 304, 411n275, 468n589, 481n662
Shantipa, 184, 422n343
shastras, conditions for composition of, 318
Shri Simha, 330, 416n307, 422n342, 459n526
Shura (Ashvaghosha and Bhawilha), 191–92, 195, 424n375
six exegetical perspectives, 333
six paramitas, 232, 251, 426n396
in Mantrayana, 92, 103, 159
six realms (classes of beings), 64, 125, 129, 135, 305
deluded perception of, 438n459
sages of awareness and, 306, 411n276
seed syllables of, 125, 167, 226, 386n161
six special features of Samantabhadra's freedom, 240, 439n464
spontaneous presence, 44–46, 132, 207, 235, 237
appearance of, 236–38, 242
dimension of, 237–40, 244, 439n460
eight doors of, 45, 46, 240, 244, 264, 282, 301
subsiding, 260–61
five kinds of, 256–57

sugatagarbha, 23, 93, 133, 385n154
    ground nature, 123, 231, 337
    nature of the mind, 87, 89, 136,
        344–45
    not expedient teaching, 187
    present in all beings, 169, 184–85, 187
    sutra vs tantra, 86, 437n454
svabhavikakaya, 132, 140, 241, 467n577
syllables, 14, 23, 72, 166, 468n583
    channels and, 10, 125, 129, 156, 166
    of purification, 140, 156, 166
    three kinds of, 388n183
    wheel of, 324, 468n587
    See also under six realms

tana and gana, 36, 197, 200, 213, 222
tantra, 89
    bipartite. See Ubhaya
    classification according to:
        capacity of beings, 96–99
        cosmic age and degree of desire,
            95–96
        social caste, 96
    father or Mahayoga, 7, 15, 18, 106–7,
        154. See also, generation stage:
        three vajra methods
    ground, path, and result, 89–93
    inner tantras, 106–7, 132, 363, 372n37,
        478n660. See also Anuttaratantra
    mother or Anuyoga, 7, 18, 106–7, 154
    nondual, 7, 19, 106, 154
    outer tantras, 99–179, 372n37,
        374n67, 478n660
    Sakya Pandita on, 378n95
    ten elements of tantric path, 351–52,
        469n606, 470n608, 477n660
    See also under Mantrayana
tathagatagarbha, 432n439. See also suga-
    tagarbha
terma, 84, 370n8, 370n11, 382n122
thögal, 268–69, 275, 300, 413n287,
    457n515
    rainbow body of great transfor-
        mation, 457n516

seven salient features of, 269
vs trekchö, 268, 457n516, 459n527
three concentrations. See under gener-
    ation stage
three doors of perfect liberation, 43,
    132, 265, 266, 416n310, 431n438
three seats. See under mandala
three-year retreat, reason for its length,
    482n667
transmission, three kinds of
    hearing transmission of spiritual
        masters, 330–31
    mind transmission of the Buddhas,
        322–4
    symbolic transmission of the Vidyā-
        dharas, 84–5, 324, 326, 467n574
trekchö, 57, 59, 132, 265–67, 268, 274,
    445n483, 455n508
    compared with thögal, 457n516
    result of, 268, 459n527
two truths
    in awareness, 257, 341, 448n490
    Madhyamaka vs Mantrayana, 342,
        437n454
    two superior truths (purity and
        equality), 89, 350, 373n29,
        472n630
twofold knowledge (of nature and
    multiplicity of phenomena), 68,
    74, 293, 296, 312, 460n533

Ubhaya (bipartite tantra), 103, 376n82,
    385n144. See also Charyatantra
uma. See central channel
universal ground, 54, 261
    alaya, 86, 451n499
    consciousness of, 261, 299, 452n499
    vs dharmakaya, 261, 279, 379n111,
        451n499
    four categories, 452n499
    of habitual tendencies, 241, 257, 303,
        453n499
    original ultimate, 453n499, 460n530
    state of delusion, 262, 277

universe, three-thousandfold, 466n564
upper door, path of. *See under* perfection stage
upward-moving wind. *See* wind(s): five main

vajra aggregate, city of, 19, 155, 478n660
vajra body (vajrakaya), 61, 278–79
  vs aggregate of, 378n99
  of great transformation, 57, 268
Vajrasana (vajra throne), 23, 166, 413n287
Vajrayana transmission lineages
  Anuyoga, 327
  Atiyoga, 328
  kahma, 84, 323
  Mahayoga, 327
  terma, 84
  See also Mantrayana; tantra
vase body, ever youthful, 44, 77, 236–38, 281, 316, 454n504
  definition, 437n455
  resultant aspect, 242
vidyādhara, 327
  definition of, 87, 430n436
  of desire and form realms, 403n248
  enjoying celestial fields, 101, 103, 402n248
  four kinds (levels) of, 153, 229
  knowledge transmission of, 324–30, 371n13, 467n574
  perceptions of, 473n634, 474n638
Vimalamitra, 165–66, 330–31, 408n265, 416n307
vipashyana (deep insight), 258, 361, 441n478, 455n511
  not present in form realm, 244
  and shamatha, training in, 269–72
visualization
  eight criteria of clarity and stability, 150–51
  firm pride or self-assurance, 399n241
  five meditative experiences of, 151, 398n238

recollection of perfect purity, 399n241
six branches of, 152, 402n246
vows
  belonging to the five enlightened families, 37, 38, 216–22, 428n414
  distinct from samaya, 26, 180–81
  enhancement of, 392n204
  foundation of tantric training, 181, 422n335
  reparation of, in Hinayana and Mahayana, 33, 40, 223
  three, 28, 43, 115, 183, 389n186

wheel of everlasting continuity, 293, 298, 337. *See also* fourth time
wind(s), 109, 155, 359–61
  basis of either delusion or wisdom, 162, 414n293
  circulation of, 94, 160, 162, 414n296
  dualistic (in roma and kyangma), 11, 129
  entry into central channel, 22, 154, 162–63, 165, 171
  five main, 21, 22, 161, 412n286
  five major and minor, 7, 45, 21, 22, 415n300
  increase and decline of number according to age, 161
  inner, 22, 162–63, 360, 415n300
  karmic wind, 140, 162, 219, 286, 360
  vs wisdom wind, 162, 414n293, 414n295
  life-wind, 156, 219, 238, 359
  outer (of elements), 18, 21, 160, 162, 415n300
  major, 160, 412n281
  minor, 161, 412n284
  quintessence of five elements, 108, 132
  secret, 22, 163, 415n300
  support of secret empowerment, 124
  transits of, 20, 158–59
  wisdom, 359–60

wind-mind, 24, 55, 129, 165, 167–69,
    263–64
  dissolves in central channel, 410n271
  dissolves into the chakras, 168,
    409n269, 411n277, 413n287
  five winds bound in, 162, 414n297
  illusory body of, 171

yakshas, 308
yogatantra, 95–98, 104–6, 118, 384n137

empowerments of, 9, 118
five factors of awakening in, 104,
    105
four powers of manifestation in, 105,
    377n91
samaya of, 189, 226
youthful vase body. *See* vase body

The Padmakara Translation Group ⌇

Translations into English

The Adornment of the Middle Way. Shantarakshita and Mipham Rinpoche. Boston: Shambhala Publications, 2005, 2010.

Counsels from My Heart. Dudjom Rinpoche. Boston: Shambhala Publications, 2001, 2003.

Enlightened Courage. Dilgo Khyentse Rinpoche. Dordogne: Editions Padmakara, 1992; Ithaca, N.Y.: Snow Lion Publications, 1994, 2006.

The Excellent Path of Enlightenment. Dilgo Khyentse. Dordogne: Editions Padmakara, 1987; Ithaca, N.Y.: Snow Lion Publications, 1996.

A Flash of Lightning in the Dark of Night. The Dalai Lama. Shambhala Publications, 1993. Republished as *For the Benefit of All Beings.* Boston: Shambhala Publications, 2009.

Food of Bodhisattvas. Shabkar Tsogdruk Rangdrol. Boston: Shambhala Publications, 2004.

A Guide to the Words of My Perfect Teacher. Khenpo Ngawang Pelzang. Translated with Dipamkara. Boston: Shambhala Publications, 2004.

The Heart of Compassion. Dilgo Khyentse. Boston: Shambhala Publications, 2007.

The Heart Treasure of the Enlightened Ones. Dilgo Khyentse and Patrul Rinpoche. Boston: Shambhala Publications, 1992.

The Hundred Verses of Advice. Dilgo Khyentse and Padampa Sangye. Boston: Shambhala Publications, 2005.

Introduction to the Middle Way. Chandrakirti and Mipham Rinpoche. Boston: Shambhala Publications, 2002, 2004.

Journey to Enlightenment. Matthieu Ricard. New York: Aperture Foundation, 1996.

Lady of the Lotus-Born. Gyalwa Changchub and Namkhai Nyingpo. Boston: Shambhala Publications, 1999, 2002.

The Life of Shabkar: The Autobiography of a Tibetan Yogin. Albany, N.Y.: SUNY Press, 1994. Ithaca, N.Y.: Snow Lion Publications, 2001.

Nagarjuna's Letter to a Friend. Longchen Yeshe Dorje, Kangyur Rinpoche. Ithaca, N.Y.: Snow Lion Publications, 2005.

The Nectar of Manjushri's Speech. Kunzang Pelden. Boston: Shambhala Publications, 2007, 2010.

The Root Stanzas on the Middle Way. Nagarjuna. Dordogne: Editions Padmakara, 2008.

A Torch Lighting the Way to Freedom. Dudjom Rinpoche, Jigdrel Yeshe Dorje. Boston: Shambhala Publications, 2011.

Treasury of Precious Qualities. Longchen Yeshe Dorje, Kangyur Rinpoche. Boston: Shambhala Publications, 2001. Revised version with root text by Jigme Lingpa, 2010.

The Way of the Bodhisattva (Bodhicharyavatara). Shantideva. Boston: Shambhala Publications, 1997, 2006, 2008.

White Lotus. Jamgön Mipham. Boston: Shambhala Publications, 2007.

Wisdom: Two Buddhist Commentaries. Khenchen Kunzang Pelden and Minyak Kunzang Sonam. Dordogne: Editions Padmakara, 1993, 1999.

The Wish-Fulfilling Jewel. Dilgo Khyentse. Boston: Shambhala Publications, 1988.

The Words of My Perfect Teacher. Patrul Rinpoche. Sacred Literature Series of the International Sacred Literature Trust. New York: HarperCollins, 1994; 2nd ed. Lanham, MD: AltaMira Press, 1998; Boston: Shambhala Publications, 1998.

Zurchungpa's Testament. Zurchungpa and Dilgo Khyentse. Ithaca, N.Y.: Snow Lion Publications, 2006.

Ekajati

Rahula

Dorje Lekpa

Shenpa Marnak